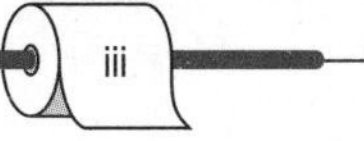

OUR "REGULA... READERS" RAVE!

Wonderful books. I buy my adult sons one of these almost every Christmas.

—Roxanne L.

Uncle John has made me the best *Jeopardy!* player in the family.

—Bear R.

Uncle John's is always a great choice for a gift when you have no idea what to buy. It's *perfect* for trivia fans.

—Rocky T.

Praise be to Uncle John! He has the uncanny ability to make boring stuff not boring. I mean, who knew a page of facts about syrup could be so interesting? Well done!

—Michelle N.

I enjoy your *Bathroom Readers* so much. I now have just over 120!

—John B.

I have just finished reading *Uncle John's Fact-tastic Bathroom Reader*, and I loved it. I'd never seen any of your previous books, but now I'm going to start searching for them.

—Brian F.

I've been a fan since your first *Reader* way back when. My favorite parts are the little factoids at the bottom of every page.

—Sheldon H.

I have been reading your books since I was a kid (thx Dad!). That's why I always seem to know so much more about so many things than my coworkers. You're my secret weapon!

—Luisa L.

I am 82 years old and love reading the *Bathroom Reader*.

—Bob A.

Great series. I enjoy reading them over and over. Thanks for the memories while sitting. Well, as you say, gotta go.

—Don E.

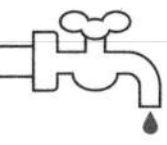

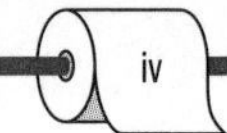

CONTENTS

Because the BRI understands your reading needs, we've divided the contents by length as well as subject.

Short—a quick read

Medium—2 to 3 pages

Long—for those extended visits, when something a little more involved is required

Uncle John's HINDSIGHT Is 20/20 Bathroom Reader

NO. 34

THE BATHROOM READERS' INSTITUTE

Portable Press
San Diego, California

Portable Press / The Bathroom Readers' Institute
An imprint of Printers Row Publishing Group
9717 Pacific Heights Blvd, San Diego, CA 92121
www.portablepress.com • mail@portablepress.com

Correspondence regarding the content of this book should be sent to Portable Press / The Bathroom Readers' Institute, Editorial Department, at the above address.

Publisher: Peter Norton • Associate Publisher: Ana Parker
Senior Developmental Editor: April Graham Farr
Copy Editor: Dan Mansfield
Production Team: Julie Greene, Rusty von Dyl

Producer, Creator, and First Wizard Deluxe: Javna Brothers LLC

Interior, Illustrations, and Infographics Designer: Lidija Tomas
Cover Illustration, Cover and Endpaper Designer: Linda Lee Mauri

Dedicated to Bo, Lou, Ivy, and Jean, B.R.I.T. (Bathroom Readers In Training)

"In retrospect it becomes clear that hindsight is definitely overrated!" –Alfred E. Neuman

Library of Congress Control Number: 2021932478
ISBN: 978-1-64517-732-6

Printed in China

25 24 23 22 21   1 2 3 4 5

* * *

SCIENCE MAGIC

At an 1898 demonstration by Nikola Tesla, onlookers observed a small boat move across the water...all by itself. Some whispered that it must be witchcraft; others suspected a tiny monkey was driving the boat. Tesla told them it was "mind power." He later filed a patent for the first radio-controlled device in history.

POST CARD

PLACE STAMP HERE.
UNITED STATES AND CANADA ONE CENT.
FOREIGN, TWO CENTS

first

To Johnny

Australia is wider than the Moon!

IS A REAL PH

POST CARD.

THIS SPACE MAY BE USED FOR COMMUNICATION.

THE ADDRESS ONLY TO BE WRITTEN HERE.

A town in Belgium once tried having cats deliver the mail! It didn't work...

THE BATHROOM READERS' INSTITUTE USA

TO: UNCLE JOHN
THE BATHROOM READERS' INSTITUTE

OM READERS' INSTITUTE

UNCLE JOHN COLLECTION ON EXHIBIT

POST CARD

ADDRE

Penguins like trumpets, but hate bagpipes!

REAL PHOT

INTRODUCTION

Another year, another *Bathroom Reader*. And, boy, what a year! As I'm writing this in early 2021—from the socially distanced safety of my home office—I'm reminded that, in tumultuous times like these, there's nothing like a brand-new edition of *Uncle John's* to take one's mind off the worries of the world and to help keep things in the proper perspective. So welcome to our 34th edition:

HINDSIGHT IS 20/20

Aside from the cheeky bathroom pun, hindsight is a valuable tool, or as we quote Kevin Kline on page 347: "It's like foresight, but without the future." On the pages ahead, we'll dive deep into the past, present, and even the future. And while you'll find a lot of strange stories and stats about the history-making year, 2020 only scratches the surface. This book is overflowing!

But that's what we do here. Ever since our first edition in the late 1980s, our primary goal has been to entertain you. And if we've done our jobs right, you'll not only learn a lot of new stuff, you'll never look at a lot of things the same way ever again. Case in point: the N95 mask, which became ubiquitous in 2020, was invented decades earlier by modifying a form-fitting bra cup. Good luck trying *not* to see that the next time you see someone wearing one. Examples of other things you'll never see the same again after reading *Hindsight Is 2020*: blueberry-flavored foods, puppy dog eyes, wraparound porches, sewing needles, stomachs, comic books, carpets, the Parthenon, *Beetlejuice*, the Coca-Cola logo, and apples.

Here are some more things to look forward to:

Hindsight: The strange history of mailing people through the mail, what life was like way back in 1994, and lots of origins—including the globe, the goblet, the GIF, velvet Elvis paintings, eyeglasses, and more.

Modern Living: Governmental "isms" defined, sarcastic online product reviews, what stuff costs on the black market, and how shibboleths divide us. Don't know what a shibboleth is? See page 58.

Science and Nature: All about rabbits and hares, the loneliest whale in the world, and why the platypus is even weirder on the inside. You'll also learn what's up with the "Barf Scientists," stroll through a poison garden, breathe the recirculated air of Biosphere2, and discover why humans love shiny things.

Pop Culture: When Eric Clapton almost joined the Beatles, when Macaulay Culkin almost starred in *The Big Bang Theory*, video games no one ever played, things that are

bigger on the inside, and the story of the worst live TV gaffe in modern history...or was it?

Eating and Drinking: Odd burgers, the benefits of a vegan diet, cocktail origins, and disgusting recipes for such culinary delights as corn s'mores and smoker's cough.

Words and Things: Aptronyms (like poker champ Chris Moneymaker), Name of the Year winners (like Crescent Dragonwagon), and words that contain "oof." Plus the difference between soup and stew, Eskimo and Inuit, and the origins of some classic insults.

Good Times! Remember those? Victorian games (like "Squeak, Piggy, Squeak!") and skateboarding lingo, like these two: "Sketchy: a trick that's done poorly or incorrectly," and "Burly: a trick that's dangerous enough to cause injury if it's done sketchily." And for the first time in our 34-year history, a page of bathroom jokes (like the constipated accountant who couldn't budget).

The Bright Side: People who found amazing stuff (a dinosaur brain fossil!), the cheerleader who saved a toddler's life, war-torn lovers who reunited after 50 years, and the inspiring tale of the "Hiroshima Trees" that still bloom today.

And a great big THANK-YOU to the dedicated staff of writers and editors at the BRI who have managed to keep it together while the world was seemingly falling apart ...and managed to create yet another masterpiece.

Gordon Javna
John Dollison
Jay Newman
Brian Boone
Thom Little
J. Carroll
Lidija Tomas
Derek Fairbridge
John Javna
Dan the Man
Gene Stone
Kim Griswell
Kathy & Tim
Shane Sevcik
Michael Ford
Gail & Gary
Mary Gabriel
Drew Papanestor
J. Cheever Loophole
Otis Criblecoblis
Thomas Crapper

And finally, thank you, dear reader. Whether you've been with us for a few years or a few decades, or if this is your first time reading Uncle John's, it's an honor to share these great stories with you.

Stay safe. And as always, go with the flow!

—Uncle John and the BRI

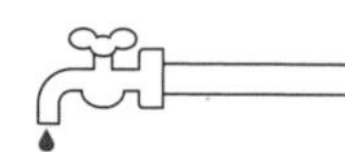

YOU'RE MY INSPIRATION

It's always interesting to find out where the architects of pop culture get their ideas. Some of these may surprise you.

STRANGER THINGS: Ever heard of the Montauk Project? It's a conspiracy theory from the early 1980s that alleged the U.S. government was performing strange experiments on children—including teleportation and time travel—in a top-secret lab in Montauk, New York. In addition to providing the foundation for the 2016 Netflix show *Stranger Things* (which had the working title *Montauk*), elements of this conspiracy theory have showed up in *The X-Files, Men in Black*, and *Eternal Sunshine of the Spotless Mind.*

"DON'T COME AROUND HERE NO MORE": This 1985 Tom Petty and the Heartbreakers top-20 hit was written by Dave Stewart of the Eurythmics ("Sweet Dreams"). Stewart came up with the title after overhearing Fleetwood Mac singer Stevie Nicks talk about the time she threw Eagles guitarist Joe Walsh out of her house: "I said, 'Don't come around here no more!' " When Petty recorded the trippy song, he took inspiration from another 1980s icon: "I saw Prince doing what looked like an attempt at psychedelia, and I loved it. It inspired me."

JOKER: Joaquin Phoenix's unconventional take on this Batman comic book villain netted him a Best Actor Oscar in 2020. "I think what influenced me the most was Ray Bolger. There was a particular song called 'The Old Soft Shoe' that he performed and...there's this odd arrogance almost to his movements...He does this thing of turning his chin up...I completely just stole it from him." (Bolger's best-known role: the Scarecrow in 1939's *The Wizard of Oz.*)

DOROTHY GALE: Maud Baum always wanted a little girl, but she and her husband, Frank, had four sons. That's why she was so distraught when her baby niece, Dorothy Louise Gage, died at just five months old in 1898. At the time, Frank was working on his book *The Wonderful Wizard of Oz*, and named the main character Dorothy Gale to console his grief-stricken wife. Maud's mother, suffragist Matilda Gage, provided much of Dorothy's personality.

SCHITT'S CREEK: In 2012, Daniel Levy was watching a lot of reality shows like *Real Housewives* and *Keeping Up with the Kardashians* when he wondered, "What would these families look like if it were to go away...would there be love there, and what would those bare-bones relationships look like?" Those questions sowed the seed for his critically acclaimed sitcom about a Kardashian-like family that goes broke and has to live in a run-down motel.

First word of astronaut Pete Conrad, when he became the third man to walk on the Moon (1969): "Whoopee!"

TASTES LIKE "BLUEBERRY"

A lot of packaged foods come in blueberry-flavored varieties enticing consumers with pictures of plump fruit on the packages. But actual blueberries aren't shelf-stable, so here's what food manufacturers pass off as "blueberries" in various items.

Quaker Blueberries & Cream Instant Oatmeal. It contains "blueberry flavored fruit pieces," which are made up of dried figs, corn syrup, starch, sugar...and a hint of blueberry juice concentrate.

Blueberry Bagels. One of the United States' most popular breakfast spots, Panera Bread, sells blueberry bagels. It uses a faux-blueberry concoction called "blueberry-flavored bits," made from sugar, corn syrup, flour, food coloring, and raw blueberries. Except these are "infused blueberries," which are actual whole berries that have been fortified with sugar, artificial berry flavoring, and sunflower oil.

Blueberry Cereal. In 2010, General Mills was sued by a consumer group over its misleading claims about its Total Blueberry Pomegranate cereal. The box and advertising materials promised real pomegranate taste, but it was actually just flavoring chemicals—there were no actual blueberries *or* pomegranates (or fruit derivatives) in the cereal. The suit was dropped in 2011; the cereal was discontinued shortly thereafter.

Kellogg's Special K Blueberry Bars. These also are made with "blueberry-flavored fruit pieces," but a different and more robust recipe that more closely mimics the look of full, whole blueberries. These consist of cranberries masked with sugar, sunflower oil, grape juice ("for color"), and a bit of blueberry juice concentrate.

Blueberry Muffin Mix. Pillsbury's has little blue dots in it, which are just clumps of sugar, binder, and blue food coloring. The ingredient list on Jiffy's enduring blueberry muffin mix doesn't mention blueberries, or anything that could even be construed as berries, leading us to guess that the berries inside are just sugar and binders.

Blueberry Mini Wheats. This cereal from Kellogg's has a blueberry-flavored frosting and little pieces of blueberries. According to the ingredient list, those fruit bits are actually "Blueberry Flavored Crunchlets," which are made from sugar, corn, cornstarch, soybean oil, glycerin, and red and blue food coloring.

Chocolate-Covered Blueberries. One would assume that bite-sized chocolate-covered blueberries are just blueberries doused in chocolate, right? Wrong. Brookside's Dark Chocolate Acai & Blueberry morsels are a combination of blended and solidified fruit concentrates and extracts (including blueberries), bound together with corn syrup and sugar...and then covered in chocolate.

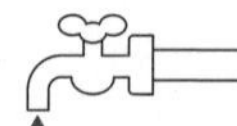

YOU BET YOUR LIFE

A true gambler will bet on almost anything: sports, awards shows, news events, even the weather. The odds of winning might be bonkers, but HEY! I've got a hunch! Here are some people who made wagers on bizarre future events and won...and others who risked everything and lost.

★ In 1989, a man from Wales placed a £30 wager with sports bookies Ladbrokes, betting that three predictions would come to pass. The man (his name wasn't released in press reports) wagered that upon the dawn of the new millennium—on January 1, 2000, 11 years after he made the bet: 1) the band U2 would still be together, 2) pop star Cliff Richard would earn a knighthood, and 3) the long-running British TV soaps *EastEnders, Neighbours,* and *Home and Away* would all still be on the air. Ladbrokes gave odds of all that coming true at 6,479 to 1, and on January 2, 2000, had to pay the man £194,400 ($290,000) because his predictions proved accurate.

★ Rory McIlroy is a really good golfer. He's won dozens of professional tournaments, including majors like the U.S. Open and the PGA Championship. His father and first golf coach, Gerry McIlroy, so believed in his son's talents that in 2004, when the future star was just 15 years old, he placed a £200 ($341) bet with a gambling house that Rory would win the British Open within 10 years' time. The odds were 500 to 1 against him. But in 2014, McIlroy won the tournament...and his father won £100,000 ($171,000).

★ Ashley Revell earned his living as a professional gambler, so he probably should have known better than to risk everything on a single spin of the roulette wheel. Acting on a drunken dare from friends in 2004, he sold off most of his possessions, including his house, car, and Rolex watch, and then flew to Las Vegas. He took all the cash he'd earned by selling his worldly goods—$135,000—to the casino at the Plaza Hotel. He exchanged his money for chips, and bet all of it on red at roulette. With odds virtually 50-50, the ball stopped on 7 red, doubling Revell's money.

★ A man who identified himself only as "Big Matt" on a gambling forum told the tale of how a can't-miss bet went very wrong during a soccer match in the 2008 Africa Cup of Nations. In the first round of the tournament, Angola was leading Mali, 4–0, with only 12 minutes left to go in regulation play. It seemed impossible for Mali to stage a comeback, so Big Matt bet on Angola to win.

Most requested item at the Vatican City Pharmacy: hemorrhoid ointment.

The payoff wasn't very big, but even so, it seemed like a sure thing, so Matt bet everything he had—$5,600. Bad move. Mali rallied hard and quickly, leading to a final score of 4–4. Big Matt lost every penny and had to drop out of college because he'd wasted his student loan gambling on the game.

★ In November 2013, two of the English Premier League's powerhouses squared off in a match between Manchester United and Arsenal. Two friends from the Iganga district in eastern Uganda made the match a little more interesting. Henry Dhabasani was so certain Arsenal would win that he told his friend Rashid Yiga he'd hand over his two-room house if they lost. Yiga, confident in a Manchester United victory, put his Toyota on the line...as well as his wife. Final score: Manchester United 1, Arsenal 0. Dhabasani lost. The next day, Yiga and his friends (all fellow Manchester United fans) went over to Dhabasani's house and threw him out, along with his family.

★ Frederick W. Smith founded Federal Express in 1971 with a $4 million inheritance and more than $90 million in venture capital. Building up the infrastructure for an international shipping company is expensive, and after settling up everything, Smith realized that he'd spent virtually all his capital, with only $5,000 in operating funds left in the bank. Not knowing what else to do, Smith took that five grand, hopped on a cheap flight to Las Vegas, and put everything that remained in FedEx's coffers on the blackjack table. He walked out of the casino $27,000 richer, which was enough money to keep the company running for another week, allowing Smith some breathing room to hit up investors for more operating capital.

Smith hopped on a cheap flight to Las Vegas and put everything that remained in FedEx's coffers on the blackjack table.

★ Pete Edwards is proudly Welsh, and loves his national soccer team. He was also so convinced that his grandson, Harry Wilson, would one day play for the Wales squad, that he went into a bookmaker in his hometown of Wrexham in 2000 and bet £50 (about $70) that Harry Wilson would, one day, hit the field in a game for the team. At the time, Harry was nowhere near to having a career as a soccer player. Reason: he was only three years old. But he did eventually play, and he got pretty good—so good that he landed a spot on the roster of the Wales national team as a 16-year-old in 2013. Three minutes before the end of a World Cup qualifying match against Belgium, Harry Wilson entered the game. His grandfather's bet, estimated at odds of 2,500 to 1, paid out £125,000 (roughly $171,000).

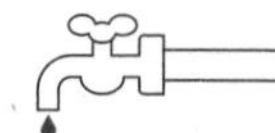

OOPS! LIVE TV EDITION

These days, thanks to screengrabs and snarky social media users, live TV flubs can take on a life of their own.

LIFE'S A GLITCH: More than three million viewers tuned in to BBC News' live coverage of the October 2018 royal wedding of Princess Eugenie of York (tenth in line to the throne). When Eugenie arrived at Windsor Castle and emerged from her car, one of the commentators, fashion stylist Alex Longmore, said, "What a beautiful dress. Absolutely fitting her." A few seconds later, as the princess was walking up the steps, the subtitles read: "What a beautiful breasts. Absolutely fitting her." The BBC blamed the mistake on a glitch with their automated subtitle service, which they boasted "produces accuracy levels in excess of 98% but, as with all broadcasters, there are instances—particularly during live broadcasts—when mistakes happen."

CAUGHT SHORT: In April 2020, ABC News reporter Will Reeve was delivering a report on *Good Morning America* about drones that will fly medication to seniors. Due to the COVID-19 pandemic, Reeve (son of late *Superman* actor Christopher Reeve) presented the report from his home office. When Reeve set up the camera, he used a wider angle than necessary so that the graphic that's displayed across the lower portion of the screen wouldn't cut off. What he didn't realize was that when the director cut to a split screen with him and the hosts in two windows, that graphic went away. The report itself went off without a hitch, but afterward, the segment went viral. Why? Because Reeve wasn't wearing pants. (He had shorts on.) He later explained himself on Twitter: "Trying to be efficient, I got ready for a post-GMA workout a little too soon this morning. The camera angle, along with friends, family, and several hundred strangers on social media made me rethink my morning routine."

REDDIT ON THEIR FACE: In July 2020, Fox News host Martha MacCallum was covering civil unrest in Seattle. While reporting about rumored infighting in the citizen-controlled Capitol Hill Autonomous Zone (CHAZ), the news channel displayed a post from Reddit. Believing it to have been posted by an occupier, MacCallum read it aloud: "I thought we were an autonomous collective. An anarcho-syndicalist commune at the least, we should take it in turns to act as a sort of executive officer for the week." In case you don't recognize that, it's from a scene in the 1975 comedy *Monty Python and the Holy Grail,* in which two muddy peasants tell a confused King Arthur why they didn't vote for him. The Reddit post included the entire scene, but MacCallum only read the above part aloud, which was highlighted for viewers at home—emphasizing the words "anarcho" and "commune." Despite

There are more cows in New York State than in Wyoming.

taking a drubbing from the press, and on social media, MacCallum and Fox News declined to comment. But Monty Python veteran John Cleese, who wrote and starred in that movie, tweeted, "BREAKING: No one @FoxNews has ever seen @montypython & The Holy Grail. 😂 #runit #goodjournalism #factchecking."

SPIDER-FLOP: Despite having hit her head pretty hard on the pavement, *Good Morning America* reporter Sarah Haines was able to laugh it off. Spider-Man was, understandably, much more concerned. He was supposed to swoop in (on his "web") and catch Haines as she "fainted." That's how they rehearsed it. But when it came time to do the bit live during the Times Square 2013 New Year's Eve celebration—to promote the upcoming movie *The Amazing Spider-Man 2*—things didn't go as planned. The actor playing the wall-crawler landed fine, but when he looked at the camera, he paused like a deer in the headlights...and didn't notice Haines falling backward onto the pavement until it was too late to catch her. "No injuries," she tweeted later, "but I have never felt LESS graceful."

BOTTLE ROCKET: Jacob Strickling, described in press reports as an "Australian science teacher," is known for his "Make Science Fun" books. In 2017, Natarsha Belling of the morning news show *Studio 10* served as Strickling's unwitting assistant for a demonstration in a Sydney park. Building on the Mentos-and-Diet Coke experiment, Strickling replaced the Mentos with liquid nitrogen. After launching a couple of plastic Diet Coke bottles, Strickling asked Belling if she'd like to "have a go."

"No," she said quickly. Then she asked, "Is it safe?"

"You've just seen me do it twice without injury."

Very tentatively, Belling held the half-full Coke bottle while Strickling poured the liquid nitrogen through a funnel. She asked, "And then what do I do with that?"

"Just sort of face it toward the sky, not toward the cameras."

"Upside down?"

"Upside down," he said as the bottle was getting full.

"I don't know how to do it!"

"I've done it twice," he said. "Weren't you watching?"

"I wasn't watching!" she yelled as the bottle started to invert and then launched like a rocket out of her hand, missing her face by mere millimeters. The area was blanketed in liquid nitrogen as a tree branch fell right next to Belling. There were some screams and nervous laughter from the crew.

Then Strickling exclaimed, "Didn't I tell you that this was gonna be the best live television ever?"

Belling, covered in debris, put her hand to her head and said, "I can't hear out of my right ear." (Her hearing returned later.) As a slow-motion replay shows, she was very lucky to still have her face intact. As soon as Belling regained her composure, she ended the report. "It was nice meeting you," said Strickling.

**Most dangerous high school sport: cheerleading.
It accounts for nearly 65% of all catastrophic injuries in high school athletics.**

MY NAME IS MY DESTINY

The term aptronym *was coined by humorist Franklin P. Adams to describe the amusing situation when a person's name is "apt" for his or her line of work or behavior—like toilet pioneer Thomas Crapper, for example. Here are some more.*

Emily Wines: San Francisco–based master sommelier

Ashley Green: Works for the Northeast Organic Farming Association of Vermont, certifying produce as organic

Patrick Godley: Seattle-area Catholic priest

Richard Chopp: Austin, Texas, urologist who specializes in performing vasectomies

Francine Prose: American novelist

William Wordsworth: English Romantic poet

Willie Thrower: NFL quarterback

Early Wynn: Major League Baseball pitcher who won a game on opening day...twice

Thomas File: U.S. Census Bureau employee who compiled election statistics

Rich Fairbank: Billionaire and CEO of Capital One, a credit card and banking company

Dan Price: CEO of credit card processing service Gravity Payments

Sara Blizzard: Meteorologist for the BBC

William Headline: CNN's Washington, D.C., bureau chief

Chris Moneymaker: The 2003 World Series of Poker champion

Marina Stepanova: Russian Olympic hurdler

Jason Baer: Vice president of Vermont Teddy Bear Co.

Rosalind Brewer: Starbucks executive

Russell Brain: Neurologist

Jack Armstrong: Major League Baseball pitcher

Tim Duncan: NBA star

Lake Speed: NASCAR driver

Lance Bass: Singer with the boy band NSYNC; he sang the bass parts

Larry Speakes: White House press secretary under President Ronald Reagan

Christopher Coke: Convicted Jamaican drug lord and cocaine trafficker

White tea, black tea, green tea, and oolong tea all come from the same plant.

STREET TALK

We all live, work, drive, and walk on these every day, so it's time we learned just what the difference is between a road, a street, a lane, and all the other words that mean pretty much the same thing and are often used interchangeably... but which actually have slightly different definitions.

Road. The most general classification, it refers simply to a stretch between two fixed points.

Way. A relatively short street that tees off of a road.

Street. It's a road–specifically, a public road–with buildings on both sides of the driving area.

Avenue. Similar to a street, except that it runs perpendicular to, or crossing through, a street. It may or may not have buildings on one or both sides.

Boulevard. A street that's long and very wide, and with trees on both sides. A true boulevard is so wide that it has a median strip in the middle, and that has trees on it, too.

Lane. A narrow road in a rural or suburban area.

Place. A road with no throughway–a dead end.

Court. A circular or looped road with no throughway.

Drive. A long road that was built into the natural geographic features of the land, such as a road that winds around a mountain or a body of water.

Beltway. A highway that surrounds a city or metropolitan area.

Terrace. A type of drive that follows the natural rise of a hill as it reaches the top of the slope.

Esplanade. A road or path (often for cars, but almost always for pedestrians) that runs parallel to the ocean or another large body of water.

Parkway. A busy major road that's been well decorated with trees, landscaping, and green spaces.

Frontage road. Also called service roads or access roads, these run parallel to major thoroughfares, such as highways and busy streets.

Highway. A highly trafficked, high-speed road that connects one population center to another with few traffic lights or stop signs to slow down traffic.

Freeway. A highway with at least two lanes going in both directions, and with its traffic flow controlled by access ramps.

Interstate. Any part of the federally funded system of highways.

Turnpike. A section of highway or freeway that requires a toll to be paid.

Causeway. A raised road that runs directly over water or swampland.

DE POEZENBOOT (THE CAT BOAT)

Here's the story of one of the most unconventional, most popular, and *most adorable tourist destinations in Amsterdam.*

THE CAT LADY

One morning in 1966, Henriette van Weelde, a woman living in Amsterdam, the capital of the Netherlands, noticed a stray cat with kittens sheltering under a tree in front of her house. Perhaps if the mother cat had been alone, van Weelde would have left it to fend for herself, but the sight of it with kittens moved her to take the animals in and care for them.

A short time later she took in another stray...and then another, and another. Soon she developed a reputation around the neighborhood for taking in sick and abandoned felines, and people started bringing her even more cats to take care of. Two years after taking in that first mother and kittens, her house was overrun with cats. Now what?

Van Weelde lived on one of Amsterdam's famous canals, the Herengracht, which is lined with houseboats. One day when she was looking at the boats tied up outside her home, she thought: Why not turn one into a cat shelter? And that's what she did. In 1968, she bought an old Dutch sailing barge, ripped out the original interior, and replaced it with one better suited to serve as a cat sanctuary. Part of the barge was enclosed, providing shelter in cold or wet weather, and there was also an open area where the cats could lounge in the sun when the weather was nice.

BUT WAIT! THERE'S MORE

The *Poezenboot,* or Cat Boat, as it came to be known, attracted a lot of interest. Result: people brought van Weelde even *more* cats to care for. By 1971, the boat had reached full capacity...so van Weelde bought a second boat and parked it next to the first. Fortunately for her, the boats attracted not just curiosity-seekers and cat lovers who wanted to visit the cats, but also volunteers to help care for them, plus contributions of money, cat food, kitty litter, and other supplies from the public. Most importantly, the boats attracted people who wanted to *adopt* cats. Every time one of the Cat Boat cats found a new home, that created room for van Weelde to take in another stray.

Over the years the Cat Boat evolved from a makeshift, one-person operation into a full-fledged and well-organized charitable foundation, one that provided food, medical care, and temporary housing for the cats most suitable for adoption, as well as forever homes on the Cat Boat for wild cats who were not. In 1979, van Weelde

First casualty of the first British bombing raid over Berlin in World War II: an elephant at the Berlin Zoo.

replaced the original Dutch sailing barge with a newer boat that was converted into a cat shelter by a shipyard, and was much nicer for the cats. The Cat Boat Foundation also grew, and it soon introduced a spay and neuter program for the public, one that charged a nominal fee for cat owners who could afford to pay, and no charge for owners who couldn't. After microchipping of cats became available in the 1990s, the foundation added this service as well. Now when cats arrive at the shelter, they are scanned for microchips, and if one is found, the owner is contacted and can be reunited with their cat the same day.

STILL AFLOAT

Harriet van Weelde passed away in 2005 at the age of 90, but as of 2020 the Cat Boat Foundation is still going strong, though now it's down to one boat after city officials required it to downsize in 2006. With one boat, the foundation can care for up to 50 cats at a time, including 14 who live there permanently.

Social media has helped the charity to develop a worldwide following via Twitter, Facebook, Instagram, and the foundation's own website, turning the Cat Boat into what is arguably the world's most popular cat sanctuary. So many visitors to Amsterdam want to visit the Cat Boat that the foundation has had to set up a reservation system to handle them all. On the website you can watch live video streams of the cats at play, schedule your visit to the Cat Boat, view photos and profiles of individual cats up for adoption and, if you live in the Netherlands, adopt a cat or two (or more). If you don't live there but still want to help out, you can sponsor Kairo, Cypie, Samus, Icey, or any of the other cats who've made the Cat Boat their forever home. Sponsors of permanent residents receive a photo of their cat and information about its history and personality, and each December they are sent an update and a new photo of their cat.

The Cat Boat has evolved quite a bit since that morning in 1966 when Henriette van Weelde found the mother and kittens sheltering under a tree outside her house, but today the mission of the organization she founded is unchanged: "Our goal," says the foundation, "is simple: to help as many cats as possible."

* * *

GEOGRAPHY QUIZ

Q: What do Russia, Mongolia, Kazakhstan, Kyrgyzstan, Tajikistan, Afghanistan, Pakistan, India, Nepal, Bhutan, Myanmar, Laos, Vietnam, and North Korea have in common?

A: They all border China.

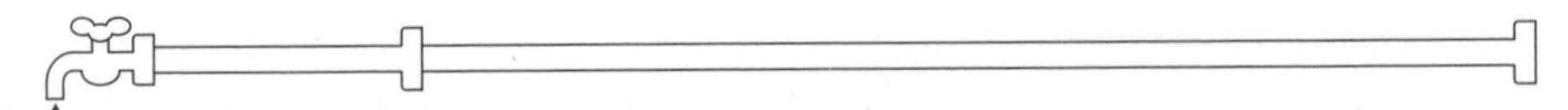

Q. Can you name the two countries that have a map on their flags? A. Cyprus and Kosovo.

KITSCHY ART ORIGINS

"Kitsch" is hard to define. It's art, but it's meant to be decorative, and it's often sentimental, sappy, spiritual, lurid—anything but subtle. Kitsch is the kind of art that some people consider tacky or cheesy, yet there's something charming about these distinctive contributions to the culture, many of which can be found right now in a thrift store near you.

PLASTIC PINK FLAMINGOS

The United States' post–World War II housing boom and the rapid growth of suburbia meant that millions of Americans suddenly had homes with front lawns. A company called Union Products of Leominster, Massachusetts, catered to these homeowners, offering dozens of plastic sculptures of animals and cute characters that they called "lawn ornaments." In 1957, Union hired a 19-year-old art school graduate named Don Featherstone to design and create prototypes for even more. His first plastic sculptures for Union Products: a little girl holding a watering can, a little boy playing with a puppy, and a duck. The duck sold so well that by the end of the year, his bosses asked Featherstone to design another bird, but something more exotic: a flamingo. (Why a flamingo? Union found that its pink products were selling particularly well, and flamingos are pink.) Featherstone went to work, but couldn't find any live flamingos to use as models (as he'd done with ducks), so he based his design on pictures in *National Geographic.* One major place where Featherstone diverged from nature: He made the legs thinner and rod-like, so that they could be used to stick the finished plastic version into the ground. The first pink flamingos, now the definitive lawn ornament, went on sale in 1958 and cost $2.76. It's estimated that 20 million of the birds have been sold since then (not including all the knockoffs made by other companies).

SEVEN-DAY CANDLES

Also known as *veladoras* (Spanish for "candle"), these eight-inch-tall glass jars filled with wax are adorned with vivid images of Jesus, the Virgin Mary, or Catholic saints, painted in a style reminiscent of Mexican folk art. They're commonly marketed to members of the predominantly Catholic Latino community and sold in Mexican grocery stores in the United States for a couple of bucks. The idea of putting religious art on the outside of a jar candle dates back to the late 1940s. According to Sister Schodts Reed (she's not a nun—"Sister" is her given name), her father-in-law Peter Doan Reed, came up with the idea. His company, the Reed Candle Company of San

The U.S. Postal Service processes 160 billion pieces of mail each year, and it photographs every single one of them.

Antonio, Texas, started out in 1938, making two-inch-tall, unadorned votive candles (encased in glass and so named for their use in Catholic prayer, or "vows"). But a decade later, he decided to focus more on the religious aspect by printing images of religious figures and prayers on the sides of the jar. And by making them extra-large, the candles would burn for a week, promising value to customers, and something more: "That way, they have a silent prayer that is continuing even after they are done praying," Sister Reed told the *Chicago Tribune*. Along with hundreds of other companies in the United States and Mexico, Reed Candle Company produces 350 different seven-day candles.

VELVET PAINTINGS

Have you ever driven by a roadside "art sale" and seen a bunch of faces of Elvis or John Wayne staring back at you from black backgrounds? The black background makes the colors pop and gives the subjects—unicorns, matadors, movie stars, landscapes, dogs, clowns, even Jesus—an eerie glow. Velvet likely originated in the Kashmir region of the Indian subcontinent, and so did velvet paintings. Religious leaders used velvet canvases for portraits of Hindu deities, and after Italian explorer Marco Polo visited the area in the late 13th century, he brought velvet paintings back to western Europe, where the idea was borrowed by the Catholic Church. Velvet paintings fell in and out of favor over the years, but reemerged strongly in the early 20th century. During the Depression, itinerant sign painter Edgar Leeteg moved from California to Tahiti. There he bought up a store's stock of unsold velvet canvas and, reminded of the velvet paintings of religious icons that hung in his St. Louis church as a child, he set out to master the form, painting idealized scenes of tropical life and Polynesian women. Leeteg started churning out hundreds of paintings a year, and they sold well, both to locals and to American servicemen stationed in the South Pacific before, during, and after World War II. "Velvets," as collectors call them, really gained popularity in the United States with the Polynesian-inspired tiki bar fad of the 1950s. After the owner of the 7 Seas tiki bar in Hollywood bought a bunch, every other tiki establishment in the country had to have one, too. By the time the tiki craze died off in the early 1960s, the velvet painting industry had moved to Mexico, where the paintings were—and still are—produced assembly-line style.

HUMMEL FIGURINES

Perhaps you've seen a small ceramic statue of a German kid on your grandma's mantel, or in her curio cabinet. That could very well be a Hummel figurine—a craze in the mid-20th century that sprouted from the mind of a nun. In 1927, 18-year-old Berta Hummel enrolled in the Academy of Applied Art in Munich, Germany, where

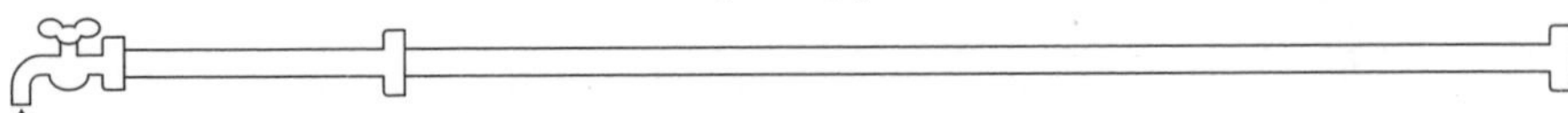

"Upside down" spelled upside down is "umop apisdn."

she developed an affinity for drawing cherubic children in nostalgically pastoral poses—sitting by a well, carrying a fishing pole, or walking through the woods, for example. After completing her artistic training, Hummel decided to take a different career path, joining the Convent of Siessen, a Franciscan order that advocated art as a form of praising God. In 1931, Hummel became a full-fledged nun, adopting the name Maria Innocentia and living in a remote convent in the German countryside, much like the ones she liked to draw.

Inspired and encouraged to continue making her illustrations of children, Hummel sold her work to a few postcard publishers. Hummel's postcards caught the eye of Franz Goebel, who ran a porcelain company called W. Goebel Porzellanfabrik. He so enjoyed them that in 1935, he signed Hummel to an exclusive deal that would allow his company to transform her drawings of cute children doing rustic things into porcelain figurines. When he took his collection of Hummel figures to the Leipzig Trade Fair in 1935, Goebel found buyers throughout Europe and in the United States, particularly Marshall Field's department stores, where they immediately became a sensation. Goebel hired a team of sculptors and painters to make figurines based on Hummel's drawings, and before long had to bring in designers to come up with new ideas in the style of Sister Maria Innocentia Hummel, who died in 1946 at age 37.

Production and sales of Hummel figurines stalled during World War II, but picked up again in the early 1950s thanks to American soldiers stationed in West Germany who bought Hummels and sent them back home as gifts. At the same time, they sold briskly to Germans, in part because the cute little kids depicted evoked nostalgia for a simpler time, before the war. Today, Hummel Manufaktur churns out about 20,000 figurines a year, which start in price at €100 (about $120). But figurines made in the 1930s and 1940s are worth a lot more. The active community of Hummel collectors might pay as much as $1,000 for an early model. (So you might want to check Grandma's mantel to see if she's got one of those.)

The cute little kids depicted evoked nostalgia for a simpler time, before the war.

* * *

WHAT A BABE

In 1914, teenage baseball prospect George Herman Ruth signed his first professional contract, with the then minor-league Baltimore Orioles. Ruth was 19, and at the time, Maryland state law held that the age of legal adulthood was 21. Ruth would need an adult to co-sign his contract, and since he was raised in an orphanage, Orioles owner Jack Dunn became the ballplayer's legal guardian. Teammates took to calling Ruth "Dunn's new babe" as a joke and, over time, the nickname was shortened to "Babe."

ON LANGUAGE

A few words about a few words.

WHAT ABOUT BLURPLE? September 1 is "National No Rhyme (Nor Reason) Day," which is exactly what it sounds like. How does one observe this holiday? According to *NationalDayCalendar.com*, on the first day of the month, "Make a list of words that you believe cannot be rhymed, and check if you are correct. Use #NoRhymeNorReasonDay to post on social media." The two most famous, of course, are "orange" and "purple." Here are a few more: "chimney," "woman," "chaos," "circle," "bulb," "eighths," and "month."

USE DISCRETION, NOT DISCRETENESS: Why do "discreet" and "discrete" have related but different definitions? Both words came from the Latin *discrētus*, which means "distinct, separate," but they took distinct, separate paths to English. "Discrete," the lesser used of the two, still means "a separate, distinct part of a whole," like this page is a discrete part of this book. "Discreet" (it means "careful" or "unobtrusive") comes to English via the French *discret*, which altered the Latin meaning to "discerning, wise"—as in, one who is discerning is also careful not to draw undue attention.

THREE WORDS THAT CHANGED MEANING: To *broadcast* once meant to sow seeds in a sweeping motion. To *dribble* once meant to shoot an arrow short or wide of its target. *Infant* once meant "unable to speak" and referred to a mute child of any age.

THINGS KIDS SAY: Are you an old fuddy-duddy who cringes at the sound of a youthful slang term? According to British linguist Tony Thorne, young people's use of their own slang "may signal a high level of intelligence" because "people who use language in a complex way need to have a heightened awareness of language, and how it works." (Now tell those little geniuses to get off your lawn.)

THESAURUSES FOR ALL! It's interesting, fascinating, captivating, absorbing, enchanting, beguiling, bewitching, enthralling, enrapturing, entrancing, and spellbinding. What is? The fact that English has more synonyms than any other language in the world—which also isn't surprising considering it is made up of words borrowed from so many other cultures. (Interestingly, one of the rare nouns in the English language that has no synonyms is..."synonym.")

HANGERS-ON: Some words can't stand on their own. For example, "nines" and "grabs" exist only in the idioms "to the *nines*" and "up for *grabs*." These are called *fossil words*—their original meaning is obsolete, but they've managed to hang on as a relic in an idiom or phrase. Other phrases with fossil words: "*beck* and call," "*eke* out," "the whole *shebang*," and "good *riddance*."

The oldest boomerang on record, made 23,000 years ago from a mammoth tusk, was discovered in a cave in Poland.

LUCKY FINDS

Ever find something valuable? It's one of the best feelings in the world. Here's another installment of one of our favorite Bathroom Reader topics.

JUST ANOTHER DAY AT WORK

The Find: Rare pieces of tanzanite

Where They Were Found: Tanzania

Story: What with the COVID-19 pandemic and global social unrest, a lot of people didn't have a great 2020. Not Tanzanian miner Saniniu Lazier. The self-employed digger finds precious gems and sells them to the government of Tanzania, which happens to be the only place in the world where the rare gemstone tanzanite can be found. It's so rare that geologists think the natural supply of it may be completely tapped out within 20 years. Maybe, but if so, Lazier just discovered the mother lode. In June 2020, he found two massive chunks of tanzanite, one weighing 20.2 pounds and the other 12.7 pounds. Total value: $3.4 million. After his find, Lazier told reporters that he wanted to use the money to throw a party for his 30 children and also build a school in his village. A couple of months later, he added "build a hospital" to his to-do list...because he'd found *another* massive piece of tanzanite. This one came in at 14 pounds, with a value of about $2 million.

ROCK ON

The Find: A big diamond

Where It Was Found: A state park

Story: Crater of Diamonds State Park in Arkansas is a tourist attraction with an alluring hook. Whatever shiny rocks visitors find, they can keep—even precious gems. Since the first diamonds were discovered at the site in 1906, more than 75,000 of those particularly attractive gemstones have been uncovered. Kevin Kinard, who lives about two hours from the Crater of Diamonds, has been visiting the park regularly for decades. Ever since he went there on a second-grade field trip, he's been going back, hoping to strike it rich. On Labor Day 2020, the 33-year-old traveled to the park and gathered up everything that looked interesting. "Anything that looked like a crystal, I picked it up and put it in my bag," he told reporters. Then he found a marble-sized crystal. "It looked interesting and shiny. I just thought it might've been glass," he said. It wasn't. At the end of the day, Kinard took it to the park's Diamond Discovery Center, where he learned that his "marble" was the real deal—a diamond. Not only that, it weighed 9.07 carats, making it the second-biggest diamond ever discovered at Crater of Diamonds.

A QUEEN'S RANSOM

The Find: A cache of special coins

Where They Were Found: A crumbling shack

Story: In 2019, an elderly, former London maintenance worker passed away, leaving his family to sift through the contents of his home, a waterlogged, rat-infested shack in the Gloucestershire countryside. The man was a hoarder, but the family knew he had a coin collection, so they invited auctioneer and coin expert John Rolfe to investigate the house. One rainy day, Rolfe drove several hours to the tiny house and started rummaging around, using only the flashlight on his phone...which caught a glimmer of gold. And then lots more. "It was mind-blowing. I felt like a pirate in a grotto," Rolfe told reporters. He found coins in drawers, in cupboards, under furniture, and even in a sugar bowl on a table. Unlike the rest of the trash-filled house, almost all the coins were in impeccable condition and sealed in plastic casings. The deceased seemed to favor commemorative coins, including a set of gold pieces issued for the Queen's Jubilee in 2002. After he'd collected every coin he could find, Rolfe auctioned them off in February 2020. Total haul: £80,000 ($109,000). Among the most valuable items were the jubilee set, which fetched £5,000 ($6,750), and a gold set marking the 150th anniversary of the death of the Duke of Wellington, which netted £3,400 ($4,650).

THERE'S GOLD IN THEM THERE YARDS

The Find: Some old coins

Where They Were Found: Under a tree

Story: In 2013, a middle-aged couple from northern California (no other details were released to the media) were taking their dog for a walk one day on their few acres of rural property, as they'd done many times before, when they noticed a rusty old can sticking out of the ground near a large, old tree. They did a little digging and found literal buried treasure—six canisters containing a total of 1,427 coins, all dating from 1847 to 1894. They took the coins to the nearest expert appraiser, the Professional Coin Grading Service in Santa Ana, California, which determined that all of the coins were uncirculated and were in mint or perfect condition. Total face value of the coins: a whopping $27,000. But considering how old, rare, and well-preserved they were, they were worth considerably more than that—somewhere in the neighborhood of $10 million. "I don't like to say 'once-in-a-lifetime' for anything, but you don't get an opportunity to handle this kind of material, a treasure like this, ever," the couple's representative, numismatist Don Kagin said. "It's like they found the pot of gold at the end of the rainbow."

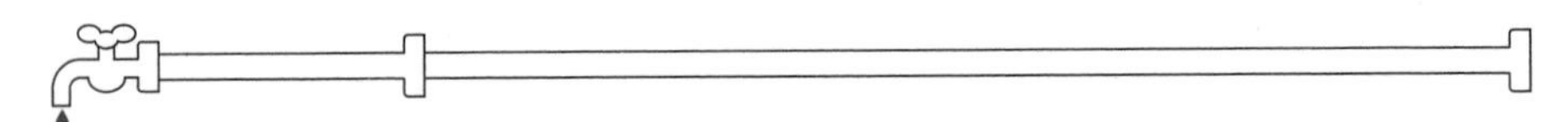

The world's biggest employer of musicians: the U.S. Army.

ENTER THE GIF

Sometimes, when commenting on a social media post, mere words will not suffice. Neither will an emoji. No, to truly convey how utterly ridiculous that post was, you need to search the animated GIFs menu for...for...there it is: "Picard Facepalm." Here's the loopy history of a little file format that made a big impact.

SMALLER IS BETTER

In 1987, the World Wide Web was still a few years away. Steve Wilhite was a developer at CompuServe, a pre-email computer service provider that allowed users to share files. It was agonizingly slow. Wilhite, whose specialty was image compression, was working on a faster way to load a color weather map when, he says, "I saw the format I wanted in my head, and then I started programming." When he was done, he'd invented a new image file format (like JPG and PNG) that reduced the file's size with minimal data loss. Wilhite named his invention Graphics Interchange Format, or GIF for short. His first GIF was a photo of a plane...but that was just a still image.

ON THE MOVE

A few years later, three computer scientists—Abraham Lempel, Jacob Ziv, and Terry Welch—created an algorithm that allowed programmers to create short animation and video clips by converting each frame to a GIF image. It supported only 256 colors and had no sound, but it took up a fraction of the space of a standard video file. The GIF might have been nothing more than a digital footnote had the ability to create animated GIFs not been included on an early internet browser called Netscape Navigator (which later became Firefox). Netscape came standard with Windows 95, which sold 40 million copies in its first year. Because GIFs run on an infinite loop, early website designers used them to create text and graphics that pulsate and change colors and do other garish things. (One of the worst GIF offenders: the Bathroom Reader's first website.)

But in 1999, following a prolonged copyright dispute that resulted in tech companies and GIF patent holders charging royalties, designers revolted (November 5, 1999, was "Burn All GIFs Day"). They abandoned the GIF in favor of more

DID YOU KNOW?

According to the search engine Giphy, the most-used GIFs of 2020 included "Billie Eilish at the BRIT Awards," "Happy Dance" (Elmo from *Sesame Street*), and "Dumpster Fire" (a cartoon dumpster fire). The #1 GIF of 2020: "Thank You," a cartoon doggy wearing a nurse's hat, wagging his tail, captioned: "Grateful for all the selfless humans on the frontlines helping keep everyone safe." It got more than 1 billion views.

How are baby eels made? No one knows—no human has ever seen eels reproduce.

sophisticated programs like Flash and JavaScript, and better image formats like JPG and PNG (which for a time people called "PING," short for "PNG Is No GIF!"). Once again, the GIF nearly became a digital footnote until...

THE DANCING BABY

One of the first—and creepiest—internet memes was the "Dancing Baby," a 3-D rendered animation of a diapered infant doing the cha-cha. Created in 1996 as a demonstration of a sophisticated animation program, the dancing baby didn't go viral until a year later when a Web developer used it as a demonstration of how to compress a large video file into a compressed GIF format.

So even though the GIF had fallen out of favor with website builders, the dancing baby helped launch a generation of short, looping videos that have inhabited the internet ever since. Few web users had the skills or the computing space to handle Flash, so the GIF was able to hang on as an easy way to create engaging content, especially since the program was ruled fair use. In 2013, a searchable database called GIPHY debuted; in 2020, it was purchased by Facebook for $400 million. Today, "reaction GIFs"—like the one of Homer Simpson slowly backing into a hedge—are as ubiquitous as hashtags and emojis. (And they're a lot more fun in comment threads.)

IS IT PRONOUNCED "GIF" OF "JIF"?

The matter could have been laid to rest years ago, except for GIF inventor Steve Wilhite. He won a Lifetime Achievement Award at the 2013 Webby Awards for his contribution to computing...but not for his contribution to linguistics. His standard argument: "The *Oxford English Dictionary* accepts both pronunciations. They are wrong. It is a soft 'G,' pronounced 'jif.' Like the peanut butter. End of story." Except that Wilhite is in the minority. Most people follow the line of thinking that says that if the first word of "GIF" is "Graphics," then GIF must begin with a hard "G."

* * *

THE CELEBRITY COLOR GAME

Jack **Black** + Betty **White** = Macy **Gray**

Vida **Blue** + Jason **Orange** = Judge Joe **Brown**

The **Yellow** Kid + DJ **Orange** Julius = **Amber** Tamblyn

Seth **Green** + James **Brown** = **Olive** Oyl

Jack **White** + Alton **Brown** = Amy **Tan**

Blue Öyster Cult + **Red** Hot Chili Peppers = Deep **Purple**

Simply **Red** + **White**snake = **Pink** Floyd

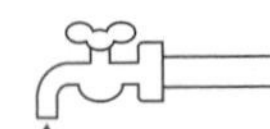

Maker city: 70 percent of all patents ever awarded in the UK have gone to inventors living in and around the city of Birmingham.

MILLION-DOLLAR GUITARS

Both electric and acoustic guitars can be expensive, costing from a couple hundred to a few thousand dollars. And the price tag goes up considerably if the instrument was played by a famous musician. Here are some of the most expensive guitars ever sold.

THE BLACK STRAT

As lead guitarist of Pink Floyd in the 1970s, David Gilmour almost always played a 1969 Fender Stratocaster with a black body, appropriately nicknamed "the Black Strat." It can be heard on Pink Floyd's landmark, best-selling albums, including *Animals, The Dark Side of the Moon, Wish You Were Here,* and *The Wall.* Gilmour didn't use it much after the 1980s, and a couple of decades later, he was ready to unload it. Gilmour, who reunited with Pink Floyd for one night only at 2005's Live 8 event for climate change awareness, got deeply involved with environmental charities, and in 2019 he decided to sell it off with the proceeds going to ClientEarth, a charity that promotes legal action to combat climate change. "I can let go of it," Gilmour told reporters before the sale. "Fender have made replica ones that they sell, and I have two or three of those that are absolutely perfect." When Christie's auction house sold the guitar, the winning bid came from Jim Irsay, a Pink Floyd superfan and owner of the NFL's Indianapolis Colts. Irsay paid $3.975 million for the Black Strat, along with $175,000 on the Pink Floyd-branded case Gilmour carried the instrument around in for a decade, plus a 1969 Martin D-35 acoustic guitar used on the 1975 song "Wish You Were Here."

KURT COBAIN'S ACOUSTIC

As the front man of Nirvana, Kurt Cobain didn't play a lot of acoustic guitars. His band's sound was loud, and reliant on volume and distortion, and better served by electric guitars, which Cobain routinely smashed or destroyed during performances. When Nirvana agreed to play on acoustic instruments on MTV's *Unplugged* in November 1993, it was a major departure, and one that produced the hit album *MTV Unplugged in New York.* For the TV show taping (one of Cobain's final performances before his death by suicide in April 1994), he used a 1959 Martin D-18E. The guitar was already a gem before Cobain played it—the C. F. Martin company made only 302 of the D-18E in the late 1950s and early 1960s, and Cobain's was the seventh one completed. In June 2020, Julien's Auctions in Beverly Hills, California, sold off the guitar, with opening bids starting at $1 million. When the gavel went down, the instrument had been sold to Peter Freedman, founder of a microphone manufacturing company, for $6 million—the most ever paid for a guitar at an auction.

Beeturia is a harmless condition where eating beets turns a person's urine pink or red. About 14% of people are susceptible.

THE STUDIO GUITAR

In the mid-1960s, a Decatur, Alabama, musician named Tommy Compton saw an ad in a newspaper offering a 1957 Les Gibson Goldtop guitar and amplifier for $250. In 1968, Duane Allman, at the time a studio musician and member of a band called Hourglass, came to town and so admired Compton's Goldtop that he asked if he could borrow it. Compton let him...and Allman never gave it back. (Although when Compton's father threatened to have Allman arrested, he sent the family a Wurlitzer electric piano and the parties called it even.) It's that instrument, nicknamed "the Studio Guitar," that Allman used on the first two Allman Brothers Band albums (including the songs "Midnight Rider" and "Whipping Post") and when he played on the Derek and the Dominos recording sessions that produced "Layla." At a show in Daytona, Florida, in 1970, Allman traded the Goldtop to Rick Stine, guitarist of a local band called Stone Balloon that opened for the Allman Brothers, for a 1959 cherry sunburst Les Paul (plus $200 and an amplifier). The Studio Guitar changed hands a few more times, ultimately coming to reside at the Allman Brothers Band Museum in Macon, Georgia, where it was occasionally loaned out to top-tier musicians, such as Billy Gibbons of ZZ Top and Kirk Hammett of Metallica. In 2019, the online classic rock memorabilia auction site Gotta Have Rock and Roll sold the Goldtop to a party who wished to retain their privacy. Price: $1.25 million.

KEITH RICHARDS'S LES PAUL

In 1961, John Bowen, guitarist for a band called the Kinsmen, purchased a 1959 Les Paul Standard (sunburst) electric guitar at Farmers Music Store in Luton, England, just outside of London. A year later, Bowen traded it to another music store, Selmer's (for a Gretsch Country Gentleman). That's where Keith Richards, who was playing around town with his new band, the Rolling Stones, picked it up. That instrument became the definitive guitar for the definitive guitarist of the British Invasion, and Richards played it on the Rolling Stones' first tour of the United States in 1964, which included an appearance on *The Ed Sullivan Show.* Richards used the guitar in the Stones' recordings of hits like "Get Off of My Cloud," "The Last Time," "Let's Spend the Night Together," "Time Is on My Side," and "Satisfaction." Around 1966, Richards started playing a Les Paul Custom and loaned his Standard (also called the "Keith-Burst") to Eric Clapton, but in 1967 Richards sold it to Mick Taylor of John Mayall's Bluesbreakers...two years before Taylor joined the Rolling Stones. In 1971, the guitar disappeared—Taylor can't remember exactly, but thinks it might have been stolen after a gig at the Marquee Club in London, or from Keith's home in Nellcote, France, where the band was recording *Exile on Main Street.* At any rate, Cosmo Verrico of the glam rock band Heavy Metal Kids somehow acquired it, and in 1974 sold it to Whitesnake guitarist Bernie Marsden, who sold it a week later to Mike Jopp of the

Weird math trick: Percentages are reversible. 25% of 16 is 4; 16% of 25 is also 4.

band Affinity. Jopp kept it until 2003, then sold it to a private collector who in turn auctioned it off at Christie's in New York in 2004. And *that* owner sold it to another private collector for around $1 million.

REACH OUT TO ASIA

More than 230,000 people died in the December 26, 2004, Indian Ocean earthquake and tsunami. Recovery and rebuilding efforts continued well into 2006, which is when a one-of-a-kind electric guitar was auctioned off to raise money for relief efforts. A standard-issue, white Fender Stratocaster, the instrument hadn't been owned by any notable guitarists, nor was it used on any classic songs—but it had been autographed by just about every major classic rock guitarist (and then some) alive at the time. The guitar bore the signatures of Keith Richards, Brian May (Queen), Eric Clapton, David Gilmour, Jimmy Page, Jeff Beck, Ray Davies (The Kinks), Mark Knopfler, Pete Townshend, Ronnie Wood (Rolling Stones), Tony Iommi (Black Sabbath), Ritchie Blackmore (Deep Purple), Mick Jagger, Sting, and Paul McCartney. In an auction at the Ritz-Carlton Hotel in Doha, Qatar, Her Highness Sheihka Al-Mayassa bint Hamad bin Khalifa Al-Thani (part of Qatar's ruling family) paid $2.8 million for it.

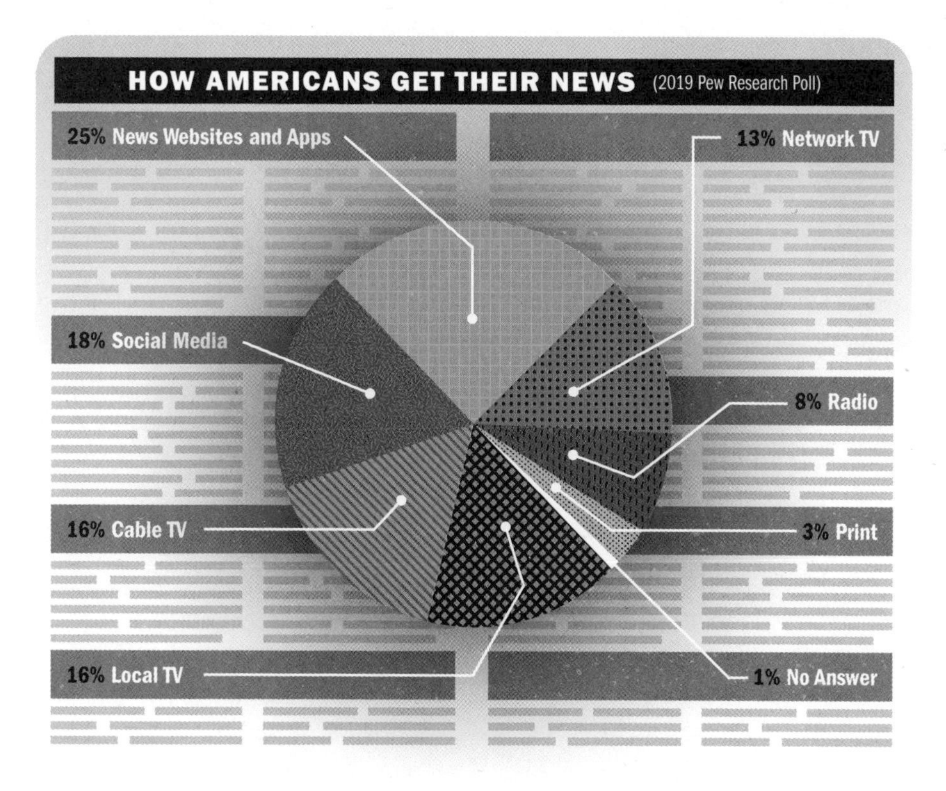

TELEPHONE POLE FACTS

The humble telephone pole—as you've never known it before.

• There are about 180 million telephone poles (aka power poles or utility poles) in the United States.

• Every telephone pole has a unique identifying number located on the "pole tag" near the bottom of the pole. The tags are most commonly made of aluminum or stainless steel.

• Height of telephone poles in residential neighborhoods: 30–60 feet. Along highways: 60–120 feet. Depth of poles in the ground: about 6 feet. Poles are typically about 125 feet apart in towns and cities, and up to 300 feet apart in rural regions.

• Most telephone poles are made from wood. The favored lumber type is coastal Douglas fir, a tall, straight-growing, knot-free evergreen species native to western North America. Another favorite choice: southern yellow pine, found across the southeastern United States.

• The life span of a wooden telephone pole is 25 to 50 years, depending on a number of factors, especially climate and the prevalence of woodpeckers in any given pole's location. (Really.)

• Most telephone poles are joint-use poles, meaning they are used for multiple services—including electrical power, telephone, and cable TV transmissions.

• Typical wire configuration of a joint-use pole: The three topmost wires—usually running across a horizontal crossarm at the very top of a pole—are the primary wires, or primary conductors. They carry primary electric power from electrical substations, and are the wires that carry the most powerful current—which is why they're at the top of the pole.

• Below the primary wires are the secondary wires—the wires that carry power meant for homes and businesses. The lowest wires on a pole are communication cables: wires that carry telephone and cable TV services. (A single neutral or static wire—part of a pole's electrical safety system—can be found either above the primary wires or between the primary and secondary wires.)

• Don't forget the transformers—the gray, barrel-shaped devices you see attached to some telephone poles, usually located between the primary and secondary wires, with wires running to and from each one. The transformer's job: to reduce the voltage coming from the primary lines to the secondary lines, to a level that is usable and safe for homes and businesses.

• All poles also have what is known as a communication worker safety zone: a wire-free area of at least 40 inches between the secondary wires and the communication cables, which allows technicians to do work away from powerful electrical wires.

HAMBS ACROSS AMERICA

How do you like your burger? With cheese or without? Ketchup? Mayo? Different regions of the United States have different ways of cooking, topping, and serving the humble hamburger.

BREADED HAMBURGER

During the Great Depression, lunch counters stretched their meat dollar by adding bread to hamburger patties. Ever since then, Snappy Lunch in Mount Airy, North Carolina (the inspiration for Mayberry in *The Andy Griffith Show*), has kept the breaded burger alive. Locals call it a breaded hamburger, a no-burger, or an old-fashioned, but the Snappy Lunch menu lists the sandwich—made from crumbled biscuits, bread crumbs, and beef, in that order—as just "hamburger." (An all-meat burger at Snappy Lunch is called a "burger with meat.") The hamburger, which resembles a crab cake, is served topped with coleslaw, mustard, onion, tomato, and chili sauce.

OKLAHOMA ONION BURGER

In Oklahoma, Depression-era cooks and diners made the meat go further with the help of onions—lots and lots of onions. The onion burger is served in restaurants all across the state—from old-timers such as Sid's Diner in El Reno and the Hamburger Inn in Ardmore, to newcomers like Tucker's Onion Burgers in Oklahoma City. Here's how it's made: First, a large pile of very thinly sliced white onions is put on the grill with a small portion of chopped beef smashed into it with the back of a spatula (it's also known as a Smash Burger). The onions and meat mix together, grilling the burger and imparting the flavor of the onions, which get crispy and caramelized.

BUTTER BURGER

Wisconsin is America's dairy capital, and Wisconsinites proudly consume a lot of butter. In the mid-20th century, dozens of Milwaukee restaurants offered the butter burger. Today, the last restaurant that sells this old-fashioned local treat is Solly's Grille. What's a butter burger? Exactly what it sounds like. It's a small cheeseburger on a bun that, upon being removed from the grill, is topped with about three tablespoons of butter. The butter then melts all over the burger (and all over the diner's hands).

The butter melts all over the burger (and all over the diner's hands).

STEAMED CHEESEBURGER

Only about half a dozen eateries in a 25-mile radius around Meriden, Connecticut, serve the "steamer," a burger first popularized in the 1950s by Ted's Restaurant, a lunch counter that once stayed open until 4:00 a.m. to cater to the area's factory

Packaged meat is treated with carbon monoxide to keep it looking red and "fresh."

workers. Ted's and its handful of competitors cook their burgers in custom-made metal steaming cabinets. Inside each cabinet are 20 small stainless-steel trays into which patties are placed to steam until they're warm and gray. Once the patty is cooked, it's put on a bun and served with a steamed slice of Vermont cheddar cheese poured on top.

THE JUCY LUCY

This burger is sold in bars and restaurants all over Minnesota's Twin Cities, but Matt's Bar in east Minneapolis stakes a claim as the creator. According to local lore, it started in 1954, when a customer asked the cook to make him something different, and the cook (his name was Matt) grilled two burger patties and crimped them together on the ends with a slice of American cheese folded and hidden on the inside. The heat from the burgers melted the cheese and turned it into hot goo. When he bit into it, the patron reportedly remarked, "Now that's a juicy Lucy!" (It's unclear why the preferred spelling went from "juicy" to "jucy.")

GUBERBURGER

The Wheel Inn drive-in restaurant created a sandwich not seen on many menus outside of its point of origin in Sedalia, Missouri. Peanuts are sometimes called "goobers," and from that comes the name Guberburger—the Wheel Inn's burger consisted of a salted patty on a toasted bun, topped with lettuce, tomato, mayonnaise, and creamy peanut butter. (Yes, peanut butter.) Unfortunately, the Wheel Inn closed in 2013, so if you really want to taste a Guberburger, you'll have to make one at home.

DEEP-FRIED BURGER

Deep-frying is a cooking method strongly associated with the American South. In 1912, Dyer's Burgers in Memphis started a burger tradition that embraced that Southern tradition: They deep-fry beef hamburgers...in beef fat. They pound a quarter-pound patty until it's paper-thin and about eight inches wide, then place it into a skillet full of beef tallow accumulated from the thousands of other burgers cooked over the years. (They strain it daily.) It takes only about a minute to fry. For cheeseburgers, the cheese is prepared separately, but it's also deep-fried in a skillet full of grease.

LOOSEMEATS

An Iowa loosemeats sandwich consists of steamed, salted, crumbled ground beef cooked in an iron skillet, then heaped onto a hamburger bun, and "doped" with mustard and pickle. It's ground beef on a bun, but it's not in the form of a patty, so Iowans don't consider it a hamburger—it's a loosemeats sandwich, also referred to as a "tavern," or a Maid-Rite, after the small Midwestern chain that serves up thousands of them every day.

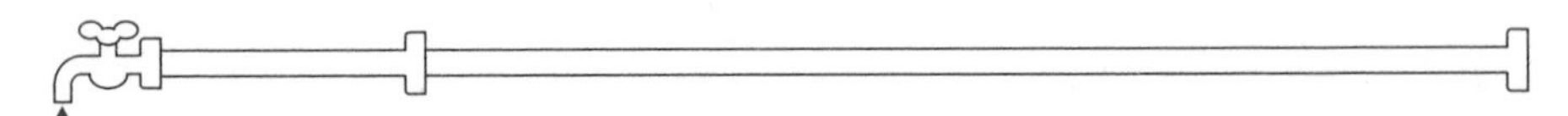

THE KID IS IN THE MAIL

Just because you're not supposed *to send human beings in the mail doesn't mean people* didn't, *at least not in the "good old days."*

SPECIAL DELIVERY

On January 1, 1913, the U.S. Post Office launched the Parcel Post Service, which allowed customers to mail parcels weighing up to 11 pounds. Before that, if you wanted to send something heavier than 4 pounds, you had to hire a private delivery company to do it. And if you lived in a small town or some other place where there weren't any such companies, you either delivered the parcel yourself...or you were out of luck.

The Parcel Post Service proved to be so popular that the maximum weight limit was raised to 50 pounds, greatly increasing the variety of items that could be sent in the mail. Including...kids? There wasn't anything in the postal regulations that said you *could,* but then again, there wasn't anything in the regulations that said you *couldn't.* Within weeks of the service being introduced, some parents gave it a try.

SIMPLER TIMES

Mailing a kid in those days wasn't considered nearly as impersonal or dangerous as it might be today. In those days more people lived in small towns, had done so their entire lives, and knew everyone else in town, including the mail carrier. And they lived close to other relatives. In such a place and time, if someone wanted their child to visit a relative who lived nearby, it wouldn't be unheard of to ask a trusted mail carrier to accompany the child if no one else was available. In the rare cases in which a child actually was "mailed" to another destination, this is often what happened: the mail carrier picked up the child—with the proper postage attached—at one address on their mail route, and either dropped them off at another address on the same route, or took them to the post office, where they were either picked up by a family member or handed off to another mail carrier, who saw them to their final destination.

In the early 20th century, a lot of mail traveled by train in special railway mail cars attached to passenger trains. Train tickets weren't cheap, and the temptation to have children declared as "freight mail" so that they could be sent by cheaper postage rates instead of by paying for a passenger ticket, was considerable. There were instances when parents did manage to pull this off. The child rode in the mail car with the postal employees, who then saw them to the local post office when they arrived at their destination.

RETURN TO SENDER

Not surprisingly, the U.S. Post Office didn't much care for the practice, and in June 1920, the assistant postmaster in charge of the Parcel Post Service specifically forbade

it on the grounds that children "did not come within the classification of harmless live animals which do not require food or water while in transit." The change in regulations didn't stop the practice entirely, but by the late 1920s, the golden age of sending kids through the mail was over.

Here are some of the most famous cases:

James Beagle (Glen Este, Ohio). A few weeks after the Parcel Post Service began operations in 1913, Jesse and Mathilda Beagle mailed their eight-month-old son to his grandmother's house about a mile away in Batavia. Both homes were on the route of mail carrier Vernon O. Lytle. Jesse weighed in at 10¾ pounds, just under the 11-pound limit for parcels mailed by Parcel Post. His parents paid 15¢ in postage and insured the boy for $50.

Charlotte May Pierstorff (Grangeville, Idaho). On February 9, 1914, four-year-old Charlotte was mailed from her parents' home to her grandparents' home 73 miles away. Charlotte traveled by train; she rode in the mail car with her mother's cousin, a postal clerk who worked on the train.

Edna Neff (Pensacola, Florida). Neff, who was six years old, may hold the record for the longest trip of a child sent through the mail. On March 27, 1915, she climbed aboard a mail train in Pensacola and was transported some 720 miles to the post office in Christiansburg, Virginia, where her father lived. She weighed just under 50 pounds. Cost of postage: 15¢.

Maude Smith (Jackson, Kentucky). On August 31, 1915, three-year-old Maude was mailed from Caney, Kentucky, to her home in Jackson, 25 miles away. The girl traveled by mail train; a shipping tag with 33¢ in postage was sewed to her pink dress. Printed on the tag were the words "To Mrs. Celina Smith, care of Jim Haddix, Jackson, Ky., from R.K. Madden, Caney, Ky." Aboard the train, the postal clerk, J. T. Sebastian, attached his own note to the child's dress. It read "Baby received 8:15 by postmaster in person. I doubt the legality of the sending, but it was put on the train and I must deliver and report."

Russell Nickerson (Pontiac, Michigan). Nickerson, who was four years old in 1927, was perhaps the luckiest kid to be sent through the mail, because he was sent by *air mail*, at a time when few people had ever traveled by airplane. Dressed in a sailor suit with a mail tag and postage attached, he climbed aboard the mail plane in Pontiac and, sitting in a passenger seat next to the pilot, he was delivered to Detroit following an 18-minute flight.

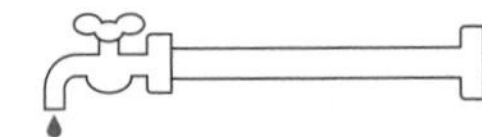

Number of Leonardo da Vinci paintings that have survived to the present day: 15.

THE DIFFERENCE BETWEEN...

And now Uncle John helps you navigate life's subtle nuances. For example, do you know the difference between...

...SOUP AND STEW? Soup is primarily liquid. It consists of a broth combined with other ingredients, such as meat and vegetables, or it can be a liquefied blend of all of its parts. Stew is much more about the meats and vegetables—large chunks with just enough water to submerge the ingredients. That's what "stewing" is—cooking solid ingredients in liquid that, over time, heats up in a pot for long enough to cook them in their own gravy.

...HERBS AND SPICES? Both enhance the taste of food and both come from plants—the difference lies in the part of the plant from which the flavoring agent originates. Herbs are the leaves of a plant, so rosemary, sage, mint, thyme, cilantro, and parsley would fall into this category. Spices are derived from any other edible parts of a plant, such as roots, bark, buds, or seeds. Cinnamon, for example, is a spice because it's made from bark. Other spices include cloves (dried flower buds), black pepper (seeds), and ginger (root).

...A FRIAR AND A MONK? Both terms refer to a man who has joined a religious order affiliated with the Roman Catholic Church and who has taken vows of poverty, chastity, and obedience. The difference is in where they live and how they move about the world. The word "monk" comes the Greek word *mono*, meaning "alone," which fits because monks live in isolation from the rest of the world, left alone to pray in their monasteries. Friars (from the French *frère*, meaning "brother") travel throughout their community, proselytizing and soliciting donations for the church and for charitable causes.

...DINNER AND SUPPER? Today, the terms are used interchangeably to describe a big meal that comes at the end of the day. Historically, though, they meant different things. Dinner described the largest meal of the day, regardless of when it was served—it could come first thing in the day, midday, or in the evening. Supper was a smaller meal that came only at night.

...PROFANITY, VULGARITY, AND OBSCENITY? Historically and grammatically speaking, profanity refers to anything that offends religious sensibilities, such as blasphemy or affronts to God. Obscenity pertains to the expression of sexual content in a way deemed indecent or offensive, while vulgarity is just coarse language, or swear words.

...A HORSE AND A PONY? A pony is not a baby horse—it's a different, smaller animal. A horse's height is measured in hands; one hand equals four inches. An equine that is at least 14 hands and 2 inches tall at its withers (shoulder blades) is a horse. Anything less than that, and it's a pony.

DUSTED!

When food is produced or stored in enormous quantities, things can quickly go wrong in a very big *way, thanks to something very* tiny: *dust.*

LARGER THAN LIFE: In 1874, a businessman, politician, and former Civil War general named Cadwallader C. Washburn built what was then the world's largest flour mill on the bank of the Mississippi River in Minneapolis, Minnesota. The Washburn "A" Mill, as it was called, was a marvel of 19th-century technology. In an era before electricity was available, the mill relied on waterpower provided by the Mississippi. Part of the river was diverted into a channel that ran beneath the mill and into waterwheels that turned the giant millstones and ground the wheat into flour. The factory was so large that it could grind enough wheat to fill dozens of railcars each day—about as fast as the railroads could deliver it.

Because powerful blasts of air were used to separate an undesirable part of the grain called the *middlings* from the rest of the flour, the air inside the mill was full of flour dust. The dust made the air difficult to breathe, but that wasn't the only danger: under the right conditions, clouds of flour dust can be more explosive than gunpowder.

BIG BANG THEORY: The reason something as seemingly innocuous as ordinary flour is potentially so explosive is that, like a leaf or a sheet of paper, flour particles have a lot of surface area relative to their volume. Why this matters: when any flammable material burns, it burns only on the surface, because only the surface is in contact with oxygen in the air that's needed for combustion to take place. Flour particles have so much surface area that if they come in contact with a spark or flame, a great deal of the particle will burn all at once. If airborne flour particles are present in just the right concentration, a flame can spread rapidly from one particle to another. The result can be catastrophic.

How catastrophic? Both the United States and Russia have developed what are called *thermobaric,* or "heat pressure," bombs that rely on the same physical principle: the bombs disperse fuel particles into the air to create a giant cloud of combustible material, then ignite the fuel. The American bomb is called the Massive Ordnance Air Blast, or MOAB, and is nicknamed the "Mother of All Bombs." It and its Russian equivalent, the four-times-as-large "Father of All Bombs," are the most powerful non-nuclear weapons ever made.

DUST TO ASHES: If Cadwallader Washburn didn't appreciate just how dangerous it was to have great clouds of flour dust inside his giant mill, he got quite an education

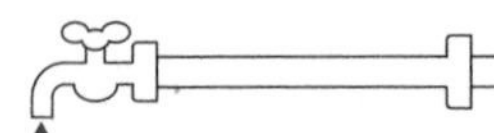

on the evening of May 2, 1878. About an hour after mill workers left for the day and a night-shift skeleton crew arrived, three massive explosions rocked the mill in rapid succession, demolishing the seven-story building and killing all 14 workers inside. The explosions—which were heard 10 miles away—and the fires that they ignited destroyed five other nearby mills, killing another four people. The cause of the explosions was determined to be airborne flour dust that had somehow come into contact with an ignition source, either an open flame or sparks created by two millstones scraping against each other.

Whatever else his faults, Cadwallader Washburn was no quitter. He quickly resolved to rebuild his flour mill bigger and better than before...and he succeeded on both counts: Two years later a larger, safer flour mill opened on the same site. The new mill could grind more than 100 boxcars of wheat into flour daily, and it boasted state-of-the-art dust collectors and ventilation systems to keep flour dust out of the air. The giant mill remained in operation for 85 years, finally closing in 1965. By then Washburn's company had merged with others to form General Mills, makers of Cheerios, Gold Medal Flour, and more than 90 other consumer food brands.

MORE DUST BUSTERS

- **The Douglas Starch Works (Cedar Rapids, Iowa).** In its day, it was the world's largest cornstarch factory, consisting of 36 buildings crowded onto a 10-acre site. Early in the evening of May 22, 1919, a cornstarch explosion leveled the plant, killing 43 people and injuring 30 more. The blast shattered windows all over downtown Cedar Rapids and damaged or destroyed more than 200 homes.
- **The Continental Grain Elevator (Westwego, Louisiana).** Two days before Christmas 1977, a grain dust explosion ripped through a 25-story grain elevator, destroying 48 of the 73 concrete grain silos at the site and crushing a two-story office building under falling debris. Thirty-six people were killed and another 20 were injured, making this the deadliest grain elevator explosion in modern history. Many of the victims were there on their day off, picking up their Christmas turkeys. The source of ignition was never officially determined.
- **The Imperial Sugar Refinery (Wentworth, Georgia).** In February 2008, a powerful explosion of sugar dust tore through an enclosed conveyor belt at the refinery. This initial blast lofted tons more sugar dust into the air, which then detonated in a series of massive secondary explosions that destroyed the sugar silos and other buildings at the site. Fourteen workers were killed; it took firefighters more than a week to extinguish all the burning sugar. A federal investigation into the disaster found that plant managers were aware of the hazard, but "did not promptly act to remove all significant accumulations of sugar and sugar dust" from the facility. The initial explosion is thought to have been sparked by an overheated bearing on the conveyor belt.

MOUTHING OFF

TWO KINDS

Which one are you?

"There are two kinds of people in the world—those who walk into a room and say, 'There you are!'—and those who say, 'Here I am!'"

—Abigail Van Buren

"The world is divided into two types of people: those who love to talk, and those who hate to listen."

—James Thorpe

"THERE ARE TWO KINDS OF PEOPLE, THOSE WHO FINISH WHAT THEY START AND SO ON."

—Robert Byrne

"There are two kinds of people: those with open minds and those with closed minds, and never the two shall meet."

—Bill Purdin

"There are two kinds of people in the world, those who believe there are two kinds of people in the world and those who don't."

—Robert Benchley

"There are two kinds of artists left: those who endorse Pepsi and those who simply won't."

—Annie Lennox

"MANKIND IS DIVIDED INTO TWO GREAT CLASSES: HOSTS AND GUESTS."

—Max Beerbohm

"There are two kinds of teachers: the kind that fill you with so much quail shot that you can't move, and the kind that just gives you a little prod behind and you jump to the skies."

—Robert Frost

"There are three kinds of men. The one that learns by reading. The few who learn by observation. The rest of them have to pee on the electric fence for themselves."

—Will Rogers

PLEONASMS

What's a pleonasm? A phrase that is unnecessarily redundant, making the same point twice. Examples: "true fact" (if it is a fact, it's already true) and "end result" (a result is, by definition, at the end). Get it? Here's a list of pleonasms. Consider it a free gift.

- First and foremost
- Warn in advance
- Evolve over time
- Revert back
- Lag behind
- Proceed ahead
- Continue on
- Chase after
- Kneel down
- Rise up
- Hoist up
- Uphill climb
- Overexaggerate
- Historic milestone
- Major breakthrough
- Few in number
- Sum total
- Tiny bit
- Cameo appearance
- Live studio audience
- Spliced together
- Added bonus
- Green in color
- Ultimate goal
- Safe haven
- 5:00 a.m. in the morning
- MSM media
- ATM machine
- PIN number
- LCD display
- UPC code
- d-CON Kills Bugs Dead
- Minestrone soup
- Polar opposites
- Foreign imports
- Overused cliché
- Prior experience
- Past history
- Future plans
- Palm of the hand
- Interact with each other
- Pair of twins
- Brief summary
- Self-confessed
- Indicted on charges
- Sworn affidavit
- Cash money
- Exact same
- Circle around
- Frozen ice
- Completely full
- Join together
- Close proximity
- Tuna fish
- Empty space
- Period of time
- Different kinds
- Close personal friend
- Pick and choose
- Basic fundamentals
- All-time record
- Reduce down
- From whence
- Manually by hand
- Might possibly
- Postpone until later
- Two equal halves
- Protest against
- Skipped over
- Temper tantrum
- Regular routine
- Passing fad

9/11 FRAUDSTERS

One of the odd quirks of human nature is that even in a tragedy as horrific as the 9/11 attacks in 2001, a few people, either because of greed or mental illness or both, will try to exploit the catastrophe for their own benefit.

SUGEIL MEJIA

Her Story: Just three days after the attack, when first responders at Ground Zero were still desperately searching through the rubble for anyone who might still be alive, a "nurse" dressed in surgical scrubs approached a police officer named Ian Sinclair at St. Vincent's Hospital in New York. The woman—Mejia—told him that her husband, a Port Authority police officer, was buried under the rubble at Ground Zero and was still alive. He had his cell phone with him and had called Mejia telling her he was trapped with five Port Authority officers and five NYPD officers beneath the North Tower. Officer Sinclair rushed Mejia to Ground Zero. On the way over, she continued to talk to her husband on the phone...or at least that's what she led Officer Sinclair to *believe* she was doing.

The Truth: Searchers at the site were energized by the news that 11 victims might still be alive, but hours later, Mejia's story fell apart during police questioning. She admitted "she was not a nurse, was not married to a police officer, did not know anyone trapped under the rubble, [and] had not received calls from anyone in the area, and her claims were based on her desire to be near Ground Zero," according to press reports. Her entire story was a lie; no survivors were found.

What Happened: According to her lawyer, Mejia claimed she wasn't in her right mind when she perpetrated the hoax—she said she'd lost a close friend in the terrorist attack, which made her act irrationally. Mejia was arrested that same day and was charged with reckless endangerment, obstructing fire operations, and filing false police reports. In January 2002, she pled guilty to the reckless endangerment charge and was sentenced to three years in prison.

RICARDO FRUTOS

His Story: In October 2001, Frutos, a middle school teacher from Utah, presented a birth certificate to the City of New York Department of Records that he claimed belonged to his brother "Hector." He used it to file for a death certificate for Hector, whom Frutos said had been in one of the World Trade Center towers on 9/11 and had died in the attack. Frutos also claimed that his niece and her husband had been killed. On the basis of these claims, he collected more than $47,000 from the American Red Cross.

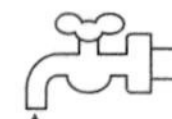

The term "jet black" comes from jet, a black gemstone that results when fossilized wood changes under extreme pressure.

The Truth: When Frutos was unable to provide any further documentation to prove that his brother really existed and had died on 9/11, the city probed deeper into his claims and discovered that Hector's birth certificate was, according to the New York District Attorney's Office, "an exact copy of the defendant's own birth certificate... with the name 'Hector' substituted for the defendant's own name." Frutos did have a brother named Alberto who went by the nickname Hector, but Frutos's ex-wife admitted to investigators that Alberto was "alive and living in Argentina." Frutos's claims about his niece and her husband were also proved false.

What Happened: In June 2002, Frutos pled guilty to third-degree larceny and was sentenced to three years in prison. Unlike many of the 15 other defendants who were charged with defrauding 9/11 charities out of more than $760,000, Frutos was not ordered to repay the stolen money, because, said a spokesperson for the District Attorney's Office, "he didn't have any assets to make that promise to pay anything back."

CYRIL KENDALL

His Story: Kendall, 61, claimed to be the father of 13 children, the youngest of whom was 29-year-old Wilfred, who was interviewing for a job on the 91st floor of the North Tower when American Airlines Flight 11 struck the building. On the basis of this claim, Kendall collected $119,000 from the Red Cross and another $40,000 from several other charities, including money to pay for the burial of his dead son.

Kendall really did have 12 other children, but not a 13th.

The Truth: Kendall really did have 12 other children, but not a 13th. Investigators determined that the photo of "Wilfred" that he provided to charities to collect the money was actually a photo of himself as a young man, and the birth certificate he presented was a forgery. Wilfred Kendall did not exist.

What Happened: In 2003, Kendall was convicted of grand larceny and fraud and sentenced to 20 years in jail. He was released from prison in 2011 and was deported back to his home country of Guyana in South America. At last report, he had not repaid any of the stolen money.

SCOTT SHIELDS

His Story: Shields claimed that he and his golden retriever, Bear, had been part of the search-and-rescue crew at Ground Zero, and that Bear had found more victims than any other search dog on the site. He achieved quite a bit of notoriety from these claims. He also told both the Red Cross and the Federal Emergency Management Agency that he lived near the World Trade Center before the attacks, and collected nearly $50,000 in rental assistance from them.

The Truth: Shields and Bear had indeed showed up at Ground Zero in the hours following the attacks, but they didn't get to stick around long: after it became clear that "Bear was not a trained rescue dog and might mislead emergency workers," the NYPD ordered both Shields and his dog to leave the scene. Shields had also lied when he said he lived near the World Trade Center at the time of the attacks. He actually lived with his sister in Greenwich, Connecticut.

What Happened: In March 2008, Shields pled guilty to conspiracy to defraud the United States, theft of government funds, and mail fraud. The charges could have landed him in prison for 35 years, but the judge sentenced him to just eight months. His sister, Patricia, was charged with being a co-conspirator and received the same sentence. The pair were also required to pay back the money they received from the Red Cross and FEMA for housing assistance.

TANIA HEAD

Her Story: If you were one of the people who took a VIP tour of the visitor center at Ground Zero between 2005 and 2007, there's a good chance the tour was led by Tania Head, president of the World Trade Center Survivors' Network support group and, she claimed, someone who had lived through the attacks. "I was there at the towers. I'm a survivor. I'm going to tell you about that," she would tell visitors as she led them around the center. Head claimed she was on the 78th floor of the South Tower when United Airlines Flight 175 flew into the building, which would have made her one of only 19 people at or above the point of impact to make it out of the building alive. She had a badly scarred arm that she said was injured on 9/11, and she claimed to have been engaged to one of the people who died in the North Tower.

The Truth: Head's story held up until 2007, when the *New York Times* attempted to verify various claims she'd made, and her entire story fell apart. A subsequent investigation by a Spanish newspaper found that Head was actually in Barcelona studying for her master's degree on 9/11 and did not visit the United States for the first time until 2003, two years after the terrorist attacks. In Barcelona, she'd told some classmates that her arm had been burned in a car crash; she told other people that the injury was from a horse-riding accident.

What Happened: Because Head had volunteered her time with the survivors' group and received no other money for her 9/11 activities, she was not charged with any crimes.

* * *

Random fact: The world's oldest tree species is *Ginkgo biloba*, which is native to China. Fossil evidence puts it at about 200 million years old.

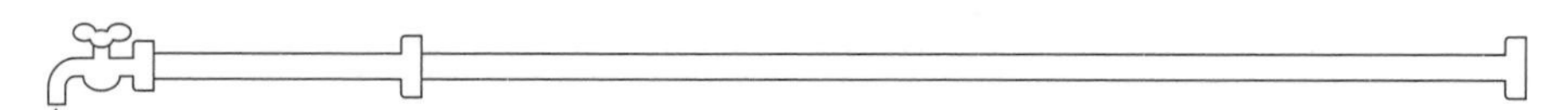

KNOW YOUR FANGS

Q: What did the vampire say when his girlfriend asked him what he wanted for his birthday?
A: Fang you very much! Now, let's learn all about fangs.

FANG BASICS

Simple definition: A fang is a long, pointy, and specialized tooth found on the jaws of many different kinds of animals. We've all seen them. When your cat or dog yawns, those prominent and pointy teeth that stand out from all the rest are the animals' fangs. (And you may even have had a personal experience with them—if you've ever been nipped by a cat or dog, what you felt on your skin were its fangs.) Which animals have them? Which don't? And how do those different animals use their fangs? Those are good questions, and—fangfully—we have the answers!

MAMMAL FANGS

Domestic cats and dogs are examples of carnivorous mammals, or mammals whose diet consists of the flesh of other animals, either exclusively or along with other foods. Other examples include minks, skunks, badgers, wolves, leopards, and bears, and some marine mammals, such as seals and sea lions. All of these animals have fangs—specialized versions of mammal canine teeth, not unlike human canines, except that on these animals, evolution has rendered them significantly longer and sharper than the teeth around them. There are always four—two protruding down from the upper jaw, and two up from the lower jaw—and they are always located at the front of the mouth. The carnivore's fangs are, quite simply, the tools used by these predators to catch, hold, and kill prey, and to help tear apart the flesh of their victim once it is dead. The fangs are also used, when necessary, for defense.

- Fangs are also found on some noncarnivorous mammals, such as gorillas and orangutans, which have a diet that is about 97 percent plant-based (the other 3 percent is mostly insects). These fangs are used primarily to intimidate enemies and rivals, such as when a gorilla opens its mouth and pulls back its lips to display its large and dangerous-looking fangs. And, as with carnivores, they're also used for defense, especially during mating battles.
- Fruit bats are another example of noncarnivorous fanged mammals. The diets of these unique creatures consist entirely of plant-based foods such as fruit, flowers, and nectar. Their fangs are used to open hard fruit husks, and to help these bats hold pieces of fruit in their mouths while in flight.

KILLER FANGSSS...

Probably the scariest fangs in the animal kingdom belong to venomous snakes. These fangs are highly specialized killing tools, essential components in the reptiles' venom

The Macy's red star logo was inspired by a tattoo the founder, R. H. Macy, got when he was a sailor.

delivery system. The fangs come in three varieties, corresponding to the three families of venomous snakes: the vipers, the elapids, and the colubrids.

- Vipers are found in the Americas, Africa, Eurasia, and South Asia, and include rattlesnakes, cottonmouths, and puff adders. They have *solenoglyphous* (pipe grooved) fangs, the most sophisticated in the snake kingdom. Solenoglyphous fangs are long, backward-curving, super-sharp, and hollow, and they are positioned near the front of the snake's mouth. Most importantly, these fangs are hinged, and therefore retractable: when not in use, they are folded into pockets in the snake's upper jaw.
- Each fang has a tiny slit opening located on the front side, very near the tip. That's where the venom comes out! (This is also true of elapid fangs.)
- When in use, a viper's fangs are pivoted down out of their pockets and into striking position just before the snake clamps down on its prey, creating a puncture that goes deep beneath the skin. Simultaneously, specialized muscles squeeze two venom glands located behind the snake's eyes, sending venom surging into its fangs, and out through their tiny slits. Once venom is delivered, a viper quickly lets go of its prey, retracts its fangs back into their pockets, and lets its deadly venom do its work, after which it tracks down its stricken victim and eats it.

KILLER FANGSSS, II

Elapids are venomous snakes found in the same regions as vipers, as well as in Australia (which has many deadly venomous snakes—but no vipers). They include cobras, taipans, and coral snakes, and they all have *proteroglyphous* (forward grooved) fangs. These fangs are not hinged—they are rigid, and always in striking position, and because they cannot be folded up and put away when not in use, they are considerably shorter than viper fangs.

- Like the vipers, elapid fangs are hollow, and connected to venom glands in the snake's skull. But because they're not as long as the fangs of vipers, and therefore cannot inject their venom as deeply as vipers do, most elapids tend to remain gripped to their prey after striking, grinding their fangs into their victims' flesh, and staying with the prospective meal until the venom has done its job.
- You've heard of spitting cobras? These snakes actually do "spit" their venom from their fangs. They use specialized muscles to powerfully squeeze their venom glands, forcing venom to squirt out of the slits on their fangs—as far as six feet. (Some vipers can also "spit" venom in this way.)

KILLER FANGSSS, III

The third kind of venomous snake fangs are known as *opisthoglyphous* (rearward grooved) fangs, and they are found on what are known as "rear-fanged" snakes, so named because their fangs are in the rear of their mouths, behind their other teeth.

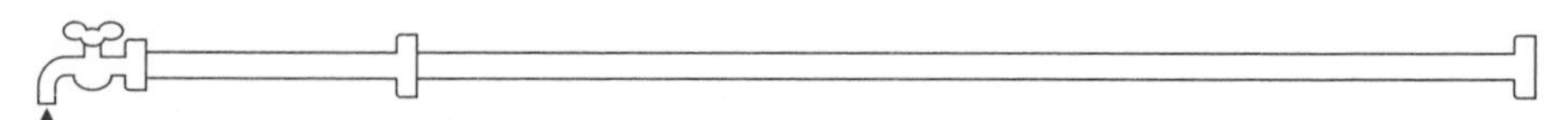

These primitive fangs are found in members of the loosely defined family of snakes known as colubrids, which includes boomslangs, king snakes, and even the common garter snakes found throughout North America. Unlike vipers and elapids, these snakes' relatively small fangs are not hollow. Instead, each fang has a narrow groove running along its length.

When it's ready for *envenomation* (injecting venom into its victim), a rear-fanged snake must chew on its prey until it is deep enough in the snake's mouth to make contact with the fangs, then emit venom from primitive venom sacs, which simply run down the grooves in its fangs and, hopefully, into whatever the snake is chewing on. Because of this, colubrids are generally not considered dangerous... except for a few species, notably the African boomslang, which has been known to cause human fatalities.

BITING FACTS

- All spiders have fangs, too. They're very hard and very sharp, and almost all of them can inject venom into prey—or you—via those fangs.
- Other mammals with enlarged canine teeth include hippos, walruses, wild boars, warthogs, and musk deer, although these specialized teeth are commonly referred to as tusks rather than fangs. (Bonus fact: The tusks of elephants are actually enlarged incisor teeth, not canines.)
- Other fanged mammalian carnivores that do not use their fangs to kill and eat prey: the three species of true vampire bats, which use their tiny but very sharp fangs to make tiny cuts in the skin of their prey to draw blood—the only food these creatures ever eat.
- Famous extinct fanged animal: the saber-toothed cat, which prowled the Americas between 10,000 and 2.5 million years ago. How long were their fangs? Up to eight inches.
- The Gaboon snake, a viper found in sub-Saharan Africa, has fangs that can grow to two inches long—the longest fangs of any snake.
- Burrowing asps are snakes that hunt and eat underground creatures such as moles and lizards. There's not always room for them to open their mouths and strike at prey in that confined environment, so some of these snakes have developed a peculiar fang ability. A burrowing asp can stick *one* of its fangs out of the side of its mouth—while its mouth is closed—and stab its prey with sideways thrusts of its head.
- Interesting viper fang fact: vipers shed and regrow their fangs every six to eight weeks.

* * *

"Always carry a flagon of whiskey in case of snakebite,
and furthermore always carry a small snake."

—W. C. Fields

MEET GODFREY SITHOLE

This page about an organization that locates and recognizes the funniest real names in the United States is dedicated to Uncle John's travel agent, Anita Mandelove.

AND THE NAME OF THE YEAR IS...

In 1982, some residents of a University of Pennsylvania dormitory posted some funny athlete names on a door and asked fellow students to vote for their favorite. The winner of the first annual Name of the Year contest: boxer Hector "Macho" Camacho. One of those Penn students, author Stefan Fatsis, kept up the tradition for decades. Fatsis adopted an NCAA Tournament–style bracket system in 1998, and when he got tired of running the contest in 2012, a group of Northwestern University students, led by Sam Gutelle, took it on the following year. The Name of the Year has one main rule: the names have to be real (but they no longer have to be athletes).

1985 ☛ Godfrey Sithole
1989 ☛ Magnus Pelkowski
1990 ☛ Otis Overcash
1991 ☛ Doby Chrotchtangle
1992 ☛ Excellent Raymond
1993 ☛ Crescent Dragonwagon
1994 ☛ Scientific Mapp
1996 ☛ Honka Monka
1997 ☛ Courage Shabalala
1998 ☛ L.A. St. Louis
1999 ☛ Dick Surprise
2000 ☛ Nimrod Weiselfish
2001 ☛ Tokyo Sexwale
2002 ☛ Miracle Wanzo
2003 ☛ Jew Don Boney Jr.
2004 ☛ Jerome Fruithandler
2005 ☛ Tanqueray Beavers
2006 ☛ Princess Nocandy
2007 ☛ Vanilla Dong

From 2008 to 2011, the public chose one winner; the NOY's "High Committee" chose another.

2008 (vote) ☛ Spaceman Africa
2008 (committee) ☛ Destiny Frankenstein
2009 (vote) ☛ Barkevious Mingo
2009 (committee) ☛ Juvyline Cubangbang
2010 (vote) ☛ Steele Sidebottom
2010 (committee) ☛ Nohjay Nimpson
2011 (vote *and* committee) ☛ Taco B.M. Monster
2012 ☛ No vote held
2013 ☛ Leo Moses Spornstarr
2014 ☛ Shamus Beaglehole
2015 ☛ Amanda Miranda Panda
2016 ☛ Pope McCorkle III
2017 ☛ Kobe Buffalomeat
2018 ☛ Jimbob Ghostkeeper
2019 ☛ Pope Thrower
2020 ☛ Mathdaniel Squirrel

Q&A: ASK THE EXPERTS

Everyone's got a question they'd like answered—basic stuff like "Why is the sky blue?" Here are a few questions, with answers from the world's top trivia experts.

SOUND OFF

Q: *Why do so many recorded pieces of music fade out instead of just end?*

A: "The fade-out—the technique of ending a song with a slow decrease in volume over its last few seconds—became common in the 1950s and ruled for three decades. Back when recording was strictly mechanical, in which the vibrations of sound waves directly created the grooves on discs or cylinders, it took heroic efforts to end a recording with a fade. Advances in technology played a big part in the rise of the fade-out. Electrical recording emerged in the 1920s, allowing studio engineers to increase or decrease amplification. And achieving the effect became even easier when magnetic tape recording became widely available in the '40s and '50s. Many early fade-outs were added simply because engineers were short on time: To meet the demands of radio, or the limited runtime of one side of a vinyl single, they had to make the record fade out early. [It was good for songwriters too. Rather than having to write an ending, they could simply repeat their catchiest hook on the fade-out, giving the listener the impression that song continued on.]" (From *Slate*)

THE SWEET LIFE

Q: *How come you can eat a huge meal and be totally stuffed, but dessert (for which you'll "make room") can still be appealing?*

A: "The sugar in sweet foods stimulates a reflex that expands your stomach, which is a very flexible organ. When you consume a large meal, the walls of the upper section of the stomach relax to make room for the food. How full you feel depends on the pressure inside the stomach, which in turn is linked to how much the stomach has expanded to tackle the food. First, the sight and smell of food, and the process of chewing and swallowing it have an effect. Second, the actual pressure of food against the stomach wall has an important—and obvious—impact. And third, the duodenum 'tastes' the components of the food. All this information goes to the brain through particular nerves, and a message is sent out again from the core of the brain stem, which oversees the relaxation of muscles in the stomach wall. And so to dessert: glucose—or sugar, if you will—stimulates this relaxation reflex." (From *Science Norway*)

Icelandic version of "the cherry on top": ***Rusinan I pylsuendanum*****,**
or "the raisin at the end of the sausage."

THE COLD HARD TRUTH

Q: *Why is grape-flavored ice cream virtually nonexistent?*

A: "Using grapes as an ice cream base presents logistical problems. 'Making ice cream at home, you can get fruit like grapes pretty close to a puree, but when you are using it as a base on a large scale, that's when you run into problems,' says Sean Greenwood, Ben & Jerry's PR lead. Grapes have high water content. When using such a watery base to make ice cream, the results often come peppered with chunks of ice. Which equates to some pretty bad ice cream. 'Jerry and Ben will sometimes talk about the old days, making melon ice cream, or cantaloupe ice cream, and how good that was. But then, they were doing it on a two-gallon batch. To try to do that on a massive scale is much more challenging.' For something like popsicles—which are predictably icy and often artificially flavored—this is fine. But for a big company, it presents a nearly insurmountable engineering hurdle." (From *Thrillist*)

THIS IS AN EMOTIONAL MOMENT

Q: *What causes a "lump" in your throat when you get upset and are about to cry?*

A: "It has to do with how the nervous system deals with stress. That part of the nervous system is called the autonomic nervous system. It controls bodily functions that we do not consciously control, such as digesting food and pumping blood through the heart. However, the autonomic nervous system is also important in dealing with emotional states. When we experience emotions such as grief or sorrow, the autonomic nervous system responds as it would to anger or fear by increasing the flow of oxygen through the body. To increase oxygen intake, the autonomic nervous system makes us breathe faster, and expands the glottis, the opening in the throat that allows air to flow from the larynx to the lungs. The expansion of the glottis in and of itself does not create a lumpy feeling...until we try to swallow. Since swallowing involves *closing* the glottis, this works against the muscles that open it in response to crying. We experience the resulting muscle tension as a lump in the throat." (From *Indiana Public Media*)

* * *

STRANGE DEATH CUSTOM

It's nice to be rich, even in the afterlife. When a wealthy person died in 18th-century Scotland, their family would place a piece of bread on the body and then pay a poor man to eat it, believing that the bread would transfer the sins of the deceased into the pauper.

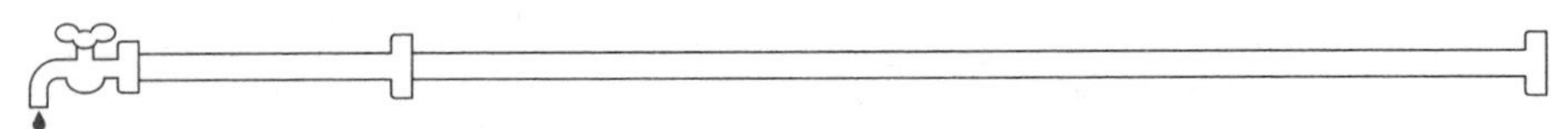

FIRST DRINKS

Care for a nice, cold, intoxicating glass of trivia about big firsts in booze history?

First cocktail: The term "cocktail" was coined in the early 1800s, and first appeared in print in 1806 in the New York newspaper *The Balance, and Columbian Repository*, describing a mix of water, sugar, bitters, and an alcoholic spirit—a drink referred to today as an old-fashioned.

First Cocktail Guide: By 1862, there were hundreds of mixed drink recipes, so barkeeps and home imbibers alike needed to keep track. That year, New York City's Jerry Thomas published *Bar-Tender's Guide*, the world's first definitive guide on cocktails.

First person to drink in space: *Apollo 11* astronaut Buzz Aldrin, a devout Catholic, administered communion to himself during his trip to the Moon. That included a sip of sacramental wine.

First dry state: In 1851, Maine outlawed the consumption and sale of alcohol, jump-starting the temperance movement which, in 1919, successfully led to the passage of the 18th Amendment to the U.S. Constitution barring the manufacture and sale of booze nationwide (also known as Prohibition).

First winery in the United States: In the 1830s, Nicholas Longworth started making, bottling, and selling sparkling wine from Catawba grapes on his vineyard in Cincinnati, Ohio.

First commercial brewery in the United States: The Stone Street Brewery on Brewers Street (later renamed Stone Street) in Lower Manhattan was opened by the Dutch West India Company in 1632. The oldest beer company still operating in the United States is D.G. Yuengling & Son, founded by David Yuengling in Pottsville, Pennsylvania, as the Eagle Brewery in 1829.

First cocktail party: The first time a group of adults gathered with the express purpose of chatting while sipping alcoholic beverages and referred to it as a cocktail party was on a Sunday afternoon in St. Louis in May 1917. Socialite Clara Bell Walsh invited 50 guests into her home for an hour of cocktail consumption before lunch was served.

First beer advertising on TV: The Narragansett Brewing Company of Cranston, Rhode Island, sponsored some early experimental broadcasts of Boston Red Sox games in 1945, but because TV advertising was so new, the team ran Narragansett Beer's ads for free. The first paid beer commercial aired in St. Louis in 1947. Hyde Park Brewery produced ads featuring a cartoon character named Albert the Stick Man, who could always get out of trouble by drinking a bottle of delicious Hyde Park Beer.

IRONIC, ISN'T IT?

There's nothing like a good dose of irony to put the problems of day-to-day life into proper perspective.

Irony Busters: *Ghostbusters* was a massive hit movie, the second highest-grossing film of 1984. In 1986, Columbia Pictures developed an animated cartoon spin-off called *The Real Ghostbusters.* None of the movie's main cast—Dan Aykroyd, Harold Ramis, and Bill Murray—wanted to reprise their roles for TV...except Ernie Hudson. A veteran voice actor before he landed his breakout live-action role as Winston Zeddemore in *Ghostbusters,* he did audition for the animated series. "I went in to read the material, and the guy said, 'No, no, no, that's all wrong! When Ernie Hudson did it in the movie...' And I'm like, 'Well, wait a minute: I am Ernie Hudson!'" It didn't matter. Producers ultimately cast Arsenio Hall instead.

An Irony He Couldn't Refuse: Francis Ford Coppola's 1972 film *The Godfather* is regarded as one of the finest ever made. Coppola hired Mario Puzo, author of the novel on which the movie was based, to co-write the screenplay. It was the first time Puzo had ever attempted that kind of writing, but he won an Academy Award for Best Adapted Screenplay, a feat he repeated with his next work, *The Godfather Part II.* Then Puzo started to get nervous. After his two Oscars, "I went out and bought a book on screenwriting because I figured I'd better learn," he told NPR's *Fresh Air.* "And then in the first chapter—the book said, 'Study *Godfather I.* It's the model of a screenplay.' "

Pungent Irony: Letetia Ware was once the president of the Australian Garlic Industry, a trade group that regulated and advocated for strong standards in locally grown garlic. Ware had particular—and very public—animosity for anyone growing garlic from bulbs imported from outside Australia. "There are many countries around the world that are using chemicals, herbicides, fungicides that would be restricted or prohibited in Australia," she told reporters in early 2019. In late 2019, Ware was arrested on ten charges of illegally importing more than 2,000 garlic bulbs. She entered a guilty plea, and was fined $2,000 and sentenced to 11 months in prison.

Suspicious Irony: One day in October 2019, a passenger waiting for a Manhattan-bound commuter train in New Rochelle, New York, noticed several suspicious-looking objects around the station. The six-foot-tall pillars, covered in electronic doodads and features, looked oddly out of place so, adhering to the "if you see something, say something" dictum, the passenger reported it to the Metropolitan

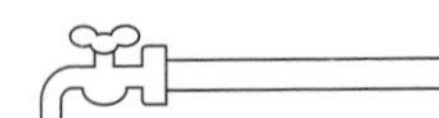

Enough instant ramen is sold each year to provide 12 packets for every man, woman, and child on Earth.

Transportation Authority. Police arrived to remove the objects from the train platform, but were stopped by the MTA, which quickly identified them as their own machines. They were part of the Help Point Communication System, which the MTA described as "a technology program that puts subway customers in touch with Transit personnel via an interactive communications device"—in other words, a way for riders to report suspicious objects.

Dig This Irony: The state of Colorado offers a service called Colorado 811. Residents call 811 before they begin a construction or digging project and officials come to the site to mark any underground utility lines or pipes, ensuring that construction workers won't strike or damage them. In April 2020, the Colorado 811 service went nonoperational for about half a day. Reason: a construction crew was doing some digging near Denver and accidentally cut the underground fiber line that carries the Colorado 811 hotline.

Ironic Failure: In the early 1970s, an English man named Stephen Pile founded the Not Terribly Good Club of Great Britain. Despite the cheeky name, it was a business organization with an earnest purpose: to unite people who've experienced extreme failure in their lives or industry, and to share the lessons they learned with others. In 1979, Pile compiled the best tales of misfires and defeats, along with many from history, into *The Book of Heroic Failures.* It became a best-seller, which led to the Not Terribly Good Club receiving a whopping 20,000 membership applications. Soon thereafter, Pile shut down the failure club because of its overwhelming success.

Pile shut down the failure club because of its overwhelming success.

Giving Irony a Shot: In April 2017, a National Rifle Association employee was hospitalized for treatment of a minor gunshot wound. The man had been taking a gun safety course. At the conclusion of the session, he tried to place his handgun into a waist holster and accidentally discharged the weapon, firing a bullet into his own leg.

Irony at Work: New York City isn't just the most populous city in the United States, it's also a major travel destination, and the area employs an army of restaurant, service, hotel, and hospitality workers. When the COVID-19 pandemic led to stay-at-home orders and government-ordered temporary closures of thousands of "nonessential" businesses in 2020, many of those workers were left unemployed. There was at least one industry that grew, however. New York City's had so many jobless benefit claims that the government's unemployment division had to hire dozens of processors.

Orville Wright piloted the first fatal plane crash in 1908.
He lived, but passenger Thomas Selfridge died.

MOUTHING OFF

INSTRU-MENTAL

If cynical comments about instruments is music to your ears, this page is for you.

"An oboe is an ill wind that nobody blows good."

—Bennett Cerf

"WELCOME TO HELL. HERE'S YOUR ACCORDION."

—Gary Larson, *The Far Side*

"Brass bands are all very well in their place—outdoors and several miles away."

—Thomas Beecham

"A gentleman is someone who knows how to play the banjo and doesn't."

—Mark Twain

"I play the harmonica. The only way I can play is if I get my car going really fast, and stick it out the window."

—Steven Wright

"WHEN YOU PLAY A 12-STRING GUITAR, YOU SPEND HALF YOUR LIFE TUNING IT AND THE OTHER HALF PLAYING IT OUT OF TUNE."

—Pete Seeger

"I wanted to play saxophone, but all I could get were a few squeaks."

—Stevie Ray Vaughan

"I understand the inventor of the bagpipes was inspired when he saw a man carrying an indignant, asthmatic pig under his arm. Unfortunately, the man-made sound never equaled the purity of the sound achieved by the pig."

—Alfred Hitchcock

"Sometimes the nicest thing to do with a guitar is just look at it."

—Thom Yorke

THE BLACK MARKET

The phrase "black market" conjures up an image of someone buying contraband cigarettes, or a phony passport from a shadowy figure in a back alley of Tangiers. You can still buy those things through illegal (or not completely legal) channels, except that it's mostly done online these days. The black market lives on the "dark web," a difficult-to-access sector where anything can be had or sold for the right price...if you know where to go, that is.

HUMAN BODY PARTS

★ **Kidneys.** They are the most transplanted organ, and so the legal waiting list to get one can be very long, leading some people to pursue alternate means of acquisition. Three-quarters of the worldwide illegal organ trade is for kidneys, and one can cost, on average, about $260,000.

★ **Livers.** Second to kidneys in terms of demand, trade, and price, a brand-new (well, *slightly* used) liver costs $157,000 on the black market.

★ **Hearts.** The next most expensive organ that can be procured from shady individuals: a human heart. One of those runs around $120,000.

★ **Spleens.** If you don't have a spleen, the liver can take over most of its functions as part of the immune system. That means a spleen on the black market runs a relatively cheap $500.

ORGANIC SUBSTANCES

★ **Blood.** It is literally the lifeblood of life, and a pint of the red stuff in illegal markets costs a mere $330.

★ **Sperm.** In 2004, Canada passed the Assisted Human Reproduction Act, which outlawed the selling of sperm at a profit. Virtually all sperm banks shut down in the Great White North, leading to a big black market semen trade. Ninety percent of this biological material in Canada is traded via black market channels like secret deals or quasi-legal arrangements with American for-profit sperm banks.

★ **Snake venom.** It's used mainly to make antivenin, or the antidote to potentially fatal snakebites. It's very difficult to get venom from a snake without getting bitten by a snake, so the venom is very rare. How rare? A liter runs a bit over $215,000.

★ **Breast milk.** Only about 25 percent of new moms breastfeed their babies. The rest use powdered formula, but not always by choice. Mothers who want to breastfeed but are prevented from doing so for any number of medical reasons may seek out the breast milk via the black market. Cost: usually somewhere between $1 and $2 per ounce.

EXOTIC ANIMALS

★ **Tigers.** Various species of tigers are threatened if not endangered, so they're not legally allowed as pets in most of the world. But if the rich and powerful want one,

they can get one via the black market. Cost of a live tiger: $50,000.

- ★ **Elephants.** Transporting it from its natural habitat in Africa or Asia and getting it to your house is a whole different set of troubles and expenses, but if you want an elephant, you can get one if you've got about $30,000.
- ★ **Komodo dragons.** These giant reptiles can grow to 10 feet long and weigh more than 300 pounds, and are native to Indonesia. Because they're on the endangered species list, the sale and purchase of Komodo dragons (and their skins) is illegal worldwide. Still, if you do know where to find one, it'll run you around $30,000.
- ★ **Chimpanzees.** They are small and are used widely in medical testing, so there are a lot of chimps out there. Cost: a mere $50.

ODDS AND ENDS

- ★ **Laundry detergent.** Big bottles of detergent are among the most shoplifted items in American grocery and big box stores. Reason: It's expensive, and it can be sold for less on the black market. What's more, thieves can water down the detergent to increase the supply, and sell it to more people. A container of Tide that might cost $20 at Target winds up half water and sells on the black market for $10 to $15.
- ★ **MDMA.** You can purchase controlled substances through some guy on the street or on some dark channels of the internet, but either way it's going to be expensive. Methylenedioxymethamphetamine is a club drug that leads to a sense of euphoria, which is probably why it's commonly known as ecstasy. It costs about $35 for a single tablet dose. (The same pill costs only $4.50 in China.)
- ★ **Cannabis.** It's legal for medicinal and/or recreational use in more than 30 states, but those who live in the states where it's not still have to buy it from a dealer. Prices run as low as $100 per ounce.
- ★ **Murder.** Not only can goods be procured through illegal channels—services can be found, too. The most illegal service of all, murder, can be arranged for a price. The average cost of a hit man on the black market runs about $25,000 (and that's for just one job). But beware: Most—if not all—hitmen on the dark web are scam artists. They take the money but never kill anyone.

* * *

A FEW MORE ITEMS YOU CAN BUY ON THE BLACK MARKET

- Crude oil
- Rhino horn
- Human hair
- Botox
- Baby formula
- Netflix memberships
- Teeth
- Fake diplomas
- Ultra-realistic silicone masks
- Grocery coupons
- Flight attendant uniforms
- Four Loko (a banned alcohol-spiked energy drink)

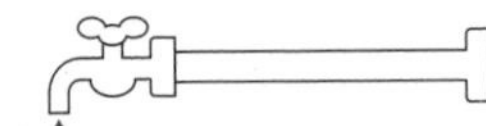

THE JACK-IN-THE-BOX BANDITS

From our "True Crime" files comes this tale of three clever crooks who did their best work at 30,000 feet. But would they get away?

HEADING EAST

On the morning of May 14, 1980, three men—Lloyd Santana, David McCulley, and William DeLucia—boarded Eastern Airlines Flight 82 in Los Angeles. A few hours later, the flight landed in Atlanta. Santana was going to catch a connecting flight to Kansas City later that day, and David McCulley got off in Atlanta. So did William DeLucia, but the odd thing was that nobody other than Santana and McCulley even knew he was on the flight: DeLucia was stowed away in the cargo hold, hidden inside a giant shipping crate marked "MUSICAL INSTRUMENT" and "FRAGILE: THIS SIDE UP."

The three men were the so-called Jack-in-the-Box Bandits, co-conspirators in what has been described by postal investigators as one of the cleverest cases of mail theft they'd ever seen. Both McCulley and DeLucia worked for a now-defunct TWA airline; DeLucia worked as a ramp serviceman and was familiar with airline cargo operations. The two men saw to it that when DeLucia was checked in as cargo, he was loaded into a cargo hold where valuable certified mail from the U.S. Postal Service was also carried.

The crate DeLucia was traveling in looked a lot like an ordinary "roadie case" that professional musicians use to transport equipment on concert tours. But it was anything but ordinary: it was designed so that DeLucia could unlock it from inside and let himself out when the plane was in flight. Then, working with a flashlight in the dark cargo hold, he would rifle through the certified mail, opening any parcel that looked like it might contain something valuable. He stuffed these items not into his own crate, but into four empty suitcases that Lloyd Santana had checked onto the flight as his luggage. When the plane began its descent into Atlanta, DeLucia would climb back inside his crate. After the plane landed, Santana and his suitcases full of stolen loot would continue on to Kansas City. McCulley would go to the baggage claim area and collect his own luggage *and* the crate with DeLucia in it. He had the claim checks for both.

...ONE SMALL PROBLEM

The scheme was nearly perfect, and postal inspectors believe it was used to steal certified mail on earlier flights. But this time things didn't go according to plan:

In 1980, 13-year-old Kamala Harris led a successful protest to allow kids to play on the lawn of her apartment building.

When DeLucia's crate was being unloaded, one of the latches broke and his feet popped out.

When DeLucia's crate was being unloaded, one of the latches broke and his feet popped out. He was quickly discovered and held for questioning. This was where the genius of putting the stolen mail in Santana's empty suitcases instead of into DeLucia's crate came into play. Now that he'd been caught, DeLucia could claim that he'd stowed away aboard the plane to win a bet that he could smuggle himself from L.A. to Atlanta without being detected. Even if investigators realized that some of the certified mail in the cargo hold was missing, by the time they did, it was likely that Santana and his suitcases would already be on their way to Kansas City. There'd be no proof left on the plane that DeLucia had anything to do with the mail theft, or that Santana was in on the plot. DeLucia would only be charged with stowing away aboard an aircraft, and the mystery of what happened to the stolen mail would remain unsolved.

QUICK THINKING

That wasn't quite how things worked out, though. As soon as DeLucia was discovered, the Eastern Airlines investigators did a thorough search of the cargo hold and realized immediately that some of the certified mail was missing. They raced to the baggage claim area to see if any accomplices were waiting there to claim DeLucia's crate. When McCulley tried to claim it (and his luggage), the investigators pulled him aside for questioning.

While McCulley was being questioned, someone made off with his luggage. The investigators searched the area, and soon found the luggage in the possession of... Lloyd Santana. He too was detained. A quick look at the passenger list revealed that he'd been aboard the flight, and that he'd checked four suitcases onto the plane. Those suitcases were located and, after a search warrant was obtained, opened. *Voilà!* More than $350,000 worth of rare coins, jewelry, gold bullion, and even some narcotics stolen from the certified mail parcels was found inside.

OUT OF THE CRATE...AND INTO THE CAN

DeLucia was charged with stowing away aboard an aircraft and mail theft, and McCulley and Santana were charged with aiding and abetting mail theft. All three men were found guilty. DeLucia and McCulley were sentenced to seven years in prison and five years' probation; Santana got six years in prison and five years' probation.

If you ever happen to visit Washington, D.C., and you have some time left over after visiting the city's more famous landmarks and museums, pop down to the Smithsonian Institution's National Postal Museum, just opposite Union Station. There, proudly displayed in the Postal Inspection Service exhibit, is the shipping crate with the faulty latch that caused the Jack-in-the-Box Bandits to come completely unsprung.

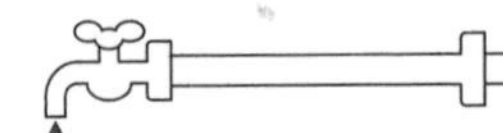

FIRST LADIES

"Each one of us has a fire in our heart for something," said U.S. Olympic hero Mary Lou Retton, adding, "It's our goal in life to find it and keep it lit." Here are some history-making women who found it and kept it lit.

♀ **First Female Athlete to Appear on a Wheaties Box:** At the 1984 Summer Olympics in Los Angeles, 16-year-old Mary Lou Retton made history as the first American of *either* sex to win the all-around gymnastics gold medal, along with four other medals (more than any other athlete in those games). Along with her fierce competitive streak came a sunny disposition that earned the 4' 9" Retton the title "America's Sweetheart," as well as a coveted spot on the front of a Wheaties cereal box. The tradition of putting athletes on the "Breakfast of Champions" packaging goes back to 1934, when baseball's Lou Gehrig appeared on the box front. On the back was the first woman ever to be on a Wheaties box: aviation pioneer Elinor Smith, who a decade earlier, at age 16, had become the youngest licensed pilot in the world. Although a few more women would appear on the back of boxes and on commemorative bowls, it would take Wheaties 50 years to put a woman on the front.

♀ **First Mom in Space:** Dr. Anna Lee Fisher, a physician and chemist, was eight and a half months pregnant when NASA selected her to be the sixth woman in space. (She helped NASA design a space suit that better fit the female anatomy.) She gave birth to her daughter, Kristin, in July 1983; 14 months later, Dr. Fisher flew on the space shuttle *Discovery.* Kristin Fisher grew up to be a national TV journalist. In 2019, she was raising a baby of her own when she told the *Washington Post,* "I always grew up thinking I could have a demanding full-time job and be a mom. The example that [my mom] set for me, it was never a question. It wasn't until I got pregnant...that I started thinking, 'How did she do this?' "

♀ **First Female Comic Book Writer:** In the early 1940s, the nascent comic book industry was run by men. There were some women staffers who contributed to storylines, but they were mostly uncredited. The female comic book writer from this era who had the most impact on pop culture was DC Comics editor Dorothy Woolfolk, who contributed to several early *Wonder Woman* and *Superman* storylines from 1942 to 1944. Her biggest contribution came after pointing out that Superman's invulnerability made him boring; she suggested adding a crippling metal from his home planet that would make it more of a fair fight. Result: Kryptonite. Unfortunately, she didn't last long at DC. According to comic book historian Sara Century, Woolfolk was fired for her outspoken feminist views. "Jarringly, the editor

that replaced Dorothy on *Wonder Woman,* Robert Kanigher, immediately murdered an analog of her on-panel. 'Dottie Cottonman, woman editor' is shot by a sniper...in one of the most unquestionably tasteless scenes ever to appear in a comic, which is definitely saying something." Woolfolk went on to be a successful novelist, penning the Donna Rockford Mystery series for Scholastic in the 1970s and '80s.

♀ **First Female College Football Players:** At least four women have played college football at smaller colleges, the first being Oregon's Willamette University soccer player Liz Heaston. In 1997, when all the football team's placekickers were injured, Heaston suited up and kicked two field goals. The first (and so far, only) woman to play in the NCAA's elite Power Five conferences is Vanderbilt University soccer goalkeeper Sarah Fuller. She suited up in 2020, when COVID-19 restrictions grounded all the football team's placekickers. The team was 0–8 that year, and despite Fuller's locker-room pep talk at halftime, the offense failed to give her the opportunity for a field goal or an extra point. She only got to kick off to start the second half. Nevertheless, that kickoff made history. A few games later, Fuller got another shot and became the first woman to score in Power Five game. "I just want to tell all the girls out there," she said, "that you can do anything you set your mind to, you really can."

♀ **First African American Woman to Star in a Non-servant Role on a TV Show:** That awkward headline was how most obituaries remembered Diahann Carroll upon her passing at age 84 in 2019, but she had many more firsts than that. Until Carroll (born Carol Diann Johnson in 1935) starred in the NBC sitcom *Julia* from 1968 to 1971, black women on TV had been subjugated to mammy, nanny, and servant roles. That's why Nichelle Nichols made history in 1966 as Lt. Uhura, a female African American senior member of the bridge crew on CBS's *Star Trek,* but her name didn't even appear in the opening credits. Two years later, during the height of the civil rights movement, Carroll landed the lead role of Julia Baker, a widowed nurse whose husband was killed in Vietnam, leaving her to raise their son on her own. The role earned Carroll a Golden Globe, making her the first black actress to get one. Also a talented singer, Richard Rodgers (of Rodgers & Hammerstein fame) wrote a Broadway role especially for Carroll in 1962's interracial romance musical *No Strings,* for which she became the first black woman to win a Tony Award. The barrier she was perhaps most proud of: In 1984, Carroll starred on the prime-time soap opera *Dynasty* as the diabolical nightclub singer Dominique Deveraux. Carroll had requested to join the hit show after noticing a general lack of racial integration in soap operas, so she told her manager, "I want to be the first black b*tch on television."

* * *

"The most effective way to do it, is to do it." –**Amelia Earhart**

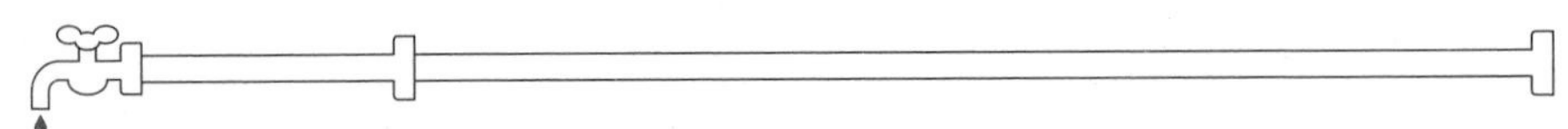

1980s car fact: Fewer than 9,000 DeLoreans were ever made.

THE POISON GARDEN

Some people plant gardens to raise food, others plant gardens to grow flowers. Here's a story about a garden that will just kill you.

REST IN PEACE

In 1995, an English aristocrat named Henry Percy, the eleventh Duke of Northumberland, passed away unexpectedly at the age of 42. The duke died childless, which meant that his title as well as the ducal estate passed to his younger brother Ralph. Now, suddenly, Ralph was the twelfth duke and sole heir to a family fortune worth hundreds of millions of dollars. The ducal estate included Alnwick Castle in Northumberland, the second largest inhabited castle in England after Windsor Castle, one of the residences of Queen Elizabeth.

Taking care of an enormous castle set on 100,000 acres of land takes money, and even though they were now quite wealthy, the new duke and his wife wanted to find ways to generate income. One thing they did was make Alnwick Castle available to film and television crews for on-location filming. Parts of it have served as the exterior and interior of Hogwarts School in the Harry Potter films, and as Brancaster Castle in the PBS period drama *Downton Abbey.*

GOING GREEN

Another project that was of particular interest to Ralph Percy's wife, Jane, was developing a public garden on the estate. Jane Percy's mother operated a similar garden in Scotland called Kailzie Gardens, and Jane believed that something like that on the castle grounds would help attract visitors. Ralph Percy set aside 42 acres and £9 million (about $12 million) in seed money for the Alnwick Garden, and over the next several years Jane oversaw further development of what has become the largest public garden built in the UK since World War II. Features include a rose garden with 3,000 rose bushes, a Japanese cherry orchard containing more than 300 rare Taihaku cherry trees, a Serpent Garden with wandering hedges and water sculptures, a bamboo labyrinth made from 500 live bamboo plants, numerous topiary plants, and the largest treehouse in Europe. The first phase of the garden opened in 2001.

But the most famous feature of the park, and one that Jane Percy included because she thought children would find it interesting, is the part that you might think would be the *least* suitable for children: the Poison Garden, home to some 100 species of plants that are deadly to human beings.

She got the idea for the Poison Garden after visiting Italy's Padua Botanical Garden, which opened in 1545. At the time, she was considering adding an "apothecary garden," or garden of medicinal plants, to the Alnwick Garden. The

Corn prices fell so far during the Great Depression that it was cheaper for farm families to burn it in place of coal.

Padua Botanical Garden has such a collection of plants, but it also has a collection of poisonous plants, and when Percy saw those, she was fascinated. "I thought, 'this is a way to interest children,' " she told *Smithsonian* magazine. "Children don't care that aspirin comes from the bark of a tree. What's really interesting is to know how a plant kills you, and how the patient dies, and what you feel like before you die." Percy took the idea home with her, and a 14-acre Poison Garden was added to the estate in 2005.

COME RIGHT THIS WAY

Alnwick's Poison Garden looks like something you might see next to the Haunted Mansion in Disneyland: It's enclosed behind black iron fencing and secured by two large locked gates, each of which features a white skull and crossbones and the warning "THESE PLANTS CAN KILL" in large white lettering. The fencing is decorative, but it also serves an important function, keeping people out of the garden and away from the nightshade, belladonna, and other dangerous plants except during guided tours. Only then are the gates unlocked and opened so that carefully supervised groups of no more than 20 guests can be admitted to look at the plants. And looking is all that's permitted: visitors are cautioned against touching, tasting, or even smelling the plants. Children must be accompanied by adults at all times. The danger is very real—in the summer of 2014, a few visitors got too close to some of the more aromatic plants and passed out from the fumes.

GARDEN VARIETY

The 100 species of plants on display at the Poison Garden include:

- *Brugmansia,* or angel's trumpet, a genus of several flowery shrubs that are related to deadly nightshade (also in the garden), and just as lethal when ingested. Eating the plant can cause dry mouth, constipation, tremors, headaches, hallucinations, delirium, paralysis, and death. The scent of some species of *Brugmansia* is said to be a powerful aphrodisiac.
- *Datura,* or devil's trumpet, a flowering plant also known as devil's weed and hell's bells. Both the seeds and flowers contain psychoactive substances that can cause delirium, hallucinations, psychosis, and death.
- *Ricinus communis,* the plant that is used to produce castor oil. The seeds (commonly called castor beans), as well as the leaves and stems of the plant, contain ricin, a toxin so potent that a few grains of it, in its purified form, are enough to kill a human being. Castor oil is extracted from the seeds using a heat process that destroys the ricin, rendering the oil safe for human consumption. But don't even think of eating the seeds raw! Their exterior is very tough, so they might just pass through your system undigested without releasing the ricin. Then again...they might not.

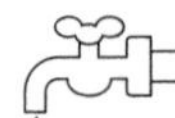

They haven't found one yet, but astronomers theorize that just as there are black holes from which light cannot escape, there are white holes that spit it out.

- *Helleborus,* a genus of perennial flowering plants. Consumption of black hellebore can cause tinnitus, vertigo, stupor, thirst, vomiting, anaphylactic shock, bradycardia (a slowing heart rate), and death from cardiac arrest.
- *Prunus laurocerasus,* also known as common laurel, cherry laurel, or English laurel, a plant that is commonly used for hedges in English gardens. Many visitors to the Poison Garden are shocked to see a plant they recognize from their own gardens included in the collection, but the laurel seeds and leaves contain cyanide. Cuttings of the plant emit fumes that can be deadly.

  "We've had visitors that go through our poison garden and say, 'Oh, yeah, I've got a laurel hedge and I put it in my car. And I've got to drive three miles to the dump. And as I go, I always get a headache.' That's because your brain is getting starved of oxygen," head gardener, Trevor Jones, told the London *Daily Express* in 2019. "That's what cyanide does. We had one gentleman that admitted he actually crashed his car on the way to the dump. He hit a lamppost, didn't know why, but then after a bit of further examination decided that yes, it was the cyanide building up in the back of his car."
- Intoxicating plants. The Poison Garden has special permission to include cannabis, coca (used to make cocaine), and opium poppy plants (used to make morphine and heroin) among its collection, as part of an anti-drug education program that is of special importance to Ralph and Jane Percy: Ralph's older brother Henry, the eleventh duke, had a drug problem. When he died in 1995, leaving Ralph the dukedom, the cause of death was determined to be cardiac arrest caused by an accidental overdose of amphetamines. The Percys have even hired actors to pose as heroin addicts outside the Poison Garden to warn kids about the dangers of substance abuse.

The Percys have even hired actors to pose as heroin addicts.

MAKING A KILLING

The Alnwick Garden was controversial from the moment it was conceived until well after it opened in 2001; stuffy traditionalists were appalled by things like the giant treehouse, the bamboo labyrinth, the Poison Garden, and the actors hired to pose as drug addicts. But these and other features have been very popular with visitors: when the garden opened in 2001, it was expected to attract 60,000 visitors the first year, but more than 330,000 people came to see it. Today the gardens and the castle attract as many as 800,000 visitors annually, though how much of this is due to the Poison Garden and how much is due to the popularity of the Harry Potter films and *Downton Abbey* creating interest in Alnwick Castle is unclear. Whatever the reason, the Alnwick Garden is now the third most popular public garden in the UK and one of the biggest tourist attractions in northern England.

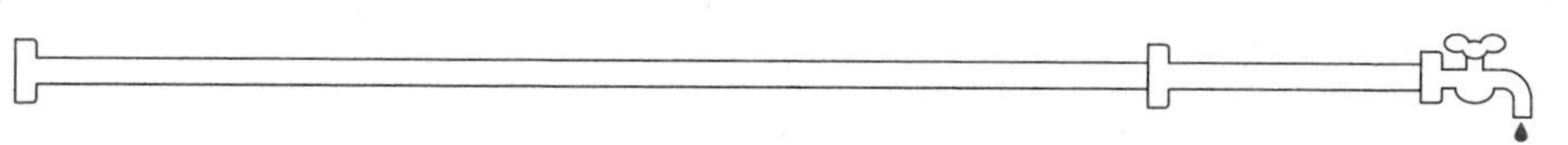

FIRST DRAFTS

Some movies are so embedded in our minds and in the culture that it's hard to believe they could have turned out a lot differently, had writers and directors gone with their earliest ideas.

Anchorman (2004)

Plot used: A TV news team in 1970s San Diego, led by local celebrity anchorman Ron Burgundy (Will Ferrell), find its male-chauvinist worldview turned upside down when beautiful and talented female newscaster Veronica Corningstone (Christina Applegate) arrives on the scene.

Plot abandoned: In Ferrell and director Adam McKay's first version of the script, the news team is flying to a TV news convention in 1976 when arrogant Ron convinces the pilot to let him take control of the jet. Result: They crash in the mountains, but not before clipping a cargo plane full of orangutans and Ninja throwing stars. The movie then follows the news anchors' quest to return to civilization while fighting off throwing star–wielding orangutans.

Back to the Future (1985)

Plot used: Teenager Marty McFly (Michael J. Fox) accidentally drives the DeLorean time machine of his friend, scientist Doc Brown (Christopher Lloyd), back to 1955, where he must ensure his own parents get together and fall in love, so as to not jeopardize his own future existence.

Plot abandoned: Marty works for Doc in his videotape bootlegging business. He's so depressed that he contemplates suicide and climbs into what he thinks is a suicide machine Doc has built in a car wash, but which is actually a time machine. After Marty goes into the past, Doc gets him back to the future by building a new time machine in a refrigerator that's propelled back to the present via the power of a military nuclear bomb test.

Beetlejuice (1988)

Plot used: When Adam and Barbara Maitland (Alec Baldwin, Geena Davis) die in a car accident, their ghosts return to their home and enlist the help of an undead boogieman named Beetlejuice (Michael Keaton) to help them scare off the Deetzes—a yuppie family (Jeffrey Jones, Catherine O'Hara) that moved in after the Maitlands died.

Plot abandoned: In Michael McDowell's original script, the Maitlands' death scene is long and involved: they're depicted drowning—in graphic detail. They do hire Beetlejuice, who doesn't so much haunt the house's new residents as he does try to kill them. (Also, he propositions the Deetzes' daughter, Lydia (Winona Ryder), before he brutally murders her.) Bonus: Before director Tim Burton cast Michael Keaton as

Paul Revere was one of the first odontologists in colonial America—he replaced patients' missing teeth with ivory or animal teeth.

Beetlejuice, the character was envisioned as an evil, Middle Eastern lounge lizard type. Burton's first choice for the role: Sammy Davis Jr.

Jaws 2 (1978)

Plot used: In this sequel to the monster hit about a bloodthirsty shark that terrifies and attacks the beach town of Amity, a bloodthirsty shark terrifies and attacks the beach town of Amity.

Plot abandoned: Steven Spielberg directed the first *Jaws,* and he later made several World War II movies, including *Saving Private Ryan.* Those two paths nearly converged with his initial plans for *Jaws 2*—a full-length version of the story shark hunter Quint (Robert Shaw) tells in the original movie, about sharks that attack the crew of the USS *Indianapolis* after a torpedo strike took out the ship during World War II.

Monsters, Inc. (2001)

Plot used: A parallel universe of monsters subsists on energy derived by collecting human child screams, so monsters regularly visit the human realm to scare kids. They travel through portals in children's bedroom closets, one of which is accidentally left open, making it possible for one kid to cross over into monster land.

Plot abandoned: Pixar screenwriter Pete Docter's first idea for the movie was about a thirtysomething man who finds his childhood notebook, full of drawings of everything that terrified him when he was little. The pictures come to life and torment him, forcing him to confront his fears and overcome them.

Pretty Woman (1990)

Plot used: Wealthy businessman Edward (Richard Gere) hires charming, winsome Hollywood Boulevard prostitute Vivian (Julia Roberts) to help stave off his loneliness. Improbably, they fall in love...and live happily ever after.

Plot abandoned: In the original script, titled $3,000 (after Edward and Vivian's negotiated price for her services), the couple's magical week together ends with Edward driving Vivian back to the spot he picked her up, throwing some money at her, and driving off alone. End of movie.

Freddy vs. Jason (2003)

Plot used: Freddy Krueger from *A Nightmare on Elm Street* and Jason Vorhees from *Friday the 13th* team up for a killing spree, until Jason oversteps his bounds and kills too many of Freddy's earmarked victims, leading to a standoff.

Plot abandoned: The first draft of the script ends with the two murderous demons squaring off in a boxing match in hell. Serial killer Ted Bundy serves as the ring announcer, while some of hell's most notable residents cheer them on, including demons, zombies, Lee Harvey Oswald, and Adolf Hitler.

Most frequently purchased condiment in the U.S.: mayonnaise.

...W YOUR SHIBBOLETHS

Shibboleth is one of those words that appears in print just often enough that it looks kind of familiar when you see it, but not often enough that many people know what it means. Here's a primer.

SPLIT ENDS

The story of the "modern" usage of the term *shibboleth* is as old as the Old Testament—more specifically, as old as the book of Judges, which relates a story about two warring tribes of Israel: the Gileadites and the Ephraimites. Sometime between 1370 and 1070 BC, the Gileadites defeated the Ephraimites in battle. Afterward, the surviving Ephraimites tried to flee back across the river Jordan to safety. But the river was guarded by Gileadite soldiers, who had orders not to let them escape. To determine who was and who wasn't an Ephraimite, the guards ordered anyone wanting to cross the river to say the Hebrew word for "ear of corn," *shibboleth.* Reason: the two tribes spoke different dialects of Hebrew and pronounced the word differently. In the Gileadite dialect the word sounded like "shibboleth." But in the Ephraimite dialect it was pronounced "sibboleth," because the "sh" sound was not used in that dialect. So if you pronounced the word as "sibboleth," you were out of luck. According to Judges 12:6:

> Then said [the guards] unto him, Say now Shibboleth: and he said Sibboleth: for he could not frame to pronounce it right. Then they took him, and slew him at the passages of Jordan: and there fell at that time of the Ephraimites forty and two thousand.

MODERN TIMES

Today the word "shibboleth" means anything—the pronunciation of a word, a bit of knowledge, or anything else—that distinguishes one particular group of people from other groups, and which can be used to determine who is a member of that group and who is not. Here are some more recent examples:

The Parsley Massacre: The Caribbean island of Hispaniola is divided between the nations of Haiti in the west and the Dominican Republic in the east. Coexisting has not always been easy. In the 1930s, the Dominican Republic was ruled by a brutal dictator named Rafael Trujillo, who was determined to rid the country of Haitians who lived on the Dominican side of the border. In the fall of 1937, he sent troops into the border region to root out the Haitians who lived there, and either kill them or force them back over the border into Haiti.

The Parsley Massacre gets its name from the story that Dominican soldiers used sprigs of parsley to determine whether someone was Haitian or not. When they suspected someone was a Haitian, the story goes, the soldiers held up some parsley

Whether by accident or design, Jenga blocks aren't uniform—they vary slightly, so that some are easier than others to slide out of the tower.

and asked them to pronounce the Spanish word for it: *perejil*. If the person rolled their r's when saying it, they were presumed to be native Spanish speakers, and therefore Dominicans, and left alone. Haitian people spoke either French or Haitian Creole and did not roll their r's. If a person pronounced the word *perejil* without rolling their r's, they were presumed to be Haitian and killed.

The story is widely believed, but unverified; whether sprigs of parsley were used or not, it's estimated that in a little over a week, Dominican soldiers killed between 1,000 and 30,000 Haitians. They dumped many of the bodies in the Massacre River, named for an earlier unrelated massacre. More than 80 years later, the Parsley Massacre continues to cast a shadow over the relations between the Dominican Republic and Haiti.

The Battle of the Bulge: In the runup to Germany's last major offensive of World War II, Adolf Hitler gave orders for English-speaking German soldiers to form a special unit called Panzer Brigade 150. Members of the brigade would pose as American and British soldiers, wearing captured uniforms and driving captured tanks, jeeps, and trucks. Their mission: to sneak behind enemy lines to sow chaos and confusion ahead of the German offensive. This effort, known as Operation Greif, fizzled out not long after it began; the Germans managed to send fewer than 50 Panzer Brigade 150 soldiers into the field, not the 3,300 they had hoped for. But as soon as the United States and its allies caught wind of Operation Greif, they became obsessed with ferreting out any "Allied" troops who were actually English-speaking Nazis in disguise.

One of the most effective means for doing this was through the use of shibboleths that quizzed soldiers on information that Americans were likely to know, and that German soldiers were not. Soldiers were asked the names of state capitols, the name of President Franklin D. Roosevelt's dog (Fala), and other trivia that only real Americans would know. Baseball was a popular topic: soldiers were asked which teams played in the 1944 World Series (the St. Louis Browns and the St. Louis Cardinals), and which team won (the Cardinals).

Not every American serviceman followed baseball closely, though. One brigadier general named Bruce Clarke was detained for half an hour and nearly arrested as a German infiltrator after he mistakenly identified the Chicago Cubs as belonging to the American League. "Only a kraut would make a mistake like that!" his questioner exclaimed. The last major German offensive ultimately failed in what became known as the Battle of the Bulge, and at least 17 German soldiers who were captured wearing U.S. and British uniforms were executed by firing squads.

Draft Dodgers: As long as the United States has had a border with Canada, young American men seeking to avoid the military draft have fled to Canada to escape it. Then, having established a safe haven in Canada, it wasn't unheard of for the draft dodgers to sneak back south of the border posing as Canadians. One method the

In 1966, the Soviet Union detonated an atomic bomb to extinguish a fire in a natural gas well that had been burning for nearly three years.

U.S. Border Patrol used to detect Americans who were pretending to be Canadians was to ask them to quickly recite the letters of the alphabet. Canadians pronounce the letter z as "zed." If a so-called Canadian slipped up and used the American pronunciation "zee," they had some 'splaining to do.

The Vietnam War: U.S. servicemen who were captured by the North Vietnamese as prisoners of war were often kept alone in solitary confinement cells in POW camps. The prisoners couldn't see one another, but they could hear other prisoners in the surrounding cells. And though communicating was forbidden and anyone caught doing so was severely punished, the prisoners developed a means of secretly communicating with one another by tapping in code on the walls of their cells. This created a new problem: how could the POWs be sure that the person in the next cell really was an American POW, and not a North Vietnamese guard pretending to be a POW? The POWs tapped out the first five notes of the musical riff "shave and a haircut," and waited to see if the person in the next cell tapped back the two-note reply, "two bits." The Vietnamese soldiers were not familiar with "Shave and a Haircut," and thus would not know that the correct response was to tap twice.

AS LONG AS WE'RE ON THE SUBJECT...

The "Shave and a Haircut" riff is popular in many parts of the world. The sound is the same, but the riff translates differently in different languages. Some examples:

- **Mexico:** it translates as an obscenity against a person's mother—"*chinga tu madre, cabrón*" ("go _____ your mother, a___hole!") that is so insulting that even tapping out the riff is considered offensive.
- **Netherlands:** "*Die zien we nooit meer, te-rug.*" ("We shall never see them, again.") A humorous way of remarking upon someone or something that has suddenly disappeared and is unlikely to return.
- **Spain:** "*Una copita...de Ojén.*" ("A shot of schnapps.")
- **Iceland:** "*Saltkjöt og baunir...túkall.*" ("Salt meat and split peas...two krona.")
- **Ireland:** "How is your aul' one? Game ball!" (A slang expression that translates as "How's your mother? She's OK!")
- **Italy:** "*Ammazza la vecchia...col Flit!*" ("Kill the old lady...with Flit!") Back when the pesticide DDT was still legal, Flit was a popular insecticide.
- **Sweden:** "*Kvart över elva...halv tolv.*" ("A quarter past eleven, half twelve [eleven-thirty].")

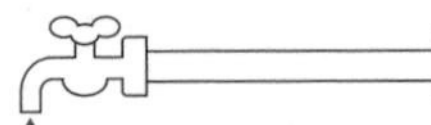

Why do baby owls sleep face down? To rest their heavy heads—they can't hold them upright when they're sleeping.

BASEBALL BIZARRE

Step up to the plate for these odd goings-on from a sport that makes you hit a round ball with a round stick and then run around a diamond.

THEY WORE SHORT SHORTS

In 1976, the Chicago White Sox ditched their long pants for three games. Why would they do such a thing? Blame owner Bill Veeck, a brilliant promoter, best known for the stunt of sending in 3'7" Eddie Gaedel to pinch hit in a game in 1951. (Gaedel's strike zone was so small that he walked in four pitches.) Veeck's replacement uniform for the Sox: knee-high white socks, tight blue shorts. Why shorts? "If it's 95 degrees out," said Veeck, "an athlete should be glad to put on short pants and forget his bony knees." Veeck also explained that the "Hollywood shorts" weren't just for comfort—his wife said they had "understated elegance." The players had mixed reactions; most chalked it up to the owner's eccentricities (Veeck also made the team wear leisure suit–style uniforms that summer). "I'm just happy to be here," remarked pitcher Jesse Jefferson. "I'll wear anything." Maybe Veeck was on to something. The White Sox won two of those three games. Even more impressive: They went eight for eight in stolen base attempts, with no reports of skinned knees.

He also made the team wear leisure suit–style uniforms that summer.

STRANGER IN THE NIGHT

In the 12th inning of a tie game in June 1999, New York Mets manager Bobby Valentine was ejected after vehemently questioning an umpire's decision. Valentine had called for a pitchout; the umpire ruled it a balk. Valentine went ballistic. "I asked him if I could get thrown out for what I was thinking and he said no," Valentine later recalled. "Then I told him what I was thinking, and he threw me out." A few minutes later, Valentine was sitting in the team clubhouse when veteran players Orel Hershiser and Robin Ventura hatched a plan to get him back out there. It worked, sort of.

Valentine did return to the dugout—but not in uniform. He was wearing a T-shirt, a low hat, sunglasses (during a night game), and a thick black mustache made from two pieces of tape (the tape that players use to keep the sun out of their eyes). Hershiser stood on the top step of the dugout in front of Valentine, blocking him from the umpires' view...but not from the TV cameras. The announcers started laughing as the camera zoomed in on the strange, mustachioed man in the dugout. "Well, Bobby's gone incognito! Sorry, Skip. We got you." Result: the Mets won the game, and Valentine was fined $5,000. "I think I did a lot of things in my life that were kind of important," he said recently, "but probably the one line that I get asked the most is, 'Hey, where's your mustache and glasses?' "

Around 30 shots were fired at the gunfight at the OK Corral. It was over in 30 seconds.

CAP'S BIG ADVENTURE

Few pitchers, past or present, were more superstitious than Mike Cuellar, who helped lead the Baltimore Orioles to three consecutive World Series from 1969 to 1971. On one road trip, when the team arrived in Milwaukee, the Cuban-born southpaw told manager Earl Weaver that he couldn't pitch the next day. Reason: he'd left his lucky ballcap at home. Cuellar pleaded with Weaver; his nine-game winning streak was at stake! With overnight delivery more than a decade away, "We had to call the clubhouse man back in Baltimore," recalled Weaver, "to airmail that [bleeping] hat to us." It took two planes, but they got it there just in time. Then Cuellar took one look at it and moaned, "They sent my practice cap!" He lasted only three innings.

BREAKING THE NEWS

On Friday evening, June 3, 2016, at the conclusion of a Miami Marlins home game, fans were making their way out of the ballpark when the digital scoreboard displayed a photograph of Muhammad Ali along with the caption "1942–2016." Photos of the scoreboard were soon on Twitter, sending news outlets into a frenzy. Was the boxing legend and civil rights activist really dead? Two hours and five minutes after the scoreboard memorial, Ali's family confirmed that he had died of a respiratory condition after decades of battling Parkinson's disease. Then the news broke all over the world. So how did the Marlins know? Ali had a special relationship with the franchise, and had thrown out the first pitch at their new stadium four years earlier. When pressed for an explanation, team president David Samson explained, "We were informed by someone close to the family that he had passed away. We wanted to get a tribute out as soon as we possibly could." That marked the first—and most likely only—time that a major news story first broke on a baseball scoreboard.

SHAME ON YOU, MR. MET!

After a particularly painful home loss during the New York Mets' disappointing 2017 season, Mr. Met, the team's baseball-headed mascot, was walking toward a tunnel door below a group of fans, many of whom had booed the team that night. They asked Mr. Met to stop for a high-five. He kept walking, so they asked louder. Then Mr. Met turned around, put his left arm across his chest to brace his right arm, which he held up and—with his oversized, three-fingered white glove—flipped them the bird. A video of the exchange went viral (one fan reportedly had made comments about Mr. Met's mother), but it was the still image of the grinning mascot's lewd gesture—which was almost immediately all over the internet—that sent the Mets' front office into damage control mode: "We apologize for the inappropriate action of this employee. We do not condone this type of behavior." A day later, according to the Associated Press, "a Mets official reported that the employee who wore the Mr. Met costume Wednesday night will never wear it again."

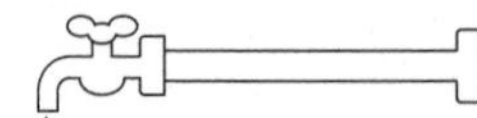

Even if a wasp doesn't sting you, it may drop pheromones on you to alert other wasps to the danger.

NOVEL NOVELS

The first Uncle John's Bathroom Reader *was called* Uncle John's Bathroom Reader *and it came out in 1988. Here are some other "firsts" from the world of books.*

First horror novel: Mary Shelley's *Frankenstein*, published in 1818, often gets the credit as the first horror tale—it's the story of a monster made out of dead people's body parts that terrorizes a community. But in 1764, British author Horace Walpole published *The Castle of Otranto*, the first "gothic" novel, named for the spooky, imposing architectural style of the Middle Ages. This dark tale of murder, death, and the supernatural inspired Shelley, who wrote the first horror story involving monsters.

First detective novel: It was *The Notting Hill Mystery*, published in serial form in 1862, then as one volume in 1865. It's by an author named Charles Felix, about whom little is known, but the book laid out most of the tropes of detective and mystery books. An eccentric private investigator looks into the bizarre death of a baroness at a country estate after the incompetent police are baffled, and he has to wade through numerous red herrings and false leads. (We'd tell you whodunnit, but the book is still in print and we don't want to spoil the fun.)

First science-fiction novel: In second-century Greece, Assyrian writer Lucian of Samosata published *A True Story*. Far from actually being true, it is a surprisingly modern sci-fi tale involving robots, aliens, and space travel.

First postapocalyptic novel: Mary Shelley followed *Frankenstein* with the first piece of science fiction set in a dystopian, far-off future. The 1826 book *The Last Man* takes place in the year 2100. A man named Lionel Verney is the only human left on earth, wandering around a devastated England after a series of plagues has wiped out humanity. Sometimes it's not easy being new—*The Last Man* sold so poorly that it wasn't reprinted until 1965.

First young adult novel: Maureen Daly's 1942 romance novel *Seventeenth Summer* is widely regarded as the first fiction book published for (and marketed to) teenagers, specifically teenage girls. It's about a summer romance that develops between 17-year-old Wisconsin girl Angie Morrow and 17-year-old high school basketball star Jack Duluth, who both have to go their separate ways in the fall.

First movie novelization: Narrative novels based on movies were a big part of every film's marketing campaign in the 1970s and '80s. (The book versions of *Star Wars* and

First expansion team to win a championship in its inaugural season: the Chicago Fire (Major League Soccer, 1998).

E.T.: The Extra-Terrestrial sold particularly well.) But novelizations have been a part of the movie industry almost since its inception. Thomas Edison, credited with helping to invent cinema, also helped invent the novelization. In 1912, his movie company released the serialized melodramatic film *What Happened to Mary*. Around the time each episode hit movie theaters, the same content in written form (by author Robert Carlton Brown) was published in *Ladies' World* magazine. The chapters were then collected and published together in 1913.

First educational book for kids: Bohemian educator Jan Amos Comenius published the first edition of the *Orbis Pictus* ("World in Pictures") in 1658. The book, geared at children under the age of six, featured illustrations of people, nature, and scenes from everyday life, along with text that identified the objects in those pictures, making it the first book aimed at teaching kids to read. Initially printed in Latin and German, it quickly spread around Europe, and was translated to English in 1659 and other European languages in the 1660s. It was the primary learn-to-read text throughout the continent for more than 200 years.

First modern-day kids book: In 1744, British publisher John Newbery printed *A Little Pretty Pocket-Book, intended for the Amusement of Little Master Tommy and Pretty Miss Polly*. It's all explained right there in the very long title (which was the style for books at the time): this was a product meant solely for kids, and solely for their entertainment (not for educational purposes).

First fantasy novel: Inspiring later writers such as C. S. Lewis and J. R. R. Tolkien, Scottish author George MacDonald wrote the first tale of mystical, magical worlds—sort of like fairy tales for adults—in 1858. *Phantastes* (it's pronounced "fantasties") concerns Anodos, a young man who is whisked away to a surreal, dreamlike forest called Fairy Land, where he tries to find a beautiful fairy woman and not run afoul of moving statues, evil trees, and medieval knights.

DID YOU KNOW?

The first contemporary American book to sell a million copies in the United States: *Uncle Tom's Cabin; or, Life Among the Lowly* by Harriet Beecher Stowe. Published in 1852, the novel presented a realistic picture of slavery and helped fuel the anti-slavery movement that would culminate in the practice being outlawed (and the Civil War being fought over it) in the 1860s.

First autobiography: Celebrity memoirs are usually big sellers, because regular people love to read about big stars owning up to their misdeeds and scandalous behavior. When the theologian Saint Augustine of Hippo wrote the first self-penned biography, or memoir, in the year 400, he was giving the people what they wanted. The volume's title: *Confessions*.

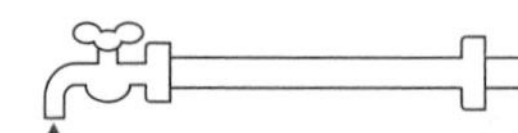

It ain't meat, but it ain't cheap: "edible" gold is considered a vegan food.

WHAT GOES UP...

The business of "controlled demolition" of structures that need to be torn down is an exact science...but not every practitioner has mastered that science, as any number of YouTube videos will attest.

STRUCTURE: An 11-story office building in Dallas, Texas, that was built in 1971 and, for a time, served as headquarters of the Southland Corporation, owners of the 7-Eleven convenience store chain

PLAN: By 2020, the building was empty and ready to be torn down to make way for The Central, a $2.5 billion mixed-use development that would include hotel and condo high-rises, plus restaurants, retail spaces, and a park. In February 2020, the building was wired with explosives that, when detonated, would cause the building to implode and collapse onto itself.

WHAT HAPPENED: The explosives were set off and the entire building came crashing down...except for the central core, which housed the stairwell and elevator shafts. It plunged about 40 feet into the basement, then tilted to one side and stubbornly stayed put.

Nondescript in life, the building gained fame in near-death as the "Leaning Tower of Dallas," as the video of the failed demolition went viral. Throngs of locals made their way to the site to take selfies, many posing to look as if they were holding the building up or pushing it down. More than 1,500 people signed a petition to have the wrecked edifice preserved as a UNESCO World Heritage Site. Within days, the Leaning Tower even had its own Twitter account.

AFTERMATH: The demolition contractor spent two weeks whacking the tower with a wrecking ball until it finally fell over. "Its 15 days of existence inspired many to stay strong when others try to knock you down," one Dallas funeral home posted on Facebook. "May its legacy never be forgotten."

STRUCTURE: A 275-foot smokestack that was part of Ohio Edison's Mad River Power Plant in Springfield, Ohio. It was scheduled to be demolished in November 2010.

PLAN: Explosives were set into the base of the tower that would cause it to topple over in one big piece to the east, where land had been cleared to give it a place to fall.

WHAT HAPPENED: After the explosives were detonated, the tower did topple over in one big piece, but in the wrong direction, crashing to the southeast instead of the east. It hit some 12,500-volt power lines on the way down and demolished several buildings, including one housing backup generators. "It just started leaning the other way and I thought, 'Holy cow'...It was terrifying for a little bit," Springfield Township's fire chief, John Roeder, told reporters.

In space, it's a meteoroid. In the atmosphere, it's a meteor. If it makes it to the ground, it's a meteorite.

No one was hurt, but 4,000 utility customers lost power for much of the day, and Ohio Edison and its sister company FirstEnergy suffered what they say was $19 million in damages. They sued the contractor, Advanced Explosives Demolition, Inc., for negligence, alleging that the company set up the explosives incorrectly and failed to cut steel reinforcing bars that would have caused the tower to fall where it was supposed to. For its part, Advanced Explosives Demolition blamed an undetected crack on the south side of the smokestack for the mishap.

AFTERMATH: The parties in the lawsuit settled out of court shortly before the case went to trial; details of the settlement were not made public.

STRUCTURE: A 175-foot silo in Vordingborg, Denmark, that was being torn down to make room for new homes, businesses, and a hotel

PLAN: Like the smokestack in Ohio, this silo was supposed to fall in one piece in a particular direction, where land had been cleared. After six months of preparation work, the demolition took place in April 2018, as hundreds of spectators looked on.

WHAT HAPPENED: The silo toppled in the opposite direction from where it was supposed to go, crashing on top of a library, demolishing a corner of the building, and sending library books and papers flying.

AFTERMATH: The library was closed during the demolition, and no one was hurt during the accident. "I simply do not know how it could have gone so bad," project leader Kenneth Wegge told reporters. "We do not know what went wrong. We are currently investigating."

STRUCTURE: An 80-year-old flour factory in the city of Çankiri in northern Turkey in 2009

PLAN: The demolition company knocked out much of the wall on one side of the 80-foot-tall building, then rigged the explosives so that the building would fall over on that side.

WHAT HAPPENED: Normally when explosives are used to knock down structures onto one side, as was planned for the flour factory, the idea is that force of falling over will cause the building to collapse into rubble, making the rest of the demolition project that much easier. That was what happened with both the smokestack and the silo mentioned above, and that was what was supposed to happen here as well. But the old building must have been a lot sturdier than anyone realized, because when it tumbled over onto its side, it remained intact and kept right on tumbling rather than breaking apart; it rolled out into the street and finally came to a rest upside down on its roof.

AFTERMATH: The flour factory came within yards of slamming into a residential building on the other side of the street. Had it struck the building, the casualties might have been much worse. Fortunately, there were no reports of injuries.

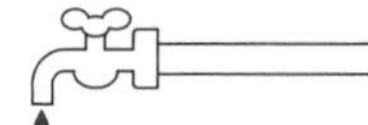

SURVIVAL STORIES

Never underestimate the power of the human spirit.

TIMBER!

If a tree falls on you and there's no one around to hear your cries for help, will you be rescued? Jonathan Ceplecha knew he would be found eventually—he just had to stay alive. In August 2020, a large oak tree fell on Ceplecha while he was cutting it down on the outskirts of his Redwood Falls, Minnesota, property, where he lived alone. The tree broke both of the 59-year-old U.S. Army veteran's legs and twisted his back, leaving him pinned in an awkward, painful position. With no phone and no one even close to earshot, Ceplacha spent the next four days (and cold nights) stuck there. He ate any insects that got too close, and drank sweat and rainwater to stay alive. To stay sane, he prayed a lot, and, as his son later wrote on a GoFundMe page (for his medical bills), he "tried to distract himself from panic by meditating and inventing rhythms to follow from dawn to dusk." Four days after getting stuck, Ceplecha was found by his ex-wife, who searched the property after he'd been reported missing from work. It took rescuers two hours to extract him from the tree, but at last report he was going to make a full recovery.

HAVE A NICE FALL

In November 2019, Ryan Cairnes did a few things right and a few things wrong when he went rock climbing in Washington's Cannon Mountains. His first goof—even though he's an experienced climber with sturdy gear—was going to the remote and rugged area by himself. So there was no one there to grab Cairnes's line when "something just let loose" and he started sliding down the steep, rocky mountainside. "There was no part me inside that said I was going to live," the 36-year-old Microsoft manager from Seattle later told reporters. "I just said, I'm falling off a cliff. And people die when they fall off cliffs." Cairnes didn't die, but after the minute-long fall of 300–400 feet that ended with him landing on a boulder, he'd fractured his neck, sternum, kneecap, and left ankle, and he'd injured some ribs. Fortunately, his head was okay (though his helmet did take quite a beating). Cairnes's second big mistake: He didn't have an emergency beacon. Unable to walk and in excruciating pain, he spread out his orange tent on the ground, hoping a helicopter would fly over and see it. No one came. One of the things he did right was to bring a zero-degree-rated sleeping bag, which kept him from freezing to death at night. The next day, a helicopter did fly near Cairnes, but it kept going. That's when he realized he'd have to get out of there on his own. Using a walking stick to pull himself along the ground, he traveled about 200 feet per hour, at around a 6,000-foot elevation, until he finally

No Major League Baseball player had worn the jersey numbers 86, 89, or 92 until the 2020 season, when all three were issued for the first time.

made it to a trail. The other thing he did right: He'd texted his mom in Pennsylvania before he left, telling her the general area he was going to be in, and when he'd return. So when he didn't text her, she called the authorities, who sent out a search-and-rescue team. They found Cairnes weak but alert on the trail. Remarkably, he only had to spend a few days in the hospital, but he's still perplexed by his survival: "I hit it with so much force," he said, "I don't know why I'm here."

THE MISSING WEEK AND A HALF

Having been diagnosed with dementia, Linda Field was not supposed to be driving. In October 2019, the 62-year-old grandmother was sitting on her porch in Porter, Texas, while her daughter, Laura Bereta, warmed up her Ford Explorer, getting ready to pick up her son from school. Bereta went back in the house for a minute, and while she was gone, Field got in the car and drove away. With little fuel and no money, Bereta thought her mom would return soon. But minutes turned to hours, and then to days, and then she remembered her mom saying she wanted to go to Montana. A Silver Alert was issued (for missing people with a medical condition), and the search area grew wider. After a week of sleepless nights for Bereta, her mother's whereabouts were still unknown...even to her mother. When Field regained her senses, she was alone in a strange forest with no clue how she got there. She wandered until she found a creek, and—to this day, it's unknown exactly what she did with her time, other than praying and drinking creek water—she spent the next ten days there until someone spotted the Ford Explorer on the side of the road, about an hour north of Porter. A few hours later, search-and-rescue dogs located Fields, weak but alive. The dogs pulled her on a sled a mile back to the road, where she was transported to a hospital. "I knew I was going to be found," Field later said. "It was God's time." But Bereta still wonders what her mom did in those woods for a week and a half. "I don't think we'll ever know the whole truth."

GRAB A CHAIR AND POP OPEN A COLD ONE

On September 8, 2020, Don Myron was one of millions of Oregonians displaced by catastrophic wildfires that were fed by a historic 36-hour windstorm. Myron, who lived along the Little North Santiam River in a forested canyon near Salem, was faced with a choice: evacuate that afternoon, even though the fire was still 15 miles away, or stick around and try to save his home. In a decision he now regrets, he stayed. He watered everything he could and braced himself. Day turned to night. Still no flames. Just when he thought he might be okay, the sky turned orange. With burning branches starting to fall on his house, Myron, 56, could see that both sides of the river were burning, so he jumped in his car and drove the opposite way...and was soon blocked by fallen limbs. He returned home—on a flat tire—and got there just before the flames did. He got back in his car and looked at his home in the rearview mirror

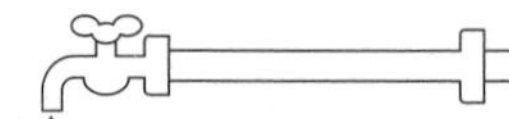

for the last time. He made it a little farther before getting blocked again. As he later told the *Salem Statesman Journal*, he said to himself, "Don, you've got to pull over and get the hell down to the river and under the bridge." Standing under that bridge in waist-deep water kept him safe for an hour until the vegetation caught fire and forced him out. Surrounded by intense heat and flames, and with incessant winds howling all around him, Myron was able to reach a wide part of the river, where he came across three chairs and a case of Rolling Rock beer on the bank. There was one beer left. He grabbed one of the chairs (and the beer) and made his way to a rocky outcrop in the middle of the river. For the next few hours, Myron used the plastic chair to shield himself from the torrents of flying embers. Then the smoke started to overtake him, so he had to crouch down under the chair at the water's surface and breathe through a T-shirt. He did that for several hours until he saw what he thought was the fire surging again, but it turned out to be the light of dawn. With the flames still smoldering in the burnt-out forest, Myron made it back to his car, which was charred but drivable, and found his way to safety. He later learned that if he hadn't been stopped by the downed branches, he would have driven right into a firestorm that had killed two people in their car. Myron credits that plastic chair with "saving my butt." When asked about the beer, he replied, "Hell yeah, I drank it."

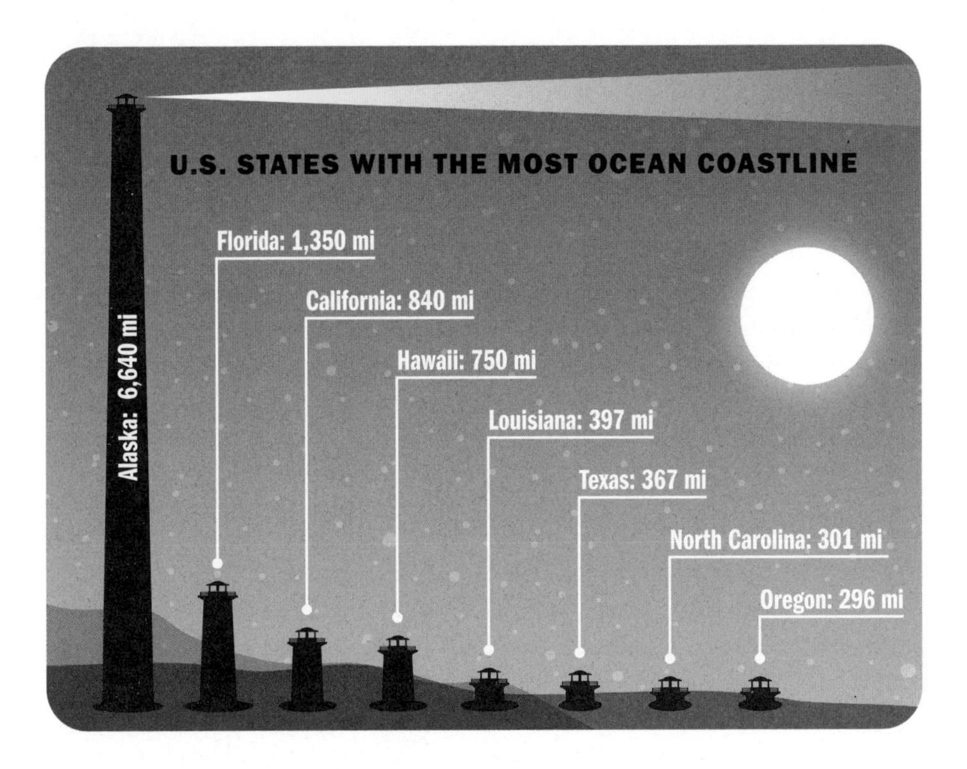

As a kid, Christopher Walken worked as a lion tamer in a circus. He says his lion, Sheba, was tame "like a dog."

THERE'S A MUSEUM FOR THAT

Sometimes it seems like there's no subject too odd, too obscure, or too insignificant for someone to build an entire museum around it.

BREAD: The Museum of Bread Culture (Ulm, Germany)

Details: The world's largest bread museum was founded in 1955 by the Eiselen family, who earned their dough selling bakery supplies. The museum features more than 18,000 artifacts organized into exhibits that cover every period of bread making, from the flatbreads made by hunter-gatherers 12,000 years ago to the gourmet breads of the present day, plus advances in bread technology, millers' guilds, and other topics. What won't you find? Actual bread, "reflecting the museum founders' firm belief that bread is not a museum artifact, but a food, freshly baked each day," explains the museum's website. (There is plenty of *fake* bread in the exhibits.)

Be Sure to See: The exhibit on medical uses of bread, such as treating wounds by rubbing them with moldy bread, a precursor to penicillin. (*Eww!*)

BARBED WIRE: The Devil's Rope Museum (McLean, Texas)

Details: If you've ever spent your days pondering the myriad uses and types of barbed wire (more than 2,000 kinds!), then this is the place for you. This tribute to barbed wire, which has been wrapped around ranches since 1874, is housed in an old bra factory. Inside, visitors learn that the wire was dubbed "devil's rope" because it injures so many people, livestock, and wild animals. Its other notable roles: caging prisoners, transmitting telephone signals, and planting crops—with a machine that ran along fences and dropped seeds at each barb. The museum has snagged unique samples of foreign wire crafted from camel hair and cactus stickers, as well as rare Cocklebur and Dodge Star wires, worth hundreds of dollars...*per inch.*

Be Sure to See: Barbed wire historian Delbert Trew's demonstration of a barbed wire–making machine that's homemade from windmill parts.

HAIR CLIPPINGS: The Chez Galip Hair Museum (Avanos, Cappadocia, Turkey)

Details: In the basement of Galip Körükçü's pottery and ceramics studio is a dim, cavelike room. Its walls and ceiling are completely covered in locks of women's hair, along with each owner's address and sometimes their photo. The creepy room isn't a serial killer's tribute to his victims; it's merely part of a tradition started in 1979. Körükçü was sad that his friend was returning to France, so she clipped a lock of her hair as a memento and wrote him a note with her address. After he hung both on

Technically speaking, snakes have belly buttons, because they grow inside an egg and are attached to the yolk by an umbilical cord. But the place where the cord was attached is not typically visible.

his wall, other customers noticed and followed suit. Since then, more than 16,000 women have left part of their hair in Körükçü's care.

Be Sure to See: The do-it-yourself hair clipping station with scissors, notepads, and tape to leave your donation. No men's hair, though! This one's just for the ladies.

ART THAT'S "TOO BAD TO BE IGNORED": The Museum of Bad Art (Somerville, Massachusetts)

Details: Bad art may be in the eye of the beholder, but these pieces all have what the museum describes as "a special quality that sets them apart...from the merely incompetent." Screwed-up proportions? Uncontrolled paintbrush (or even crayon) strokes? One-dimensional objects? All are welcome! Rescued from thrift stores or trash bins, most of these disasterpieces are attributed to Anonymous. The curator makes up fun titles and descriptions, and places art into categories such as "Poor-Traits," "In the Nood," and "Oozing My Religion."

Be Sure to See: "Safe at Home," a scene on a baseball diamond in which a hooved and headless beast is swallowing a Red Sox player with deformed hands who may have been running in the wrong direction around the bases (it's, uh, confusing).

MORE ODD MUSEUMS

- **The International Cryptozoology Museum** (Portland, Maine). Learn all about famous Cryptids like Bigfoot and the Loch Ness Monster, as well as more obscure ones like the Montauk Monster, the Chupacabra, and the Orang Pendek.
- **The National Poo Museum** (Isle of Wight, UK). This museum is full of "poo globes," specimens of animal dung enclosed in solid resin globes; they resemble crystal balls except that they're full of poo. Also on display: fossilized turds and a shoe that a cat pooped in. The museum's mission: "break down the taboo around poo."
- **Meguro Parasitological Museum** (Tokyo, Japan). An entire museum dedicated to the study of parasites, with hundreds on display, including the world's longest tapeworm (nearly 29 feet) and a turtle's head "overtaken by parasites."
- **Museum of Broken Relationships** (Zagreb, Croatia). "A collection of items left over after relationships have disintegrated," including love letters, a wedding dress, a vial of tears, a prosthetic leg, and edible underwear that was still uneaten when the relationship ended.
- **The National Mustard Museum** (Middleton, Wisconsin). Everything you've ever wanted to know about mustard, with 5,624 examples on display, a number of which can be purchased from the museum's mustard vending machine.
- **The Museum of Death** (New Orleans, Louisiana). Smack dab in the French Quarter, this museum's collection of artifacts from cannibals, serial killers, head shrinkers, famous murderers, and gruesome autopsies is enough to put you off your Cajun food.

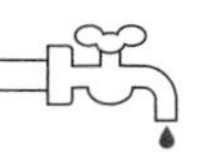

Baby giraffes rest their heads on their own rear ends when they lie down to sleep.

FLOP.COM

In the late 1990s and early 2000s, companies populating cyberspace grew at a tremendous rate—and enjoyed skyrocketing stock prices. Then the "dot-com bubble" burst, and a lot of companies went out of business. One reason why: Their names often didn't adequately describe what they were selling. Can you match the names of these long-gone dot-bombs with what they actually offered? (Answers are on page 405.)

1. *Boo.com*
2. *LastMinute.com*
3. *Kozmo.com*
4. *TheGlobe.com*
5. *Pseudo.com*
6. *iWon.com*
7. *Chemdex.com*
8. *Freei.com*
9. *Ritmoteca.com*
10. *Flooz.com*
11. *Gadzoox.com*
12. *Pixelon.com*
13. *Radvision.com*
14. *WebVan.com*
15. *Pets.com*
16. *Broadcast.com*
17. *AltaVista.com*
18. *StartUps.com*

a) Streaming video
b) Chat rooms for college students
c) Clothes and cosmetics
d) Seller of online-only currency
e) Internet service provider
f) Plane tickets and hotel booking
g) Grocery delivery
h) Online TV network
i) Internet-based telephone service
j) Video games and a cash lottery
k) Online music store
l) Home delivery of sundries
m) Online data storage
n) Laboratory equipment
o) Internet-based radio
p) Search engine
q) Dog and cat food
r) Internet business consultants

JUST PLANE WEIRD

If you happen to be reading this in midair, you might want to turn to another page and save this one for when you're safely back on the ground.

GOING NOWHERE

In 2020, worldwide restrictions, lockdowns, and stay-at-home orders aimed at curtailing the spread of the COVID-19 virus severely cut down on millions of people's ability to travel. In September, Australian carrier Qantas Airlines offered a solution for anyone who missed the airplane experience: a special seven-hour-flight... to nowhere. The round-trip flight was scheduled to depart Sydney Airport on October 10, and land back at Sydney Airport later that same day. Travelers would have an opportunity to see (from the air) Australian points of interest such as the Great Barrier Reef and the Uluru rock formation, and they'd still get to sleep in their own beds that night. So how many tickets did they sell? Of the 134 seats available on the Boeing 787 flight, all 134 seats were sold...in 10 minutes. Cost: $566 for coach, and $2,734 for first class. "It's probably the fastest selling flight in Qantas history," a spokesperson told reporters.

IT'S A GIRL

"Gender reveal parties" started as a fad in the late 2000s, and are now a common celebration during pregnancy. After parents-to-be learn the sex of their gestating infant, they throw a big bash to announce whether they're having a boy or girl, and the "reveal" involves the sudden appearance of something blue (for a boy) or pink (for a girl). In September 2020, expectant parents (their names weren't included in news accounts or the National Transportation Safety Board's report) in Turkey, Texas, held an unusual gender reveal party. For their gender reveal, they hired a local crop-dusting company to fly over a nearby field, where the pilot flew at a low altitude and dropped 350 gallons of pink water. (It's a girl!) But immediately after it discharged the water, according to the NTSB, the crop duster "aerodynamically stalled, impacted terrain, and came to rest inverted." In other words, the plane crashed. The pilot and passenger suffered only minor injuries.

HIDING OUT

An October 2020 American Airlines flight from Dallas to Miami had already been delayed 90 minutes (a catering truck had struck the plane's cargo door) when a flight attendant noticed that a passenger was missing. There was one empty seat on the plane despite the manifest listing a completely full plane with everyone checked

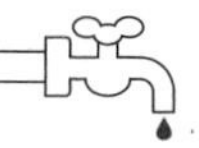

First disposable single-use camera: the Photo-Pac, in 1948. (It bombed.)

in. An announcement was made asking the missing woman to come forward, and warning that the plane couldn't leave until she was located, but no one responded. Finally, a flight attendant spotted the unaccounted-for individual crawling out from under a seat in first class and attempting to sneak back to her seat in coach. She'd been hiding in an alcove outfitted with a TV console—an empty space large enough to hold a bag or, apparently, a human being—that was in front of a seat occupied by a friend of hers. The captain returned to the gate and the women, who were doing this as a stunt for their YouTube channel, were told that they would have to leave the plane. When they refused, protesting (loudly) that they were being mistreated and disrespected, and that they'd done nothing wrong and had paid for their seats, security guards forcibly removed them from the plane.

WHEN DRUGS DRAG

A small, lightweight plane chartered by a private party was headed from the town of Mareeba in Far North Queensland, Australia, to Papua New Guinea in August 2020. Although the pilot kept the aircraft at a low altitude to avoid radar detection, authorities still noticed and figured the plane was being used for some kind of drug smuggling operation. After six days spent looking for the plane in the jungles of Papua New Guinea, government officials finally found it, crashed at the end of a rural airstrip outside Port Moresby. Though the plane was pilotless and empty, their suspicions had been correct: The plane was being used to smuggle drugs into Australia. How do they know? The pilot turned himself in to authorities and told them that the smugglers had stuffed the plane with 500 kilograms of cocaine—about $80 million worth of the stuff—which made the plane too heavy...and it crashed immediately on takeoff.

THE SHAPE OF THINGS

Until November 2020, soccer star Artyom Dzyuba was the captain of Russia's national team. Then he was fired amidst the embarrassing fallout when a videotape featuring the athlete performing a lewd act was leaked to the media. Fans across Russia protested Dzyuba's dismissal, including one pilot working for Pobeda Airlines, a subsidiary of Russia's national carrier Aeroflot. On an eastbound flight from Moscow to Yekaterinburg carrying more than 100 passengers, the pilot (unnamed in news reports) deviated from the usual, approved flight path and employed a roundabout course that, when plotted on a map or air traffic controllers' monitors, formed the shape of human male genitalia—a show of solidarity with Dzyuba's video, which featured a lot of that. The Rosaviatsia, Russia's federal transportation agency, recommended that the pilot be reprimanded for his unauthorized rerouting, and that the head of Aeroflot offer his resignation.

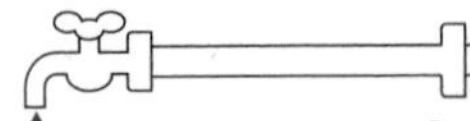

Loudest animal on Earth: the sperm whale, whose clicks register 230 decibels, much louder than a shotgun blast (165 dB).

SMARMY REVIEWS

Sure, everyone's a critic, but some folks make an art of it. These are real product reviews we found online.

A lift-the-flap book for toddlers, *Where Is Baby's Belly Button?*
"Everything falls apart the second you realize that the belly button was in plain sight all along. There is no conflict, there is no character development, and there is scarcely any plot...One of the worst pieces of literature I have ever read."

The book *Crafting with Cat Hair: Cute Handicrafts to Make with Your Cat*
"My wife has made all of the Christmas gifts for our friends and family. She has made 4 pairs of socks, 2 scarves, 3 hats, a toaster cozy, slippers, a winter jacket and carpeted the family room."

A banana slicer
"One of the greatest inventions of all time. My husband and I would argue constantly over who had to cut the day's banana slices. It's one of those chores NO ONE wants to do! You know, the old 'I spent the entire day rearing OUR children, maybe YOU can pitch in a little and cut these bananas?'...The minute I heard our 6-year-old girl in her bedroom, re-enacting our daily banana fight with her Barbie dolls, I knew we had to make a change...THANKS BANANA SLICER!"

Googly eyes stickers
"Best pasties ever. Made the strip club look like sesame street 'after dark'."

"Vintage" Casio calculator watch
"It's like an Apple Watch only it costs under $20...Doesn't send text messages, but you can write such words as 'BOOBS', 'BOOBLESS', 'BEES', and 'SHOE'. So if you're a man of few words and your friend is right next to you, it's basically the same as iMessage."

T-shirt with an image of wolves howling at the Moon (worn on *The Office* by Dwight, who calls it "suggestive to women")
"It's like a redneck magical pumpkin that doesn't end at 12am. Once I apply the magical wolves fabric to my chest, my mullet grew like Odin's beard, my rusted T-top Firebird turned sweet candy apple red and my White Snake tape started playing its body moving melodies once again."

Sugar-free gummy bears, which, according to reviewers, cause gastrointestinal issues
"My friend hasn't been practicing social distancing during the pandemic, so I bought him a bag of these gummies for his birthday. It's now been 10 days since he left the house out of fear of pooping himself again."

Ford's Theatre, reviewed by "Abe L."
"Was murdered here. Would not recommend."

Yosemite Sam's full name: Samuel Michelangelo Rosenbaum.

UFO Detector
“Critical Flaw. If you’re hiding in a hedge waiting for a UFO to make an appearance, bear in mind that nothing attracts attention like a beeping plastic cylinder with sixteen flashing LEDs.”

Pillowcase with Nicolas Cage’s face and “See you in my dreams” printed on it
“I bought one for all my loved ones for Christmas. They were at a loss for words. So much in fact, I haven’t heard from any of them since Christmas. Totally worth the money.”

White air mattress with brown cover
“I ordered this when I was high because I thought it was a giant ice cream sandwich. It’s not. It’s a bed and not the $150 ice cream sandwich I wanted.”

A grandmother’s review of the animated film *Zootopia* (2016)
“I started out hopeful that it was going to be good. Then it kept getting darker and then ‘nude’ animals entered...Not appropriate and suggestive.”

The book *How to Avoid Huge Ships*
“WHY NO KINDLE EDITION??????? Given that there is a huge ship bearing down on me RIGHT NOW I am extremely disappointed that I cannot get inst–”

***Star Wars* (1977) on DVD**
“the phantom menace was better. this movie was the worst by far, there was only one light saber fight, and they didnt even do any spins and stuff.”

Bic for Her pens
“Comes without instructions! We are frantically waiting for the plus or minus sign to appear, but...nothing. My wife peed on all sixteen of them and none seem to work.”

The book *A Million Random Digits,* which is just lists of numbers
“Still a better love story than *Twilight*.”

A “Daddle”—a saddle for kids to ride on their dad
“Please note that this Daddle is Western Style and will not be appropriate for those trained in the English Father Riding Method.”

A Playmobil Airport Security Check Point playset

A Luke Skywalker Ceremonial Jacket with Medal of Yavin
“Chick Repellent. I was tired of getting hit on by beautiful women every time I went out in public, and then I bought this jacket. Problem solved.”

A cat door
“I hate my wife’s cat but it made my wife pretty happy that the cat can come into our bedroom at-will now and claw the dogs while they sleep.”

A black and silver casket
“Its Great. No complaints from Grandpa.”

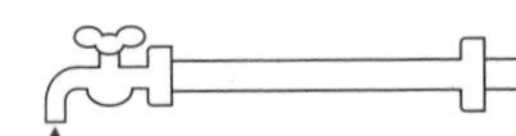

Oldest musical instruments ever found:
the Geisenklösterle flutes, carved from bird bones and mammoth ivory,...

MIGALOO AND SPLASHY PANTS

Most whales will live out their entire lives without attracting the attention of human beings, perhaps without ever even being seen by one. And then there are whales like these two.

MIGALOO

Background: Migaloo is a white humpback whale, first spotted in 1991 off Byron Bay, New South Wales, in southeastern Australia, by community volunteers conducting a whale count. He was estimated to be three to five years of age.

Whale of a Tale: White whales are extremely rare, and as soon as the sighting was announced to the public, the whale began to attract a large following. A whale that popular needs a name, and it was decided that the elders of an aboriginal collective in Hervey Bay, Queensland, should be the ones to name it. They settled on "Migaloo," which means "white fella" in several aboriginal languages.

The first photographs of Migaloo were taken through a telescope from more than three miles away. From that distance it wasn't possible to tell if he was *all* white, or just *mostly* white, with darker markings somewhere on his body. It wasn't until another sighting in Hervey Bay in 1993, that scientists were able to confirm he was, in fact, all white, and it wasn't until 1998 that he was recorded singing, which means he is a male, since only male humpbacks sing. DNA tests conducted in 2011 confirmed that Migaloo is a true albino, which means that he has no pigment in his skin at all.

Keep Your Distance: Australian law protects all whales from humans getting too close, but public interest in Migaloo is so great—he was struck by a boat in 2003—that special legislation had to be passed to keep people even farther away from albino whales than from ordinary whales. The legislation requires that boats and other watercraft keep more than 550 yards away, and airplanes flying overhead cannot approach lower

DID YOU KNOW?

- When whales "sleep," only one half of their brain is asleep at any time. The other half remains awake to enable the whale to surface periodically for air.
- One way that scientists determine a whale's age is by analyzing the wax in its ears. The earwax can also reveal the toxins that the whale has been exposed to.
- Closest living land mammal relative of whales, porpoises, and dolphins: the hippopotamus.

...were discovered in a prehistoric German cave and are 42,000 years old.

than 2,000 feet. Failure to obey these restrictions can result in a fine of AU $16,500 (about $12,000). The law is renewed every year.

Update: As of 2020, Migaloo is in his mid-30s and has been spotted more than 50 times—he's hard to miss! And he has a traveling companion. Quite often when he's spotted, an ordinary male humpback (named Milo) is seen swimming nearby. Migaloo is not the only albino whale in the sea: another white humpback whale, named Bahloo, was spotted near the Great Barrier Reef in 2008, and a white humpback calf called Migaloo Jr. was spotted near the reef in 2011. It's not known whether any of the whales are related to each other, though Migaloo may be Migaloo Jr.'s father. Bahloo has black spots on its head and tail, which means it's not a true albino.

MR. SPLASHY PANTS

Background: In 2007, the anti-whaling group Greenpeace launched a campaign to raise awareness of the Japanese government's plan to hunt 50 endangered humpback whales each year for what it claimed were "scientific research purposes." As part of the campaign, Greenpeace tagged 20 humpback whales with satellite tracking devices, then organized an online poll to name some of the tagged whales.

Whale of a Tale: Greenpeace accepted 30 suggestions from the public, then called for a vote. Though the organization hoped that some of the more serious names like Aiko, Shanti, or Libertad would be popular, someone suggested the name "Mr. Splashy Pants," and it won more than 78 percent of the vote. "Humphrey," the second most popular name, got less than 3 percent. Greenpeace wasn't happy with the results, but it bowed to public sentiment and named one of the whales Mr. Splashy Pants. Smart move: The whale with the silly name generated so much news coverage—and so much negative publicity for the whale hunt—that the Japanese government abandoned its plans to hunt humpback whales.

"Humphrey," the second most popular name, got less than 3 percent.

* * *

"Consider the subtleness of the sea; how its most dreaded creatures glide under water, unapparent for the most part, and treacherously hidden beneath the loveliest tints of azure. Consider also the devilish brilliance and beauty of many of its most remorseless tribes, as the dainty embellished shape of many species of sharks. Consider, once more, the universal cannibalism of the sea; all whose creatures prey upon each other, carrying on eternal war since the world began."

—**Herman Melville, *Moby-Dick***

WELCOME TO MIANUS

Some towns have names that were perfectly acceptable when they were founded, but have taken on alternate meanings since then. Result: A bunch of places that sound like their names should be unprintable.

Shitterton (England)

Sexmoán (The Philippines)

Thong (England)

Beaver Lick (Kentucky)

Weener (Germany)

Penistone (England)

Gofuku (Japan)

Erect (North Carolina)

New Erection (Virginia)

Cockington (England)

Big Beaver (Saskatchewan)

Three Way (Tennessee)

Colon (Michigan)

Fanny Mountain (Alaska)

Windy Passage (Alaska)

Shitagoo Lake (Quebec)

Mianus (Connecticut)

Ballplay (Alabama)

Horneytown (North Carolina)

Poop (Mexico)

Pis Ris River (Nicaragua)

Bum Bum Island (Malaysia)

Peculiar Knob (Australia)

Lovely Bottom (Australia)

Bowels of the Earth (New Zealand)

Leakesville (Mississippi)

Buttzville (New Jersey)

Pee Pee Township (Ohio)

Organ Cave (West Virginia)

Goshen Hole (Wyoming)

Rectum (The Netherlands)

Crap (Albania)

Anus (France)

Boysack (Scotland)

Ta Ta Creek (British Columbia)

Weiner (Arkansas)

Hoars Addition (Delaware)

Slickpoo (Idaho)

Bonus: The sign welcoming visitors to Shitterton was (understandably) stolen so many times that in 2016, residents pitched in to buy one too difficult to abscond with: It's a 1.5-ton stone with "Shitterton" carved into it.

OOF!

A few obscure words that contain, in order, the letters "o-o-f." Most of these probably won't be accepted in a game of Scrabble, but they are real words nonetheless. (Note: "Oof" is also the sound Uncle John made when he saw this article.)

OOF/OOFTISH. Slang terms for cash or money. (Archaic British English, derived from the Yiddish *oyf tish,* meaning "on table," used by gamblers demanding to see fellow gamblers' money "on the table.") Bonus: "Ooftish" is the title of a 1938 poem by Irish writer Samuel Beckett.

OOFY. Slang for rich or wealthy. (Archaic; see above.)

FOOFARAW. A great deal of fuss over a trivial matter, e.g., "The staff made a great foofaraw over Uncle John's tight leather pants." Also refers to excessive and flashy frills, e.g., "Jay's neighbors are always amused by the blow-up Santas and other holiday foofaraw he puts up every year." (First appeared in the mid-1800s in the American West, and was spelled "fofaraw," "forfarraw," and "froufraw." Possible origins for the word include the Spanish *fanfarrón,* meaning "braggart," and *froufrou,* a French word that describes extravagant frills, derived from the rustling noises made by a frilly-layered dress.)

BOOFHEAD. Slang term for a fool or buffoonish person. "Meaghan told Chris she was tired of her job at the bus company because her coworkers were a bunch of 'obnoxious boofheads.'" (Australian English)

SHADOOF. An ancient device used to fetch water from a well, river, or other water source, consisting of a long pole with a heavy weight at one end and a bucket attached to a rope at the other. The pole itself is suspended from a wooden frame, allowing the bucket to be pulled down into the water. The counterweight at the other end of the pole then allows the bucket to be easily lifted out of the water. Shadoofs, also known as counterpoise lifts, well poles, and well sweeps, are still used today.

WITLOOF. From the Dutch *witloof,* meaning "white leaf," this variety of chicory is also called Belgian endive. The plant, with its firm white and yellowish leaves that grow in a tight, cone-shaped bundle, was developed in Belgium in the mid-1800s, and is widely cultivated for food around the world today.

LOOF. Slang term for the palm of the hand, or the whole hand. (Scottish English)

COOF. A stupid person, a dolt, an idiot: "Oy! Reginald, you coof, stop sticking your loof in the fire!" (Scottish English)

KLOOF. A deep ravine or glen, e.g., "Reginald, you absolute coof, keep your loof on the handrail or you'll fall into the kloof!" (British English, from Afrikaans)

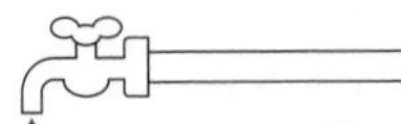

TIBOTIs

*A TIBOTI (**T**hing that **I**s **B**igger **O**n **T**he **I**nside—an acronym we made up for this article) is a seemingly normal object that can be viewed in its entirety, but on the inside, it is impossibly vast. It's time to leave logic behind and explore some spacious settings from the bottomless depths of pop culture. Physics be damned!*

THE TARDIS

On the Outside: The Doctor's space-time ship on *Doctor Who*, which premiered on the BBC in 1963, looks like a typical British blue police box (a telephone booth used for calling police, common in the UK in the 20th century).

On the Inside: There's a cavernous control room with blinking lights, knobs, and a doohickey that goes up and down—all of which perform, as the Tenth Doctor (David Tennant) explains, "wibbly-wobbly, timey-wimey stuff." Astonished first-time passengers are further amazed to find that the ship's control room doors lead to a library, a costume shop, gardens, swimming pools, squash courts, a cricket pavilion, and many other things mentioned but rarely seen.

Details: The TARDIS (short for *Time And Relative Dimension In Space*) once had the ability to change into any shape by use of a "chameleon circuit," which the Doctor lost long ago (and doesn't seem very eager to find). In real life, the reason the Doctor travels in a blue police box is because the BBC didn't have the budget to build him a spaceship in 1963. The original TARDIS prop was borrowed from the set of a police show called *Dixon of Dock Green*.

THE WEASLEYS' TENT

On the Outside: It looks like a "shabby, two-man tent" that Ron Weasley's family borrows to take to the Quidditch World Cup in *Harry Potter and the Goblet of Fire*, by J. K. Rowling. But once activated via the Extension Charm spell—"*Capacious extremis!*"—the tent makes a magical transformation.

On the Inside: There are multiple levels, a small kitchen, living room, a wood-burning stove, bunk beds, and a bathroom.

Details: The Extension Charm shows up often in the Potterverse. It's been used to add more seating to Mr. Weasley's flying Ford Anglia, to hide a large professor inside a small trunk, and to hide Harry and his friends inside a handbag. And in Rowling's Potter spinoff *Fantastic Beasts and Where to Find Them*, those beasts can be found inside Newt Scamander's suitcase...until they get out.

SNOOPY'S DOGHOUSE

On the Outside: A red doghouse, only seen from the side, in Charles Schulz's *Peanuts* comic strip that ran from 1950 to 2000

On the Inside: Snoopy's got a lot going on in there. His most prized possession was his Van Gogh painting, tragically lost when the doghouse burned down in a 1966 strip. (He replaced it with an Andrew Wyeth painting.) Over the years, the doghouse also contained a Ping-Pong table, a grandfather clock, a library, a science lab, an exercise room, a servant's entrance, bunk beds, a picture of Tiny Tim, and a ceiling mural painted by Linus—none of which we've ever seen.

Details: Why can't we see the inside of Snoopy's doghouse? "It's too fantastic," Schulz explained. "No one could draw what we've said is down there." Instead, he used the contents to reveal more about the beagle's personality. In the beginning, the doghouse was shown at an angle, making it possible to see a bit inside. But a year into the strip, Schulz drew it from the side for the first time. Charlie Brown walks past, sees an antenna mounted on top, and observes, "Everyone is buying television sets these days." That was the first hint that there's more in Snoopy's doghouse than meets the eye.

OSCAR THE GROUCH'S GARBAGE CAN

On the Outside: It's a metal garbage can on top of a crate, located right next to the front stoop at 123 Sesame Street, on the PBS children's show that premiered in 1969.

On the Inside: One of most memorable sight gags on *Sesame Street* is when Oscar's herd of pet elephants stick their trunks out of his garbage can. All the viewer can see is the trunks; what's going on inside is left to the imagination. Also mentioned but never seen in the garbage can: an Olympic-sized swimming pool, an ice-skating rink, a pastry kitchen, a piano, an art gallery, goats, a horse, and a dolphin.

Details: Originally, Oscar was going to live in a manhole, but co-creators Jim Henson and Jon Stone didn't have a trapdoor under the stage. Solution: They put Oscar's garbage can on top of a crate large enough to fit puppeteer Caroll Spinney, who performed both Oscar and Big Bird from 1969 until 2018. There's a fan theory that Oscar actually lives in an underground lair beneath his garbage can, but that's disproven every time Oscar and his can are carried around by Bruno the Trashman (also played by Spinney, who operated Oscar through a hole in the back of the can). Even more mind-blowing: Oscar sometimes walks around with his feet sticking out of the bottom of the can. So where are the elephants?

MAGRATHEA

On the Outside: It's an Earthlike planet.

On the Inside: It's a planet-making *factory*, more vast than a solar system.

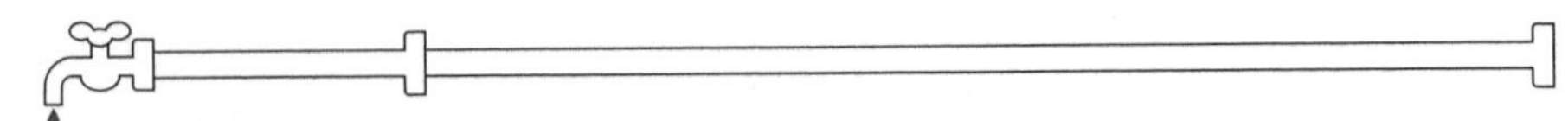

Who is Joseph Fourestier Simpson? He invented the carnival game Skee-Ball in 1908.

Details: The entry for Magrathea in *The Hitchhiker's Guide to the Galaxy* says it was created long ago when "hyperspatial engineers sucked matter through white holes in space to form it into dream planets—gold planets, platinum planets, soft rubber planets with lots of earthquakes." The planet-making factory features heavily in Douglas Adams's *Hitchhiker's* books, TV show, and movie. Adams never quite explained how Magrathea can be so vast inside, but in the book, a planet factory worker named Slartibartfast notes that it gives "the impression of infinity far better than infinity itself."

MARY POPPINS'S MAGIC CARPETBAG

On the Outside: Just what it sounds like—a top-opening handbag made of carpet

On the Inside: It contains everything that a supercalifragilisticexpialidocious nanny might need, including "an apron, a packet of hairpins, a bottle of scent, a small folding armchair, a packet of throat lozenges, a large bottle of dark red medicine, seven flannel nightgowns, one pair of boots, a set of dominoes, two bathing caps, one postcard album, one folding camp bedstead, blankets and an eiderdown."

Details: Author Helen Lyndon "Ginty" Goff (whose pen name was P. L. Travers) grew up in Australia in the early 1900s. She and her sisters were raised by their great aunt Ellie (after their alcoholic father died of tuberculosis), and Ellie was the inspiration for Mary Poppins. Like Mary Poppins, she had a carpetbag that seemed to young Ginty to hold far more than it should have been able to. As Mary Poppins (Julie Andrews) advises in the 1964 Disney movie, "Never judge things by their appearance. Even carpetbags. I never do."

AND FINALLY: A REAL TIBOTI?

Can something like a TARDIS exist in real life? Possibly. Some astrophysicists suggest that it would have to be connected to a wormhole, or maybe multiple wormholes, each one leading to another room in the TARDIS. Scientists know that wormholes exist, even though no human has ever seen one. Another theory was proposed by an astrophysicist named Erin MacDonald in the blog *Technically Fiction*. She says the TARDIS could be a *tesseract*, a special kind of cube that contains a fourth dimension inside. What is that dimension? The fourth dimension is usually assumed to be time. But MacDonald says *this* fourth dimension would be a space dimension. Partial explanation (sort of): If you were to look at a three-dimensional cube straight-on, it would appear as a two-dimensional square until you moved to the side and could see the third dimension. With a tesseract, you wouldn't experience the fourth dimension until you entered...and encountered a world many times bigger than what it appeared to be on the outside.

We'd love to fit in a few more, but this is the real world, and we're out of space.

THE STADTTEMPEL

If you ever happen to visit Vienna, Austria, take some time to visit the Stadttempel, the only synagogue in the city that wasn't destroyed during the Holocaust.

OUT OF SIGHT

In the early 1820s, the Jewish community in Vienna decided to build a synagogue in the center of the city, to provide a house of worship for the city's growing Jewish population. Vienna was then the capital of the Austrian Empire, whose official state religion was Roman Catholicism. Although Jews and non-Catholic Christian denominations within the empire had enjoyed freedom of religion since the 1780s, their right to worship was limited. For example, they were allowed to build churches and synagogues, but the buildings could not open onto, or be visible from, public streets. Nor could the buildings have steeples, bells, or any other exterior features that would call attention to their religious purpose.

With these restrictions in mind, Jewish leaders set to work planning what would become known as the Stadttempel, or City Prayer House. They hired one of Vienna's most prominent architects, Joseph Kornhäusel, who had designed palaces for Austria's royal family, the Habsburgs, as well as the royal family of Liechtenstein. Kornhäusel came up with a design for a synagogue that would be surrounded by two five-story apartment buildings, one on either side of the synagogue, that would hide the synagogue from view. The Stadttempel would be physically attached to one of the apartment buildings and right next to the other; all three buildings would be constructed at the same time.

HIDDEN BEAUTY

That layout hid the synagogue from view on the street, but how would worshippers enter unseen? The entrance to the neoclassical Stadttempel would be down a narrow, alleylike side street called the Seitenstettengasse. The entrance was of necessity modest, with Hebrew lettering above the doors offering the only hint as to what lay beyond. Once inside the building, a visitor may as well have been in one of the grand ballrooms in the palaces that Kornhäusel had designed: The Stadttempel's large main hall was oval-shaped and over two stories tall, with a domed ceiling painted sky blue with gold stars to mimic the actual sky. Surrounding the main floor, where the men worshipped, were the women's galleries on two levels—set apart from the central hall by 12 Ionic stone columns that circled the room. The setting was magnificent, and also well hidden. If you didn't wander down the narrow Seitenstettengasse and poke your head through the right set of doors, you would never have known the synagogue was there.

The melody from the *Flintstones* theme song was derived from a section of Beethoven's *Piano Sonata no. 17*.

NIGHTMARE YEARS

Ironically, the religious discrimination that resulted in the Stadttempel being constructed in this fashion—surrounded by and structurally attached to apartment buildings instead of as a freestanding structure—is the only reason it survives today. The synagogue opened in 1826 and served as the spiritual heart of Vienna's Jewish community for just over a century. Then, in March 1938, Adolf Hitler annexed Austria in what was called the *Anschluss* (union). On November 9 of that year, the Nazis orchestrated what would come to be known as *Kristallnacht* (Night of Broken Glass), a *pogrom,* or violent attack, on Jewish communities in every part of the Third Reich, which now included Austria. Synagogues in virtually every city and town were ransacked by the Nazis and then burned to the ground; firefighters were instructed to prevent the fires from spreading to surrounding buildings, but they had strict orders to let the synagogues burn.

In Vienna alone, 92 of the 93 synagogues and Jewish prayer houses were destroyed by arson in a single night. Only the Stadttempel survived, and only because it was structurally attached to one apartment building and smack dab against another—there was no way to burn it down without the fire spreading to those buildings and beyond. The Nazis ransacked the Stadttempel but left it standing. Damaged but not destroyed, it survived the war.

A NEW BEGINNING

On May 7, 1945, Nazi Germany surrendered unconditionally, bringing the war in Europe to an end. After the war, the damage to the Stadttempel was repaired, and it served as the community center for the tiny remnant of Vienna's Jewish community that had survived the Holocaust. About 192,000 Jews had lived in Austria before the Anschluss; afterward, between 1938 and 1941, more than 135,000 were forced by the Nazis to emigrate abroad. Few would ever return. Most of the 57,000 Jews who were unwilling or unable to leave Austria were subject to forced deportation. About 35,000 Jews from Vienna alone were later "deported" to ghettos and ultimately to concentration camps. All but about 2,000 were murdered in the Holocaust. At war's end, the Jewish community in Vienna numbered only 4,000 people, and many of those people emigrated to Palestine, the United States, and other places after the war, causing the community to shrink further.

In the decades since then, Vienna's Jewish community has slowly grown to an estimated 15,000 people, including many émigrés from the former Soviet Union. The Stadttempel is still the main synagogue of Vienna and the heart of the city's Jewish community, as well as one of its few surviving links to the community's pre-war past. It is also home to a memorial for the more than 65,000 Austrian Jews who perished in the Holocaust. Its stark beauty serves as a silent witness to its own tragic past.

2012 Land Rovers sold in Dubai came with a desert survival guide made out of edible paper and ink.

MIS-MAPPED FOODS

Just because a food is named for a place doesn't mean it comes from there.

Philadelphia Cream Cheese: This Kraft Foods product isn't made in the City of Brotherly Love, and it never was. Naming it "Philadelphia" was a marketing ploy. In 1880, New York–based cheese men Alvah Reynolds and William Lawrence teamed up to promote their line of cream cheeses by calling it Philadelphia Cream Cheese. At the time, Philly was America's dairy capital and renowned for its top-quality cheeses.

Chicken Kiev: This entrée was named after the capital city of Ukraine and is that nation's national dish...although it was created someplace else. In the early 1900s, European royalty and elites considered French food to be the peak of cuisine, and Russia's Empress Elizabeth sent her chefs to France to learn the proper techniques. One dish they brought back was *côtelettes de volaille,* chicken breast stuffed with herb butter. Its popularity spread through Russia but wasn't widely known in the former Soviet republic of Ukraine until after World War II, when it was served to victorious military leaders.

Hawaiian Punch: Before it was a sugary fruit-flavored drink for kids, Hawaiian Punch was marketed as a thick, gooey, fruit-flavored topping for ice-cream sundaes. That's what inventors A. W. Leo, Tom Yeats, and Ralph Harrison intended when they concocted it in 1934 in a garage in Fullerton, California. The original ingredient list included the juices of five fruits shipped in from Hawaii—orange, passion fruit, papaya, guava, and pineapple.

German Chocolate Cake: In 1852, American chocolatier Sam German went to work for the Baker's Chocolate Company, where he invented a product the company named after him—German's Dark Chocolate (named not for bakers, but for company founder Dr. James Baker). It wasn't a big seller until the 1950s, when a recipe for "German's Chocolate Cake" appeared in homemaking magazines. The dessert calls for coconut, nuts, and the chocolate devised by a man named German, who was actually born in England.

Denver Omelet: This diner classic is made with eggs, ham, cheese, diced green peppers, and diced onions. Restaurants in Denver may have appropriated it, but the dish started as a version of the Chinese dish egg foo young, introduced to the United States by Chinese railroad workers in the late 1800s. That entrée consists of eggs, ham, and whatever vegetables are available. Workers ate it on bread to make it more portable, and American cooks later adapted it into an omelet (with toast on the side).

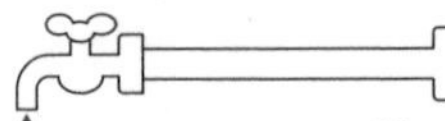

Denali Flavors: This company produces a line of "Alaskan Classics" ice cream flavors named after animals native to the state, including "Moose Tracks," "Bear Claw," and "Caramel Caribou." Denali is the name of a prominent national park and mountain in Alaska, but Denali Flavors bases its operations a few thousand miles away in Michigan.

Lima Beans: This starchy green bean is native to western South America and was domesticated by Indigenous people around 2000 BC. That's where modern-day Peru is located, and its capital city is Lima. The "Lima" in "Lima beans," however, is pronounced "lye-mah," while the city's name is pronounced "lee-mah."

Fig Newtons: The popular fig-paste cookies are named after Newton, Massachusetts, but they didn't originate there. They were invented and first manufactured in 1891 by the now-defunct Kennedy Biscuit Company in the nearby town of Cambridge. At the time, Kennedy named most of its cookies and crackers after Boston-area places. Only Fig Newtons have survived to the modern day (though Nabisco, which owns the brand, dropped "Fig" from the name in 2012 and now simply calls them "Newtons").

DID YOU KNOW?

Twenty-eight states have an "official state beverage," and thanks to aggressive lobbying by the dairy industry in the 1980s, milk is the official state beverage of 19 of those states. Some others include tomato juice (Ohio), apple cider (New Hampshire), cranberry juice (Massachusetts), and the soda Moxie (Maine).

Baked Alaska: This showstopper of a dessert consists of layers of ice cream placed over sponge or pound cake and topped with meringue, which is then browned with a torch or in the oven. Although the dish is served as cold as Alaska, it wasn't created there. In 1876, Delmonico's Steakhouse in New York City whipped it up in honor of Alaska, on the occasion of the U.S. government purchasing the territory from Russia.

Moscow Mule: The cocktail, consisting of lime juice, ginger beer, and vodka served in a copper mug, isn't from Moscow, or anywhere else in Russia. The drink's creators (who devised it in New York in the 1940s) gave it the "Moscow" as a reference to the fact that it contains vodka, a spirit closely associated with Russia. (It most likely got the "mule" part from the kick provided by the ginger beer.)

German Pancakes: This breakfast treat is like a sweetened pancake in the form of a ball or popover. One might also see it on a diner menu as a Dutch Baby, and yet the dish didn't originate in Germany or the Netherlands. Manca's Café, a Seattle restaurant, originated the Dutch Baby in the 1940s, and at one point owned a trademark on the term.

Puppy pregnancy syndrome is a condition where, after getting bitten by a dog, the patient thinks they're pregnant with puppies.

KARENS

Now for some thoughtful quotations to remind us that women named Karen have a lot more to say than "I demand to speak to your manager!"

"There is no ascent to the heights without prior descent into darkness, no new life without some form of death."

—**Karen Armstrong**, author

"Rationalization may be defined as self-deception by reasoning."

—**Karen Horney**, psychoanalyst

"CULTURE INFORMS PERSPECTIVE, AND THE WORLD IS A COMPLICATED PLACE. TELLING THE STORY ON STAGE INCREASES UNDERSTANDING."

—**Karen Zacarias**, playwright

"It is a mistake to do nothing just because you think you can only do a little."

—**Karen Duffy**, author

"It's so much easier to throw rocks than it is to govern."

—U.S. Rep. **Karen Bass** (D-CA)

"The best things in life are often waiting for you at the exit ramp of your comfort zone."

—**Karen Salmansohn**, author

"The irony is that the more we fight age, the more it shows."

—**Karen DeCrow**, attorney

"Eventually you love people—friends or lovers—because of their flaws."

—**Karen Allen**, actor

"*There is no pot of gold at the end of the rainbow.*"

—**Karen Black**, actor

BEHIND THE HITS

Ever wonder what inspired your favorite songs? Here are the inside stories of some popular tunes.

The Artist: Queen

The Song: "Under Pressure" (1981)

The Story: In 1981, Queen retired to Mountain Studios in Montreaux, Switzerland, a recording facility owned by the band. One of the songs they started working on was called "People on the Streets," centered on a propulsive, two-note riff devised by bassist John Deacon. One day, Queen took a break and went out for pizza, but when they returned to the studio to lay down "People on the Streets," Deacon couldn't remember the riff. After several hours of trying, drummer Roger Taylor figured it out. The song remained unfinished when who should drop by the studio but David Bowie, who lived nearby, off Lake Geneva. After drinking a lot of wine, Bowie had an idea: He and Queen singer Freddie Mercury would do "People on the Streets" as a duet, but they'd record their parts separately and wouldn't be allowed to hear each other's takes. Mercury agreed to it, but then Bowie cheated—he secretly listened to Mercury's recordings so he could sing the perfect counterpoint. Mercury was angry at being misled, but his animosity didn't last—renamed "Under Pressure," the song hit #1 in the UK and #29 in the United States.

The Artist: The 5th Dimension

The Song: "Aquarius / Let the Sunshine In" (1969)

The Story: *Hair* was Broadway's first "rock" musical. The show, a series of sketches and musical numbers about 1960s hippies and the anti–Vietnam War counterculture movement, opened off-Broadway at the Public Theatre in New York City in 1967 before moving to Broadway in 1968, where it became a massive hit. That same year, pop vocal group the 5th Dimension booked a string of shows in New York. One day, lead singer Billy Davis Jr. left his wallet in a cab. It was discovered by the next passenger, who tracked down Davis to return it. The Good Samaritan happened to be a *Hair* producer, and invited Davis and the rest of the group to attend a performance. The band so loved "Aquarius," the show's opening number about how, according to the astrological calendar, the Earth was about to enter a period of love and understanding, that they decided to record a cover version. Only problem: their producer, Bones Howe, felt the song was subpar—nothing more than a half-finished introductory number—and needed some additional material. So Howe went and saw *Hair,* and found what he was looking for: The ending of the song "The Flesh

First sporting event ever filmed: an 1894 boxing match between James Corbett and Peter Courtney at Thomas Edison's studio.

Failures," which featured the cast ecstatically imploring the audience to "let the sunshine in," over and over. But no one could figure out how to connect the two dissimilar songs, until studio drummer Hal Blaine came up with a percussive bridge. "Aquarius / Let the Sunshine In" went to #1 in April 1969, and it's the last show tune to top the pop chart.

The Artist: The Andrea True Connection

The Song: "More, More, More" (1976)

The Story: Andrea Truden, who used the stage name Andrea True, worked in several different fringes of the entertainment industry in the late 1960s and early 1970s. She wrote music for commercials, performed as a nightclub singer, appeared as an extra in Hollywood films, and starred in more than two dozen adult films under the names "Inger Kissin," "Rose Stevens," and "Sandra Lips." In 1975, Truden went to Jamaica to film a TV commercial, but when she tried to return to New York, authorities wouldn't let her leave the country with the money she'd just earned there—it was a response to American sanctions levied on Jamaica after the election of socialist-leaning Prime Minister Michael Manley. Truden had to spend her money in Jamaica or forfeit it, so she used it to record a demo of a disco song written by her friend Gregg Diamond. The tune: "More, More, More," a breathy, hypnotic, and seductive track memorable for its repeated refrain of "How do you like it? How do you like it?" When they returned to the United States, Truden and Diamond expanded the demo into a fully produced song, adding studio musicians and calling the project "The Andrea True Connection." It hit radio and dance clubs in early 1976, where it became a smash hit, reaching #4 in the United States and #1 in Canada.

The Artist: Oasis

The Song: "Wonderwall" (1995)

The Story: Oasis was supposed to be "the next big thing"—Generation X's version of the Beatles. Like the Fab Four, they were from northern England and crafted catchy pop-rock. Its members were also unabashed Beatles fanatics, lacing songs with references to the band, most notably on its first worldwide hit, the ballad "Wonderwall," named for *Wonderwall Music,* George Harrison's first solo album. When Oasis guitarist/songwriter Noel Gallagher first came up with the song, he titled it "Wishing Stone," but then changed it because he thought a nonsense word would be more of a conversation starter. Gallagher told British music magazine *NME* that he wrote the love song for his then-girlfriend, Meg Matthews, who became his wife in 1997. But after they divorced in 2001, he changed his mind, telling BBC Radio, "The meaning of that song was taken away from me by the media who jumped on it, and how do you tell your missus it's not about her once she's read it

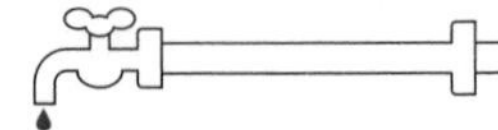

is?" The real meaning: It's not about a lover-as-savior, but "an imaginary friend who's gonna come and save you from yourself." Oasis never reached Beatlemania-levels in the United States—"Wonderwall" was the group's only top-10 hit in America.

The Artist: Lee Ann Womack

The Song: "I Hope You Dance" (2000)

The Story: In 1999, Tia Sillers was in a rut bordering on depression. The Nashville songwriter had sold only a handful of songs over half a decade and was considering giving it up. Then she broke up with her boyfriend, and to take some time to reflect on her life, she rented a house on the Gulf of Mexico. At first, the many beach walks she took didn't help—the ocean made her feel insignificant and inconsequential. Then a lyric popped into her head: "I hope you still feel small when you stand behind the ocean"; the "I hope" part was at the forefront of her mind because of her mother's frequent phone calls damning Sillers's ex, saying things like "I hope he never finds anyone that will ever love him." When Sillers returned to Nashville, she got a call to participate in a songwriters' retreat in the Rocky Mountains, to fill in for a last-minute no-show. There, on a mountain hike she came up with the line "I hope you never fear those mountains in the distance." Over the next few days she developed a long list of "I hope" statements—wishes a parent has for a child as they make their way in the world. Songwriter Mark D. Sanders helped Sillers to develop it into a song, and they sold "I Hope You Dance" to rising country star Lee Ann Womack, who took it to #1 on the country chart and #14 on the pop chart. "I Hope You Dance" was also published as a book, with its lyrics accompanied by photographs, and that sold two million copies, helped in part by Oprah Winfrey recommending it on her talk show. Winfrey had been turned on to the song by her friend, poet Maya Angelou, who said, "I didn't write this, but if I ever did write a song, this is exactly what I would say." When Angelou died in 2014, Womack sang "I Hope You Dance" at her funeral.

* * *

THE FIRST 30 ROCK AND ROLL HALL OF FAME INDUCTEES

★ **1986:** Buddy Holly, Chuck Berry, Elvis Presley, Fats Domino, James Brown, Jerry Lee Lewis, Little Richard, Ray Charles, Sam Cooke, and the Everly Brothers

★ **1987:** The Coasters, Eddie Cochran, Bo Diddley, Aretha Franklin, Marvin Gaye, Bill Haley, B. B. King, Clyde McPhatter, Ricky Nelson, Roy Orbison, Carl Perkins, Smokey Robinson, Big Joe Turner, Muddy Waters, and Jackie Wilson

★ **1988:** The Beach Boys, the Beatles, the Drifters, Bob Dylan, and the Supremes

Youngest country in the world in 2020: Niger, whose citizens have a median age of 15.3 years.

TICKLE YOUR FANCY

Uh-oh, here comes Uncle John with a TICKLE ATTACK...of ticklish trivia.

- Why are humans ticklish? Scientists say it's a deeply embedded defense mechanism. The most ticklish parts of the body—the ribs and under the arms—are located where the skin covers the body's most vulnerable organs. To provoke laughter when those areas are tickled demonstrates submission...and gets the tickler to stop it.
- Another school of thought: Tickling and the response it causes is a form of nonverbal communication between infants and parents. According to sociologists, that kind of tickling creates stronger social bonds.
- In the 1940s, Antioch College scientist Clarence Leuba conducted one of the first scientific studies related to tickling: he tickled his two infant children while wearing a mask, so that they couldn't see his face and read his "cue" to laugh. Both babies laughed, suggesting it is a natural, not a learned, response.
- Humans aren't able to laugh as a result of being tickled until they're about six months old.
- There are two kinds of tickling. *Gargalesis* is the type that makes you laugh when someone touches ticklish body parts. *Knismesis* describes tickling caused by a light, feathery touch on the skin, the kind associated with tingling or itching.
- *Knismesis* was likely borne out of a survival instinct. Perceiving slight stimuli in sensitive areas made early humans more aware of threats, such as an animal predator sneaking up on them, or a disease-carrying bug on their arm.
- According to a 1997 University of California–San Diego study in which 72 students were tickled, the most ticklish places on your body are your underarms, your waist, your ribs, and the bottoms of your feet.
- The phrase "tickled pink" dates to the 1920s, and means "delighted," evoking the feeling of laughing so hard over a tickle attack that one's face gets flushed.
- Why can't you tickle yourself? Because part of the tickle response is the brain's quick reaction to a sudden, surprise stimulus. If you know the surprise is coming, your brain doesn't act in the same way. Self-tickling is just regular touch.
- Some people with schizophrenia *are* able to surprise themselves with a self-tickle. Neurologists aren't sure why this is the case, beyond a disconnect in the brain that sometimes makes it hard for people with that particular condition to differentiate between self-generated and externally generated touch.

STALL OF FAME: CANINE EDITION

We're always amazed by the way people—and in this case, a dog—make their mark (so to speak) with bathrooms, toilets, etc. To honor them, we created Uncle John's Stall of Fame.

HONOREE: Juliana, a Great Dane living in the English city of Bristol during World War II

Notable Achievement: Saving her owner's house by "spending a penny" in just the right spot at just the right time

True Story: Bristol was and is a major port city in the southwest of England. During World War II, it was home to a bustling harbor, shipyards, a warplane factory, and other military targets. Just six miles upstream from the mouth of the river Avon, it was also an easy site for German bombers to find, and as a consequence, it was the fifth most heavily bombed British city during the war. How heavily? More than 80,000 buildings in the city were destroyed in the air raids.

One building that wasn't destroyed was the house that Juliana, a Great Dane, lived in with her owners. That's thanks entirely to the massive dog...and her massive bladder. During one air raid in April 1941, an incendiary "bomblet" (one segment of a large cluster bomb that scattered the smaller bomblets across a wide area) crashed through the roof and landed inside the house. The bomb likely would have burned the house down, save for the fact that Juliana promptly peed on it, extinguishing the fire before it could spread. For her heroic pee, er, deed, she was awarded a medal by the UK's Blue Cross animal charity. Three years later, in November 1944, she was awarded a *second* Blue Cross medal after she alerted her owners to a fire that had started in their shoe shop.

Aftermath: The reason we know all this is only because Juliana's second Blue Cross medal, along with a beautiful painted portrait of the very good girl, surfaced in September 2013 when auctioneers were clearing a house owned by a relative of Juliana's owners, who had died. The relative had inherited both the portrait and the medal from Juliana's owners, and when that relative passed away, the items were put up for auction as part of the estate sale. The auction house publicized Juliana's story in order to drum up interest in the auction...and it worked. Sold together as a single lot, the portrait and the medal were expected to sell for about £60 (about $95) but ended up fetching £1,100 (more than $1,700) from the winning bidder (who preferred to remain anonymous).

Nirvana front man Kurt Cobain (1967–94) owned only one car in his lifetime: a blue 1965 Dodge Dart.

Note: Juliana's *first* Blue Cross medal, the one that recognized her for peeing on the incendiary bomb, may still be out there somewhere. If it ever surfaces, this unique piece of World War II memorabilia could be worth a small fortune.

THREE MORE WINNERS OF THE BLUE CROSS MEDAL

- Rip (1945). This mixed-breed terrier mutt, a stray, was taken in by a London air raid warden named E. King during the war in 1940. Rip received no formal training, but when he accompanied King on his rounds following air raids, he proved so adept at finding people trapped beneath the rubble—more than 100 in all—that the government launched a program to train additional search-and-rescue dogs to assist in the work. In addition to his Blue Cross medal, he was also awarded the Dickin Medal, another prize recognizing bravery in animals, in 1945. When his Dickin Medal was put up for auction in 2009, it sold for £24,250 (more than $35,000).
- Jake (2007). When terrorists bombed the London Underground and city buses on July 7, 2005, Jake, a cocker spaniel trained by London's Metropolitan Police Service to sniff out explosives, searched the tube tunnels for secondary bombs. In the process, he cleared the way for paramedics to quickly reach and evacuate the wounded who'd been aboard the subway trains when the bombs went off.
- Daisy (2014). A ten-year-old Labrador, Daisy was specially trained to use her strong sense of smell to detect the scent of chemicals given off by cancerous cells. This enabled her to detect the presence of cancer in human beings simply by smelling their breath, skin, or a urine sample. Over the years, she sniffed for cancer in 6,500 cases, and detected cancer in just over 550 of them, including in her owner, Dr. Claire Guest. "Daisy kept nuzzling and pawing at my chest one day, which really alarmed me. I got it checked out and was told I had early stage breast cancer," Dr. Guest said in 2014. "Fortunately, I was able to have it removed...but if it wasn't for Daisy it would have gone undetected for much longer and could have been more serious."

"Daisy kept nuzzling and pawing at my chest one day, which really alarmed me."

THEY'RE CREEPY AND THEY'RE KOOKY

The first names of 29 distant relatives who were mentioned—but never seen—on the 1960s sitcom *The Addams Family*: Bleak, Bleep, Blink, Blob, Cackle, Caliban, Clot, Creep, Crimp, Cringe, Curdle, Droop, Farouk, Fungus, Goop, Gripe, Grisly, Grope, Imar, Turncoat, Manuel, Melancholia, Nanook, Plato, Slimey, Slosh, Slump, Trivia, and Vague.

BAFFLING HEADLINES

We've found so many awkward and obliviously obvious news headlines over the years that we're beginning to wonder if the headline writers are doing it on purpose.

Forecasters Call For Weather On Monday

THURSDAY IS CANCELED

Bridge Closure Date: Thursday Or October

Voters To Vote On Whether To Vote

Northfield Plans To Plan Strategic Plan

Shell Found On Beach

Clown Commits Fu King Robbery

City Plans Its First Dog Park, Archery Range

Deceased Drummer Dead

Breathing Oxygen Linked To Staying Alive

Lindsay Lohan Bitten By Snake On Holiday In Thailand

Scientists To Kill Ducks To See Why They're Dying

Study Shows Frequent Sex Enhances Pregnancy Chances

NASA Fixes Broken Hubble Telescope By Turning It Off And On Again

Man Crashes Car, Lights Cigarette From Its Flames

Kansas City Police Need Your Help Tracking Down A Giant, Inflatable Colon

Boy Paralyzed After Tumor Fights Back To Gain A Black Belt

President Obama Aging Only As Fast As The Rest Of Us, Researcher Finds

Maine Officials: Getting Lobsters Stoned Before Killing Them Is Now Illegal

Study: Our Cats Understand Us, But They Don't Really Care

Michael Jackson's 1993 Super Bowl halftime show was watched by more people than the 1993 Super Bowl.

"ESKIMO" OR "INUIT"?

There are names that cultures give to themselves, and names that are bestowed upon them by others. This is the story of both.

SHE NETS A SNOWSHOE: In the United States, "Eskimo" has long been a catch-all term to describe any Indigenous person from the Arctic Circle. The mere mention of it brings to mind the stereotypical image of a Native person wearing a fur parka, sitting in front of an igloo, eating seal meat. This image was perpetuated by the 1922 silent film *Nanook of the North*, directed by Robert Flaherty, a groundbreaking but wildly inaccurate documentary about an Arctic family, portrayed as much more primitive than they were in real life. The word "Eskimo" was already around, but thanks to the movie, it entered common usage in the 1920s—in particular with the Eskimo Pie and Eskimo kiss. Since then, linguists, etymologists, and anthropologists have put forth several theories as to the word's origin. Here are the three main ones:

- The word entered English in the late 1500s, from the Danish *Eskimo* or the Middle French *Esquimaux* (plural), both of which probably derive from an Algonquian word meaning "eaters of raw meat."
- An earlier theory—that doesn't seem to hold much merit today—is that "Eskimo" isn't Indigenous at all; it comes from the Latin *excommunicati.* Not being Christian, the Natives were described as the "Excommunicated Ones."
- In the 1980s, R. H. Ives Goddard III, senior linguist in the Department of Anthropology at the Smithsonian Institution in Washington, D.C., presented new findings: The word originated from the Montagnais (Innu) word *ayaškimew,* which means "she who nets a snowshoe." A far cry from "flesh eating," lacing snowshoes was and still is a crucial skill and respected art.

Even though the word's roots come from First Peoples, "Eskimo" is still classified as an *exonym*—a name that was assigned to them by another culture.

INUIT AND INNU: The "Innu" that Goddard referred to is not, as you might think, a shortened form of "Inuit." They are two distinct groups. The Innu Nation, also called Montagnais, is from a region that comprises parts of Quebec and Labrador in eastern Canada, and there are only about 3,200 members of that group, compared to about 180,000 Inuit. According to the *Canadian Encyclopedia*:

> It is possible that the term [ayaškimew] was used generally by the Innu to describe the Mi'kmaq [who inhabited Canada's Atlantic Provinces including parts of Quebec and Maine] and was later transferred to Inuit upon contact between the two groups. As the word came into use in Ojibwe, its original meaning may have

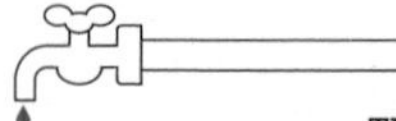

The only people in the UK who can legally eat swan: fellows of St. John's College (Cambridge University), and members of the Royal Family.

become blurred, as the *ashk-* prefix can also mean raw or fresh in Ojibwe. French explorers and settlers translated the word to *esquimaux,* the Danish spelling.

Ojibwe is a language spoken by people of that name who live in south-central Canada and the northern parts of the U.S. Midwest.

The word "Inuit" means "people." The language it's spoken in is called Inuktitut by culturally similar groups from Canada, Denmark, Russia, and the United States. Both Inuit and Innu are *autonyms,* names a culture gave to themselves...kind of.

NAMING RIGHTS: In the late 1970s, Indigenous leaders from all over the Arctic Circle met in Alaska for the Inuit Circumpolar Council, where they decreed that they were collectively to be referred to as Inuit, and that Inuit means "indigenous members of the Inuit homeland recognized by Inuit as being members of their people and shall include the Inupiat, Yupik (Alaska), Inuit, Inuvialuit (Western Canada), Kalaallit (Greenland), and Yupik (Russia)."

Despite the decree not mentioning "Eskimo"—thereby rejecting it as an acceptable name—the use of that word persists. And the debate continues as to whether "Eskimo" is pejorative. Either way, it does seem to be on the outs: In 2020, the Edmonton Eskimos, a Canadian football team, announced that they would find a new name. Also that year, after nearly a century, Eskimo Pie was changed to Edy's Pie. As far as proper usage goes, when in doubt, use "Inuit," not "Eskimo," but only for the plural. The singular is "Inuk." According to *National Geographic*'s style guide, "the word *Inuit* means 'people,' so avoid using 'people' with Inuit."

LANGUAGE LESSON: On the outs or not, the word "Eskimo" does live on in the linguistics term "Eskimo-Aleut languages" (which comprise the Yupik language group and the Inuit language family). There are some Indigenous peoples—including the Yupik in Alaska and Russia—who are called Inuit even though that name doesn't appear anywhere in their language (which, in that case, makes it an exonym). Many Yupik still refer to themselves as Eskimo.

Ironically, because it came from the Ojibwe language (before the French corrupted it), "Eskimo" was never a word in any of the Eskimo-Aleut languages; rather, it's from the Algonquin language family found throughout much of eastern Canada, parts of the midwestern United States, and several northeastern states that border the Atlantic.

All of that may seem confusing, but it's actually a simplified explanation. Linguistics is very complicated, especially when there are so many groups of people and so many similar names for the same things. We've only scratched the surface about Inuit, Eskimo, and Algonquin. There are hundreds more language families and groups around the world, many of them extinct or in danger of going extinct. For more stories of Indigenous words that live on in English, turn to page 330.

Otters can smell underwater objects by exhaling bubbles onto the surface of the object, then sniffing them back in again.

CAINE MEETS WAYNE

Here's a classic tale of an up-and-coming young actor crossing paths with a Hollywood legend, who gave him some advice he never forgot.

THE BIG TIME

In March 1966, a British film called *Alfie* opened to rave reviews in the UK. It would soon be a hit in the United States as well and prove to be a breakthrough role for its star, an unknown 33-year-old actor named Michael Caine. On the strength of this performance and one the previous year in another British film called *The Ipcress File*, the American actress Shirley MacLaine lobbied (successfully) to have Caine cast as the male lead in her next movie, a heist film called *Gambit* that would soon begin filming. It was Caine's first Hollywood movie.

As production of *Gambit* got underway, Universal Pictures flew Caine out to Los Angeles and put him up in a luxurious suite in the Beverly Hills Hotel. He was supposed to start work on the film immediately, but MacLaine was busy finishing up another movie, and when it fell behind schedule, Caine was stuck cooling his heels at the Beverly Hills Hotel for more than a week with nothing to do but order room service on Universal's dime. This was his first trip to the United States, and he didn't know anyone in town. The cockney kid from east London was still starstruck, so he spent his days sitting in the hotel lobby, hoping to spot any movie stars who might be at the hotel.

DROPPING IN

Caine was sitting there one day "star-spotting," as he called it, when he heard a helicopter approach and make a noisy landing on the lawn next to the hotel, throwing the place into chaos. "A porter told me [that] was strictly illegal," Caine wrote in his 2010 memoir *The Elephant to Hollywood*. "We stood at the door to see who had dared break the law so flagrantly and out of the swirling cloud that had been whirled up came the figure of John Wayne."

In the mid-1960s, "the Duke," as he was known, was one of Hollywood's biggest stars. He'd been filming a western on location and was still dressed for the part as he strode up to the front desk and registered for a room. As he was collecting his room key, he looked over in Michael Caine's direction and saw that Caine was staring at him. A look of recognition came over Wayne's face and he called out to Caine, "What's your name?"

When Caine introduced himself, Wayne asked him, "Are you in that movie *Alfie*?"

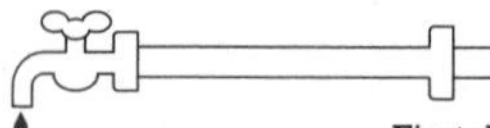

First department store Santa: James Edgar, who dressed up as Santa in his own Edgar Department Store in Boston (1890).

Caine answered yes, to which the Duke replied, "You're gonna be a big star, kid, and if you want to stay one, remember to talk low, talk slow, and don't say too f***ing much."

MAKING A SPLASH

Then Wayne looked down at Caine's suede shoes and offered Caine one more piece of advice: "Never wear suede shoes," he said.

"What?" Caine asked him.

Wayne repeated, "Never wear suede shoes."

"Why not?"

"Because I just told you, you're going to be a big star, and you're going to be in the Gent's toilet taking a pee, and the guy next to you is going to be taking a pee, and he'll recognize you and say, 'Michael Caine!' Then he'll turn to face you and he'll pee all over your shoes."

"I threw my suede shoes away," Caine says.

EPILOGUE

Caine and Wayne traveled in different circles, but they managed to keep in touch over the years, and Wayne served as a sort of mentor, giving Caine acting tips and career advice. In the late 1970s when Caine's wife Shakira suffered a health crisis and was admitted to the UCLA Medical Center, Caine discovered that John Wayne was in the hospital room next door, where he was being treated for the cancer that would ultimately claim his life in June 1979. Caine says that when he went to visit his wife each day, he also spent time with Wayne, accompanying the ailing star as he slowly walked up and down the hospital corridor dressed in a bathrobe, cowboy hat, and cowboy boots, swearing and cursing as he went.

"When Shakira was well enough to go home, I went in to see him for the last time," Caine remembered. " 'I won't be getting out of here,' [Wayne] said as I got up to go and then, seeing I was close to tears, 'Get the hell out of here and go have a good time!' I left before he could see me cry."

* * *

NOW *THAT'S* HINDSIGHT

The modern "mooning" fad began at American college campuses in the early 1960s. "Three or four boys will crouch down in a car," wrote *Look* magazine, "lower their trousers and, at a signal, push their bare bottoms out of every available window." In 1966, *Esquire* added, "There are even some girls who enjoy throwing a moon now and then, just for the hell of it, or maybe to strike a blow for academic freedom."

Cremains aren't ashes—they're pulverized bone fragments that weren't consumed during cremation.

GOVERN-MENTAL: KNOW YOUR -*ARCHIES* AND -*OCRACIES*

Winston Churchill once described democracy as "the worst form of government except for all those other forms that have been tried from time to time." Here's a look at some of the alternatives, including a form of democracy you may not realize exists.

PURE DEMOCRACY

You probably know what *representative democracy* is, since you almost certainly live in one. In a representative democracy, the people elect representatives to make legislative decisions for them. A *pure* or *direct democracy* is a system of government in which the people *do not* elect representatives, and instead retain all decision-making power for themselves.

Believe it or not, a few such pure democracies do exist in the world. Two of them are in Switzerland, in two states, or *cantons*, named Glarus and Appenzell Innerrhoden. In these two places, decisions are made by having all eligible citizens meet periodically in a giant, open-air meeting called a *Landsgemeinde*, where a series of ballot questions are discussed and then voted on. The citizens vote by raising their hand or voter identification card. Some 4,000 citizens typically participate in the Landsgemeinds in Appenzell Innerrhoden; in Glarus the number is closer to 5,000. Votes are decided by majority rule, and in the case of close votes it's the job of an official called the *Landammann* to figure out which side of an issue won the day. If pure democracy sounds appealing, be careful what you wish for: If there are more than a couple of ballot items to discuss and vote on, a Landsgemeinde meeting can drag on for more than 4½ hours.

ARISTOCRACY

Can you guess the meaning of the Greek words *aristos* and *kratos*, which are the roots of the English word *aristocracy?* They mean "best" and "power"—an aristocracy originally meant a government led by a small group of only the best or most qualified people. Plato, Aristotle, and other ancient Greek philosophers considered aristocracy a superior alternative to both monarchy ("one rule"), which is rule by a single individual, and democracy ("people rule"). The Greek philosophers had little faith in the ability of common people to govern themselves.

As originally conceived, each generation of aristocrats would be carefully selected and appointed to the ruling class based on their intelligence, leadership skills, and

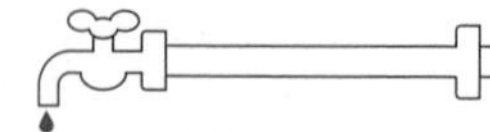

There are 5,000 French loan words in Turkish, making Turkish easier to learn if you're fluent in French.

other qualifications, rather than inheriting the job from their parents—a *meritocracy,* in other words. In time, of course, aristocracies became known for being exactly the opposite: a privileged group of people who inherited their wealth, titles, and the right to rule from their parents, whether they were the people best suited for the job or not.

OLIGARCHY

Oligarchy ("few rule") is a concept similar to aristocracy in that it, too, means rule by a few, but not necessarily the *best* few. Any "few" will do: It could be rule by the very rich (a *plutocracy*), religious leaders (a *theocracy*), or the well-educated, political elites, the military, or even corporate leaders. Any power structure or system of government that concentrates power into the hands of a small number of people can be considered an oligarchy.

KAKISTOCRACY

This is a form of government that no one wants to live under. Whether anyone actually *does* live under such a government is a matter of opinion, and open to interpretation: a *kakistocracy,* from the Greek words for "worst" and "power," is a government made up of the people least suited for the job of running the government, either because they are unqualified, incompetent, or corrupt. The *worst few,* in other words. (Not to be confused with an *ochlocracy,* which means "mob rule.")

DIARCHY

If *monarchy* means "rule of one," what's a *diarchy?* You guessed it: "rule of two"—a government that has two monarchs co-ruling at the same time. Great Britain became a temporary diarchy in 1689 after King James II was deposed in favor of his daughter Mary II; she refused to take the throne as queen unless her husband, William of Orange, was crowned King William III as well. The diarchy lasted until Mary's death in 1694, when it reverted to a monarchy with only William III remaining on the throne.

One of the few remaining constitutional diarchies in the world is the tiny principality of Andorra, nestled in the Pyrenees mountains between Spain and France. It has two heads of state—"co-princes"—at any one time: 1) the bishop of Urgell in Spain, appointed by the pope; and 2) the president of France, who inherited the job from the kings of France after the French monarchy was abolished in 1792. The president of France/co-prince of Andorra is the only co-head of state of an independent country that is elected by citizens of another independent country.

AUTOCRACY

Autocracy is an extreme form of monarchy that places absolute power in the hands of a single ruler, the *autocrat.* Prior to the Russian Revolution of 1905, the Russian Empire was an autocracy ruled by hereditary monarchs known as *tsars,* sometimes spelled *czars.* The tsar was seen as a father figure (or when a female *tsarina* occupied

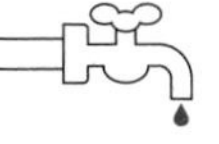

The members of Duran Duran once won a Duran Duran lookalike contest.

> **The Russian people had no individual rights, and no say in the running of the government. Even their own personal property was considered the property of the tsar.**

the throne, a mother figure) for the entire Russian people, who in the eyes of the law were little better than children. Like children, the Russian people had no individual rights, and no say in the running of the government. Even their own personal property was considered the property of the tsar and could be reclaimed by him at any time. The Russian Revolution of 1905 ended autocracy by placing the first limits on the tsar's power in the form of a written constitution that required him to share power with an elected national assembly called the Duma. This reformed system of government lasted just 12 years before the tsar himself was overthrown in the Russian Revolution of 1917.

KLEPTOCRACY

If you know what a kleptomaniac is, you know what a *kleptocracy* is: it's a government run by people who, rather than use their power to serve their fellow citizens, use it to enrich themselves through embezzlement, kickbacks, bribe-taking, and anything else they can think of to line their own pockets and those of their political cronies.

Most countries use the Indigenous Tupi (Brazil) word: ananas. *But the Spanish and English speakers thought they looked like pinecones...and apparently still do.*

ANIMAL IN THE NEWS

Some wild news from the wild kingdom.

A VERY GOOD BOY

Thousands of neighborhoods across the world have been gifted with "little libraries"—small covered boxes on residential side streets, offering books for neighbors to read and return, based on the honor system. In 2019, Andrew Taylor, a 59-year-old toolmaker in Kaiapoi, New Zealand, took that concept to a different audience: dogs. After trimming the branches in his yard one day, he realized that he had a lot of sticks that his dog, Bella, would love...and so would all the neighborhood canines. Taylor sanded them down until they were smooth, then loaded them into a handmade box. A new dog park had just opened up nearby, and that soon became the home of what the box said was a "Stick Library," just for dogs. (He also engraved "PLEASE RETURN" onto the box, to encourage the dogs to return the sticks when they were done, so that others got a chance to play with them.)

EIGHT ARMS TO SCARE YOU

On February 1, 2019, police rushed to a home in Wanneroo, a suburb of Perth, Australia. They were responding to an emergency call placed by a passerby who heard what seemed to be the shrieking cries of a toddler and the voice of an adult man shouting, "Why don't you die?" About 20 minutes later, the Wanneroo Police updated its online call log to explain what had happened. No toddler had been attacked, it turned out, but there was a death involved. The homeowner, a man with a "serious fear of spiders," had been trying desperately and without success to exterminate one of the creatures. It was he who had shrieked; he later apologized to police for any inconvenience he'd caused.

TOUGH TO SWALLOW

In 2020, scientists exploring the Tanque Loma—a pit in southwestern Ecuador where a number of large mammal fossils dating back as far as 2.6 million years had been discovered previously—uncovered 575 bones, comprising nearly complete skeletons of 22 giant ground sloths. Scientists dated the fossils as somewhere between 18,000 and 23,000 years old, and found them all in a single, parallel layer, clumped closely together. The condition and proximity of the bones suggests that all 22 sloths died around the same time. Preserved vegetation in the vicinity—some of which had

Don't let the movies fool you: In the Old West of the 1860s–1880s, about 1 in 4 cowboys was Black.

already been digested and excreted—helped scientists determine the cause of death. The Tanque Loma was once a marshy watering hole where sloths would gather to rest, drink...and defecate. The water became so polluted with the sloths' own feces that when they returned to the marsh for water, they drank their own waste and poisoned themselves to death.

THE EGLE HAS SPLASH-LANDED

In July 2020, the Michigan Department of Environment, Great Lakes, and Energy released a drone into the wilderness of the state's Upper Peninsula to study the shoreline erosion of Lake Michigan, near the town of Escanaba. Just seven minutes into the flying robot's survey, reception between the device and drone pilot Hunter King grew inconsistent, and the machine started to spin and twirl out of control. Then when he looked at a video monitor of the drone's progress, the flying machine was gone, and King watched an eagle soar away. Two birdwatchers later reported that they saw an eagle attack something, not knowing what it was. State officials put two and two together and determined that the eagle had attacked the drone operated by the environmental agency, whose acronym is...EGLE. The drone fell into Lake Michigan and was recovered about a month later.

* * *

ANTI-COSTUMES

Young people in Japan recently started an odd Halloween fad. Instead of monsters, witches, and superheroes, they don the costumes of everyday people in specific everyday situations. Here are the descriptions of some we found online:

- "Person who refused a bag but their item ended up not fitting in their purse"
- "PE teacher who usually wears jerseys wearing a suit at the graduation ceremony"
- "A guy eavesdropping on a fight he heard on the train"
- "Person who is quietly despairing over the lack of seats with power outlets in a cafe they popped into"
- "Person who is dressed up only because they're about to get a photo ID picture taken"
- "Someone in a thrift store but you don't know if they're a customer or staff"
- "Person who finished their popcorn even before the movie started"
- "The woman looking for a seat at a crowded food court"
- "The guy waiting for his girlfriend by the shopping mall restroom"
- "The guy who had to work during vacation"
- "Someone who isn't aware their phone flashlight is on"

Forget "happily ever after." Some old German fairy tales end with "If they haven't died, then they are still living today."

UNCLE JOHN'S PAGE OF LISTS

Random bits of information from the BRI's bottomless files.

5 TV Characters and Their Pet Fish

1. Captain Picard and Livingston (*Star Trek: The Next Generation*)

2. Arnold and Abraham (*Diff'rent Strokes*)

3. Stanley and Dennis (*Stanley*)

4. Tony and Kate (*NCIS*)

5. Ricky and Orangie (*Trailer Park Boys*)

8 Strange Things Left in Ubers

1. Dog tuxedo

2. Handmade cat puppet

3. Full set of 18-karat gold teeth

4. Louboutin heels

5. Deer antlers

6. Shopping cart

7. Fish tank with fish

8. Bejeweled Elvis cape

5 Nicknames of NASCAR Champion Kyle Busch

1. Wild Thing

2. Candy Man

3. KFB

4. Shrub

5. Rowdy

6 Most Common Mexican Boys' Names (1930–2008)

1. José Luis

2. Juan

3. Miguel Ángel

4. José

5. Francisco

6. Jesús

6 Sets of Celebrities Born the Same Year

1. Patrick Stewart and Ringo Starr (1940)

2. Tom Hanks and La Toya Jackson (1956)

3. Paul Giamatti and Vin Diesel (1967)

4. Eminem and Jennifer Garner (1972)

5. Macaulay Culkin and Kim Kardashian (1980)

6. Justin Bieber and Dakota Fanning (1994)

5 "Authentic" Rock Stars (According to the Who's Pete Townshend)

1. Mick Jagger

2. David Byrne

3. Debbie Harry

4. Joni Mitchell

5. Neil Young

6 Most Common Mexican Girls' Names (1930–2008)

1. María Guadalupe

2. María

3. Juana

4. María del Carmen

5. Margarita

6. Verónica

7 Types of Diversity in the Workplace (Workable.com)

1. Cultural

2. Racial

3. Religious

4. Age

5. Sex/Gender

6. Sexual orientation

7. Disability

10 Most Popular Sandwiches in the U.S.

1. Grilled cheese

2. Grilled chicken

3. Turkey

4. Roast beef

5. Ham

6. BLT

7. Club

8. Bacon

9. Peanut butter and jelly

10. Pulled pork

The oceans of the world contain about 20 million tons of gold... suspended in seawater. Each gallon contains 3.4 billionths of a gram.

LUCKY FINDS

Ever find something that's of great value? Whether it's monetary or sentimental, it's a wonderful feeling. Here's a BRI staple from our "It Could Happen to You" files.

DIGGING UP THE PAST

The Find: A class ring that went missing from a bathroom 44 years ago

Where It Was Found: In a garden, 34 miles away

The Story: KC Curiel was weeding her garden in Newberg, Oregon, in the fall of 2018 when she felt something hard in the topsoil. She dug it up, and found an old class ring with a blue stone. It was too dirty to read the inscription, so Curiel took it to a jeweler for cleaning. The best they could make out, it belonged to someone named Lori "Hill" or "Hitt." Curiel posted a photo of the ring on some local Facebook groups, but noone claimed it.

Nearly a year later, Samantha Swindler, a reporter for the *Oregonian,* came across Curiel's post and decided to look into it. Utilizing some local contacts and Ancestry.com, she discovered a Forest Grove High School Class of 1975 graduate named Lori Gregory (maiden name: Hitt) living in a nearby town.

"I was flabbergasted," said Gregory after she was contacted by Swindler. She'd saved up to buy the class ring and was devastated to lose it. "I was a senior in high school. I had gone into the bathroom...set it down on the sink...When it dawned on me that I didn't have my ring anymore, I went back and it was gone." Gregory and her ring were reunited in a Cornelius, Oregon, parking lot in November 2019.

One question remained: How did the ring travel 34 miles away? According to Swindler's article, "KC's husband...does landscape work...and routinely brings home dirt to add to the garden at home. Most recently, he had brought home a pile from outside Newberg's Momiji Sushi Bar, a site that had been a fast food restaurant back in the 1970s. Maybe it flew off someone's hand years ago?" Only the ring knows for sure.

OUT OF THE BOX

The Find: An 18th-century Chinese vase

Where It Was Found: In a shoebox in an attic

The Story: A French family (names not released) decided to get rid of some stuff that had belonged to their grandparents. Among the items was a small vase that

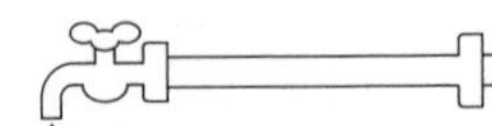

looked like it might be worth something. According to Olivier Valmier, an Asian arts expert at Sotheby's in Paris, "The seller took the train, then the metro, and walked on foot through the doors of Sotheby's and into my office with the vase in a shoebox." Valmier deduced that the small porcelain vase (painted with a forest scene) was from the Qing dynasty. Very rare and in perfect condition, it had been made for the Qianlong emperor, who ruled China for most of the 18th century. When the vase went up for auction in June 2018, it was estimated to sell for €500,000 ($590,000). After an unprecedented 20-minute bidding war, the vase was sold to an anonymous Asian firm for 16.2 million euros ($19.11 million). But even if it had no monetary value, the seller wouldn't have kept it: "We didn't like the vase too much, and my grandparents didn't like it either."

SOFT TISSUE

The Find: A piece of a fossilized dinosaur brain

Where It Was Found: On a beach

The Story: In 2004, a fossil hunter named Jamie Hiscocks was exploring an area of shoreline in Sussex, England, after a winter storm had left new deposits in the sands. Among his finds that night was a "misshapen pebble" that most people wouldn't even look at twice. Hiscocks suspected it was worthy of studying, so he took it to Oxford University. Twelve years later, in October 2016, the Geological Society of London finally published the groundbreaking findings: This misshapen pebble is the only known dinosaur brain fossil in the world. Researchers can tell that it's brain tissue because of the corrugated surface and traces of tiny blood vessels and meninges, the brain's protective outer layer. The fossil was determined to come from an iguanodon, a 30-foot-long dinosaur from the Cretaceous period, about 130 million years ago.

"The chances of preserving brain tissue are incredibly small, so the discovery of this specimen is astonishing," said researcher Alexander Liu of Cambridge's Department of Earth Sciences. This particular fossil went through a specific set of circumstances to end up this way, starting with the dinosaur dying with its head underwater. "Now that we know that these soft tissues can be preserved," said Liu, "people can go back in museum collections and look out for them, reexamine them, see if it is more common." If more brains are found, Hiscocks's lucky find could settle the birds vs. reptiles dinosaur debate once and for all. Modern reptiles have tiny brains, whereas birds' brains fill up the skull cavity. Scientists aren't sure whether this fossilized brain filled up its host's skull, because the iguanadon likely died upside down and its brain may have "spread out on the roof of the skull," making it seem larger than it actually was. But proof that birds did evolve from dinosaurs could be resting in some university drawer or on some museum shelf, just waiting to be rediscovered.

LIFE IN 1994

It's always good to remember that what seems permanent today, is actually fleeting. Want proof? Here's a look at daily life back in the days of beepers, grunge, and Crystal Pepsi.

COSTS IN THE KITCHEN

- A loaf of bread: **$1.59**
- A dozen eggs: **87¢**
- A pound of ground beef: **$1.48**
- A McDonald's Big Mac: **$2.30**
- A "tall" (small) coffee at the rapidly expanding Starbucks Coffee chain: **$1.25** (There were 425 Starbucks stores in 1994. There were more than 30,000 in 2020 in more than 70 countries. Bonus: 1994 is also the year the company opened its first drive-thru.)
- A 12-pack of Coca-Cola, or Diet Coke: **$3.99**
- A pound of bacon: **$1.99**
- A gallon of milk: **$2.88**
- A pound of butter: **$1.60**
- A box of cereal: Perhaps something new to stores, like Pop-Tarts Crunch or Reese's Peanut Butter Puffs? It could cost about **$2.90**.
- Tomatoes: **$1.30** a pound for old-fashioned vine-ripened tomatoes, although the newly available Flavr Savr—the first FDA-approved genetically modified food in the U.S.—went for **$2** a pound.
- A 16-ounce jar of peanut butter: **$1.85**
- A pound of margarine: **$1.15**
- A six-pack of beer: Regular domestic beer, such as Miller Lite or Coors, or something newer, like Bud Ice or Zima, would set you back about **$5.80**.

WHAT PEOPLE EARNED

- Average yearly income for an American worker: about **$26,900**
- Average yearly salary for a construction worker: **$28,307**
- For a retail employee: **$14,385**
- For a doctor: **$186,000**
- Federally set minimum wage: **$4.25** an hour

BOOKS

- Among the best-selling books of 1994: John Grisham's legal thriller *The Chamber*, Michael Crichton's sexual harassment saga *Disclosure*, Robert James Waller's romance *The Bridges of Madison County*, and the spiritual self-help novel *The Celestine Prophecy* by James Redfield.
- Awards for fiction: Philip Roth's *Operation Shylock* won the Pen-Faulkner, Annie Proulx's *The Shipping News* won the Pulitzer Prize, and William Gaddis's *A Frolic of His Own* won the National Book Award.

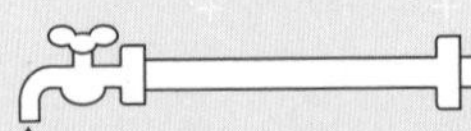

The E's have it: "E" is the most commonly used letter in English...as well as in Norwegian, Dutch, French, and Italian.

AROUND THE HOUSE

- Shoes: The latest, hottest Air Jordans from Nike ran a steep **$80**. (Today they can sell for as much as **$4,000** on eBay.)
- Online services: If you wanted to use your computer to "go online" or "surf the web," as people were starting to do in large numbers in 1994, you had to sign up with a service provider. The big three: America Online, CompuServe, and Prodigy. They all charged **$9.95** a month for five total hours of dial-up internet access.
- A first-class postage stamp: **29¢**
- A 46-inch big-screen TV with picture-in-picture: **$1,700**
- Home computer: A PC for the whole family, including a monitor, mouse, keyboard, printer, and a tower with a disk drive and a newfangled CD-ROM drive, would run you about **$2,000**.
- Newspaper: The price of a weekday edition of the *New York Times* went up for the first time in years, from **50¢** to **60¢**.
- A new three-bedroom home, on average: **$129,900**
- A standard Ford F-150 pickup truck, the best-selling vehicle in America in 1994: **$12,866**
- A gallon of gas to put in it: **$1.11**
- Annual health insurance coverage for a family of four: **$450**
- Toys: Mighty Morphin Power Rangers action figures, depicting color-coded teenagers who control giant robots and fight alien monsters, were the hottest toys of the year. A set of all six would cost **$60**, or **$9.99** per figure.
- *Uncle John's 7th Bathroom Reader*: **$9.95**

TELEVISION

- *Friends*, *ER*, and *Touched by an Angel* all debuted in the fall of 1994. The most-watched show on TV: *Seinfeld*
- Weirdest TV event of the year: the O.J. Simpson car chase. Rather than surrender to police, on June 17, Simpson and a friend, Al Cowlings, fled in Cowlings's white Bronco. They drove on Highway 405 at 35 mph for several hours, followed by police cars, helicopters...and the news media. The chase was broadcast live on all three TV networks and CNN for more than an hour. All regular programming was interrupted (including game five of the NBA finals), as 95 million viewers were glued to the screen, watching the low-speed chase, which ended with Simpson quietly surrendering.

NAMES

- The most popular names for baby boys born in the United States in 1994: Michael, Christopher, and Matthew. For girls: Jessica, Ashley, and Emily.

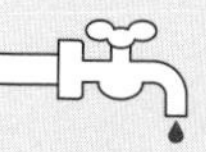

MUSIC

- Swedish dance-pop quartet Ace of Base had the number-one single of the year, "The Sign," as well as the top-selling album, *The Sign.* (Average cost of an album on CD that year: about $16.) Other big hits that year included Boyz II Men's "I'll Make Love to You," and Tim McGraw's "Don't Take the Girl." The biggest story in music in 1994: the suicide of Nirvana's Kurt Cobain.

MOVIES

- For the first time, two movies in a single year had box office grosses exceeding $300 million: the animated *The Lion King* and the Americana epic *Forrest Gump.* The latter won Best Picture at the Academy Awards over such classics as *Pulp Fiction* and *The Shawshank Redemption.* It cost about $4 for an adult to see them in the multiplex...the same as it cost to rent a VHS copy of a movie at Blockbuster Video.

SPORTS

- After three straight NBA titles with the Chicago Bulls, Michael Jordan retired, leaving the door open for the Houston Rockets to become the NBA champions. In football, the Dallas Cowboys won their second consecutive Super Bowl (handing the Buffalo Bills a record fourth loss in the big game), and in baseball, no World Series was played for the first time in major league history, due to a players' strike.

VITALS

- Life expectancy for an American male born in 1994 was estimated at 72.4 years, and for females, 79 years.
- Population of the United States: 263.4 million

* * *

DOWNERS

"You fall out of your mother's womb, you crawl across open country under fire, and drop into your grave." —**Quentin Crisp**

"If you live long enough, you'll see that every victory turns into a defeat." —**Simone de Beauvoir**

"Whenever a friend succeeds, a little something in me dies." —**Gore Vidal**

"Hell is other people." —**Jean-Paul Sartre**

"The meaning of life is that it stops." —**Franz Kafka**

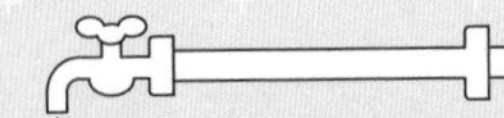

Why do Julia butterflies irritate the eyes of turtles and make them "cry"? So they can drink the tears.

THE SURGEON AND THE GUINEA PIG

Uncle John has unearthed a lot of odd medical stories over the years, but this one has got to be one of the strangest ever. (Warning: It's not for the faint of heart...or stomach.)

AS GOOD AS DEAD

In June 1822, Alexis St. Martin, a 20-year-old French-Canadian trapper working near Fort Mackinac in the Michigan Territory, was gravely injured when someone accidentally fired a musket loaded with "powder and duck shot" less than three feet behind him. The powerful blast, similar to buckshot from a shotgun, struck him in the back and then exited his chest a few inches below his left nipple, leaving an exit wound about the size of a man's fist.

The injury was horrific: two of St. Martin's ribs were broken and both his left lung and his stomach were punctured. Tattered pieces of both organs poked out of the wound in his chest. None of St. Martin's friends thought he had long to live. Neither did the U.S. Army surgeon from Fort Mackinac, Dr. William Beaumont, who treated St. Martin: he predicted the young man would be dead within 36 hours.

Beaumont gently poked the lung and stomach tissue back into St. Martin's chest, cleaned his wounds, and applied poultices (soft, moist masses of herbs and other plant materials) to ease soreness and inflammation, hoping to make his patient as comfortable as possible until he passed away. But the unfortunate St. Martin couldn't have been very comfortable, because the poultices were about as close to anesthesia or painkillers as he was going to get. Although morphine, one of the earliest painkillers, had recently been developed, it was not yet in widespread use. St. Martin couldn't even take *aspirin* for his agonizing pain. That drug would not be introduced until the late 1890s.

HANGING ON

The 36 hours came and went. Somehow, St. Martin did not die. He developed a high fever, and his wound became fetid. And he had labored breathing and a bad cough caused by the injury to his lung. He was also restless and still in excruciating pain. Beaumont responded by administering a cathartic solution (a laxative), and he bled St. Martin as well.

The cathartic had no effect. As soon as St. Martin swallowed the solution, it poured out of the hole in his stomach and spilled down the front of his chest. But Beaumont believed that bleeding 18–20 ounces (about 1¼ pints) of blood from St. Martin—after he'd already lost copious amounts of blood when he was shot—*had* done

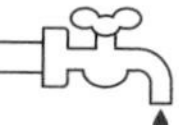

Bad news: Technically, cannibalism isn't illegal in the U.S.
Good news: Obtaining, possessing, and abusing dead bodies is.

some good, by giving the young man "relief," as he put it. What it really did, most likely, was rob St. Martin of what little strength he had left, leaving him *too weak* to be restless and bringing him even closer to death. And yet he fought on.

THE RIGHT MAN FOR THE JOB

Laxatives and bleeding aside, Beaumont may well have been one of the best physicians in the country to be looking after St. Martin, but not because he'd gone to an elite medical school. He hadn't gone to *any* medical school. Like most aspiring doctors in his day, he'd learned his profession by apprenticing with a practicing physician for about two years. Then when the War of 1812 broke out, Beaumont joined the U.S. Army and served as an assistant surgeon, where he gained considerable experience treating wounded soldiers. The standard of care for trauma patients wasn't great in 1822, but it was (hopefully) better than nothing. Now Beaumont drew upon his wartime experience as he tried to save St. Martin's life.

The moist poultices that he applied to St. Martin's wounds seemed to help, and as the days passed, the young man's injuries slowly healed. On the 11th day, his fever subsided and his wounds assumed a "healthy" appearance, as Beaumont noted. St. Martin still couldn't eat normally: anything he ate spilled out of his stomach and down the front of his chest. Intravenous feeding hadn't been invented yet, so Beaumont resorted to feeding St. Martin with food enemas, or as he put it, "by means of nutritious injections per anus."

ON THE MEND

Finally, on the 17th day, St. Martin's chest wound healed to the point that the young man could tolerate having "firm dressings...[and] compresses and adhesive straps" placed over the opening to his stomach, sealing it temporarily and enabling him to eat normally, at least when the bandages were in place.

The road to full recovery would be long and full of complications. By the fifth week, scar tissue had formed over the chest wound and had begun to contract, both of which were signs of healing. But the opening in St. Martin's stomach was not mending properly: instead of closing up, the stomach tissue attached itself to the skin at the opening of the wound and bonded with it, creating a *fistula,* or direct passage from the stomach to the surface of St. Martin's chest. The opening was about ¾ inch in diameter, or about as wide as a human finger.

THANKS...BUT NO THANKS

The fistula could have been corrected with surgery. All Beaumont needed to do was make an incision to separate the stomach tissue from the skin tissue, then suture the stomach closed before sewing the skin closed as well. But by that time, St. Martin had

X-Files star David Duchovny auditioned for all three male parts on *Full House*.

endured all the painful medical procedures without anesthesia that he could stand, including surgeries to remove duck shot and at least five procedures on his damaged ribs. He refused to submit to any more operations and was determined to make do by plugging the fistula with bandages. Beaumont tried repeatedly to close the fistula without resorting to surgery, to no avail. "After trying all the means in my power for eight or ten months to close the orifice...I gave it up as impracticable," he wrote.

"I can look directly into the cavity of the Stomach and almost see the process of digestion."

CAUSING A FLAP

By June 1823, one year after the shooting, St. Martin's injuries had largely healed—except for the fistula, which he still refused to let Beaumont operate on. The young man was able to walk and could perform light tasks, but he was not up to returning to his old job as a trader for the American Fur Company, so out of pity, Beaumont hired him as a household servant.

Then in the winter of 1823–24, a "fold or doubling" of tissue formed at the opening of the fistula, creating a flap that sealed the stomach and kept food and liquids in without the use of bandages. But it was only a flap. Beaumont discovered as much when he pressed on the tissue with his finger and it opened, allowing him to poke around the interior of St. Martin's stomach and even peek inside. "I can look directly into the cavity of the Stomach and almost see the process of digestion," he wrote. "I can pour in water with a funnel, or put in food with a spoon, and draw them out again with a siphon."

LOVE AT FIRST SIGHT

Living as we do in an age of X-rays, endoscopes, ultrasounds, CAT scans, MRIs, and other forms of medical imaging, it can be difficult to understand just how remarkable it was for Beaumont to be able to look inside the stomach of a living human being and watch it function. No one had ever before been able to do this, and no one knew for sure how the stomach did its job. Some scientists theorized that digestion was a mechanical process, something akin to kneading dough. Others believed chemical action was responsible. Still others believed that the stomach used high temperatures to digest food, in much the same way that firewood is consumed in a fire. And then there was the spiritual school of thought, which held that digestion was a miraculous process, one that mechanical and chemical explanations were inadequate to describe.

Another unknown was how much work the stomach really did. Was it entirely responsible for digestion, or did it just do a little bit of the work before passing semidigested food onto the intestines, where the process continued? Once again, no one knew for sure.

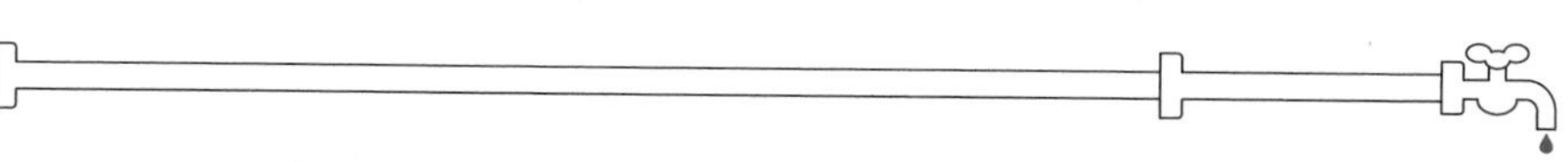

Praying mantises have been known to catch and eat hummingbirds—especially their brains.

IN THE FLESH

Beaumont realized that he was in a unique position to put these theories to the test by experimenting on St. Martin as if he were a lab rat or a guinea pig. That would certainly be unethical today, but in the 1820s it was something that Beaumont had no qualms about doing. How much he pressured St. Martin to cooperate is not known, but the young man owed his life and now his livelihood to Beaumont, and may have felt obliged to consent to the experiments. Whatever the case, he agreed to participate.

After digesting that bit of gruesome imagery, you may need a few moments to catch your breath and regain your composure. No? Well, then turn to Part II on page 249.

* * *

THE FIRST WOMAN TO...

...fly solo around the world: Jerrie Mock. In 1964, she flew her Cessna, called *Spirit of Columbus*, from Ohio...to Ohio in 29 days, 11 hours, and 59 minutes.

...be elected as a head of state: Khertek Anchimaa-Toka, who was elected as the chair of presidium in the now-defunct Tuvan People's Republic in 1940.

...be elected governor of a U.S. state: Nellie Tayloe Ross. She became Wyoming's first (and so far, only) female governor in 1925.

...host a syndicated daytime talk show: Sally Jesse Raphael. Her long-running half-hour talk show debuted on a local St. Louis station in 1983. (Oprah was the first to go national in 1986.)

...earn a medical degree in America: Elizabeth Blackwell. When she applied to New York's Geneva Medical College (now called Hobart) in 1859, all 150 male students voted to accept her.

...climb Mt. Everest: Japanese mountaineer Junko Tabei, who reached "the roof of the world" in 1975.

...compete in a NASCAR event: Sara Christian, at the first ever NASCAR Cup Series race (then called "Strictly Stock") in 1949. Christian competed against 32 other drivers and came in 14th.

...win a Tony Award for Best Musical Score: Although a few had won with a male collaborator, a woman didn't win it by herself until 2013 when '80s pop icon Cyndi Lauper took home the award for her original score to the musical *Kinky Boots*.

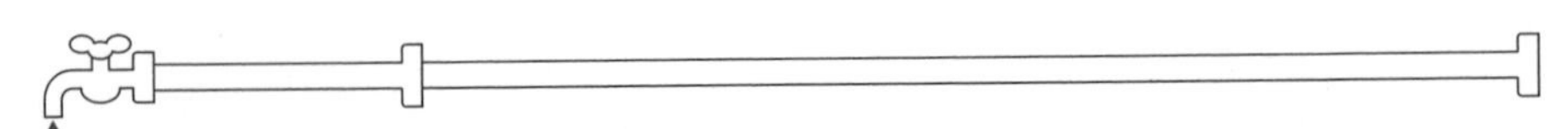

Oldest federal law-enforcement agency in the U.S.: the Postal Inspection Service (1772).

RIDING THE CONCRETE WAVE

Skateboarding, which only began in the 1950s, is now an Olympic sport. And like all sports, it has a colorful language all its own.

REGULAR FOOT: A skater who normally skates with their left foot forward

GOOFY-FOOT: A skater who normally skates with their right foot forward

SWITCH STANCE: When a regular footer skates goofy foot, or a goofy-footer skates regular foot

OLLIEING: The basis of most tricks: a jump that's executed by the skater popping the tail of the board against the ground with their rear foot while jumping and controlling the nose of the board with their front foot as the skateboard lifts into the air

OLLIE NORTH: An ollie in which the skater lifts their front foot forward off the nose of the board

ACID DROP: Skating off the end of an object and free-falling to the ground to land on the wheels

AM: An amateur skater

FLIP: Rotating the board in midair along its lengthwise axis; can also refer to the skater flipping head over heels

TRUCK: The metal assemblies that connect the axles and wheels to the actual board or "deck" of the skateboard; the truck assembly is what enables skaters to turn

GRIND: Any trick where the truck makes contact and "grinds" along the edge of an obstacle

SLIDE/BOARDSLIDE: Similar to a grind, except that the deck, not the truck, slides perpendicularly along the edge of the obstacle

LANDING BOLTS: When a skater executes their trick perfectly, landing on the top side of the board on the bolts that secure the trucks to the deck

SCORPION: Wiping out so bad that the skater's feet nearly touch the back of their head

PUSHING: Moving the skateboard forward by pushing against the ground with the rear foot

INDY GRAB: A trick where the skater grabs the middle of the board between their toes with their back hand in midair

FAKIE: Rolling backward on the skateboard

MANUAL: When the skater shifts both feet over the rear wheels and skates with the front wheels off the ground

POLE JAM: Riding up and off a pole that's sticking diagonally out of the ground

BRAIN BUCKET/SKID LID: A helmet

Since 1980, about 40% of the top honors in men's long distance running have gone to Kenyans from a single tribe, the Kalenjin.

NOSE SLIDE: A board slide performed on a curb, bench, or other obstacle, on the front or nose of the deck

MONGO PUSHING/MONGO-FOOT: Moving the skateboard by pushing with the front or "incorrect" foot

NOSE GRIND: Grinding on the front truck, with the tail of the board pointing up

NOSE PICK: Coming to a stop while in the nose grind position

SNAKE: Someone who cuts another skater off or cuts in line at the skate park where people are lined up to skate a particular obstacle

JUDO: When the skater grabs the board near the front wheel and kicks their front foot forward; resembles a judo kick

FUNBOX: A box-shaped structure with a flat top and ramps, rails, or other features, used to perform tricks on

BOMB A HILL: Skate down a big hill, generally on a longboard, a skateboard with a larger deck

CARVING: Skating in a long, curving arc

SPEED WOBBLE: At a certain speed, a skateboard will begin to oscillate and become unstable

DEATH WOBBLE: An unrecoverable speed wobble that causes the skater to crash

WHEEL BITE: When the skater shifts so much weight to either the left or right side of the board that the board rubs against a wheel and stops it from rotating

FOCUS: When a skater breaks a skateboard in half

SHIFTY/9090: When the skater shifts the board 90 degrees along its vertical axis and brings it back to the starting position without removing their feet from the board

CHRIST AIR: Posing in a crucifix position in midair, while holding the board in either the left or right hand before landing with feet back on the board

LINE: A series of tricks performed consecutively

SKETCHY: A trick that's done poorly or incorrectly

BURLY: A trick that's dangerous enough to cause injury if it's done sketchily

RIPPER: A consistently good skater

SACK IT: A crash where the skater's testicles make contact with the rail or other obstacle

KICK TURN: When the skater turns by shifting their weight to the back of the board to lift the front wheels off the ground, then pivots their body to the left or right

TIC-TACKING: Propelling forward by executing a series of short kick turns

GROM/GROMMET: A young skater

DARKSIDE: The underside of the board, or when the board is upside down

DOG PISS: Kicking off with the rear foot in a manner that resembles a dog relieving himself

AIR WALK: Grabbing the nose or front of the skateboard and kicking both feet out in midair, then putting them back on the board before landing

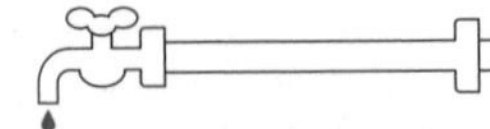

DUMB CROOKS

Here's proof that crime doesn't pay.

IN THE FLESH: Donald Murray's fifteen minutes of fame began in December 2019 when he showed up on an episode of the TV show *Live PD.* As cops pulled him over for driving without headlights, he crashed into a tree and escaped on foot. The Terre Haute, Indiana, fugitive evaded capture until the following February, when he led police on a high-speed chase that ended with charges including "felony resisting, reckless driving, possession of methamphetamine, maintaining a common nuisance, and auto theft." Aiding in Murray's capture...and the reason his *Live PD* appearance went viral: the large tattoo on his forehead that reads "Crime Pays."

CHARGED WITH A CRIME: Early one morning in September 2020, a thief from Fife, Scotland, described in local press reports as a "yob," attempted to steal some copper wire from a power station. First, he had to get past the pesky outer safety casings emblazoned with the words "CAUTION: LIVE WIRES. DANGER OF DEATH." Once inside, the thief attempted to steal the exposed wire but received 11,000 volts of electricity instead. When he regained his senses, he called an ambulance and was arrested at the hospital. Meanwhile, more than 400 homes in the area were without power for an hour. "This guy should be dead," said a police spokesperson.

ANYONE SEEN MY METH PIPE? In December 2019, Marvin Cumberworth went into a store in North Vernon, Indiana, to return a cell phone. A short time later, an employee was going through the box and found what police described as "a glass smoking device commonly used to smoke methamphetamine." After a brief investigation—brief because Cumberworth, 50, had left his contact info—he was arrested. He explained that he sold meth to "supplement my income."

FAR FROM SUPERMAN: Clark Kent hid his true identity with a pair of thick-rimmed glasses. Unfortunately for David Springthorpe, 30, of Derbyshire, England—who was wanted for shoplifting—the thick-rimmed glasses he wore as a disguise failed to conceal his distinctive neck tattoo and his abnormally large left ear. Police easily located Springthorpe on a Derbyshire sidewalk one afternoon in November 2019 and arrested him. They called the disguise "cunning" but "not quite cunning enough to evade capture."

LEAVING HIS MARK: A 22-year-old Pennsylvania man named Nicholas M. Mark walked into Pizza D'Oro in North Catasauqua in August 2020 to apply for a job. After Mark filled out an application, he grabbed the tip jar (which contained over $200) and darted out. An employee gave chase but stopped when Mark produced a

knife. So the thief escaped? No. Not only was Mark's name and address on his job application, he also left behind a backpack that had more identifying info, along with some drug paraphernalia.

APPLY HERE: Alberto Saavedra Lopez had seemingly gotten away with stealing $5,000 from a bank he used to work at in Cottonwood, Arizona. He moved to Phoenix and, although he was wanted in connection with the bank theft, he evaded capture for two years. Then, in 2018, Lopez moved back to Cottonwood and applied for a dispatch job...at the police department. A background check revealed his fugitive status, so police asked Lopez, 32, to come in for a job interview. As soon as he arrived, he was arrested. A police spokesperson said he was "out of the running" for the job.

GRAND THEFT WORK TRUCK: A Florida man, identified by Polk County police only as "Kevin," stole a work truck from a Circle K parking lot in 2018. After nearly running over the driver in his escape attempt, an APB was issued for the truck—which was pretty easy to find. Kevin used his own ID to cash some business checks that he'd found in the truck. Officers found the truck parked in his yard. At first, Kevin insisted that he couldn't steal the truck because he didn't know how to drive. He did, however, admit to knowing that the truck was stolen. Then, according to a Polk County Facebook post: "When asked why he didn't report the truck as being stolen to the cops, Kev said it was because he does not like the police. That hurts, Kevin." (His rap sheet with 48 felonies might explain his disdain.)

MORALITY TEST: Klaid Karpuzi had just been released from a New Port Richey, Florida, jail for auto theft when he saw a car in the detention center parking lot with the engine running and no one inside it. At least he *thought* there was no one inside it (the windows were tinted). So Karpuzi, 41, sauntered over, circled the car, and then tried to open the passenger door...only to discover an off-duty deputy in the driver's seat. She escorted Karpuzi right back inside. When he was released a second time, he didn't try to steal a car.

WHAT TIME IS IT? "Time for some wake and bake ☺," read the text that Emanuel (last name not released) sent to the Henry County Police Department in April 2019. A few minutes later, an officer texted back, "Good morning, Emanuel! Do you live in Henry County, GA?" (He was asking because marijuana use is still illegal in Georgia.) "Just jokes," Emanuel responded. "Alright," came the officer's reply, "well don't try becoming a comedian. Have a great day, Emanuel!"

Emanuel: "Don't tell me what to do! Thanks!"

Officer: "You have the right to remain silent."

The Police Department posted the odd exchange on Facebook. It's unclear whether Emanuel remained silent.

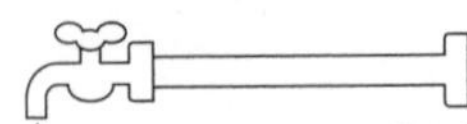

Fred Astaire took up skateboarding as a hobby when he was in his seventies. He gave it up after he fell and broke his wrist.

RANDOM ORIGINS

Once again, the BRI asks—and answers—the question: Where does all this stuff come from?

CHICKEN NUGGETS

Food scientist Robert C. Baker devised the chicken nugget at a lab at Cornell University in the early 1960s. He discovered that by grinding chicken with vinegar and salt, it dried out the meat, which made it stick together in a nuggetlike form. It worked even better when he added grains and milk as binding agents and then breaded the chicken concoction like a piece of traditional fried chicken. Test marketed in upstate New York, Baker's "Chicken Sticks" sold 200 boxes in six weeks. Although he had a hit on his hands, Baker (and Cornell) didn't patent the recipe, instead mailing the recipe to about 500 industrial, packaged, and frozen food companies. They sold moderately well in various forms until 1977, when Congress issued its *Dietary Goals for the United States*, which advised that Americans faced increased risk of cancer and stroke because they ate too much red meat. The alternative: chicken, and easy-to-prepare chicken nuggets. The meaty morsel was firmly ensconced in Americans' dietary habits in the early 1980s when Chick-Fil-A introduced the Chicken Nugget to its menu in 1982 and McDonald's unveiled the Chicken McNugget in 1983.

HIGH HEELS

Today, high heels are almost exclusively associated with women's fashion—according to sociologists, they elongate legs in a way that the human brain finds attractive. And yet this very feminine (and primarily ornamental) shoe began as practical work shoes for men. Butchers in ancient Egypt wore history's first high-heeled shoes on the job. The blood of butchered animals would drain out onto the ground. By wearing tall shoes with high heels, butchers could avoid getting their feet soaked in animal blood. Ancient Greek stage actors—all men—later wore high-heeled shoes to make themselves taller, instantly lending stature when they were playing gods and kings. Horseback troops in the ancient Persian army wore high heels to prevent their feet from slipping out of the stirrups. By the 1500s, aristocratic and wealthy European men had adopted the shoe style, and it wasn't until the 1630s that women, primarily in France and England, started wearing them too. Women adopted male fashions and behaviors so as to be taken more seriously—to be seen as equals to men. Some of the "manly" things that French and English women did: they smoked pipes, added epaulettes to their clothes, and wore high-heeled shoes.

Some species of moles have toxic saliva that they use to stun, but not kill, worms, which they store to eat later.

BLUE SCRUBS

Up until the early 20th century, surgeons in the operating room (along with nurses across the medical field, and for many more decades) wore white scrubs (as in "scrubbed," meaning clean), which conveyed a sense of hygiene and purity—important in medical situations. Infections incurred during surgery were very common and often deadly in the age before widespread use of antibiotics and proper cleaning techniques. In 1914, French surgeon René Leriche decided to change the color of his scrubs to cut down on cross-contamination—he dyed his gowns, masks, caps, and patients' bedsheets blue. That way, medical teams could easily identify and dispose of germ-covered items—the blue ones—and not accidentally reuse them elsewhere in the hospital and infect patients. The idea of blue scrubs soon spread from France to the rest of Europe, but not to the United States until the 1970s. Hospitals realized that the combination of white scrubs and bright white lights in a surgical environment led to eye strain and headaches for doctors. The solution: a shade called "Ciel Blue," followed by the addition of green scrubs in the late 1970s, both of which are easier on the eyes.

DISGUSTING JELLY BEANS

Thanks to one notable fan—President Ronald Reagan—jelly beans enjoyed a big pop-culture moment in the 1980s, followed by a demand for "gourmet" jelly beans, such as those produced by candymaker Jelly Belly. Today the company offers dozens of traditional and nontraditional flavors, such as cherry, lemon-lime, peach, buttered popcorn, mixed berry smoothie, and toasted marshmallow. It also produces really gross jelly beans. That started as a tie-in with the Harry Potter films of the early 2000s. The wizards and witches in the Harry Potter stories eat Bertie Bott's Every Flavour Beans, which include *every* flavor. Ambrose Lee, head of Jelly Belly's research-and-development team, was charged with making a series of pizza-flavored beans for the Bertie Bott's line. His initial attempt failed miserably. "People were actually trying to run away from the lab," Lee told *Confectionery News*. One executive said they tasted *almost* like human vomit. So Lee added some other flavorings, so as to perfectly nail the flavor of barf. That, in turn, led to the development of other Potter flavors, such as rotten egg, earwax, sardines, and worms. After the Potter line ended, Lee headed up the team that made BeanBoozled, a game that challenges consumers to buy a box and play flavor roulette—they might get a tasty flavor or they might get one of Lee's horrible ones, such as dirty dishwater, stinky socks, spoiled milk, toothpaste, dog food, dead fish, lawn clippings, baby wipes, skunk, moldy cheese, and booger.

"People were actually trying to run away from the lab."

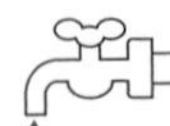

The tradition of leaving out milk and cookies for Santa started in the U.S. during the Great Depression as a way to teach kids to share with others.

RAIDERS OF THE LOST APPLES

In the 19th century, Americans grew thousands of different varieties of apples; today just 15 varieties make up more than 90 percent of U.S. apple production. The Lost Apple Project aims to save as many "lost" varieties as possible before they disappear forever.

NEIGHBORLY

Not long after he retired to a small town near Spokane, Washington, in 2006, Dave Benscoter was asked by a neighbor to help her pick apples from an old orchard on her property. He agreed, but soon realized that the apples were too high for him to reach. The orchard, originally planted around 1915, was badly overgrown. Benscoter offered to come back and prune the trees, so that in future years, the apples would be lower on the tree and easier to reach.

Working on his neighbor's trees got Benscoter interested in learning about old apple varieties, sometimes called "heritage apples," the majority of which are now presumed to be lost. He had no idea what kinds of apples were planted in his neighbor's orchard, and neither did she. Nor did anyone else they asked. Benscoter began to wonder how many of the "lost" varieties were actually alive and well, long forgotten but still thriving in old orchards like the one on his neighbor's property.

SOUTH BY NORTHWEST

Over the next several years, Benscoter immersed himself in the subject of heritage apples, reading anything he could get his hands on. That included plenty of books. One that caught his attention was *Old Southern Apples,* by Creighton Lee Calhoun. The first half of the book was devoted to varieties that are still grown in the southern United States, and the second half listed varieties that were lost and presumed extinct.

He also discovered a 1904 article from a newspaper called the *Colfax Gazette* that listed the prizewinning apples in that year's Whitman County Fair in eastern Washington. As he studied the article, he realized that *every* apple entered in the fair had won a prize of some kind, and the names of all the varieties were listed. That meant that the article, and similar ones published in other years, provided fairly comprehensive lists of the varieties of apples that were growing in the area at the time.

Even better, when Benscoter made note of some unfamiliar varieties mentioned in the article and looked them up in *Old Southern Apples,* he discovered that three of the varieties—Lankford, Walbridge, and Babbitt—were listed as lost, at least in the South. But since they'd also been planted in eastern Washington, it was possible

Jane Jetson had Judy Jetson when she was 18 (and George was 25).

that some of the trees there might still be alive. He was particularly interested in the Walbridge apple, because it had a distinctive appearance—red with dark crimson stripes—that he thought he would recognize if he ever came across it. So in 2014, he started a group called the Lost Apple Project and set out to find the Walbridge and other lost varieties.

APPLE COUNTRY

Eastern Washington turns out to be a great place to look for lost apples. So are parts of Oregon and Idaho. Washington has been the heart of the U.S. apple industry for more than a century, and people have been planting apple trees in great numbers in the state since not long after the passage of the Homestead Act of 1862. That law enabled homesteaders to stake a claim on a 160-acre plot of frontier land and eventually claim ownership, provided that they built a home, added a well or made other improvements to the land, farmed it for five years, and paid an $18 fee (about $460 today).

Apple orchards were a common feature on homestead farms. They could be planted in spots not suitable for plowing, such as on steep hillsides or down in ravines, or along a water source such as a stream or a creek. Some varieties produced fruit as early as July, and others ripened in the late fall and kept well through the winter. Apples were an important source of food in hard times: Even when wheat, corn, and other crops failed, apple trees could be counted on to provide something for homesteaders to eat for much of the year. In times of plenty, the apples could be made into hard cider and sold for a good price, and apple vinegar could be used to preserve other foods by pickling. Apples were so important that each homesteading family was advised to plant at least *one hundred* apple trees of different varieties—some that ripened early, some that ripened late, some that were good for eating raw, others that were good for cooking, and still others that were good for making cider—to provide for their needs throughout the year.

MIXING IT UP

In the early years, homesteaders planted many different apple varieties, not knowing which ones would thrive in the local climate and which would not. Some 250 varieties were planted throughout the Pacific Northwest. Over time, as it became clear which ones did the best, the number of varieties planted declined. But the old trees weren't always chopped down—they were often left in place and ignored in favor of newer trees. As farms changed hands over the years, precisely *which* varieties had been planted was forgotten. Many small farms were eventually abandoned, but their apple orchards survived. Even today, more than 150 years after the oldest trees were planted, many are still alive and producing apples. These are the apples that Dave Benscoter

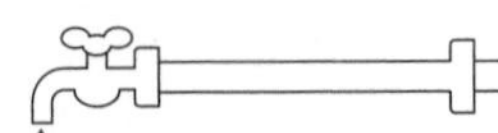

wanted to find and identify. And he's not alone. In 2017, the Lost Apple Project attracted the interest of E. J. Brandt, another retiree. Brandt looks for lost apples in northern Idaho, where he lives, and Benscoter searches in eastern Washington.

PAPER CHASE

Before he retired, Benscoter worked as an agent for both the FBI and the IRS Criminal Division. Some of the skills he used to hunt criminals and tax cheats are the same ones he uses to hunt lost apples. "It's like a crime scene," he explained to the *New York Times* in 2017. "You have to establish that the trees existed and hope there's a paper trail to follow." Benscoter pores over old nursery catalogs, newspaper articles and advertisements, county fair records, sales receipts, and any other evidence he comes across that might identify which farmer purchased which varieties of apple trees. Then he looks up the farmer, using old property records to figure out the location of their homestead, and drives out to the property to see if there are any old apple trees still growing there.

NERO APPLES AND ROBERT BURNS

Some of his best information comes from the descendants of homesteaders and the people who operated commercial orchards in the 1800s. Benscoter found his first "lost" apple variety, the Nero, in Whitman County, Washington, in 2014, when his paper trail led him to a homesteader named Robert Burns. In 1894, Burns planted hundreds of fruit trees, including more than 400 apple trees, on a steep hill called Steptoe Butte, 40 miles south of Spokane, Washington. When Benscoter looked up Burns's name on Find a Grave, a website that identifies where people are buried, he saw that one of Burns's descendants had left a detailed family history on the site. Benscoter contacted the descendant through the website, and they sent him information that helped him find the Nero apple tree on the old Burns homestead.

Steptoe Butte turns out to be an especially good place to look for heritage apples. Over the years, Burns and a neighboring homesteader named James Davis planted more than 800 apple trees on the slopes of the butte and in the surrounding ravines. The Burns family is long gone from the homestead; they left in 1899, and Davis soon followed. But more than a century later, hundreds of the trees the two homesteaders planted are still alive and producing apples. The Lost Apple Project has already found four varieties there long thought to be extinct: Nero, Arkansas Beauty, McAfee, and Dickinson—and there may be others. *(Part II of the story is on page 272.)*

* * *

"Write a wise saying and your name will live forever."

—**Anonymous**

...slow, distinct manner of speech to a childhood speech impediment—
he couldn't fully move his lower jaw.

UNPLAYED VIDEO GAMES

The multibillion-dollar video game industry churns out thousands of titles a year. Every so often, a few widely hyped games wind up being canceled just before they're scheduled to hit stores. Here are a few notables.

Six Days in Fallujah (2009)

Combat video games are an especially popular genre, delivering a realistic soldier's point of view in wars both fictional (*Halo* troops fight on distant planets) and historical (*Call of Duty: WWII*). In 2009, publisher Atomic Games used the real-life approach with its *Six Days in Fallujah.* Lacking the historical perspective that comes with setting a game in a long-since-over war, this game concerned the ongoing U.S. military operations in Iraq—specifically, the events of 2004, when a group of Iraqi insurgents attacked a convoy of American soldiers and then killed a contingent of private-sector employees of Blackwater Security. Only five years gone, that tragedy was still painfully fresh in people's minds, and the families of the troops who died protested the release of the game. "These horrific events should be confined to the annals of history, not trivialized and rendered for thrill-seekers to play out," one grieving parent told reporters. A month after *Six Days in Fallujah* was announced, Atomic canceled it.

Xpo-ferens Columbus (1992)

In 1992, Americans celebrated the 500th anniversary of Christopher Columbus's arrival in the New World with large and boisterous Columbus Day festivities across the United States, especially on the East Coast. Hollywood got in on it with two Columbus films, *Christopher Columbus: The Discovery* and *1492: Conquest of Paradise.* Both flopped, but at least they made it to the public—unlike Misawa Entertainment's bizarre video game *Xpo-ferens Columbus.* Named after the Greek-Latin mixture in which Columbus signed his name, this title for the Super Nintendo and the Sega Genesis was set in 1492 and found Columbus sailing not to America but on a quest to discover gold. Also, his ship, the *Santa Maria,* can fly and shoot off "energy bullets" to repel dragons, woolly mammoths, and sea monsters. Although *Xpo-ferens* appeared in Misawa's 1992 catalog, programmers missed their deadlines, forcing the time-sensitive title into early 1993. Then the company started going out of business…and the Columbus game never set sail.

Thrill Kill (1998)

One of the hottest game types of the 1990s was also the most controversial: ultra-violent, super-gory, hand-to-hand combat titles like *Mortal Kombat* and *Street Fighter.* (The former allowed players to rip out the opposing character's spine upon victory.) Parents groups loudly protested the games, but that only made kids want to play

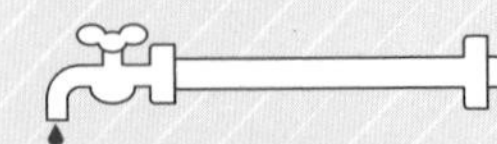

the games more, and prompted video game companies to make titles even more brutal, such as *Thrill Kill.* The premise: It takes place in hell, where eight of the most despicable people who ever lived compete in a fighting tournament, and the winner gets to come back to life and return to Earth. The level of violence is high—one character can shove a cattle prod into opponents' throats, another drinks blood from the severed heads of the defeated, and another beats people with their own severed arms. The Entertainment Software Rating Board, which rates games for consumers, gave *Thrill Kill* an AO, or "Adults Only," prompting most major American retailers to refuse to stock it. That (not the protests) led *Thrill Kill*'s publisher to pull the game before its scheduled release.

DID YOU KNOW?

If a game receives an "AO" or "Adults Only" rating from the Entertainment Software Rating Board (ESRB), it might as well have never been released—it's a commercial kiss of death for any game in an industry that caters to teens and kids. Fewer than 30 games have ever been rated AO, including a video-game adaptation of the 1972 best-selling book *The Joy of Sex* (the first game to get an AO), *Playboy: The Mansion*, and *Hatred* (because the main character murders everyone he sees).

The Grape Escape (1990)

The California Raisins were a huge fad in the 1980s. As is the case with most crazes, in retrospect it's hard to understand why Americans became obsessed with Claymation raisins that sang Motown songs in ads for the California Raisin Advisory Board to the point where the raisins got their own TV specials, a Saturday morning cartoon, an album, T-shirts, lunchboxes, and toy lines. Nintendo wanted a piece of the pie, and announced that it would bring *California Raisins: The Grape Escape* to its Nintendo Entertainment System. Big problem: Nintendo planned to release the game in 1990, by which point the California Raisins fad had come and gone. But that wasn't the only reason it canceled the game. By the time this NES title was ready to hit the market, Nintendo would have already released its next-generation Super NES, making the NES (and all its games) obsolete.

Propeller Arena (2001)

Flight simulators are another popular style of video gaming, providing players an exciting experience approximating taking the controls of an airplane. The 2001 Sega Dreamcast game *Propeller Arena* re-created the cockpit of a fighter jet. Not only did gamers get to pilot a plane, they could engage in dogfights with as many as three other players. Scheduled to hit stores in early fall 2001, *Propeller Arena* was one of the last games planned for release on the Dreamcast, but it wound up never shipping to stores. Just a few days after the events of September 11, 2001, in which terrorists hijacked planes and crashed them into the World Trade Center, Sega thought making *Propeller Arena,* a game about purposely crashing airplanes, seemed tasteless and offensive, so they pulled it.

FIRSTS IN ADVERTISING

This page is brought to you by advertising. Advertising. Yes, advertising. That name again? Advertising. Try some today!

★ **First ad of any kind in the English language.** In 1476, William Caxton, an enterprising publisher who operated in the Westminster area of London, printed a handbill announcing the release of a new prayer book and posted it on church doors around the city.

★ **First newspaper advertisement.** The first paper in the United States to sell space to advertisers was the *Boston News-Letter.* Its first edition, on April 24, 1704, included an ad looking for someone to buy a 20-acre estate for sale on Long Island's Oyster Bay in New York.

★ **First American magazine ad.** In January 1741, jack-of-all-trades Benjamin Franklin started up a general-interest magazine called, appropriately enough, *General.* The inside cover featured the first magazine advertisement in America—touting the next issue of *General.*

★ **First celebrity endorsement.** In 1760, British pottery maker Josiah Wedgwood ran newspaper ads boasting that his products were so good that he enjoyed an official royal commission—in other words, he touted an endorsement by Queen Charlotte.

★ **First billboard.** Also called outdoor advertising or large-format advertising, the first billboards went up in New York City in 1835. A promoter named Jared Bell produced 50-square-foot ads around Manhattan touting the arrival of a traveling circus called "The Great Wallace Shows."

★ **First product placement.** The act of allowing sponsors to advertise their products within a work of narrative fiction, such as a movie or TV show, began with books. French adventure novelist Jules Verne had already enjoyed such massive success with *Journey to the Center of the Earth* and *Twenty Thousand Leagues Under the Sea* that his 1873 book *Around the World in Eighty Days* was guaranteed to be a smash hit and attract lots of readers. So Verne happily made overtures to Peninsular and Oriental Steam Navigation Company, a large international shipping firm, and wrote references to one of their ships, the *Carnatic,* into the novel. Whether Verne received payment for the mention is unknown.

Catnip equivalent for dogs: anise, which has a taste similar to licorice. Anise is also used on fishing lures to attract fish.

★ **First advertising mascot.** After founder Henry Seymour named his oats company Quaker (because he thought the religious sect conveyed a sense of purity), he had an artist draw up a picture of a stern Quaker man, who appeared on all packaging and—though he's become less stern-looking over the years—still does to this day. Quaker filed the first ever trademark for an ad mascot in 1877. (Fun fact: according to Quaker, his name is Larry.)

★ **First direct marketing campaign.** The ad industry's term for the coupons and postcards you receive from local businesses is "direct marketing." A less flattering name for it: "junk mail." Sears, Roebuck & Co., America's most dominant retailer at the time, tried it in 1892. The company mailed out 8,000 postcards offering customers a few items for purchase by mail—sort of like a miniature, one-page catalog—and received 2,000 responses.

★ **First radio ad.** In 1922, AT&T, which had established a few radio stations on the East Coast, announced that it would begin "toll broadcasting," or selling airtime to whoever wished to buy it. The first company to respond to the pitch: a New York–area real estate management firm called the Queensboro Corp. The company paid $200 to air a 15-second ad four times on New York station WEAF, alerting the public to the apartments available in its new housing complex in Queens.

★ **First commercial jingle.** Radio advertising took off fast. Only four years after its introduction, the first memorable bit of music written and recorded specifically to sell a product—a jingle—debuted. On Christmas Eve 1926, a Minneapolis radio station broadcast a commercial for Wheaties, which included an a cappella quartet called the Wheaties Quartet singing about the goodness of the breakfast cereal.

★ **First pop song used in an ad.** Using familiar songs in lieu of creating original jingles is a common practice in commercials today. (Think of those Chevy truck ads that started to run in 1991, scored with Bob Seger's "Like a Rock.") The pioneer in this: General Motors. A 1928 Oldsmobile radio ad took the melody of a 1905 song called "In My Merry Oldsmobile" and added new lyrics with a harder sell.

★ **First sponsored TV broadcast.** In the early decades of television, programs were sponsored by a single company, and there would be breaks in the shows, during which a pitchman would flog the wares of that company. The first program to do this: a 1946 NBC travelogue called *Geographically Speaking,* sponsored by pharmaceutical company Bristol-Myers.

Over the centuries, Iran (Persia) has had 59 different capital cities.

★ **First TV commercial.** On July 1, 1941, NBC's flagship affiliate, WNBT in New York, broadcast a baseball game between the Brooklyn Dodgers and Philadelphia Phillies. Just before, the screen bore a primarily still image of a clock showing the time, along with the Bulova Watch logo and the words "Bulova Watch Time." At the time, only 7,500 New York City homes had a TV set.

★ **First spam email.** Before the internet was available to the public, it existed as a computer network called ARPANET, primarily for use by American government agencies and employees. In 1978, a computer equipment company employee named Gary Thuerk used ARPANET's electronic communication function (email, as it would later be called) to send an unsolicited message to 397 accounts, inviting them to a product demo of a new computer.

★ **First all-ad TV network.** On August 1, 1981, Music Television—MTV—debuted, broadcasting a 24-hour-a-day schedule of music videos, which are essentially ads for records, provided (and paid for) by musicians' labels. It also has commercial breaks, and the first ad in the first break was for a 3-ring binder called "The Bulk."

★ **First internet banner ad.** Those big advertising rectangles that lurk at the top of many websites were birthed on October 27, 1994, on HotWired.com, the online version of the tech magazine *Wired.* It was for AT&T, and played into the company's then-current campaign promising futuristic technologies, ending with the tagline "You will." The banner ad read: "Have you ever clicked your mouse right here? You will."

* * *

KNITTING LINGO

- **FART:** An acronym for "fiber acquisition road trip," or a drive to another town specifically to hit up its yarn stores
- **FO:** A "finished object"
- **UFO:** An "unfinished object"
- **Body bag:** A knitter's collection of UFOs
- **Frogging:** Ripping out stitches after a mistake
- **Frog pond:** A knitter's bag where they keep projects they haven't gotten around to frogging yet
- **Stash:** A knitter's collection of yarn
- **SEX:** "Stash enhancement experience," or buying yarn
- **KIP:** Knitting in public
- **Tink:** Knit spelled backward; it means to reverse progress one stitch at a time to fix mistakes

The negatives of *Gone With the Wind*, *The Wizard of Oz*, and *Star Wars* are stored in a salt mine 650 feet below Kansas.

UNCLE JOHN MOONS YOU

Strap into your rocket ship for some history, facts, and theories about our own Moon, the moons of our celestial neighbors, and even moons in other solar systems.

First Words Spoken on the Moon: Contrary to popular belief, they weren't Neil Armstrong's famous quotation, "One small step for a man, one giant leap for mankind." Six hours earlier, right after *Apollo 11*'s lunar module touched down on July 20, 1969, the actual first words that were spoken on another celestial body came from pilot Buzz Aldrin, who said to Mission Control: "Contact light." (A blue light came on to tell the astronauts that the lunar module's contact probe had touched the surface, and they could safely turn off the engines.)

The Impact of Galileo's Discovery: In 1610, Italian astronomer Galileo Galilei was viewing Jupiter through his new 20-power telescope when he discovered "four planets, never seen from the beginning of the world up to our own times." They weren't planets, they were the four largest moons of Jupiter, what we now call the Galilean moons: Io, Europa, Ganymede, and Callisto. Seeing the moons revolving around Jupiter helped confirm Nicolaus Copernicus's earlier theory that the Earth revolved around the Sun, and not vice versa. After Galileo published his findings in *Siderius Nuncius* (*The Starry Messenger*), the Catholic Church charged him with heresy and banned his works on scriptural grounds, arguing that Earth was the center of the universe. Nearly 400 years later, Pope John Paul II expressed "formal regret" on behalf of the Church and admitted that Galileo was right.

"Irregular" Moons: Astronomers have discovered 79 moons around Jupiter (called the Jovian moons), but there might be a lot more. And they're doing something odd. In our solar system, the planets' moons all orbit in the same direction. Astronomers estimate there could be as many as 600 smaller "irregular" satellites orbiting Jupiter...in the opposite direction. It's theorized that these space rocks were wayward asteroids that got caught in the planet's gravity, but why they're orbiting backward remains a mystery.

Exomoon: Astronomers search for *exoplanets*—planets outside of our solar system—using essentially the same method Galileo used when he discovered Jupiter's moons: by observing one pass in front of a larger object. (That's called a *transit*.) Exoplanets are identified when their transit dims a star, prompting astronomers to "zoom in" to get a closer look. In 2018, while using the Hubble Telescope to observe an exoplanet in the constellation Cygnus (about 8,000 light-years away), they observed "little deviations and wobbles in the light curve" of the gas giant. Those deviations, say the scientists, were most likely caused by the first exomoon ever identified.

What Our Moon Is Made Of: Not cheese...but it's not a solid chunk of rock, either. The push and pull of gravity between the Moon, Earth, and the Sun is why our planet has a spinning, molten core at its center, which in turn causes the tides, plate tectonics, and volcanism (and life). Those same forces are at work deep inside the Moon. That's why NASA astronomers say the Moon has a solid, iron-rich inner core and a fluid, primarily liquid-iron outer core. The evidence? Moonquakes, detected by seismographs left on the lunar surface by the Apollo crews in the early 1970s, have left long fault lines—called *scarps*—all over the Moon's surface. In addition, as the Moon continues to cool off from its original formation, Researchers say it is "shriveling like a raisin."

The Rings of Mars? Saturn, Jupiter, and Neptune have rings. (So does Uranus.) Mars doesn't...yet. Mars was once assumed to have acquired its two potato-shaped moons, Phobos and Deimos, from the asteroid belt. But new studies of the satellites' circular orbits point to a more violent origin: Mars used to have one larger moon that was smashed in two by an asteroid. What's more, Phobos's orbit is degrading and in about 100 million years, the 17-mile-wide moon will get so close to Mars that gravity will tear it into millions of pieces—leaving a flat, rocky ring around the red planet.

Life on Moons: According to scientists, several of the Earthlike moons that orbit the gas giants (Jupiter, Saturn, Neptune, and Uranus) are better candidates than Mars for supporting life.

- Titan: Saturn's largest moon is the only other body in the solar system with a thick atmosphere and lakes, rivers, and seas. It's not made of the same stuff as Earth, so the Titans could be methane-based life-forms.
- Enceladus: Saturn's icy moon has geysers that indicate it has a subsurface ocean.
- Europa: Jupiter's moon contains more water than Earth; it's trapped under miles of ice, kept in liquid form by the gas giant's constant tugging.
- Ganymede: This Jovian moon is the largest satellite in the solar system (it's bigger than Mercury), and like Earth, it has a protective magnetic field to shield its inhabitants from the Sun's harmful rays.
- Io: The moon closest to Jupiter is the most volcanically active body in the solar system. Why is that important? The most habitable areas on *our* planet—the ones that have an abundance of flora and fauna—are located in volcanically active regions. So, who knows who or what could be inhabiting Io—or perhaps another distant moon—gazing up at their own night sky, pondering the existence of life on Earth.

During World War I, the U.S. War Industries Board asked women to stop wearing corsets to free up metal production. It saved enough to build two battleships.

20 USES FOR SILICA GEL PACKS

You know those little packets you have to remove before you eat beef jerky, or else risk dying? Those packets (also called sachets) contain tiny grains of silicon dioxide, technically called silica xerogel, *that serve as a desiccant, drawing water molecules to them (through the paper) and away from whatever they're packed with. Manufacturers include them in boxes of electronics, in the pockets of leather jackets, and with vitamins, shoes, pepperoni, or anything else that needs to be kept moisture-free. They help dry out whatever's nearby, so here are a few ways you can use them around your house.*

1. De-odorize your gym bag. When you throw sweaty socks or wet towels in your bag, toss in a couple of silica gel packets to stave off mildew and odors.
2. Prevent rust. Place silica packets in your toolbox, tackle box, gun safe, or behind tools hanging on the wall.
3. Avoid condensation on windows or car windshields by putting silica packets at the bottom of the glass.
4. If your cat or dog eats dry food, store it in a plastic or glass container with a packet taped underneath the lid.
5. Preserve your baseball card, comic book, or coin collection. Slip desiccant packets into the album's plastic sleeves.
6. Store guitars or other musical instruments with silica packets to help keep them from warping.
7. Drop silica gel packets into your camera case, laptop bag, or even between your phone and its case to keep out moisture.
8. Flower and vegetable seeds eventually lose their ability to germinate, but you can extend their viability by keeping them in a cool, dry place...with a silica packet.
9. Prolong the life of your jack-o'-lantern. To slow down rotting, put silica packets inside the hollowed-out pumpkin. (And use a battery-operated candle to prevent a fire.)
10. Protect photos, important documents, and scrapbooks. Damage caused by humidity in your attic or garage may be avoided if you throw some silica packets into the storage box.
11. When not in use, a hearing aid can be kept with a silica packet to dry it out. (Ear wax...yech.)

12. Freshen up musty books. Put books that need to be rejuvenated in a plastic bag with silica gel packets for a couple of days.

13. Prevent tarnish. Nestle silica packets alongside watches, jewelry, holiday ornaments, or other shiny items.

14. Use silica packets to ensure your medicine cabinet or vitamin stash stays dry.

15. Make homemade potpourri. Warning: do this *only* if you can keep it securely away from kids and pets. If you can, carefully tear open two or three silica packets, and without touching the beads, pour them into a small dish. Add a drop or two of essential oil, and place it near the source of an unwanted odor (the bathroom).

16. Prevent powdered laundry or dish detergent from clumping with a few silica packets.

17. Did you drop your phone in the toilet? While you *can* use rice to try to dry it out, the grains might get lodged in the charging port, headphone jack, or other slots. Instead, fill a bag with enough silica packets to bury your phone. Wait 24 to 48 hours before turning it on. Then sanitize.

18. Preserve leather by stowing shoes and jackets with silica packets inside.

19. Got boxes of cassettes, VHS tapes, or even 8-tracks that you're definitely going to "do something with soon"? Transfer them to plastic bins with silica packets before humidity destroys them forever.

20. You can reuse silica gel packets even after they've become damp with use. Just lay them in the hot sun for a few hours.

Bonus fact: You can use silica packets for many things, but not everything. In case you've never noticed, they have a warning—DO NOT EAT—printed on them. The reason isn't because you'll get silicon poisoning, as many people assume. Silica is not digestible, and cannot break down in your body. It can, however irritate your digestive tract. And if the silica is coated with cobalt chloride, which is toxic, eating it can cause nausea and vomiting. So leave the silica in the pouch, and keep the pouch out of your mouth!

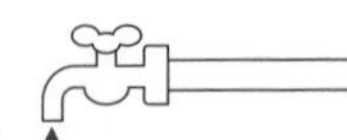

Sammy Davis Jr. claimed to be addicted to *Pac-Man*. He played for hours on end.

WHEN WORLDS COLLIDE

According to scientific estimates, there are nearly eight million animal species on Earth. Here are some strange-but-true tales about what happens when one of those species (us) runs afoul of a few of the others.

BITE ME

In September 2019, a camel named Caspar—described as a "gentle giant" by his keepers at the Tiger Truck Stop petting zoo in Gross Tete, Louisiana—got into a tussle with Gloria Lancaster, 68, her husband Edmond, 73, and their little dog, Baby Girl, 14. After finishing dinner at the truck stop, the Florida couple let Baby Girl, who is deaf, run around outside the camel enclosure while Edmund was tossing doggy treats *into* the enclosure. Predictably, the dog ran in after them. With no way for Baby Girl to hear their calls (and no staffers around to help), the desperate couple crawled under the wire fence to retrieve her. As Edmund swatted his ball cap to distract Caspar, Victoria tried to get the dog. She wasn't fast enough. The 600-pound camel knocked her to the ground and then sat on top of her. Edmund tried to push Caspar off, but the camel wouldn't budge. Pinned beneath the crushing weight, Gloria couldn't even move her arms. "Get the dog," she shouted. "Get out of here! I'm already dead." But then, dangling right in front of her face, Gloria saw a way out: "I bit his balls to get him off of me," she later told police. According to the *Advocate* (Baton Rouge), Gloria was treated at the hospital for "non-critical injuries to her abdomen, neck, shoulder, arm, and head." Caspar was treated with antibiotics and was reported to be doing fine. The Lancasters were charged with criminal trespassing and violating the leash law. When asked by police why he threw doggy treats to the camel, Edmund answered, "I wasn't thinking."

OUTFOXED

"Thinking back on it now, the fox was a mangy, stanky fox," said Eliza Ruth Watson, 37. She was gardening in her yard in Gray, Maine, in April 2020, when she saw the small predator slinking near her chicken coop. She ran toward it, yelling and waving her arms, expecting it to run away, as all the other foxes had. It didn't. Instead, it darted right at her, snarling and biting, and before Watson knew it, she was fighting off the bleeding fox with her feet. (It was literally bleeding.) Then the crazed animal jumped into the air and bit at her hands, which were somewhat protected by gardening gloves. Watson finally managed to pin down the fox by its neck. It squirmed relentlessly as she carried it to a large pot used for scalding chickens. She threw the fox into the pot and slammed the lid. But the fox sprung right back out and scratched her and bit her some more before she could properly secure the lid. Later,

Subway's ham, salami, and bologna are all turkey-based. "Real" salami is only used in the Italian sandwiches.

at the hospital, Watson's wounds were cleaned, and she was given a series of rabies shots. "I don't think I could have handled it any differently," she said. "It's not like alligator wrangling where you can position yourself to get the alligator a certain way. I've never had to wrestle a fox before."

GOD SAVE THE QUEEN

By the time Carol Howarth (who was shopping in Haverfordwest, Wales, in May 2016) returned to her car, the swarm of bees was no longer there. Swarm of bees? A concerned citizen named Tom Moses explained to her that he and several other people had gathered to watch a "brown splodge" of bees grow larger and larger on the back of her unattended car. Fearing that "someone might do something stupid and get hurt...or hurt the bees," he called in local beekeepers to remove the swarm, which they did. Mostly. Howarth thanked Moses and drove away, having seen not even one single bee...until the next morning when she went out to her car and saw, to her shock, that the swarm was back. Reason: The beekeepers had failed to get the queen. Result: 20,000 bees followed the car all over town and then to Howarth's residence. Later that day, a beekeeper removed the hive–queen included–and Howarth got on with her buzzy life.

LIFE AND DEATH IN THE FAST LANE

Despite their humdrum name, brown snakes kill more Australians per year than any other snake species. In June 2020, Jimmy Canhan, a 27-year-old *tradie* (a "tradesman" in Australia), nearly became a snake-death statistic himself when a brown snake crawled into Canhan's *ute* (a "utility vehicle," or small truck) on his last job of the day. Later, as he was driving on Queensland's Dawson Highway, it was "like something out of the Chamber of Secrets was sitting on my passenger seat, it was massive," he later told a newspaper reporter. "It just unfurled like this octopus as soon as it knew I knew it was there, and it was on!" The brown snake quickly wrapped itself around Canhan's leg and started striking at his seat. The more Canhan moved, the angrier the snake became. Canhan struck back, using a "work knife and my seat belt" to kill the snake. Then he started shaking and was afraid he'd been bitten. Knowing he only had minutes before the powerful venom kicked in, he sped away for the nearest hospital...and got pulled over for speeding. When the officer approached the vehicle, Canhan was babbling about "a brown snake or a tiger snake, it's in the back of the ute...I think it's bitten me!" The officer walked to the back, saw the dead snake, and remarked dryly, "Oh, that one." The good news is that Canhan hadn't been bitten but was merely in shock. Nor did he get a speeding ticket. The bad news is that after the police body cam footage went viral, Canhan was fired from his tradie job for using his company car on personal business. (He'd been driving to visit his daughter when the snake struck.) Still, he's grateful to be alive. "It was him or me."

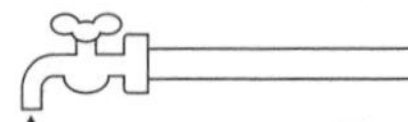

The Nobel Prize for Economics is awarded by the Bank of Sweden, not the Nobel Foundation. So technically, it's not a "real" Nobel Prize.

OL' BLUE EYES IS BACK

When Frank Sinatra visited Australia in 1974, his concert tour generated plenty of headlines...but not the kind that he or anyone else would have wanted.

BEWITCHED

Even superstars can fall into a rut, and in 1970 Frank Sinatra fell into one of his: his album *Watertown* flopped, never climbing higher than #101 on the music charts. That September, he pulled out of a three-week singing engagement at Caesars Palace in Las Vegas, after a Caesars executive pulled a gun on him at the gaming tables when he demanded to play baccarat at $16,000 a hand (the house limit was $2,000 a hand).

Sinatra didn't miss the work: after more than 30 years in the business, he was tired of singing the same old songs to audiences who weren't interested in his new material. In June 1971, he announced his retirement and walked off of the stage for good.

"For good" didn't last long, though. Two years later, Sinatra came out of retirement after deciding the quiet life wasn't for him. He recorded a new album called *Ol' Blue Eyes Is Back* and promoted it with a TV special by the same name. Then in January 1974, he embarked on a concert tour of the United States, Europe, Asia, and Australia.

UNDER MY SKIN

This was not a happy time for the Chairman of the Board: he was in his late fifties, and past his prime. He was restless. He was insecure about his fading looks. He was unsure about his singing voice, because his vocal cords were acting up. And he was angry at the press. After years of infuriating newspaper stories about his three failed marriages, his many extramarital affairs, his alleged mob ties, and other things he didn't want to talk about, Sinatra refused to hold press conferences or speak to reporters at all during his concert tour. And he was still smarting at the fact that *The Godfather,* the biggest film of 1972, had featured a sobbing Sinatra-esque crooner named Johnny Fontane who relies upon the Godfather's muscle to revive his flagging career. Perhaps because of his frustration, Sinatra was chain smoking and drinking as much as two bottles of Jack Daniels a day.

THE LADY IS A TRAMP

These and other resentments were swirling in Sinatra's mind when he arrived in Australia in July 1974 to perform five concerts: two in Melbourne, followed by three in Sydney. He stopped over in Sydney the night he arrived and was mobbed by reporters who followed him from the airport to his hotel. Nonetheless, Sinatra appeared to be in good spirits...until he opened a newspaper at the hotel and saw an

Only recorded instance of sky pirates: when the German zeppelin L23 captured the Norwegian sailing ship *Royal* in 1917.

article detailing his alleged mafia ties and featuring photos of several of the women he'd been linked to over the years under the headline "Sinatra's Molls."

He was still seething the following day when he flew to Melbourne for his first concert there. As had become his custom, he sang a few opening numbers, then took a break to give his vocal cords a rest as he sat on a stool onstage drinking tea with honey and chatting with the audience. Normally he used the time to establish a friendly rapport with his fans, but on this occasion, he attacked the press. "They keep chasing after us," he complained. "We have to run all day long. They're parasites who take everything and give nothing. And as for the broads who work for the press, they're the hookers of the press. I might offer them a buck and a half. I'm not sure."

RING-A-DING-DING!

Americans might have been used to this kind of language from Sinatra, but in Australia it was shocking and insulting. The morning after the concert, the Australian Journalists Association demanded that he apologize for his remarks, especially for his crack about female reporters being buck-and-a-half hookers. Sinatra refused, whereupon the Australian Theatrical and Amusement Employees' Association, which provided musicians as well as lighting and staging crews for Sinatra's concerts, ordered its members to stand down until Sinatra apologized. Once again, he refused.

With no one willing to work the second Melbourne concert, it had to be canceled. Sinatra still refused to say he was sorry: his lawyer, Mickey Rudin, released a statement threatening that "Unless within 15 minutes Mr. Sinatra had an apology for '15 years of sh*t' from the Australian press, he would be leaving the country within an hour."

At that point, the Australian Transport Worker Union got in on the act, refusing to refuel Sinatra's jet or provide services to any commercial flight that Sinatra boarded. Then the Australian Council of Trade Unions (ACTU), headed by a man named Bob Hawke, upped the ante by forbidding any member of *any* trade union from serving Sinatra until he apologized. This included restaurant waiters, kitchen staff, limousine drivers, and hotel maids, to name just a few. "If you don't apologize, your stay in this country could be indefinite," Hawke warned Sinatra. "You won't be allowed to leave Australia unless you can walk on water."

OH! LOOK AT ME NOW

Sinatra and his entourage managed to sneak aboard a flight back to Sydney by buying their tickets under assumed names. But they had to carry their own bags, because no porters would assist them, and they had to hail their own taxis, because the limousine service that had been arranged for the concert tour refused to shuttle them around. That night, Sinatra cooked pasta in his hotel room for himself and his cronies after the restaurant refused to serve them dinner. As he and the others sat around eating

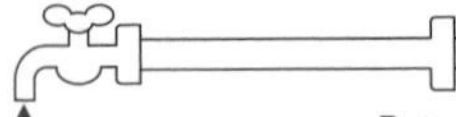

Bats eat so many insects in the U.S. each year that if you tried to kill that many bugs with pesticides, you'd need about $23 billion worth.

their pasta, Sinatra said to John Pond, the hotel's director of public relations, "Well, John, how the hell are we gonna get out of this enchilada? Got any ideas?"

Pond used his connections to put in a call to Australia's prime minister, Gough Whitlam, but Whitlam refused to intervene, insisting that the ACTU's Bob Hawke was the only man that could resolve the crisis. But Hawke refused to take the call. Three days passed before he finally went to Sinatra's hotel to negotiate an end to the standoff. In the meantime, Sinatra explored other options for getting out of Australia: he'd recently performed a concert in Japan for the U.S. Navy, and was friendly with an admiral who commanded an aircraft carrier in the Pacific. He considered asking the admiral to sail into Sydney Harbour and evacuate him by helicopter from the roof of his hotel. Sinatra was also friends with Jimmy Hoffa, the head of the Teamsters Union; maybe the Teamsters could put pressure on the Australian unions by refusing to unload Australian ships in American ports until Ol' Blue Eyes was allowed to return home. Neither of these ideas went anywhere.

REGRETS, I'VE HAD A FEW

When Bob Hawke finally arrived at Sinatra's hotel, the singer refused to meet with him. Sinatra remained holed up in his hotel suite while Mickey Rudin met with Hawke to hammer out some kind of deal with the labor leader to end the crisis. Once again, Hawke demanded an apology from Sinatra. Once again, Rudin refused on behalf of his client. Sinatra had never apologized to anyone in his life, Rudin explained, and he wasn't going to start now.

The negotiations dragged on for nearly eight hours before the two men finally worked out an agreement. Sinatra wouldn't apologize, but he would sign a statement regretting that his fans had been inconvenienced by the cancellation of the Melbourne concert. The statement would also say that while both sides had a right to speak their minds, they also had a job to do and it was time to get back to work. Sinatra did make one gesture of conciliation: he allowed one of the upcoming Sydney concerts to be televised so that fans who missed out on seeing him live in Melbourne could at least watch him on television.

After the agreement was finalized, Sinatra emerged from his hotel room to shake Hawke's hand; then *Hawke,* not Sinatra, went downstairs and read the statement to the assembled reporters. With that, the stalemate came to an end. Sinatra performed the remaining concerts without incident, then returned home to the United States. "A funny thing happened in Australia," he said later. "I made one mistake: I got off the plane."

DID YOU KNOW?

Sinatra's ill-fated Australian tour was the subject of the 2003 film *The Night We Called It a Day,* starring Dennis Hopper as Frank Sinatra, Melanie Griffith as his soon-to-be wife Barbara Marx, and Portia de Rossi as the female reporter he calls a hooker.

SIGNS AND WARNING LABELS

These are all real. We're doomed.

A WHITE TRAFFIC SIGN AT AN INTERSECTION:

**"RIGHT LANE
MUST
RIGHT LEFT"**

IN A RESTAURANT, ON A COFFEE CONDIMENT STAND:

**"Please Don't Touch Yourself
Ask Your Server For Help."**

A SIGN AT AN ATHLETIC FACILITY:

**"Notice: Exorcising of Dogs Not
Allowed on the Course Area"**

PAINTED WITH STENCILED LETTERING ON A ROADWAY:

"RIGHT TRUN ONLY"

OUTSIDE A FAST-FOOD RESTAURANT:

**"NOW HIRING
2 FISH SANDWICHES
FOR $3.29"**

OUTSIDE A FAST-FOOD RESTAURANT DRIVE-THROUGH:

"No Checks Excepted"

IN AN OFFICE BUILDING:

**"ELEVATOR Out of Service
Please Use Elevator"**

IN ANOTHER OFFICE BUILDING:

**"ATTENTION: Please Make Sure
Elevator Is There Before Stepping In"**

ON A SIDEWALK AT AN INTERSECTION:

"STOP HERE WHEN FLASHING"

ON THE PACKAGING OF AN ELECTRIC DRILL SOLD AT A HARDWARE STORE:

**"CAUTION: This Product Not
Intended For Use as a Dental Drill"**

OUTSIDE A GAS STATION CAR WASH:

**"WASH & VACUUM
SENIOR CITIZENS
$15.95"**

AT A LIBRARY:

**"The library will be closed
July 4th for the 4th of July."**

OUTSIDE A COMMUNITY CENTER:

**"SMOKING
BARE FEET PETS
PROHIBITED IN BUILDING"**

A WARNING LABEL ON A BOX OF RAT POISON:

**"Has been found to cause
cancer in laboratory mice."**

AT A GROCERY STORE DELI:

**"Steamed Broccoli
Ingredients: Broccoli, Salt, Pepper, Steam"**

OUTSIDE AN ELECTION POLLING PLACE:

**"No Campaign Materials or Clothing
Allowed Inside Polling Place"**

A LABEL ON A CHOPPING BOARD SOLD AT A DISCOUNT STORE:

**"WOOD CHOPPING BOARD
Wipe clean only, wipe up spills immediately
to avoid staining. Do not soak.
Do not use as a chopping board."**

Poll results: 11 percent of Americans think HTML is a venereal disease. (It's a computer language.)

THE MAN WHO DOVE OUT OF HIS WHEELCHAIR

Here's one of the more unusual medical tales we've come across recently.

NUMB

In 1996, an accountant named Mark Chenoweth, 34, of Stoke-on-Trent, England, was in a business meeting with one of his clients. The meeting itself was uneventful, but when Chenoweth got up to leave, he discovered that he could not feel his legs. He could still move them and was able to walk—barely—but he had no sensation below his waist. This was a moment that Chenoweth had been dreading for some time. He was born with spina bifida, a congenital defect of the spine in which one or more vertebrae fail to close properly, leaving the spinal cord exposed and often protruding in a small bulge or sac at the base of the spine.

The meeting itself was uneventful, but when Chenoweth got up to leave, he discovered that he could not feel his legs.

Because the spinal cord is not protected by the spine, it can be damaged over time. This had been happening to Chenoweth over much of his life. A surgical procedure performed shortly after birth had provided some protection to his spinal cord, and he walked normally until the age of 12. Then he began to lose mobility. The problem worsened in his 20s, and now at the age of 34 he'd hit a new low with the loss of all feeling in his legs. Some sensation returned over the next few weeks, but his physical condition continued to deteriorate until he was forced to use a wheelchair to get around.

STUCK

When Chenoweth went to a medical specialist to see if anything could be done, the physician explained that he had a "tethered" spinal cord, which means that instead of moving freely as a spinal cord should, his was tethered, or stuck, at one point, and the tension it created at that specific location was causing nerve damage and paralysis. In 1997, Chenoweth underwent surgery that doctors hoped would repair the problem and restore some leg function, but his condition did not improve. He was now a paraplegic, with very little hope that he would ever walk again.

Chenoweth and his wife, Denise, had been planning a vacation to the Greek island of Rhodes, hoping to celebrate Chenoweth regaining function in his legs after his surgery. Even though their hopes were now dashed—or perhaps because they were—they decided to take the vacation anyway, and in the summer of 1998 they packed up Chenoweth's wheelchair and went. One sunny afternoon they were sitting

Generalissimo Jimi: According to his sister, Jimi Hendrix never lost a game of Risk.

poolside at their hotel in Rhodes when some instructors from a local scuba diving company dropped by, hoping to drum up business. The idea was to give tourists a free introductory lesson in the hotel pool, and if they enjoyed the experience, they could pay for a dive in the sea. The diving instructors walked right past Chenoweth, assuming that a man in a wheelchair would either be uninterested or unable to go scuba diving. But he *was* interested, and after wheeling after the instructors to get their attention, he slid out of his wheelchair into the pool, where he received a full scuba diving demonstration using goggles, a respirator, and an oxygen tank.

FLOATING

After months of suffering one crushing disappointment after another, culminating with the realization that he was going to spend the rest of his life in a wheelchair, the sensation of floating freely in the pool and breathing underwater was wonderful. Chenoweth was hooked on scuba diving from the start. He tried to schedule diving lessons in the open sea, but that required clearance from a doctor...and none of the doctors he visited in Rhodes were willing to sign off on giving permission for a man in a wheelchair to swim in the ocean. Chenowith returned home, determined to find a doctor who would give him clearance so that he could take scuba diving lessons on his next vacation.

FIBBING

It took a little doing to find such a doctor, despite the fact that Chenoweth fudged some of the details of his medical history that had doctors concerned. But after several tries, he finally found a doctor who signed the forms. In October 1998, he and his wife traveled to Menorca, an island off the east coast of Spain. His first two dives were to a depth of 12 meters (about 40 feet), and then the third was to a depth of 17 meters (just shy of 56 feet).

As a paraplegic, Chenoweth had required quite a bit of help getting suited up before his dives, and when he returned to the boat after the third dive, he was doubtless expecting to need more assistance unsuiting once he was back on the boat. But after he was pulled aboard, he noticed something strange: his legs were no longer numb. He could feel them, and when he tried to lift them, they actually moved. Even better, when he tried to stand up, he was able to do so, for the first time in more than a year. When the boat returned to port and Chenoweth arrived back at the hotel, Denise was shocked to see him *walking* into the hotel—a bit wobbly to be sure—instead of using his wheelchair.

REPEATING

Chenoweth's improvement in leg function lasted for about four days; then his paralysis returned, and he went back to using the wheelchair. It was a disappointment,

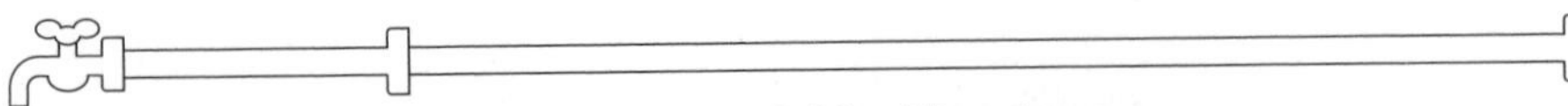

DNA testing has revealed that falcons are more closely related to parrots than they are to other birds of prey.

but he was certain that scuba diving had something to do with his improvement, and he hoped that when he went diving again, he would walk once again. Sure enough, when he and his wife traveled to South Africa five months later and he went scuba diving—again to a depth of 17 meters—he was able to walk again. But just as before, only for three or four days.

For the next several years, Chenoweth kept at it, scheduling scuba diving sessions each time he went on vacation, and each time he dove he was able to walk again. He noticed that he had to dive at least 17 meters to regain the use of his legs. If he dove 16 meters or less, there was no improvement at all. And as he became certified to dive to ever greater depths, he discovered that the deeper he went, the longer he retained the use of his legs. If he dove to 30 meters (about 100 feet), he regained the use of his legs for two to three months. When he dove to 40 meters (130 feet), he was able to walk for four months. If he dove to 50 meters (165 feet), he was able to walk for eight months. And since he scheduled his diving trips an average of once every six months, once he was able to dive to 50 meters, he was able to walk all of the time. He put his wheelchair away, and there it stayed.

WONDERING

By 2007, Chenoweth had completed 300 dives and was walking better than ever. And yet even after all that time, no one knew for certain what it was about scuba diving that restored his leg function, and whether other people paralyzed by spina bifida would have the same experience. One theory was that the compression that results from diving to great depths was somehow relieving the strain on his spinal cord; another theory was that because he breathed high concentrations of oxygen on his deep dives, the extra oxygen in his bloodstream was helping marginal cells in his spinal cord function better. No one knows for sure. What is certain is that somehow the nerve cells that were assumed to be damaged beyond repair were working again—that's all anyone knows. "It was lucky that I didn't just go down to 16 meters on my first dive or else I'd never have found out," he told a reporter in 2007. "I'm just so thankful I went that extra bit deeper, otherwise I'd still be in that wheelchair."

TOO SOON?

The first movie ever made about the sinking of the *Titanic* was *Saved from the Titanic.* It starred Dorothy Gibson, an actress who had survived the disaster by boarding the first lifeboat to flee the ocean liner. In the film, Gibson wore the same dress she'd had on the night of the sinking. The movie was released on May 14, 1912, just 29 days after the real *Titanic* sank.

MOUTHING OFF

ON BEING SHY

Are you shy? You're not alone: according to surveys, around half of all adults say they are too.

"A struggle with shyness is in every actor, more than anyone can imagine."

—Marilyn Monroe

"The way you overcome shyness is to become so wrapped up in something that you forget to be afraid."

—Lady Bird Johnson

"PEOPLE ASSUME YOU CAN'T BE SHY AND BE ON TELEVISION. THEY'RE WRONG."

—Diane Sawyer

"Shyness is when you turn your head away from something you want."

—Jonathan Safran Foer

"The very best way to overcome shyness is to get interested in other people. Do something for other people. Practice deeds of kindness, acts of friendliness, and, almost miraculously, your timidity will pass."

—Dale Carnegie

"The bashful are always aggressive at heart."

—Charles Horton Cooley

"A lot of vices that I've had over the years were always to make up for some sort of character deficiency, one of them being shyness."

—Slash

"Shyness has a strange element of narcissism, a belief that how we look, how we perform, is truly important to other people."

—Andre Dubus

"The shell must break before the bird can fly."

—Alfred Tennyson

"The flower that smells the sweetest is shy and lowly."

—William Wordsworth

MOUTHING OFF

"SO AM I"

If you yourself are shy and are worried that it will keep you from succeeding, take heart. Here are some successful folks who overcame it.

"I AM AN INTROVERT; PRIVATELY I AM VERY SHY, AND I DON'T SPEAK UNLESS I HAVE TO."

—Greta Thunberg

"My first language was shy. It's only by having been thrust into the limelight that I have learned to cope with my shyness."

—Al Pacino

"I WAS JUST GENUINELY SHY. I'D ALWAYS BEEN A SHY KID."

—Elton John

"I know this sounds strange, but as a kid, I was really shy. Painfully shy. The turning point was freshman year, when I was the biggest geek alive. No one, I mean no one, even talked to me."

—Jim Carrey

"I am quite shy and people think I'm aloof."

—Kristen Stewart

"Even though I was very shy, I found I could get onstage if I had a new identity."

—David Bowie

"I was just so blatantly shy throughout my life."

—Danny Aiello

"People are always saying that I must have been the class clown, with all these voices. No, I was way too shy to be the class clown; I was a class clown's writer."

—Tom Kenny, voice of *SpongeBob SquarePants*

"When I was young, all I wanted and expected from life was to sit quietly in some corner doing my work without the public paying attention to me. And now see what has become of me."

—Albert Einstein

COUNTRY? *WHAT* COUNTRY? I DON'T SEE ANY COUNTRY.

Just because a country appears on the map, that doesn't mean that other countries acknowledge that it exists. The phenomenon may be more common than you realize. Here are a few examples–some from the present, and some from the past.

ISRAEL

Not Recognized By: More than 30 countries around the world as of 2021

Details: One of the best-known examples of a country that is not recognized by other countries, the state of Israel was founded in 1949 in the face of vehement opposition from Arab and Islamic states that refused to acknowledge its right to exist. Most of those countries continue to do so today, as do Cuba, North Korea, Venezuela, and Bhutan. Thirteen refuse to admit travelers carrying Israeli passports into their country, and six will not even admit travelers whose non-Israeli passports show "evidence of travel" to Israel, i.e., passport stamps or visas issued by Israel. As of 2021, Israel has established diplomatic relations with four Arab states: Egypt (in 1979), Jordan (1994), Bahrain (2020), and the United Arab Emirates (2020).

CZECHOSLOVAKIA / THE CZECH REPUBLIC AND SLOVAKIA

Was Not Recognized By: Liechtenstein

Details: During World War II, Liechtenstein, the tiny European country named for the princely House of Liechtenstein that has ruled it since the early 1800s, remained neutral and stayed out of the war. Czechoslovakia was not so lucky: it was occupied by Nazi Germany from 1938 until the Germans surrendered in 1945. After the war, Czechoslovakia accused Liechtenstein of collaborating with the Germans. It retaliated by categorizing Liechtensteiners living in Czechoslovakia as Germans, then it confiscated their property and expelled them from the country as it did all ethnic Germans. The property seizures included the vast holdings of the House of Liechtenstein itself: 13 castles and palaces and more than 618 square miles of territory–an area *ten times* the size of Liechtenstein–that had been the property of the princely family since the 13th century.

In response, Liechtenstein refused to reestablish diplomatic relations with Czechoslovakia, which had lapsed during the German occupation. When Czechoslovakia split into the Czech Republic and Slovakia in 1992, Liechtenstein refused to recognize those two countries as well. The Czech Republic and Slovakia, in turn, did not recognize Liechtenstein. It wasn't until 2009 that the countries

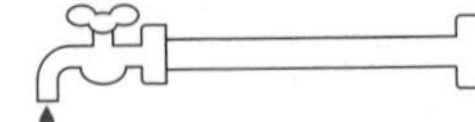

reestablished diplomatic relations, though the Liechtenstein family is still trying to get their castles, palaces, and land back. No luck so far, though. The Czech Republic did offer to return the castles and the palaces *without* the land, but Liechtenstein turned down the offer.

ITALY

Was Not Recognized By: The Vatican, from 1870 to 1929

Details: Today Italy is one country, but for most of the 1800s the Italian peninsula was a hodgepodge of several independent states, including one halfway down the peninsula called the Papal States that was ruled by the pope. Between 1859 and 1870, these independent states were joined together, some voluntarily, and others by force, to create the Kingdom of Italy.

The Papal States, with Rome as its capital, was one of the countries that had to be taken by force. After a series of military defeats, by 1870 the reigning pope, Pius IX, had lost all of his territory except for the Vatican quarter of Rome; the rest of the city was captured by the Italians.

The first pope without a country in more than 1,000 years, Pius refused to acknowledge the new Italian state.

The first pope without a country in more than 1,000 years, Pius refused to acknowledge the new Italian state or even step foot outside the Vatican onto the streets of Rome, lest that be interpreted as an endorsement of the new status quo. Instead, he remained a self-proclaimed "prisoner in the Vatican" for the rest of his papacy. So did his four successors, Popes Leo XIII, Pius X, Benedict XV, and Pius XI. The crisis wasn't resolved until 1929, when Pope Pius XI signed a treaty with the Kingdom of Italy, led by the fascist dictator Benito Mussolini, that established Vatican City as an independent state. Only then did the popes venture out of the Vatican into the rest of Rome and beyond.

BELIZE

Was Not Recognized By: Guatemala

Details: Guatemala's dispute with Belize, its neighbor to the east, dates back centuries before either country *was* a country. The first permanent English settlement in what is now Belize was founded in 1717, but Spain claimed sovereignty over that part of the Yucatán Peninsula as early as 1494...even though it had no settlements there. In the early 1800s, Spain's territories in Central America proclaimed their independence. The new nation of Guatemala saw itself as the inheritor of all Spanish possessions in the area and thus claimed Belize as part of its own territory. But in 1859, Guatemala renounced its claim after the British agreed to build a road through Belize connecting Guatemala to the coast. Three years later,

Only person to ever play himself on Star Trek:
Stephen Hawking, on *Star Trek: The Next Generation* (1993).

Belize was formally incorporated into the British Empire as the colony of British Honduras. Only problem: the road was never built, so Guatemala reasserted its claim over the territory, and when British Honduras became the independent nation of Belize in 1981, Guatemala refused to recognize it. It finally did so in 1991, but without renouncing its territorial claims; then in 1999 it revised its claim to include only the southern half of Belize. Twenty years later, the citizens of both countries voted to refer the issue to the UN's International Court of Justice, and that's where the issue stands as of 2021. Because Guatemala has never actually controlled the disputed territory, the court is expected to decide in favor of Belize.

ARMENIA

Not Recognized By: Pakistan

Details: Armenia was part of the Soviet Union until it gained independence when the Soviet Union broke apart in 1991. Its neighbor, Azerbaijan, is another former Soviet republic. The Armenians who live in Azerbaijan—in the ethnic Armenian enclave called Nagorno-Karabakh—have been struggling to break away and join Armenia since the late 1980s. At times, the conflict has exploded into open warfare between Armenia and Azerbaijan. As of 2020, Nagorno-Karabakh is still a part of Azerbaijan, and because Pakistan strongly supports Azerbaijan in the conflict, it does not recognize Armenia as an independent state; it is the only country in the world that refuses to do so.

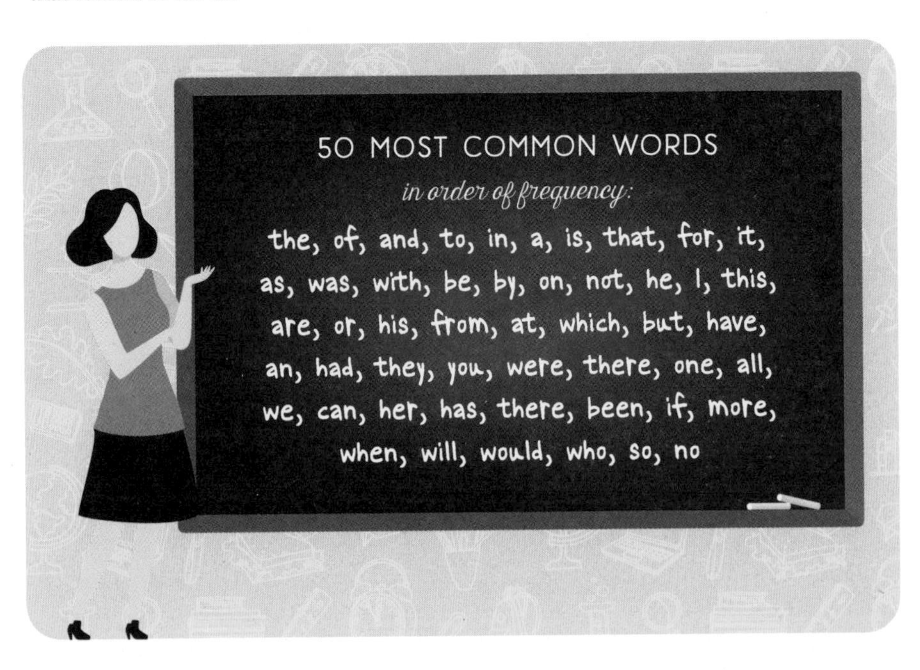

50 MOST COMMON WORDS
in order of frequency:
the, of, and, to, in, a, is, that, for, it,
as, was, with, be, by, on, not, he, I, this,
are, or, his, from, at, which, but, have,
an, had, they, you, were, there, one, all,
we, can, her, has, there, been, if, more,
when, will, would, who, so, no

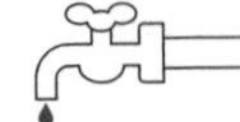

More people speak English as a second language (1.1 billion) than speak it as their native language (360 million).

BATHROOM HUMOR

Roll on up and grab a stool! The potty jokes are about to commence.

"Thank you for calling the Incontinence Hotline. Can you hold, please?"

I've run out of toilet paper and have started to use old newspapers instead. The *Times* are rough.

Customer: Do you have any talcum powder?
Pharmacist: Yes we do. Walk this way.
Customer: If I could walk that way, I wouldn't need talcum powder.

Q: What do you get when you drop a laxative into holy water?
A: A religious movement.

Did you hear about the truck full of toilet paper that lost control and crashed in the forest? Investigators found it by following the skid marks.

Q: What does an Australian do when he runs out of TP?
A: Bidet, mate!

What's the difference between a shower curtain and toilet paper? If you don't know, stay out of my bathroom.

Q: What should you do if you find a grizzly bear using your toilet?
A: Let him finish.

A boy asks his mom where poo comes from. "Uhh," she says, "the digestive system breaks food down, and the part that comes out of your butt is poo." Perplexed and disgusted, the boy slowly asks, "And Tigger?"

Pharmacist: Why is that customer leaning against the wall with a panicked look on his face?
Clerk: He has a bad cough, but we're out of cough syrup, so I gave him a laxative.
Pharmacist: A laxative? To treat a cough? What were you thinking?
Clerk: Well, just look at him. He's afraid to cough.

The other day I was on the toilet when I ran out of TP. I had to shimmy with my pants down to get another roll. Luckily, I didn't have to go that far. The grocery store is just around the corner.

An elderly couple is sitting in church when the husband leans over to the wife and whispers, "Oh no. I just had a very long, silent fart. What should I do?" "Replace the battery in your hearing aid, dear."

Q: Why did the toilet paper roll down the hill?
A: To get to the bottom.

I got in touch with my inner self today. That's the last time I use 1-ply.

Did you hear about the constipated accountant? He wasn't able to budget. It really added up. He was able to work it out with a pencil in the end.

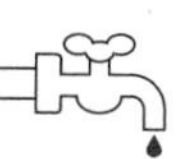

Most orbiting space junk travels at 18,000 mph...about seven times faster than a rifle bullet.

ODD BOOKS

Every well-stocked library or bookstore has its share of unusual books. Here are some of the stranger ones we wish we had on our shelf.

BOOK: A Christian prayer book from the 1600s
DETAILS: This "book," made for Francesco Morosini, the guy who blew up the Parthenon (page 157), was hollowed out to house a concealed pistol mechanism. To fire it, all Morosini had to do was point the top of the closed book in the direction he wanted to shoot, then pull the silk bookmark that poked out of the bottom of the book. It was never fired. Today it's on display in the Museo Correr in Venice.

BOOK: *The Complete Works of Sebastião Barradas, Volume III*
DETAILS: This 17th-century book has a secret compartment containing four small glass bottles and ten drawers labeled with the German names for poisons such as hemlock and belladonna—suggesting that it was used to kill people. There's no evidence that it was actually used for this purpose; the bookseller who offered it for sale in 2019 suspects the book was made as a novelty item. If you want to buy it, the asking price alone might kill you: $11,000.

BOOK: *Shadows from the Walls of Death* (1874)
DETAILS: In the late 19th century, wallpaper was made using arsenic. Breathing the air inside a room decorated with the wallpaper could be hazardous to a person's health, and small children had died from licking wallpaper containing the toxic substance. To warn of the danger, in 1874 a Michigan physician and chemistry professor named Dr. Robert Kedzie published this book, with 86 sheets of arsenic-laden wallpaper bound into it. Kedzie distributed the book free to public libraries across Michigan...but the books themselves were so dangerous that most libraries threw them out. Only four copies survive. The pages of Michigan State University's copy have been sealed in plastic to prevent the arsenic from poisoning readers.

BOOK: *Narrative of the Life of James Allen* (1837)
DETAILS: In the 1830s, Allen was a "highwayman"—a thief on horseback who robbed travelers. In 1834, he tried to rob a man named John A. Fenno, who fought back. This must have made quite an impression on Allen, because three years later when he was incarcerated in the Massachusetts State Prison and near death, he dictated his life story to the warden and asked that it be made into a book bound in his own skin and presented to Fenno as an apology. The warden complied; the book, bound in skin taken from Allen's back, was donated to the Boston Athenaeum library in 1905. Scientific tests have confirmed that the "leather" is indeed of human origin.

The Apollo astronauts planted more than just flags on the Moon: they also left behind 96 bags of human waste.

THE TREES OF HIROSHIMA

The hibakujumoku *trees of Hiroshima brought hope to a community at its darkest hour, and they continue to spread hope today.*

DOWNFALL

Shortly after 8:15 a.m. on August 6, 1945, the United States dropped an atomic bomb on Hiroshima, Japan. The blast laid waste to the city in seconds, obliterating everything within a one-mile radius of the hypocenter and igniting fires all across the city. Those fires quickly combined into a single massive firestorm that, over the next several hours, reduced the ruined city to ash. A second atomic bomb was dropped on the city of Nagasaki on August 9, and six days later, on August 15, the Japanese government surrendered unconditionally. World War II was over.

The sudden end of the war likely spared the lives of hundreds of thousands of Allied servicemen—not to mention a million or more Japanese soldiers and civilians—because now, the long-anticipated Allied invasion of the Japanese mainland would not take place. But the price paid by people living in Hiroshima and Nagasaki was horrific: As many as 225,000 people died in the bombings, and hundreds of thousands more were severely injured. In the years to come, additional thousands would die from these injuries or from illnesses caused by exposure to radiation.

SCORCHED EARTH

The world that the Hiroshima survivors found themselves living in after the bomb was dropped was remarkably colorless. The cityscape was a palette of blacks, whites, and grays, as if the survivors were living inside a fireplace, or in a black-and-white photograph. Very little vegetation within a few miles of the hypocenter survived. Some of the sturdiest tree trunks were still standing, but they were charred black and had lost most of their limbs. Many were little more than sticks or stumps poking up from the ground. Farther out from the hypocenter, trees were scorched on the side that had faced the atomic blast but showed little or no damage on the side facing away.

The devastation was so complete that it seemed like decades might pass before anything grew in Hiroshima again. How *could* anything grow there? That's why it came as a shock when, just two months after the bombing, some of the charred, limbless trunks within about a mile of the hypocenter began sprouting new buds.

More plants—many more—sprouted the following spring. Even in places where there seemed to be no vegetation left at all, new growth appeared where plants destroyed in the blast once stood—on root systems that had survived belowground.

RENEWAL

These first bits of color in the blackened city, and the hardy plants that

In 1979, U.S. president Jimmy Carter was fishing near his hometown of Plains, Georgia, when his boat was attacked by a swimming rabbit.

produced them, provided inspiration to the survivors as they set about what must have seemed like the impossible task of rebuilding their shattered lives. "We were told nothing would grow for 75 years," says Akio Nishikiori, an architect and Hiroshima survivor who was in the second grade when the bomb was dropped. "However, the trees put out new shoots! Everyone was really moved to see the green leaves."

The leaves grew in size and number, adding more color to the city from one day to the next. Soon flowers began to bloom. The new growth was a welcome diversion and a symbol of hope: a reminder that survival against all odds was possible, and that life would eventually get better.

As the years passed and a new Hiroshima slowly rose from the old city's ashes, the more than 170 surviving trees closest to the epicenter of the blast—weeping willows, fig and cherry trees, ginkgo biloba, as well as eucalyptus, bamboo, and more than 30 other species of plants—came to be revered by the survivors, who named them *hibakujumoku,* or "A-bombed trees." Great care was taken to make sure the *hibakujumoku* were not harmed as the city rebuilt. Most trees were left where they stood, but some were carefully moved to new locations when there was no alternative. In a few places, buildings were built *around* the trees rather than risk moving them. Cutting them down or harming them in any way was out of the question.

The *hibakujumoku* were lovingly tended to. Each one was entered into an official city registry and given its own plaque to call attention to the fact that it had survived the atom bomb. Dozens of similar trees in Nagasaki are similarly cared for.

MESSENGERS

The *hibakujumoku* are beloved in Hiroshima, but they are also a part of the fabric of everyday life, something the next generation of locals didn't see as all that remarkable. That began to change in 2011, when Tomoko Watanabe, the daughter of a nurse who had survived the bombing of Hiroshima, pointed out some of the trees to a friend, Nassrine Azimi, who worked for the United Nations. Azimi believed that the trees might have a new purpose—to serve as messengers of peace and resilience while also warning of the dangers of nuclear proliferation.

RETURN TO SENDER

As far back as the 1950s, when Hiroshima was rebuilding and remaking itself into an international "city of peace" similar to Geneva, Switzerland, the city had solicited donations of plants and trees to plant in its Peace Memorial Park and other places around the city. Donors from all over the world contributed seedlings to plant in Hiroshima. Now, Azimi thought, it would be possible to do the reverse: take seeds from the *hibakujumoku* and send them all over the world. Just as the parent plants had provided hope to the survivors after the war, now offspring grown from their seeds could spread the message of Hiroshima and Nagasaki to other parts of the world.

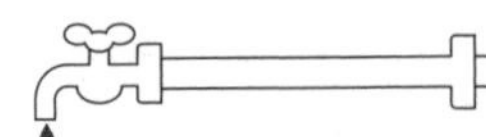

Only country that protested Hitler's takeover of Austria in 1938: Mexico.

In 2011, Azimi and Watanabe, with support from the United Nations, formed a nonprofit group called Green Legacy Hiroshima to do just that.

HARVEST

Green Legacy Hiroshima works with an arborist named Chikara Horiguchi, who has looked after the *hibakujumoku* for more than 30 years. Horiguchi keeps careful track of when each of the more than 160 trees are producing seeds. When the time is ripe—so to speak—for a particular tree, Green Legacy Hiroshima organizes teams of volunteers to collect its seeds. Once they have been collected, Horiguchi cleans the seeds and stores them away.

When Green Legacy Hiroshima receives a request from one of its international partners for some of the seeds, the organization researches the climate of the partner's country to determine which of the more than 30 species of *hibakujumoku* are most suitable for that climate. Then it researches the plant quarantine laws for that country to ensure that the proper procedures are followed when packing and shipping the seeds abroad. Green Legacy Hiroshima doesn't, as a rule, send the seeds to individuals. Instead, it prefers to send them to universities, botanical gardens, schools, urban parks, and other such groups that have the ability to care for the trees for many years to come. To date, the organization has sent seeds to more than 100 partner organizations in 36 countries around the world.

PASS IT ON

Once the partner organization receives its seeds and plants them, it can distribute the seedlings as it sees fit. In 2017, for example, Green Legacy Hiroshima sent ginkgo, persimmon, and camphor seeds to the Oregon Department of Forestry and Southern Oregon University in the town of Ashland at the behest of 85-year-old Hideko Tamura Snider, a Hiroshima survivor who was now living in southern Oregon. Snider was ten years old when the bomb was dropped. Her mother, other family members, neighbors, and friends all died in the bombing, and she witnessed horrific scenes that remained with her for the rest of her life. After moving to Oregon in 2003, Snider founded a nonprofit organization called the One Sunny Day Initiative to promote nuclear nonproliferation, peace, and reconciliation. In 2017, she helped arrange for the *hibakujumoku* seeds to be sent to Oregon. "I cannot grow my mother. But the tree, I can grow," she told NBC News in 2019.

The seeds were germinated by the Oregon Department of Forestry, and in the spring of 2020, more than two dozen saplings grown from the seeds were distributed to schools and towns all over Oregon and northern California for planting. Snider hopes the trees will serve as a warning of the horrors of war, she says, as well as a reminder that there is life and hope after a disaster in which everything seems lost: "The trees are saying, 'Look, look, life is wonderful.' "

If all the blood vessels in the human body were stretched into a line, it would be nearly 100,000 miles long, enough to circle the equator four times.

NCIS, STARRING HARRISON FORD

Some actors are so closely associated with a specific role or TV series that it's hard to imagine he or she wasn't the first choice. But it happens all the time.

***Baywatch*, starring Tom Selleck**

Fresh off an eight-year run as the frequently shirtless Hawaii-based detective Thomas Magnum on *Magnum, P.I.*, Tom Selleck was offered the lead role of Mitch Buchannon on a show about Southern California lifeguards. Selleck turned it down, not wanting to get typecast and viewed as capable of only playing shirtless hunks. Several other 1980s TV notables failed *Baywatch* auditions, including Lorenzo Lamas of *Falcon Crest*, Tom Wopat of *The Dukes of Hazzard*, and William Katt of *The Greatest American Hero*. After reading the script, David Hasselhoff of *Knight Rider* initially passed on the role...and then accepted it. Good move: *Baywatch* became the most popular show in the world.

***The Dukes of Hazzard*, starring Dennis Quaid**

Tom Wopat portrayed Luke Duke, a reformed bootlegger and backcountry good old boy, for seven seasons, from 1979 to 1985. Wopat had never landed a main role in anything prior to *Dukes*, and he beat out some slightly more experienced actors to get the role, including Gerald McRaney (who would go on to star on CBS's *Simon & Simon* a year later), and future movie star Dennis Quaid. Producers actually did offer the part to Quaid, who said he'd accept on one condition: that his wife at the time, *Halloween* actress P. J. Soles, was cast as Daisy Duke. She bombed her audition and didn't get the part, so Quaid backed out.

***NCIS*, starring Harrison Ford**

Mark Harmon has played the stern, man-of-few-words naval investigator Leroy Jethro Gibbs for nearly two decades, and is a producer on multiple *NCIS* shows—but he wasn't the first choice for the role. When the show was in development in the early 2000s, the show's creators pursued legendary film star Harrison Ford, who was experiencing a downturn in his career at the time. There was still something of a stigma attached when a movie star deigned to do television, however, so Ford passed.

***The West Wing*, starring Sidney Poitier**

Casting someone to play the president of the United States in *The West Wing* proved difficult—the actor had to command respect and carry an inspirational air, all the while adhering to the show's politically neutral (sort of) tone. Creator Aaron Sorkin's

U.S. Senate sessions used the same gavel from 1789 to 1954, when Richard Nixon broke it during a debate on nuclear power.

first choice for the president: Sidney Poitier. But the Oscar winner wanted too much money, so producers walked away from Poitier and over to another Academy Award winner: Jason Robards. At the time, Robards was nearly 80 and in poor health (he died in 2000, about a year after the show premiered), so Sorkin went after Martin Sheen, who he'd worked with on the film *The American President* and figured would be too busy to accept the role. He wasn't, and he accepted the offer.

The Big Bang Theory, starring Macaulay Culkin

When TV producer Chuck Lorre (*Two and a Half Men, Dharma and Greg*) was putting together a show in the mid-2000s about nerdy, sci-fi loving roommates who were also genius researchers at Caltech, one of the actors he pursued was former child star Macaulay Culkin. He'd just appeared in two well-received indie movies, *Saved!* and *Party Monster*, ending a decade-long hiatus since his successes in *Home Alone* and *Richie Rich*. Culkin turned down what would become a TV mega-hit. The reason: He thought the show's premise was awful. On *The Joe Rogan Experience* podcast, he described the pitch he was given as "these two astrophysicist nerds, and a pretty girl lives with them. Yoinks!" Culkin didn't say whether producers wanted him to play Sheldon (ultimately portrayed by Jim Parsons) or Leonard (Johnny Galecki), but did mention that he had to turn down the offer two more times.

The King of Queens, starring Megan Mullally

Mullally had bounced around Hollywood since the early 1980s, landing mostly guest-star roles on TV shows and a few lead roles in little-seen series that were quickly canceled. In 1998—and about to turn 40—she auditioned for two roles: as Carrie Heffernan, exhausted wife of a buffoonish delivery driver played by Kevin James on CBS's *The King of Queens*, and Karen Walker, a blousy, kooky, perpetually drunk wealthy lady on NBC's *Will and Grace*. Mullally won both parts, and had to choose. She went with the latter, but she probably would have succeeded in either role. *The King of Queens* (starring Leah Remini as Carrie) ran for nine years; *Will and Grace* ran for 11, and it won Mullally two Emmy Awards.

The Golden Girls, starring Elaine Stritch

Stritch was primarily known for her work on the stage—she's a Broadway legend and four-time Tony Award nominee closely associated with the works of Stephen Sondheim. She dabbled in TV, including a recurring role on *30 Rock* as the bitter mother of Jack Donaghy (Alec Baldwin) toward the end of her life. In her 2002 one-woman show filmed for HBO, *Elaine Stritch at Liberty*, she discussed how she botched her big chance to break into television when she "blew" her audition to play Dorothy Zbornak on *The Golden Girls* in 1984. She asked the casting director if she could improvise, and did so, changing the line, "Don't forget the hors d'oeuvres" into "Don't forget the f***ing hors d'oeuvres." *Maude* star Bea Arthur got the role instead.

New theory: The Milky Way is warped,
giving it a shape like a Pringles potato chip or a "flattened letter S."

STRANGE TWISTS OF FATE

There's really no way to explain luck—some people just get lucky. And fortunately for the folks below, they got lucky when it truly counted.

MESSAGE IN A BOTTLE

On Father's Day weekend in 2019, Curtis Whitson took his girlfriend and 13-year-old daughter on a hiking trip to the scenic Pfeiffer Big Sur State Park in California. Seven years earlier, he'd hoofed it up to the top of a 40-foot waterfall overlooking Arroyo Seco Canyon and got back by rappelling down the falls with a rope system someone had installed, and he wanted to repeat the experience with his family. Only problem: When he got to the top of the waterfall, the rope was gone, and the conditions on the hiking trail were too unsteady to go back the way they came in. Miles away from the park's campground and way out of cell phone service range, Whitson used the only option available to him. He took a piece of paper from a notepad his girlfriend had in her bag (which she used for keeping score in card games), and wrote, "We are stuck here @ the waterfall. Get help please." Then he put the distress note in a green water bottle—a Father's Day gift he'd received that day—carved "HELP" onto the side, and tossed it into the waterfall, where it was carried downstream. A few hours later, some other hikers found the message and called authorities. The California Highway Patrol located Whitson and his party around midnight, and airlifted them safely out the next morning.

"We are stuck here @ the waterfall. Get help please."

IN OTHER NEWS

Victoria Price is an investigative reporter for WFLA-TV in Tampa, Florida. Following an on-air appearance relaying news about the COVID-19 pandemic in June 2020, she received an email from a viewer. The person had suffered from a form of throat cancer after a malignant tumor was discovered on her neck, and she noticed something similar on Price. "She saw a lump on my neck," Price later tweeted. "Said it reminded her of her own. Hers was cancer. Turns out, mine is too." Price visited a doctor, and tests confirmed that she had cancer. In July 2020, she underwent surgery to remove the tumor, along with her affected thyroid and some lymph nodes. "I will be forever thankful for the woman who went out of her way to email me, a total stranger," Price said. "She had zero obligation to, but she did anyway."

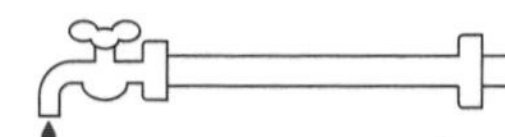

The state of Tennessee allows miniature horses to be used as service animals.

LUCKY TICKET

In August 2020, a man from Alpena County, Michigan (he wished to stay anonymous in media reports), went to the Corner Depot, a local convenience store, as he'd done many times before, to buy a scratch-and-win lottery ticket. The one he usually played was out of stock, so, on a whim, he decided to try a different one. "I saw the Emerald 10's ticket and decided to give it a try," the man told reporters. He scratched some numbers off the Emerald 10's game and thought he'd won $1,000. Pleased, he started working on another ticket he'd bought, but something on the Emerald 10's drew his attention. "All the zeroes caught my eye. When I focused in on the prize amount, I couldn't believe it." He hadn't won $1,000 from a lottery ticket he'd bought only because the one he'd wanted was unavailable—he'd won $1,000,000.

OH, WELL

A couple in Fuliudian, a village in the Henan province of China, had an abandoned—and dangerous—well in their yard, and they planned to have it filled in with concrete. Until they could get around to doing that, though, they just boarded up the opening with wooden planks. That apparently wasn't enough of a safety measure, because in August 2020, their 28-year-old son (named in news reports as Liu) stepped on the wooden well cover...and broke right through it. Most people would have plunged down the well and been injured, or possibly killed. That's not what happened to Liu. The heavyset man, who various news agencies reported weighed between 300 and 500 pounds, found himself wedged in the opening of the well—his large belly prevented him from falling any further. He patiently waited in the well as five firefighters got him unstuck by putting a rope around him and pulling. Liu was unharmed.

BAD NEWS, GOOD NEWS

In the fall of 2005, after passing a basic training course, 21-year-old Shayna Richardson was ready for her first solo skydive. Richardson lived in Joplin, Missouri, but couldn't make her jump there—she was banned from her home facility because she'd started a relationship with her instructor, Rick West. So Richardson and West went to nearby Siloam Springs, Arkansas, where they would both skydive solo jumps. But Richardson's jump didn't go according to plan. Due to what was later judged an equipment failure, her parachute didn't open. Richardson's hair-raising 3,000-foot plummet ended when she landed in a parking lot...face first. Astonishingly, she survived the impact, but not without injury—she lost six teeth, broke a leg, and shattered her pelvis; she immediately underwent surgery, and doctors installed 15 steel plates. That's not the end of Richardson's amazing luck: While treating her, doctors discovered something about her that even she didn't know—she was pregnant. In 2006, Richardson gave birth to a healthy baby boy.

Flower power: Impressionist Claude Monet painted more than 300 pictures of the same lilies that grew in a pond behind his house.

LADIES AND GENTLEMEN... SNOT!

What's the hardest part about forming a heavy metal band? Learning how to play the guitar fast and loud? Developing a good menacing guttural scream? Nah. It's picking a cool, dangerous, and appropriately metal name. Here are a few real examples.

Iron Reagan
Suffocation
Night Demon
Brutal Sphincter
Thrown Into Exile
Municipal Waste
Kataklysm
Lake of Blood
Knock out Monkey
DevilDriver
Killdozer
Lacerated Entrails
Kingdom of Sorrow
Skeletonwitch
Black Spiders
Apocalyptica
Rigor Mortis
Joyless
A World of Illness
Within Chaos
iwrestledabearonce
3 Inches of Blood
1,000 Funerals
Black Tide

DragonForce
Hades
Bleeding Through
Full Blown Chaos
Killswitch Engage
Bury Your Dead
Lady Beast
Every Time I Die
No One
Kill Everything
I Am Destruction
Slaves on Dope
Pushmonkey
Coal Chamber
Snot
Iberian Wolves
Hammer of the Witches
Life of Agony
Yoda's Eye
Monster Voodoo Machine
Anal Vomit
Landfill
Yawning Void
A Waste of Talent

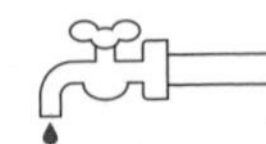

Bats have nothing to do with it: *Batology* is the study of berry plants.

EDIFICE WRECKED: THE PARTHENON

The Parthenon in Athens is nearly 2,500 years old and in ruins, so it's easy to assume that the structure crumbled slowly over the centuries due to exposure to the elements, earthquakes, etc. Think again...

TOP OF THE HILL

If you've ever been to Athens, the capital of Greece, you could hardly have missed the Parthenon: it's the classical Greek temple that towers above the Acropolis, the walled hilltop fortress that overlooks the rest of the city. Constructed between 450 BC and 437 BC, the Parthenon was built to honor Athena, the goddess of wisdom and warfare, for whom the city of Athens was named. The Greek word *parthenos* means "maiden" or "virgin," and was often used to describe Athena, who, according to legend, remained perpetually a virgin.

The Parthenon is considered by many to be the high point of classical Greek architecture. Nothing built before or after was as beautiful or as skillfully made. It occupies a plot of land just over 23,000 square feet in area, about half the size of a football field. Today it's in ruins, but when it was intact, 46 columns, each standing 34 feet tall, surrounded the exterior of the temple: 17 along each side and six more at either end. Atop the exterior columns sat long, horizontal stones (called *lintels*), topped at either end of the temple by triangular *pediments*, which provided support for a sloped roof made of marble tiles. The lintels and pediments were decorated with some of the finest statuary and stone carvings ever produced in ancient Greece.

Within the space surrounded by the exterior columns, masonry walls enclosed an area called a *cella*. The cella was divided into two chambers, the larger of which contained a gold and ivory statue of Athena that stood nearly 40 feet tall and was the focal point of the temple.

THE GREAT TURKISH WAR

The Parthenon served as a temple to Athena for nearly a thousand years. Then in the late sixth century AD, it was converted into a Christian church. (What happened to the statue of Athena is a mystery. It may have been destroyed in a fire in the cella sometime around 165 BC, or it may have been taken to Constantinople—modern-day Istanbul—where it was later destroyed. No one knows for sure.) The Parthenon remained a church for nearly another thousand years until Athens fell to the Ottoman Turks in 1458. They converted the Parthenon into a mosque.

Two hundred and twenty years later, Athens, like much of the rest of Greece, was still a territory of the Ottoman Empire. But the Republic of Venice was determined to recapture the city for Christendom. By September 1687, the Venetians had already clawed back some territory in the south and west of Greece, and Athens was next on the list. On September 21, the Venetian fleet arrived in the port of Piraeus, southwest of Athens. There, a military force of nearly 10,000 soldiers led by Francesco Morosini disembarked and marched into Athens, where they took up positions all around the Acropolis, into which the Ottoman Turks had retreated. Over the next few days, the Venetians shot cannons at the walls of the Acropolis in an attempt to blast an opening into the fortress. They also fired an estimated 2,000 mortar shells into the Acropolis itself, doing untold damage to the temples and other classical Greek buildings inside the fort.

For decades, the Turks had stored gunpowder inside the Parthenon and at least one other temple inside the Acropolis, apparently in the belief that the Christians would never risk damaging these sacred buildings by firing on them. So...were the Turks correct? According to a German mercenary soldier named Sobievolski, who fought on the Venetian side, "After receiving the information [that the gunpowder was in the Parthenon], most of the mortars directed their fire *at* the temple."

BOOM AND BUST

On the night of September 26, the Venetians struck the fatal blow—what Morosini called a "fortunate shot"—when a mortar shell crashed through the roof of the Parthenon and landed on the gunpowder, igniting it. The resulting explosion—greeted by triumphant cheers from the Venetian soldiers who witnessed it—tore through the center of the temple, blasting out the walls of the cella, knocking down 14 columns and causing the marble roof to collapse. Some 300 Turks were killed in the explosion, and the fire it started spread through the Acropolis, destroying many wooden buildings before it finally burned itself out. The temple that had stood for more than two thousand years was all but destroyed.

THE LONG AND SHORT OF IT

The Ottoman Turks surrendered two days later. Athens was now in the hands of the Venetians, but they didn't hold it for long: A few months later, they beat a strategic retreat southward and Athens again fell to the Ottomans, who held on to it until the early 19th century, finally losing it for good (so far) in 1833. After that, the city became part of an independent Kingdom of Greece, which became the Republic of Greece in 1974.

The Venetians' occupation of Athens may have been temporary, but the damage they did to the Parthenon was permanent...and ongoing. As soon as the temple was

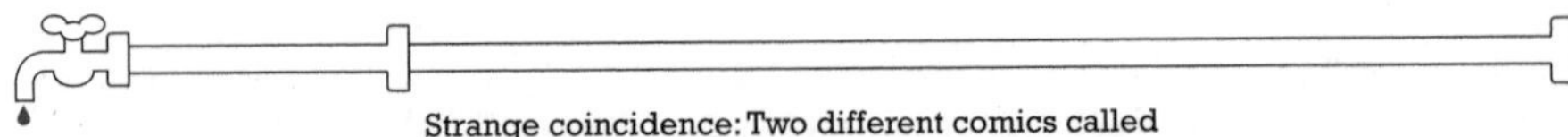

Strange coincidence: Two different comics called *Dennis the Menace* debuted in the U.S. and UK on the same day in 1951.

blown up, it lost the aura of being a sacred site, a holy place—something that had protected it from vandalism and pilfering for centuries. Now it was just a plain ruin, and people felt free to haul away stones for use as building materials, and to loot any statues, carvings, or other valuable objects they found. Morosini himself was the first looter. He had his eye on a statue of the sea god Poseidon and a horse from Athena's chariot, both of which decorated one of the pediments which still rested high atop some columns that had not been knocked over. But when Morosini tried to lower the statues to the ground, the rope snapped, and they crashed to earth and were smashed to pieces. The Ottomans weren't much better: for years afterward, they sold interesting bits pulled from the rubble of the Parthenon as souvenirs to Western tourists.

In the early 19th century, the British ambassador to the Ottoman Empire, Thomas Bruce, 7th Earl of Elgin, removed about half of the remaining marble statues and sculptures that had decorated the pediments, lintels, and other parts of the Parthenon. Elgin claimed to have obtained permission from the Ottoman government to remove the sculptures, but no proof exists that he did. He sent the pieces back to Britain, where he planned to use them as decorations inside his home. But when his marriage failed and an expensive divorce nixed those plans, he sold them to the British Museum to raise some quick cash, albeit less money than he'd spent procuring them and getting them back to Britain. The "Elgin marbles," as they are known, remain in the British Museum to this day; the British government has repeatedly refused Greek requests to return them to Greece.

PUTTING IT BACK TOGETHER

The first serious attempt to stabilize and repair the Parthenon came in 1898. Fortunately for the restorers, in 1674, just 13 years before the temple was destroyed, a French draftsman named Jacques Carrey visited Athens and over a two-week period made detailed drawings of the statues and other carvings that decorated the Parthenon. More than 50 of his drawings have survived, and they provide the only accurate, though incomplete, record of the sculptures and other carvings that were either destroyed by the Venetians in 1687 or stolen afterward.

The restorers of 1898 may have *attempted* to stabilize the Parthenon, but when another major restoration effort began in 1975, civil engineers discovered that much of the original repair work did more harm than good and had dangerously destabilized parts of the temple that were still standing. The work would have to be undone and then carefully rebuilt, this time correctly. This and other problems caused the work to drag on well past the original completion date of 1985. How far past? Nearly half a century after the work began, it still continues, and the end is nowhere in sight.

BUILDING BLOCKS

One of the factors that has slowed down the work is the restorers' determination to reuse as many of the original materials as possible. Centuries of scavenging and looting aside, more than 300 years after the Parthenon was destroyed, hundreds of giant marble blocks still lay scattered around the site, many of them right where they landed when the temple blew up. More than 700 blocks have been identified as belonging to the temple walls, and computer modeling that began in the late 1990s and other techniques have made it possible to determine the precise location of where 500 of the blocks were placed when the walls were constructed. The restorers are returning these blocks to their original places as the walls are repaired. Work to determine the position of each of the remaining 200 blocks—and other pieces as well—will likely continue for decades.

THE NEXT BEST THING

Dying to see an intact Parthenon but don't want to wait that long? Don't worry: There's a full-scale replica of the Parthenon in Nashville, Tennessee, a city known as the "Athens of the South." Built in 1897 as part of the Tennessee Centennial Exhibition, this Parthenon was originally made of plaster, wood, and brick, and was supposed to be torn down after the exhibition. But people really liked the building, and tearing it down would have cost a lot of money...so it was left standing. By 1920, the original materials were so damaged by weather that the building was redone in concrete. More than a century later, the concrete version endures, and is used as an art museum. Keep your fingers crossed! As of this writing, neither the Venetians nor anyone else has tried to blow it up.

* * *

NO FOOLING

The mineral pyrite is known as "fool's gold" because it looks like gold, but it's worthless, right? Not so, say researchers at the University of Minnesota, who have been testing pyrite for use in solar cells. Those experiments haven't yielded much success, but as a side experiment, they subjected pyrite to a process called *electrolyte gating*—which in simple terms means they added an electric charge. Result: For the first time ever, an entirely nonmagnetic material became magnetic. More testing is required, but if all goes well, pyrite could one day become quite valuable as a material for magnetic data storage devices. "Frankly," said lead researcher Chris Leighton, "we're pretty surprised it worked."

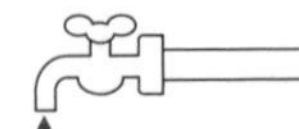

If you're a girl, there's a good chance you spent a lot of time with Barbara Millicent Roberts as a kid. (That's the Barbie doll's full name.)

THE BIRDS

We share the planet with our feathered friends...and mostly stay out of each other's way. But as these stories illustrate, when territorial borders become blurred, birds rule.

MINE!

The headline from *HuffPost UK* tells the story: "Seagull Steals Pensioner's Dentures After She Took Them Out to Have a Biscuit." The *pensioner* ("senior citizen" in the UK) was Renee A'Bear, 92. She was eating her *biscuit* ("cookie" in the UK) outside of a Sussex, England, nursing home in 2013 when the gull swooped in, grabbed the dentures from the bench, and flew away. "Poor Renee came in crying her eyes out and absolutely distraught at having lost her teeth," said manager Linda Stevens. A'Bear's caregivers tracked the dentures to a nearby roof. They gave them a thorough cleaning and returned them to their relieved owner.

BARFLIES

Everyone in the tiny Australian Outback town of Yaraka (population: "fewer than 20") loved Carol and Kevin...until the three-year-old emus took over the local pub. The emus (slightly smaller cousins of the ostrich) had become something of a tourist attraction after they were found as abandoned eggs in 2017. Their keeper, Leanne Byrne, told Australia's ABC News that she and the pub's owners were pretty sure five-foot-tall birds couldn't climb the three steps to the patio. Wrong. The clever birds learned quickly, and were soon sauntering around the patio, snatching bread and fries off customers' plates. They also made their way through an open door *into* the pub. The worst part, said Byrne, was that "they're a tad incontinent." Pub owners Gerry and Chris Gimblett put up a sign that reads "Emus have been banned from this establishment for bad behavior." "We're not quite sure whether they're able to read or not," remarked Gene, "so we've had to put a bar across the door as well." (Your move, emus.)

SIMMER DOWN, PEACOCK!

In springtime, when a male peacock is ready to mate, he emits a piercing call to invite females to his "harem," where he will try to impress them with his majestic tail feathers. In 2020, a peacock in Victoria, British Columbia, chose the entrance of an apartment building as his harem. At first, tenants were able to walk around the posturing peacock's impressive plumage, but when hens began arriving from a nearby park, Pea (as tenants named him) became nearly impossible to have around. "I like to say he set up a brothel or a Studio 54," tenant Susan Simmons told a reporter. "He'd do his little glitter dance and all the girls would come around." Then the situation

Fight Foods: The Pittsburgh, Pennsylvania, restaurant Conflict Kitchen serves dishes from countries where the U.S. is currently involved in a conflict.

became dangerous: the "sex-crazed peacock" (as he was referred to in headlines) clawed a woman in her 90s. Animal control officers captured Pea and drove him all the way to the other side of the park...apparently unaware that peacocks can fly. Pea was back in a few hours. Then they put him in "peacock jail" for two weeks until the mating urge waned and he was able to, as Simmons put it, "simmer down."

NO EGRETS

The six-month siege began in March 2017 when a few pairs of mating egrets and herons constructed nests in a large oak tree that towers over the Witrykus home in Brentwood, California. As spring turned to summer, several more of the three-foot-tall wading birds arrived, until there were 40 of them. Then they had chicks—lots of chicks. "It was like...*Star Wars* with all the characters that make the funny sounds," said Danielle Witrykus, who lives there with her husband and two young children. But it got a lot less funny as summer wore on. The noise never ceased and the backyard became buried beneath rotting bits of fish, rodents, and songbirds. Worst of all: the bird droppings. "The smell was overwhelming," said Witrykus. Even the sidewalk beyond the fence was covered with feces. That happened to be where the tree's trunk was, making this the city's responsibility. But when the family complained that they were being "held prisoner" in a "hazardous environment," Brentwood officials said there's nothing they could do: herons and egrets are protected species in California, so it's against state law to remove an active nest. Witrykus was "beyond frustrated." So was Brentwood's mayor, Robert Taylor, who told California Fish and Wildlife to find a way around the bureaucracy to help this desperate family. "Not a Band-Aid approach," he barked, "we need to fix it!" They got their fix...eventually. Shortly after the migratory birds abandoned the tree in October, the city cut it down.

FLIGHT OF THE FIREHAWK

The 2019–20 Australian bush fire season was among the worst ever—it burned 72,000 square miles of wilderness and destroyed nearly 6,000 structures. Seventy-five people lost their lives, but an estimated 3 *billion* animals died in the fires. And some of those fires were actually spread by birds. Known in northern Australia as "firehawks," three raptor species—whistling kites, black kites, and brown falcons—were seen picking up burning sticks and depositing them in dry areas. The activity wasn't confirmed by ornithologists until the 2010s, but Aborigines have long known about the firehawks' odd behavior—it's a hunting tactic. In his 1962 autobiography, an Indigenous doctor named Phillip Waipuldanya Roberts wrote: "I have seen a hawk pick up a smoldering stick in its claws and drop it in a fresh patch of dry grass half a mile away, then wait with its mates for the mad exodus of scorched and frightened rodents and reptiles."

What's *koagulationsvitamin*? The German name for vitamin K, which is how vitamin K got its name.

HAVE A HEART

A perfectly functioning, state-of-the-art, implantable, self-powered artificial heart is the ultimate in medical technology. Here's a look back at how far engineers, doctors, scientists, surgeons, and patients have come toward making that a reality.

1937 Vladimir Demikhov, a Russian scientist known for performing pioneering heart and lung transplants on dogs in the 1940s (and surgically creating a two-headed dog in the 1950s) builds and implants the world's first artificial heart in a dog. Demikhov's device consists of two diaphragm pumps and an electric motor. The dog survives with the fake heart for a little more than two hours.

1949 Drs. William Sewell and William Glenn at the Yale School of Medicine construct an artificial heart pump out of parts from an Erector Set and other cheap mechanical toys. Implanted into a dog, it works for about an hour.

1952 At Michigan's Wayne State University, Dr. Forest Dodrill and Dr. Matthew Dudley build a makeshift mechanical external heart to use on 41-year-old Henry Opitek during his heart surgery. It successfully pumps Opitek's blood and keeps him alive while the doctors operate on his real heart.

1956 Paul Winchell, a popular ventriloquist best known for hosting TV shows in the 1950s and '60s (and as the voice of Tigger in Disney's *Winnie the Pooh* cartoons), uses his medical training to build a mechanical, implantable artificial heart. In 1963, his is the first man-made heart to earn a U.S. patent. Assisting Winchell in his development: Dr. Henry Heimlich, creator of the Heimlich maneuver used to assist choking victims. This heart is just a prototype, however, and is never mass-produced or surgically inserted into anyone.

1957 Internal medicine pioneer Dr. Willem Kolff—he also designed an early heart-lung machine to assist doctors during heart surgery, and built the first functioning artificial kidney—implants a rough prototype of an artificial heart pump into a dog at the Cleveland Clinic. The dog survives...for 90 minutes.

1964 Similar to NASA's directive to put a man on the Moon by 1970, the National Institutes of Health's National Heart, Lung, and Blood Institute

If you laid all the viruses on Earth end to end, they'd stretch 100 million light-years. (And you'd have to wash your hands when you were done.)

launches the Artificial Heart Program, aiming to surgically implant a workable synthetic heart (with a power source) into a human by the end of the decade.

1966 Dr. Michael DeBakey of Houston's Baylor College of Medicine successfully installs a partial artificial heart. It's an external pump that bypasses (and does the work of) the left ventricular chamber of the heart.

1966 Dr. Adrian Kantrowitz performs the first permanent implantation of a partial mechanical heart, a left ventricular assist device, at Maimonides Medical Center in Brooklyn.

1967 It's not an artificial heart, but it's a major moment in heart surgery history when South African surgeon Dr. Christiaan Barnard performs the first successful human heart transplant. The recipient, 54-year-old Louis Washkansky, lives for 18 days with his new heart. Also in 1967, Dr. Willem Kolff starts the Division of Artificial Organs at the University of Utah. The program will come to employ more than 500 doctors and engineers to build multiple artificial heart prototypes. Among them: the Jarvik 5, named for project leader Robert Jarvik. After a calf (named Lord Tennyson) lives for nine months on the Jarvik 5, the device is rebuilt and renamed the Jarvik 7.

1969 Drs. Domingo Liotta and Denton Cooley replace a patient's heart with a mechanical heart at the Texas Heart Institute in Houston while they wait for a human heart to transplant. After 64 hours, the pneumatic-powered heart is removed and replaced by a donor heart. (The patient dies after 32 hours.)

1981 Dr. Kolff's lead surgeon, Dr. William DeVries, files for FDA approval to surgically insert the Jarvik 7 into a human being.

1982 After receiving approval from the FDA, the Division of Artificial Organs implants the Jarvik 7 into congestive heart failure patient Dr. Barney Clark (a dentist). Clark remains bedridden, however, connected to a 400-pound external pneumatic compressor that powers the pumping of the artificial heart. He survives for 112 days and suffers from severe confusion, bleeding episodes, and at one point asks to have the heart removed so that he can die naturally.

1983–85 Dr. William DeVries implants the Jarvik heart into four other patients. The most successful surgery of the bunch is performed on William Schroeder, who lives for 620 days with his artificial heart (and all the

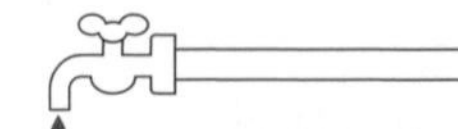

external machinery). DeVries and his associates also implant the heart into patients awaiting heart transplants—the Jarvik is then removed when their new heart arrives.

1994 The left ventricular assist device, an artificial implant that takes over some of the heart's natural functions and which has been used experimentally since the 1960s, receives FDA approval for mainstream surgical use.

2000 Doctors in Israel place the latest edition of the Jarvik heart, the Jarvik 2000, into a patient. It's the first artificial heart that generates a pulse on its own (without an external power source).

2001 The Jarvik program rebrands as SynCardia and introduces the improved Jarvik 2000, called the SynCardia Total Artificial Heart. It's only meant as a temporary solution, and since its creation, it has served as a stopgap solution between removal of a failed heart and transplant of a new, biological one.

2006 The FDA grants limited approval to Abiomed's AbioCor, an implantable artificial heart. It was only ever used on 15 patients, 14 in a preapproval clinical trial and one after. It didn't effectively prolong the lives of any of those patients, and Abiomed soon thereafter discontinued the product.

2020 SynCardia's Total Artificial Heart is the only commercially and medically available artificial heart in the United States. But it remains indicated only for use as a temporarily implanted medical device for patients imminently awaiting a heart transplant. And it is not fully self-contained—its use requires a backpack-sized air compressor that pumps the heart (which pumps the blood). Still, it does keep someone with a bad heart alive a little bit longer. With the incredibly slow progress on artificial hearts over the years, it turns out that transplants of actual human hearts are the way to go when replacing a bad ticker, and artificial hearts are an important and valuable tool that extends the lives of heart patients until they can get that new heart they need. And with all the improvements scientists are making in nanotechnology, who knows? Maybe someday in the not too distant future we'll be able to have artificial hearts (and kidneys and pancreases) installed at the neighborhood body shop.

* * *

"I don't believe in astrology. I'm a Sagittarius and we're skeptical."

—Arthur C. Clarke

Tipping point? According to one estimate, the combined weight of all human-made objects now exceeds the combined weight of all living things on Earth.

MUSIC AND INDUSTRY

Can you match the world-famous musical act to the giant company that originated in the same city? And then guess the city? Sounds easy, but...

(Answers are on page 405.)

1. Pearl Jam
2. The Supremes
3. Aerosmith
4. Jefferson Airplane
5. The Who
6. Chuck Berry
7. ABBA
8. Prince and the Revolution
9. Alice Cooper
10. The Ramones
11. ZZ Top
12. Bob Seger and the Silver Bullet Band
13. Elvis Presley
14. TLC
15. R.E.M.
16. The Beatles
17. Rush
18. Kansas
19. U2
20. Chicago

a) Guinness
b) JP Morgan Chase
c) Federal Express
d) Starbucks
e) Ford Motor Company
f) Zaxby's
g) Coca-Cola
h) Rice-A-Roni
i) University of Phoenix
j) Motown Records
k) Enron
l) 3M
m) Sears-Roebuck
n) Payless Shoes
o) IKEA
p) Anheuser-Busch
q) Royal Bank of Canada
r) Samuel Adams
s) Unilever
t) Twinings Tea

* * *

"All the good music has already been written by people with wigs and stuff."

–**Frank Zappa**

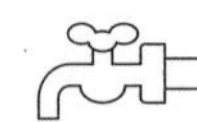

The Moscow subway has a ticket machine that accepts payment in squat thrusts. (30 squat thrusts and you ride for free.)

FOOD FLOODS

A little bit of food is a good thing, a lot of food can be a bad thing, and a wall of food rushing toward you at 35 miles an hour is a really *bad thing.*

THE LONDON BEER FLOOD (1814)

Story: In the early 1800s, breweries fermented their beer in enormous wooden vats that were like giant barrels—vertical planks held in place by horizontal bands of iron circling the outside of each vat. On October 17, 1814, a band on one of the vats at London's Horse Shoe Brewery slipped out of place. Bands had slipped before, but the brewers had always managed to put them back in place, so the situation wasn't considered an emergency. This time was different. About an hour later the tank suddenly burst, destroying neighboring vats and releasing, according to one estimate, close to 400,000 gallons. A 15-foot-high wave of the beer (it was porter) slammed into the rear wall of the brewery, demolishing it with such force that bricks from the wall were thrown onto the roofs of adjacent buildings. The beer then roared into a neighboring slum, flooding the underground cellars where many poor families lived. Two houses were completely destroyed and other buildings, including (ironically) a pub, were damaged. Considering the scale of the disaster, it's a wonder that only nine people were killed—eight who drowned, and a ninth who was crushed when her house collapsed on her. No brewery workers died.

Aftermath: A coroner's inquest later ruled the tragedy to be an "act of God," which meant the brewery's owner, Meux & Co., was not responsible and therefore did not have to pay compensation to the victims. One good thing did come out of the disaster, though: breweries began replacing wooden vats with stronger concrete vats. If you happen to visit London in October, the Holborn Whippet tavern near the intersection of Tottenham Court Road and Oxford Street, where the Horse Shoe Brewery once stood, sells a special porter each year to commemorate the anniversary of the flood.

THE DUBLIN WHISKEY FLOOD AND FIRE (1875)

Story: Sometime in the evening of June 18, 1875, a fire erupted at Malone's Malt House and an adjacent warehouse in the Liberties section of Dublin, Ireland. These buildings contained more than 5,000 wooden barrels filled with whiskey and other liquors, and when the fire reached them they began to burst, accelerating the intensity of the fire because the whiskey was flammable. As the blaze grew out of control, the burning whiskey spilled onto Mill Street and streamed more than a quarter mile down the street, igniting buildings and anything flammable in its wake. Fearing that pouring water on the burning whiskey would cause the fire to spread, firefighters battled the blaze by shoveling sand and manure onto the street in an attempt to dam the whiskey

Hugh Hefner's father, an accountant, refused to loan his son $1,000 to start *Playboy* magazine. (He thought it was a bad business investment.)

and soak it up before it spread any farther.

Aftermath: No one died in the fire, but 13 died afterward...from *alcohol poisoning.* Crowds of Dubliners, unwilling to let the whiskey go to waste even if it was on fire, descended on the neighborhood and scooped up the burning whiskey with their cupped hands, hats, boots, or whatever was available, then blew out the flames and drank more than was good for them. The lord mayor of Dublin shrugged off the fatalities, saying they would have happened "in any city where there was a tendency to indulge immoderately in drink." Nearly 150 years later, the fire remains one of the most destructive in Dublin's history.

THE BOSTON MOLASSES FLOOD (1919)

Story: On January 15, 1919, a giant steel storage tank near the Boston waterfront failed, releasing 2.3 million gallons of molasses and sending a 25-foot-high wave of the syrup roaring through the surrounding streets at a speed of about 35 miles per hour. The wave slammed into nearby buildings with enough force to demolish them. The molasses then flowed through the city streets, covering an area of several blocks in up to three feet of the sticky goo.

Have you heard the expression "as slow as molasses in January"? Much of the molasses in the tank had recently been heated to make it easier to offload from a ship, and it was still warm when the tank collapsed. This made the molasses more fluid, which is what allowed it to flow through the streets as quickly and with as much force as it did. But within minutes of the collapse, exposure to the wintry Boston air caused the molasses to cool and thicken to the consistency of tar, trapping its victims like mice in a glue trap. This greatly complicated rescue efforts: emergency teams struggled to wade through the knee-deep syrup to reach and extract the people stuck in it. Twenty-one people were killed and another 150 were injured. Several horses also died after getting trapped in the muck.

DID YOU KNOW?

Molasses is a by-product that results when sugarcane is refined to make sugar. The juice from the sugarcane is harvested and then boiled, which causes the sugar to crystallize. The crystallized sugar is removed, and the thick, dark syrup that remains is molasses. Brown sugar is sugar that hasn't had all of its molasses removed, or that has had some molasses added back to the white sugar.

Aftermath: It took a crew of several hundred people many weeks to clean up the molasses. Much of the work was done by blasting it with fire hoses, and so much of it drained into Boston Harbor that the water remained brown for months. After three years of court battles, the owner of the tank, the United States Industrial Alcohol Company, was ordered to pay more than $600,000 in damages, the equivalent of more than $9 million today. The victims' families received $7,000, or more than $100,000 today. The flooded neighborhood was said to smell like molasses for decades afterward, especially on hot days.

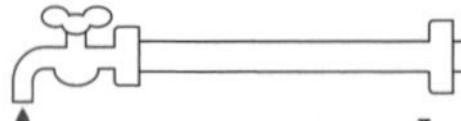

Australia chose the town of Dalgety as its capital in 1903, only to change its mind and pick Canberra. Population of Dalgety today: 205.

ANY RESEMBLANCE TO ACTUAL PERSONS...

Any similarity to actual people, living or dead, is purely coincidental...except these fictional characters who really were inspired by someone real.

Fictional Character: Moby-Dick

Inspired by: Mocha Dick

Story: The title character in Herman Melville's 1851 novel *Moby-Dick* is a massive white whale that takes revenge on whalers, destroying their ships in a matchup of man vs. nature that seems too allegorical to be real. But there actually was an albino sperm whale that battled sea captains in the early 1800s. Called Mocha Dick, after Mocha Island off the coast of Chile where it was first sighted, the white whale was an astounding 70 feet long (average length of a whale: 40–50 feet). Although the creature was often targeted by whalers, it managed to demolish 20 ships and escape another 80 of them. Incredibly, Mocha Dick survived with 20 harpoons in its back, which one writer called "the rusted mementos of many a desperate encounter." That's where Melville got the name of his whale. But Melville's story is based on an even bigger 85-footer that—allegedly unprovoked—sank the American whaling ship *Essex* in 1820. One of the ship's eight survivors wrote an account of the tragic ordeal (including cannibalism), which motivated Melville to write his novel about a ship captain named Ahab who seeks vengeance on a whale.

As for Mocha Dick, in 1838, it attacked a whaling ship that had killed a calf. During the struggle, Mocha Dick was harpooned, and the helmsman was knocked overboard. Unlike Captain Ahab in Melville's novel, the helmsman survived; unlike the whale in Melville's novel, Mocha Dick did not.

Fictional Character: Olivia Pope, lead character in TV's *Scandal*

Inspired by: Judy Smith

Story: Smith is a Washington, D.C. lawyer, former deputy press secretary for President George H. W. Bush, and a crisis-management expert who helps famous clients navigate embarrassing situations. Her agents thought her unique job would make for good TV, so they set up a meeting with award-winning writer/producer Shonda Rhimes. That's how Rhimes's hit show *Scandal* (2012–18) was born, with Kerry Washington starring as Olivia Pope, a character modeled on Smith. Both Smith and Pope are African American women who held top communications jobs in the White House and run crisis-management firms. But there the similarities end.

Unlike Pope, Smith never disposed of dead bodies, committed murders, or broke any laws on behalf of the administration. Another difference: Smith stresses that she did *not* have an affair with the president. In fact, when she learned about that plot in *Scandal*, she immediately called President Bush to give him talking points for the press. When asked about their "romance," he put the matter to rest with her help. As Pope would say, "It's handled."

Fictional Character: Mary of "Mary Had a Little Lamb"

Inspired by: Mary Sawyer

Story: The nursery rhyme is about Mary Sawyer, a girl from Sterling, Massachusetts, who was around nine years old in 1815. When the little girl heard that an abandoned lamb had been left for dead, she begged her parents to let her nurse it to health. The white lamb grew attached to her, and one morning the animal followed Mary to the schoolhouse, where she wrapped it in a blanket in an attempt to hide it. Depending on which account you believe, her teacher was either alerted by the "baa" sounds or the lamb hopped out and followed Mary when she was called to the front. In any case, the lamb was ejected from class but waited patiently outside for its owner. The full 24-line poem recounts these events and offers lessons about trust, love, and kindness. Although the author is disputed, Mary Sawyer claimed an older student wrote the first half and that the teacher, Sarah Josepha Hale, expanded it. In 1830, Hale published it under her own name.

Fictional Character: Delphine LaLaurie in TV's *American Horror Story*

Inspired by: Madame Marie Delphine LaLaurie, a New Orleans socialite

Story: In season three of the critically-acclaimed FX drama, a rich woman portrayed by Kathy Bates performs sadistic experiments on slaves in her attic and even develops a beauty balm made from human pancreas. It might seem too over-the-top to be true—except that there really was a New Orleans socialite named Madame LaLaurie, and she was a reputed serial killer who owned more than 50 slaves in the early 19th century. Rumors of LaLaurie's "barbarous treatment" of her slaves were common throughout the city, although no one knew the full extent of her depravity. The worst acts took place in a torture chamber in her attic. After investigators found her responsible for the death of a young girl who'd fallen off the roof while fleeing a whipping, LaLaurie simply paid the fine and continued her reign of terror. That is, until 1834, when a cook who was tied to a stove rebelled and set the house on fire. LaLaurie saved herself, but she left everyone else caged inside. Only after rescuers broke into the slave quarters did they discover the unspeakable acts that had taken place there—many of them too horrible for *American Horror Story* to delve into. Even so, LaLaurie's portrayal sparked controversy for turning the serial killer into a sympathetic character for much

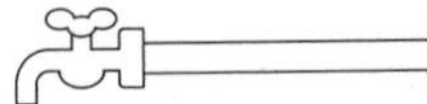

Disney's Mary Poppins books (to tie-in with the 1961 movie) have outsold the original P. L. Travers Mary Poppins novels by five to one.

of the season. In real life, LaLaurie got away and most likely spent the rest of her life in Paris. But she did get her comeuppance on the show, which ended with her spending eternity in a special hell all her own.

Fictional Character: Tony Stark/Iron Man

Inspired by: Howard Hughes

Story: Stan Lee of Marvel Comics referred to eccentric billionaire Howard Hughes as "one of the most colorful men of the time. He was an inventor, an adventurer, a ladies' man, and a nutcase." After being orphaned at age 18, Hughes inherited millions. The following year, 1926, he became a movie producer, and in the 1930s, he founded an aircraft company and later bought a controlling interest in Trans World Airlines. Hughes set world records while flying planes he designed, and developed top-secret weapons, becoming a major supplier for the U.S. military. He was even part of a cover story for the CIA to recover a nuclear-armed Soviet submarine that had sunk. All of the intrigue surrounding Hughes made him a good candidate for comic books. In 1963, Stan Lee and his team created Tony Stark (and his superhero alter ego, Iron Man), a wealthy weapons maker whose parents died and whose father, in a nod to Hughes, is named Howard.

Bonus fact: Sometimes art imitates life *and* life imitates art. Engineers at several defense contractors were inspired by Stark's inventions and have worked for years to develop a bulletproof exoskeleton. Raytheon introduced its version, the XOS 2, nicknamed "the Iron Man suit," in 2010 (to coincide with the release of *Iron Man 2*).

Fictional Character: Miss Piggy

Inspired by: Peggy Lee

Story: Norma Deloris Egstrom was a sultry-voiced jazz singer who first found fame in the 1940s under the name Peggy Lee. The blonde Midwesterner was an independent woman who married and divorced four times, and had a string of hit records (including "Why Don't You Do Right," "Mañana," "Fever," "Is That All There Is," and one with a refrain in French—"C'est Magnifique"). She was nominated for 12 Grammy Awards (she received two) and an Academy Award (for her performance as an alcoholic singer in *Pete Kelly's Blues*). In 1974, designer Bonnie Erickson created a puppet pig who left the Midwest to become a singer on *The Muppet Show.* The diva pig speaks French phrases and wears gowns, gloves, and jewels. The puppet's name: Miss Piggy Lee. Erickson had memories of her mother listening to the vocalist and meant the character to be a tribute to Lee. But Lee didn't take it that way. Rumor has it that she threatened to sue over the name. "Nobody wanted to upset Peggy Lee," Erickson says, "especially because we admired her work." Accordingly, the name was shortened.

BIG-TIME IMPOSTORS

Do you have what it takes to make it in this world? We're not referring to athletic ability, superior intellect, a fancy college degree, or even a killer instinct. We're asking: Do you have the skills to fake *your way to glory? These people did.*

THE FAKE FOOTBALL PLAYER: In 1923, football enthusiast Ollie Kraehe scraped together enough money to start a team in his hometown, St. Louis, and join the fledgling NFL. He wasn't just the owner and coach of the St. Louis All-Stars, Kraehe also played for the team, because he was having a hard time recruiting players to a brand-new, unproven team that couldn't pay much. Unable to attract many fans and quickly running out of money, Kraehe needed a big attraction. That's probably why he jumped at the chance to sign Dolly Gray, who represented himself to Kraehe as having been an all-American—one of the country's best college players—at Princeton University the previous year. Kraehe immediately signed him up. But after inserting Gray into three games and noticing that he didn't play very well, Kraehe did some research and found that nobody named Dolly Gray had been an all-American for Princeton in 1922, or ever. Not only that, nobody by that name had *ever* played for Princeton.

Kraehe didn't confront or expose the phony football star. Instead, he sold Gray's contract to the rival Green Bay Packers and used the cash to keep the All-Stars afloat. But once more, Gray performed poorly, and after Packers coach Curly Lambeau confronted Kraehe after a game with the All-Stars, the St. Louis coach admitted that Dolly Gray wasn't really a collegiate standout. He told Lambeau that the whole thing had been a prank, and that he'd give him his money back (eventually).

So what happened to Dolly Gray? Nobody knows. When the team had boarded a train in Wisconsin for its game against the All-Stars, Gray got off somewhere along the way and was never heard from again.

THE FAKE PLAYER, REFEREE, CHEERLEADER, AND EMMY WINNER: For a seven-year period between 1979 and 1986, Michigan insurance adjuster Barry Bremen made a hobby out of appearing in public, high-profile places where he had no business being. His first stunt: At the 1979 NBA All-Star Game at the Silverdome outside of Detroit, he put on a Kansas City Kings uniform and joined the players in their pre-game shoot-around. He got in a couple of drills before Kings all-star Otis Birdsong called him out, because he didn't recognize him. Two years later, Bremen crashed the 1981 NBA All-Star Game, this time posing as a member of the Houston Rockets. For game five of that year's NBA Finals at Boston Garden, Bremen donned a referee's uniform and snuck onto the court, where he stood next to the game's real officials during the national anthem.

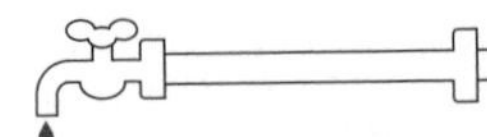

Bremen liked baseball, too. In 1979, dressed in a New York Yankees uniform, he snuck onto the field for Major League Baseball's All-Star Game at the Seattle Kingdome. He shagged fly balls for nearly 30 minutes and almost made it into a group photo with a bunch of star players before security realized he shouldn't be there and "escorted" him from the field. (He repeated the stunt at the 1986 All-Star Game—this time wearing a New York Mets uniform—once again engaging in pre-game warm-ups, until he was spotted by National League manager Tommy Lasorda.)

Perhaps Bremen's most outrageous stunt was when he snuck on the field during a Dallas Cowboys game and pretended to be a member of the Dallas Cowboys Cheerleaders. He'd prepared extensively for the stunt, losing 23 pounds to slim his body down to cheerleader shape, rehearsing cheerleader and drag routines, and squeezing himself into a custom-made uniform (along with a blond wig and fake breasts). After one cheer, Cowboys security guards hog-tied and handcuffed him, and threw him out of the stadium. Then the Cowboys sued him for trespassing.

He'd prepared extensively for the stunt, losing 23 pounds to slim his body down to cheerleader shape.

Bremen's last big stunt was at the 1985 Emmy Awards. He paid $300 for a ticket, rented a tuxedo, and waited. When Betty Thomas of *Hill Street Blues* was announced as the winner of Best Supporting Actress in a Drama, he beat her to the stage and told presenter Peter Graves that he was accepting the award on Thomas's behalf. He later told reporters that he'd picked Thomas because he thought she wasn't in attendance. (She was.) After being arrested for attempting to steal an Emmy, Bremen was fined $175 and publicly apologized to Thomas.

THE FAKE RESTAURATEUR: In the early 2010s, freelance writer Oobah Butler supplemented his journalism income by getting English restaurants to pay him for writing positive reviews and posting them on the travel website TripAdvisor. He didn't have to actually dine at the establishments, just compose glowing prose about them. That gave him the idea of writing fake reviews for a restaurant that was also fake. So, in April 2017, he created a website for The Shed at Dulwich, a high-end eatery in the Dulwich neighborhood of London. To make the website look real, he set up a phone number for The Shed and posted photos of some of its culinary offerings. (The entrees were fake, too, made out of soap, shaving cream, and other inedible household items.) Apparently it all looked legitimate, because TripAdvisor accepted Butler's application to have The Shed listed among its London restaurants. Then, over the next six months, Butler asked friends to post positive reviews on TripAdvisor to increase The Shed's ranking. It worked: On November 1, 2017, The Shed at Dulwich became the #1 rated restaurant (out of more than 18,000) in all of London. Two weeks later, Butler opened the establishment for real, but for one night only. He took reservations for 20 unsuspecting guests and served them microwaved frozen meals.

In France, it's illegal to keep the cremains of loved ones at home.

ROBOTS IN THE NEWS

We must become aware of what's going on in the world of robots...before they rise up and kill us all.

MEDI-BOT: In 2020, engineers at Purdue University revealed that they'd developed a small robot that can do backflips, turning end over end as it travels. How small? It's as thin as a human hair. Why does it do backflips? Because the point of this robot is to transport drugs through the human colon. After someone swallows medication along with this tiny robot, the machine flips over and over, side-stepping organs as it transports medicine from the digestive system to where it needs to go. This way, the medicine doesn't barrel through the human body and run into sensitive tissue, which is how drugs cause side effects such as stomach bleeding or organ interference. Because it's too small to house a battery, this robot works via magnets on the outside of the body. "When we apply a rotating external magnetic field to these robots, they rotate just like a car tire would to go over rough terrain," project lead David Cappelleri said in *Micromachines*. Scientists can then use those magnets to guide the robot to the part of the body where the medicine needs to go.

TONGUE-BOT: Researchers in South Korea have created a robotic version of a chameleon. No, it doesn't change colors at will, but like the lizard, it has a lightning-fast tongue that can grab objects and retrieve them. The robot, called Snatcher, consists primarily of a two-foot-long tongue. The device resembles a tape measure. The long metal "tongue" (which actually was repurposed from a tape measure) shoots out at tremendous speed, grabs objects with a hook, then retracts just as quickly. As it stands right now, Snatcher's researchers hope the device can be used to help people with mobility issues—it can grab objects and turn off light switches. In the future, engineers want to add the Snatcher technology to drones, which they believe will open up commercial opportunities such as delivering packages.

DANCE-BOT: Nantes, France, is home to SC-Club, a nightclub that features 10 human female pole dancers. As of 2019, it added two performers to its roster—both of them robots. The bots are made to look somewhat humanoid, with white plastic female mannequin parts covering the machinery on their torso, arms, hands, and legs. The robots have high-heeled shoes instead of feet and closed-circuit TV cameras instead of heads. (What the cameras "see" is broadcast to monitors around the SC-Club.) British artist Giles Walker crafted the robots both to dance and to "play with the notion of voyeurism."

The Library of Congress routinely receives requests for *The President's Book of Secrets*, a fictional book from the 2007 movie *National Treasure: Book of Secrets*.

THE LINGUISTIC ETHER

Why do some words and phrases catch on while others don't? There are no set rules. Our language changes all the time depending on taste and trends, and what's happening all around us. As anthropologist Dr. Christine Mallinson puts it, "We repeat what we hear in the 'linguistic ether.'" That elegant phrase inspired this article.

Hello? Hey, y'all. Did you know that the word "hello" only dates back to the 1830s? Before that, the most common English greeting was "Good day." "Hello" was adapted from the similar-sounding "hallo," or "halloo," or "hullo," and it originally meant "Hey!" as in, "Halloo! How much longer will you be in there?" Then, on July 18, 1877, when Thomas Edison created the first sound recording machine, he loudly exclaimed, "Hello!" into the device. When Alexander Graham Bell invented the telephone, his choice for a standard greeting was "Ahoy." Edison, the superior marketer of the two, pushed for "Hello," and it caught on quickly. It first appeared in print as a greeting in Mark Twain's 1880 short story "A Telephonic Conversation," in which he writes of the newfangled technology: "I notice that one can always write best when somebody is talking through a telephone close by."

OMG! You might think this shortening of "Oh my God!" was coined in the early 2010s by texting teenagers. According to the *Oxford English Dictionary*, its digital debut occurred in 1994 in an internet forum when an excited soap opera fan typed "OMG what did it say?" But the exclamation is much older than that. Its first known print appearance was in a 1917 letter from retired British admiral Lord Fisher to Minister of Munitions (and future prime minister) Winston Churchill. Fisher concluded sarcastically with: "I hear that a new order of Knighthood is on the tapis – O.M.G. (Oh! My God!) – Shower it on the Admiralty!!"

Drama + Comedy. Whichever clever wordsmith coined "dramedy" wasn't clever enough to take credit for it. Until etymologists uncover new evidence, the origin will remain "unknown." What is known is that television had featured shows that combined drama and comedy for decades—starting with Jackie Cooper's *Hennesey* in 1959, followed by *M*A*S*H*, *All in the Family*, and *Eight Is Enough* in the 1970s. However, the portmanteau didn't show up until the following decade. Here's an early mention from a 1987 *South Florida Sun Sentinel* article by TV critic Bill Kelley about a show called "*Hooperman*, starring John Ritter as a San Francisco cop," which "inaugurates a new form—the so-called 'dramedy,' a half-hour program mixing elements of sitcom humor with straight drama." That excerpt proves the word was already in use, but who called it that first? (If it was you, give us a call!)

WWWebsites. Today, the internet goes by many names: the web, the Information Superhighway, the Net, online, cyberspace, and others. Back in 1990, internet inventor Tim Berners-Lee considered several official names for his new browser. Among the finalists were "The Information Mesh," which he rejected because it sounded too much like "mess." "The Information Mine" was also rejected because it abbreviated to "TIM," which the humble software developer felt was egotistical. And he rejected "Mine of Information," or "MOI" ("me" in French), for the same reason. Ultimately, he settled on this one: "World Wide Web," which is why websites now start with "www" and not "tim" or "moi."

Verbing the nouns and nouning the verbs. "Just Google it!" "Beer me!" "Let's party!" If it feels like nouns are undergoing verbification at an alarming rate, it might comfort you to know that *verbification* (a word coined in the 1870s) has actually played a huge part in forming our language. Even William Shakespeare did his fair share of verbifying, such as in this line from *Love's Labour's Lost*: "But now to task the tasker." And 400 years before Facebook, the Bard wrote, "And what so poor a man as Hamlet is / May do, to express his love and friending to you." Conversely, a lot of nouns began as verbs. That's what allows us to meet for a drink, have a catch, go for a walk, or get the runs.

Listen up! English used to have a gender-neutral pronoun for "you people": ye—as in "Hear ye, hear ye." That phrase fell out of use long ago without a real replacement. The closest we have today is the standard callout: "Hey, you guys." Two replacements that have been bandied about: the gender-neutral phrases "Howdy, folks" and "Hey, y'all"—both of which have been used for more than a century in the American West and South (respectively), but neither has caught on en masse...yet. ("Guy," by the way, is an *eponym*, a word named after a real person, in this case Guy Fawkes, a British revolutionary. And while the plural "guys" is considered gender-neutral, the singular "guy" is not.)

Goodbye. The next time you hear someone complain about the word-shortening words like "gonna," "splain," or "prolly" (which actually dates to the 1940s), remind them that there are no language overlords dictating how words are added to the Linguistic Ether. Half a millennium ago in England, someone was probably complaining, "What is this 'goodbye' I'm hearing people say? Everyone knows the proper phrase is 'God be with ye.'" But it sounded similar to the widely accepted phrase "Good day," which is why, according to etymologists, it caught on. The original term was a blessing, similar to the Spanish *adiós* and the French *adieu*, both of which translate literally as "to God," but functionally mean "farewell." Goodbye!

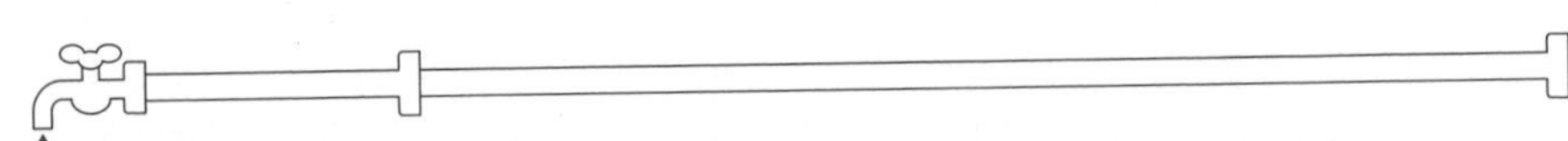

HOT COCKLES, ANYONE?

Liven up your next shindig with these real (and really weird) British party and parlor games from the Victorian Era (1837–1901).

ARE YOU THERE, MORIARTY?

Players: Two or more

Details: The players, blindfolded, stand face to face, and hold hands as they would if they were shaking hands. The first player says, "Are you there, Moriarty?" The second player responds in the affirmative, and the two then take turns swinging a rolled-up newspaper at the other person, who attempts to duck and wiggle out of the way while still holding hands with their opponent. The winner is whoever strikes the other one first. The winner then takes on the next opponent, and so on.

SCULPTOR

Players: Four or more

Details: Everyone stands perfectly still, except for the person who is "it"—the Sculptor. The Sculptor then walks around the group and manipulates everyone's bodies into silly positions and their face into odd expressions. Those being sculpted are not allowed to laugh or smile. If they do, they become the new Sculptor and the game starts over.

SNAPDRAGON

Players: As many as possible

Details: It is generally played on Christmas Eve, the most common occasion on which a large bowl of brandy would be available, and involves dropping a handful of raisins into the reservoir of booze. Players take turns fishing raisins out of the brandy and eating them as quickly as possible. What's so hard about that? The bowl of brandy is set on fire before the raisin-grabbing begins.

THE BELLMAN

Players: Five or more

Details: All but one member of the party puts on a blindfold. The one seeing person becomes the Bellman, and zigzags across the room, every so often ringing a bell. The blindfolded players then run around and, based on where they think the sound of the bell is coming from, try to grab the Bellman (and not run into each other, or the furniture, or the fireplace).

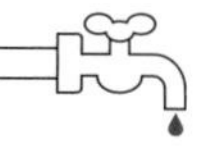

A giraffe's tongue is, on average, 21 inches long.

HOT COCKLES

Players: Four or more

Details: Various versions of this game were played from medieval times to the Victorian era. In one version, a player hides their face in the lap of another player. Then, other party guests take turns slapping them about the head and face. The object: The person getting beaten up has to guess which strike came from which person.

SQUEAK, PIGGY, SQUEAK!

Players: Six or more

Details: One player is selected to be the Farmer. They sit down on a pillow and are blindfolded, while everyone else sits in a circle around them. Then the Farmer stands up, spins around to the point of dizziness, and places the pillow in the first lap they can find in such a state. Then the Farmer sits on that pillow and commands, "Squeak, piggy, squeak!" The person whose lap the Farmer occupies then squeals like a pig. If the Farmer correctly guesses whose lap they're in, they win, and the "piggy" becomes the Farmer in the next round.

BULLET PUDDING

Players: The more, the merrier

Details: This game is like Jenga, except that you play with flour instead of blocks. Find a large serving tray, the kind you'd use to present an Easter ham or a Christmas goose, for example. Then get four or five one-pound bags of flour, and have your guests assist you in using it to build as tall of a white, dusty, powdery mountain as possible. At the very top of this approximately two-foot-tall mountain of flour, gently place a single bullet. Now the game truly begins: Each player takes turns poking their finger into the flour, hoping to dislodge enough flour to destabilize the mountain but keep that bullet at the summit. Whoever finally makes a false move and causes the bullet to fall inside of the flour pile has to retrieve that bit of live ammo...by plunging their face into it (no hands allowed) and fishing it out with their teeth.

SARDINES

Players: As many as possible

Details: It's a very physical variation of hide-and-seek. Rather than have everyone hide and one person seek, Sardines requires just one guest to hide, and all the others to find them. The twist: As soon as they locate the hiding party, they have to squeeze into the secret spot with them, and so do the next person and the next person—like a can of sardines. The last "seeker" loses, and becomes the first to hide in the next round.

Why did Jack Johnson, the first Black world heavyweight boxing champ (1908–15), take up boxing? He thought bicycle racing was too dangerous.

CLASSIC ROCK ALMOSTS

From the mid-1960s to the early '80s, classic rock ruled the FM radio dial. This was a storied time in music history, but if not for a few twists of fate, some of those stories could have gone much differently. It's high time to take a long, strange trip back to what might have been.

Eric Clapton almost replaced George Harrison in the Beatles.

Story: Clapton was only 18 years old and already one of England's best guitarists when he met the Fab Four in 1964. He was adored by all four Beatles and soon became close friends with lead guitarist George Harrison. Clapton played the solo on Harrison's "While My Guitar Gently Weeps" for 1968's *The White Album* and Harrison co-wrote "Badge" with Clapton for the 1969 Cream album *Goodbye.*

But by then, the Beatles could barely stand each other. John Lennon was spending most of his time with his wife Yoko Ono, Paul McCartney was butting heads with his bandmates over the business side of things, Ringo Starr quit and then reluctantly returned, and Harrison was frustrated because he was allowed to contribute only a few songs per album.

Then came the 1970 *Let It Be* sessions, which were being filmed for a documentary. At one point, off camera, Harrison and Lennon got into a fistfight. Later, during rehearsals (and on camera), McCartney was patronizingly directing Harrison, who barked back, "I'll play whatever you want me to play, or I won't play at all." At lunch, Harrison announced, "Put an ad in, and get a few people in. See you 'round the clubs." Then he quit the Beatles.

Harrison barked back, "I'll play whatever you want me to play, or I won't play at all."

"Let's get Eric," Lennon said a bit later. "He's just as good and not such a headache." That afternoon, the remaining Beatles "jammed violently" (as Starr later described it). Ono sat on Harrison's abandoned cushion and screamed into his microphone. "I think if George doesn't come back by Monday or Tuesday," Lennon reiterated, "we ask Eric to play."

Clapton's latest band, Blind Faith, had called it quits a few months earlier, so he was available. He was aware of what Lennon had proposed, but he was never formally offered a spot in the Beatles. It didn't matter, because ten days later, Harrison returned.

Why It Didn't Happen: As far as McCartney was concerned, it was John, Paul, George, and Ringo...or nothing. As for Clapton, "I don't think I could have been brought in because I was too much a mate of George's." But that's not the only reason he stayed away: "There were times when [the Beatles] was like the closest-knit family you've ever seen," recalled Clapton, "but the cruelty and the viciousness was unparalleled."

Somebody call a doctor! Half the PhDs issued in the U.S. are fake (about 50,000 in all).

Aftermath: In April 1970—just a few months after Harrison returned—McCartney released a solo album, and announced that the Beatles had broken up for good. A year later, Lennon wrote Clapton a letter practically begging him to...re-form the Beatles? "Eric, I know I can bring out something great, in fact greater in you than has been so far evident in your music. I hope to bring out the same kind of greatness in all of us, which I know will happen if/when we get together."

But Clapton didn't need the Beatles. He went on to form Derek and the Dominos before embarking on a very successful solo career. He remained friends with Harrison, even after running off with Harrison's wife Pattie Boyd in one of rock 'n' roll's most sordid love triangles (but that's another story).

Paul McCartney almost appeared on Pink Floyd's *The Dark Side of the Moon.*

Story: Released in 1973, Pink Floyd's breakout album introduced FM radio mainstays "Time," "Money," and "Brain Damage/Eclipse." Along with its distinctive triangle-and-prism cover, *Dark Side* is known for its extensive use of sound effects (like the cash register at the beginning of "Money") and its spoken word parts (like a line at the end of that song, "That geezer was cruising for a bruising"). For the spoken parts, lyricist and bass player Roger Waters created a set of flashcards with questions like, "When was the last time you got violent? Were you in the right?" and "Does death frighten you?"

As Waters recalled years later, "We would scour Abbey Road Studios for willing guinea pigs, bring them to the studio, sit them down, roll tape, and then ask them to respond to each card in order." For example, the maniacal laughter that opens the album belonged to Floyd's road manager Peter Watts (father of actress Naomi Watts), and the final line—"There is no dark side in the moon, really; as a matter of fact, it's all dark"—was provided by Abbey Road's Irish doorman, Gerry O'Driscoll.

It just so happened that Paul McCartney and Wings were down the hall recording the album *Red Rose Speedway.* Wings guitarist Henry McCullough provided one of *Dark Side*'s best-known lines (also at the end of "Money"): "I don't know, I was really drunk at the time." Paul and his wife Linda also participated in the Q&A sessions, but their answers didn't make the final cut.

Why It Didn't Happen: According to Floyd guitarist David Gilmour, Paul and Linda were "much too good at being evasive for their answers to be usable." As Waters put it, "He was trying to be funny...He was the only person who found it necessary to perform." Exactly what McCartney said has been lost to history, but for some reason he gave cheeky responses (like he did in the early Beatles days) instead of the raw, honest admissions Waters was hoping for.

Aftermath: McCartney has never given his side of the story, but to put things in perspective, this took place in 1972, when Pink Floyd was still just an art-house group with a dedicated following but no big hits. And McCartney was, well, Paul McCartney. It's a good bet that if the former Beatle had had any inkling that *Dark Side* would launch Floyd to superstardom and spend a record 18 years on the Billboard 200—selling 45 million copies and counting—he would have taken the session more seriously.

The Dark Side of the Moon was almost called *Eclipse (A Piece for Assorted Lunatics).*

Story: Pink Floyd spent an entire year working on their seminal 1973 album about universal themes like time, money, war, and lunacy. From the beginning, Roger Waters wanted to call it *Dark Side of the Moon,* but those plans hit a snag in 1972 when Medicine Head, an up-and-coming British blues-rock band, released an album called... *Dark Side of the Moon.* Garnering praise and support from influential rockers like John Lennon and Pete Townshend, it looked like Medicine Head's *Dark Side* would propel them to fame. Floyd guitarist David Gilmour later said that they were *very* annoyed, not at Medicine Head directly, but because "we had already thought of the title." There wasn't much they could do about it, though, so Waters renamed the album *Eclipse (A Piece for Assorted Lunatics).*

Why It Didn't Happen: Despite critical praise, Medicine Head's *Dark Side of the Moon* flopped, so Floyd quietly reclaimed the title and hoped no one would say anything. No one did. Waters ended up using the name "Eclipse" for the album's final track, which was originally called "End."

DID YOU KNOW?

David Bowie was well ahead of his time when it came to music, fashion, and...the internet? His 1996 song "Telling Lies" was the first released solely online (300,000 people each spent around 11 minutes to download it). A year later, he launched the first internet subscription service, Bowienet. "I don't think we've seen the tip of the iceberg," he said at the time. "We're on the cusp of something both exhilarating and terrifying."

Rick Wakeman almost joined *Ziggy Stardust and the Spiders from Mars.*

Story: In 1969, Wakeman was 20 years old and training to become a concert pianist in London when he decided to quit school to become a session musician because it paid better. "One Take Wakeman," as he came to be called, quickly gained a reputation not just for his virtuoso playing but for his composing and arranging prowess. One of his first jobs—for which he received £9 ($21.50)—was playing the Mellotron on David Bowie's first hit single, "Space Oddity" (the one that begins "This is Ground Control to Major Tom"). That session made Wakeman a Bowie fan for life.

Over the next two years, while playing in a folk-rock band called the Strawbs, Wakeman did session work for other top-tier acts such as Cat Stevens (he played the piano intro on "Morning Has Broken"), T. Rex, Elton John, and the crowning

achievement of his early career: playing piano on Bowie's "Life on Mars?" All the while, Wakeman was feeling stifled by his folk-rock band; he wanted to play in a progressive rock band like the one that the Strawbs had recently opened for, Yes.

Formed in London in 1968, Yes hit it big in 1971 with *The Yes Album* (featuring "I've Seen All Good People" and "Starship Trooper"). What Wakeman didn't know at the time was that Yes was feeling stifled by their keyboardist, Tony Kaye, who was reluctant to expand beyond a Hammond organ. Then Yes's Chris Squire (bass) and Jon Anderson (vocals) read an interview in *Melody Maker* magazine, in which Wakeman predicted that keyboards would become "almost the orchestral part of a band." That's exactly what Yes wanted.

In July 1971, Wakeman auditioned for Yes. They clicked immediately; by the end of that first jam session, Wakeman and the band had worked out the foundations for what would become two of Yes's biggest hits, "Roundabout" and "Heart of the Sunrise."

Later that day, Wakeman received an offer that any other keyboardist in England would have jumped at: to join Bowie on his next concept album, *The Rise and Fall of Ziggy Stardust and the Spiders from Mars.* "I sat up nearly all night thinking about it," Wakeman recalled. "It was one of the most difficult decisions of my career."

Why It Didn't Happen: "If I joined Yes—and David was much bigger than Yes at the time—I thought, at least I'll be able to...put in some of my own thoughts and music, and I could grow with it. So, I called David up and said, 'I'm going to join Yes.'"

Aftermath: The decision paid off. Wakeman's contributions to Yes's next two albums, *Fragile* and *Close to the Edge,* helped make them huge hits both critically and commercially. Wakeman has been involved with Yes (on and off) ever since, while also releasing more than 90 solo albums. (Though not as well known in the U.S., he's a household name in England.)

Wakeman admits to having "some regret" that he didn't play on *Spiders from Mars,* which spawned two of Bowie's biggest hits—"Suffragette City" and "Starman"—and sold 7.5 million copies. "The truth of the matter is," Wakeman said in 2016 following Bowie's death, "David was undoubtedly the most influential person I've ever worked with, but when I told him I was joining Yes, he said, 'You've made absolutely the right decision.'"

5 FAMOUS CHRISTMAS SONGS WRITTEN BY JOHNNY MARKS

- "Rudolph, the Red-Nosed Reindeer"
- "I Heard the Bells on Christmas Day"
- "Run Rudolph Run"
- "Rockin' Around the Christmas Tree"
- "A Holly Jolly Christmas"

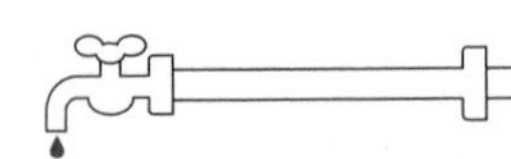

THE SCIENCE OF STINK

Everything you've never wanted to know about smells you never want to smell.

The Smell: "Old man smell"

The Science: Johan Lundstrom of the Monell Chemical Senses Center in Philadelphia proved in a 2012 study that the long-speculated idea of "old man stink"—the distinctive aroma associated with old folks and old folks' homes—is real. First, he collected odor samples from volunteers in their 20s, 40s, and 70s. Then he placed those samples in jars and had young volunteers grade the odors. Without fail, they could consistently identify the "old people" samples. The actual chemical reason isn't yet clear, but Lundstrom believes that the odor comes "from a complex interaction between skin gland secretions and bacterial activity." The reason for the smell, according to one theory: It's an evolutionary tactic, developed to discourage people from trying to breed with anyone too sickly or elderly to produce quality genetic material.

The Smell: Human feces

The Science: The main contributor to this odor is *skatole,* an organically occurring compound that was discovered in 1877 by German physician Dr. Ludwig Brieger. Here's where it comes from: In mammals, the amino acid *tryptophan,* found in the digestive system, helps break down food. What cannot be used by the body becomes waste (poop) and the tryptophan becomes indoleactic acid, of which skatole is a byproduct. Turns out there's a lot of it in feces—enough to generate that familiar smell.

Bonus: Scientists can now synthesize skatole in a lab. Why would anyone want to do that? Because in small amounts, skatole smells like flowers, and it's used to enhance the pleasant odors of essential oils.

The Smell: Death

The Science: As a dead body decays and decomposes, it breaks down thanks to aggressive bacteria, which consume the body's cells at a rapid rate. In 1885, Dr. discovered that as those bacteria help a corpse disintegrate, they create two waste products: the noxious-smelling chemical compounds *putrescine* (as in putrid) and *cadaverine* (as in cadaver).

Bonus: Cadaverine is also produced (in trace amounts) by live humans. It's one of the compounds that gives urine its smell.

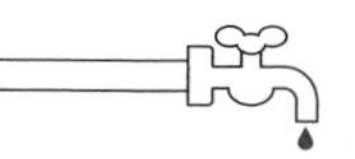

NICE STORIES

Every now and then we like to lock our inner cynics in a box and share some good news.

IT WAS A PIECE OF CAKE

In 1991, a struggling musician named John McCrea was at a garage sale in Sacramento, California, when, on a whim, he bought a three-foot-tall tree sapling for $7.00. McCrea took it to his apartment building and, not having a yard, he planted the tiny tree in a median. Not long after, his alternative rock band CAKE (named for caked mud, not the dessert) made it big with their album *Fashion Nugget*. McCrea moved to Los Angeles and forgot about the tree until he visited his old haunts many years later. Much to his surprise, the tree was nearly 30 feet tall. "It just blew my mind, and it just dwarfed my sense of time," he said. "And I guess it occurred to me that everyone should have some sort of experience that does that." So, since the early 2000s, McCrea has given away a tree at nearly every CAKE concert. First, he chooses a young tree that's native to the region in which they're playing. (According to the band's publicist, "More often than not, we've given away fruit-bearing trees—always based on the USDA Plant Hardiness Zone Map.") The tree spends most of the concert on stage, and then McCrea asks if anyone would like to take it home. In some cases, the audience member he chooses will have to tell a joke or "do a little dance," but every tree bearer must meet three criteria: They have to have a good place to plant it, be able to take care of it, and promise to send CAKE photos of its progress. As of 2021, the band estimates it has gifted more than 2,000 trees. "Although there is no way we're going to save the world by giving away a few trees," says McCrea, "it's just something that I think, maybe if a few more people can have that experience, it probably is a good thing."

NOT A BOBBER JERKER

One day in July 2020, Joseph Feeney of Wisconsin received the "phone call of a lifetime" from an old friend named Thomas Cook, who reminded him of a handshake deal the two men had made back in 1992—that if either one of them ever won the lottery, they'd split the winnings. Well, guess what Cook had in his hands? A $22 million winning Powerball ticket. "Are you jerking my bobber?" asked Feeney. Cook wasn't jerking his bobber (a fishing idiom, if you're unfamiliar). At a press conference, Cook said that it had never occurred to him to not honor the deal. "Handshake's a handshake," he said.

RESCUE CAT

"This is so cliché, but so very true for me," said Bridgid Staub. "I may have saved her life by adopting her, but she has very much saved my life as well!" Staub had

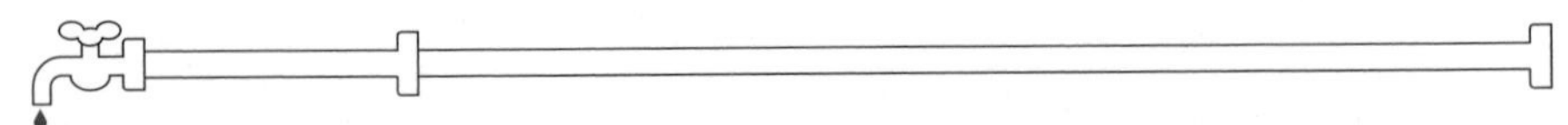

just returned home from a month in the hospital after combating a serious illness. Feeling there was something lacking in her life, she went to her local animal shelter in San Antonio, Texas, and asked for the cat that had been there the longest. Out came Cali. Staffers said they didn't know how old Cali was—she'd come in as a stray. She was elderly, mostly toothless, deaf, and she'd been there for many months because no one had wanted her. But when Staub introduced herself to the "beautiful calico cat with huge green eyes," Cali instantly took to her, pushing up against her to be petted. "This made me smile for the first time in a while," she wrote on the cat adoption website Love Meow. Although Cali had trouble sleeping the first night, Staub reported that by the next day she was right at home, living in the lap of luxury for perhaps the first time in her life.

DESK JOB

In October 2020, when COVID-19 had forced millions of schoolkids to adapt to remote learning from home, one of the difficulties for many was the lack of a separate space for the student and their supplies. Faced with that issue, a building inspector named Mitchell Couch of Lemoore, California, decided to build a simple, yet functional, desk for his daughter. It didn't take the skilled carpenter too long, and the wood and hardware only cost about $20. He posted a photo of the desk on social media, and soon started to receive requests for directions. So Couch decided to make a YouTube tutorial, telling viewers: "You can get a sheet of plywood and...a few 2×4's to make the legs. Some glue and some nails and you put it together. They're super strong." Within hours of its upload, the tutorial "went crazy." Couch awoke to more than 200 requests for blueprints. Then a friend who owns a grocery store paid for enough supplies for Couch to build 40 desks, resulting in even more publicity. Within a few weeks, his tutorial had received 30,000 views, giving thousands of students a much-needed classroom away from home.

PASSING IT FORWARD

Allen took to social media to try and find the "nice guy named Dave" who "helped pull me out."

On January 12, 2019, a winter storm hammered Kansas City as the Chiefs players were trying to make their way to the stadium for an NFL playoff game. Offensive lineman Jeff Allen was navigating the icy roads when his truck got stuck in a snowbank. He tried pushing it out, but it wouldn't budge. And no one around could help him because they were all stuck as well. He was running out of time. That's when a stranger drove up in a Chevy Suburban. He parked safely on the shoulder and started pushing people's cars off the road. He ran over to Allen and started digging out the front tire, and before Allen knew it, his truck was free. He thanked the man, who said his name was Dave, and was back on the road. He got to the game on time, and the Chiefs won. Afterward, Allen took to social media to try

When Wendy's founder Dave Thomas finally earned his GED in 1993, his class voted him "Most Likely to Succeed."

and find the "nice guy named Dave" who "helped pull me out without knowing I was a player." He had free tickets to the upcoming AFC Championship game against the New England Patriots. The next day, Allen posted an update: "Despite the recent influx in people changing their name to Dave in the KC area lol, I was actually able to track down the Dave that helped me thanks to the power of social media and #ChiefsKingdom. Thanks for your kindness." The kind stranger, Dave Cochran, was bewildered at first. And his story touched a lot of people because, as it turned out, he lives in that Suburban, telling reporters, "That's right, I'm homeless." He said he would have helped Allen if he were a "normal person" and not a pro football player. But he's sure glad he did. He'd lived in Kansas City his whole life and had never been to a game. Now he got to see them play the NFL's most notorious team (the Chiefs lost in a nail-biter). Cochran told 41 Action News, "Call me soft if you want to, home boys, but I started bawling." After the story ran, the station reported that "people from all over the country are reaching out and asking, 'How can we help Dave?' " The *Kansas City Star* later reported that Cochran was a recovering addict and ex-convict who was already putting his life back together when the incident happened. The show of support overwhelmed him: "We've got a lot of caring, good-hearted people in Kansas City. I want to use this to build myself up. I want to give back."

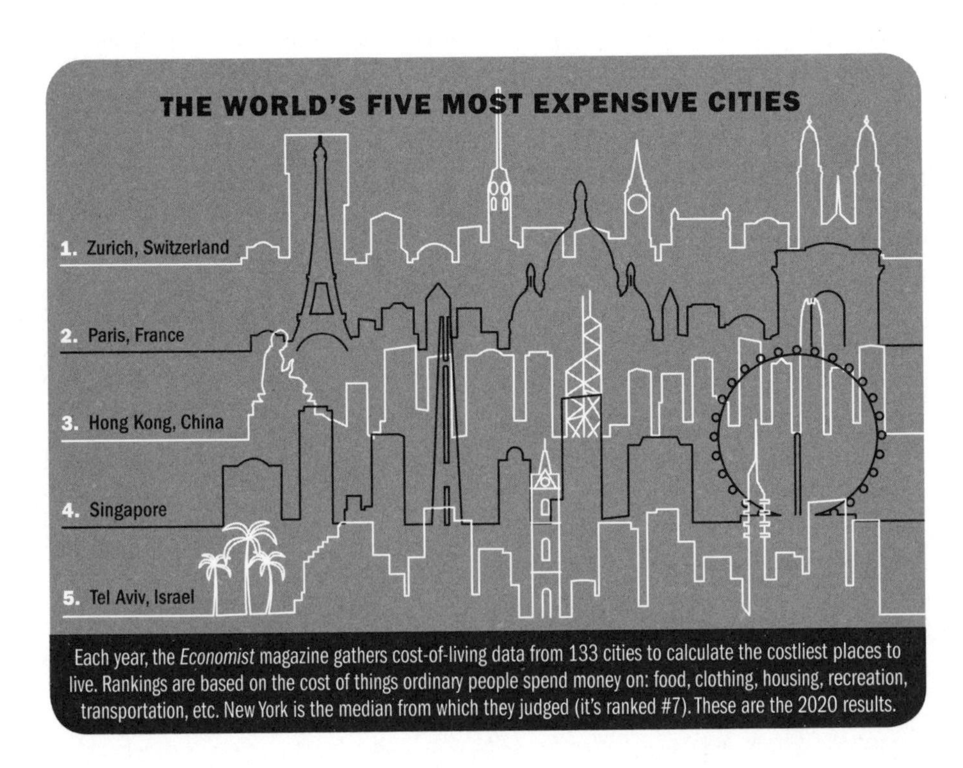

THE WORLD'S FIVE MOST EXPENSIVE CITIES
1. Zurich, Switzerland
2. Paris, France
3. Hong Kong, China
4. Singapore
5. Tel Aviv, Israel

Each year, the *Economist* magazine gathers cost-of-living data from 133 cities to calculate the costliest places to live. Rankings are based on the cost of things ordinary people spend money on: food, clothing, housing, recreation, transportation, etc. New York is the median from which they judged (it's ranked #7). These are the 2020 results.

BEFORE A/C WAS COOL

Have you ever wondered how people kept cool in their homes in the bad old days before air-conditioning? So did we. Here are some cooling features of old homes that most new houses don't have.

SHOTGUN HOUSES: Shotgun houses got their name from being one room wide the entire length of the house, usually no more than 12 feet across at any point. There's no hallway—the only way to move from one end of the house to the other was by walking through the rooms. Such simple construction meant it was possible to position the doors and windows on one side of the house so that they lined up with the doors and windows on the other side, maximizing the amount of cross ventilation and air circulation whenever there was a breeze. The front and rear doors and the doors connecting one room to another were also lined up, which may explain how the homes got their name—if all these doors were open, the joke went, you could fire a shotgun through the house without hitting anything. Shotgun houses were originally popular in both middle- and lower-class neighborhoods, particularly in Southern states, but they later fell out of favor and were stigmatized as "shotgun shacks"—houses fit for only the poorest of the poor.

THICK WALLS: Today, air-conditioning and central heating make it possible to build exterior walls cheaply, by constructing a lumber frame out of two-by-fours and covering this frame with a thin layer of exterior siding on the outside, and a thin layer of drywall on the inside. This leaves lots of hollow spaces—often filled with insulation—inside the walls. In the old days, it made more sense to build exterior walls out of brick or stone, and to make them good and thick. This was because brick and stone walls have a high *thermal mass,* which means that the materials can absorb a tremendous amount of heat without transferring it to the interior of the house. When the sun goes down, the walls slowly release the heat absorbed during the day back into the house, keeping it warmer on chilly nights than it would be otherwise. Bonus: brick and stone walls are also extremely fire-resistant.

WRAPAROUND PORCHES: For people who could afford larger homes, covered porches that wrapped around two or more sides of a house were popular. They provided plenty of extra space to sit outside when it was hot and stuffy inside. Also, the porches functioned like awnings and kept direct sunlight from shining in, making it less likely that the house would become that uncomfortable in the first place. Protection from sun and rain meant that windows could be kept open much of the time, allowing air to circulate inside the home.

Neil Armstrong took fabric and a piece of propeller from the Wright brothers' first airplane with him to the Moon.

TREES: Today, landscaping is something that is often considered separately from the construction of a house. Not so in the old days: because the Sun rises in the east and sets in the west, trees were often planted on the east and west sides of houses as they were being constructed, so that when the trees grew to maturity they would provide shade and prevent sunlight from striking large parts of the house. Bonus: When the trees shed their leaves in the fall, as the weather cooled and the need for shade disappeared, so did the shade itself—allowing sunlight to enter and warm the home in the colder, darker winter months.

ATTICS AND DORMER WINDOWS: Building an attic onto a home provided an unoccupied space for hot air to rise into, and it also protected occupants from the heat that radiated into the house when sunlight struck the roof. Putting openings in the roof in the form of dormers, cupolas, or even towers in really elaborate homes gave the hot air in the attic a means of exiting the house. As hot air flowed up and then out of a home, cooler air was pulled in through windows on the lower floors.

TRANSOM WINDOWS: Many older homes were built with higher ceilings than homes typically have today; this allowed hot air to rise above people's heads, where it was less noticeable. Transom windows, which were windows placed above doors, could be opened to allow this hot air to be blown out as cool evening breezes flowed into the house.

SLEEPING PORCHES: If you've ever lived by a lake, along a river, or by the sea, you know that being near a large body of water can really make the evenings cool and pleasant, even on hot summer days. (Large bodies of water absorb tremendous amounts of heat and have a moderating effect on the climate.) People living in warm climates preferred to sleep outside much of the year. Converting a portion of a wraparound porch into an open-air bedroom was common, as was designing and constructing homes with special enclosed balconies off the bedrooms on the second floor.

SHUTTERS: The exterior shutters on Uncle John's home, like those on a lot of homes built in the last 50 years, were purely decorative. They didn't open and close, so technically they weren't really shutters at all—they just *looked* like shutters. Real shutters are mounted on hinges and can be swung open and shut as needed. Closing them in the summer keeps the sunshine out and keeps interiors dark and cool. Louvered shutters allow air to pass through an open window without letting the sunshine in. Keeping shutters open in the winter lets in the sunshine when it's needed most. (What did Uncle John do about his shutters? He found the fact that they didn't do anything so annoying that when he had his house painted, he took them all down and threw them away.)

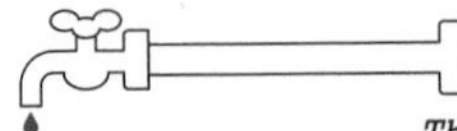

The Wolf of Wall Street, a movie about financial fraud, was financed using money stolen from the Malaysian government.

PORTRAIT OF AN ARTIST: PIERRE BRASSAU

Here's the story of an unknown abstract "artist" who put one over on the critics in the mid-1960s.

THE EYE OF THE BEHOLDER: Abstract art first appeared in the late 19th century. It was a style that broke from traditional imagery and did not attempt to depict subjects as they appear in the real world. Although the movement came to dominate the Western art world by the 1950s, it still wasn't everyone's cup of tea. Great works of abstract art are very sophisticated, and clearly demonstrate an artist's skill. But to some viewers, these works can seem simple, even primitive. An abstract painting, for example, may consist of little more than paintbrush strokes smeared seemingly at random across a canvas, and it can be difficult to distinguish between such a painting and the work of a child. Or at least that's what some skeptics of modern art argued. They questioned whether artists who produced such "simplistic" works had any real skill, and whether the artwork had any true artistic merit.

One such skeptic of abstract art was Åke "Dacke" Axelsson, a journalist who wrote for the Swedish tabloid newspaper *Göteborgs-Tidningen* in the mid-1960s. He wondered if art critics would be able to tell the difference between abstract paintings produced by skilled artists and those produced by someone who had never held a paintbrush before. He decided to find out.

THE ACID TEST: Axelsson commissioned several paintings from just such an inexperienced painter. He arranged for four of them to be shown alongside the work of legitimate abstract artists in an exhibition at an art gallery in Göteborg. To conceal the true origin of the paintings, Axelsson signed them himself, using the name "Pierre Brassau," whom he claimed was an abstract artist from France.

The exhibit was held, local art critics showed up, and not only were they unable to distinguish Pierre Brassau's work from those painted by real artists, at least one critic, Rolf Anderberg of the morning paper *Göteborgs-Posten*, said that Brassau's paintings were the best in the show. "Brassau paints with powerful strokes, but also with clear determination," Anderberg wrote. "His brush strokes twist with furious fastidiousness. Pierre is an artist who performs with the delicacy of a ballet dancer." A second critic hated Brassau's primitive style: "Only an ape could have done this," he observed.

Little did he know...

CREATURE FEATURE: Once the art critics' reviews were in, Axelsson revealed the true identity of Pierre Brassau—he was a four-year-old West African chimpanzee named Peter who lived in the zoo in Borås, Sweden. His painting style was primitive because he was a *primate*.

It had taken a bit of effort for Axelsson to teach Peter how to paint: when first presented with brushes, canvas, and paints, he sat on the canvas and ate the paint. (Cobalt blue was especially tasty.) But by coaxing Peter, giving him a few demonstrations, and rewarding his efforts with bananas, Axelsson eventually did teach the chimp to pick up the brushes, dab them in paint, and apply the paint to the canvas. Peter produced several paintings before Axelsson selected the four he thought were the most impressive and exhibited them at the gallery.

So how did the art critic Rolf Anderberg respond when he learned that the painter he'd praised so effusively was a chimpanzee? He replied that Peter's work was "still the best painting in the exhibition." He wasn't alone. An art collector snapped up one of the four paintings for $90, the equivalent of about $750 today. Two of Peter's paintings are still at the Borås zoo: they're hanging in the zoo offices and are shown to the public by appointment.

MONKEY SEE, MONKEY DO...

Peter isn't the only animal who learned how to paint. Here are three more examples:

- **Congo,** a chimpanzee living in the London Zoo in the mid-1950s. Congo was introduced to drawing with pen and paper at the age of two, and soon graduated to painting. Over the next two years he produced more than 400 drawings and paintings, many in a style that has been described as "lyrical abstract impressionism." Pablo Picasso was a fan and hung one of Congo's paintings in his studio. In 2005, three of the paintings sold for more than $25,000, about twenty times the estimated sale price.
- **Banghi,** a chimpanzee living in a zoo in Saxony-Anhalt in eastern Germany in 2005. Does this story sound familiar? One of Banghi's paintings was presented to the director of the State Art Museum, Dr. Katja Schneider, who mistook it for the work of the modernist painter Ernst Wilhelm Nay (1902–68), one of the most important German painters of the postwar period. Not many of Banghi's paintings survive: her mate Satscho often destroyed them as soon as she finished painting them.
- **Pigcasso,** a female pig rescued from a South African slaughterhouse in 2016. Joanne Lefson, Pigcasso's owner, says that when the pig came to live at the farm sanctuary she operates, the porker became fascinated with the paintbrushes used to paint the barn. Lefson showed her how to put paint on canvas, and she's been creating art ever since. Her paintings sell for as much as $4,000 apiece; in 2020, one of them was turned into a limited-edition Swatch wristwatch. "Pigcasso is definitely an abstract expressionist," Lefson says. "You can't exactly define what she's painting, but I can tell you that her style slightly changes depending on her mood, like any great artist."

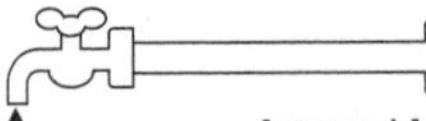

1st president to be photographed in office: William Henry Harrison (1841).
1st to have his voice recorded: his grandson, Benjamin Harrison (1889).

THE SHELL STATION

Read these facts about snails...very slowly.

- Snails are mollusks, which means they're shellfish, in the same family as clams and oysters. The largest mollusk group—comprising 80 percent of all mollusk species—are gastropods, or snails and slugs.
- What's the difference between a snail and a slug? The shell. A gastropod with a prominent outer shell is a snail; one without is a slug.
- As they age, snails don't abandon their old shells and grow new ones. Rather, the shell grows along with the rest of the snail, and they have it for their entire lives. (The reason you find empty snail shells in your garden is because predators eat only the soft tissue inside, and leave the inedible shell behind.)
- There are three types of snails: land snails, sea snails, and freshwater snails.
- Most land snails are hermaphroditic (meaning they have male and female parts)...but they still need to mate with another snail in order to breed.
- Land snails hatch from eggs. A newborn land snail's first meal? The shell of the egg from which it just hatched.
- Land snails secrete a layer of mucus that dries and covers their entire shells to help prevent the snail's soft tissue from drying out. It's called the *epiphragm.* That's also the main function of an anatomical structure called the *operculum,* found in many sea snails and freshwater snails. Centuries ago, people gathered operculums and used them (ground-up) in the production of incense.
- The mucus that doesn't prevent drying is spread on the ground as a snail travels. It helps them move, as they use it to glide across surfaces with the aid of a footlike appendage (called a "foot") that contracts and expands.
- Smallest land snail: *Angustopila dominikae.* It is around 0.03 inches tall, small enough to crawl through the eye of a needle.
- Largest land snail on record: the giant African land snail. It will top out at 15 inches long and weigh as much as two pounds.
- Snail shells are made primarily of calcium carbonate, making it molecularly nearly identical to limestone.

- Reason the common garden snail is so common: it breeds a *lot.* One snail may lay as many as 400 healthy eggs in a year. A single batch, or *clutch*, contains about 100 eggs, of which only half successfully hatch and produce baby snails.

- Common land snails have two sets of tentacles. The upper tentacles hold a snail's eyes, and the lower ones their olfactory organs, or smell receptors. One organ snails lack: ears, or any sort of hearing mechanism.

- Largest sea snail: the Australian trumpet. It can be as long as 35 inches and weigh around 40 pounds.

- Life span of a snail in the wild: two to five years. Life span of snails in captivity: as long as 15 years.

- Snails have a long, narrow tongue called a *radula* that's covered in thousands of tiny, jagged, toothlike nubs. Instead of chewing, it rips and shreds food into tiny bits that the snail can consume.

- Are snails really as slow as we think? Yes. Garden snails can crawl at a rate of 45 meters per hour. That's 0.027 miles per hour. At that pace, it would take a garden snail just under 12 years to crawl from Los Angeles to New York.

- The plough snail, a species of sea snail, is *much* faster. It can extend its foot out to work like a sail and ride the waves, or it can crawl along the ocean's surface at a lightning-fast 0.06 mph.

* * *

ART IMITATES LIFE

In 2020, curators at the British Library were scrolling through digitized historical texts from the early 1400s when they came across a painted scene that looked vaguely familiar. It depicted two men in a sword fight—one of the men's legs has fallen off, and he's using it as his sword. The other swordsman is using his own decapitated head as a shield. The bloody (and bizarre) confrontation is reminiscent of the classic scene in 1975's *Monty Python and the Holy Grail*, in which King Arthur (Graham Chapman) cuts off all the limbs of the Black Knight (John Cleese), setting up two of the most-quoted lines in movie history, "'Tis but a scratch!" and "It's only a flesh wound!" It's unlikely that the Pythons could have seen the ancient text, so it appears to be a case of art unknowingly imitating life. (What was their inspiration for the scene? They were poking fun at American director Sam Peckinpah's ultra-violent Westerns.)

CHALICE, TUMBLER, TANKARD & STEIN

Do you know the proper definitions of different types of drinking cups and other kinds of vessels? No? Well, bottoms up!

CHALICE/GOBLET: A goblet is any drinking cup that consists of a relatively large bowl attached to a stem and a foot, or base. A chalice is a special goblet, often of elaborate ornamental design, commonly used for religious and other ceremonial purposes, and usually to hold sacramental wine. Example: a chalice made from either gold or silver, and filled with wine symbolizing the blood of Christ, is used during the ritual of the Eucharist in Christian churches. A goblet, on the other hand, can hold any drink—hot or cold, alcoholic or nonalcoholic.

TUMBLER: A flat-bottomed drinking glass, usually with a heavy base. Tumblers can be tall or short, but perhaps the best known variety is the whiskey tumbler (also known as a rocks glass)—a short, broad, thin-walled, and heavy-based glass vessel made for sipping whiskey or whiskey-based drinks, often "on the rocks" (with ice cubes). Etymologists indicate that the term "tumbler" came about in the mid-17th century, referring to glasses with rounded bottoms. You had to empty your drink before putting the glass down, or it would tumble over and spill.

TANKARD: A tall, broad, one-handled, hinge-lidded drinking vessel, made from metal such as silver or pewter, often with a glass base. Tankards were popular with beer drinkers across northern Europe and in the British Isles from medieval times until the 18th century. (A beer stein is similar to a tankard, but is more commonly made of ceramic stoneware, elaborately designed, and associated with Germany. The tankard is more associated with Great Britain.)

Tankard Hall of Fame: The Langstone Tankard—a large vessel that was unearthed by a metal detector in a Langstone, Wales, bog in 2007. It is composed of six wooden staves held together by circular bronze bands—like a small barrel—with a copper handle. It held approximately four pints of beer or cider, or whatever its owners drank, and is roughly 2,000 years old.

FLUTE/TULIP/COUPE: There are three primary types of stemmed glasses used for drinking champagne. The coupe, also known as a champagne saucer, is a short-stemmed glass with a wide and shallow bowl. The flute has a tall, narrow body with straight or nearly straight sides and a narrow opening. And the tulip is a sort of combination of the other two, with a tall profile like the flute but with a wider,

rounded body, and a larger opening than the flute. (A champagne tower is a pyramid-shaped construction made up of several levels of champagne glasses stacked upon each other until there is a single glass at the top. Often seen at ceremonies such as weddings, they are made using champagne coupes.)

CARAFE: A tall container, usually made of glass, typically used for pouring water or wine. There is no standard design for carafes—except that they are without handles and are most commonly the size and shape of wine bottles, but with larger openings for easy pouring.

SNIFTER: Also known as a brandy glass, a cognac glass, or a balloon glass, a snifter has a short stem and a large, rounded bowl with a narrow opening. You hold the bowl of the glass in your hand, transferring heat from your hand to the liquid inside, and the design of the bowl traps the aromas of the drink for the nose to enjoy while sipping the drink. It's most commonly used for distilled spirits such as brandy, cognac, and whiskey, but is also used for strong beers.

DECANTER: A tall glass container (often crystal glass) with a wide or even bulbous body and a narrow neck, used to decant wine for serving. Wine is carefully poured from a bottle into a decanter, leaving any sediment from the wine in the bottle, allowing only the "clear" wine to be served. Decanting also allows wine to aerate, or breathe, meaning the wine is exposed to oxygen, which enhances the taste of certain wines, and also softens the sharpness of more astringent wines. Decanters often come with stoppers, usually also made of glass, to seal the decanter for the storage of wine that is not consumed. (Decanters are also used to store distilled spirits, such as whiskey and brandy.)

FLASK: When you hear the word "flask," you might think of a laboratory flask. The most common of those is an Erlenmeyer flask, with a wide, round base, tapering sides, and a narrow cylindrical neck. But there's another kind of flask: the hip flask—a small, flat-bodied container made of pewter or glass, that holds a small amount of liquor. The earliest known portable alcohol container—from ancient Greece—was the wineskin, made from an animal bladder and cured with beeswax. The modern version was "invented" by 19th-century soldiers who realized that the metal container they carried gunpowder in could also carry alcohol. The hip flask was favored by the wealthy until Prohibition took effect in the U.S. in 1920. As soon as the sale of alcohol became illegal, sales of hip flasks skyrocketed to the point that some states banned them. They're curved so they fit the contour of the human body, and are thus easier to conceal.

* * *

"To succeed in life, you need three things: a wishbone, a backbone, and a funny bone."

—Reba McEntire

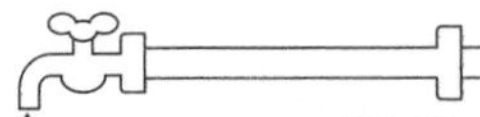

Worldwide, in 1800, only 50 cities had more than 100,000 people.
Today in China alone, there are more than 100 cities with a population over one million.

AFTERLIFE IN PRISON

As if the idea of prisons isn't scary enough, some of the world's oldest and most imposing penitentiaries are also rumored to be occupied by ghosts. Whether you believe in ghosts or not, the stories can make for interesting reading.

FACILITY: Eastern State Penitentiary, Philadelphia, Pennsylvania (1829–1971)
DETAILS: Eastern was one of the strictest prisons in history when it opened its doors in 1829. Upon arrival, prisoners were hooded and then sent to their cells, where they'd spend 23 hours a day alone and in total silence. When they were out of their cells, they wore their hoods and were not allowed to communicate with other inmates.
GHOST STORIES: Prison locksmith Gary Johnson claims to have seen spectral figures of prisoners several times, and on one occasion, he says, one of them reached out and tried to grab him. Inmate Joseph Taylor, who bludgeoned a guard to death in 1884, can supposedly still be spotted wandering the grounds. Legendary gangster Al Capone served eight months at Eastern in 1929; he is said to have asked a guard to help him get rid of the ghost that wouldn't leave his cell—one of the victims of the St. Valentine's Day massacre that Capone orchestrated.

FACILITY: Alcatraz Federal Penitentiary, San Francisco, California (1934–1963)
DETAILS: Alcatraz is an isolated concrete behemoth set on an island in the middle of San Francisco Bay. Today "the Rock" is operated by the National Park Service and is open for tours.
GHOST STORY: The inmates are long gone, but the ghosts may still be around. In 2010, a team from the TV show *Ghost Hunters* captured what it says are recordings of an eerie human whisper. The whisper says something like "Harry Brunette 374"—the name and prisoner number of a bank robber who did time on the Rock. A team from the TV show *Ghost Lab* captured what they claim is another human voice in the prison's lowest level of basement cells, nicknamed "the Dungeon," calling out "I want you" and "I got you now." Tourists visiting the prison have reported hearing a woman crying in the Dungeon. Their accounts are all very similar: they say the crying suddenly stops, followed by a cold wind sweeping through the area.

FACILITY: Idaho State Penitentiary, Boise, Idaho (1872–1973)
DETAILS: One of the most infamous of the Idaho State Penitentiary's 13,000 total residents was a man named Raymond Allen Snowden, nicknamed "Idaho's Jack the Ripper." In 1956, he murdered a woman named Cora Dean after a tussle, stabbing her 35 times. Convicted of that murder, Snowden confessed to more killings but was sent to the gallows in October 1957 before he could be tried for those crimes. Prison

authorities botched his execution: the noose didn't break his neck, and Snowden was slowly strangled for 15 minutes before he finally perished.

GHOST STORY: Since the prison was decommissioned and converted into a museum in 1973, many guests have reported hearing the ghostly gasps of a man unable to breathe near where Snowden died. He may also haunt the cigar store in downtown Boise near where he ditched the knife he used to murder Cora Dean, and which was used to convict him at his trial. The owner of the cigar store has reported hearing ghostly footsteps that he believes are Snowden's.

FACILITY: Burlington County Prison, Mt. Holly Township, New Jersey (1811–1965)

DETAILS: Robert Mills designed the Washington Monument as well as New Jersey's Burlington County Prison, a gray brick institution that opened in 1811 and was America's oldest operating prison when it closed in 1965.

Visitors claim to have spotted unexplainable green orbs floating in the air.

GHOST STORY: Since opening to the public in 1966, the prison (now a museum) has been beset with all kinds of strange events and possible paranormal activity. Visitors claim to have spotted unexplainable green orbs floating in the air, and when the facility was renovated in the 1990s, construction workers reported tools disappearing, then showing up later in locked cells. The earliest reported ghostly event at the prison dates back to 1833. Convicted murderer Joel Clough spent his last night alive in a solitary confinement cell, and then after his execution, he was buried in the prison yard. A few days later, guards and prisoners heard odd sounds coming out of the solitary confinement cell where Clough was last seen alive, such as moaning and chain rattling, along with the smell of Clough's cigarette.

FACILITY: Ohio State Reformatory, Mansfield, Ohio (1896–1990)

DETAILS: This prison is so intimidating that it was used as the grim backdrop for the 1994 movie *The Shawshank Redemption.*

GHOST STORY: Late at night, the sounds of unoccupied cell doors flinging open, and the sad cries of the imprisoned, are said to be a common occurrence. Visitors checking out the prison's chapel have reported the sensation of feeling grabbed even though nobody is there, while the facility's former offices are the place to hear spooky footsteps, human murmurs...and see shadows of human figures when there are no living people around to cast them.

RANDOM FACT

The summit of Mt. Everest has about as much area as two ping-pong tables.

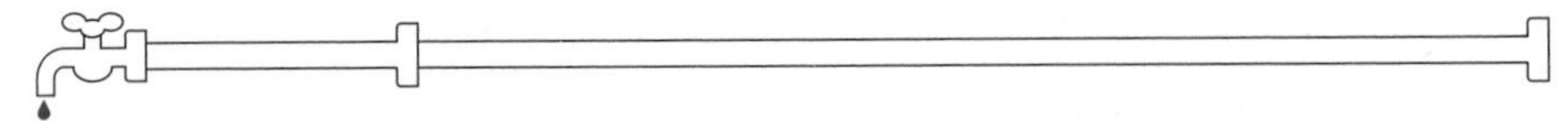

"ACTION-PACKED STORIES!"

There's nothing like flipping through a crisp, new comic book to make you feel like a kid again—that glossy cover featuring your favorite superhero in peril; the cheap, pulpy pages; the speech balloons' distinctive, hand-scripted, italicized text; and each panel advancing the narrative in a way that only comic books can. Now it's time to pull the covers over your head, turn on your flashlight, and read about the visionary writers and artists—and the guileless businessmen—who brought us the characters that have come to dominate popular culture.

WHO INVENTED THE COMIC BOOK?

The origin of the comic book isn't quite as dramatic as a bite from a radioactive spider, nor was it as quick. In fact, an entire century elapsed between the 1837 publication that historians call the first comic book and the first one that included *all* the essential elements—*Action Comics #1,* issued in 1938, which introduced Superman and ushered in the Golden Age of Comic Books. In between, the art form grew up in spits and spurts in newspapers, pulp magazines, and dime novels. Here's how this indomitable 20th-century art form came to life.

INNOVATION: A book that consists solely of illustrations in boxes (later called "panels"), with several per page, each one with a caption that keeps the story going
Origin: *Histoire de M. Vieux Bois* (1837), by Swiss caricaturist Rodolphe Töpffer
Story: In 1827, Töpffer invented the single-panel cartoon—a simple drawing inside a square border anchored by a humorous caption. Originally created as gifts, his "little follies" were adored by his friends, including writer Johann Wolfgang von Goethe, who liked Töpffer's *Faust* parody (called *Dr. Festus*) so much that he helped convince the reluctant artist to publish a collection. Considered the first comic book, *Histoire de M. Vieux Bois* was instantly popular throughout Europe...and widely imitated, often even plagiarized. When it was translated into English, it was retitled *The Adventures of Mr. Obadiah Oldbuck* and sold in the United States from the 1840s to the 1870s, where Töpffer inspired a new crop of cartoonists.

INNOVATION: A larger-than-life folk hero on newsprint
Origin: The modern version of Santa Claus, created by Thomas Nast in the 1860s
Story: It might seem like a stretch to connect Santa Claus to Superman, but when you think about it, they have a lot in common: Both wear strange costumes and fly around the world at great speeds. Heroes of the working class, both were used as recruiting tools—Santa for the Union Army in the Civil War, and Superman for the Allies in World War II.

During Nast's 25-year stint at *Harper's Weekly*—which included the Civil War and the Reconstruction era—he invented the political cartoon. His pro-Union, abolitionist

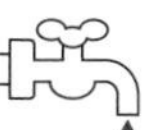

stance helped elect Presidents Abraham Lincoln and Ulysses S. Grant, and his anti-corruption crusade helped take down the powerful "Tweed Ring," the group of politicians, led by William "Boss" Tweed, that controlled New York City in the 1860s.

Nast based his Santa Claus on a Dutch gift-giving folk hero called Sinterklaas, who was derived from the third-century Greek "protector of children" Saint Nicholas. Unlike the stodgy, Old World versions of St. Nick, Nast drew Santa as a jolly old man with a red suit, red cheeks, a white beard, and a sack of presents who lives at the North Pole (down the street from Superman's Fortress of Solitude?).

So when it comes to the evolution of the comic book, Nast not only established the newspaper cartoon as a reputable art form, he showed that when times are dark, Americans would eagerly rally around a hero.

INNOVATIONS: Recurring characters, merchandising tie-ins, and speech balloons
Origin: The Yellow Kid
Story: The first newspaper comic strip to feature recurring characters was *The Little Bears,* which ran from 1893 to 1897. But the first recurring character to really catch on was the Yellow Kid, who appeared in Richard Outcault's cartoon *Hogan's Alley.* This oddball New York City slum boy debuted in Joseph Pulitzer's *New York World* in 1894. Two years later, *New York Journal* owner William Randolph Hearst hired Outcault away at a much higher salary. The rivalry between the moguls helped make the Yellow Kid a sensation. The first comic character with a line of merchandising, his simplistic catchphrases—such as "Well Hully gee, here's to you"—were printed en masse on gum and cigarette packets and toys. He was even the main character in the first publication ever to be called a "comic book": 1897's *The Yellow Kid in McFadden's Flats,* a 196-page book made of cheap "pulp" paper that consisted of black-and-white reprints of *Hogan's Alley.*

INNOVATION: Panels of various shapes and sizes
Origin: *Little Nemo in Slumberland,* created by Winsor McCay
Story: By the turn of the century, the artistry of the comic strip was steadily evolving. One of the most influential was *Little Nemo,* about a boy whose nightly slumbers are filled with fantastical dreams. The strip debuted in the *New York Herald* in 1905, and then, as he had done with *Hogan's Alley* a few years earlier, William Randolph Hearst purchased it for the *New York American* in 1911. Winsor McCay was one of the first comic strip artists to vary the size of his panels to improve pacing; he'd sometimes make the middle panel a large circle. In fact, his full-page, color strips look more like they belong in a comic book than a newspaper. Among those influenced by *Nemo* were future Superman cocreators Jerry Siegel and Joe Shuster. (Also a pioneer of animation, McCay made a 1914 short, *Gertie the Dinosaur,* considered the first true cartoon.) In 1912, another New York newspaper, the *Evening Journal,* became the first one to dedicate an entire page to comic strips. The rest would soon follow suit.

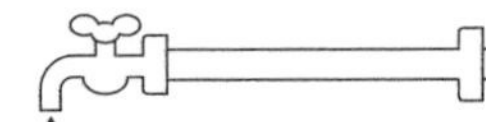

INNOVATION: The first comic character with super strength
Origin: *Hugo Hercules* (1902), created by Wilhelm Heinrich Detlev Körner, which ran for five months in the *Chicago Tribune*'s "Sunday Funnies"
Story: Imagine Clark Kent, but without the Superman costume. That was Hugo Hercules. The 17 strips that Körner drew featured the good-natured Hugo using his super strength to impress people—mostly girls—and occasionally to help those in need. The strange strip didn't really catch on (and Körner quit the comics to become a painter), but *Hugo Hercules* did reach a lot of readers. And it foreshadowed one of comicdom's most enduring images: a man lifting a car over his head.

INNOVATION: Comic strips in a standalone book
Origin: *Funnies on Parade*, a collection of color reprints of popular strips
Story: While working at Eastern Color Printing in Waterbury, Connecticut, in 1933, Max Gaines was tossing out some Sunday newspaper inserts when he stopped to read the comic strips. That gave him an idea: What if these unused broadsheets were bound into a small booklet? He shared his idea with the sales manager, Harry Wildenberg, who immediately saw dollar signs. The result: *Funnies on Parade*—32 pages of color reprints of strips like *Keeping Up with the Joneses, Mutt and Jeff*, and *Joe Palooka.* Wildenberg sold the booklets in bulk to companies like Kinney Shoes and Canada Dry beverages, which used them as giveaways for sending in a proof of purchase. Though still not a true comic book, *Funnies on Parade* was the first publication to start to look like one.

INNOVATION: Comic books sold in retail stores
Origin: *Famous Funnies*, another collection of comic strip reprints
Story: A year later, in 1934, Eastern Color Printing partnered with Dell Comics (which had been printing comic book–like Sunday inserts for newspapers since 1929) to produce *Famous Funnies: A Carnival of Comics.* At 36 pages, it was the first comic book made especially for retail. (They were sold at Woolworth's.) The first print run was 35,000, and it sold out in a few days.

INNOVATION: Modern comic book dimensions and issue numbers
Origin: *New Fun #1*, a "BIG COMIC MAGAZINE" featuring a strip about a cowboy called Jack Woods on the cover, important to collectors as the very first issue from the company that would become DC Comics
Story: Comic books were successful, and with success comes competition. Result: Depression-weary Americans, ever on the lookout for cheap entertainment, suddenly had a lot of comic books to choose from—although they were still just reprints of previously published comic strips. That would soon change. Of the dozens of fledgling comic book publishers that popped up, none had a greater impact than Malcolm Wheeler-Nicholson's National Allied Publications, which released *New Fun #1* in 1935.

New Fun was the first comic book to have (close to) the dimensions that are still used today: 6⅝ inches wide by 10¼ inches high. It's also among the first with an issue number. This practice came from two predecessors of the comic book—dime novels and pulp magazines, which used open-ended sequential numbering, rather than the periodic volume numbers of newspapers and magazines. The assumption of open-ended numbering was that collectors would know that they had every issue. (Unintended benefit: Early issues could become worth a lot of money.)

INNOVATION: Original material
Origin: *New Fun #1*
Story: Most importantly, *New Fun #1* was the first comic book to consist of all-new material. This wasn't because the publisher, Wheeler-Nicholson, was a visionary—he was simply too late to purchase the rights to any existing comic strips. So he hired young writers and artists (for less money) to create original stories. But those early comic books—featuring little-known characters like Don Nogales, Cattle Rustler, and gas station pals Jigger and Ginger—failed to entice newsstand owners to replace the popular (and profitable) *Famous Funnies*. For his books to succeed, Wheeler-Nicholson was going to need some better material.

INNOVATION: Superheroes
Origin: "The Reign of the Superman," a short story by 17-year-old Jerry Siegel
Story: In the 1930s, with the Great Depression in full swing and fascism on the rise in Europe, America was in need of a hero. The unlikely duo that delivered it were two best friends, writer Jerry Siegel and illustrator Joe Shuster. Like Thomas Nast, their families had fled persecution in Europe. The two Ohio teens met in high school and bonded over a mutual love of fantasy and science-fiction characters like Little Nemo, Buck Rogers, and Flash Gordon, and pulp magazines like *Amazing Stories* and *Weird Tales.*

In his first incarnation, the Man of Steel was a bald villain with superpowers.

In his first incarnation, called "The Reign of the Superman," the Man of Steel was a bald villain with superpowers. His name was lifted from George Bernard Shaw's 1903 play "Man and Superman" (itself inspired by Friedrich Nietzsche's philosophy of the *Übermensch*, or "Superman"). Siegel and Shuster developed the character into a newspaper comic strip, but editors weren't interested, so they remade "The Superman" in the vein of two of their favorite characters: a good guy, like Tarzan, but with super strength, like Popeye. Superman continued to evolve, but neither newspaper editors nor comic book publishers showed much interest. One rejection letter from Tip Top Comics called Superman "an attractive idea because of its freshness and naïvité, but still a rather immature piece of work."

As Siegel and Shuster refined the character, they were also defining what the comic book would become: "I tried to incorporate what was so popular in the pulp

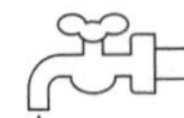

field into the comics field," explained Siegel. "I used a great number of captions along with dialogue balloons, visualizing the way a pulp comic should be. I feel now that we were pioneering, and that much of the stuff that followed was influenced by the way we handled our very early work, like Slam Bradley, especially." Who's Slam Bradley? A larger-than-life character who fights crime.

INNOVATION: Larger-than-life characters who fight crime
Origin: *Detective Comics #1* (1937), which boasted on the cover: "Brand-new! Action-packed Stories in Color!"
Story: Comic books still weren't taking off. One reason: They were just newspaper comic strips bound together in a booklet that featured mostly benign characters, a far cry from the hard-boiled detectives of dime novels, which always sold well. But there was one comic strip character that brought the pulp to newsprint: Dick Tracy, a detective created by Chester Gould that debuted in the *Detroit Mirror* in 1931. Although Dick Tracy would eventually get his own comic book (featuring reprints of the strips), he's always been known primarily as a newspaper character.

Over at National Allied, Malcolm Wheeler-Nicholson hired young writers and illustrators, including Siegel and Shuster, to create Dick Tracy–esque characters. Like every other editor, Wheeler-Nicholson had rejected Superman, who didn't fit in with his new line, *Detective Comics.* He did like Slam Bradley, though. The fist-fighting private eye, created by Siegel and Shuster, was the forerunner of Superman in many ways—strong, clever, and always looking out for the little guy. Another Siegel-and-Shuster creation: Doctor Occult, a mad scientist with special powers who actually predates Superman as the first true superhero to appear in a comic book.

Wheeler-Nicholson, it turned out, wasn't a very good businessman. Mired in debt, he lost control of his own company before *Detective Comics #1* hit newsstands in March 1937. The men who drove him out: his partner, Jack Liebowitz, and his distributor, Harry Donenfeld. They changed the name of the company to National Comics Publications and came up with the idea for a new line called *Action Comics.* Now they just needed some comics with action.

According to legend, an editor named Sheldon Mayer was standing next to Max Gaines at National Comics, looking through a pile of unused strips, when he stopped on Superman. Mayer instantly fell in love with it. Gaines was also a fan, but he'd been unable to sell Superman to newspapers. Gaines took the completed comic strips upstairs to show to Donenfeld...who hated them. The character, he said, was "too fantasy" for his tastes. But they needed pages, and Donenfeld agreed that a cover featuring a caped man lifting a car over his head might be good for sales. Boy, was he in for a surprise.

What happened next? Fly over to page 305 to find out! (If you can't fly, take your invisible jet.)

The first time President Zachary Taylor ever voted was in 1848, when he voted for himself for president. (He won.)

MYTH-CONCEPTIONS

"Common knowledge" is frequently wrong. Here are some examples of things that many people believe...but according to our sources, just aren't true.

MYTH: The official residence of Britain's prime minister is 10 Downing Street in London.
TRUTH: Technically, that is the address of the official living quarters provided to the First Lord of the Treasury, not the prime minister. They are two separate and distinct positions...although by tradition, the same person holds both offices simultaneously.

MYTH: On average, humans accidentally swallow about eight spiders a year. (They crawl into our mouths while we sleep.)
TRUTH: In 1993, a writer named Lisa Birgit Holst wrote an article for *PC Professional* about how it's incredibly easy to spread misinformation, positing that if a fact is interesting enough, people will share and reprint it without verifying if it's true or not. As an example, Holst cites the "fact" that humans swallow eight spiders a year. Turns out it's a made-up fact, as is "Lisa Birgit Holst"—an anagram for "this is a big troll."

MYTH: Ohio has been a state since 1803, one of the first to join the union after the original colonies.
TRUTH: Statehood was approved by the Ohio state convention in 1802, and in 1803, Congress and President Thomas Jefferson did approve the action. Only thing: Congress skipped a necessary part of the statehood process—it never ratified the state's constitution. It wasn't until 1953, when the state was celebrating its sesquicentennial (its 150th birthday), that some teachers researching documents related to statehood noticed the discrepancy. That year, on August 7, Congress finally passed a law that officially made Ohio a state.

MYTH: Clinical depression is caused by a chemical imbalance, specifically a low level of serotonin in the brain.
TRUTH: There's no evidence that depression has anything to do with serotonin. Neuroscientists actually aren't sure what, physically, causes the condition, or how antidepressant drugs alleviate it.

MYTH: According to Greek mythology, the world's evils were unleashed after Pandora opened a forbidden box where all the bad stuff had been restrained.
TRUTH: The idea (and the phrase) "Pandora's box" is the result of a mistranslation. According to the ancient Greek writer Hesiod in *Works and Days*, Pandora was the first

human woman and gave the world all of its problems by opening a cursed *pithos*, or a large jar. When the Dutch scholar Erasmus translated the Pandora myth into Latin in the 16th century, he changed the Greek *pithos* to the Latin *pyxis*, which means "box."

MYTH: Capping the Cold War–era "Space Race," the United States beat the Soviet Union to the Moon when *Apollo 11* touched down on the lunar surface in July 1969.
TRUTH: The Soviets won the early stages of the Space Race. They were first to launch a satellite (*Sputnik* in 1957), first to send a man into space (Yuri Gagarin in 1961), and first to reach the Moon, too. In February 1966—more than three years before American astronauts Neil Armstrong and Buzz Aldrin made it there—the USSR's unmanned *Luna 9* became the first spacecraft to successfully land on the Moon.

MYTH: Michael Jordan, regarded by many as the greatest basketball player of all time, didn't make his high school basketball team.
TRUTH: Although Jordan's experience is often used as an encouraging example of why a person should keep trying and never give up on their dreams, it's not true. In 1978, sophomore Michael Jordan tried out for the varsity squad at Emsley A. Laney High School in Wilmington, North Carolina, and didn't make the varsity team. But not because he wasn't good enough—coaches picked Leroy Smith over Jordan because Smith was nine inches taller. Also, the varsity team was reserved for upperclassmen (like Smith), not sophomores (like Jordan). The future superstar spent the season on the junior varsity team, and a year later, as a junior, he made varsity.

MYTH: The logo of the Walt Disney Company is founder Walt Disney's actual signature.
TRUTH: Many examples of Disney's signature remain from various company documents, and it varies wildly, mostly because the busy executive authorized assistants to sign contracts and forms on his behalf. But even the real Disney signature evolved over time. The "Walt Disney" used by the company today dates to 1984, nearly 20 years after Walt Disney (the person) died—it's a stylized, artist-rendered version of Walt's signature from the 1940s.

* * *

HISTORY QUIZ

Q: Why is the following sentence so important? "The one of Ombos has handed over the two realms to his son, the King of Upper and Lower Egypt, Peribsen."

A: According to linguists, these words—written in hieroglyphs and discovered in the nearly 5,000-year-old tomb of an Egyptian monarch named Seth-Peribsen—comprise the earliest known full sentence ever written down.

Athletes who finish 4th through 8th place in the Olympics receive a paper "Olympic diploma," but no medal.

WHEN GOOD PIPES GO BAD

Plumbing is like a lot of modern conveniences: you don't appreciate how good you've got it until something goes wrong.

UP IN THE AIR

In January 2018, a Norwegian Airlines flight took off from Oslo, bound for Munich, Germany. Just 20 minutes into the journey, the toilets all malfunctioned, forcing the plane to turn back. It wasn't the first time a flight has had to return to the airport because of a plumbing issue, but what made this incident unusual was the fact that there were 85 plumbers aboard the flight, on their way to a plumbers' convention. There wasn't much they could do: "We would have liked to fix the restrooms, but unfortunately it had to be done from the outside," Frank Olsen, head of the plumbing company Rørkjøp joked to Norway's *Dagbladet* newspaper. "We did not take the opportunity to send the plumber out."

After landing in Oslo, the toilets were fixed (by a maintenance crew working for the airline, not the plumbers on the plane) and the flight departed again, finally arriving in Munich 3½ hours late. "So many plumbers on an aircraft and it has to turn back due to toilet trouble," said plumber Hans Christian Ødegård. "It's enough to make you laugh."

DOWN BELOW

In 2019, the Louis Armstrong New Orleans International Airport had to push back its plans to open its new $1.3 billion airport terminal building from February to May. It was the third time that the opening—originally scheduled for May 2018—had been delayed. Latest reason: Inspectors found 126 ruptures in the brand-new, never-used sewer lines that ran beneath the terminal building.

If you've ever been to New Orleans, you know that it's a low-lying, swampy kind of place. That's because almost all of the city is at or below sea level. For this reason, the airport's building engineers expected anything set into the soil would sink, or "subside," as it's called in the industry, as the soil compressed. The terminal building sat atop hundreds of giant pilings that had been driven deep into the ground, so it was not going to subside. But the sewer pipes laid in the dirt beneath the foundation might, if nothing were done to prevent it. So they did something: The pipes were secured to the foundation using steel straps called "hangers." Only problem: instead of attaching the $6 hangers every *two* feet along the pipe as the building inspector, James Mohamad, had advised, the building contractor got approval to save $22,000 in materials, plus the installation cost, by installing the hangers every *three* feet. That

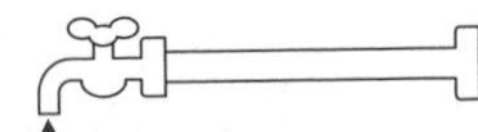

may not sound like much of a difference, but it was enough to cause the sewer pipes to rupture in 126 places as soon as the soil began to subside.

The only solution: cut giant holes into the concrete foundation and repair each break in the pipe. "We warned them what was going to happen," Mohamad told WWJ-TV News. "They're spending more money in repairs than if they would have listened to us from the get-go." The terminal building finally opened in November 2019, eighteen months behind schedule...and more than $300 million over budget.

UP AND DOWN THE STREET

One of the more irrational—and yet somehow understandable—responses to the outbreak of the 2020 COVID-19 pandemic was the way people in many parts of the world hoarded toilet paper. Nowhere in the world did this make less sense than in the United States, which manufactures nearly all of its own TP domestically. Global trade slowed to a crawl? International borders sealed? Still gotta go to the bathroom? Not a problem, because your TP comes from any one of dozens of paper mills operating inside the United States. But the rolls still disappeared from store shelves as hoarders stocked up. Many people who ran out of TP after the hoarding started couldn't find it anywhere.

What followed was what the *New York Times* called a "coast-to-coast surge in backed-up sewer lines and overflowing toilets," as people made do with whatever was on hand—napkins, paper towels, and coffee filters, plus all those "flushable" disinfecting wipes used to sanitize doorknobs and countertops—then flushed them down their toilets. Plumbing systems aren't engineered to handle these items, no matter how similar they may appear to toilet paper, which breaks down into non-clogging paper fibers as soon as it gets wet.

"Toilets are not trash cans," the Environmental Protection Agency tweeted in March 2020, at the height of the crisis. "Please remember napkins, paper towels, and so-called 'flushable' wipes can all clog your pipes." The problem resolved itself within a few weeks as soon as toilet paper returned to store shelves and the non-hoarders got a chance to buy it again.

ALL OVER THE PLACE

In 1993, a man named Jack Charles Du Mars and his wife, Rosanne Irving, bought a 19th-century brick mansion in the small town of Moravia, in the Finger Lakes region of upstate New York. It was a beautiful old three-story building, built in the Second Empire style at the end of the Civil War. But it needed work. Du Mars and Irving set about the task of fixing up the place and turning it into a home that they could live in when they retired.

Only Disney Princess with a star on the Hollywood Walk of Fame: Snow White.

Everything went smoothly...until one cold day when they turned on the building's antiquated steam heating system, and pipes burst all over the house. Steam and water went everywhere, destroying the ceilings and walls on all three floors as well as in the basement. There was so much water damage that the entire building had to be gutted down to the bare studs, though the wood floors and stairwells survived.

"That set us back in a different direction," Du Mars told NewYorkUpstate.com. "When we purchased the property, we weren't counting on having it stripped down to its bare bones and have to rebuild it." Nonetheless, they held on to the house until 2020...then threw in the towel and put the place up for sale. Asking price: $75,000, making it one of the cheapest mansions for sale anywhere in America. Are you in the market for a fixer-upper? This gutted edifice could be yours. All it needs is walls, ceilings, plumbing, wiring...

* * *

NOT-SO-DUMB PREDICTIONS

In 1964, science-fiction author Isaac Asimov envisioned life in 2014.

- "Robots will neither be common nor very good in 2014, but they will be in existence."
- There will be "few routine jobs that cannot be done better by some machine than by any human being. Mankind will therefore have become largely a race of machine tenders."
- "By 2014, only unmanned ships will have landed on Mars, though a manned expedition will be in the works."
- "As for television, wall screens will have replaced the ordinary set."
- "Communications will become sight-sound and you will see as well as hear the person you telephone. The screen can be used not only to see the people you call but also for studying documents and photographs and reading passages from books."
- "Vehicles with 'Robot-brains'...can be set for particular destinations...without interference by the slow reflexes of a human driver."
- "Not all the world's population will enjoy the gadgety world of the future to the full. A larger portion than today will be deprived and although they may be better off, materially, than today, they will be further behind when compared with the advanced portions of the world. They will have moved backward, relatively."
- *One prediction that Asimov (and everyone else) got wrong:* "There will be increasing emphasis on transportation that makes the least possible contact with the surface. There will be aircraft, of course, but even ground travel will increasingly take to the air a foot or two off the ground."

VIDEO TREASURES: DIRECT-TO-DVD

Before the pandemic of 2020, when a movie skipped a theatrical release and headed straight to DVD or other home viewing formats, it was a signal that the film wasn't very good. But that wasn't always true. Here are some gems that, for whatever reason, never got a chance to shine on the big screen. So if you're looking for something offbeat to stream, give these a look.

I COULD NEVER BE YOUR WOMAN (2007)

Starring: Michelle Pfeiffer, Paul Rudd, Tracey Ullman, and Saoirse Ronan in her feature film debut

Plot: Mother Nature (Ullman) helps an older professional woman (Pfeiffer) find love with a younger man (Rudd) as she's trying to guide her 13-year-old daughter Izzie (Ronan) through adolescence.

Details: The film was written and directed by Amy Heckerling, who also directed the 1982 coming-of-age hit *Fast Times at Ridgemont High.* To keep the film's budget under control, Michelle Pfeiffer accepted a reduced salary in exchange for a healthy chunk of the film's gross profits. But MGM Studios, which had a deal to distribute some of Heckerling's films, backed out of distributing this one because it didn't want to share the profits with Pfeiffer. No other studios were interested, so it went straight to a DVD release. MGM filed for bankruptcy in 2010.

RIPLEY'S GAME (2002)

Starring: John Malkovich, Dougray Scott, Ray Winstone, and Lena Headey

Plot: When an associate from the Berlin underworld asks Tom Ripley to kill a rival, Ripley recommends a dying art-framer for the job.

Details: If you enjoyed Matt Damon's performance in *The Talented Mr. Ripley* (1999), here's your chance to see John Malkovich playing the same character. Film critic Roger Ebert called *Ripley's Game* his favorite Ripley film; he considered the film's straight-to-DVD release as "a shameful blunder." This movie is the second film adaptation of the 1974 Patricia Highsmith novel *Ripley's Game*; the first was the 1977 film *The American Friend*, starring Dennis Hopper and Bruno Ganz.

RED ROCK WEST (1993)

Starring: Nicolas Cage, Lara Flynn Boyle, J. T. Walsh, and Dennis Hopper

Plot: A contemporary "Western film noir" movie about a drifter (Cage) who wanders into the small town of Red Rock, Wyoming. There he's mistaken for a hit man, "Lyle from Dallas," whom a local bartender (Walsh) has hired to murder his wife (Boyle). After taking money to do the hit and warning the wife that her husband is trying to have her killed, the drifter attempts to flee town, only to run into the real Lyle from Dallas, who has just arrived.

Details: The film generated some buzz at the Toronto International Film Festival, but because it wasn't quite a Western, and wasn't quite film noir either, Columbia TriStar decided not to risk an expensive theatrical release for fear that it might never find an audience. It was sent straight to HBO and home video instead. One art-house theater owner in San Francisco was so impressed with *Red Rock West* when he saw it in Toronto that he showed it at his own theater. It went on to have limited runs in Los Angeles and New York City, but it was never shown in theaters anyplace else in the United States. Filmed for $7 million, the film made just over $2.5 million at the box office.

SPINNING BORIS (2003)

Starring: Jeff Goldblum, Anthony LaPaglia, and Liev Schreiber

Plot: When Russian president Boris Yeltsin's approval rating drops into the single digits, three American campaign consultants (Goldblum, LaPaglia, and Schreiber) travel to Russia to help him win reelection.

Details: The film is based on a true story. In 1996, three Republican consultants—George Gorton, Joseph Shumate, and Richard Dresner—were hired by Yeltsin's campaign manager to right his struggling campaign. The consultants stayed on even after Yeltsin fired his campaign manager. Yeltsin did win reelection, though how much of his victory is due to the consultants is debatable.

RUN RONNIE RUN! (2002)

Starring: David Cross, Bob Odenkirk, Jill Talley, Ben Stiller, and Jack Black

Plot: Redneck Ronnie Dobbs (Cross), whose only claim to fame is that he has been arrested on a true-crime reality show called *Fuzz* more times than anyone else, lands a TV show of his own called *Ronnie Dobbs Gets Arrested* and finds real stardom.

Details: The character of Ronnie Dobbs first appeared in comedy sketches on the cult HBO comedy series *Mr. Show*. Bob Odenkirk (*Breaking Bad, Better Call Saul*) plays the infomercial presenter who turns Ronnie's life into a reality show. Co-writers Cross and Odenkirk had full creative control at first, but that was withdrawn after creative disagreements with both the director and the studio, and they had no say in the final cut. Result: the studio sat on the movie for two years before releasing it as part of a 2-for-1 DVD set along with *The Real World: Cancun*. Cross and Odenkirk have since disowned the film, but it did get a respectable 71 percent on Rotten Tomatoes, and it's worth watching for the cameos alone: Garry Shandling, Patton Oswalt, Mandy Patinkin, Sarah Silverman, John Stamos, Kathy Griffin, Jeff Goldblum, and many more.

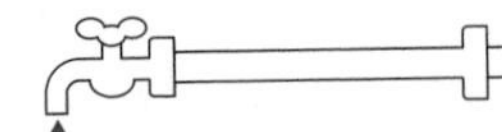

World's largest bat: the giant golden-crowned flying fox, with a 5½-foot wingspan.

MACY'S PARADE BALLOONS

Since it started in the 1920s, the Macy's Thanksgiving Day Parade has included balloons based on characters from comic strips, cartoons, and marketing campaigns. Here are most of the balloons that have sailed down New York's Fifth Avenue on Thanksgiving morning.

The Katzenjammer Kids (1929) • Joe Jinks (1930) • Barney Google (1930) • Boob McNutt (1930) • Felix the Cat (1932) • Gulliver from *Gulliver's Travels* (1933) • Mickey Mouse (1934) • Donald Duck (1935) • Pinocchio (1937) • Uncle Sam (1938) • Ferdinand the Bull (1938) • The Tin Man from *The Wizard of Oz* (1939) • Superman (1940) • Howdy Doody (1949) • Mighty Mouse (1951) • Popeye (1957) • Bullwinkle J. Moose (1961) • Dino, the Sinclair Oil mascot (1963) • Elsie the Cow from Borden Dairy (1963) • Linus the Lionhearted (1964) • Underdog (1965) • Smokey Bear (1966) • Snoopy (1968) • Weeble (1975) • Kermit the Frog (1977) • Olive Oyl (1982) • Woody Woodpecker (1982) • Yogi Bear (1983) • Garfield (1984) • Raggedy Ann (1984) • Betty Boop (1985) • Spider-Man (1987) • Ronald McDonald (1987) • The Snuggle Bear (1987) • Big Bird (1988) • The Quik Bunny (1988) • The Pink Panther (1988) • Woodstock from *Peanuts* (1988) • Bugs Bunny (1989) • Clifford the Big Red Dog (1990) • Bart Simpson (1990) • Babar the Elephant (1991) • Goofy (1992) • Beethoven from the movie *Beethoven* (1993) • Sonic the Hedgehog (1993) • Rex from *We're Back! A Dinosaur's Story* (1993) • Izzy, the 1996 Atlanta Olympics mascot (1993) • Barney the Dinosaur (1994) • The Cat in the Hat (1994) • Dudley the Dragon (1995) • SkyDancer toys (1995) • Macy's mascot Eben Bear (1995) • Rocket J. Squirrel (1996) • Peter Rabbit (1996) • Arthur Read from PBS's *Arthur* (1997) • Nickelodeon's Rugrats (1997) • Babe the Pig from *Babe: Pig in the City* (1998) • Wild Thing (1998) • Dexter from *Dexter's Laboratory* (1998) • Honey Nut Cheerios Bee (1999) • Blue from *Blue's Clues* (1999) • Jeeves from the website AskJeeves (2000) • Cassie from PBS's *Dragon Tales* (2000) • Curious George (2001) • Pikachu (2001) • Jimmy Neutron (2001) • Cheesasaurus Rex, the ad mascot of Kraft Macaroni and Cheese (2001) • Little Bill from Nickelodeon's *Little Bill* (2002) • Mr. Monopoly (2002) • Super Grover from *Sesame Street* (2003) • Chicken Little (2004) • M&M's Red and Yellow (2004) • SpongeBob SquarePants (2004) • Scooby-Doo (2005) • Dora the Explorer (2005) • Mr. Potato Head (2005) • JoJo from *JoJo's Circus* (2005) • Abby Cadabby from *Sesame Street* (2007) • Hello Kitty (2007) • Shrek (2007) • The Smurfs (2008) • Buzz Lightyear (2008) • Horton the Elephant (2008) • The Pillsbury Doughboy (2009) • Greg Heffley from *Diary of a Wimpy Kid* (2010) • Po from *Kung Fu Panda* (2010) • Julius the Sock Monkey (2011) • The Elf on the Shelf (2012) • Toothless from *How to Train Your Dragon* (2013) • Characters from Cartoon Network's *Adventure Time* (2013) • Thomas the Tank Engine (2014) • Paddington Bear (2014) • The red Mighty Morphin Power Ranger (2014) • Eruptor from the video game *Skylanders* (2014) • Scrat the Squirrel from *Ice Age* (2015) • Red from the *Angry Birds* game app (2015) • Charlie Brown (2016) • Trolls (2016) • Olaf from *Frozen* (2017) • Jett from *Super Wings* (2017) • Chase from *Paw Patrol* (2017) • The Grinch (2017) • Goku from *Dragon Ball* (2018) • Gary the Snail from *SpongeBob SquarePants* (2019) • Dr. Seuss's *Green Eggs and Ham* (2019) • The Boss Baby (2020) • Red Titan from *Ryan's World* (2020)

I'M STILL STANDING

What's the oldest building in your town? In your state? Many old buildings have faded into history, but that doesn't mean they don't still have stories to tell.

THE FAIRBANKS HOUSE (Dedham, Massachusetts)

Claim to Fame: The oldest timber frame home still standing in North America

Story: An English colonist and builder of spinning wheels named Jonathan Fairbanks immigrated with his wife and six children to the Massachusetts Bay Colony in 1633, just 13 years after the *Mayflower* brought the Pilgrims to the New World. Fairbanks settled in the town of Dedham on 12 acres of land, where from 1637 to 1641 he built a house for his family. His descendants lived there for eight generations and more than 260 years. In 1904, the last resident, a woman named Rebecca Fairbanks, moved out and the family began operating the house as a museum. Few improvements were made to the house over the centuries. Though rooms were added, the house remains in largely the same condition that it was in in the 1600s. It is still open to the public and still owned by the Fairbanks family through a corporation they set up. If they hang on to the house until 2041, it will have been in the family for 400 *years*. In all that time, the property has never once had a mortgage taken out against it.

THE LENT-RIKER-SMITH HOUSE (Queens, New York)

Claim to Fame: It's a Dutch Colonial farmhouse that dates back to the days when New York actually *was* a Dutch colony called New Amsterdam. The farmhouse is the oldest house in the state—and perhaps the country—that is still lived in as a private residence, instead of being operated as a museum.

Story: If you're a New Yorker, you know that Rikers Island is the home of the city's main jail complex. The island is named for the Riker family, which arrived in New Amsterdam in the late 1630s. In 1656, a member of the family named Abraham Riker built the farmhouse in what is now Jackson Heights, in the borough of Queens, just across Bowery Bay from Rikers Island. The house remained in the extended families of Riker and one of his descendants, Abraham Lent, for 300 years, at times serving as a tavern, a boardinghouse and, legend has it, a brothel.

In the mid-20th century, when the last Riker to live in the house died, his personal secretary, William Gooth, bought the property to save it from being cleared and redeveloped. When Gooth died in 1975, the property was sold to the tenant who rented the house, a man named Michael Smith. He and his wife Marion spent the next 25 years restoring the house to its original appearance. Michael Smith died in 2010, but Marion is still living there and still opening the place up for private tours that include the house, the Riker family burial plot, and the rest of the one-acre lot, which is all that remains of the original Riker farm. The burial plot contains more than 130 graves, including dozens of Rikers, as well as several members of the Smith family.

ST. BERNARD DE CLAIRVAUX CHURCH (North Miami Beach, Florida)

Claim to Fame: The oldest building in the state of Florida (sort of)

Story: The oldest building in Florida that was *constructed* in Florida is the Castillo de San Marcos, the Spanish fortress that has guarded the approach to St. Augustine since 1695. But St. Bernard de Clairvaux Episcopal Church in North Miami Beach was built around 1141—in *Spain.* The building served as a monastery near Segovia in northern Spain for 700 years before falling on hard times. During a period of social upheaval in the 1830s, the monastic community was forcibly disbanded, and the building was sold.

Nearly a century later, it was being used as a granary and a stable when the American newspaper baron William Randolph Hearst passed through Segovia in 1926, fell in love with the place, and bought it. Hearst had the monastery dismantled stone by stone and smuggled to the United States in 11,000 packing crates. But then the Great Depression hit and Hearst, financially strapped, could not afford to have the monastery rebuilt. The crates were still locked away in his warehouse when he died in 1951. The following year, they were purchased by two Florida entrepreneurs who had it reassembled in North Miami Beach as a tourist attraction. That flopped—and in 1964, a philanthropist purchased the monastery for a fraction of its actual value and donated it to the Episcopal Church, which still owns it today.

Hearst had the monastery dismantled stone by stone and smuggled to the United States in 11,000 packing crates.

THE LANE HOUSE (Edenton, North Carolina)

Claim to Fame: The oldest house in North Carolina

Story: Most old houses fade into obscurity but are not completely forgotten. The Lane House *was* completely forgotten—no one realized how old it was until 2013, when owners Steve and Linda Lane were having it renovated so that they could rent it out. At the time the house was estimated to have been built around 1900, but as the renovators began tearing out wallboards and other, more recent additions, they exposed timber framing, ceiling joists, and other features that made them suspect that the house was much older. The Lanes brought in an expert who studied the tree rings in the timber framing and determined that the house was built in about 1719 (*who* built it may never be known). That makes it the oldest house in North Carolina that is still standing—unless, of course, there are even older houses out there waiting to be rediscovered.

QUOTES FOR MARXISTS

And by Marxists, we mean Groucho, Chico, and Harpo! Honk-honk!

Chico: "The garbage man is here."
Groucho: "Well, tell him we don't want any."

—*I'll Say She Is*

"Ice water? Get some onions—that'll make your eyes water!"

—Groucho, *The Cocoanuts*

"Mustard's no good without roast beef."

—Chico

Leo: "Well, if you fellows don't mind, I'm going to wash up."
Chico: "Yeah, go ahead. The rest of us are already washed up."

—*Room Service*

"Remember, men, we're fighting for this woman's honor—which is probably more than she ever did."

—Groucho, *Duck Soup*

"I would like the west better if it was in the east."

—Chico, *Go West*

Prosecutor: "War would mean a prohibitive increase in our taxes."
Chico: "Hey, I got an uncle lives in Taxes."
Prosecutor: "No, I'm talking about taxes—money, dollars!"
Chico: "Dollars! There's-a where my uncle lives! Dollars, Taxes!"

—*Duck Soup*

"Why don't you bore a hole in yourself and let the sap run out?"

—Groucho, *Horse Feathers*

"I wasn't kissing her. I was whispering in her mouth."

—Chico

"I could dance with you till the cows come home, but I would rather dance with the cows till you come home."

—Groucho, *Duck Soup*

Groucho: "What are the requirements for an umpire?"
Jack Powell: "An umpire must have honesty, integrity, good eyesight, and plenty of intestinal fortitude."
Groucho: "Wouldn't it help if you knew a little about baseball?"

—*You Bet Your Life*

"I don't have a photograph. I'd give you my footprints, but they're upstairs in my socks."

—Groucho, *The Groucho Phile*

"I bet your father spent the first year of your life throwing rocks at the stork."

—Groucho, *At the Circus*

"I am the most fortunate self-taught harpist and non-speaking actor who has ever lived."

—Harpo

"Be open minded, but not so open minded that your brains fall out."

—Groucho

"Those are my principles, and if you don't like them...well, I have others."

—Groucho

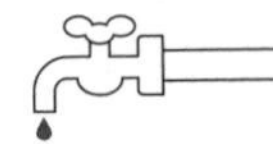

An oil tycoon named Armand Hammer once tried to buy the company that makes Arm & Hammer baking soda.

UNCOMMON ORIGINS OF COMMON PHRASES

If you're going through a difficult phrase, Uncle John is here to help.

PATIENT ZERO

MEANING: The first person to be infected with a disease

ORIGIN: "In the tortuous mythology of the AIDS epidemic, one legend never seems to die: Patient Zero, a.k.a. Gaétan Dugas, a French Canadian flight attendant who supposedly picked up HIV in Haiti or Africa. Dugas was once blamed for setting off the entire American AIDS epidemic, which traumatized the nation in the 1980s. But after a new genetic analysis of stored blood samples, bolstered by some intriguing historical detective work, scientists in 2016 declared him innocent. The researchers also reported that originally, Mr. Dugas was not even called Patient Zero—in an early epidemiological study of cases, he was designated Patient O, for 'outside Southern California,' where the study began. The ambiguous circular symbol on a chart was later read as a zero, stoking the notion that blame for the epidemic could be placed on one man." (From the *New York Times*)

TO BE ON CLOUD NINE

MEANING: Perfection, paradise

ORIGIN: "The encyclopedic if little read *International Cloud Atlas* runs to two volumes, but virtually all of the cloud types—mammatus, pileus, nebulosis, spissatus, floccus, and mediocris are a sampling—have never caught on with anyone outside meteorology and not terribly much there. Incidentally, the first, much thinner edition of that atlas, produced in 1896, divided clouds into ten basic types, of which the plumpest and most cushiony-looking was number nine, cumulonimbus. That seems to have been the source of the expression 'to be on cloud nine.'" (From *A Short History of Nearly Everything,* by Bill Bryson)

KEEP YOUR SHIRT ON

MEANING: Stay calm, don't lose your temper

ORIGIN: "The stiff, starched shirts worn by American men back in the mid-19th century when this expression originated weren't made for a man to fight in. Therefore, men often removed their shirts when enraged and ready to fight, a practice reflected in the old British expression *to get one's shirt out*, 'to lose one's temper.'" (From *The Facts on File Encyclopedia of Word and Phrase Origins*, by Robert Hendrickson)

Do you agree? According to one study, Oregonians talk faster than people of any other state. New Yorkers were #38.

THE BITTER END

MEANING: The actual, horrible, unfriendly finish

ORIGIN: "It's a nautical term. The 'bitt' end (or bitter end) refers to the final part of the anchor rope near to where the rope is fixed to the ship's deck. Usually marked with colored rags, the bitter end gets its name from the bollards (or bitts) on the deck to which the anchor rope was tied. When the sailors lowering the anchor came across the rags on the bitter end, they knew there was no more rope left, meaning the water was too deep to set anchor. To go to the bitter end means to go to the very end (i.e., right to the last few yards of the anchor rope)." (From *Grammar Monster*)

WILLY-NILLY

MEANING: To perform an act lazily or sloppily

ORIGIN: "'Like-it-or-not-here-it-comes' was the original meaning, and it comes from the 17th-century phrase *will ye, nill ye,* a shortened form of *be ye willing, be ye unwilling.* Both of these mean 'whether you like it or you don't like it' (*ye* is an archaic form of 'you'). There's also a Latin version of this that comes up now and again: *nolens volen,* 'unwilling, willing,' that some people think might have been the true origin of willy-nilly, but no one knows for sure." (From *The Complete Idiot's Guide to Weird Word Origins,* by Paul McFederies)

IN ONE FELL SWOOP

MEANING: All at once

ORIGIN: "It conjures up an image of a bird of prey swooping down on its target. It is one of Shakespeare's creations. In the Bard's 1606 play *Macbeth,* the character Macduff, learning his wife and children have all been killed, cries out, 'What, all my pretty chickens and their dam, at one fell swoop?' The word 'fell' has been used since then to mean 'evil' or 'deadly.'" (From *Red Herrings & White Elephants: The Origins of the Phrases We Use Every Day,* by Albert Jack)

BALLS TO THE WALL

MEANING: A particularly intensive and enthusiastic effort

ORIGIN: "This phrase sounds as if it is a reference to a part of the male anatomy. The original usage has nothing to do with anatomy, coming rather from the world of aviation. On an airplane, the handles controlling the throttle and the fuel mixture are often topped with ball-shaped grips, referred to by pilots as (what else?) *balls.* Pushing the balls forward, close to the front wall of the cockpit, results in the highest volume and richest mixture of fuel going to the engines and therefore the highest possible speed." (From *Word Myths: Debunking Linguistic Urban Legends,* by David Wilton)

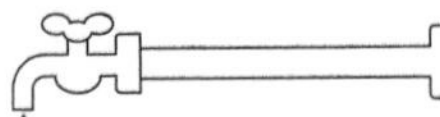

The world's factory: China produces more toys, clothing, concrete, steel, and fertilizer than any other country.

THE WEIRD CRIME BLOTTER

In the American legal system, you're considered innocent until proven guilty. But if we can't call them criminals, we can at least preemptively call them out when their illegal acts are undeniably strange.

CRIMINAL: James Johnson
CRIME: Drug possession
CRIME STORY: One day in May 2018, Johnson aroused the suspicions of the staff at a Travelodge hotel in Eastleigh, Hampshire, UK, when they saw him entering his room wearing a bra over his shirt and carrying a bag of potatoes. They called the police, who searched Johnson's room and found a large stash of hallucinogenic drugs and a bathtub full of potatoes. When the judge asked why he'd done it, Johnson said, "It felt like the right thing to do at the time."

CRIMINAL: Mack Samuel Stokes
CRIME: Public lewdness
CRIME STORY: Stokes, 48, of Athens, Alabama, was arrested for washing a mirror in the front yard of his home in September 2019. He was naked at the time.

CRIMINAL: Marcus Davis
CRIME: Felony firearm possession
CRIME STORY: In January 2020, Davis was hospitalized after suffering a gunshot wound to his groin. When local police in Portland, Oregon, investigated, Davis claimed that he'd been waiting for a bus when a homeless man shot him after an armed robbery went awry. That was a lie—Davis had accidentally shot himself (in the groin), then hid the handgun. The gun had been reported as stolen, and Davis was already on parole for a federal drug offense. Altogether, that added up to a six-year prison sentence.

CRIMINAL: Gianfranco Fernandez
CRIME: Battery and resisting arrest
CRIME STORY: Fernandez was blocking the flow of traffic on a busy road in Orlando, Florida, one day in July 2020. His method: Doing cartwheels in the road (and also lying down). Sheriff's Department officials managed to grab Fernandez and pull him to safety, only for him to break free and go back onto the road, where he evaded recapture (temporarily) by doing more cartwheels.

Odd astronomy fact: All disk-shaped galaxies, no matter their size or mass, complete a single rotation roughly once every billion years.

CRIMINAL: Name unknown; the man remains at large
CRIME: Theft
CRIME STORY: In February 2020, security cameras captured footage of a man who walked into a Tim Hortons donut shop outside of Calgary, Alberta, and placed a rubber chicken on top of the charity donation box that was on the counter. Then he picked up the chicken *and* the box, and walked off.

CRIMINAL: Jerry Ray Benton
CRIME: Malicious damage to property
CRIME STORY: Union, South Carolina, police answered a call from a woman who claimed her home and property had been vandalized. The cops noticed a toilet seat on the ground, next to the woman's Toyota Camry, which was scratched. The victim explained that her ex-husband, Benton, 60, had been verbally harassing her for weeks, but now, she saw him outside, throwing a toilet seat at her house. He missed, striking the car instead.

CRIMINALS: Leng Sreyka, Chan Leakena, and Chun Ren
CRIME: Vandalism
CRIME STORY: These three friends–Leng and Chan, two women who work for a TV station in Kampong Speu, Cambodia, and Chun, their male friend, a motorcycle driver–were riding on Ren's bike through a village while simultaneously drinking coconut milk straight out of the coconuts. When they were done with the coconuts, they threw the spent husks at a moving car, where the husks passed through an open window and landed inside. The driver gave chase and cornered them a few miles away, and then summoned the police.

CRIMINAL: Linda Evans (not the *Dynasty* actress)
CRIME: Disorderly conduct
CRIME STORY: After an evening of drinking one night in March 2019 at his trailer in Mountain Home, Arkansas, Gary Bean, 69, became belligerent and started throwing things. His partner, Evans, 49, called 911 to ask for the police's help in subduing Bean. Baxter County Sheriff's deputies soon arrived, and entered Evans's name in their system. Turns out there was an outstanding warrant for *her* arrest on an old charge. When the officers told Evans they'd be arresting her (and Bean, when they discovered a bag of illegally obtained prescription painkillers on him), she grabbed a nearby bottle of vodka and chugged it before surrendering herself. The couple were driven to the sheriff's office, and while Evans was being booked, she grabbed a police officer's groin.

* * *

"For the powerful, crimes are those that others commit." –**Noam Chomsky**

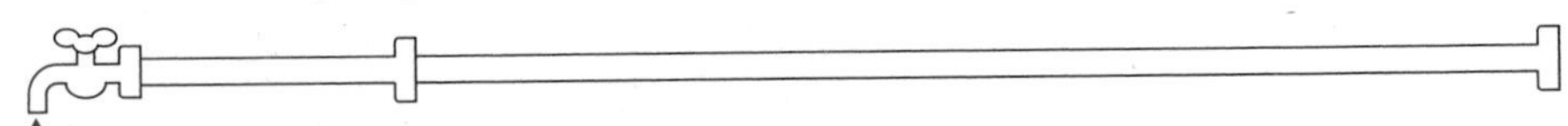

According to the manufacturer, the plural of LEGO is "LEGO bricks."

THE LONELIEST WHALE IN THE WORLD

Here's the strange tale of the whale that sings just a little bit off-key.

PITCH (IM)PERFECT

In 1989, scientists monitoring whale songs in the northern Pacific Ocean detected a whale song different from any they'd ever heard before: a single whale, believed to be a male, singing at a higher pitch—52 hertz—than other whales. That sound has been described as being "just above the lowest note on a tuba." Blue whales and fin whales typically sing much lower than that, in the 15–20 hertz range, right at the limit of what humans are able to hear. The strange whale's calls were also shorter in duration and more frequent than the calls of other whales. Because of the unusual pitch of its song, the whale was given the name "the 52-Hertz Whale."

OH, SOLO ME-O

The same whale was recorded every year for the next 26 years, though after 1992 the pitch of the song dropped to 50 hertz, suggesting that the whale had matured into adulthood and, like human males, his voice had grown deeper. He was unlike any other whale in the world: "In spite of comprehensive careful monitoring year-round, only one call with these characteristics has been found anywhere, and there has only been one source each season," the scientists wrote in 2004.

The 52-Hertz Whale wasn't just unique, he was all by himself—no other whales were ever detected in the same vicinity, and his movements, according to the scientists, "appeared to be unrelated to the presence or movement of other whale species." It isn't clear what species of whale the 52-Hertz Whale is, either: he could be a blue whale, or a fin whale, or maybe a hybrid of two species of whale and, if so, most likely a blue whale and some other species, perhaps a humpback. His high pitch could be the result of some kind of deformity, or he could be deaf, and thus unable to adjust his singing to match the singing of other whales of his species. No one knows for sure. He has been heard in the Pacific Ocean as far south as Baja California, and as far north as

DID YOU KNOW?

The largest animal in the world produces the largest babies in the world:

- Female blue whales typically breed once every three years and have one calf at a time. The calf will gestate inside the mother's womb for about a year before the mother gives birth.
- Baby blue whales are about 23 feet long at birth; they weigh nearly 6,000 pounds—as much as an adult hippo.
- Over the first six to seven months, the calf will gain up to 250 pounds a day by drinking as much as 150 gallons of its mother's milk daily.

According to a 2008 University of Colorado analysis, 15% of the particulate matter found in the New York City subway system are flakes of human skin.

the Aleutian Islands off Alaska. No matter where he traveled, no other whales were heard responding to his calls.

When an article about the 52-Hertz Whale was published in a scientific journal in 2004, the story was picked up by the media. It soon captured the attention of the public, which was fascinated by the idea of a one-of-a-kind whale, all by himself in the deep blue sea. What kind of whale was he? Could other whales even hear him? And if they could hear him, would they want to interact with such a strange-sounding whale? This and other speculation earned the 52-Hertz Whale the nickname "the loneliest whale in the world."

SOLO NO-MO?

If the whale ever really was lonely, his luck appears to have changed around 2010. That year, John Hildebrand, a scientist at the Scripps Institution of Oceanography, detected more than one whale singing at this unusual pitch for the very first time. "You could see it on two widely separated sensors at the same time, so that suggests it's not just a single animal. It may be *multiple* animals," he told BBC Earth in 2015. After more than 20 years of being the only whale of his kind, the 52-Hertz Whale was no longer quite so unique.

Who are these new whales? Are they the 52-Hertz Whale's siblings? His offspring? His cousins? Unrelated hybrid whales? No one knows for sure, but now there's at least a chance that the world's loneliest whale won't be so lonely anymore.

SPACE INVADERS
The total mass of all the space objects in Earth's orbit is 9,700 tons.
That's about the same as 62 Statues of Liberty.

WHAT AM I?

Are you clever enough to solve these riddles nineteen?
If not, turn to page 405 to find out what they mean.

1. My belly is a boat. My feet are paddles. My throat is a trumpet.
2. I spend most of my day at the window, only going to the table for my meals.
3. When I grow to capacity, I shrink until I am reborn.
4. I have cities but no houses, mountains but no trees, and rivers but no fish.
5. I fly with no wings, cry with no eyes, and wherever I go, darkness follows.
6. Always on my way, I never arrive today.
7. I am a bird. I am a fruit. I am a person.
8. I can grow, but I am not alive. I cannot breathe, but I need air to survive.
9. Yellow I live without arms or legs, in a room of black with walls of blue. My food is light. My spirits haunt me, yet I am controlled by you.
10. Chase me all you want, in any direction you want, but I'll always be about three miles away.
11. I am the leader of fashion, but I am always out of date.
12. If you don't have me, you don't want me. If you do have me, you wouldn't part with me for the world.
13. Your bottom is our top.
14. I can be green, or I can be sweet. Take away all but one of my letters and I sound the same.
15. I turn without moving.
16. I build up castles and tear down mountains. I make some people blind and help others to see.
17. Look at my rings and you'll know my age, but only after I'm dead.
18. I run but never walk.
19. I have a head and a tail but no legs.

TP, FYI

A few random facts about that soft white roll of paper sitting a foot away from you.

During World War II, British troops received a daily ration of three sheets of toilet paper. American troops got 22.

Until the Cold War ended in the late 20th century, Soviet-bloc troops weren't issued toilet paper at all. Many soldiers wound up using whatever they had on hand, which included official documents...some of which were classified. During the Cold War, American troops routinely raided waste facilities to retrieve those, um, used documents.

Toilet paper was first packaged and marketed in 1857 by businessman Joseph Gayetty, who marketed the rough, scratchy tissue as "the greatest necessity of the age!" (But it's not an American invention: wealthy people used thin paper for TP in China as far back as the sixth century AD.)

Toilet paper isn't always white, and it isn't always two-ply. A company called Renova sells a line of black, three-ply TP. It costs about $20 for a three-roll tin, which is also black and adorned with the slogan, "The Sexiest Paper on Earth."

An estimated 5 percent of Americans suffer from *perianal dermatitis,* a particular kind of skin irritation also known as "polished anus syndrome." How do you get it? By wiping with toilet paper so vigorously and so much that it abrades the skin.

What's the difference between two-ply and one-ply toilet paper? Two-ply paper isn't just one-ply doubled up. Generally speaking, one-ply is made from 13-pound thickness paper and two-ply consists of two layers of 10-pound thickness paper.

All told, the world uses the equivalent of 27,000 trees' worth of toilet paper... every day.

Despite utilizing a lot of trees, toilet paper *can* be environmentally friendly. In 2012, the large UK supermarket chain Sainsbury's discovered that if it shrunk the size of the cardboard roll in its store-brand toilet paper from 123 millimeters to 112 millimeters, they could fit far more rolls into a shipping container, and more rolls into its trucks. From that one move, Sainsbury's was able to cut its truck fleet by 500, which reduced carbon emissions by 140 tons per year.

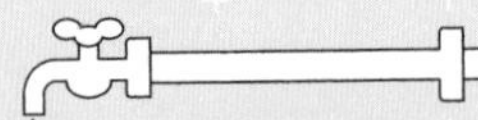

In Greece, the sewer pipes are so small and narrow that they can easily get clogged by flushed toilet paper. The solution: You're not supposed to flush your used TP in Greece. It's customary to just toss it in the garbage instead.

Costco's biggest-selling product is toilet paper. In an average year, they move $400 million worth.

Americans spend $6 billion a year on TP, the most of any country on Earth.

About 75 percent of the world's population doesn't use toilet paper. Not because they don't want to—TP is prohibitively expensive for people in developing countries.

The average American TP user goes through 57 squares a day, which works out to 50 pounds a year per person.

The average roll of toilet paper weighs 227 grams, or eight ounces.

According to studies, 31 percent of people look down at the toilet paper after they've used it.

The Soviet Union didn't begin to produce or sell toilet paper until 1969, when the nation's first TP factory was built. Before that, Soviet citizens made do with other kinds of paper, such as the rough and scratchy gray paper used as packing material.

In 2009, the Japanese company Nakabayashi began selling a machine that can turn office waste paper into brand-new toilet paper. It can make two rolls an hour out of 1,800 sheets of standard-sized paper. Cost: $95,000.

Today it makes cell phones and other consumer electronics, but when the Finnish tech company Nokia started out in 1865, one of its first products was a high-end, three-layer toilet paper.

Among the 75 European and American products banned by the government of Iran: premium toilet paper. Reason: it's considered luxurious and decadent. (There's a big secondary market for smuggled TP in Iran.)

According to studies, 7 percent of people who stay in a hotel or motel will swipe a roll of toilet paper from the room.

What is *acartohygieiophobia?* The fear of running out of toilet paper.

Pablo Picasso was born on October 25, 1881, the day before the shoot-out at the O.K. Corral.

OOPS!

Everyone makes stupid mistakes from time to time, so go ahead and feel superior for a few minutes.

A Bridge Too Wobbly

On Saturday, June 10, 2000, more than 80,000 people celebrated the opening of the London Millennium Footbridge, the first pedestrian bridge built across the river Thames in more than a century. But something wasn't right. The 2,000 people who could fit on the 1,050-foot-long footbridge were having trouble keeping their footing. As more people matched each other's footsteps, the sway got even worse. Result: three hours after it opened (and two years after construction began), the steel suspension bridge was closed for 10 minutes. This time, officials let even fewer people on... but the bridge started swaying again. What happened? All those pedestrians had unwittingly participated in a physics demonstration of *synchronous lateral excitation*, which causes sway to increase when everyone gets in lockstep. The "oops" part: Similar suspension pedestrian bridges have exhibited this type of behavior before, but for some reason, the engineers didn't take it into account during their $24 million construction project. Originally estimated to be closed for a few weeks, the London Millennium Footbridge ended up being closed for two years and cost $6.6 million to repair. It's much more stable now, thanks to a complex system of dampers that absorb the footsteps, but Londoners still call it the "Wobbly Bridge."

Hospital Hijinks

A "kindly grandfather," as he was described in news reports, wanted to thank the nursing staff at Warrington Hospital in Cheshire, England, for their hard work. So he brought them a half of his grandson's red velvet birthday cake. Although the nurses later said that they noticed an "odd smell" coming from the cake, it was still cake...so they ate it. Later on, the shift got weird. According to an anonymous staffer, the cake "was full of funny stuff and had them all relaxed." That funny stuff turned out to be cannabis that had been baked into the 18-year-old grandson's cake. At first, hospital officials denied that anyone had been affected, but the source maintained that several nurses were "off their faces." The cake was later "destroyed" by police, who chalked it up to "genuinely an error by all parties." The grandfather was not charged.

I'm Dreaming of a Hot Christmas

On a bright Christmas morning in 2019, 12-year-old Cayden Parson of McKinney, Texas, got just what he'd asked for: a magnifying glass! Keeping alive a longstanding

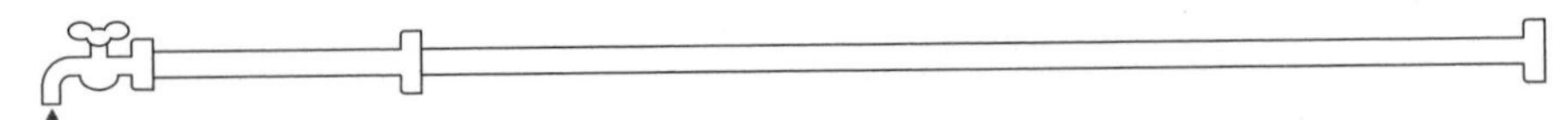

French name for AA batteries: *mignon*, which means "cute."

tradition, Cayden and his siblings took the glass out to the driveway to try to burn a hole in a newspaper under the midday sun. Cayden's dad, Justin, wasn't too concerned. "The trick with a magnifying glass is you can burn and scorch stuff, but it's actually really hard to start a fire," he told the *Washington Post.* Cayden's mom, Nissa-Lynn, described what happened next: "Everything was under control, until the boys came running into the house telling us that the lawn was on fire and the Christmas lights were melting." Apparently, the newspaper had ignited rapidly and Cayden let it out of his grip; the wind took it to the grass. The family of seven, reported the *Post,* "rushed outside in their matching Christmas pajamas" and got the fire out before it did any serious damage. "Instead of a tragedy," said Nissa-Lynn, "it will now be a Christmas to remember."

Blunt Got What?

When British singer James Blunt ("You're Beautiful") was in college in the mid-1990s, he was one of only three men in his sociology major. The other 170 students were women, most of whom were vegetarians. "So out of principle I decided I'd become a carnivore and just lived on mince, some chicken, maybe with some mayonnaise," Blunt recalled in 2020. Thinking it would prove his manliness, he kept to that diet for two months, but instead of attracting women, he got scurvy. Though commonly associated with seafarers of old, scurvy can affect anyone who eliminates vitamin C from their diet. Some symptoms: "exhaustion, spontaneous bleeding, swelling, pain in the limbs, and sometimes ulceration of the gums and loss of teeth." To rectify the situation, Blunt said he drank "copious amounts of orange juice," which led to acid reflux. "Food's not necessarily my forte," he admitted.

But instead of attracting women, he got scurvy.

President Football Man

In 2014, a "reputable and highly recommended merchandising company in Dorset" (which went unnamed in press reports) was tasked with creating a set of commemorative mugs for England's World Cup soccer team. An intern (aka scapegoat) reportedly used Google to search for royalty-free images of all the players. When he typed in defender Chris Smalling's name, the first photo that popped up was of U.S. president Barack Obama. (The two men do resemble each other.) The intern chose that image. He later said he was "more of a rugby fan" (and obviously not interested in American politicians). After they were inspected and approved by the reputable company's managers, 2,000 Chris Smalling mugs were issued with Barack Obama's face on them. When the goof went public, the intern was reportedly demoted (what's below an intern?). As for the mugs, they've become collector's items, selling for up to $150 each.

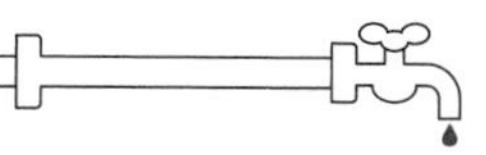

Dream Chaser

In September 2020, Dylan Harraway, an 18-year-old aspiring rapper from Virginia, went to a tattoo parlor (which he declined to name for fear of embarrassing them) and had the words "Dream Chaser" inked onto his forearm in large cursive letters over an elaborate background. The phrase is an homage to Harraway's hip-hop hero, Meek Mill, who founded Dream Chasers Records. The $200 "sleeve tattoo" took two hours. "I thought it looked great when I first saw it," Harraway said. But later, "I was very angry." Why? "I didn't notice until my friend told me it was backwards. So now I can only read it through a mirror and nobody can see it." It's unclear whether or not the tattoo artist knew he was doing it backward; Harraway described the parlor as "very clean and professional." The good news is that, after a video of the goof went viral, a "tattoo artist to the stars" named Bang Bang from New York offered to fix it free of charge.

Walk Off

The score was tied at 1–1 in a May 2010 baseball game between the Los Angeles Angels and the Seattle Mariners. In the bottom of the 10th inning, with the bases loaded, home-team hero Kendrys Morales stepped up to the plate. The Angels slugger was an "emerging superstar" who'd famously arrived in America after 12 escape attempts from Cuba. With his young career already off to a great start, here was a chance to keep it going with one swing of the bat. On the first pitch, Morales hit a walk-off grand slam to win the game! As he jubilantly ran the bases, his teammates gathered at home plate and started jumping up and down. When Morales approached home plate, he raised his fist and leapt high in the air toward the scrum. He landed awkwardly on home plate and crumbled to the ground. A few minutes later, to the silence of the stunned crowd, Morales was carried off on a stretcher. His broken ankle kept him out the rest of the season and most of the following one. After returning, he was never able to play at the level he once did. But he did improve in one way: "No more jumping, no celebrations."

* * *

BASKETBALL, NORTH KOREAN STYLE

North Korean leader Kim Jong-il was a big basketball fan, and in 2006, he ordered the implementation of some new rules to make the sport more exciting in the country. Among them: a slam dunk is worth three points (as opposed to two everywhere else), a missed free throw leads to a point subtracted from the team's total, a three-pointer is worth four points if it's a "swish" and doesn't hit the rim at all on its way in, and any basket made in the last three seconds of a game is worth eight points.

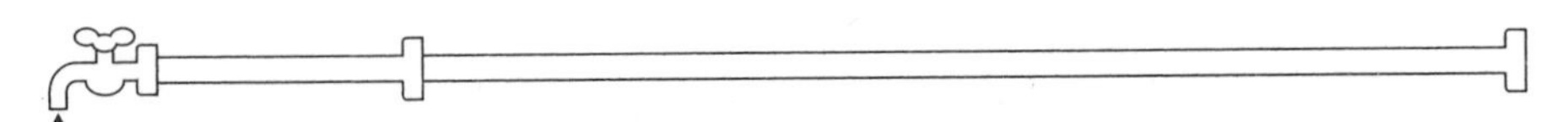

Most educated religious group in the U.S.: Hindus. 77 percent have college degrees.

MAKE YOUR OWN CANOLA OIL

Here's the latest installment of Uncle John's DIY manual–projects no one will ever attempt at home, but it's still interesting to know how they're done, just in case.

Background

Canola oil is one of the most commonly used vegetable-based cooking oils. But while sunflower oil comes from sunflowers and coconut oil comes from coconuts, there's no such thing as a canola plant. The oil is derived from the seeds of the *Brassica* plant, a relative of the turnip, Brussels sprout, and mustard. *Brassica* seed was once known as rapeseed (*rapum* is Latin for turnip) and its oil was marketed as rapeseed oil. Then, when the government of Canada, where the plant is abundantly grown and cultivated, decided that marketing a product with "rape" in its name was problematic, it came up with the far more innocuous name "canola oil." "Can" refers to Canada and "ola" is short for "oil, low acid."

What You Need

- Canola seed pods
- Several bowls
- Large wooden mallet
- Oil press
- Hexane
- Ventilator mask
- Centrifuge
- Sodium hydroxide
- Thermometer
- Freezer
- Double boiler

What to Do

1. Bright yellow canola plant flowers bloom in the summer, then die off, shedding numerous scratchy, pale yellow seed pods, each about an inch and a half long. Collect a few hundred of these after your canola flowers have died off.
2. Carefully peel open each seed pod. Remove the seed inside. It's black and round–about the same size and color as a peppercorn. Keep the seeds in a bowl, and discard all the dried pods.

3. Lay out the seeds in a single layer on a durable surface. Now take a large mallet and smash the whole lot until every seed is crushed and flat, when it takes on a chunky, flaky consistency.
4. Place the flaked canola seeds into an oil press, carefully collecting every drop.
5. Slightly less than half the inside of a canola seed consists of oil, but flaking and then pressing them will only yield about 75 percent of the usable oil within. To extract the rest from the seemingly spent seed flake, submerge the material in a hexane solution. (Note: Hexane is an industrial solvent and a neurotoxin, so wear a ventilator mask during this step, because inhaling it can cause severe brain damage.)
6. Oil floats on top of watery liquids like hexane, so skim the oil off the top of the bowl. Combine this oil with that obtained from the press earlier.
7. You'll notice this raw canola oil isn't particularly appetizing because it's cloudy and full of impurities. That means you'll need to refine it. To do that, place the oil in a centrifuge and spin it at a high speed for 20 minutes in a chemical bath of sodium hydroxide, which is also more commonly known as lye.
8. Again, skim the oil off the top of the chemical solution.
9. The canola oil will now be noticeably clearer but you'll still see some chunky ribbons throughout. Those are waxes, which need to be removed. Place a thermometer in the oil and chill it in a freezer until it reaches 40°F. This will solidify the wax, but not the oil. Then you can easily remove the separated, solid wax and dispose of it.
10. Canola oil has a neutral taste, but in its natural state (and in its refined state) it has a nasty, putrid stench. To remove the odor and make it more palatable for kitchen use, place the refined canola oil in the top part of a double boiler. Fill the bottom portion with water and let it boil. The heat and steam will remove the gross smell from the oil.
11. Let the oil cool.
12. Pour it in a pan, turn on the heat, and make yourself some hashbrowns.

* * *

"A human being should be able to change a diaper, plan an invasion, butcher a hog, conn a ship, design a building, write a sonnet, balance accounts, build a wall, set a bone, comfort the dying, take orders, give orders, cooperate, act alone, solve equations, analyze a new problem, pitch manure, program a computer, cook a tasty meal, fight efficiently, die gallantly. Specialization is for insects."

–Robert A. Heinlein

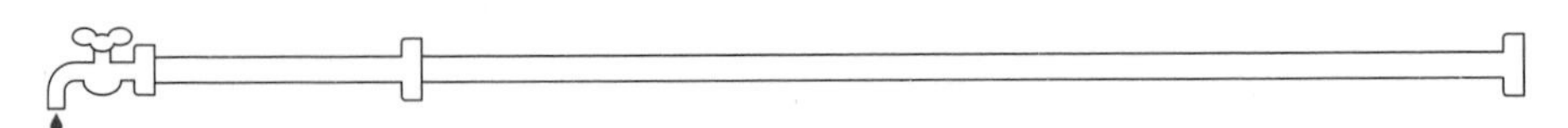

Weight of a teaspoonful of a neutron star: about six billion tons.

GOVERN-MENTAL: KNOW YOUR -*ISMS*

Lots of people throw around words like federalism, socialism, fascism, capitalism, and Marxism, but how many people know what they really mean? Here's a primer.

REPUBLICANISM: (Not to be confused with the Republican Party.) A system of government in which the power is held in the hands of the citizens and their elected representatives. The head of state is elected or nominated, and therefore is not a king or monarch who rules for life by hereditary right. Republics get their name from the Latin phrase *res publica*, which means "thing of the people" or "public matter." In a republic, the country and its government belong to the people and are not the property of the rulers.

FEDERALISM: A political system consisting of two levels of government with equal status, if not equal power: the central or *federal* government, and the regional governments, which can be states, provinces, territories, or some other political unit. The United States of America is a *federal republic*, a federation of states with a republican form of government.

CONFEDERALISM: *Confederalism* is a form of government in which the federal government is subordinate to the regional governments. During the American Civil War, the secessionist Confederate States of America ceded less of their power to the Confederate central government than they had to the federal government when they were still part of the United States.

ANARCHISM: A belief system that calls for the abolishment of all governments and nation-states, and the reorganization of society on a completely voluntary basis, with no force or coercion used to compel people to do anything they don't want to do. Such an existence would likely be chaotic, which is why the words "chaos" and "anarchy" are often synonymous.

LIBERTARIANISM: A belief system that emphasizes the liberty of the individual above other concerns, with little to no involvement of the state in the lives of citizens. Libertarianism is similar to anarchism, and at times in history the two terms have been used interchangeably. Where they came to differ is where they place their emphasis: Libertarianism stresses the liberty of the individual, while anarchism focuses more on dismantling the systems and institutions that are barriers to individual liberty. That could be why, even though their goals are nearly identical, anarchism has become synonymous with chaos, and libertarianism has not.

Can you name the two First Ladies not born in the U.S.?
1. Louisa Adams (England); 2. Melania Trump (Slovenia).

CAPITALISM: You probably know this one already: capitalism isn't a form of government per se, it's an economic and political system in which most or all of a country's trade and industry are privately owned and operated for the purpose of generating profits for the owners.

MARXISM AND COMMUNISM: The political and economic theories of Karl Marx (1818–83) and Fredrich Engels (1820–95) view social change as taking place in the form of class struggle in response to exploitative economic conditions that exist in capitalist societies. Marx and Engels predicted that the inequities of capitalism would inevitably reduce the *proletariat*—the workers who produce goods and services—to a state of poverty over time, causing them to rise up against the wealthy *bourgeoisie*, or owners of the "means of production," and replace the capitalist system with *communism*—an egalitarian society in which there are no social classes, all property is publicly owned, and each worker is paid according to their abilities and needs.

COLONIALISM: When a country tries to extend its sovereignty over other territories and exploits them economically. In the process, the colonizing country will often impose its language, religion, form of government, and other components of its culture onto the colonized peoples.

SOCIALISM: Socialism is a catch-all word that can mean different things to different people. The classical definition of socialism is a political and economic philosophy that advocates for large sectors of the economy being publicly owned and/or regulated by the government and managed by workers for the public good. In Marxist theory, after capitalism is overthrown it is replaced with a transitional society and economy called socialism that will eventually evolve into communism.

TOTALITARIANISM: A system of government that is undemocratic, dictatorial, and that requires the complete subservience of individuals to the state. Opposition parties are prohibited, and both public and private life is tightly controlled using government surveillance, mass censorship, state-controlled mass media, secret police, and other tools of oppression. Totalitarian states recognize no limits to their power—their authority is *total*, hence the name.

FASCISM: A form of right-wing totalitarian state that emerged in Italy in the early 20th century. Italian fascists, led by Benito Mussolini, advocated for the complete mobilization of society along military lines to prepare for armed conflict and to manage economic difficulties if they arose. Economic policy was directed toward achieving national self-sufficiency through protectionist and interventionist policies, which propped up domestic industries by stifling competition from abroad. The Italian Fascist government, which allied itself with Nazi Germany during World War II, lasted until July 1943, when it collapsed after the tide of the war turned against Italy.

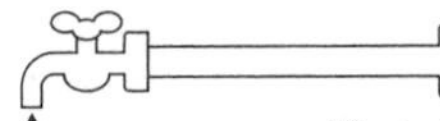

Musical anhedonia is a neurological disorder in which the sufferer is incapable of enjoying music. An estimated 3–5% of humans are affected by it.

STONEHENGE FOR SALE

Ever wonder how parks, monuments, and other public tourist attractions become public? Somebody has to give them to the public. Here's the story of a historic treasure that almost wasn't.

THIS ROCKS

Stonehenge—the mystical arrangement of huge stones, located in the English countryside near Salisbury, about 90 miles west of London—is an ancient monument, believed to have been used as part of an ancient Druidic religious rite. In the early 1800s, the estate on which Stonehenge stands was purchased by a prominent aristocrat, Sir Edmund Antrobus, 1st Baronet, and it became the seat of the Antrobus baronetcy.

Thousands regularly visited the site, as they had since the Middle Ages, to observe and speculate on how and why prehistoric peoples built it...and that took a toll. By the turn of the 20th century, Stonehenge had fallen into disrepair. Not only had tourists taken to chipping off chunks of the rocks to take away as free souvenirs, in 1900, one of the vertical stones fell over, and one of the horizontal lintels atop it fell and broke in half. Authorities had to step in, fencing off Stonehenge and charging an admission fee of one shilling (the equivalent of about $6 in today's money), with the fees going to maintenance expenses under the watchful eye of agents of the Antrobus family.

Then, in the fall of 1914, 27-year-old Lt. Edmund Antrobus, the sole heir of Sir Edmund Antrobus (the 4th Baronet), died in the first few weeks of World War I. When Sir Edmund died the following year, the estate passed to his brother, Sir Cosmo, who decided to divide the property into lots and put it up for sale. That land, including the portion on which Stonehenge sat, was offered as part of an auction on the afternoon of September 21, 1915, at the Palace Theatre in Salisbury, the closest city to Stonehenge, about 10 miles away from the monument. The auction was well publicized and every seat in the theater was occupied, presumably because interest in buying lot 15—Stonehenge—was that high.

DID YOU KNOW?

There's a full-sized replica of Stonehenge in Maryhill, Washington, right along the Columbia River. Unlike the real Stonehenge, we know exactly who built this one, and why. Railroad tycoon Sam Hill founded Maryhill, and in 1918, he used some of the land to erect a concrete version of Stonehenge as a tribute to the soldiers who died in World War I—the first such monument in the United States.

HARD SELL

That wasn't the case, though. The general public wasn't interested in buying Stonehenge—they were merely curious to see who would actually fork over the cash to purchase what the auction catalog called

"a place of sanctity dedicated to the observation or adoration of the sun," constructed by ancient Druids approximately 5,000 years earlier. Auctioneer Sir Howard Frank opened bidding at £5,000. A few bidders swiftly drove up the price to £6,000...and then interested parties stopped raising their paddles. This left Sir Howard bewildered. "Gentlemen, it is impossible to value Stonehenge," a contemporary news article claimed he said. "Surely £6,000 is poor bidding, but if no one bids me any more, I shall set it at this price. Will no one give me any more than £6,000 for Stonehenge?" A few more bidders begrudgingly put in bids before the auction stalled yet again. Finally, Sir Howard called it for lot 15. The final sale price of Stonehenge: £6,600—about £680,000 or $880,000 today. That's a lot of money, but is that how much Stonehenge is worth? In 2010, the UK government placed a value of £51 million on Stonehenge, so the buyer got quite a deal in this real estate transaction.

That lucky buyer was Cecil Chubb. That's the name of the local lawyer ("barrister" to the British) who forked over £6,600 for Stonehenge. When he arrived at the auction that day in 1915, he hadn't intended to buy it. He was on a casual errand—his wife, Mary, had sent him to buy a set of modestly priced dining room furniture also on the auction block that day...which he neglected to purchase. When asked by reporters why he decided to bid on Stonehenge, Chubb said, "While I was in the room, I thought a Salisbury man ought to buy it."

VERY GIFTED

Chubb's plans for Stonehenge: to protect it from falling into further disarray, and to preserve it for the item of historical importance and curiosity that it was. However, that notion lasted just three years. Mary Chubb was reportedly furious that her husband had sunk so much money into Stonehenge, and just three years later, Cecil Chubb washed his hands of the affair, donating it, free of charge, to the government and people of England. "I became the owner of it with a deep sense of pleasure," Chubb said at the time, "but it has been pressed upon me that the nation would like to have it for its own." Chubb officially signed over Stonehenge in a 1918 ceremony. No money changed hands, but the Chubbs did get a title for their trouble, and were thereafter referred to as Sir Cecil and Lady Mary Chubb. Around Salisbury, the locals called him "Viscount Stonehenge."

And speaking of no money changing hands, one of the Chubbs' conditions of the donation was that it wouldn't cost anything to visit Stonehenge. Admission fees weren't charged and still aren't, and the site is managed by the nonprofit English Heritage organization. Chubb, it turns out, did keep his promise to preserve Stonehenge. That might not have happened had the second-place bidder, Isaac Crook, won the 1915 auction. Crook was a sheep farmer who lived close to Stonehenge, and he wanted to use the land for livestock grazing.

Can you name the three Simpsons characters, other than the Simpsons themselves, with the most lines of dialogue? 1) Mr. Burns; 2) Moe the Bartender; 3) Ned Flanders.

CHRIS "NICKNAME" BERMAN

For 40 years, sportscaster Chris Berman has been known for the punny nicknames he gives to athletes...like these.

- Mike "Pepperoni" Piazza
- Willie "Lost in the" Mays
- Darryl Strawberry "Shortcake"
- Todd "Highway to" Helton
- Todd "Which Hand Does He" Frohwirth
- Albert "Winnie the" Pujols
- John "I Am Not a" Kruk
- Walt "Three Blind" Weiss
- Wade "Cranberry" Boggs
- Sammy "Say It Ain't" Sosa
- Tom "Leave It to" Seaver
- Chuck "New Kids on" Knoblauch
- Eddie "Eat, Drink, and Be" Murray
- Al "Cigarette" Leiter
- Ozzie "Like a" Virgil
- David "Supreme Court" Justice
- C. C. "Splish Splash I Was Taking" Sabathia
- Alan "Have Gun, Will" Trammell
- Bill "Hard a" Lee
- Roberto "Remember the" Alomar
- Todd "Smack Crackle" Van Poppel
- Bobby "Bad to the" Bonilla
- Moises "Skip to My" Alou
- Rollie "Chicken" Fingers
- Dwight Gooden "Plenty"
- Jim "Pork Fried" Rice
- Dave "Parallel" Parker
- Jeff "Brown Paper" Bagwell
- Lance "You Sunk My" Blankenship
- Mark "Tossed" Salas
- Todd "Mercedes" Benzinger
- Kelly "Churchill" Downs
- Jerry "Rolls" Reuss
- Mark Carreon "My Wayward Son"
- Bert "Be Home" Blyleven
- "Fettuccine" Alfredo Griffin
- Franklin "Ticket" Stubbs
- Danny "Dung" Heep
- Bernard "Innocent Until Proven" Gilkey
- Scott "Supercalifragilisticexpiali" Brosius
- Carlos "One if by Land, Two if by Sea, Three if" Baerga
- Mike "Nova" Scioscia
- Brook Jacoby "Wan Kenobi"
- Jim "Washer and" Dwyer
- Todd "Caribbean" Cruz
- Gary Redus "A Bedtime Story"
- Bill "Hello" Dawley
- Glenn "Old Mother" Hubbard
- Erik "Look, Mom, No" Hanson
- Rick "See Ya Later" Aguilera

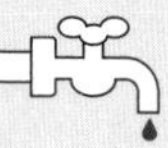

Beaver teeth never stop growing. They are sharpened as they wear down, and they're covered with a coating of iron that helps prevent tooth decay.

INITIAL STATES

North Carolina's license plates proclaim it "first in flight," because it was the site of the Wright brothers' inaugural airplane flight in 1903. But it turns out that every single state has a claim to fame and historical status as the first in the country to do...something. (Although we doubt any of these will ever show up as a slogan on a license plate.)

- **ALABAMA:** The first and, so far, only state to decree an alcoholic spirit as its official state drink. As of 2017, the state drink of Alabama is the locally produced Conecuh Ridge Whiskey.
- **ALASKA:** In 2016, the state passed a law requiring judges in divorce cases to consider the well-being of the pets from an ended marriage, including awarding custody rights.
- **ARIZONA:** It's the first state to make proper sun safety a part of its official public school curriculum. A program called SunWise holds an annual sun safety and skin cancer awareness poster contest and passes out thousands of containers of sunscreen.
- **ARKANSAS:** The first state to require all students in its public and charter high schools to learn computer science: isn't California, home of Silicon Valley. It's Arkansas, where the law passed in 2019.
- **CALIFORNIA:** State legislators approved the Cruelty-Free Cosmetics Act in 2018, which, when it went into effect in 2020, made California the first state in the country to ban the sale of any cosmetics whose safety was tested on animals.
- **COLORADO:** For the first time, in the midterm elections of 1894, a state elected not one but three women to its state house of representatives. More than 25 years before women earned the right to vote in federal elections, Colorado's citizens (men *and* women) voted to make lawmakers of Clara Cressingham, Frances Klock, and Carrie C. Holly.
- **CONNECTICUT:** As the popularity of that newfangled contraption, the automobile, started to spread at the turn of the 20th century, Connecticut enacted the first law to limit the speed of motorized vehicles. In 1901, drivers faced a speed limit of 15 mph on country roads, and 12 mph in cities.
- **DELAWARE:** In 2012, the state outlawed parental corporal punishment. The law defines illegal child abuse as anything that causes physical "pain"...including spanking.
- **FLORIDA:** It's a simple task today. You go to the Department of Motor Vehicles to renew your driver's license, get your photo taken, and get a new card all in one visit. Result: instant photo ID. In 1973, Florida became the first state to issue instant photo driver's licenses–and in color, too.
- **GEORGIA:** The University of Georgia, established in the city of Athens in 1785, is the first state college (meaning one funded at least in part by public funds) in the country.

- **HAWAII:** The state consists of five counties, which are governed by councils, and in 2015, all of them worked in concert to ban disposable plastic shopping bags at stores. That made Hawaii the first state to say *aloha* to the single-use carry-out sacks.

- **IDAHO:** By the late 1920s, more states required clearly placed license plates on cars. In 1928, Idaho became the first state to put a graphic to its plates, in addition to numbers and letters. The image: a potato.

- **ILLINOIS:** It was a great day for lazy Illinois gamblers on March 25, 2012, when their state became the first to authorize the sale of lottery tickets over the internet.

- **INDIANA:** While other states house male and female convicts in separate parts of the same prisons, Indiana was home to the first incarceration facility just for women—the Indiana Women's Prison, which opened in 1873.

- **IOWA:** The U.S. Supreme Court formally legalized interracial marriage on a national level when it overturned a state law with the *Loving v. Virginia* ruling in 1967. That was more than a century after Iowa became the first state to do so, back in 1851.

- **KANSAS:** Long before the passage of the 18th Amendment to the Constitution in 1919 made the production and sale of alcohol illegal in the United States, many cities, counties, and states outlawed booze. The first entire state to go dry: Kansas, in 1881.

- **KENTUCKY:** They figure prominently in the works of Charles Dickens, but debtors' prisons were a real thing in both the United States and the UK. Those with tremendous debts (and their families) were sent to work camps to pay off what they owed in the form of hard labor. In 1821, Kentucky became the first U.S. state to ban debtors' prisons.

- **LOUISIANA:** When Louisiana joined the Union in 1812, it immediately became the first state in which English was not the predominant language of its citizens. Because it had been both a French and Spanish colony, more people spoke French and Spanish than English.

- **MAINE:** This state was online before it was cool. In 1996, an educational initiative made it the first state to get all of its libraries and schools hooked up to the internet.

- **MARYLAND:** It's the first state to put a law protecting bees on the books. In 2016, Maryland banned *neonicotinoids*, a type of industrial pesticide whose use is linked to the global decline of bee populations.

- **MASSACHUSETTS:** Over the past several years, many states have legalized marijuana for both medicinal and recreational use, reversing laws banning it that had been in place for decades (or longer). The first state to outright ban marijuana in all its forms: Massachusetts, in 1911.

- **MICHIGAN:** Not only was Michigan the first U.S. state to get rid of the death penalty in 1847, it was the first English-speaking government in the *world* to do it.

The Canary Islands aren't named after birds. The name is from the Latin for "island of dogs." (But the birds are named after the islands.)

- **MINNESOTA:** It's the first to regulate smoking. The state's Clean Indoor Air Act of 1975 didn't ban smoking in public places, but it did require the creation of "No Smoking Areas" in all public places statewide.
- **MISSISSIPPI:** Around 1900, Mississippi became the first state to allow prisoners serving long sentences to have conjugal visits with spouses. (The state government repealed the law in 2014.)
- **MISSOURI:** George W. Bush established the first new presidential cabinet-level agency in decades when he helped form the U.S. Department of Homeland Security in November 2002. Meant to bulk up the fight against terror after the events of September 11, 2001, it followed a model set out at the state level by Missouri. Just two weeks after 9/11, the state created its own Office of Homeland Security.
- **MONTANA:** Montana built the first luge course in all of North America, not just the United States, in 1965. It stood over the Lolo Hot Springs resort, near the state's western border.
- **NEBRASKA:** In 1974, Nebraska became the first state to finish construction on the portion of the Interstate Highway System within its borders. The 455-mile, four-lane segment became part of Interstate 80, which runs across the entire country, starting in Teaneck, New Jersey, and ending in San Francisco. The highway was not completed in full until 1986. (Last state to finish construction: Utah.)
- **NEVADA:** As a way to combat the rising rate of needle-drug users testing positive for HIV, the state set up a program in 2017 in which new syringes could be obtained by enrolling in a special program that provides an electronic card to access a series of self-operated kiosks. This makes Nevada the first state in the country with syringe vending machines.
- **NEW JERSEY:** The first (and so far, only) National Marbles Tournament takes place here. It's been held annually since 1922 in Wildwood, which also happens to be the site of the National Marbles Hall of Fame.
- **NEW HAMPSHIRE:** It's the birthplace of the taxpayer-funded library. The Peterborough Town Library, free to the public, opened in 1833.
- **NEW MEXICO:** Most states have some kind of law that requires motorcycle riders to wear a helmet while operating their vehicle. In 2007, New Mexico became the first state to include motorized tricycle riders in those laws.
- **NEW YORK:** Legislation passed in 2019 makes New York the first state in the union where it's illegal to declaw a pet cat.
- **NORTH CAROLINA:** This state pioneered allocating public funds to support fine art. It's the first state to use taxes to fund a theater devoted to American plays (Playmakers Theatre, 1923), the first to support a symphony orchestra (1932), and the first to publicly fund art museums (1956).

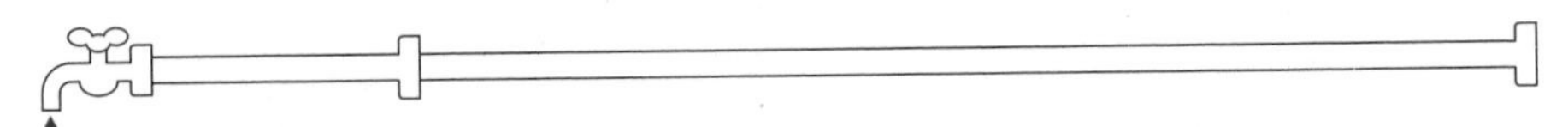

- **NORTH DAKOTA:** In 2015, it became the first state to allow government law enforcement agencies to use armed, unmanned drones. (They're armed with tasers, not bullets.)
- **OHIO:** Lawmakers here were among those who caught cryptocurrency fever in 2018. That year, Ohio became the first state to let some types of businesses (23 specific ones) pay taxes with the internet-based, nongovernmental form of money called bitcoin.
- **OKLAHOMA:** The death penalty is still on the books as a punishment for first-degree murder in several states. Largely gone are the firing squads, hanging gallows, and even electric chairs of the past. In 1977, Oklahoma became the first jurisdiction and U.S. state to use a lethal injection as its means of executing prisoners convicted of capital crimes.
- **OREGON:** In 2000, it became the first state to completely do away with in-person voting. Out went voting booths and in came a vote-by-mail system.
- **PENNSYLVANIA:** To ensure there would be nothing "sacrilegious, indecent, or immoral" presented in the emerging medium of silent film, Pennsylvania became the first state to establish a movie censorship board, in 1911.
- **RHODE ISLAND:** As a result of a ballot measure approved by voters in 2020, it became the first state to change its name. Before that, the state's full name was "the State of Rhode Island and Providence Plantations." The citizens voted to drop "and Providence Plantations" due to its connotations with slavery.
- **SOUTH CAROLINA:** Checks and balances were pioneered here. In 1776, the brand-new state became the first to grant its governor the power to veto, or reject, bills passed by the legislature.
- **SOUTH DAKOTA:** Many jurisdictions no longer celebrate Columbus Day, the holiday on the second Monday in October that commemorates Christopher Columbus's "discovery" of America. But as a different view of history has become more widely acknowledged—that Columbus helped unleash a genocide that took the lives of countless native peoples—more places have dropped "Columbus Day" in favor of "Indigenous Peoples' Day." South Dakota started it all in 1990, officially renaming the holiday Native Americans' Day.
- **TENNESSEE:** In 1978, Tennessee became the first state to make automobile child restraints—baby seats, safety seats, and booster seats, depending on the age and size of the child—legally mandatory.
- **TEXAS:** In the midst of a fight against an outbreak of the mosquito-carried Zika virus in 2016, Texas became the first state to distribute mosquito repellent, for free, to Medicaid recipients.
- **UTAH:** As of 2016, Utah was the first state with a registry of convicted white-collar criminals.

In 2017, Virginia became the first state to allow remote-controlled delivery robots to use city streets and sidewalks.

Why do mice, squirrels, porcupines, foxes, wolves, and coyotes eat deer antlers and elk antlers? They're high in calcium and protein.

- **VERMONT:** In the U.S., a public school education is such a normal part of life that it's taken for granted. In 1777, Vermont was the first state to not only offer education but to codify laws that required the government to fund schooling for all kids.

- **VIRGINIA:** "Virginia is for lovers," so the state tourism campaign slogan goes, but it's also for robots. In 2017, the state became the first to legally allow remote-controlled delivery robots to use city streets and sidewalks.

- **WASHINGTON:** In 2019, it became the first state to allow "human composting," an alternative to burial or cremation, in which the body is converted into "useful" soil. The family can either keep the soil or donate it for use in tree planting.

- **WEST VIRGINIA:** Pioneering the concept of inaccurate price tags, West Virginia became the first state to institute a sales tax, back in 1921. (Today, 45 of 50 states have a sales tax. The five that don't: Alaska, Delaware, Montana, New Hampshire, and Oregon.)

- **WISCONSIN:** It's the site of the first state-sponsored car race. In 1878, the state legislature allocated $10,000 to whoever could build an automobile that could travel the 135 miles between Green Bay and Madison on its own internally generated power. Alexander Gallagher of Oshkosh built a car and made the trip over the span of several days, because he averaged a speed of 6 mph and had to stop along the way to make repairs.

- **WYOMING:** It's the first (and only) state with a monument built to honor a prostitute. The Mother Featherlegs Monument, near the town of Lusk, was erected in 1964 to honor Charlotte Shepard (aka Mother Featherlegs), a lady of the night murdered in 1879.

* * *

A "BATHROOM READER" THAT'S ALL BATHROOM...AND NO READER

When well-to-do people traveled in the 1700s, they often brought their chamber pots with them, along with a portable toilet chair called a "close stool" to set the chamber pot in. Even in those days people could be squeamish about being seen with such objects, so sometimes the close stools were disguised to look like something else.

A "book" titled *Histoire des Pays Bas* ("*History of the Netherlands*") published around the year 1750 is just such an object: It's a collapsible close stool that when folded up looks like a book about the size of a large coffee-table book. Whenever nature called, the owner opened the cover, unfolded the boards inside, and *voilà!–Histoire des Pays Bas* was transformed into a close stool with a large round hole in the seat and a shelf below it to hold the chamber pot. The title of the book is intended as a sly joke: the "Netherlands" is a reference to the owner's nether regions. If you want your own copy, it's going to cost you a potful of money: A London bookseller named Daniel Crouch Rare Books put theirs up for sale in the fall of 2020. Asking price: $8,341.62. As of this writing, there were no takers.

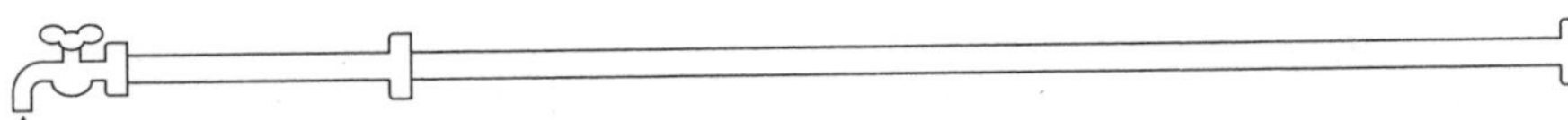

Longest nontechnical word in many English dictionaries: *floccinaucinihilipilification*...

RANDOM ORIGINS

Once again, the BRI asks—and answers—the question: Where did all this stuff come from?

AUTO-TUNE

In 1995, an oil-industry engineer, Dr. Andy Hildebrand, was at a trade show and asked some friends, "What should I invent?" A colleague's wife jokingly answered, "Well, Andy, why don't you make a box that would have me sing in tune?" Hildebrand thought it was a "lousy idea" at first. The consensus back then was that correcting pitch in real time is something only a supercomputer could do. But a few months later, Hildebrand changed his mind. He realized he was uniquely suited to solve this problem—the self-described "practitioner of digital signal processing" had studied violin and has a PhD in research engineering. After two years of writing mathematical formulas in notebooks and creating computer algorithms, he invented Auto-Tune.

Hildebrand explains it for laypeople: "When you're processing pitch, you add wave cycles to go sharp, and subtract them when you go flat. With autocorrelation, you have a clearly identifiable event that tells you what the period of repetition for repeated peak values is. It's never fooled by the changing waveform. It's very elegant." In 1998, Cher became the first singer to use Auto-Tune—albeit for its opposite effect, to create a robotic tone—on her Grammy-winning song "Believe." A year after that, T-Pain became the first rapper to feature it heavily. Then it showed up on Radiohead's 2001 album *Amnesiac.* Today it's estimated that 99 percent of all pop songs use at least some Auto-Tune. Hildebrand knows a lot of people don't like his invention but, as he points out, "If you're going to complain about Auto-Tune, complain about speakers, too. And synthesizers. Recording the human voice, in any capacity, is unnatural." And, he notes, "Haters will be haters."

THE N95 MASK

In the late 1950s, a New York design consultant named Sarah Little Turnbull was caring for ill family members when she noticed that doctors' masks were difficult to tie on, and difficult to keep on. What if, instead of fabric and string, masks were made out of a form-fitted bra cup, like the one she had recently developed for 3M? That's how Turnbull first came across a material that the manufacturing conglomerate had developed called Shapeen, a "non-woven" fabric that can be molded to any shape. Working with 3M's "melt blowing" fabrication process, Turnbull's bra-inspired face mask debuted in 1961. It attached to the head with an elastic band and had an aluminum nose clip to keep it snug. The bubble shape made it easier to breathe, but it still wasn't as effective as cloth masks were at blocking pathogens, so 3M branded it as a disposable dust mask. Approved by OSHA in 1972, the N95 as we know it today—based on Turnbull's original design with thicker mesh and a respirator—blocks 95 percent of airborne particles, hence the name. The mask has since become an integral tool not just for doctors but for everyone from factory workers, artists, mechanics, and more. Five years after Turnbull's death in 2015, N95 masks were found to block the COVID-19 virus. Result: Production of the masks in the United States alone exceeded 180 million per month in late 2020.

A MOMENT OF SILENCE

Six months after World War I ended, Edward Honey, an Australian-born journalist living in London, was trying to find an appropriate way to celebrate victory while also honoring the dead. Unable to come up with a suitable word or phrase, it dawned on him that there's one thing *everyone* understands: silence. "I would ask for five minutes, five little minutes only. A very sacred intercession," he wrote in an article for the *London Evening News* in May 1919. "Can we not spare some fragment of these hours of Peace, rejoicing for a silent tribute to these mighty dead?" That November, on the first Armistice Day observed in England, King George V decided to turn Honey's idea into a national custom. However, during rehearsals at Buckingham Palace, organizers realized that five minutes is a *very long* time to stand silently. So it was shortened to two minutes (that's how long they figured an old lady could hold out).

Over the next few years, more countries—the first being South Africa—began observing similar ceremonial silences. Two minutes is still observed every Armistice Day in England and Australia. Busy Americans have shortened it to one minute, and it's become the go-to custom for remembrance. Why? On the "socially awkward" scale, a moment of silence is pretty low. You don't have to be religious, nor do you really have to even know the person being honored. Whether it's for disaster victims, or it's the first day back at work after Brett from marketing's unfortunate golf cart mishap, all you have to do is stand there with your head down and keep quiet for 60 seconds. As for Edward Honey, four years after he wrote his article, he died at age 36, never having gotten to see his "very sacred intercession" become an enduring, worldwide tradition. Let us observe a moment of silence for him.

* * *

BLECCH NO MORE

Did you hate Brussels sprouts as a kid but enjoy them now? You didn't change. In the 1990s, researchers found better-tasting, less-bitter heirloom varieties and cultivated them.

Scurryfunge is an Old English word that means to run around quickly cleaning your house while guests are on their way over.

WATER, WATER, EVERYWHERE

Here at the BRI, we're positively swimming in trivia about bodies of water.

- **SALTIEST LAKE:** What's the difference between a sea and a lake? They're both large bodies of water surrounded by land, but seas eventually let out into the ocean, and lakes do not. Another difference: seas are at ocean or "sea level," at an elevation of 0. Lakes can be found at any elevation—above or even below sea level. Because it doesn't empty into an ocean and because it sits below sea level, the Dead Sea, despite its name, is actually a lake. It's also the saltiest large body of water on Earth—10 times saltier than the oceans.
- **LARGEST LAKE (SURFACE AREA):** The saltwater Caspian Sea is another sea that's not really a sea, but geologically speaking, a lake. It's also the lake that takes up more area of the Earth's surface than any other. It covers 143,200 square miles. The largest lake in the United States and Canada—and the largest freshwater lake (meaning non-salty) on the planet—is Lake Superior, one of the Great Lakes in the Upper Midwest, covering 31,700 square miles.
- **MOST VOLUMINOUS LAKE:** Lake Baikal, found in southeastern Siberia, contains more water than any other lake. It holds 5,521 cubic miles of water, which amounts to one-fifth of all surface freshwater on the planet, which is more than all five of the Great Lakes put together.
- **DEEPEST LAKE:** Lake Baikal is also the deepest lake on Earth. At its least shallow point, it's 5,300 feet deep, which is just over a mile. That part of the lake also dips 4,000 feet below sea level, which gives Lake Baikal the designation of being the lake with the lowest elevation in the world.
- **HIGHEST LAKE:** The lake at the highest elevation on the planet is Lake Titicaca, which straddles the border between Peru and Bolivia. It's the biggest lake in South America, and has an average elevation of 12,507 feet above sea level.
- **LONGEST LAKE:** Lake Tanganyika takes up a lot of room. It spans four African countries: Tanzania, Burundi, Zambia, and the Democratic Republic of the Congo. It's the second most voluminous lake on Earth and the second deepest, but it's number one in length. On a north–south orientation, it spans 420 miles. (And it's 31 miles wide, on average.)
- **HOTTEST LAKE:** Boiling Lake sits on the small Caribbean island nation of Dominica. Aptly named, the naturally occurring highlight of Morne Trois Pitons National Park reaches temperatures of 180–197°F near the shorelines, and gets hotter the farther out one goes—so much so that scientists are unable to accurately measure its temperature.
- **PLACE WITH THE MOST LAKES:** Earth is home to approximately 1.42 million lakes—and about two-thirds of them are in Canada.

- **YOUNGEST LAKE:** Dewart Lake, located in Kosciusko County in northern Indiana. It covers an area of 551 acres and is 82 feet deep at its deepest point. It's the newest naturally formed lake on the planet, created by a receding glacier during the most recent ice age, between 12,000 and a million years ago.

- **LONGEST RIVER:** Starting in the middle of Egypt in northeastern Africa, the Nile (and its system of tributaries) runs into Lake Victoria in Uganda. That comprises 4,130 miles, making the Nile the planet's longest river.

- **WIDEST RIVER:** The Nile edges out the 4,086-mile Amazon River for world's-longest status, but the South American waterway holds claim as the widest. During the rainy months, it can expand to as much as 24.8 miles wide at some places. And in the dry months, it shrinks down to a still substantial 6.8 miles on average.

- **MOST VOLUMINOUS RIVER:** The Amazon can also boast having the most water of any river. A river's volume is measured by the rate at which it discharges water into the ocean, and the Amazon delivers 4.2 million cubic feet of liquid into the Atlantic Ocean every second.

- **SHORTEST RIVER:** By definition, a river flows from one body of water to another. So the Roe River in Montana *is* a river, albeit the world's shortest. It starts in Giant Springs and feeds into the Missouri River outside the city of Great Falls. Total length: 201 feet.

- **NARROWEST RIVER:** The Haolai River runs into Dalai Nur Lake in the Inner Mongolia Plateau in northern China. It spans a respectable 11 miles, but gets so narrow at one point it's a wonder it keeps flowing. At its narrowest, according to Chinese scientists, the Haolai River is only one foot wide.

- **HOTTEST RIVER:** The Shanay-Timpishka River, or La Bomba, is a tributary in the Amazon River system. It's very short at only four miles long, and very uncomfortable; its temperature ranges from a toasty 113°F to a nearly boiling 210°F. Heated by geothermal energy, La Bomba has a reputation for killing anything that falls into it.

- **COLDEST RIVER:** Found in the nations of Croatia and Bosnia and Herzegovina, the Upper Neretva is one of the cleanest rivers in the world, but that might be because its waters are too cold to let anything fester. In even the hottest summer months, the Upper Neretva's average temperature measures 40°F.

- **MOST POLLUTED RIVER:** According to the World Bank, the most polluted river in the world is the Citarum River, found on the island of West Java in Indonesia. It's the longest river in the most populous area of the country, and it's also where about 2,000 textile companies dump around 20,000 tons of toxic waste and 340,000 tons of waste water...every day. The water is generally a murky brown color, although chemicals can temporarily turn it red, blue, or black.

* * *

"A river cuts through rock not because of its power but because of its persistence."

–Jim Watkins

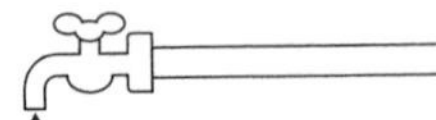

Who doesn't? According to the experts, penguins like the sound of trumpets, but hate the sound of bagpipes.

ARE YOU ON RUGS?

When we told the contractor we didn't want carpeted steps, he gave us a blank stair. (Insert groan here.) Unless you're decorating your house, you're unlikely to think much about carpets. But maybe you should. Although it was once exclusively in the homes of the wealthy, today it's everywhere, from hotels and office buildings to the most modest homes...to the rest of this article.

UNDER-STANDING HISTORY

Humans have been making floor coverings of various kinds for thousands of years—because who wants to sit or walk on a cold stone, wood, or tile floor when you can sit or walk on a bed of palm leaves, a nice, warm animal skin, or whatever else primitive peoples first used for carpeting? That primitive compulsion to make one's foundation a bit more comfortable evolved over the eons into an industry that today installs more than 14 *billion* square feet of carpeting every year in the United States alone. (That's about 500 square miles of carpeting—or about the size of the entire city of Los Angeles.) Along the way, an elaborate array of carpet-making techniques developed, involving the development of increasingly complex forms of dyeing and weaving. With that in mind, let's look down—at the carpet!—and then back at the page, and learn some carpet lingo.

PILE. All carpet is made by stitching loops of yarn into a backing material. The pile is the fabric that comprises the top, visible surface of a carpet, also known as the *face* or *nap*. There are two main types of carpet pile: loop pile and cut pile.

- For cut pile carpet, the loops are cut during the manufacturing process, so the pile is made up of individual pieces of cut yarn standing upright with ends exposed. This gives cut pile a smoother, softer look and feel than loop pile carpet, and it is the most common style of home carpeting used today. (Cut pile can come in many different pile lengths, from plush pile, which has short, densely packed, evenly cut pile, making for a smooth, velvety feel, to shag pile, which has very long pile, giving shag carpet its characteristic shaggy look.)
- Loop pile is carpet in which the loops of yarn stitched into the backing are left intact. This makes it more durable than cut pile carpet, and gives it a stiffer, more formal look. Loop pile carpet is commonly used in high traffic areas, such as hallways and staircases, and in commercial buildings.
- Another style: cut and loop pile, or cut-uncut pile, carpet that employs both cut and loop pile, in a way that creates distinctive visible patterns.

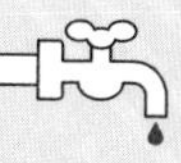

Why are black cars banned in Turkmenistan? The country's dictator, Gurbanguly Berdimuhamedow, thinks they're ugly. (He likes white cars.)

BACKING. The backing of a carpet is the fabric that makes up the underside of a carpet—the part that touches the floor—as opposed to the pile or face. On tufted carpets (see below), there are two types of backing: primary backing is the fabric that the pile yarn is attached to; secondary backing is material laminated to the primary backing, adding strength and stability to the overall carpet.

CARPET. Typically used to refer to wall-to-wall carpeting, as opposed to rug, which refers to a textile floor covering that covers just a portion of a floor.

FRIEZE. A type of cut pile carpet (pronounced "free-ZAY") made with relatively long, highly twisted yarn, creating a rough, frizzy-looking carpet. It's similar to shag carpet, but more durable and less likely to become matted down.

BERBER CARPET. Originally the name for hand-woven, low-profile, loop pile carpets made from coarse wools by Berber peoples in North Africa. Today, berber is used as a broad term for "flecked" loop pile carpets—single-colored carpets (often beige or light brown) with flecks of lighter or darker colors.

FACE WEIGHT. The weight of the fabric that makes up the face or pile of a carpet (not including the backing), normally expressed in ounces per square meter. Most carpets have a face weight between 35 and 60 ounces per square meter. Note: A higher face weight does not indicate a higher quality, especially between different types of carpet. A high-quality berber carpet, for example, can have a lower face weight than a low-quality frieze carpet, simply because the berber has a lower profile and, therefore, less yarn per square meter.

FIELD. The large, central part of a carpet.

GRINNING. A term describing carpet damage in which backing shows through damaged or deteriorated rows of carpet pile.

HAND. The feel of the carpet to your hand, e.g., a carpet can have a scratchy hand, a smooth hand, a rough hand, etc.

PILE CRUSH. The flattening of a carpet's pile due to foot traffic, furniture, etc.

PLY. Yarn is made up of individual plies, or filaments, of fiber twisted together. Two-ply yarn—made up of two plies twisted around each other—is the most common type of yarn used in modern carpets.

TUFT. A single piece of yarn in a carpet's pile.

SPROUT. A tuft of pile yarn that sticks up out of the level of the rest of the pile. (Note: Never pull on a sprout! If it's a loop cut carpet, you could end up pulling out an entire row of pile. Just use scissors to cut the sprout to proper pile height.)

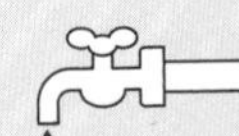

Good news? Bad news? Cancerous tumors can be destroyed by other cancerous tumors, which are called "hypertumors."

SELVAGE. The finished edge of a carpet or rug. Derived from "self-edge," it's what keeps a carpet from unraveling.

TUFTED CARPET. Carpet made on a tufting machine, rather than being woven on a loom. The machine uses rows of needles to punch tufts of pile yarn through a primary backing material. The tufts are held in place with a layer of glue, then covered with a secondary backing. Tufting machines can produce either loop pile or cut pile carpet.

ZIPPERING. A term describing what happens when a row of loop pile carpeting is pulled out of the carpet backing.

TWIST. Refers to the number of times the plies of a yarn are twisted around each other per inch. Most carpet yarns have a TPI (turns per inch) of 3.0 or 6.0. Generally, the higher the TPI, the better the carpet quality, because the more the pile yarn is twisted, the stronger and more resistant it is to traffic and pile crush.

SAXONY. A cut pile carpet style consisting of relatively long, highly twisted, densely packed yarn, all cut to the same length, resulting in a very smooth and luxurious look and feel, similar to plush but with longer threads.

LEVEL-LOOP PILE. A style of loop pile carpet where the loops are all the same height, producing an even and smooth pile texture. Another style, multi-level loop carpet, has loops of different heights, usually just two, which creates a visible pattern in the carpet's pile.

AXMINSTER CARPET. A generic term for a style of cut pile carpet made using a weaving method similar to the one that's used to produce velvet and chenille. Once considered the height of luxury, it originated in the 1750s at a carpet factory in the town of Axminster, England, and is still commonly used today. The Axminster weaving style is especially suited for creating multicolored and intricately designed carpets.

DIY TIP

If you don't have an anti-static carpet—and you have a "carpet shock" problem at home—mix one part fabric softener with four parts water in a large spray bottle, finely spray your carpet with the mix, and let it dry before walking on it. It will cut down on carpet shock for a few months.

BROADLOOM. Carpet woven on broad (or wide) looms—to reduce the number of seams in a wall-to-wall installation. Broadloom carpets come in rolls of at least 54 inches wide, and most commonly today in 12-foot-wide rolls.

ANTI-STATIC CARPET. Carpets created or treated to prevent the buildup of static electricity when you walk across them—so you're less likely to get a shock when you reach for a doorknob.

Groaner: Someone stole all the carpeting out of my house. Police think it was the work of rug addicts.

WEIRD CANADA

O Canada: land of maple trees and professional hockey players, where the mountains are capped with snow and the news stories are really, really strange.

SALT LICK CITY

In late November 2020, town officials in Jasper, Alberta, posted multiple electronic traffic signs bearing a simple and direct message: "Do not let moose lick your car." Wild moose are abundant in this part of Canada, and human civilization, with its attractive food sources (especially salt), can be irresistible to the animals. "They're obsessed with salt. It's one of the things they need for the minerals in their body," Jasper National Park spokesman Steve Young told reporters. "They usually get it from salt lakes in the park." But in winter months, the moose have collectively realized they can acquire it from mobile salt licks: cars. Highway-grade salt, used in large quantities to de-ice roads, can splash onto cars and stick there. Locals are advised to not let moose lick their cars because it sets a dangerous precedent—knowing they can get salt from automobiles attracts the animals to the road, where they can be struck and killed.

HAVE A SEAT

An officer with the Halton Regional Police Service based in Burlington, Ontario, pulled over a driver one day in December 2020. The motorist was obeying speed and other safety laws, but something appeared wrong: the driver was sitting too low in their seat. After stopping the car, the officer immediately realized the issue: the driver had replaced their car seat with a folding lawn chair. HRPS seized the vehicle and cited the driver on a charge of operating an unsafe vehicle and for not wearing a seat belt (because lawn chairs don't have seat belts).

BEARING IT

The Canadian equivalent of Veterans Day is Remembrance Day, observed on November 11 in honor of members of the country's armed forces who died in the line of duty. On Remembrance Day 2015, a polar bear was born at the Toronto Zoo, and zoo officials named her Juno, after Juno Beach, reclaimed from German forces by Canadian soldiers during the D-Day invasions of World War II. That inspired the Canadian military to adopt Juno as its mascot. When the bear made her public debut in February 2016, the Canadian Army made her an honorary private. When Juno turned five, she was promoted again. The polar bear is now a master corporal.

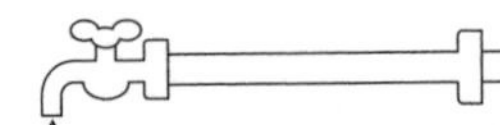

THE MAN IS IN THE MAIL

On page 27 we told you about the "good old days" when people could—legally—mail their children from one address to another. Here's the story of one adult who managed to do it too.

IF AT FIRST YOU DON'T SUCCEED...

In the Australian summer of December 1963 to February 1964, a 22-year-old athlete named Reggie Spiers tried out to qualify for the Australian Olympic team as a javelin thrower. He didn't make the cut, but rather than give up, he went to England, where the tryouts were held later, and tried again. Once again, he failed to make the team. Now he was out of the Olympics and out of luck, stuck in England with no money and no plane ticket home.

Then a British athlete and friend of Spiers's named John McSorley got him a job in the export cargo department of London's Heathrow Airport. There, Spiers earned enough money for a plane ticket back to Australia...but soon after he got the money, his wallet was stolen. He was out of luck again.

THINKING INSIDE THE BOX

"I thought, 'If the animals can do it, I can do it.' "

Spiers was desperate to get home to Adelaide, because his young daughter's birthday was just a few weeks away. He had seen, at the airport, how animals in crates were shipped COD, or "cash on delivery," which meant they were shipped first and paid for later, after they reached their destination. "I thought, 'If [the animals] can do it, I can do it,' " he told the BBC in 2015. Shipping himself as air freight was *more* expensive than buying a plane ticket (not to mention illegal), but if Spiers were able to ship himself COD, he could leave immediately and worry about how to pay for it after he got home to Australia. He decided to do it.

John McSorley had some carpentry experience and reluctantly agreed to build his friend a crate. It was five feet long, three feet tall, and two and a half feet wide, just large enough for Spiers to sit up with his legs stretched out, or lie down with his knees bent. The crate contained straps on the inside to secure Spiers in place while it was being moved. And though it looked like an ordinary nailed-together shipping crate that would need to be pried open with a crowbar, it contained secret latches inside that Spiers could use to let himself out whenever the plane was airborne and he was alone inside the cargo hold.

CRATE EXPECTATIONS

When the crate was finished, Spiers slapped a shipping label on it that described the contents as "rubberized emulsion" being shipped to a nonexistent shoe company in Perth. Spiers was scheduled to depart London in October 1964, and when the day arrived, he sealed himself inside the crate with a pillow and a blanket, some canned food and a bottle of water, plus a flashlight and an empty bottle to pee in. McSorley delivered Spiers to the airport and the crate was loaded onto an airplane bound for Paris, his first stop on the way to Perth in Western Australia.

When the plane finally took off after a 24-hour delay due to fog, Spiers was able to climb out of the crate. But he barely had a chance to stretch and then pee into a can before the plane began its descent into Paris. He quickly climbed back inside the crate, realizing only too late that he'd left the can with the pee in it on top of the crate. When the plane landed in Paris, the can o' pee was discovered by baggage handlers, who assumed it had been put there as a joke by airport workers in London. How else could it have gotten there? "They were saying some terrible things about the English. But they didn't even think about the box. So I kept on going," Spiers later told the BBC.

HOMECOMING

In Paris, the crate was transferred to a plane bound for Bombay, India. After arriving in Bombay, it spent four hours sitting on the tarmac, roasting in the hot sun with Spiers inside before it was loaded onto a plane bound for Perth. Then, after a final flight lasting more than 15 hours, Spiers was back in Australia. He'd spent more than 63 hours in transit on a journey of more than 13,000 miles.

In Perth, the crate was locked inside a bond shed, where it was supposed to sit until someone claimed it and paid the shipping charges. But Spiers let himself out of the crate, and then used some tools he found in the shed to cut a hole in the wall. He climbed through the hole, walked out of the airport, and hitchhiked the 1,300 miles back to Adelaide, arriving just in time for his daughter's birthday.

The only reason we know the story today is because Spiers never let John McSorley in England know that he'd made it home safe. After waiting for a week and hearing nothing, a panicked McSorley contacted a sportswriter with the London *Daily Telegraph* newspaper, who used his contacts in Australia to track down Spiers and confirm that he had indeed survived the trip. The *Daily Telegraph* ran the story and so did Australian newspapers, and Spiers became an instant celebrity, the very embodiment of youthful Australian pluck, daring, and resourcefulness.

NOT SO FAST

If you're getting any funny ideas about repeating Spiers's stunt, think again: repeated hijackings and bombings over the years, and especially the 9/11 attacks in 2001, have caused airlines to ramp up security dramatically. Today all air freight is carefully screened before it's loaded aboard an aircraft, and the penalties for stowing away on a plane have become much stiffer. Do yourself a favor—just buy a ticket and ride in the passenger compartment like everyone else.

Before plastics, tortoiseshell glasses really were made from turtle and tortoise shells. The trade of actual turtle and tortoise shells was banned in 1973.

RATED PG-13 FOR VERY BAD WEATHER

The Motion Picture Association of America rates every mainstream film released in the United States, giving it a G, PG, PG-13, R, or NC-17. The ratings are a quick way to advise audiences about the content of a film, as well as its age-appropriateness. But along with a letter rating, the MPAA provides the filmmakers with a brief explanation of why it gave a film that particular grade. (Why, for instance, the film got a PG-13 instead of a PG.) And some of those explanations are pretty odd.

***Team America: World Police* (2004, R)**
"Graphic, crude, and sexual humor, violent images, and strong language—all involving puppets"

***The Brady Bunch Movie* (1995, PG-13)**
"Racy innuendos"

***Twister* (1996, PG-13)**
"Intense depiction of very bad weather"

***Grumpier Old Men* (1995, PG-13)**
"Salty language and innuendos"

***The Monuments Men* (2014, PG-13)**
"Images of war violence and historical smoking"

***Much Ado About Nothing* (1993, PG-13)**
"Momentary sensuality"

***Alice in Wonderland* (2010, PG)**
"Fantasy action/violence involving scary images and situations, and a smoking caterpillar"

***Jefferson in Paris* (1995, PG-13)**
"Mature themes, some images of violence, and a bawdy puppet show"

***3 Ninjas Knuckle Up* (1995, PG-13)**
"Non-stop ninja action"

The monster in the 1954 horror classic *Creature from the Black Lagoon* was designed to look like an Oscar statue with "gills, fins, and scales."

The Skateboard Kid 2 **(PG)**
"Brief mild language and an adolescent punch in the nose"

Pink Flamingos **(1972, NC-17)**
"A wide range of perversions in explicit detail"

Matilda **(1996, PG)**
"Elements of exaggerated meanness and ridicule, and for some mild language"

Cutie and the Boxer **(2013, R)**
"Nude art images"

Mother's Boys **(1993, R)**
"Language, and for a mother's sociopathic behavior"

Blue Crush **(2002, PG-13)**
"Sexual content, teen partying, language, and a fight"

For the Moment **(1993, PG-13)**
"Sexual situations, language, and a poignant death"

Addams Family Values **(1993, PG-13)**
"Macabre humor"

Ghost in the Machine **(1993, R)**
"High-tech horror violence"

Beethoven's 2nd **(1993, PG)**
"Mild language and unsuitable teen behavior"

Little Giants **(1994, PG)**
"Kids' rude language and pranks"

Bats **(1999, PG-13)**
"Intense sequences of bat attacks, and brief language"

The Dentist **(1996, R)**
"Graphic violence including scenes of dental torture, sexuality, and some language"

Texas Chainsaw Massacre: The Next Generation **(1994, R)**
"Demented mayhem and torture, and for strong language"

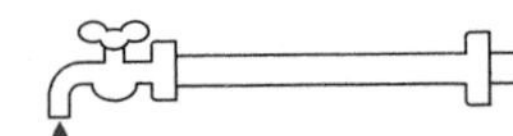

Some actual delicacies at Roman feasts: stewed snails, flamingo tongue, and dormice dipped in honey.

THE SURGEON AND THE GUINEA PIG, PART II

If you've ever wondered how doctors know what they know about the human body, this story will give you a little insight. As with the first part of the tale (on page 111), be forewarned: The descriptions are graphic and not *for the faint of heart...or stomach.*

STRINGS ATTACHED

Dr. Beaumont began his first set of experiments on St. Martin in May 1825, by tying silk strings to pieces of different kinds of food—chunks of beef and pork, slices of cabbage and other vegetables, cubes of bread, etc.—and inserting them directly into St. Martin's stomach through the fistula. He removed the foods at hourly intervals to see how long it took the stomach to digest each kind of food, and to get a better idea of precisely how they were digested.

Some experiments produced little pain or discomfort for St. Martin, but others were quite uncomfortable. "The lad complaining of considerable distress and uneasiness at the stomach, general debility and lassitude, with some pain in his head, I withdrew the strings [with chunks of raw beef, boiled beef, and stewed beef attached]," Beaumont noted during the very first experiment. "The boy still complaining, I did not return them anymore." In other experiments, St. Martin complained of vertigo, nausea, "dimness and yellowness of vision," faintness, a sinking feeling in the pit of his stomach, loss of appetite, and other symptoms. Undeterred, Beaumont plowed on.

IN THE TUBES

As he stuffed foods into St. Martin, he conducted parallel experiments in test tubes using gastric juices he'd collected from the young man's stomach. He placed pieces of the same foods into the test tubes, added the gastric juices, then immersed the test tubes in a hot water bath heated to 100°F, the temperature he'd recorded inside St. Martin's stomach by poking a thermometer through the fistula while the young man was digesting food.

Just as the food had been completely digested in St. Martin's stomach, the food in the test tubes was also fully digested, proving the theory that digestion was a chemical process involving the gastric juices, and that it took place almost entirely in the stomach. The foods digested a little more quickly in the stomach than they did in the test tubes, something Beaumont attributed to the churning motion of the stomach he'd observed during digestion. (Luckily for St. Martin, the gastric juices were also very good at killing germs and bacteria, which is how he was able to survive one invasive experiment after another.)

HE DIDN'T HAVE THE STOMACH

Beaumont experimented on St. Martin from May until August of 1825. That month he made a trip to Plattsburgh, New York, near the Canadian border, and he brought St. Martin along with him. Big mistake: The young man was from Quebec, and after four long months enduring Beaumont's experiments, the trip so close to Canada proved to be too much of a temptation. "[St. Martin] returned to Canada, his native place, without obtaining my consent," the doctor noted. "Being unable to ascertain the place of his resort, I gave him up as a lost subject for physiological experiments... He remained in Canada for four years."

It wasn't until 1829 that Beaumont discovered where St. Martin was living. He hired agents of the American Fur Company—St. Martin's employer before the accident—to go to Canada and entice him into returning. St. Martin and his family eventually did agree to join Beaumont at his new posting at Fort Crawford in Wisconsin, but only "after considerable difficulty, and at great expense to me," Beaumont complained.

Once again, St. Martin was employed as Beaumont's servant and once again he allowed himself to be subjected to medical experimentation. This time, Beaumont studied the effect that temperature, exercise, and emotions have on digestion, among other areas of inquiry. St. Martin remained with Beaumont from December 1829 until March 1831, when he went back to Canada. In November 1832, he returned to Beaumont and was experimented upon until March 1833. Then he returned to Canada, this time for good.

GOING TO PRESS

That year, Beaumont published an account of his experiments on St. Martin, and the conclusions he'd drawn from them, in a book entitled *Experiments and Observations on the Gastric Juice, and the Physiology of Digestion.* Among his 51 conclusions were that the stomach does most of the work of digestion, which is accomplished by chemical action involving gastric juices containing hydrochloric acid. The gastric juices are secreted through the lining of the stomach, but only when food is present, and only gradually and only in sufficient quantities to digest the amount of food contained in the stomach. No gastric juices are present when the stomach is empty either before or after digestion, and the lining of the stomach is coated with a layer of mucus that protects it from digesting itself while it's digesting food.

Beaumont found that vegetables are not as easy to digest as meat, and that foods high in starch, including boiled rice and bread, are some of the easiest foods to digest. "The time ordinarily required for the disposal of a moderate meal of...meat, with bread, etc., is from three to three and a half hours," he observed. People typically eat more food than they need to live, and indigestion occurs when people eat more food in a short period of time than the stomach can readily digest, he concluded. He also found that excessive alcohol consumption—St. Martin was a drinker—irritates the lining of

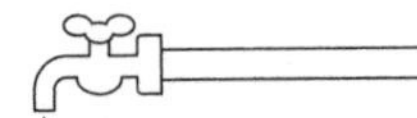

How many do you have? In the 1970s, there were about two radios for every person in the United States.

the stomach and "always produces disease of the stomach, if persevered in," the doctor wrote. (Beaumont wasn't right about everything: he also concluded that spicy mustard and other "stimulating condiments" are "injurious to the healthy stomach.")

JUST LIKE THAT

After his book was published, Beaumont was eager to continue his study of the stomach and digestive system, but to do that he needed St. Martin's cooperation. He never got it. Though Beaumont spent the next 20 years beseeching St. Martin to return to the United States and consent to further experimentation, the Canadian stubbornly stayed put on his farm in Quebec, where he fathered several more children.

Ironically, after spending so many years studying a man who had survived for so long after suffering such a grievous injury, Beaumont met his own end very quickly. One freezing-cold day in St. Louis, Missouri, in April 1853, he slipped on some icy steps and died from his injuries. He was 67. St. Martin outlived Beaumont by 27 years, dying in 1880 at the age of 78. By then he'd lived with the hole in his stomach for just over 58 years.

So was St. Martin's gunshot wound a contributing factor in his death? No one will ever know for sure: Like St. Martin himself, his family apparently had had enough of all the poking and prodding, and they refused to consent to a postmortem exam. They were so determined that St. Martin not receive an autopsy that they delayed his burial until well after decomposition set in, thinking that a rotten corpse would be less of an attraction for the "resurrection men" who plied their grisly trade digging up dead bodies and selling them to medical schools.

NOT (QUITE) FORGOTTEN

Nearly 200 years after it was published, *Experiments and Observations on the Gastric Juice, and the Physiology of Digestion* is considered a seminal work in the field of gastroenterology, the study of the stomach and intestines, as well as one of the most important medical texts written in the 19th century.

Beaumont himself is celebrated as the "Father of Gastric Physiology," a true giant in the annals of medicine. He has had an elementary school, a high school, a medical school, at least four hospitals, and even a stretch of highway named in his honor. Poor Alexis St. Martin, who suffered so mightily to advance the cause of science, is little more than an historical footnote. No schools, hospitals, or highways have been named for him. It wasn't until 1962, more than 80 years after his death, that someone even thought to erect, in the cemetery where he is buried, a modest marker describing his contribution to medicine.

St. Martin has received at least one accolade, however: inside the William Beaumont Army Medical Center in El Paso Texas, the *cafeteria* has been named in honor of the man who owes his place in history to the fact that he was shot in the stomach.

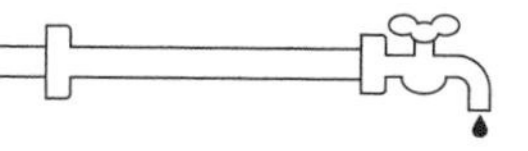

First major movie dubbed into a Native American language: *Star Wars*, in 2013.

WHALE TALE: OLD TIMER

Whale researchers can learn a lot by studying individual whales over a long period of time. Old Timer, as his name suggests, has been studied for nearly half a century.

TAIL O' THE WHALE

In the summer of 1971, a pioneering whale researcher named Charles Jurasz was whale watching in the Lynn Canal in southeast Alaska when a particular humpback whale surfaced and flapped its tail on the water. Jurasz snapped a photo of the underside of the tail as its markings were exposed; those markings have since been described as looking like "black with white shading, like dots of shaving cream left on a full beard." Jurasz filed the photograph away as part of a database he was building of humpback tail markings.

Why did he do that? Because the patterns on humpback tails are as unique as fingerprints, and they can be used to distinguish one humpback whale from another. By tracking individual whales over time, scientists can study migratory routes, reproductive trends, changes in behavior roles, and other areas of scientific interest.

DID YOU KNOW?

At more than 90 feet long and weighing more than 330,000 pounds, the blue whale is the largest animal that has ever lived on Earth—even larger than the Argentinosaurus, the largest dinosaur discovered to date. Adult blue whales weigh more than 24 times as much as the largest land animal living today, the African bush elephant. But its food is small: blue whales feed on krill, tiny shrimplike creatures that are about the size of jelly beans. A blue whale can eat as much as six tons of krill a day.

DÉJÀ VIEW

What makes this particular whale special is that it has been sighted multiple times over a longer period of time than any other humpback whale ever—more than 40 years as of 2015. Because of that, he's earned the nickname "Old Timer." After that first sighting in 1971, Jurasz spotted him again in Alaska in August 1978. Then in the winter of 1990, Old Timer was seen off the coast of Hawaii escorting a mother and calf. (Humpbacks in the northern Pacific migrate between Alaskan waters in the summer and Hawaiian waters in the winter.) In the winter of 2006, the humpback was spotted in Hawaiian waters again, this time defending his position next to a lone female from other males who were competing for her attention. This behavior confirmed that he was a male.

SOMEBODY CALL GUINNESS

Old Timer entered the record books in August 2015 when he was sighted yet again, this time in Frederick Sound, Alaska, 44 years after his first sighting, by Adam

Pack, a biologist from the University of Hawaii. Pack and a colleague were aboard a boat called the *Northern Song* when Old Timer surfaced nearby and lifted his tail out of the water, revealing his signature "dots of shaving cream" pattern. "We just looked at each other and said, 'There's Old Timer!' and we literally jumped up and high-fived right there on the front of the boat," Pack says. A photo taken that day shows that the markings on the tail are virtually identical to those in photos taken by Charles Jurasz in the 1970s.

Old Timer was about 50 years old in 2015, and since humpback whales can live to be 70–100 years of age, the prospects for more sightings in the future are good. One complicating factor, however, is the fact that the humpback whale population in the northern Pacific Ocean has rebounded tremendously since the late 1960s, when they were hunted nearly to extinction. Thanks to a worldwide moratorium on commercial whaling, the population of fewer than 1,000 whales then has grown to well over 20,000 whales today. So even if Old Timer is never spotted again, it may be good news: he's become just another face in the crowd.

MOUTHING OFF

DEAR JOHN

John Waters is the writer and director of several bizarre cult films, such as Pink Flamingos *and* Polyester, *as well as the campy hit* Hairspray. *He's picked up some wise (and very funny) lessons along the way.*

"True success is figuring out your life and career so you never have to be around jerks."

"It wasn't until I started reading and found books they wouldn't let us read in school that I discovered you could be insane and happy and have a good life without being like everybody else."

"To understand bad taste one must have very good taste."

"As far as socially redeeming value, I hope I don't have any."

"My idea of an interesting person is someone who is quite proud of their seemingly abnormal life and turns their disadvantage into a career."

"I'M SO LUCKY TO BE HAVING A HAPPY CHILDHOOD AS AN ADULT."

"I always wanted to be a juvenile delinquent, but my parents wouldn't let me."

"Cheer up. You never know—maybe something awful will happen tomorrow."

"I'D LOVE TO SELL OUT COMPLETELY. IT'S JUST THAT NOBODY HAS BEEN WILLING TO BUY."

LIFESAVERS

Now for some true stories to restore your faith in humanity, brought to you by the kindness of strangers.

GAME NOT OVER

Caroline Jackson of Widnes, England, was watching TV with her husband one evening in January 2020, while their 17-year-old son, Aidan, was upstairs in his room playing video games. "The next thing we noticed," Jackson told BBC News, "was two police cars outside with flashing lights." The officers said they received a call from America that someone at this address was having a seizure. They all rushed upstairs to discover Aidan was "extremely disoriented" and in danger of choking on his tongue. (He was prone to seizures but hadn't had one for eight months.) Good thing for Aidan that he was in the same online game as Dia Lathora, 20, of Texas. When Aidan started acting strangely, Lathora tried unsuccessfully to get his phone number. But she did have his address, so she got ahold of the Widnes police and told them she could hear him "seizing and breathing really hard and it sounds like he was choking and crying." Had Dia not called for help, Aidan could have died. "I thank her every day," said Jackson.

ALL TOGETHER NOW

In January 2020, a 25-year-old woman (unidentified in press reports) was run over by an SUV on a busy street corner in New York City. A passerby rushed over and saw that she was alive, but trapped under the vehicle. By then, a couple more people had gathered around. They tried to lift the SUV off her, but it was too heavy. Then a few more people offered to help, but they couldn't lift it high enough to safely pull her out. Then a few *more* people joined in, then a few more, until there were nearly two dozen New Yorkers surrounding the SUV. They all lifted together, and the woman was freed. An ambulance took her to the hospital, and the heroes dispersed. (The woman was later released without serious injury.)

HAIL TO THE BUS DRIVER

On a bitter cold morning in January 2019, a Milwaukee bus driver named Irena Ivic saw something very wrong: a baby, barely old enough to walk, was running down a sidewalk all by herself...on a freeway overpass. Ivic stopped the bus and, as her stunned passengers looked on, she ran over to the baby as it was running toward the road. Ivic called for him to stop. He did, and then turned around and ran toward her, and she scooped her up. "Oh my god. Oh my god," Ivic kept repeating when she got back to her driver's seat with the baby, who was barefoot and wearing only a onesie

in the subfreezing temperatures. By the time police and firefighters arrived a few minutes later, the baby had fallen asleep in Ivic's arms. (Police reported that she had gotten away from her mother, and was later returned to her father.) According to a Milwaukee County Transit System statement, Ivic isn't the only hero in their employ: "This is the ninth lost or missing child found by MCTS drivers in recent years."

No one around her knew what to do... and the boy was turning purple!

HOMECOMING HERO

Nicole Hornback and her two-year-old son Clarke were watching the 2019 Rockwall High School Homecoming Parade in Texas when the toddler suddenly stopped breathing. Hornback tried the Heimlich maneuver, but she'd never been trained, and Clarke still wasn't breathing. "Somebody help me! Somebody help me!" No one around her knew what to do, either...and the boy was turning purple! Then, from out of nowhere (actually, from a parade float), Tyra Winters swooped in and said, "I got him." Then the 17-year-old cheerleader, who was CPR-certified, gave Clarke three strong thrusts and dislodged a piece of candy from his throat. Then she jumped back on the float and continued her routine. A few weeks later, Hornback went to Rockwall High to properly thank Winters, who said she wants to be a pediatrician when she grows up. She's off to a pretty good start.

EXCESSIVE USE OF FORCE

New Jersey Transit Police (NJTP) Officer Victor Ortiz isn't a small guy—he's 5'11" and weighs nearly 200 pounds—but the unruly train passenger was much taller and outweighed him by at least 100 pounds. Ortiz, a 16-year veteran of NJTP, was patrolling Secaucus Junction after his shift had ended, waiting for his replacement (who was late), when he got a call about a disorderly passenger on the platform. Ortiz and the train conductor tried to calm the 56-year-old man, but after a brief scuffle, the man jumped onto the train tracks, laid down, and said he wanted to die...just as a train was approaching. Ortiz tried to wrestle the man off the tracks; he even managed to get one of the man's wrists cuffed, but he was just too big and too strong. With the train closing in, "There was an instance where he started to pull me in further, toward him," Ortiz told WNBC New York. He was faced with a life-or-death decision: "I'm either going to let him go and the consequences of [his actions] will be on him, or I try to pull one more time, and try to get this guy off the tracks." Ortiz decided to try. It was as tense as any action movie you've ever seen: CCTV footage shows Ortiz grabbing the man's hands and using every bit of his strength to drag him off the tracks, a split second before the train barrels through. (The man was later charged with several crimes; his condition was not reported.) Ortiz, who was scheduled for a vacation the next day, tried to downplay all the "hero" talk: "It's part of the job."

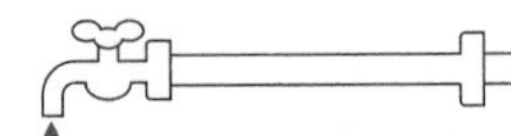

Does yours? 60 percent of American cars have at least one bumper sticker.

IRONIC FACTS

One of our all-time favorite ironic facts is that Dolly Parton once lost a Dolly Parton lookalike contest. Here are some others.

98 percent of Earth's water is undrinkable (and most of the water that is drinkable is trapped in the polar ice caps).

Cotton candy, considered one of the least healthy foods for your teeth because of its high sugar content and sticky texture, was invented in 1897 by William Morrison, a dentist.

Light and fluffy? The average cloud weighs about a million pounds.

According to experts, one of the most often misspelled words in English is the word "misspell." (Tip: it's mis + spell.)

Cindy Lauper's 1983 "feminist anthem," "Girls Just Want to Have Fun," was written by a man (country singer Robert Hazard).

Q: What does *sesquipedalophobia* mean?
A: The fear of long words.

Which young, social media–savvy celebrity holds the Guinness World Record for "fastest time to reach 1 million followers on Instagram"? That would be 94-year-old British naturalist Sir David Attenborough, who did it in 4 hours, 44 minutes when he joined in September 2020, beating the previous record holder, 50-year-old Jennifer Aniston, by 32 minutes.

"Stand by Your Man" singer Tammy Wynette was married five times.

Every time you feel physical pain, it's because your brain has alerted you to that fact, thanks to nociceptors, sensory nerve cells that produce signals that travel via nerve fibers to your brain. The ironic part: Your brain is the only organ in your body that has no nociceptors, which is why you can be awake during brain surgery and not even feel it.

A butterfly, regarded as the most beautiful insect, will never see its own wings.

Worried about getting a computer virus while online? According to security firm Symantec, "Religious websites carry three times more malware threats than pornography sites."

Felix Powell, who wrote the 1915 song "Pack Up Your Troubles in Your Old Kit Bag and Smile, Smile, Smile," later took his own life.

In an effort to protect the environment, more and more municipalities are banning the use of plastic shopping bags, but allowing the use of paper bags. Only problem: compared to a plastic bag, each paper bag requires 94 percent more water and 71 percent more energy to produce.

There's a small village in Norway that freezes over every winter. It's called Hell.

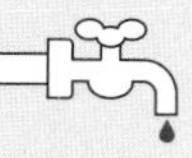

Not just a martial artist: Bruce Lee (1940–73) was an excellent dancer. In 1958, he won the Hong Kong, China, cha-cha ballroom dancing championship.

SUGARTIME

We've all had the experience of trying to finish a letter or a school paper, and finding ourselves at a loss for words. Here's a famous case of writer's block that was resolved "in the most delightful way."

SOMETHING NEW

In 1955, a polio vaccine developed by Dr. Jonas Salk became available to the public. Six years later, a new vaccine was developed by a researcher named Albert Sabin. Sabin's vaccine offered a number of advantages over Salk's: it provided longer-lasting immunity to the polio virus, and it was easier to administer because it was given orally, in droplet form, instead of by injection. That eliminated the need for sterile hypodermic needles, making the Sabin vaccine more suitable for mass vaccination campaigns.

Just as importantly, at least as far as kids were concerned, was that no shots meant no pain and no fear of needles. The vaccine did have a bitter, salty taste, but that was easily remedied by putting the vaccine on sugar cubes and having kids eat the cubes.

One kid who was more than happy to get the vaccine this way was a Los Angeles eight-year-old named Jeffrey Sherman. Like a lot of children his age, he hated getting shots. "I was big for my age and notorious for pushing over the tray of hypodermics my doctor's nurse brought in. I'd often run out and hide a couple of blocks away," he told NBC's *Today* show in 2020. The Sabin vaccine, by comparison, was a piece of cake. It was administered right at school, so Jeffrey didn't even have to go to the doctors' office to get it. The school nurse handed him a small paper cup containing a sugar cube and told him to eat it, and he did. No fuss, no muss—that was it. And now he was immune from polio for life.

A TOUGH DAY AT THE OFFICE

Years later, Sherman still remembered that when he came home from school that day, his father Robert was already home from work, which was very unusual. He almost never came home before 5:30. Even more surprising, he'd closed the curtains and was sitting alone in the darkened house.

Robert Sherman was having a bad day, the latest of many. He and his younger brother Richard were a songwriting team that had been hired by Walt Disney himself to compose songs for the movies produced by Disney's film studio. "The boys," as Disney called them, were currently working on songs for a film in production called *Mary Poppins*, based on a character in a series of children's books by British author P. L. Travers.

The boys had already dreamed up "Chim Chim Cher-ee," "Let's Go Fly a Kite," and "Supercalifragilisticexpialidocious," all of which had been approved for

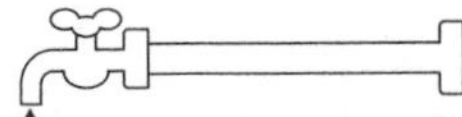

There's no such thing as native Hawaiian pottery. There's not much soil formation on the volcanic islands, so there is very little clay to work with.

the film, but the song they'd thought was the best, "Through the Eyes of Love," had been axed. Julie Andrews, the Broadway star making her feature film debut as Mary Poppins, didn't like the song, so Walt Disney told the Shermans to come up with something else.

They'd spent the last two weeks trying to build songs around familiar phrases like "a stitch in time," and "an apple a day," but nothing seemed to work. And Walt Disney was not a man who would settle for an inferior song or take no for an answer. He wanted a catchy tune that Julie Andrews could live with, and if the Shermans couldn't deliver, there was little doubt that he'd find someone who could. After spending another fruitless day batting ideas around at the studio, Robert grew so discouraged that he knocked off early and went home. That's why he was sitting in the dark that afternoon when eight-year-old Jeffrey came home from school.

JUST THE CURE

"How was school today?" Sherman called out from the dark. Jeffrey replied that he'd had a good day, and that he'd been given the polio vaccine at school.

A day with a vaccine in it was a *good* day for Jeffrey? "Didn't it hurt?" Sherman asked his son, thinking that the vaccine had been administered by injection.

"No. They dropped the medicine on a sugar cube and you just ate it," Jeffrey responded.

The house grew quiet as Sherman pondered this. "Dad stared at me a long time, and then said, 'thank you,' and went to call my uncle," Jeffrey remembered. "The next day they wrote 'A Spoonful of Sugar.' "

DID YOU KNOW?

Songwriter Doc Pomus (1925–91) was paralyzed by polio as a boy and used a wheelchair to get around. In 1957, he married Willi Burke, a Broadway actress and dancer...but was unable to dance with his bride on their wedding day. The poignant sight of her dancing with their guests inspired him to write the song "Save the Last Dance for Me," which the Drifters turned into a #1 hit in 1960.

A SONG FOR THE TIMES

Jeffrey Sherman shared his story on Twitter in the winter of 2020, during the COVID-19 pandemic. The world had been hunkered down for nearly a year waiting for life to return to normal, and the number of cases was surging to new heights. Many people were nonetheless wary of taking a COVID-19 vaccine if one became available, out of fear that the vaccine might be dangerous or—even worse—was part of some vast conspiracy that had nothing to do with the virus. Sherman says he related his childhood experience in the hope of reassuring the public that a vaccine would be a good thing, not bad. "I just want to do what I can to instill that we are all in this together, that we must trust scientists, immunologists and doctors to lead us through this dark time," he wrote. "I thought by posting what I did about this song and its background regarding the polio vaccine, I might change a few minds."

Only person to win an Academy Award and a world championship in rodeo: Ben Johnson (*The Last Picture Show*, 1971).

MORE CLASSIC ROCK ALMOSTS

More stories of how a few twists of fate almost changed the history of rock 'n' roll. (Part I is on page 179.)

THE LOVIN' SPOONFUL ALMOST BECAME THE MONKEES.

Story: For a band that no one talks about that much anymore, the Lovin' Spoonful was a very big deal in the mid-1960s. They had nine top-20 hits from 1965 to 1967. Paul McCartney said the Beatles' "Good Day Sunshine" "was me trying to write something similar to 'Daydream' " (the song that begins "What a day for a daydream"). Ray Davies of the Kinks said he was more influenced by the Spoonful than the Beatles. Eric Clapton has cited the Spoonful as having a huge impact on his band, Cream. One of the Spoonful's other big hits, "Do You Believe in Magic," lives on in numerous TV commercials and in Disney films like *Return to Never Land.*

In 1965, two Hollywood filmmakers, Bob Rafelson and Bert Schneider, set out to make a TV sitcom that would cash in on the popularity of the Beatles' zany adventures in the film *A Hard Day's Night.* The original plan was to hire an existing band, and the Lovin' Spoonful—fresh from New York's Greenwich Village folk scene—fit the bill perfectly. Taking the job would turn them into instant celebrities.

Why It Didn't Happen: Rafelson and Schneider wanted to hire their own songwriters and retain the rights to the songs. "When we were asked to be a television rock 'n' roll group, we knew it was going to be as puppets, and we still had a few things to offer," explained lead singer John Sebastian (whose 1976 solo hit "Welcome Back" was used in 2020 for an Applebee's commercial).

Aftermath: With the Lovin' Spoonful out of contention (the band lasted until 1969), Rafelson and Schneider put out a casting call in Hollywood for "folk & rock musician-singers...four insane boys, age 17–21."

STEPHEN STILLS WAS ALMOST A MONKEE.

Story: More than 400 aspiring musicians and actors auditioned for one of the two remaining spots in NBC's 1966 sitcom about a zany rock group. The first two—English singer/actor Davy Jones and former child star and singer Micky Dolenz—had already been cast through their agents. The third spot went to singer-songwriter Mike Nesmith. Other future stars who tried out included Harry Nilsson and Paul Williams. (Despite the rumor that won't seem to die, Charles Manson did not audition for the Monkees.)

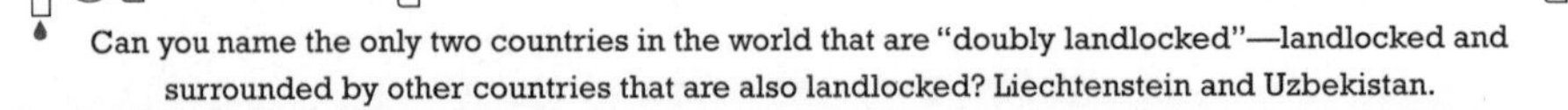

Can you name the only two countries in the world that are "doubly landlocked"—landlocked and surrounded by other countries that are also landlocked? Liechtenstein and Uzbekistan.

Stephen Stills, a 20-year-old singer-songwriter who had made a name for himself in New York's Greenwich Village folk scene, was the top prospect to fill the final spot. He had everything show creators Bob Rafelson and Bert Schneider were looking for: He could act, sing, and write catchy songs. But there were two things about Stills they didn't want.

"I want to write the songs because that's where the moola is."

Why It Didn't Happen: The story most often told is that Stills had "bad teeth and a receding hairline." While those two factors certainly didn't help his chances, there was another reason he never became a Monkee. Like the Lovin' Spoonful, who were originally offered the job but declined, Stills would have had to give up his creative freedom and his publishing rights, so he told them, "I'm not that interested in the show... mainly I want to write the songs because that's where the moola is."

Aftermath: Rafelson asked Stills if he could recommend someone with the same "open Nordic look" (but with better teeth). "I know another guy that's a lot like me," he replied, "and he might be a little bit quicker and funnier." That other guy was Stills's former Greenwich Village bandmate, a 24-year-old folk singer named Peter Tork, who was working as a dishwasher in L.A. when he auditioned for the Monkees.

Tork got the part—playing a dim-witted version of himself, which he never quite lived down—and for the next two years was one of the most famous people in the country. His made-for-TV band outsold the Beatles in that time period, but for Tork, landing the "role of a lifetime" was a double-edged sword. As he sarcastically recalled years later: "Poor Steve had to settle for the consolation prize: Buffalo Springfield and then Crosby, Stills, Nash and Young. Poor boy, he really suffered terribly for not being photogenic. And I dipped into the obscurities of Monkeedom."

Bonus fact: Rafelson and Schneider used their Monkees profits to finance a movie—the 1969 film *Easy Rider,* which brought 1960s counterculture into the mainstream, was one of the year's highest-grossing films, earned two Oscar nominations, and made Jack Nicholson a star.

PHIL COLLINS ALMOST JOINED THE WHO.

Story: From the mid-1960s to the late 1970s, the Who was one of the most respected but unpredictable bands in the world. A big reason for that went to Keith Moon, one of rock's most respected but unpredictable drummers. (The Muppets character Animal was based on Moon.) Then, in 1978, Moon died of a drug overdose, leaving the future of the band in doubt. "The Who were sleepwalking along the edge of a cliff," recalled guitarist Pete Townshend. "The band had become a celebration of itself and was slowly grinding to a halt. But no one would make a decision to call it a day."

One thing that Townshend was craving: stability. As he said in 2020, Moon's reckless abandon—both in his life and behind the kit—made him "difficult to play with." That explains why Townshend looked to fill the empty drum stool with an old friend, Kenney Jones, formerly of the Faces, who was as mild as Moon was wild.

Before the lineup change was announced to the public, however, Townshend got a proposition from Phil Collins, drummer of the progressive rock band Genesis, whose own star had been rising after taking over lead vocals from Peter Gabriel in 1975. As Collins later recalled: "I was working with Townshend just after Moon died, and I said to him: 'Have you got anybody to play the drums? Cos I'd love to do it. I'll leave Genesis.' "

Why It Didn't Happen: "And Pete said: 'F*ck, we've just asked Kenney Jones,'" said Collins, adding, "Because Kenney, unbeknownst to most people, played on stuff when Keith was too out of it. He was far too polite for the Who, but I would have done the job."

Aftermath: It's safe to say that the 1980s would have sounded a whole lot different if Phil Collins had joined the Who. Instead, he stayed with Genesis and also became one of the top-selling solo artists of the decade, with an astounding 13 top-ten songs between 1984 and 1990.

The Who didn't fare as well. Jones lasted for two studio albums—neither of which performed well—and lead singer Roger Daltrey later admitted that he never thought the staid drummer was a "good fit." The Who disbanded in 1982 after embarking on its first "Farewell Tour."

Collins did join the Who in L.A. in 1989 for a star-studded performance of the 1969 rock opera *Tommy*. And he has high praise for the man who's been drumming behind Townshend and Daltrey in recent years: Zak Starkey, son of Ringo Starr and godson of Keith Moon. "They've got a great drummer now in Zak," said Collins. "Someone with the balls that Moony had."

* * *

A FISH STORY

Peter Joyce was paddling the Waccamaw River in North Carolina on a hot summer day in 2020 when, as he later described, "I thought I heard a fish jump to my left." So he looked over to his left...just in time to see a large alligator coming at him. At full speed. With its head all the way out of the water. Before Joyce could react, the gator plowed into his kayak and capsized it, sending Joyce underwater. Luckily, Joyce was able to grab a nearby tree limb and right the boat (and himself). By that time, the gator was gone. "Turned out not to be a fish," he said.

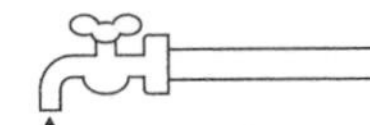

THIS IS AN INSULT!

After learning about the origins and original meanings of these common putdown words, you'll finally know what your older brother was really *calling you all those years ago.*

WIMP

"It seems to have originated in the USA in the 1920s, although it was not really used much until the 1960s. There was an earlier slang term 'wimp' which meant 'woman,' used at Oxford University in the early years of the 20th century. This could be the origin, or wimp could simply be an alteration of whimper. Like bonk, drum, and hoot, whimper is another of those words suggested by the sound it represents." (From *Oxford Dictionary of Word Origins,* by Oxford University Press)

IDIOT

"*Idiot,* meaning a very foolish or stupid person, comes from the Greek *idiotes,* 'private,' which comes from *idios,* 'own, peculiar.' In ancient Greece, concerning oneself with public business was the pet hobby of everyone. Anyone who concerned himself with his 'private' business rather than with public business was an *idiot.*" (From *Word Origins,* by Dhirendra Verma)

OAF

"Oaf goes back to Old Norse *alfr,* 'elf.' It originally meant 'elf's child, changeling,' and from this 'an idiot child,' then 'fool' or 'halfwit.' Finally, in the early 20th century, it acquired the general sense of 'large clumsy man,' a sense used by Rudyard Kipling in *The Islanders* (1903) when he called cricketers and footballers 'flannelled fools at the wicket' and 'muddled oafs at the goals.'" (From *Little Oxford Dictionary of Word Origins,* by Julia Cresswell)

NERD

"It seems likely that nerd, a term for a dull, socially inept or otherwise obnoxious person that appeared in U.S. slang in the early 1950s, was inspired by a whimsical creature called a 'nerd' that was invented by the American children's author Dr. Seuss (Theodore Seuss Geisel) and introduced by him in his book *If I Ran the Zoo* (1950): 'And then, just to show them, I'll sail to Ka-Troo and bring back an It-Kutch, a Preep, and a Prog, a Nerkle, a Nerd, and a Seersucker, too!' In thinking up the word he may have been influenced by *Mortimer Snerd,* the name of a dummy used by the American ventriloquist Edgar Bergen." (From *Word Origins,* by John Ayto)

Don't believe it? Count 'em: Total number of cups of coffee consumed on *Friends*: 1,154. Phoebe drank the most (227 cups); Rachel drank the least (138).

WEIRDO

"'Wyrd' was a noun that meant 'fate,' or more specifically, Fate. When Shakespeare called the witches in *Macbeth* the Weird Sisters, he didn't mean they were bizarre, he meant they were the Fates, the three sisters out of Greek mythology who controlled peoples' destinies. As the Fates faded from popular culture, weird came to refer to the second biggest characteristic of the witches—that they were supernatural. Of course, supernatural is often interchangeable with unnatural, which the sisters also were, and unnatural is just a more powerful word for strange or unusual, and thus 'weird' still has all of those meanings to some degree or another. The -o that turns weird into the noun weirdo is thought to come from the Middle English interjection 'o,' and over time become a diminutive suffix." (From Gizmodo.com)

MORON

"*Moron* is the name of the Fool in Moliere's *La Princesse d'Elide* (1664). In 1910, the American Association for the Study of the Feeble-Minded adopted *moron* to designate an adult of the mental age of eight to 12." (From *The Origins of English Words*, by Joseph Twadell Shipley)

GEEK

"'Geek' seems to have started out as a variant of 'geck,' which was a dialect word for a stupid or peculiar person. Coincidentally, someone is actually referred to as a 'geeke' in Shakespeare's *Cymbeline*, but this is likely just a misspelling of 'geck.' So 'geek' chugged along in the 19th century as a general term of contempt. It acquired a particular meaning in early 20th-century carnival sideshows as a person who performed sensational and disgusting acts like biting heads off chickens. So added an element of freakishness to the meaning of the word." (From *Six Words You Never Knew Had Something to Do with Pigs*, by Katherine Barber)

IMBECILE

"*Imbecile* is a word we use to castigate someone we consider to be stupid. It is a handy word for such a use as it not only covers the meaning we want to convey but also sounds impressive, too intelligent a term to be used by someone to whom it may be applied. It only acquired the specific meaning of a stupid person in the 19th century; before that it was applied to any individual who was less than perfectly well, physically as well as mentally. It came into English in the 16th century via French from the Latin *imbecillus*, meaning 'with no support,' from *baculum*, 'stick' or 'staff.'" (From *Useful Dictionary of Word and Phrase Origins*, by Martin Manser)

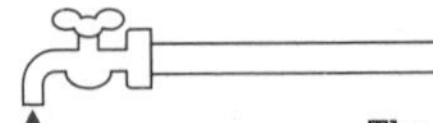

The reason old passenger ships like the *Titanic* had black hulls: they burned coal—black paint helped to hide soot and coal dust.

Q&A: ASK THE EXPERTS

More answers to life's important questions from the world's trivia experts.

IT'S A LONG STORY

Q: *How do those neck-stretching rings traditionally worn by women in some parts of the world actually work?*

A: "Yes, their necks clearly will look longer after wearing them for some time, but it's not a result of their neck bones somehow stretching out—it's because the weight and pressure of the coils pushes their collarbones down. In fact, one of the main reasons why some tribes choose to begin the practice when girls are young is because their bones are more pliant, making the desired results easier to achieve and with less pain. Wearing the rings doesn't just affect the collarbones, though. When the rings push down enough, they can actually cause the position of the rib cage to shift, as well. Typically, wearing the rings will move the rib cage and the collarbones approximately 45 degrees below where they normally sit in the body. Not only are the coils not entirely comfortable to wear, but they can also lead to permanent muscle weakness in the head when worn for long periods." (From *Urbo*)

SHINE ON

Q: *Why don't stars show up in photographs taken by astronauts in space?*

A: "Such pictures do not show stars because the stars aren't bright enough in comparison to the nearby sun and the things it shines on. Virtually all of the astronaut photos are of objects brightly illuminated by the sun. To capture them on film without overexposing the image, you need a relatively short exposure, which does not provide enough time for the film to capture images of stars." (From *The New York Times Second Book of Science Questions and Answers*)

GREEN DAY

Q: *Why is St. Patrick's Day so closely associated with drinking alcohol?*

A: "The first observation of St. Patrick's Day is said to have occurred in the ninth or tenth century. It is observed on March 17 because that was believed to be the date of St. Patrick's death. It was initially celebrated with reverence and a sort of solemn quiet, and seen more as a religious holiday. Eventually, it became a day that was celebrated with a feast. A few centuries ago, the shift toward more of a fun-filled celebration began to happen. St. Patrick's Day fell toward the middle of Lent, but Catholics were given a one-day reprieve from the usual fasting and discipline of the

season and were allowed to indulge in a wide range of food and drink, including alcohol." (From *Reader's Digest*)

WRITE ON

Q: *Why are pencils traditionally that orange-yellow shade?*

A: "Pencils have been painted yellow ever since the 1890s. And that bright color isn't just so you can find them on your desk more easily. In fact, the yellow pencil has a much deeper history than you might expect. During the 1800s, the best graphite in the world came from China. American pencil makers wanted a special way to tell people that their pencils contained Chinese graphite. In China, the color yellow is associated with royalty and respect. American pencil manufacturers began painting their pencils bright yellow to communicate this 'regal' association with China." (From *Pencils.com*)

ONE WHEEL DIFFERENCE

Q: *Why are there different styles of bicycles for men and women?*

A: "Historically, women's bikes did not feature the horizontal top tube, leaving an 'open' frame. This allowed women to step on without having to lift a leg and expose an ankle. It also better accommodated long skirts. The fact that many women's bikes are still designed like this is due less to science than to convention." (From *Cycling Science*, by Max Glaskin)

NEVER ON A MONDAY

Q: *Why are elections in the U.S. always held on Tuesdays?*

A: "In 1792, Congress mandated the first Wednesday in December as the date when the presidential electors would meet to cast their votes for president and vice president. States were required to appoint their electors within the 34 days prior to this Wednesday. But other than that, there was no national election day; each state set its own day to appoint the electors. (It would usually fall in November to comply with the 34-day rule.) Appointing the electors on different days proved to be problematic, so in 1845 Congress established a national election day—the Tuesday following the first Monday in November—on which all states must appoint their electors. Why the Tuesday following the first Monday? Because at the time, many religious people objected to traveling to the polls on Sunday, which eliminated using the first Monday of the month. (In those days, getting to a polling place could mean a full day's journey.) Simply using the first Tuesday of the month wouldn't work either, because it might fall on the first day of the month, which would cause problems for some businesses." (From *Everything You Pretend to Know and Are Afraid Someone Will Ask*, by Lynette Padwa)

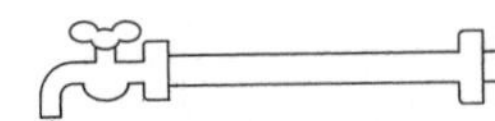

AROUND THE WORLD IN A PAGE AND A HALF

Here's how the globe came to be.

MAP MAY NOT BE TO SCALE

In fourteen hundred and ninety-two, while Columbus was sailing the ocean blue, Martin Behaim was putting the finishing touches on what is now the oldest surviving terrestrial globe in the world. In a testament to just how "dark" the Dark Ages had been in Europe (while many Asian and Middle Eastern cultures flourished), Behaim's 15th-century globe was basically a copy of one made in the second century AD by the Greek geographer Ptolemy. The first globe that historians know of was made in the second century BC by another Greek, Crates of Mallus. "We have now traced on a spherical surface," he wrote, "the area in which we say the inhabited world is situated." That world was missing half its continents, but at least the Greeks knew it wasn't flat, thanks to Aristotle, who pointed out that Earth's shadow was round during a lunar eclipse.

DID YOU KNOW?

Amid the growing popularity of globes, there was even a "pocket globe" fad. From the early 1700s until the late 1800s, globe makers created special mini globes as "large" as three inches in diameter, down to as small as an inch and a half across.

EARTH APPLES

But after the Roman Empire fell in the late 400s, for the next millennium or so, most Europeans *did* believe the world was flat. Then the Age of Discovery, which saw Europeans take to the seas in search of new trading routes, put that notion to rest (because when a ship appeared on the horizon, its mast appeared first), and by the end of the 15th century, globes had become fashionable among the aristocracy. The Holy Roman Emperor's court in Germany commissioned Behaim's "Nuremberg Terrestrial Globe." The townspeople called the 21-inch globe made of hardened strips of linen *Erdapfel*, which means "Earth apple."

Behaim was primarily a merchant, and although his résumé also includes "explorer, cartographer, and astronomer," his "Earth apple" was no more navigable than it was edible. On Behaim's globe, Europe and Africa are somewhat recognizable, but Japan is about 8,000 miles off course, and there's an ocean where the Americas should be. But what it lacked in accuracy Behaim made up for in creativity, with hundreds of notations and drawings of fantastical creatures, mythical lands, zodiac symbols, and whatever else he felt like adding.

Polish Prince Leszek the White's excuse for keeping Poland out of the Fifth Crusade to recapture the Holy Land (1217–21): "There was no wine, mead, or even beer to be had" there.

FILLING IN THE GAPS

In the wake of the voyages of Christopher Columbus, Ferdinand Magellan, Amerigo Vespucci, and others, knowledge of the Earth's geography was growing faster than mapmakers could keep up with. For the next few centuries, globes—which could take up to a year to make—were still reserved for the wealthy.

With the Renaissance in full swing in the 1560s, Flemish geographer and globe maker Gerardus Mercator used mathematics to modernize cartography. His "Mercator projection" flattened the globe to create a two-dimensional world map (the first atlas) that made navigators' jobs easier by keeping the longitude and latitude lines parallel. Mercator also made the first globe that actually resembles Earth's landforms (centuries before satellite photos proved him right).

But what really put the globe on the map, so to speak, was the Industrial Revolution. Thanks to mass production, globes could be made cheaper and in a fraction of the time. By 1900, most classrooms in Europe and America had one.

* * *

WHAT'S A PARAPROSDOKIAN?

It's a short statement with a surprising ending. (The term comes from Greek words meaning "against expectations.") It's also known as a one-liner. The most famous example: "Take my wife...please!" Here are some more.

"I haven't slept for ten days, because that would be too long."
—Mitch Hedberg

"So, this is hard to say, but: Worcestershire sauce."
—Andrew Nadeau

"Nostalgia isn't what it used to be."
—Peter De Vries

"He's a writer for the ages... for the ages of four to eight."
—Dorothy Parker

"I can picture in my mind a world without war, a world without hate. And I can picture us attacking that world because they'd never expect it."
—Jack Handey

"Spend a few minutes a day really listening to your spouse. No matter how stupid his problems sound to you."
—Megan Mullally

"When I was a kid my parents moved a lot, but I always found them."
—Rodney Dangerfield

"I used to be indecisive. Now I'm not sure."
—Tommy Cooper

"Always remember my grandfather's last words: 'A truck!'"
—Emo Phillips

"People say nothing is impossible, but I do nothing every day."
—A.A. Milne, *Winnie the Pooh*

UNCLE JOHN'S STALL OF FAME

Uncle John is amazed—and pleased—by the unusual ways people get involved with bathrooms, toilets, and so on. That's why he created the "Stall of Fame."

HONOREE: Whitney Budd of Hope, Indiana
NOTABLE ACHIEVEMENT: Flushing out hunger by spreading commodious color
TRUE STORY: Greg Potts got home from work one day in 2019 to discover that someone had left a toilet—that had been painted red like a strawberry (with the dots and all)—sitting on his front lawn. Next to the toilet was a yard sign. At the top of the sign, it said "FLUSH OUT HUNGER." Below that was "Plumbing Policy" with a fee schedule: It would cost Potts $10 for someone to come and take the toilet away, $20 to have it sent to someone else (but not anonymously), $30 to ensure the toilet never returns, and $40 for a spot on the "Party Pooper List: pre-register so it never comes to you." Potts seemed more amused than upset by his new lawn ornament. "When you drive down any street in Hope," he told reporters, "and you see a brightly painted toilet sitting in someone's yard, you gotta think...huh?"

That was the same reaction Whitney Budd received when she first proposed the fundraising toilet idea at a Students Fund of Hope meeting. "They looked at me like I had three heads," she said. The nonprofit Students Fund provides meals to kids who are behind on their school lunch accounts. The potty that Budd put on Potts's property, along with the three others she randomly placed around town that summer, bought $6,000 worth of lunches. In addition to the strawberry-themed toilet, Budd's Fruit of the Loo collection includes an avocado-themed toilet, a banana-themed toilet, and a grape-themed toilet.

HONOREE: Miroslav Bobek, director of the Prague Zoo in the Czech Republic
NOTABLE ACHIEVEMENT: Building a permanent poop exhibit
TRUE STORY: Many zoos have staged temporary poop-themed exhibits, but in May 2019, Bobek devoted an entire building to the excrement of creatures great and small. Inspired by the Prague Zoo's ongoing publication, "Encyclopedia of Excrements," the poop house features everything from pellets to mounds, from scat to cow pies, and even transports visitors back in time with its impressive collection of fossilized feces called *coprolites*. Visitors will see panda poop, lion poop, bison poop, gorilla poop, tortoise poop, and much more. Good news: All the excrement is behind glass.
Bonus: Bobek (whose surname means "goat droppings" in Czech) and the Prague

According to a study by the *National Journal*, if you're an average American, you believe you're smarter than the average American.

Zoo also deserve a spot in the Stall of Fame for developing a business selling elephant dung to local farmers and gardeners as fertilizer—in ice cream containers. Each 2.2-pound tub costs 70 koruna ($3.05). In 2016, the zoo started selling the dung to a local mill, where it's used to make paper. In yet another Prague Zoo exhibit, visitors can learn how to make their own elephant dung paper (or they can watch the first stage of the process...conducted by the elephants themselves).

HONOREE: George Frandsen, aka "King of Fossilized Feces," founder of the Poozeum
NOTABLE ACHIEVEMENT: Preserving that which was meant to be left behind
TRUE STORY: Dressed like Indiana Jones on his official Guinness World Record Facebook page, Frandsen considers himself a serious paleontologist. Except that Frandsen's most treasured finds look a lot...crappier than the average fossil. He's been collecting prehistoric poop since college. In 2014, after realizing that few natural history museums would display coprolites or acknowledge their scientific value, Frandsen founded the Poozeum, an online photo gallery that occasionally lends out samples to museums. These rocks formed as the animal's fecal matter was slowly replaced by minerals. It takes a rare set of circumstances for this to occur, which makes these rocks so worthy of study. "They're little mini time capsules," Frandsen told *Inverse* in 2016. "You look at one and learn about animal physiology, digestion, diet. Sometimes you can find pollen—you learn all about their ecosystem and the animal itself, all from this little nugget of poop. Whereas, if you find a bone, that's really neat, but it is just a bone."

The Poozeum (which bills itself as "#1 for Fossilized #2") houses Frandsen's world-record coprolite collection: 5,000 pieces and counting. The rocks, which are anywhere from 10,000 to 400 million years old, range in size from a pebble to one four-pound monster.

He looks for, as he puts it, "the proper sphincter marks."

Bonus: Frandsen points out that there are fewer than 10 verified dinosaur coprolites in collections around the world; most "dinosaur poop fossils" are actually from crocodilians. And a lot are just rocks sold by unscrupulous sellers. If you're wondering how Frandsen can tell if a specimen is real, he says that coprolites usually resemble animal turds. So he looks for, as he puts it, "the proper sphincter marks."

HONOREE: Motoki Reoga, 29, of Saitama, Japan
NOTABLE ACHIEVEMENT: Deterring bike thieves by grossing them out...and faking them out
TRUE STORY: Nearly half of all bike thefts in Japan occur when the bike is locked, so it's obvious that locks alone aren't doing the trick. In 2018, Reoga, a student at Kansei Design at Chiba Institute of Technology, came up with an ingenious

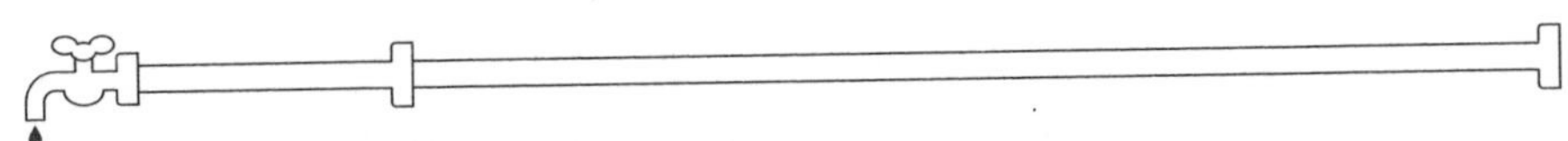

The record for the biggest "single-act, ticketed concert" in American history was set on...

invention: bird poop stickers. They look just like big splotches of fresh avian droppings, and when prominently placed on a bike seat, they encourage thieves to look elsewhere. At least, that's what Reoga predicted when he started testing the stickers. Turns out he was right. In his five-day experiment, not a single one of the unlocked "bait bikes" adorned with bird poop stickers was stolen.

HONOREES: Cheeky organizers at the 2019 Sziget Music Festival in Budapest, Hungary
NOTABLE ACHIEVEMENT: Turning a portable toilet into a secret rave
TRUE STORY: "This is why I love Sziget, just open a random toilet and there is a secret party going on," beamed one "Szitizen" who posted a video of his surprising discovery. Sziget, which began as a small college festival in 1993, now draws more than half a million music fans to the weeklong event every August. There are literally thousands of artists and DJs, but none are more exclusive than the ones you'll find in the rave toilet. Exactly which toilet, and at what time, is not announced. You have to either know someone, or just happen to find it.

On the outside, it looks exactly like any one of the other hundreds of toilets scattered around the festival, but instead of being a cramped commode, it opens into a tunnel that takes you to "the world's most exclusive bathroom party." Of course, if you actually happened to be looking for a bathroom, you'll have to turn around, make your way back out, and wait in line for a real one.

HOTEL ROOM HACKS

- If the thought of touching a hotel room remote control scares you, bring antiseptic wipes to clean that along with other surfaces. In a pinch, you can put the remote in a clear plastic bag, or in the shower cap. If you're really savvy, there are apps that will allow your phone to act as the remote.
- If you're unable to close the blinds so that they completely block the light, use the clips on one of the coat hangers (usually provided in the closet) to clip it shut.
- To keep your toothbrush off the bathroom counter, pack a clothespin to prop it up. Another trick: flip a paper cup upside down and pierce the bottom with the handle of your toothbrush, and you have a stand.
- Some hotel rooms have only one nightstand. If the person you're with commandeers the one in your room, instead of putting your personal stuff on the floor or on a chair, pull out one corner of the fitted sheet and use it as a pocket.

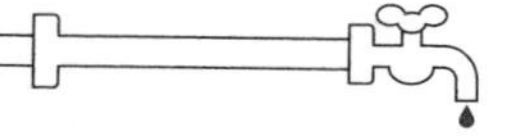

RAIDERS OF THE LOST APPLES, PART II

How many apple varieties can you name? Delicious, Macintosh, Fuji? It turns out that hundreds of varieties have been planted in the U.S., though most have been abandoned in favor of more popular types...and subsequently lost. Here's Part II of the story of one man's quest to save as many apple varieties as possible before they disappear forever. *(Part I is on page 121.)*

X MARKS THE SPOT

When Dave Benscoter's paper trail leads him to an orchard that he believes is likely to contain lost varieties of apples, he visits the site when the apples are ripe and uses GPS to map out the precise coordinates of each individual tree in the orchard. He picks the apples he cannot identify and bags them, carefully noting on the bag the GPS coordinates of the trees that produced them. Each tree that interests Benscoter gets its own bag, and he fills each bag with eight or nine apples he has picked from that tree. Later, during the winter months, he will return to the same trees and prune a few branches off of each one. This stimulates the trees to produce new shoots in the places where they were pruned. (The new shoots will come in handy later.)

Benscoter sends the apples he collects to the Temperate Orchard Conservancy in Molalla, Oregon, to see if they can be identified. Working from old agriculture textbooks and watercolor illustrations of the lost varieties, the apple identification experts at the conservancy try to find a variety that matches the size and appearance of each apple and other known characteristics, such as whether the apple ripens in the spring, summer, or fall. (Using DNA to identify apples is not an option, because there are no DNA samples from the lost varieties to compare the apples to.)

Sometimes it takes two or three years to establish definitively that an apple belongs to a lost variety. That means Benscoter has to make multiple return trips to the same tree and pick new apples each time. Drought years, like 2015, have to be skipped. That year "most of the trees I needed to return to and pick apples from only had apples the size of a Ping Pong ball or smaller," Benscoter says. "The identification experts need apples that are closer to their normal size to make a determination on what variety it is."

SHOOT 'EM UP

Most of Benscoter's apples will be identified as belonging to *obscure*, but not *lost*, varieties. Occasionally, however, an apple is confirmed as belonging to a variety that was thought to have been lost forever. In these cases, Benscoter returns to the tree that produced the apple and collects the new shoots that have grown in the places he

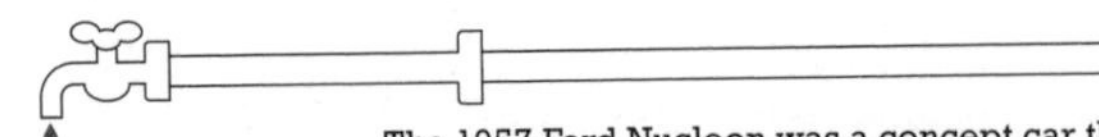

The 1957 Ford Nucleon was a concept car that would have been powered by a small nuclear reactor. It was never built.

pruned during his earlier visit. When he gets home, he grafts these shoots onto the *rootstock*—roots from other apple trees. These grafted trees will later be planted in the orchard at the Temperate Orchard Conservancy.

Why create new trees by grafting shoots cut from the tree, instead of simply planting apple *seeds?* Because seeds vary genetically from one another and are not identical to the trees that produced them, in much the same way that kids *resemble* their biological parents but are not genetically identical to either of them. Apple seeds contain a mix of DNA from both the tree that produced the apple (the "mother"), and the tree that provided the pollen that fertilized the tree (the "father"). Since the identity of the father tree is unknown, when you grow trees from seeds, you never know what kind of apples you're going to get. Trees produced by grafting a shoot onto rootstock are different: The shoot contains only the DNA of the mother tree and will grow into a tree that is genetically identical to it.

After the grafted tree grows and sprouts its own new shoots, some of the shoots are pruned and grafted onto rootstock to produce still more trees. And some of those trees will be planted at the Temperate Orchard Conservancy, adding to their collection of more than 5,000 rare apple varieties, the largest such collection in the United States. The remaining trees are sold to the public to raise money for the Lost Apple Project.

JUST GETTING STARTED

In a typical year, Benscoter and his Lost Apple Project partner, E. J. Brandt, will each log hundreds of miles driving around searching for apples. They'll submit apples picked from 200 or more trees for testing at the Temperate Orchard Conservancy in northeastern Oregon. Usually only a few apples will be identified as lost varieties, though in their best year yet, 2020, they found ten.

As of 2020, they've identified 23 once-lost varieties of apples that, thanks to the Temperate Orchard Conservancy, are on their way back from the brink and will eventually be made available to the public. Benscoter and Brandt believe there are at least 25 more varieties in eastern Washington and Idaho waiting to be rediscovered, perhaps more. One of the varieties they're still looking for: the Walbridge, the red apple with dark crimson stripes that set Benscoter on the hunt in the first place, back in 2014. But stay tuned. "We have two trees that we're looking at as possible Walbridges," he said in the summer of 2020.

SPREADING THE WORD

When Benscoter and Brandt aren't out hunting for lost apples, they speak to civic and community groups about the Lost Apple Project. Their public outreach has attracted a lot of interest in the project, and some fans of the Lost Apple Project have even started their own apple-finding groups. In June 2020, a woman in Michigan named Melissa Flora launched her own group, called the Lost Apple Project – Midwest,

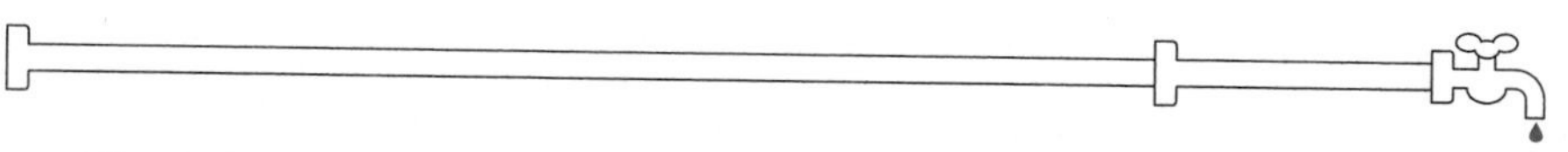

to hunt for heritage apples in the middle of the country. Within months of being founded, her group's Facebook page had nearly 300 members, many of whom were already searching for lost apples and sending in tips. Another way that social media helps in the hunt for lost apples: at certain times of the year, when a sought-after variety is thought to be ripening in a certain part of Washington, Idaho, or now in the Midwest, the Lost Apple Project will post a message on its Facebook page asking people living in that area to look for ripening apples matching the description of the missing variety, and report in if they find some.

It takes a lot of time and energy to track down and then confirm that a lost apple variety has been rediscovered, but for heritage apple lovers like Dave Benscoter, E. J. Brandt, and the people they've inspired, there's great satisfaction in saving an apple that might otherwise disappear forever. "It's a lot of footwork and a lot of book work and a lot of computer work," Brandt told Oregon's *Statesman Journal* newspaper in 2019. "You talk to a lot of people, and with that type of information, you can zero in a little bit—and then after that, you just cross your fingers and say, 'Maybe this will be a lost one.' "

Here are the names of the 23 apple varieties that have been rediscovered by the Lost Apple Project as of 2020:

Nero
Whitman County, WA, 2014

Arkansas Beauty
Whitman County, WA, 2016

Dickinson
Whitman County, WA, 2016

Ewalt
Rathdrum, ID, 2017

Flushing Spitzenburg
Rathdrum, ID, 2017

Kittageskee
Boise, ID, 2017

McAfee
Whitman County, WA, 2017

Saxon Priest
Ellensburg, WA, 2017

Shackleford
Spokane, WA, 2017

Surprise #1
Dayton, WA, 2017

Excelsior
Moscow, ID, 2018

Jackson Winter Sweet
near Waitsburg, WA, 2018

Regmalard
Troy, ID, 2018

Butter Sweet of Pennsylvania
Latah County, ID, 2019

Claribel
Latah County, ID, 2019

Colman
Latah County, ID, 2019

Fink
Boise, ID, 2019

Givens/Arkansas Baptist
Latah County, ID, 2019

Gold Ridge
Pomeroy, WA, 2019

Milalfyi
Pullman, WA, 2019

Nelson Sweet
Seattle, WA, 2019

Sary Sinap
Latah County, ID, 2019

Streaked Pippin
Waitsburg, WA, 2019

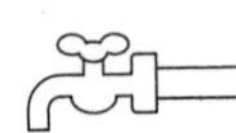

The *Guardian* asked its readers to describe 2020 in one word. The winner: "sh*t".

NUDES AND PRUDES

We're back with a regular feature—those who are fine with nudity...and those who are not—showing that hindsight may indeed be 20/20, but that doesn't mean everyone wants to see it.

NUDE

For more than 40 years, the Alpha Phi Omega (APO) fraternity at the University of Philippines has held an annual event called the Oblation Run. Wearing nothing but masks over their faces, 24 fraternity members streak across campus every December 16. The event has occurred annually since 1977 when, according to school legend, an APO member ran naked through the campus to promote a movie called *Hubad na Bayani* (Tagalog for "Naked Hero"). But the Oblation Run is no mere prank. According to the fraternity, the "Ritual Dance of the Brave," as they call it, is a political statement. For example, the 2020 theme was to bring awareness to environmental issues. In 2017, they ran "to end drug-related killings." Although one politician has decried the "blatant display of male genitals," the runs have generated little controversy...but huge crowds. "When I was a freshman," one student told the Philippines *Inquirer,* "I asked, 'Why is this happening?' But now I understand [it's] a form of protest." And that, said Oblation Runner Marco Zaplan, is what it's all about: "Naked or not, at the end of the day, we just want to magnify our advocacy."

PRUDE

It was "purely just to break up the monotony of life...and have a little fun," lamented Mike O'Neill of Sandy Springs, Georgia. He was refering to his annual Halloween display, which he'd installed in his yard several times over the years, and no one had complained. Then, in October 2019, some people in the Grogans Bluff neighborhood told their HOA that it was "offensive to small children." So the HOA president called O'Neill and told him to remove the display: a scarecrow with two large pumpkins that comprise the "cheeks" of his butt—which was facing the road and "mooning" the neighborhood. Rather than remove his work of art, O'Neill covered up the offensive gourds with a big sign that read "Censored by GBHOA."

NUDE

In July 2020, after police in Australia's Capital Territory completed their first round of compliance checks during a COVID-19 lockdown, they reported the good news: So far, everyone was following the correct pandemic protocols. Detective Superintendent Jason Kennedy told reporters that he was grateful for the "warm reception" his officers received from local citizens, but added that "some of them may need a reminder to put some clothes on before they open the door."

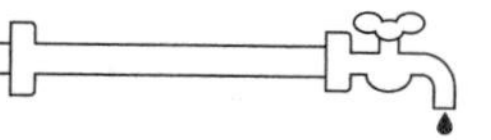

It looks like someone pasted a square piece of cardboard onto Hannah's rear end.

PRUDE

In the 1984 romantic comedy *Splash*—starring Tom Hanks as a guy who falls for a mermaid played by Daryl Hannah—there's a scene in which Hannah runs into the sea and, for a brief moment, some of her bare butt is visible beneath her long, blond hair. In 2020, when Disney (which originally released *Splash* via its more adult-oriented Touchstone Pictures) added the movie to its streaming service, Disney Plus, that scene was digitally altered. Now, when Hannah runs to the sea, her hair is longer and covers her entire derriere. And it wasn't done with the level of sophistication you'd expect from Disney—while the rest of her hair waves back and forth, it looks like someone pasted a square piece of cardboard onto Hannah's rear end. The media giant took a drubbing on social media, with most people complaining that Disney could have simply put the unaltered film onto its more adult-oriented streaming service, Hulu. As one Buzzfeed commenter put it, "I watched *Splash* with my family when I was like 5, and I was not scarred for life because I saw a butt for .5 seconds."

NUDE

In March 2019, a mysterious Florida man wearing what was described in news reports as "a headband, hot pink socks, sneakers—and a thong" became a viral sensation after a video was posted of him riding his bicycle, speeding down Interstate 95...backward while seated on the handlebars. Who was this mostly naked man? As of press time, he was still unidentified, but he obviously struck a chord with his fellow Floridians (though not with the highway patrol, who reminded the public that what the man was doing was both dangerous and illegal). One person tweeted, "I see this dude all the time. I call him, Flamboyro! The hero Miami deserves."

PROOD

"In these strange times, people are in need of extra comfort," said comedian Vanessa Bayer in an odd promotional video posted to social media in late 2020. "That's why it's always a nice gesture to send nudes so they know you're thinking of them." Then Bayer held up a box of Kraft Macaroni & Cheese and added, "Noods, I mean. Not nudes." The cheesy pun was part of Kraft's pandemic-themed promotion to celebrate National Noodle Day on October 6: Customers could send loved ones a box of mac and cheese in lieu of visiting them in person. The #sendnoods campaign had barely begun when the food brand was bombarded with complaints for "sexualizing mac 'n' cheese." "This is not okay," read one. "Don't you realize that a huge portion of the people who actually eat your mac 'n' cheese are *children*?!" Kraft removed the videos and canceled the campaign, saying in a statement, "We sincerely appreciate all of your feedback." By that point, even though the promotion was only a few days old, Kraft said that more than 20,000 people had sent their loved ones a box of noods...and cheese.

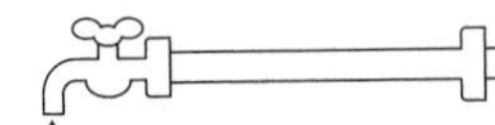

Genetically speaking, all the children of identical twins are half-siblings, not cousins.

LEAVE THE GUN. TAKE THE CANNOLI.

Some of the greatest movie scenes involve eating. See if you can match the following film quotes with the films listed at the bottom of the page. (Answers are on page 405.) Bon appétit!

1. "In prison, dinner was always a big thing. We had a pasta course, and then we had a meat or a fish. Paulie did the prep work. He was doing a year for contempt and he had this wonderful system for doing the garlic. He used a razor and he used to slice it so thin that it used to liquefy in the pan with just a little oil. It was a very good system."

2. "Bring me four fried chickens and a Coke."
"You want chicken wings or chicken legs?"
"Four fried chickens, and a Coke."

3. "Lemme have a diablo sandwich and a Dr Pepper and make it fast. I'm in a g*dd*mn hurry...[Calling out the door]: You want something?"
"Hush puppies, Daddy!"
"We got no time for that crap! Dumb somb*tch!"

4. "Now all you have to do is hold the chicken, bring me the toast, give me a check for the chicken salad sandwich, and you haven't broken any rules."
"You want me to hold the chicken, huh?"
"I want you to hold it between your knees."

5. "Come over here kid, learn something. You never know, you might have to cook for twenty guys someday. You see, you start out with a little bit of oil. Then you fry some garlic. Then you throw in some tomatoes, tomato paste, you fry it; you make sure it doesn't stick. You get it to a boil; you shove in all your sausage and your meatballs. Add a little bit of wine, and a little bit of sugar, and that's my trick."

6. "That Christmas would live in our memories as the Christmas when we were introduced to Chinese turkey. All was right with the world."

7. "I'll have what she's having."

8. "Big Kahuna Burger! That's that Hawaiian burger joint. I hear they got some tasty burgers. I ain't never had one myself. How are they?"
"They're good."
"You mind if I try one of yours? This is yours here, right? [Takes a big bite]... Mmmm! This is a tasty burger!"

9. "S*n of a b*tch demanded a second dinner. Lamb chops—extra rare."

A) *The Godfather* (1972) **B)** *A Christmas Story* (1983) **C)** *Five Easy Pieces* (1970) **D)** *When Harry Met Sally* (1989) **E)** *Goodfellas* (1990) **F)** *The Silence of the Lambs* (1991) **G)** *Smokey and the Bandit* (1977) **H)** *The Blues Brothers* (1980) **I)** *Pulp Fiction* (1994)

LO$ING CASINOS

There's a saying in the gaming industry that "the house always wins." But is it really true? Here are some concepts for Las Vegas casinos that never even made it off the drawing board.

THE BEVERLY HILLBILLIES: Max Baer Jr. starred as dim-bulb yokel Jethro Bodine on *The Beverly Hillbillies.* When the show ended in 1971, he put his business degree to use as a movie producer, earning millions. After moving to Nevada in 1978, he saw how much money he could make as a casino operator and set out to open Jethro Bodine's Beverly Hillbillies Mansion and Casino, which he claimed would embody his show's "warmth, humor, and good old-fashioned American fun." Among the plans for the casino and hotel, which would be made to resemble the Clampett's Beverly Hills mansion: a 200-foot-tall flaming oil derrick, Granny's Shotgun Wedding Chapel, a bakery called Ellie May's Buns, Jethro's All-You-Kin-Et Buffet, and hotel rooms outfitted with log bed frames and "outhouses" with beer bottle door handles. Baer's first attempt—to remodel an existing Lake Tahoe casino—fizzled when city planners refused to allow him to place a Clampett-style jalopy on the roof. An attempt to convert a Carson City Walmart in 2003 failed because of zoning issues, while a lawsuit delayed (probably forever) another try in 2007.

THE *TITANIC*: When it set sail in 1912, the *Titanic* was the largest and most elaborate steamship the world had ever seen. What's the modern-day equivalent of this top-shelf luxury liner? A Las Vegas resort outfitted with casinos, hotels, and multiple entertainment options. Well, that's what poker champ turned casino developer Bob Stupak thought. In 1999, two years after the movie *Titanic* was released, he decided to build the Titanic Resort, which would have featured all of those things (and more) in a 400-foot-long building shaped and styled like the world's most famous cruise ship...except for the one thing that makes it so famous 100 years after its one and only voyage. Yes, the Titanic Resort would have just overlooked the 1,500 people who died horrible deaths in the icy waters of the Atlantic Ocean when the liner crashed into an iceberg. Stupak's group registered trademarks on a number of tasteless Titanic-themed and iceberg-based attractions, such as the Glacier Waves Water Park, Polar Paradise nightclub, the Ice Dome Skating Rink, and the Ice Jammer, a roller coaster. Why didn't this resort ever open? In 2014, the Las Vegas City Council rejected its gargantuan building plans. (Wise move.)

THE MOON: Vancouver developer Michael Henderson wasn't a Las Vegas real-estate insider when he proposed his project for the Nevada city's popular Strip in 2002... but what he lacked in connections, he made up for in ambition. He wanted to

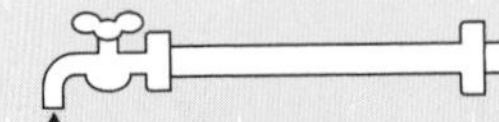

develop the largest project that Vegas had ever seen. His theme: the Moon. The hotel and casino would have offered 10,000 rooms in a giant, curving highrise tower that wrapped around the site. In the center: a giant reproduction of the Moon nearly as tall as the hotel tower. Henderson later added on to his concept, with a PGA-level golf course that would utilize a monorail instead of golf carts, plus a restaurant, a nightclub with a two-story waterfall, a hockey arena, a spa, a casino with 12,000 slot machines, the Sea of Serenity Aquatic Center and Crater Wave Pool, 80 condos, an indoor vineyard, and a moon-buggy driving course. While it would certainly have been impressive, the main reasons the Moon never landed in Vegas were size and money. There wasn't (and still isn't) enough undeveloped land on the Las Vegas Strip to house the resort, which would have cost $5 *billion,* much more than Henderson could afford.

STARSHIP ORION: International Thoroughbred Breeders (ITB), a company that operates horse racing facilities in New Jersey, decided to get into a *real* gambling-based business in 1996, announcing plans to tear down Las Vegas's old and crumbling El Rancho Casino and replace it with a new complex called Starship Orion. The 5,400,000-square-foot property would include a 2,400-room, 65-story hotel and 30,000 square feet of high-end retail stores, all with a science-fiction theme. (At a shareholder meeting, developers said the resort would feature virtual reality amusement park rides, a "galactic theater," and an "alien circus.") Another unique part of ITB's plan was to build seven independently owned and operated casinos inside Starship Orion, charging other gaming companies $100 million for the privilege of being there. ITB, which had never built a casino before, aimed to open Starship Orion in just two years' time, but the project crashed. Reason: ITB couldn't convince enough potential shareholders that the project was viable.

THE WWF HOTEL AND CASINO: In the late 1990s, the World Wrestling Federation (now known as World Wrestling Entertainment) purchased the Debbie Reynolds Hollywood Hotel for $10 million. Under the direction of executive Linda McMahon, the WWF announced that it would spend $100 million to transform the property into a monument to the company's brand of professional wrestling. The resort would have a casino, and also be home to regular, live wrestling matches, of which clips would be shown on outdoor screens that covered the building's exterior. Rooms would be themed after popular wrestling stars such as the Rock and Mick Foley. But after about a year, McMahon realized that it would take far more money and expertise than her team had to build a Vegas resort, and she sold the building for $11 million, still turning a profit. The old Debbie Reynolds Hollywood Hotel changed hands a few times, and operated as the Greek Isles Hotel and Casino and the Clarion Hotel and Casino before it was demolished in 2015.

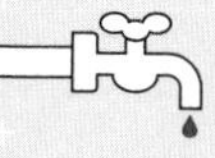

Only about 1% of an average tree—the leaf and root tips, and a thin layer of underbark—is alive. The rest is dead cells.

21 RABBITS (AND HARES)

Did you know that there are more than 60 different species of rabbits (and hares) in the world? Neither did we! Turns out there are rabbits (and hares) on every continent except Antarctica. Ear are 21 rabbits (and hares) you might or might not have hared of before.

1. **WOOLLY HARE.** A high-altitude species found in mountainous grasslands in Central Asia, Mongolia, China, Nepal, and northern India—at altitudes as high as 17,000 feet. They get their name, obviously, from their thick, woolly coats.

2. **AMAMI RABBIT.** A small, dark-furred species found only in forested regions of two small Japanese islands—Amami Oshima and Tokunoshima. They have bulky bodies, short legs, small heads with elongated snouts and short ears, and long sharp claws, which they use for digging burrows in their forest homes.

3. **VOLCANO RABBIT.** A small, short-eared rabbit species found only on the slopes of four extinct volcanoes southeast of Mexico City. It's the world's second-smallest rabbit species, weighing just 1.3 pounds when fully grown.

4. **RIVERINE RABBIT.** Also known as the bushman rabbit, this is a small, long-eared, long-bodied species found in dense bush around the rivers of South Africa's Karoo Desert. Because it has lost most of its habitat to farming, it is one of the most endangered mammals in the world, with less than 400 individuals alive today.

5. **BROOM HARE.** A very long-eared, mountain-dwelling hare, living at altitudes of up to about 6,000 feet in the summertime. Its native habitat is just a few regions of the Cantabrian Mountains in northern Spain.

6. **HAINAN HARE.** A small hare species native to grassland areas of Hainan Island, off China's southern coast.

7. **HISPID HARE.** Also known as the bristly rabbit because of its coarse, bristly fur, this species of hare is found in the southern foothills of the Himalayas in Nepal, India, and Bangladesh.

8. **SNOWSHOE HARE.** Found in forested regions across a wide swath of North America. Especially known for its fur coat, which turns a stark and solid white in winter, giving these shy creatures the camouflage they need to escape predators in the snow. It is so named for its oversized rear feet, which act like snowshoes, allowing these hares to run across deep, soft snow.

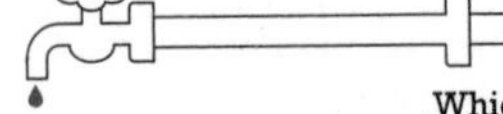

Which came first? According to scientists, the egg came before the chicken, since birds evolved from reptiles that laid eggs.

9. **BLACK-TAILED JACKRABBIT.** A very large, long-bodied, and large-eared hare native to the American West and Mexico. It is called a jackrabbit because of its large ears, which bear a resemblance to the ears of a donkey, or jackass. Bonus: jackrabbits were once known as "jackass rabbits."

10. **WHITE-TAILED JACKRABBIT.** Slightly larger and lighter-colored than its black-tailed cousin—and with a white rather than black tail—these hares are found from northern California to Wisconsin, and in south-central Canada. It is also known as the prairie hare.

11. **ANTELOPE JACKRABBIT.** These hares live only in a small area of southern Arizona, and in northwestern Mexico. They are known for their speed and their leaping ability, reaching speeds of more than 40 miles per hour and leaping more than 20 feet in a single bound—much like an antelope, which is how they got their name.

12. **ARCTIC HARE.** Very large hares—up to 28 inches in length and weighing up to 15 pounds—found only in the far Arctic north of Canada and Greenland. They are well adapted to their habitat, having exceptionally thick and dense fur that turns white in winter, and a thick layer of fat below their skin, both of which protect these hares from the extreme cold.

13. **ALASKAN HARE.** Even larger than the Arctic hare—weighing up to 16 pounds—these hardy hares live in the western part of Alaska, well down into the state's Aleutian Peninsula. These hares are easily recognizable in the winter by their white coats and distinctive black-tipped ears. It is also known as the tundra hare.

14. **PYGMY RABBIT.** The smallest rabbit species in the world, topping the scales at just one pound. The pygmy rabbit is found only in the American West, from Montana to eastern California, with a small and isolated population in Washington's Columbia Basin region. When sitting hunched up in a fuzzy ball, the pygmy rabbit is about the size of a softball.

15. **EASTERN COTTONTAIL.** The most common rabbit species in the United States, inhabiting

DID YOU KNOW?

What's the difference between rabbits and hares? Although they look similar, hares are generally larger than rabbits, with larger ears and longer legs, and their natural sitting position is more upright than a rabbit's. And while most rabbit species live in groups in burrows known as "warrens," hares tend to live solitary lives, and live and nest aboveground in shallow depressions called "forms." Another difference: rabbits are born hairless, with their eyes closed; hares are born with hair and with their eyes open. But both are hunted by the same predators—feral cats, wolves, coyotes, foxes, and birds of prey.

almost the entire eastern half of the country, and as far south as northern South America. It is known for having a bright white underside to its short tail—hence its name—which flashes when the rabbit runs. There are 20 species of cottontails in the Americas. A trait they share with hares: they don't dig burrows, preferring to nest in hollows in the ground, or in dense vegetation.

16. **OMILTEME COTTONTAIL.** A cottontail species found only in a tiny area of the Sierra Madre del Sur, a mountain range in the Mexican state of Guerrero. It is one of the most endangered rabbits in the world.

17. **BUNYORO RABBIT.** This is a medium-sized rabbit species native to rocky grasslands in central Africa, in and around Uganda. It is named after the Bunyoro kingdom, a powerful kingdom that ruled in central Africa for several hundred years, dating back to the 13th century, and which still exists today as part of the nation of Uganda. (One of the many predators these bunnies have to look out for: baboons.)

18. **NATAL RED ROCK HARE.** A gray-brown rabbit with thick, grizzled fur, a fluffy dark tail, and distinctive reddish-brown underparts found in southeastern South Africa. It is one of four species of red rock hares found in southern Africa.

19. **MOUNTAIN HARE.** Another white-in-winter hare, this one is found in the northern regions of Asia and Europe, including throughout Russia, Scandinavia, Scotland, and Ireland. They are known in Scotland as *blue hares,* for the slight blue tinge to their winter coats.

20. **ANNAMITE STRIPED RABBIT.** An extremely rare and elusive short-eared rabbit species, found only in dense forests in the Annamite Mountains, located on the Laos–Vietnam border, and only revealed to the world when a British biologist came upon carcasses of two of the creatures in a market in Laos in 1995. It has gold- and cream-colored fur ribboned with seven broad black stripes, and a rusty-red rump. Its only partner in the genus created just for them, *Nesolagus,* is the Sumatran striped rabbit, native only to the Barisan Mountains on the Indonesian island of Sumatra, and discovered around the same time as the Annamite striped rabbit.

21. **EUROPEAN RABBIT.** These small, stocky rabbits, originally native to southwestern Europe, were later introduced to the rest of Europe, as well as parts of South America, and, in the 18th century, to Australia—where the population grew to an estimated 10 billion by 1920. That number has fallen to about 200 million today, after decades of control measures such as poisoning and rabbit-proof fence construction. Bonus: all domestic rabbit breeds—more than 300 of them—in the world today are subspecies of the European rabbit.

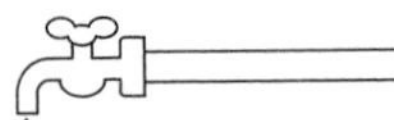

Tragic, but not as tragic as you think: 62 out of 97 people aboard the *Hindenburg* survived the explosion and crash.

CLEVER HOUSEHOLD HACKS

Not all of these tips and tricks will apply to you, but chances are, at least one of them will change your life for the better. (For Uncle John, it was the marshmallows.)

PROBLEM: Cleaning a bathtub with a scrub brush can be really hard on your back.
Solution: Use a household broom instead. Add the cleanser as usual, and let the broom's bristles do the abrasive, dirty work for you. Not only will a broom clean just as effectively as a scrub brush, it makes it easier to clean crevices and other hard-to-reach places.

PROBLEM: Your old broom is frayed, and you're too sentimental (or cheap) to let it go.
Solution: Use one or two rubber bands to train the bristles back into shape. A day should do it.

PROBLEM: You're having trouble opening a jar, or twisting off a supposedly twist-off bottle cap.
Solution: Chances are, you have an old mouse pad. Use it to grip the jar lid or bottle cap. The mouse pad will add traction and protect your fingers.

PROBLEM: Blinds and ceiling fans are really hard to clean, and when you do clean them, dust gets everywhere.
Solution: You can wrap rags around the end of a pair of tongs (one over each tong), securing them with a rubber band, and try wiping with that. You can also put on a fabric oven mitt and wipe off the blades by hand.

PROBLEM: You have to hammer a nail into a wall, and you're afraid you'll miss and damage the wall...or miss and injure your finger.
Solution: Use a clothespin to hold the nail in place. But don't clamp it directly onto the nail; most clothespins have a circular cutout to put the nail through while holding it loosely in place.

PROBLEM: Murphy's Law says that if something can get tangled, it will get tangled—whether it be an extension cord, holiday lights, string, or twine.
Solution: To keep extension cords accessible and tangle-free, coil them up accordion-style and put them in cardboard tubes—the kind you find at the center of a roll of toilet paper or paper towels. Label the tubes for an extra level of organization.

PROBLEM: You want to paint each of your toenails separately, but you don't have a foam toe separator.
Solution: Marshmallows are a good substitute (but you might want to skip eating them).

PROBLEM: A handle on a drawer or a cabinet is perpetually loose, no matter how often you tighten the screw.
Solution: Put nail polish on the screw right before screwing it in, and the knob will remain tight.

PROBLEM: Your zipper is stuck.
SOLUTION: Rub a dry bar of soap onto both sides of the zipper, and then give the tab a gentle tug. It should come right loose. (Lip balm will also work.)

PROBLEM: You've removed the cords from your computer, and you can't remember where they go.
SOLUTION: Use bread tags and a Sharpie to label the cords.

PROBLEM: You've removed the cords from your computer, and they fall behind your desk.
SOLUTION: Tape (or clip) binder clips to the back of the desk and use them to secure the cords.

PROBLEM: Right now, somewhere in the far reaches of your produce bin, a vegetable is rotting.
SOLUTION: To diminish moisture—the primary reason veggies spoil—place a clean, dry sponge into the back of the bin. It will absorb water, keeping your food fresher. Replace the sponge periodically, or use the next trick.

PROBLEM: Your sponge has a new life-form growing on it, and you're out of replacements.
SOLUTION: Experts say to change out sponges frequently because they also make for great bacteria habitat. Good news: Sponges can be washed in the dishwasher; the near-boiling water will kill most of the bacteria. Another trick is to moisten the sponge and then heat it in the microwave (on a small plate) for one minute.

PROBLEM: Plastic produce bags seem to reproduce and take over random drawers and cupboards all over the house.
SOLUTION: Rein in those bags with a pair of pantyhose. Hang the hose on a pantry door and stuff as many bags in as will fit (a lot if you use both legs).

PROBLEM: You eat some guacamole and put the container back in the fridge. When you go back for it later, it's turned brown.
SOLUTION: This discoloring is caused by oxygen in the air, which (surprise!) oxidizes it. (That's why a bitten apple turns brown.) You can stop oxidation from occurring by mimicking the shell of an avocado; gently place a piece of cling wrap on the guacamole's surface before putting the lid back on the container.

PROBLEM: You have a button-up shirt or blouse that refuses to hang on the coat hanger.
SOLUTION: Two rubber bands—one each stretched over the hanger's shoulders—will help your clothes get a grip.

PROBLEM: Dude, you spilled potpourri all over my shag carpet! Not cool!
SOLUTION: Potpourri? Well, maybe...or maybe you spilled an organic collection of leaves and flower buds. Regardless of what it was, chillax, bro. Just get a piece of nylon from some pantyhose, stretch a small section of it over the end of a vacuum cleaner hose, turn that sucker on, and collect the buds in the nylon. Then carefully place the collected "potpourri" over the bowl, turn off the vacuum, and all will be well.

"WHATEVER THE MISTAKES THAT HAVE BEEN MADE"

In 1974, Richard M. Nixon became the first and, so far, only U.S. president to resign from office. But what if he hadn't?

BACKGROUND

On August 8, 1974, as undeniable evidence piled up that his administration attempted to cover up a break-in at the Democratic National Committee headquarters at the Watergate Office Building, President Richard Nixon resigned from his post. Rather than face an embarrassing impeachment and likely conviction, Nixon walked away, delivering a short address on national television based on remarks prepared for him a few days earlier by his chief speechwriter, Raymond Price.

But that wasn't the only speech Price wrote that week–he composed another, in case Nixon decided to keep fighting for his job. Nixon never saw this other speech, which emerged in 1996, two years after the president's death, when it was sent to the National Archives among 40 million pages of the former commander in chief's documents.

Good Evening. With the deliberations of the House Judiciary Committee completed and its recommendations awaiting action by the full House of Representatives, questions have been raised about my own plans for dealing with the impeachment issue.

I have requested this time in order to tell you how I intend to proceed.

Debate on the committee's impeachment recommendations is scheduled to begin on the House floor two weeks from today—on Aug. 19.

In the wake of the Judiciary Committee's action, there has been a very substantial erosion of the political base that I would need in order to sustain my position in the House of Representatives. Therefore, at this time it appears almost a foregone conclusion that one or more articles of impeachment will be voted by the House, and that the matter will go to a trial in the Senate. It is not my purpose tonight to argue my case. There will be time for that later. Rather, I want to explain how I intend to proceed.

I also want to tell you about one new piece of evidence I have discovered, which I recognize will not be helpful to my case—but which I have instructed my attorneys to make available immediately to the Judiciary Committee.

In the past several days, I have been engaged in an intensive review of the 64 taped conversations covered by the Special Prosecutor's subpoena and the Supreme Court's recent order that they be turned over to Judge Sirica. With one exception, I have found that they bear out what I said on April 29 when I announced my decision to make public the original transcripts: that the evidence I have turned over to the Judiciary Committee tells the full story of Watergate, insofar as the President's knowledge or involvement is concerned. These 64 additional tapes are being turned over to Judge Sirica. As they become public, which they undoubtedly will, the truth of this will be evident.

The one exception is a conversation I held with H. R. Haldeman on June 23, 1972, which concerns my instructions with regard to coordination between the F.B.I. and the C.I.A. In reviewing the tape it is now clear to me that Mr. Haldeman and I did discuss the political aspects of the situation, and that we were fully aware of the advantages this course of action would have with respect to limiting the possible public exposure of involvement by persons connected with the re-election committee. Because this conversation took place just a few days after the break-in, I know it will be widely interpreted as evidence that I was involved from the outset in efforts at cover-up.

Let me take a moment to explain why I did not make this public sooner, although I should have. In May of this year I began a review of the 64 tapes subpoenaed by the Special Prosecutor, but then postponed completing it pending the decision that was finally handed down 12 days ago by the Supreme Court. In the course of that earlier partial review I listened to this tape, but did not focus on it thoroughly. I did not at the time consider it inconsistent with my past statements, nor did I have transcripts made or advise my staff or counsel about any possible concern with it.

I now recognize this as having been a serious mistake, because as a result of it my counsel, my staff, and others, including members of the Judiciary Committee, who defended my position did so on the basis of facts that were incomplete.

Let me turn now to the future.

There has been a great deal of speculation that I would resign, rather than face trial by the Senate. Some cite the erosion of my political base, and say that this either dims or dooms my chances in the Senate. Some cite the costs to the nation of more months of distraction and uncertainty. Some say I should not see the Constitutional process through, because even if vindicated by the Senate I would be so weakened politically that I could not govern effectively for the remainder of my term.

Some suggest that if I persevere, I am not only ignoring what they consider the inevitable outcome, but doing so at considerable political risk. Indeed, when I reviewed the June 23 tape, and realized the interpretations that will probably be placed on it, I seriously considered resigning.

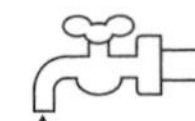

The longest family tree in the world is that of Confucius (551–479 BC), with 2 million confirmed descendants across 80 generations over 2,500 years.

I have thought long and hard about all of these questions...I have explored the questions thoroughly with my family. They share in my belief that the Constitutional process must not be aborted or short-circuited—that having begun, it must be carried through to its conclusion, that is, through a fair trial in the Senate.

If I were to resign, it would spare the country additional months consumed with the ordeal of a Presidential impeachment and trial. But it would leave unresolved the questions that have already cost the country so much in anguish, division, and uncertainty. More important, it would leave a permanent crack in our Constitutional structure: it would establish the principle that under pressure, a president could be removed from office by means short of those provided by the Constitution. By establishing that principle, it would invite such pressures on every future president who might, for whatever reason, fall into a period of unpopularity.

More important, it would leave a permanent crack in our Constitutional structure.

Whatever the mistakes that have been made—and they are many—and whatever the measure of my own responsibility for those mistakes, I firmly believe that I have not committed any act of commission or omission that justifies removing a duly elected president from office. If I did believe that I had committed such an act, I would have resigned long ago.

For me to see this through will have costs for the country in the short run. The months ahead will not be easy for any of us. But in the long run—whatever the outcome—the results will be a more stable form of government. Far more damaging than the ordeal of a Senate trial, far more damaging that even the conviction and removal of a president, would be the descent toward chaos if presidents could be removed short of impeachment and trial.

Throughout the Western world, governmental instability has reached almost epidemic proportions. In the United States, within the last dozen years one President was assassinated [JFK]; the next was in effect driven from office when he did not even seek re-election [LBJ]; and now the third stands on the verge of impeachment by the House of Representatives, confronted with calls for his resignation in order to make the process of removal easy.

This country bears enormous responsibilities to itself and to the world. If we are to meet those responsibilities in this and future Presidencies, we must not let this office be destroyed—or let it fall such easy prey to those who would exult in the breaking of the President that the game becomes a national habit.

Therefore, I shall see the Constitutional process through—whatever its outcome. I shall appear before the Senate, and answer under oath before the Senate any and all questions put to me there.

Only American president buried under the flag of another nation: John Tyler (1790–1862), whose coffin was draped with a Confederate flag.

KNOW YOUR COLUMNS

Ever walk past an old bank or government building and notice the decorative columns that appear to be holding up the structure? Columns have been a part of classical architecture for more than 4,500 years, but how much do you know about them? Here's a field guide.

FROM THE BOTTOM UP

Columns are typically comprised of three main parts:

- **The base or pedestal.** The lowest part of the pedestal, usually square or round in shape.
- **The shaft.** The main body of the column, usually cylindrical in shape. The term "column" can also be used to refer to just the shaft.
- **The capital.** The top piece, which is wider than the shaft because it supports the roof or other architectural elements.

EGYPTIAN COLUMNS

- Egyptian stone columns date back as far as 2600 BC. Many early columns had grooves carved into them, giving them the appearance of reeds bundled together. This has led to speculation that prehistoric columns, now lost, were made from actual bundles of lotus, palm, or papyrus reeds. When Egyptian architecture became more advanced, the theory goes, and the loads that the columns needed to support became too great for columns made with reeds, they were replaced with stone columns carved to give them the same look.
- The shafts of Egyptian columns are frequently decorated with hieroglyphs that have been carved into the stone and then painted bright colors. Near the top of the shaft, horizontal bands are carved into the stone to create the appearance of the bundle of reeds being tied off.
- The capital sits above these bands and is carved to look like lotus, palm, or papyrus leaves poking out from the top of the bundle.

DORIC COLUMNS (Greece)

- Doric columns, which originated in the western Dorian region of Greece, are the earliest and simplest form of Greek columns. They have no base. The earliest surviving examples of the Doric style date to the seventh century BC.
- The surface of the shaft has 20 parallel flutes or vertical concave grooves carved into it that run the length of the shaft.

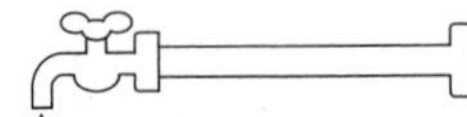

- The shaft's height is typically four to eight times its diameter, making it the squattest of ancient Greek and Roman column styles. This squatness, the ancients believed, gave it a masculine appearance compared to taller, more slender columns, which appeared more feminine. The squatness is also why Doric columns don't have a base: the base is there to provide stability to slender columns, and Doric columns are so thick that they don't need them.
- Greek and Roman columns often have a slight outward curve on their shaft (called *entasis*), and the diameter of the shaft diminishes slightly as it rises. Both of these features are there to trick the eye into seeing the columns as taller and straighter than they really are. Perfectly straight shafts can appear slightly concave (narrower in the middle) to the eye, and entasis corrects this.
- The design of a Doric column's capital is simple: it usually consists of a circular disk at the top of the column. The disk can be wider at the top than at the bottom, and a flat, square slab called an *abacus* sits on top of it.

Famous example: The Lincoln Memorial

TUSCAN COLUMNS (Rome)

- The Romans borrowed so much from the Doric style, or "order," to create the Tuscan style that it's also known as the Roman Doric order.
- The Romans did change a few of the details, though. In some cases, Tuscan columns have a flat, square stone pad as a base, or the column will sit on a taller square slab called a *plinth*. In some other cases, one or more flat, circular discs (called *tori*) can serve as the base.
- The capital of the Tuscan column is also made from tori.
- The shafts are not fluted and are usually about seven times as tall as the diameter of the shaft at the base.

Famous examples: Pre-Civil War plantations in the South. Many of these homes were built in a Greek Revival style and used simple Tuscan order columns.

IONIC COLUMNS (Greece)

- Ionic columns date to the sixth century BC. They originated in Ionia, in what is now the southwest coast of Turkey and the islands off the coast.
- The most distinguishing feature of Ionic columns are the capitals, which are carved to look like rolled-up scrolls (called *volutes*). There are two scrolls, one on either side of the column as you face the column. In the oldest columns, the scrolls are visible only from the front and the rear of the column; in later years the style of carving was changed so that scrolls were visible on four sides.

Anton syndrome is a rare disorder where blind people don't believe they're blind.

- Ionic shafts are narrower than Doric columns as well as taller, with a height that's eight or nine times the diameter of the shaft. They're slender enough to require a base, which is carved to look like two tori stacked on top of one another and separated by a narrower space called a *scotia*.
- Ionic shafts are usually fluted. If they are fluted, they're likely to have 24 flutes.
- One thing that separates Greek fluting from Roman fluting is that the Greeks didn't leave space between their flutes: they meet each other at a sharp edge. But these edges are easily damaged, and the damage is quite visible. Perhaps because of this, the Romans left uncarved spaces between the flutes on their columns. These in-between spaces are called *fillets*.

Famous examples: The Jefferson Memorial, the U.S. Treasury Building

CORINTHIAN COLUMNS (Greece)

- This style of column gets its name from the Greek city-state of Corinth, though the sculptor who is believed to have created the style in the fifth century BC was probably from Athens.
- The most prominent features of Corinthian columns are the elaborately carved capitals, which feature small scrolls that are surrounded and frequently overpowered by two or more rows of leaves from the Mediterranean acanthus plant. It can be hard to spot the scrolls unless you know to look for them, but you can't miss the leaves.
- The shafts of Corinthian columns are very slender, with a height that's ten times the diameter of the shaft. They are fluted, usually with 24 flutes.

Famous examples: The New York Stock Exchange, the U.S. Supreme Court building, the National Archives

COMPOSITE COLUMNS (Rome)

- Just as the Romans altered the Doric style to suit their tastes, so too did they mix elements from the Ionic style with the Corinthian style to create the Composite style. Put simply, the Composite style takes the large scrolls or volutes of the Ionic capital and combines them with the acanthus leaves from the Corinthian capital. The rest of the column, including the base and the shaft, is Corinthian.

Famous examples: Composite order columns are less common than other styles and were seldom used on public buildings in the United States, but one place you can see them is on the Alabama Governor's Mansion.

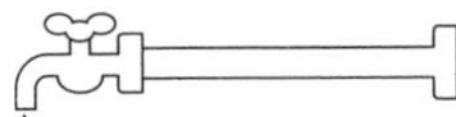

By walking on the Moon, the Apollo astronauts raised the surface temperature by 3.6°F. (They uncovered darker lunar dust, which absorbs more solar energy.)

TALK SHOW FLOPS

*There are dozens of talk shows on TV, and hundreds more that have come and gone over the years. Plenty will last for decades—*The Tonight Show, *for example. Others barely make it on the air before they get canceled.*

The Don Hornsby Show (1950)

NBC executive Pat Weaver created *The Today Show* in 1952, establishing a morning show format still used today—the same thing he'd done for late-night TV two years earlier, when he introduced American television's first bedtime programming, *Broadway Open House,* hosted by comedian Jerry Lester. *Broadway Open House* debuted at 11:00 p.m. on May 29, 1950, and aired for about a year until it was revived and rebranded in 1954 as *The Tonight Show,* with host Steve Allen. All of that may never have happened had Weaver's original plan not ended in tragedy. The first late-night show was *supposed* to be *The Don Hornsby Show,* hosted by Don "Creesh" Hornsby, a rising star on the nightclub comedy scene who specialized in playing silly songs on the piano (like Tom Lehrer or Victor Borge). But in mid-May 1950, Hornsby was diagnosed with a case of aggressive, rapid-onset polio (five years before the first polio vaccine was introduced). On May 22, the day the first *The Don Hornsby Show* was set to air, Hornsby died. He was 26 years old.

The Jerry Lewis Show (1984)

The wacky, loud comedy of Jerry Lewis—silly faces, nonsense yelling, pratfalls, broad characters—made the actor one of the most popular movie stars of the 1950s and 1960s in movies like *Cinderfella, The Bellboy,* and *The Nutty Professor.* His goofy schtick was passé by the 1980s until he enjoyed a comeback, starring as a Johnny Carson–like late-night host in Martin Scorsese's 1982 film *The King of Comedy.* Two years later, Lewis got a show for real: the syndicated *The Jerry Lewis Show,* a hastily assembled replacement for Canadian TV personality Alan Thicke's *Thicke of the Night,* which was canceled by distributor Metromedia after a year due to its routinely getting trounced by Johnny Carson. *The Jerry Lewis Show,* with its old-school Hollywood flavor (Hollywood veteran Charlie Callas served as sidekick, and Frank Sinatra appeared as a guest), didn't make it past its one-week on-air tryout before Metromedia pulled the plug.

The Las Vegas Show (1967)

In 1967, Daniel Overmyer, a tycoon who owned several TV stations around the country, attempted to create a fourth major broadcast service—the United Network. In May of that year, the network debuted its first flagship (and, ultimately, its only) program: *The Las Vegas Show,* a nightly two-hour talk show broadcast live from the

World's strongest lily pad: The Victoria water lily is large enough and sturdy enough to support an adult human.

fabulous Hotel Hacienda in Sin City. It featured an orchestra and a cast of sketch performers (including future *Laugh-In* star Jo Anne Worley), and was hosted by comic Bill Dana, in a rare gig in which he didn't play his popular Spanish-accented persona, Jose Jimenez. The United Network didn't have many stations, so *The Las Vegas Show* ran mostly on other networks' affiliates. But despite appearing on more than 100 stations, the shaky and expensive broadcasting experiment had a hard time finding advertisers, and in June 1967, after 23 episodes were produced, *The Las Vegas Show* went off the air—and so did the United Network.

The Kilborn File **(2010)**

In the 1990s and early 2000s, former sportscaster Craig Kilborn was a major player in late-night TV. In 1996, the smirking, easygoing host served as the original anchor of Comedy Central's *The Daily Show.* He jumped to network TV in 1999 when CBS selected him to host its post–David Letterman series *The Late Late Show.* On that show, Kilborn followed Letterman's lead by making a silly, experimental comedy show that skewed TV conventions. He'd end every interview with five dumb questions, make his guests play moronic party games, and once staged the slowest close-up in TV history. But by 2004, Kilborn was bored with making a talk show and he quit, not really surfacing again until 2010 with a syndicated show called *The Kilborn File*—a half-hour re-creation of all the best bits from his late-night shows, just 30 minutes long and presented at 7:00 p.m. in most cities. The ratings were so bad that the syndicator decided not to renew *The Kilborn File* past its six-week trial period.

The Orson Welles Show **(1979)**

Orson Welles was the man who once made an ultra-realistic radio adaptation of *The War of the Worlds* that caused widespread panic among listeners who thought it was a news report about an actual alien invasion. He was also the man who starred in and directed *Citizen Kane,* regarded by many critics as the best film ever made. But Welles's stellar career ended with a whimper. By the 1980s, he'd been reduced to commercial pitchman work for cheap wine and frozen peas, and voiced a character in *The Transformers: The Movie.* At least those projects were released, unlike his 1979 venture into late-night TV with *The Orson Welles Show.* The 90-minute show, directed by Welles himself (under the pseudonym G. O. Spelvin), offered a little something for everyone. He interviewed his close friend Burt Reynolds, then took questions from members of the theater-in-the-round-style audience (they were all scripted). Then he chatted with Muppet masters Jim Henson and Frank Oz, and introduced some pretaped segments featuring Kermit the Frog and Fozzie Bear. He even performed a couple of magic tricks with *Police Woman* star Angie Dickinson. Perhaps because of Welles's remarks about resenting commercial breaks, no network or programming syndicator bought the show, and it ended with that one episode, which has never been released to the public.

GOIN' VEGAN

For generations of Americans raised on burgers and bacon, a vegan diet is viewed as something only health nuts follow. But when we learned that there are more vegans in the world today than at any time in history—an estimated 78 million—we wanted to know what the hubbub is all about. So we sought out some experts: BRI stalwarts Gene Stone and Kathy Freston, the authors of 72 Reasons to be Vegan. *As the title suggests, the benefits are more far-reaching than you might realize. Bon(eless) appétit!*

WHAT IS VEGANISM?

According to The Vegan Society, an advocacy group formed in 1944, veganism is "a philosophy and way of living which seeks to exclude—as far as is possible and practicable—all forms of exploitation of animals for food, clothing, or any other purpose." The practice is older than you might think. The earliest known historical figure to forego meat was the Greek mathematician Pythagoras, who lived 2,500 years ago. But he wasn't a true vegan; he was a vegetarian. The difference? Vegetarians eat animal byproducts like eggs and dairy. A vegan diet is one that contains zero animal products—no meat, no eggs, no dairy, no honey. If you're thinking of switching to one of these diets, the benefits can go far beyond merely feeling better. Here's a primer.

IT'S GOOD FOR THE ENVIRONMENT

- A 2010 United Nations report advocated for the switch to a plant-based diet on the grounds that "raising animals for food generates more greenhouse gases than all the cars and trucks in the world combined."
- Going meatless could save enormous amounts of water, crucial at a time when nearly 10 percent of the planet's population suffers from water scarcity. According to a report in *Nature*, about 23 percent of the United States' freshwater goes to livestock. It takes 1,800 gallons of water to produce the amount of meat that the average American consumes in a year, compared to 119 gallons to grow enough potatoes for that same person.
- Animal agriculture pollutes streams and rivers due to animal waste, chemicals from fertilizers, and factory farm pollutants such as nitrogen, pesticides, antibiotics, and hormones. It's also harmful to rainforests by driving countless species extinct. In 2018, an Oxford University study reported, "A vegan diet is probably the single biggest way to reduce your impact on planet Earth, not just greenhouse gases, but global acidification, eutrophication, land use and water use...It is far bigger than cutting down on your flights or buying an electric car."
- Farmed animals occupy 45 percent of the Earth's surface. The average beef cow eats around 90 pounds of food a day, and poops 15 times a day. That's about 65 pounds

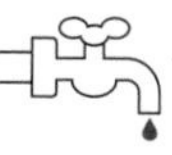

of poop a day, or close to 12 tons of poop a year. A lactating cow produces even more—nearly 27 tons a year. And that's just the cows (there are almost a billion of them at any given moment); don't forget the pigs, sheep, and chickens. In just the United States alone, livestock produce approximately 396 million tons of excrement every year.

- The animal waste is especially damaging. Unlike human poop, which gets treated at sewage processing plants, all that cattle, pig, and poultry poop is generally stored in waste lagoons or sprayed over fields as fertilizer. The toxic runoff carries nitrates, phosphorous, bacteria, and viruses that contaminate nearby groundwater, which can kill fish and harm people. In fact, large-scale industrial factory farms are one of the leading causes of drinking water contamination.
- Then there's the inhumane treatment most farmed animals receive. Without anesthesia, bulls and pigs are castrated (so they fatten up faster and become more compliant), cattle are dehorned, and hens are de-beaked. When the end comes, the animals are typically dunked in scalding water (chickens), hung up by their legs (pigs), or sliced open (cows, pigs, and chickens), often while still alive. Accounts from traumatized ex-slaughterhouse workers have told of "palpable terror in the animals" as they move down the line.

IT'S GOOD FOR YOU

- Feeling down? In addition to improving your cardiovascular health by eliminating cholesterol and animal fats from your diet, recent studies have shown that a plant-based diet can lift your spirits. The antioxidants present in many fruits and veggies help protect the body and brain from inflammation, which can negatively influence mood and energy levels, and interfere with the brain's self-repair process. A plant-based diet also helps reduce the damaging effects of a compound called *arachidonic acid*, which is found in animal foods and is linked to brain inflammation.
- A growing body of research is finding a strong link between gut health and emotional stability. The nutrients in plants support a happy *microbiome*, the genetic material of all your body's microbes—including bacteria, fungi, protozoa, and viruses. Why? Plants are loaded with "friendly" bacteria, whereas meat tends to introduce harmful microbes.
- Dr. Drew Ramsey, a Columbia University psychiatrist who studies the link between diet patterns and mental health conditions, found that low levels of twelve nutrients—including omega-3 fatty acids, B vitamins, vitamin D, iron, magnesium, and zinc—can be linked to depression symptoms; replenishing them helps prevent or relieve these symptoms. In his study ranking foods by "antidepressant nutrient score," the top scorers were plants, especially leafy greens, pumpkin, and peppers. With the exception of oysters, no animal foods scored nearly as high as plants. And

The first pressing of Madonna's *Like a Prayer* album was scented with church incense.

while key vitamins B12 and D3 aren't found in plants, vegans can get B12 from fortified foods or supplements and D3 by spending time in the sun.

- The drug Viagra was originally intended as a heart medication because it increases blood flow. It was marketed instead for its "side effect." Studies have shown that veganism increases blood flow as well, giving it the same sort of "rise to the occasion" benefits as Viagra. (And not just in men; increased blood flow in women also makes sexual intercourse more pleasurable.) Clinical studies have indicated that the saturated fat in meat and dairy clogs up the arteries going to *all* the body's organs. In other words, an apple—or a salad—a day keeps the Viagra away.

TRY GOING "VEGANISH"

Being vegan is not necessarily a white-knuckle, hard-core discipline, say authors Stone and Freston; it's about finding the foods that work for your life, cause the least suffering, and keep you feeling healthy and happy. And you don't have to go totally vegan. You can be just "veganish." The Oxford study refers to this as a "flexitarian" diet. And if humanity is to reverse the harmful effects of climate change, "The average world citizen needs to eat 75% less beef, 90% less pork, and half the number of eggs, while tripling consumption of beans and pulses [legumes], and quadrupling nuts and seeds."

One way to start is to switch up your favorite dishes to plant-based versions. Just veganize what you already love. For example, if you love pizza, buy a pizza crust, spread out the tomato sauce, sprinkle on some vegan cheese, add some olives, onions, bell peppers, or whatever other plant-based toppings you want. The point is that anything you're used to enjoying, you can still enjoy...just crowd out the animal-based ingredients with cleaner, animal-free ones.

VEGGING OUT

Need more reasons to go vegan? It's estimated that if everyone in the United States went vegan for just *one day*, we could save: 190 billion gallons of water (enough to supply all American homes for a week) and the fossil fuels equivalent to 78 million gallons of gas.

And for every person who switches to a full-time vegan diet, the world could save:

- 180,000 gallons of water each year—that's 500 gallons each day.
- 1,400 pounds of plant food otherwise fed to livestock each year—that's four pounds each day, which could feed the hungry and poor.
- Fossil fuels equivalent to 87 gallons of gas each year.
- More than three acres of land a year—that is, when you do the math, every extra day a person goes vegan theoretically saves another 375 square feet of wilderness.
- Greenhouse gas emissions equivalent to 1.6 tons of CO_2 per year—that's nine pounds each day.

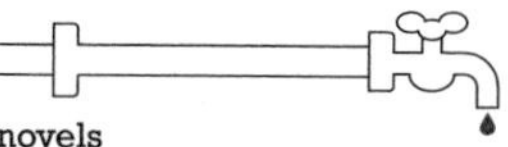

Game of PC Clones: George R. R. Martin writes his novels on a computer from the 1980s. (He hates modern spellcheckers.)

TALES FROM THE MAN CAVE

In the old days it might have been called a den. Today it's known as man cave—the place where a man can have some time to himself and retreat from his problems for awhile...or create even more problems.

WOOD-BURNING CAVE

A man (unnamed in news reports) in Rigby, Idaho, had a unique feature in the shed he'd made into his man cave: a wood-burning stove. Or at least he had one until around 3:00 a.m. one morning in October 2019, when it got a little too cold and he decided that his fire was a little too small. So he took out his gas can and poured some gas onto the fire. Bad idea. As soon as the gasoline ignited, the flame raced up the stream of fuel into the gas can. BOOM. The man dropped the gas can and ran out of the shed. By the time the fire department arrived, the man cave was fully engulfed and a total loss. Estimated damages: $1,500 for the shed, plus another $1,500 for the stuff inside the shed. The man escaped with minor burns to his fingertips.

COP CAVE

According to a grand jury indictment handed down in South Carolina in January 2020, Chester County sheriff Alex "Big A" Underwood broke the law when he built his man cave in 2017. Well, *he* didn't build it—he got his *deputies* to do it. He ordered them to convert a barn on his property into a man cave while they were on duty and supposed to be protecting and serving the community. In the process, Big A benefited from $10,000 worth of free labor paid for by county taxpayers. He was also charged with financial improprieties, including pocketing his deputies' overtime money, using county funds to take his wife to a sheriffs' conference in Reno, Nevada, and altering expense receipts to cover up the malfeasance. The 16-count indictment includes charges of criminal conspiracy, misconduct in office, embezzlement, and forgery. If convicted on all charges, Big A could spend 62 years in the "Big P"—prison.

GRAND CENTRAL CAVE

In September 2020, three employees of the Metro-North division of New York City's Metropolitan Transportation Authority were suspended without pay after it was alleged that they had converted a forgotten, unused locksmith shop below the tracks at Grand Central Station into a man cave, complete with a flat-screen TV, futon, pullout cot, microwave oven, and a fridge for beer and snacks. The three employees—a wireman, a carpenter foreman, and an electrical foreman—are believed to have used the sub-basement space to "hang out and get drunk, and party" when they were supposed to be working. Wooden cabinets in the man cave appear to have been custom-made for the purpose of concealing the TV, the futon, and the cot from prying eyes.

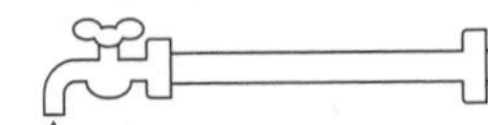

When confronted, the three employees denied knowing anything about the secret room, but investigators say their fingerprints were everywhere, as were receipts, datebooks, and other items with the defendants' names on them. And the Amazon streaming device attached to the TV was registered to the construction foreman. MTA president Catherine Rinaldi called the man cave "outrageously inappropriate" and "not consistent with Metro-North's values." If found guilty of creating the man cave, the employees could be fired from their jobs.

CAPITOL CAVE

The MTA employees weren't the first public employees in New York to turn part of their workplace into a secret man cave. In 2009, a janitor and his supervisor set up a TV, DVD player, and couches in a maintenance room in a parking garage that serves the state capitol in Albany. Prosecutors alleged that the two men, Gary Pivoda, 48, and Louis Marciano, 50, would clock in to work and then retreat to the man cave, where they either used drugs, watched TV, or slept through their shifts. They also threw all-night parties for coworkers and friends. Both men were suspended without pay following a police raid on the man cave; in a 22-count indictment, they were charged with grand larceny, official misconduct, criminal nuisance, and drug possession. They were each looking at up to seven years in prison, with an additional nine years tacked onto Pivoda's sentence for the drug dealing. In July 2010 both men pled guilty to lesser charges relating to watching TV, sleeping, and taking drugs on the job. Marciano got five years' probation and Pivoda was sentenced to a year in jail. Both men were barred from ever working for the State of New York again.

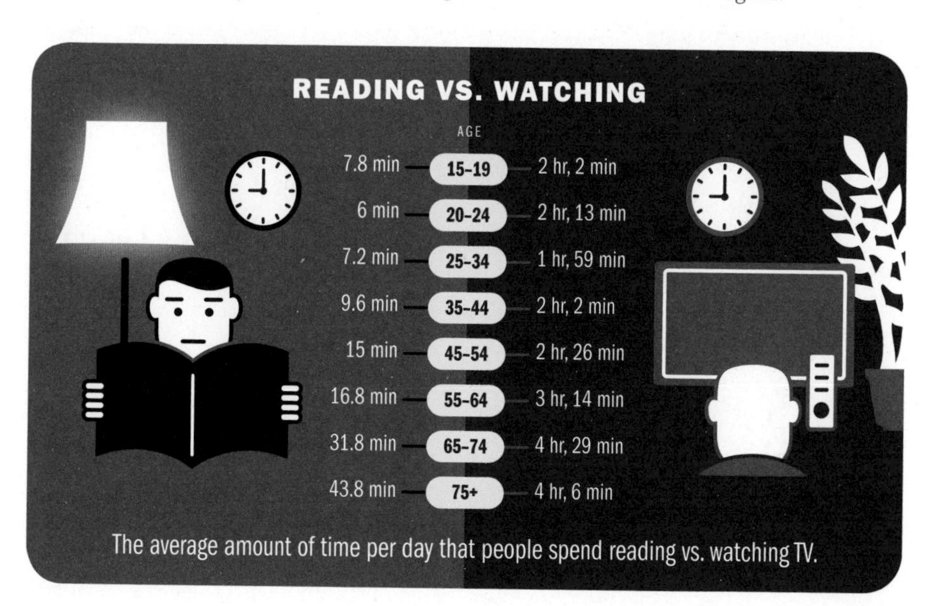

READING VS. WATCHING
AGE
7.8 min 15–19 2 hr, 2 min
6 min 20–24 2 hr, 13 min
7.2 min 25–34 1 hr, 59 min
9.6 min 35–44 2 hr, 2 min
15 min 45–54 2 hr, 26 min
16.8 min 55–64 3 hr, 14 min
31.8 min 65–74 4 hr, 29 min
43.8 min 75+ 4 hr, 6 min

The average amount of time per day that people spend reading vs. watching TV.

...he leased a new car every six months when the temporary permit expired.

DON'T LISTEN TO MY EARLY STUFF

Few rock stars have their artistic vision mapped out from the beginning. Like all artists, they evolve, and some of their early incarnations may seem a little embarrassing in retrospect.

Musician: Deborah Harry

Story: Before she formed Blondie, Harry recorded an album in 1968 as a backup vocalist in the mellow hippie band The Wind in the Willows. Among the tracks on the band's one and only album of folk pop: "The Friendly Lion," "Park Avenue Blues," and "There Is But One Truth, Daddy."

Musician: Alanis Morissette

Story: Morissette earned a Grammy nomination in 1995 for Best New Artist, but she wasn't new to Canadians. As a teenager in the early '90s, she released two albums, *Alanis* (1991) and *Now Is the Time* (1992). Both were in the vein of late 1980s teen dance pop, à la Debbie Gibson or Tiffany, with songs like "Too Hot," "Party Boy," and "Feel Your Love."

Musician: John Mellencamp

Story: Under the stage name Johnny Cougar, Mellencamp cut an album called *Chestnut Street Incident* in 1976, consisting mostly of soft-rock covers of familiar songs like "Hit the Road Jack" and "Jailhouse Rock."

Musician: Ronnie James Dio

Story: Before he was one of the most influential heavy metal singers of all time with bands Black Sabbath, Rainbow, and Dio, a teenaged Ronnie Padavona played in a 1950s doo-wop group called the Vegas Kings, which later changed its name to Ronnie and the Rumblers, then Ronnie and the Red Caps (and Padavona changed his name to Dio), before switching its sound entirely to psychedelic rock in the 1960s and changing names again to the Electric Elves.

Musician: Trent Reznor

Story: Nine Inch Nails is virtually a one-man band, a project led by producer, songwriter, and multi-instrumentalist Trent Reznor. But in the early 1980s, before he nailed down NIN's dark, metal-meets-industrial sound, Reznor played keyboards in a Pennsylvania-based New Wave band called Option 30. Their sole album includes covers of hits of the era like the Thompson Twins' "Lies" and Falco's "Der Kommissar."

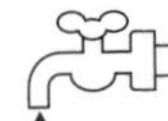

World's deepest subway station: Kiev's Arsenalna station in Ukraine is 346 feet below ground.

LUCKY FINDS

More unburied treasures from our "It Could Happen to You" files.

A SECRET MESSAGE

The Find: A medieval gold ring

Where It Was Found: First on a farm...and then inside a tin box

The Story: In 1979, Tom Clark, with the help of a metal detector, found a gold ring on a farm in South East England. "At the time," he told BBC News 40 years later, "I didn't realize the ring was anything special." But when Clark was clearing some junk from his late mother's garage in 2019, the 81-year-old former leather craftsman came across the ring in a tin. "I'd completely forgotten about it," he said. He took the ring to an expert, who dated it to 1350. It has an engraving of the god Mars, along with a Latin phrase that translates to "I hide the true message." Clark was informed that the ring could net £10,000 ($13,000) at auction, but as of last report, the "medieval treasure" had failed to sell. Still, not a bad conversation piece.

HARRY POTTER AND THE DUMPSTER OF TREASURES

The Find: Several rare books

Where They Were Found: In a *skip* (a "dumpster" in England) outside a school

The Story: In 2008, a British teacher (who went unnamed in press reports) came across a pile of books and, as she recalled, "It just seemed awful to throw them away, so I picked up about five Harry Potter books. I thought they might be useful for my children or grandchildren in the future." Twelve years later, in 2020, the 65-year-old teacher's lucky finds were among the most sought-after items at a Harry Potter online auction in Staffordshire. The best of the lot—a first edition of *Harry Potter and the Philosopher's Stone,* one of only 500 printed in its initial 1997 run—sparked an intense bidding war that ended with the book selling to a UK buyer for £33,000 ($42,600). That's more than three times its estimate, despite some damage to the binding. The teacher's other Potter novels—first editions of later installments—netted her another £10,000. "To say I'm pleased is an understatement."

DID YOU KNOW?

Most of the first 500 printings of *Harry Potter and the Philosopher's Stone* went to schools and libraries in the UK in 1997, but by this point they could be anywhere. If you think you have one, or know someone who does, check out the copyright page. If the print line reads "10 9 8 7 6 5 4 3 2 1" then you have a first edition. To find out if you have one of those lucrative 500, go to page 53 and look at Harry's list of school supplies. If the "1 wand" line is printed twice, you'll be one happy muggle.

JIMI HENDRIX IN BLACK AND WHITE

He was an anomaly among white musicians and didn't resonate for many black musicians. Here's a modern look at the life and times of a man widely regarded as rock's greatest guitarist—including his complicated relationship with race, his ever-expanding place in music history, and where he might have been headed had he made it out of his 20s.

THE STAR-SPANGLED BANNER

On a muggy Monday morning in August 1969, at the end of the three-day Woodstock Rock Festival in Bethel, New York, the weary crowd of about 200,000 was slowly making its way out when the headliner, Jimi Hendrix, finally hit the stage. "You can leave if y'all want to," he said playfully. "We're just jamming." A few songs in, during an extended version of "Voodoo Child," the other instruments tapered off, leaving only Hendrix's white Fender Stratocaster ringing out over the countryside as he launched into a soulful deconstruction of "The Star-spangled Banner," the melody interspersed with deafening feedback and distortion.

That rendition of the national anthem became the defining moment of the defining event of the 1960s counterculture movement. A little over a year later, Jimi Hendrix was dead.

PURPLE HAZE

For decades, most music writers put Hendrix alongside the Who, the Rolling Stones, Cream, and other legendary rock bands of the era. He was less likely to show up on lists that included James Brown, Aretha Franklin, Stevie Wonder, Parliament-Funkadelic, and other R&B and funk acts. But in the 2010s, as U.S. racial tensions regained an intensity not seen since the late 1960s, music historians—many of them people of color—reexamined Hendrix in relation to the tumultuous times he lived in. "Jimi's image has often been hijacked by the mainstream to paint a picture of an artist that was a pied piper for the LSD-induced flower children of the 60's," writes Corey Washington in the 2019 book *Jimi Hendrix - Black Legacy (A Dream Deferred)*. It turns out that race played a larger role in Hendrix's life than most biographers have acknowledged, including his official Biography.com entry, which barely mentions his race at all and glosses over the effect being black had on his life. Case in point, under the heading "Military Service," it reads: "In 1961, Hendrix followed in his father's footsteps by enlisting in the United States Army."

What that bio doesn't mention is *why* Hendrix joined the army: At 19, he was arrested for being a passenger in a stolen car. The judge gave him a choice—join the army, or go to prison. That's why Hendrix enlisted, not to "follow in his father's footsteps." According to Hendrix biographer Charles R. Cross, "What happened to Jimi would have never happened to a white male in that era. Jimi was run out of Seattle for being black."

LITTLE WING

Born in 1942 to a 17-year-old alcoholic mother and an overbearing father, James Marshall Hendrix grew up in Seattle's impoverished Central District, which, due to segregation, was home to more than 90 percent of the city's African American population. His lineage included both enslaved people and slave owners, and his grandmother was one-quarter Cherokee Indian. While his neighborhood was primarily African American, Hendrix attended Garfield High School, one of the country's few integrated high schools. There, the school's music programs weren't divided by race—any student could play whatever they wanted. For the rest of Hendrix's life, he never understood why music had to be so divisive.

After his parents divorced, Hendrix wanted a guitar, but his father (who'd once whipped his son for being left-handed) couldn't afford one. So the lanky, soft-spoken teenager carried around a broomstick that he *pretended* was a guitar, while wearing a Flash Gordon cape. In the midst of a very unstable childhood, those were his two escapes: science fiction and the blues. When Hendrix was 15, his mother died. (She never heard her son play.) He got his first electric guitar a year later and took right to it, figuring out Elvis Presley's "Hound Dog" by ear.

Then, in 1961, came the kicked-out-of-Seattle fiasco, and Hendrix joined the army. As a paratrooper with the Screaming Eagles 101st Airborne Division in Fort Campbell, Kentucky, Private Hendrix completed 26 jumps and spent his free time listening to T-Bone Walker and Percy Mayfield records while developing his left-handed playing technique. There are conflicting stories about Hendrix's early (but honorable) discharge from the U.S. Army, ranging from a broken ankle to a litany of "behavioral problems" to getting himself labeled a "sexual deviant" so that his superiors would kick him out. Whatever went down, it's safe to say that Hendrix and the military were not a good fit. That would become a recurring theme.

DRIFTING

Hendrix landed in Nashville, living on Jefferson Street in the city's black section, where he and some army buddies started a blues group. Money was tight, but the 20-year-old's skills were getting him noticed, and he was soon picked up by a record producer named Ed Chalpin, the first of many who would try to exploit Hendrix.

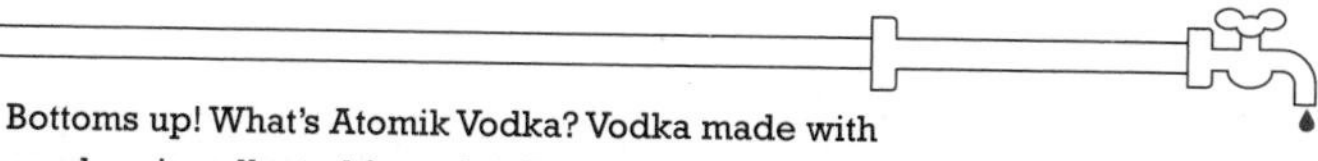

Bottoms up! What's Atomik Vodka? Vodka made with water and grain collected from the Chernobyl exclusion zone.

> **"I thought they were screaming for me," recalled Little Richard. "I look over and they're screaming for Jimi!"**

Chalpin (who specialized in recording covers of top-40 hits) signed him to a three-year recording contract with a $1 signing bonus and a 1 percent royalty rate. But they never did record an album, and Chalpin sued after his former client became famous. The case outlived Hendrix.

Chalpin did manage to get Hendrix some backup guitar jobs on the "Chitlin' Circuit"— clubs and other venues friendly to black people in the Jim Crow South. Hendrix fit in at first, wearing button-down suits and keeping his hair trimmed, but he soon started making a name for himself on stage, and not in a good way. "People would scream, and I thought they were screaming for me," recalled Little Richard years later. "I look over and they're screaming for Jimi! He'd be playing the guitar with his teeth!"

But it was by watching acts like Little Richard, Curtis Mayfield, and Ike and Tina Turner that Hendrix learned what true stage presence looked like. The work wasn't steady, though, especially after Little Richard fired him. "I'd get a gig once every twelfth of never," Hendrix said in 1967. "Sleeping outside them tall tenements was hell. Rats running all across your chest, cockroaches stealing your last candy bar out of your pocket." Musically stifled and out of money, he cut ties with Chalpin and headed north.

ELECTRIC LADYLAND

In the mid-1960s, New York City had two competing pop music scenes: Greenwich Village, a trendy folk-rock bohemia in lower Manhattan, led by Dave Van Ronk, Phil Ochs, Judy Collins, and others, including, of course, Bob Dylan; and Harlem, home of the Apollo Theater, a mecca for black R&B artists like James Brown, Marvin Gaye, Stevie Wonder, B. B. King, the Isley Brothers, and many more. Hendrix landed in Harlem. And for a while, he was fitting in, shacking up with African American socialite Lithofayne Pridgon (who would inspire his song "Foxy Lady"). Through her, Hendrix learned about Malcolm X and the Black Panthers, and he started an R&B group called the Ghetto Fighters. "He was a very progressive person," recalled bandmate TaharQa Aleem. "Influenced by the consciousness in Harlem, [he] caught the message and was even more attentive." But Hendrix's attention was focused on only one thing: his music.

After taking first place at an Apollo Theater amateur contest in 1964, Hendrix was hired as a backup player for the Isley Brothers (known for "Shout," "Twist and Shout," and "This Old Heart of Mine"). They invited him to live with them in New Jersey; that's where Hendrix acquired his famous white Stratocaster, which he restrung and flipped over to play left-handed. After his stint with the Isley Brothers, Hendrix backed up Curtis Knight and the Squires. Once again, he didn't really

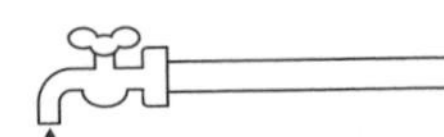

fit in with either group—he was always trying to do more with his guitar than was allowed. A black folk singer named Richie Havens (who would later open Woodstock) suggested to Hendrix that he check out Greenwich Village.

CROSSTOWN TRAFFIC

Word quickly started spreading through the Village about a young black blues guitarist named Jimmy James. He and his band, the Blue Flames, landed a residency at the Cafe Wha? on MacDougal Street. Greenwich Village, it so happened, was a big draw for British Invasion rockers and their managers looking for new talent. Several were reportedly circling Hendrix (including the Rolling Stones' manager, Andrew Loog Oldham), but he ended up signing with the first one to make him an offer: Chas Chandler, who played bass for the Animals...until Chandler quit the Animals to manage Hendrix. So did Mike Jeffrey, the Animals' actual manager, who became Chandler's partner.

But first Hendrix had to decide if he wanted to leave New York behind. He sat in with his old band, Curtis Knight and the Squires, only to receive the same "tone it down" admonishments as before. Hendrix unplugged his guitar and announced, "That's the last time I play this sh*t. I'm going to England."

ARE YOU EXPERIENCED

In September 1966, three days after Hendrix, Chandler, and Jeffrey arrived in London, Chandler approached reigning British guitar god Eric Clapton at a Cream show and told him that Hendrix was a good young player and would love to join Clapton for a blues song. Clapton happily agreed. Midway through the blues standard "Killing Floor," Clapton stormed off the stage and shouted at Chandler, "You didn't say he was that f***ing good!"

Over the next nine months in England, Chandler and Jeffrey took control over every aspect of Hendrix's career. They paired him with two white British musicians—bassist Noel Redding and drummer Mitch Mitchell—and called them the Jimi Hendrix Experience (which is when Jimmy became Jimi). They financed the single "Hey Joe," a cover song that became Hendrix's first hit. The next two singles, "The Wind Cries Mary" and "Purple Haze," made Hendrix a star. Their debut album, *Are You Experienced,* was released in May 1967, just in time for Hendrix to make his triumphant return to America for the Summer of Love. There, he debuted a fully formed stage act that merged the showmanship of the Chitlin' Circuit, the poetry of Greenwich Village, and the soul of Harlem. Hendrix definitely stood out, but he still wasn't fitting in.

Did becoming the highest-paid act in rock earn Hendrix the respect he was due? Yes and no. *Groove your way over to page 388 to read about Hendrix's final three years.*

MOOSE TONGUES AND DINGLE BELLS

Orchids are among the most delicate—and intriguing—flowers under the sun. Appropriately, many orchid breeds, cultivars, and varieties have really weird names.

Adam & Eve
Little Tarantula
Alpine Chicken
Rabbit Ears
Lizard
Donkey
Camel's Foot
Monkey Goblet
Monkey Face
Striped Tiger
Pink Bunny
Parrot's Beak
Chicken Foot
Mt. Tu-Wu Fall
Palm Polly
Bedbug
Flower in the Form of a Yellow Serpent
Angel Without Leaves
Crooked Spur
Many Swans
Shadow Witch
Praying Virgin
Aunty Rosie
Crippled Crane Fly

Clown Spikes
The Clown
Medusa's Head
Black Man's Potato
Crib of Venus
Punch & Judy
Cinnamon Bells
Cat's Face
Little Man
Old Man
Babe-in-a-Cradle
Granny's Bonnet
Ladies of the Night
Blue Fairies
Fairy Bells
Fairy's-Peach-on-the-Rock
Pixie Cups
Dancing Doll
Creeping Forest
Jack Spaniard
Wax Lip
Pink Fingers
Fried Egg
Eggs of a Bird

Jungle Cat
Bucket
Joined Pavement
Hardy Chinese
Mother-in-law's Flower
Pine Pink
Moose Tongue
Goat's Head
Goat's Mouth
Goat's Milk
Nanny-Goat
Dead-Horse
Toad Skin
Daddy Long Legs
Snake Flower
Copper Beards
Big Ears
Eyelash
Tree on Fire
Samurai
Dragon's Mouth
Large Duck
Dingle Bell
Flower of the Dead
You Will Cry

"ACTION-PACKED!" PART II

When we left off on the origin of the comic book on page 197, Clark Kent was about to change into his blue jammies for the first time. The world would never be the same.

Up, Up, and Away!

Everything changed when *Action Comics #1* hit newsstands in April 1938. Times were difficult and people needed a hero, and Superman certainly fit the bill. But according to Al Jaffee of *DC Comics News,* that wasn't the only reason he caught on: "Cynically, one might say that the early, immediate popularity of Superman was simply a matter of crafty marketing. With a tantalizingly priced 10-cent cover charge allowing for the most meager budgets even by 1938 standards, Superman's early adventures were immediately accessible to anyone looking for a fully illustrated escape into a world of fantasy before the age of television. Within six weeks of the first issue's publication, Superman had already become a household name."

Crafty marketing aside, there's another big reason for the popularity. "If you're interested in what made Superman what it is," Siegel said in 1983, "Joe and I had certain inhibitions" (they were nerds) "which led to wish-fulfillment, which we expressed through our interest in science fiction...That's where the dual-identity concept came from, and Clark Kent's problems with Lois. I imagine there are a lot of people in this world who are similarly frustrated."

An Expanding Universe

In May 1939, *Detective Comics #27* introduced Batman, created by Bob Kane. But without Superman's meteoric rise—he and Mickey Mouse had become the two most famous characters on the planet—who knows if Batman, or the comic book industry as a whole, would have ever caught on like it did. (Unfortunately for Superman creators Jerry Siegel and Joe Shuster, they were swindled out of millions in profits, but continued on as employees for meager salaries. They were finally compensated and credited for their creation with the release of 1978's *Superman: The Movie*.)

Detective Comics Inc. would later shorten its name to DC Comics and add dozens more superheroes to the cultural landscape, the most enduring being Wonder Woman, the Flash, and Green Lantern. (Less known today, but popular in their own time, were early DC characters Johnny Thunder, Spectre, Doc Strange, Guardian, and Neon the Unknown.)

The Birth of Marvel

By the end of the 1930s, the nascent comic book industry had grown to include dozens of publishers, releasing around 150 titles each month. Most failed. The one that rose above all the rest—and became DC's main competition—was originally called

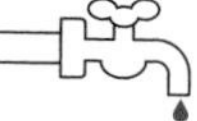

Ouch! There's a form of tinnitus (objective tinnitus) in which the ringing in the ears can be heard by others.

Timely Comics, founded by Martin Goodman, yet another former pulp-magazine publisher (and Great Depression hobo). Released in August 1939, *Marvel Comics #1* introduced the Human Torch, the Angel, the Sub-Mariner, the Masked Raider, and Ka-Zar. The following March, Timely introduced Steve Rogers's alter-ego in *Captain America #1*, created by Joe Simon and Jack Kirby.

In 1961, after years of lagging postwar sales under the Atlas Comics banner, the company officially became Marvel Comics. That year, Kirby, along with Steve Ditko and Stan Lee, launched the Marvel Universe. Lee and Kirby cowrote *Fantastic Four #1*, which introduced a new line of heroes that included Spider-Man, the Incredible Hulk, Iron Man, and the Avengers.

During World War II, each new Superman, Captain Marvel, or Captain America comic book could sell upward of 1.5 million copies each month, compared to a few hundred thousand—at best—today. What changed? By the end of the 1940s, superheroes had fallen out of favor as Old West cowboys became the next big fad (though Superman would soon find new life on TV in the 1950s, followed by the campy *Batman* TV show a decade later).

Meanwhile, Back in Riverdale...

It turned out, however, that comic books didn't really need superheroes to survive. In 1940, Walt Disney launched Disney Comics, which introduced Scrooge McDuck, created by Carl Barks in 1947. By 1960, Scrooge McDuck was the best-selling comic book in the United States. In 1941, *Pep Comics #22* introduced the teenagers Archie Andrews and his friends at Riverdale High School (created by John L. Goldwater, Bob Montana, and Vic Bloom). By 1973, Archie Comics titles were outselling Batman and Superman combined. Archie has since expanded to both the big and small screen and even Broadway.

But despite that, the comic book will always be linked to the superhero. And while superhero comic books continue to sell at a steady pace, superheroes themselves have gone mainstream. Three movies that were released in 2019—*Avengers: Endgame, Spider-Man: Far from Home,* and *Joker*—combined to haul in an unprecedented $3.2 billion at the box office.

Though critics debate the validity of the comic book as an art form (or graphic novels as true literature), there can be no denying the staying power of the characters who were brought to life on pulpy pages. So the next time you find yourself at a newsstand or in a bookstore, flip through a comic book and take a moment to appreciate what you're holding in your hands: a piece of history borne out of a time when true heroes were made.

* * *

"Most every guy wishes he could be more than he is. Who wouldn't love to fly? Who wouldn't love to be bulletproof? And X-ray eyes! I won't even get into that." —**Stan Lee**, on Superman

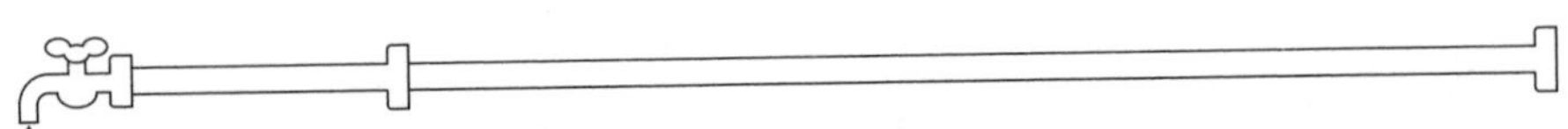

Not verry bright: The 1996 edition of *Webster's Dictionary* contained more than 300 misspelled words.

THE BARF SCIENTISTS

Believe it or not, some scientists have made their reputations with research involving vomit. Here's a look at two famous cases that prove science can be pretty interesting... even when it's absolutely disgusting.

SUBJECT: Stubbins Ffirth, a University of Pennsylvania medical student in 1803

Experiment: Prove that the deadly disease yellow fever (also called malignant fever) is not contagious

Details: In the United States, yellow fever epidemics tended to occur during the hot summer months, then fade away in fall and winter. In the tropics, where it was hot and humid year-round, yellow fever was a problem year-round. This caused Ffirth to conclude that the disease was not contagious, but rather was something akin to heatstroke, caused by overexposure to hot weather.

To prove his theory, Ffirth exposed animals, and then himself, to black vomit (caused by bleeding in the gastrointestinal tract) that in severe cases was one of the main symptoms of the disease. It's such a common feature that in Spanish countries yellow fever is known as *vómito negro* (black vomit). Ffirth made cuts in his skin and rubbed the vomit into the wounds. He also put drops into his eyes. And he heated vomit in a skillet and inhaled the fumes, then converted a small room into what could be called a "vomit sauna," by placing a dish containing six ounces of vomit on a stove that heated the room to 100°F. "For two hours I remained in the room thus heated, breathing in the air filled with the vapor produced by the evaporation, and very frequently held my head over the dish inhaling it as it arose," he recounted in a book describing his experiments. Finally, Ffirth *drank* some of the nasty stuff:

> I took half an ounce of the black vomit immediately after it was ejected from a patient, and diluting it with an ounce and a half of water, swallowed it; the taste was very slightly acid...No more effect was produced than if I had taken water alone...I thought of desisting from any further experiments; but upon mature consideration I thought it best to continue them, which I did, repeating them a great number of times...I increased the quantity I took internally from half an ounce to two ounces, drinking it at length without dilution.

Having satisfied himself that vomit did not transmit disease, Ffirth moved on to similar experiments with the blood, saliva, sweat, bile, and urine collected from yellow fever sufferers. When these, too, failed to make him sick, he concluded that "malignant fever is not a contagious disease; that it never has been, and from the established laws of nature, never can be."

Aftermath: Ffirth was wrong. Yellow fever *is* a contagious disease, but it is not

Dieticians recommend an intake of 2,000 calories per day.
At Thanksgiving dinner, you'll eat about 3,000 calories.

transmitted by exposure to vomit or bodily fluids. And even if it were, Ffirth had collected his black vomit from patients in the late stages of the disease, when they were no longer contagious. All of his breathing, drinking, and rubbing vomit into his wounds and eyes had been for nothing. It wasn't until nearly a century later that a U.S. Army surgeon named Walter Reed proved that the disease is a virus, transmitted through the saliva of mosquitos after they've bitten an infected human or animal.

SUBJECTS: Ten patients suffering from pernicious anemia, a disease in which the body fails to produce enough red blood cells, in the late 1920s

Experiment: Prove that pernicious anemia is caused by an inability to absorb certain nutrients from food as it is being digested

Details: The patients were fed regurgitated pieces of raw beef that had been partially digested by the creator of the experiment, William Castle, who did not suffer from pernicious anemia. Castle suspected that the patients were lacking something in their digestive system that prevented them from fully breaking down meat into the nutrients that the body needed to create red blood cells. Castle thought he could prove this theory by partially digesting the meat himself, using his own gastric juices—which were not deficient—then extracting the contents of his stomach and feeding them to his patients. If the patients got well, that meant that their digestive juices were *not* able to release certain nutrients from the meat, but Castle's *were.* He theorized that the patients' gastric juices lacked something he called an "intrinsic factor."

Each morning over the course of the experiment, Castle consumed 300 grams (a little over half a pound) of *raw* ground beef, then waited an hour before vomiting up the contents of his stomach by "pharyngeal stimulation" (sticking his finger down his throat). He adjusted the acidity level of the vomit by adding hydrochloric acid, then ran it through a blender and poured it through a fine sieve before feeding the resulting liquid to his unsuspecting patients through a tube. Patients in the control group were fed *un*regurgitated ground beef that had been prepared in a similar fashion.

Result: Patients who were fed Castle's regurgitated beef got better, while those in the control group did not, proving Castle's theory correct. Later studies showed that the "intrinsic factor" his patients lacked was a protein that, when absent, prevented the absorption of vitamin B12, which the body needs to produce red blood cells.

Once vitamin B12 has been absorbed from food, it is stored in the liver—not just in humans but in other animals as well. Until the vitamin was isolated and identified in the late 1940s, people suffering from pernicious anemia had to eat half a pound of raw or lightly cooked liver *every day,* or drink the equivalent in the form of raw liver juice or liver juice concentrate, just to get enough vitamin B12 to be healthy. If they didn't, they could die. Once vitamin B12 in pure form became available in the 1950s, treatment was as simple as getting regular B12 injections.

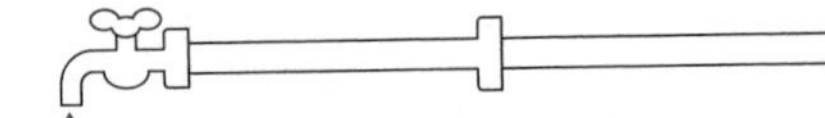

IMPONDERABLES

Some questions have no answers, but we ask them anyway.

"If a book about failures doesn't sell, is it a success?"

—Jerry Seinfeld

"IF LOVE IS BLIND, WHY IS LINGERIE SO POPULAR?"

—Dorothy Parker

"HOW COME YOU NEVER SEE A HEADLINE LIKE 'PSYCHIC WINS LOTTERY'?"

—Jay Leno

"The only mystery in life is why the kamikaze pilots wore helmets."

—Al McGuire

"Do Transformers get car or life insurance?"

—Russell Howard

"WHY DO THEY CALL IT RUSH HOUR WHEN NOTHING MOVES?"

—Robin Williams

"IF EVOLUTION REALLY WORKS, HOW COME MOTHERS ONLY HAVE TWO HANDS?"

—Milton Berle

"If one synchronized swimmer drowns, do the rest drown too?"

—George Carlin

"Why is there so much month left at the end of the money?"

—John Barrymore

"You can't have everything. Where would you put it?"

—Steven Wright

"If you can't live without me, why aren't you dead already?"

—Cynthia Heimel

"When I hear someone sigh that life is hard, I am tempted to ask, 'Compared to what?'"

—Sydney Harris

STRANGE ANIMAL SCIENCE

We live in a world full of very strange creatures. We're not referring to your Aunt Tillie or your Cousin Fred (although they may, in fact, be very strange). We're talking about animals—and the fascinating discoveries being made about them. Here's the latest research.

DRAGON'S BLOOD

Though they aren't really dragons, Komodo dragons do seem like ancient mythical beasts. They are the world's last species of big lizards—growing up to 10 feet long. They hunt large prey such as water buffalo, and can eat 80 percent of their body weight in one sitting. Most interesting to scientists, Komodo dragons pack a deadly venomous bite and can have 80 types of bacteria in their mouths, yet they are immune to bites from other Komodos. Most likely that's because their blood is full of antimicrobial peptides, which are proteins that fight bacteria. In 2013, researchers discovered more than 200 unknown peptides in Komodo blood and have been investigating their properties ever since. The goal? To develop new antibiotics that might help heal infections in humans. And they've made progress. In 2017, one of these peptides was used to create a synthetic protein that cured mice of the antibiotic-resistant super bug known as MRSA. So who knows? Maybe someday soon, when you tell the druggist you need something to treat an infection, he'll recommend using dragon's blood.

SOLAR-POWERED SLUGS

Though it's only five millimeters (0.2 inch) long, the *Costasiella kuroshimae* sea slug has a distinctive look. The creature went viral on social media in 2020 because in close-up shots, it clearly has the face of...a cartoon sheep—so much so that it's been nicknamed the "leaf sheep" or "Shaun the sheep," after the title character of an animated TV show. But it has another unique characteristic: it's one of the only animals on the planet that can perform photosynthesis. Using the chloroplasts in the green algae they eat, the slugs transform light into food energy just as plants do. Some can live for months on sunlight alone. (If you haven't yet, do an online search for photos of the leaf sheep—it's incredible.)

MAD HATTERPILLAR

In *Alice in Wonderland*, the Mad Hatter wears a tall hat and confuses everyone with nonsensical riddles. The real-life *Uraba lugens walker*, also known as the "mad hatterpillar," perplexes predators with its tall, bizarre "hat"—a stack of heads. The

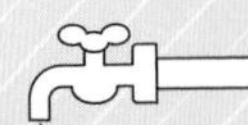

Australian insect lives on eucalyptus trees, where it must fend off wasps, spiders, and birds. One of its defense mechanisms is the stinging hairs that cover its body; another is its ability to vomit a foul green liquid that repels predators. But its nickname comes from the fact that each time it grows larger and sheds its skin, it keeps its old head, which sits on top of its new, bigger head. Ultimately, *Uraba lugens walker* can have seven heads, stacked up to a half-inch tall. An experiment published in the journal *PeerJ* in 2016 showed that caterpillars with their tower of heads are more than twice as likely to survive than those who had it removed. The heads make the insect look bigger and more intimidating, and they offer a false target for predators. Attackers often home in on the dead heads, allowing many caterpillars to survive and transform into moths.

NOW YOU SEE IT, NOW YOU DON'T

A species that the media is calling a "ghost" frog was rediscovered in Chile in 2020. Originally identified in 1935, the two-inch-long frog was found by researcher Frank Gregory Hall in warm water at 10,000 feet altitude. Since then, searches for *Telmatobius halli,* also called Hall's water frog, yielded no results. More than 80 years later, it was finally spotted by Chilean scientists in a hot spring in the high-altitude Atacama Desert. The frog is so rare because it inhabits water in the desert, which is hard to come by, and it cannot live on dry land for even five minutes. As water sources diminish, only time will tell whether this ghost will disappear forever.

LAND SHARKS

As if nightmares created by *Jaws* weren't bad enough, a 2020 study catalogued four new species of sharks that can chase you out of the water. Called epaulette sharks, not only can they swim, but they can also "walk" across land using the fins on their undersides like feet. With this discovery, there are now nine known species of walking sharks. All four new species live in shallow coral reefs near northern Australia, Papua New Guinea, and Indonesia. But the three-foot-long walkers won't "chase" you (probably). Throughout their lifetime, they travel no more than a mile from home, and they generally walk only from one tide pool to another. That way they can hunt small fish and crustaceans under rocks and in spots inaccessible to swimmers. The study's lead author, Dr. Christine Dudgeon, posits that originally the sharks may have been separated from the main population and ended up in isolated areas. There, they had to evolve new abilities to survive. Now it's normal for the shark pups to learn to walk and to slow their heart rate and breathing while they wander around terrorizing prey. Dudgeon adds, "We believe there are more walking shark species still waiting to be discovered."

Not only can they swim, but they can also "walk" across land using the fins on their undersides like feet.

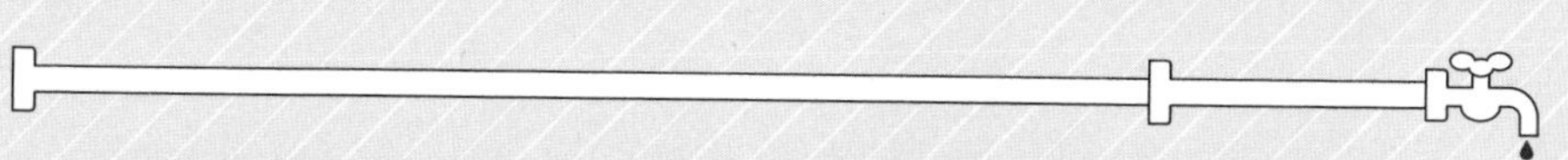

WE'RE STILL OPEN!

Discovering a great new restaurant you've never tried before is one of the best parts of eating out. And if that new place is a gem that's been around forever, so much the better.

THE WHITE HORSE TAVERN (Newport, Rhode Island)

Claim to Fame: Oldest tavern and restaurant in the United States, more than a century older than the country itself

Story: The original building in which the tavern is still located was built by an Englishman named Francis Brinley in 1652. But it was another man, William Mayes, who added on to the place and turned it into a tavern in 1673. One of the largest buildings in the colony, over the years the tavern did double duty as a city hall, a courthouse, a boardinghouse, and even the meeting place of the Rhode Island General Assembly until the Assembly's own Colony House building was constructed in the 1730s. During the Revolutionary War, the tavern was used to provide lodging for Hessian mercenaries fighting for the British. The tavern remained in Mayes's family until 1895. By the early 1950s, the 300-year-old building had changed hands a number of times and was in derelict condition. It was in danger of being demolished...until a preservation group stepped in and restored it to its former glory. The White Horse reopened in 1957 and has been serving rum drinks, seafood, and colonial cuisine to the public ever since.

ANTOINE'S (New Orleans, Louisiana)

Claim to Fame: Oldest family-run restaurant in the United States

Story: Antoine's, a Louisiana Creole restaurant, was founded in New Orleans's French Quarter in 1840 by 18-year-old Antoine Alciatore, a French immigrant. When Alciatore fell ill in 1874, his wife, Julia, took over; she passed the business on to their son Jules in 1887. (Jules is the guy who, one day when he ran out of escargot in 1899, substituted oysters covered in green sauce and bread crumbs and called the dish "Oysters Rockefeller.") Jules ran the restaurant until 1934, and succeeding generations of the family have been stepping up ever since. In 2005, the restaurant passed to Rick Blount, Antoine Alciatore's great-great-grandson. As of 2020, he's still running the place—180 years after it first opened its doors.

JONES BAR-B-Q DINER (Marianna, Arkansas)

Claim to Fame: Believed to be the oldest family-run, African American-owned restaurant in the United States

Story: Jones Bar-B-Q got its start in about 1910, when a man named Walter Jones,

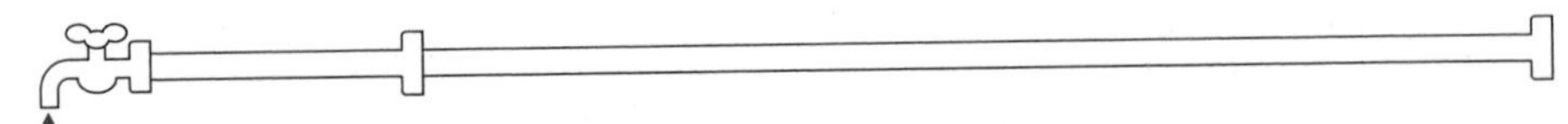

who had learned from his uncle Joe how to smoke meat, began selling barbecue off of his back porch on Fridays and Saturdays. The food was delicious, and the business grew. Jones later opened a takeout restaurant called The Hole in the Wall (so named because customers ordered their food and received it through an actual hole cut into the wall). In 1964, Walter's son Hubert took over the business, renamed it Jones Bar-B-Q, and opened the diner that is still serving customers today. Now it's run by Hubert's son and daughter-in-law, James and Betty. If you're ever passing through Marianna and want a taste of what the locals say is the best barbecue in the state, you'd better get there early: Jones opens for business at 6:00 a.m. and closes as soon as the meat runs out. On busy days, it's closed by 10:00 a.m.

LOUIS' LUNCH (New Haven, Connecticut)

Claim to Fame: Possible birthplace of the hamburger, and the oldest burger joint in America

Story: When Louis' Lunch opened for business in 1895, one of the items offered was a plate of ground beef cooked medium rare. Around 1900, a customer in a hurry wanted his lunch to go and told owner Louis Lassen to "slap a meatpuck between two planks and step on it!" Serving ground beef between two slices of toasted white bread seemed like a good idea, so Lassen added the sandwich to the menu. Four years passed before hamburgers found widespread fame when food vendors (independently of Lassen) began serving them up at the 1904 St. Louis World's Fair.

It took another 15 years for someone to invent the hamburger bun. Lassen ignored it then, and more than a century later, his restaurant still ignores them. Today Lassen's great-grandson, Jeff Lassen, runs the place with his wife Kerry. He still grinds the meat fresh each day, still grills the beef patties on a vertical grill that dates to 1898, and still serves the meat on white bread toasted on a gas toaster that's more than 90 years old. Toast, he says, "makes the taste of the burger come out." Cheeseburgers have been on the menu since the 1950s, and you can order your burger with onions and tomatoes. But if you want condiments, you'd better go someplace else. At Louis' Lunch, the meat is what it's all about. A "NO KETCHUP" sign is prominently displayed in the restaurant; mustard and mayo are frowned upon as well. If you try to sneak in your own, you may be asked to leave.

PEKIN NOODLE PARLOR (Butte, Montana)

Claim to Fame: The oldest Chinese restaurant in the United States

Story: In 1911, a Chinese American man named Hum Yow moved from California to Butte, Montana. There, he and a relative named Tam Kwong Yee opened a restaurant called the Pekin Noodle Parlor in the city's China Alley neighborhood. At the time, Butte was home to a community of hundreds of Chinese immigrants and Chinese Americans, many of whom were descended from people who came to Montana in the 19th century to work in the mines or to build the transcontinental railroad. By the late 1870s, people of Chinese ancestry made up nearly 10 percent of the population of the Montana Territory. But prejudice against the Chinese, which included decades-long boycotts of Chinese-owned businesses, caused the Chinese community in Butte to dwindle to fewer than 100 people by the mid-20th century. One business that managed to hold on was the Pekin Noodle Parlor, which is still doing business in the same location. Today it's run by Tam Kwong Yee's great-grandson, Jerry Tam.

PAPA'S TOMATO PIES (Robbinsville, New Jersey)

Claim to Fame: The oldest pizzeria in continuous operation in the United States

Story: If you've ever eaten at Lombardi's Pizza in Manhattan's Little Italy neighborhood, you know that they claim to be the oldest pizzeria in the United States. And in a sense they are, because when they opened in 1905 they were the first and only pizza restaurant in the country. But the original Lombardi's went out of business in 1984, and it wasn't until a decade later that the grandson of the founder, Gennaro Lombardi III, opened his own pizza place a block away and named it after his grandfather's place.

The oldest pizzeria that has never closed its doors—though it has moved a few times—is Papa's Tomato Pies, which first opened in Trenton, New Jersey, in 1912. Founded by Giuseppe "Joe" Papa, a 17-year-old immigrant from Naples, it was only the third pizzeria in the entire United States, and the second in Trenton. (Joe's Tomato Pies, where Giuseppe Papa learned the business, opened in Trenton in 1910 and went out of business in 1999.) Papa's is the only one of the original three that has never stopped making pizzas. Today Giuseppe's 73-year-old grandson Nick Azzaro is the owner, and he still makes them his grandfather's way—cheese and toppings on the dough first, then tomatoes or sauce. Unless, of course, you order the mustard pie: then the mustard goes on first.

Food for thought: A pizza is its own pie chart that updates in real time, always showing how much pizza you have left.

* * *

COUNTRIES THAT CONSUME THE MOST COFFEE PER CAPITA

1. Finland
2. Norway
3. Iceland
4. Denmark
5. The Netherlands

25. United States

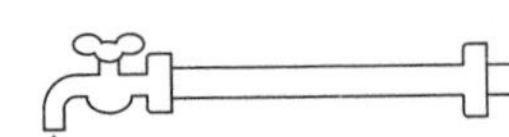

IT'S A WEIRD, WEIRD WORLD

Here's proof that truth is stranger than fiction.

A LITTLE NIGHT MUSIC

Michigan-based funk band Vulfpeck has recorded several studio albums and EPs, as well as a special project called *Sleepify,* released exclusively to the streaming music service Spotify in March 2014. *Sleepify* isn't really an album, though. In fact, it isn't really anything—it consists of 10 tracks, each about 30 seconds, and they're all complete and total silence. Shortly after *Sleepify*'s release, the band asked its fans to put the album on when they went to bed at night, and to set it to play on a loop. Reason: the constant play drove royalty revenues of about $20,000 to Vulfpeck...and it would've been more had Spotify not caught on. In April 2014, Spotify banned *Sleepify,* citing content violations. Nevertheless, the album generated enough money that when Vulfpeck embarked on a Sleepify Tour in the fall of 2014, it didn't have to charge admission to any of the shows.

THE DEVIL IS IN THE DETAILS

Death Angel has been one of America's most prominent thrash metal bands since the early 1980s, giving fans just what they want: loud, fast, angry songs, with themes of death, Satan, and other dark stuff. In March 2020, Death Angel was in the middle of a European tour when the rapid spread of COVID-19 forced them to cancel the tour and return home to San Francisco. On the flight back, drummer Will Carroll started exhibiting symptoms of the illness, and after he tested positive, he became so sick that doctors put him in a medically induced coma to give his body the chance to recover. Twelve days later, on March 30, 2020, Carroll woke up. His first words: "Am I still in hell?" According to Carroll, he'd experienced some terrifying visions in his comatose state, including a meeting with Madam Satan, who punished him for his slothful ways by turning him into a blood-vomiting monster resembling Jabba the Hutt from *Star Wars.* Apparently, an audience with Satan will change a person. "I'm still going to listen to satanic metal," he told the *San Francisco Chronicle,* "but I don't think Satan's quite as cool as I used to."

HE'S A MAGIC MAN

Ian Brackenbury Channell used to teach sociology at Australia's University of New South Wales. When he was laid off in the early 1970s, the college's vice chancellor

Botanically speaking, an avocado is a berry. So is a banana. (Their seeds are enclosed in a fleshy pulp.)

offered him a unique (and paid) position, created just for him: official university wizard. Channell took the job, and served for two decades, until 1990, when the prime minister of New Zealand asked Channell to become the official wizard of the entire country. He accepted, and he takes the salaried position (about $10,000 a year) seriously, roaming the city of Christchurch wearing a black robe, pointy hat, and long white beard, and carrying a staff. (He even legally changed his name to "The Wizard.") The 88-year-old's official duties: "provide acts of wizardry and other wizard-like services for the city of Christchurch."

NICE JOB, BOB

A man whose name was given only as "Bob" in news reports landed a job as a code developer for a digital infrastructure company, and it paid six figures. For several years, his work was exemplary, and according to his performance reviews, he was regarded as probably the best coder in the firm. Then something seemed amiss. The security team at the company (also unnamed) noticed that its private network was somehow being accessed remotely from China—with Bob's username and password, which otherwise existed only on a secure thumb drive that Bob was supposed to keep on his person at all times. An investigation revealed that no hacking had occurred. Bob, it turned out, had mailed his thumb drive to China, where he'd outsourced his job to another coder, paying him about a fifth of his own salary. A look at Bob's computer revealed what Bob did all day while someone else did his work: surf Reddit, take lunch, watch cat videos, buy things on eBay, update Facebook, go home.

HEY, WATCH IT

An Indonesian man named Muhammad Didit runs a YouTube channel called Sobat Miskin Official. He has a respectable 53,000 subscribers who regularly view his videos depicting life in a rural Indonesian village and tasting strange food combinations. In 2020, one of his videos went viral: two hours and 20 minutes of Didit doing... nothing at all. For the entire video, he sits on the floor in front of a bare mattress, staring into the camera. In the video's description, he explains that "some elements of Indonesian society" were complaining about a lack of educational content in YouTube videos, so he responded by making his video devoid of *all* content. He had planned it to be only ten minutes long, but he ended up sitting there longer than expected. It's Didit's most-watched YouTube video, with four million viewers willing to watch him sit quietly for 140 minutes.

* * *

"What would life be like without coffee? But then, what is it even with coffee?"

—Louis XV

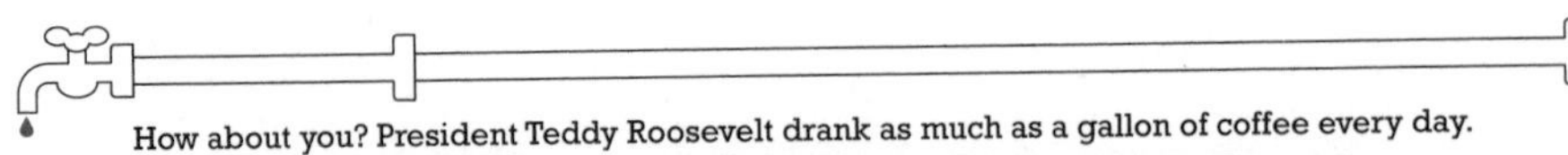

How about you? President Teddy Roosevelt drank as much as a gallon of coffee every day. He added five to seven lumps of sugar to each cup he drank.

TERRIBLE TYPOS

Behold the power of the written wrod.

WHAT A LOAD

After record rainfalls in 2011, the Iowa Farm Bureau issued a report that was shared by dozens of news outlets, mostly with somber headlines such as "Iowa Farm Bureau: Flooding caused $207M in crop losses." But not WWDC-FM. The alternative rock station—also known as DC101—ran the story on their home page with the headline "Farm Bureau estimates crap damage at $207 million from Missouri River flooding," followed by the lede, "The figure doesn't include damage to roads, buildings, or soil loss." (Soil loss? Eww.)

WIND INSTRUMENT

There was an unfortunate misprint in the sheet music to John Williams's *Jurassic Park* theme. At the top of the page, the first letter of "Bass" didn't print. What was left says "ASS CLARINET." (Below, it says, "Forcefully.")

FLY PROUDLY, MOSQUITO

In January 2021, Mississippi unveiled its new state flag, featuring a magnolia flower. But it was almost a mosquito. After the previous flag (the last to have a Confederate battle emblem) was retired, the state held a design contest for a new one. Among the 147 finalists—out of 3,000 entrants—was a white flag with a giant mosquito on it, submitted by Thomas Rosete, a deckhand on the Yazoo River, where the pesky bugs are rampant. His flag, which he intended as a joke, went viral and was threatening to take the lead in contest voting when it was suddenly pulled from contention. Why? "The mosquito flag advanced," wrote an official, "due to a typo in a list of flag numbers submitted by one commissioner." The removal irritated many Mississippians, one of whom commented, "It's so bad it's good. I would proudly fly the mosquito."

PROCLA...PROCLO...WHATEVER

The following text message was sent to Washington nursing home residents in July 2020:

> "Special Announcement: Govener Inslee Proclomation
> for Long term care – Re - opening"

How many errors can you count? There are three: "governor," "proclamation," and "reopening." A short time later, they sent out a new text that fixed the goofs...sort of:

> "Special Announcement: Governor Inslee Proclamantion –
> Long term Care Reopening Plan"

Voyager 2 launched before *Voyager 1*, but *Voyager 1* reached Jupiter and Saturn sooner.

THINKING OUTSIDE THE BOX

"For some things in life, there will never be an app." Next to that tagline was a photo of a silver convertible. Beneath that was printed: "The new Boxter. Porsche of London." This ad appeared on billboards throughout London, Ontario. Porsche of London might want to invest in an app—a *spelling* app. The car they're trying to sell is spelled "Boxster."

HIDDEN IN PLAIN SIGT

Product labels are a team effort. The text is written, then reviewed and finalized by copyeditors before being sent to a graphics team to design the label. Then it typically undergoes revisions and is checked and rechecked by editors before getting final approval. But apparently that didn't happen to packages of Made with Plants brand Madras curry. It said "MADRAS CURRY" in block letters on the top of the package, and on the side, in the same large block letters, it said "MADRS CURRY." When a local news station asked company cofounder Cale Drouin to explain the glaring error, he said, "The good news is that what we might lack in typing skills, we more than make up for in our culinary skills!"

MAYBE NO ONE WILL NOTICE

In August 2013, after Nike issued "retro full-zip" sweatshirts for each NFL team, Tim Williams, digital content manager at Pittsburgh's CBS affiliate, informed the apparel giant (via Twitter) that they should take a second look at their "Seatlle Seahawks" shirts. No one from Nike replied, so Williams tweeted several more times over the next few weeks, which got retweeted, and so on. Then came all the headlines: "Nike spells 'Seatlle' Wrong!" Finally, Nike responded: "We have removed them from sale and apologize for the error."

REATED OUT

The writer of this news headline, which appeared in the *Yuma Sun* in July 2020, could very well be a product of said school system: "Arizona reated third worst school system in America."

WHAT'S HAPPENING?

This perplexing police report from California's *Red Bluff Daily News* probably contains several typos...but we're not sure. To our eye, it actually transcends the typo and approaches something more akin to abstract poetry, so that's how we'll present it.

"Animal Douglass Street"
About 5:20 p.m. Wednesday
it was reported
a man in a loose dog
a days prior
and it had turned vicious.

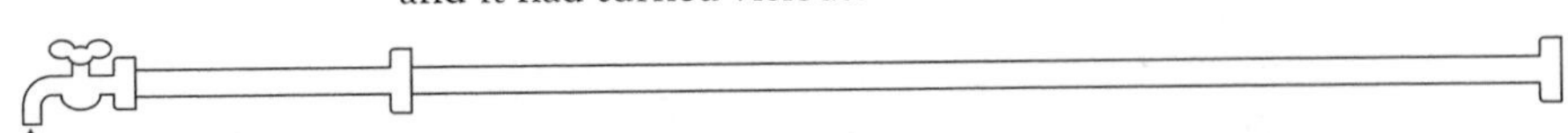

Brawwwk!? There are three times as many chickens on Earth as there are humans.

AND THE WINNER ISN'T...

In December 2015, during the finale of the Miss Universe Pageant—which aired in 190 countries—first-time host Steve Harvey committed the most embarrassing gaffe in the recent history of live television. But was it really Harvey's fault?

THE GAFFE

The top three Miss Universe contestants were called to the front of the stage. After comedian and game show host Steve Harvey announced that Miss USA had come in third place, the two finalists, Colombia's Ariadna Gutiérrez and the Philippines' Pia Wurtzbach, clung to each other as they awaited the outcome. "And the winner is..." (looonnnng dramatic pause) "...Colombia!"

Harvey's first mistake was mispronouncing it "Co-*lum*-bia." His second mistake: The winner was actually Miss Philippines. It said so right on his card. No one on stage knew that yet, so the music started playing as Gutiérrez was given her sash and bouquet to the cheers of the crowd. Then she hugged Wurtzbach, who walked to the rear of the stage to join the 78 other contestants. Gutiérrez was crowned by the previous year's winner, Paulina Vega. She too was Colombian, making this a rare repeat win and a huge source of national pride for their country. Harvey abruptly left the stage as the celebration continued.

Roughly four minutes later, Harvey slowly walked back out and the music stopped. "Okay, folks. Uhh..." Gutiérrez was still smiling and waving a small Colombian flag. "There's...I have to apologize." Another dramatic pause—this one *not* rehearsed. Gutiérrez stopped smiling and stared at Harvey. "The first runner-up is Colombia," he said. "Miss Universe 2015 is Philippines." The crowd erupted in boos and screams as a stunned Wurtzbach was led back to the front of the stage, where Harvey said to her, "Miss Philippines, take your first walk as Miss Universe." The most painful moment came when Vega removed Gutiérrez's crown and placed it on Wurtzbach, who later said she "wasn't sure what was going on."

THE FALLOUT

Harvey's gaffe became a bigger story than the pageant itself. (The five-and-a-half-minute YouTube clip has amassed nearly 5.5 million views.) Some people—including one of the pageant's own judges, gossip maven Perez Hilton—accused organizers of staging the mistake as a publicity stunt, which they flatly denied.

The next day, a Colombian law firm threatened to sue the Miss Universe Organization to get Gutiérrez's "rightful title" back. She said in an interview, "In four minutes, they destroy your dreams, they throw it in a bag, and they throw it in

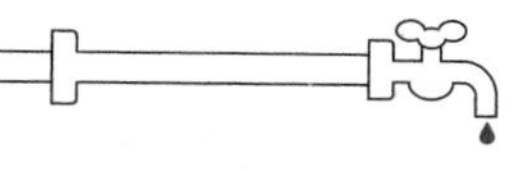

the trash." People in her home country burned effigies of Harvey. He said his family received death threats.

THE APOLOGY TOUR

The morning after, Harvey tweeted, "I want to apologize emphatically to Miss Philippians and Miss Columbia. This was a terribly honest human mistake, and I am so regretful." A few minutes later (after more than 30,000 retweets), he deleted that tweet and put up a new one with both countries' names spelled correctly. A few weeks later, Harvey invited both women on his syndicated talk show. He told Gutiérrez "just how sorry I am." After chiding him a bit—"You need to learn to read"—she said she forgave him, even though "it was the worst night of my life, but also the best." (Gutiérrez did okay: Two years later, she landed the coveted role of Lola, Xander Cage's girlfriend in *XXX: Return of Xander Cage.*) Harvey repeatedly asked Wurtzbach for forgiveness as well, until she finally said, "Steve, don't beat yourself up for this anymore. Let's move forward. Let's be happy."

THE CARD

So, whose fault was it? Pageant organizers released a vague statement that read, in part, "Unfortunately, a live telecast means that human error can come into play." But they fell short of blaming the error on any specific human. A short video taken from the crowd during the immediate aftermath appears to show Harvey telling someone, "The Teleprompter said, 'Miss Universe—Colombia.' " But no one else saw that, and the winner's name was only on the card. A few minutes after that clip, Harvey held it up to the TV camera and said, "This is exactly what's on the card. I will take responsibility for this. It was my mistake." Here's what it looked like ("elminination" spelling mistake included):

MISS UNIVERSE 2015 ELMININATION CARD – *SHOW* FINALS 3 TO 1

2nd Runner Up USA

1st Runner Up COLOMBIA

MISS UNIVERSE 2015

PHILIPPINES

THE BLAME GAME

After initially taking full responsibility, a month after the pageant, Harvey said on a radio show: "Now, when the mistake was made, when I said the wrong woman's name, I can only give information I had...I said the name that was on the card. When I walked off, everything was cool." Not long after, he said on the *Today Show*: "I was ashamed for the mistake, but I was also a little bit angry at the mistake. A lot of people could have stepped up and said, 'I played a role in this, too, you know.' "

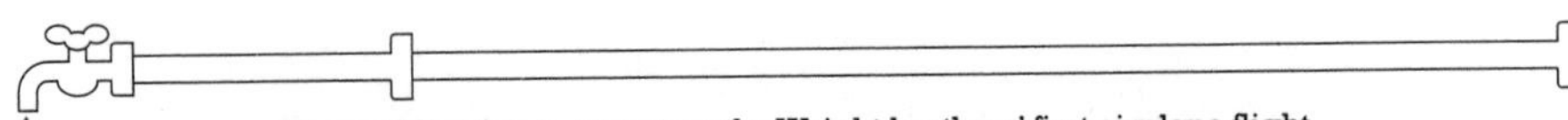

First publication to report on the Wright brothers' first airplane flight in September 1904: the January 1905 edition of *Gleanings in Bee Culture*.

No one else did. Then he admitted, "Had I taken a moment to look at the card, but I was trying to keep it down so nobody saw the winner. I blew it."

A year later, Harvey went on *The Tonight Show* and told Jimmy Fallon that he was just doing what the director had instructed: "I read the teleprompter" (which had on it "Miss Universe 2015 is") "but the guy in my ear said, 'Read the next name now, now.' I said, 'Miss Colombia.' Crowd goes crazy. He goes, 'Great job, Steve.' " Backstage, it was "four minutes of pure hell" before taking "the most gut-wrenching walk I've ever had in my life."

"But the guy in my ear said, 'Read the next name now, now.' I said, 'Miss Colombia.' Crowd goes crazy. He goes, 'Great job, Steve.' "

THE THUMB

Four years after the debacle, in January 2019, Harvey gave a much more detailed account on Dr. Phil's podcast. There'd been a last-minute change. Originally, only two finalists were supposed to be brought out front, and only two names were supposed to be on the card. "We rehearsed it that way, I can't tell you how many times." But then: "The lady that used to run the old pageant, she decides we're not doing that. So, she puts a third name on the card, don't tell nobody. Little do I know, on this card, this woman done put the winner in the corner."

Then came the real villain: "My thumb is on the name of the winner. I never saw the third name because we never looked for it." A still image confirms that Harvey was holding the card in his right hand, with his thumb covering the winning country. Result: When he held up the card, he only saw two countries. (Of course, that still doesn't explain how the host of the world's biggest beauty pageant didn't know that "1st Runner Up" means second place.)

During those "four minutes of hell" backstage—during which Harvey reportedly unleashed a barrage of profanities—the producers told him they were going to wait until the next day to announce the error and crown Miss Philippines, but Harvey insisted that it be done immediately. "I went out there, man, and I took all that heat... It was so nasty, man. It got ugly." In addition to the death threats, Harvey said he was treated like a punching bag by the press, and that he's become a punchline for talk show hosts.

THE GAFFE, PT. 2

Despite the controversy (or perhaps because of it), Harvey was asked to host Miss Universe again. The next year, he asked Miss Colombia, Andrea Tovar, what the citizens of her country thought of him. Her reply: "A lot of people hate you." (Awkward silence.) "But you know I love you!" (Laughter.)

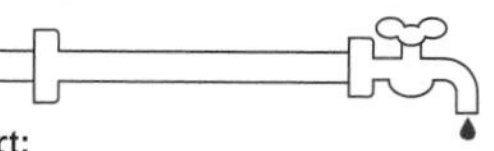

Only sports team named in honor of another sport: The NBA's Indiana Pacers, named for the Indy 500 pace car.

Harvey brought up the gaffe at every subsequent pageant (he's still the host), and in 2019, when an eerily similar gaffe occurred, he made it clear who he blamed for what happened back in 2015. The gaffe happened during the National Costume Show, a previously held portion of the pageant wherein each contestant modeled an elaborate costume representing her country. The lone contestant on stage was Miss Malaysia, Shweta Sekhon, who was wearing an ornate wedding gown and standing in front of three tables of sweets and treats. Harvey walked up to Miss Malaysia and said, "Here's a look at the winner, Miss Philippines." Meanwhile, Miss Philippines, Gazini Ganados (the actual winner of the costume segment), was still backstage. But her photo was being displayed on the giant screen behind Harvey, who was gushing about Sekhon's ensemble: "This is it, right here. I thought I had on something fly [he was wearing a shiny, golden blazer] but, girl, you just, wooo! Cakes and oranges and potato chips! That's a lot. And..." Sekhon stopped smiling and pulled Harvey's microphone—arm and all—over to her and said tersely, "It's not Philippines, it's Malaysia!" Then she resumed smiling.

Harvey yanked the microphone back and said, "Okay, well, let me explain something to you," he pointed forward, "I just read that in the teleprompter." Then he glared offstage, "Y'all got to quit doing this to me. I can read!" Then, to the audience: "See, this what they did to me back in 2015. Played me short like that!" Producers later blamed Sekhon for interrupting Harvey before he was able to announce the actual winner, but they didn't inform her beforehand (and she didn't find out she hadn't won the costume contest until four hours later on Twitter). That wasn't even the biggest story to come out of that year's pageant: Afterward, Harvey was widely criticized for making "tasteless" Colombian drug cartel jokes—to Miss Colombia—in reference to the death threats he'd received four years earlier. No, Steve Harvey was far from over it.

* * *

PREHISTORIC HINDSIGHT

In 2021, a British paleobiologist named Jakob Vinther announced the discovery of the first well-preserved dinosaur butthole. Technically called a cloacal vent, the butthole belonged to a dog-sized Triceratops-like dinosaur called a Psittacosaurus. Bonus: There's a fossilized dinosaur poop still inside it! Vinther and his fellow researchers at the University of Bristol are studying the rare 100-million-year-old soft-tissue fossil to help determine whether birds did indeed evolve from dinosaurs—but this specimen is neither avian nor crocodilian. "It's its own cloaca," says Vinther, "shaped in its perfect, unique way."

Erotomania is a psychological disorder where the patient thinks a famous person is in love with them and sending them coded love messages.

TECH FLOPS

For every successful bit of consumer technology like a DVD player or an iPhone, there are a lot more that don't become a must-have gadget.

NEXUS Q

Small digital media players like Roku, Apple TV, and Amazon Fire connect to your TV and allow viewers to watch streaming services such as Netflix and Hulu. They are very popular, and very lucrative for the manufacturers. So why doesn't a giant like Google have one? It did. Google planned to have one of the first on the market in 2012. The Google Nexus Q hooked up to almost any television and allowed users to stream videos and music...but only from services owned by Google, which at that time consisted of YouTube and the obscure Play Music and Play Video. Even weirder about the Nexus Q: it was about the same size, shape, and color as a Magic 8-Ball. The cost: $299, plus $399 for speakers, and another $49 for the cables and cords necessary to use it. Shortly after it started taking preorders for the Nexus Q, Google delayed its launch because market research revealed that consumers were unimpressed with the device. The company ultimately decided not to let the Nexus Q hit stores.

ATARI LYNX

Home video games debuted in the late 1970s. Trips to the arcade to pump quarters into stand-up machines offering *Pac-Man* and *Space Invaders* were no longer necessary for gamers who could now get their fix at home by connecting an Atari 2600 or Intellivision to their TV set. After a video game industry crash in 1983 in which leader Atari nearly went out of business, the industry was revived by the next-generation graphics of the Nintendo Entertainment System, a cultural phenomenon in 1987. In 1989, Nintendo expanded into handheld gaming with its Game Boy, a gray brick with a two-inch, monochromatic screen that played interchangeable cartridges. At the same time, Atari made one last stab at restoring its relevance, introducing its own pocket video game system—the Lynx. Technologically, the Lynx was superior to the Game Boy in every way: its screen was backlit, it played full-color games, and its graphics were rendered in 16 bits while the Game Boy had an 8-bit system. But Nintendo led the video game world and could devote far more money to marketing. Nintendo even had its own magazine (*Nintendo Power*) and a Saturday morning cartoon show (*Captain N*). Atari was viewed as passé, and it certainly didn't help that ten times more games were available for the Game Boy than for the Lynx, a unit that ate up a fresh load of AA batteries in about an hour. (It also

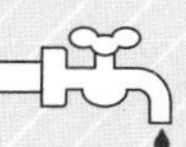

cost twice as much as a Game Boy—$180 vs. $90.) The Lynx hung around in stores until 1995, and was discontinued about the time that Nintendo unveiled the next-generation, full-color Game Boy. By that point, 119 million Game Boys had been sold, compared to 3 million Lynxes. By 1998, Atari as an independent company was finished, having been acquired by Hasbro.

PONO PLAYER

Music has gone through a lot of delivery methods over the last 40 years, from records to cassettes to compact discs to digital song files streamed to your smartphone. While it's certainly convenient to have access to thousands of songs via a phone or MP3 player, it's not ideal for hard-core audiophiles. Reason: making a digital music file involves audio compression, eliminating a lot of the nuance and layers in a recording that a discerning ear can hear on vinyl or CD. In 2012, after hundreds of millions of people started listening to music on iPhones and iPods, rock legend (and fidelity hound) Neil Young announced that he was coming out with Pono, a digital music player that he'd helped develop himself. What made the Pono line different: using a computer app like the iTunes Music Store, buyers could download noncompressed, super-high-quality "lossless" music files. It took three years for Young and his associates to raise the $6 million financial backing necessary to bring the little yellow PonoPlayer to market. After just two years, the $400 PonoPlayer and the PonoMusic Store were discontinued after attracting only around 20,000 customers.

HP TOUCHPAD

In 2010, Apple Computer combined its Macintosh computers with its iPhone to create the iPad, a tablet-style computer. It looked like a giant iPhone but had the functionality of a desktop Mac, only with a touchscreen display. Within a year, Apple had sold 15 million iPads and popularized the concept of tablet computers. PC manufacturer Hewlett-Packard wanted in on the market and, in July 2011, released its own take on the technology with a device called the HP TouchPad. At a price of $499 for the basic model (one with twice the hard drive space cost $100 more), the TouchPad was cheaper than an iPad...but it was harder to find. One reason: HP didn't roll out a marketing plan beyond an announcement at a press conference six months before the device was commercially available. By that time, the iPad 2 was already available for sale at hundreds of Apple Stores. After about seven weeks on the market, only 25,000 of the 270,000 HP TouchPads manufactured had been sold, prompting Hewlett-Packard to discontinue the product and discount unwanted units to $99. (At the new, lower price, they sold out almost immediately.)

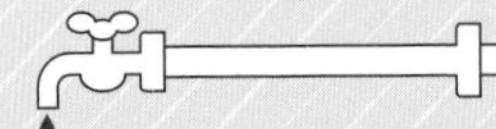

THE LAW OF THE TONGUE

Whale hunting is frowned upon today, but for many Indigenous cultures, it was a way of life. Here's a fascinating tale from a bygone era.

EAST OF EDEN

The seaside town of Eden, in the Australian state of New South Wales, was a center of whaling activity long before the first Europeans arrived in the late 1700s. The Aboriginal Yuin people hunted humpback and southern right whales there for centuries, assisted by some remarkable helpers: orcas (or killer whales), which the Yuin believe are their reincarnated ancestors. It's not clear when or how this cooperative relationship developed, but at some point in the distant past, orca pods began "herding" migrating whales close to shore in a place called Twofold Bay, in much the same way that sheepdogs herd sheep. They kept the whales confined to a small area of shallow water until the Yuin whalers could get to the whales and kill them. Afterward, to repay the orcas for their help, the Yuin would leave the dead whales' carcasses in the water for a day or more, so that the orcas could eat the lips and tongue, which for them were the choicest parts. They would not eat any other part of the whale.

This unique hunting partnership between humans and orcas did not exist anywhere else in the world. It continued after the first Europeans to arrive in Australia began whaling in the same waters. The Yuin worked alongside white colonists in whaling boats, which were little more than large rowboats, and they showed the new arrivals how the orcas helped in the hunt. Though the white Australians had first viewed the orcas as a nuisance, they quickly learned to treat them with respect. And just like the Yuin, the white Australians learned to recognize individual orcas by their unique markings. They gave them names like Hooky, Humpy, Cooper, Flukey, and Jackson. The orcas were as beloved as pets and the whalers never harmed them. The "law of the tongue," as it came to be known, was sacrosanct: any time a whale was captured and killed, it was tied to a buoy or anchored in Twofold Bay for a day or two so that the orca pod could feast on the tongue and lips. Only after the orcas finished was the whale brought ashore so that the whalers could collect the blubber and bones, which—to the humans—were the most valuable parts.

ON CALL

This relationship was so well developed that the whalers who lived in Eden never had to go out looking for whales. Instead they could stay close to home, almost like firefighters waiting for a fire alarm, while the orca pod hunted for humpback and southern right whales offshore.

When the pod found a whale and penned it in somewhere along the shoreline, one of the orcas would split from the pod and swim to the whaling station on the shore of Twofold Bay, where it would leap out of the water and slap its tail on the surface to attract the whalers' attention. As soon as the whalers heard the splashing, they knew that a whale had been caught. They ran to the whaling boats, and the orca would lead them out to wherever the rest of the pod had cornered the whale.

LAWLESS

This cooperative relationship remained in place until about the mid-1920s, when a wealthy retired sheep farmer named John Logan went hunting for whales aboard his motor yacht the *White Heather* with a friend named George Davidson, and Logan's young daughter Margaret. That afternoon, a much-loved whale named Old Tom, thought to be the leader of the orca pod, pushed a small whale to the surface near the *White Heather*, and Logan succeeded in harpooning and killing it. But there was a storm coming in, and this was late in the whaling season, which typically ran from May to October.

Logan was worried that if he left the dead whale tethered to a buoy overnight, it might break loose in the wind and waves and be carried off by the storm. There wasn't enough time left in the season to catch another whale. Logan decided to bring the whale ashore that same day, violating the centuries-old Law of the Tongue and depriving Old Tom of his share of the hunt. When Davidson pointed this out, Logan replied, "Bugger Old Tom!" and began towing the whale to shore.

TUG OF WAR

Old Tom wasn't going to give up his share of the whale without a fight: he grabbed onto the tow rope and tried to stop the *White Heather* from taking the whale away. But he was not successful and, even worse, he lost a few of his teeth in the struggle. Logan's daughter Margaret recalled that when her father realized that Old Tom had been injured, he exclaimed, "Oh God, what have I done?"

Old Tom wasn't going to give up his share of the whale without a fight.

Logan had a veterinary background, and he understood that this kind of injury could be deadly to an orca. Just as he feared, the injury to Old Tom's mouth became infected and developed into an abscess that never healed. Eating became painful, and over the next few years the orca slowly starved to death. When Old Tom's body washed ashore in September

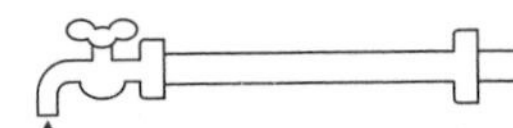

1930, Logan was so overcome with guilt that he had it rendered at the whaling station so that he could save the skeleton, and he founded a museum in Eden to house it. The Eden Killer Whale Museum, a memorial both to Old Tom and to Eden's unique whaling history, is still open today, and if you ever get a chance to visit, you'll see that Old Tom's skeleton is still displayed there.

END OF AN ERA

Eden's whaling industry was already in decline by the mid-1920s; men throwing harpoons from rowboats could not hope to compete against modern motorized whaling ships shooting exploding harpoons from giant deck guns, not even when the orcas did most of the work. And then the orcas stopped doing the work: Around the time Old Tom died, his pod left Twofold Bay and never returned. It's not clear what happened to them after that. They may simply have gone someplace else. If so, their descendants may still be alive today. It's also possible that they were killed off by Norwegian whalers operating off the coast who, like the first European whalers in Australia, saw orcas as a nuisance. Whatever the case, by 1930, the orcas were gone from Twofold Bay, and Eden's whaling industry was dead. The unique cooperative relationship between killer whales and humans, which had existed for hundreds—if not thousands—of years exclusively in this one place on Earth, disappeared forever.

* * *

ACCORDING TO THE LATEST RESEARCH: CHEESE PREFERS HIP-HOP

Researchers: Swiss cheese maker Beat Wampfler and the music department at Bern University of the Arts

What They Did: In 2018, Wampfler exposed nine 22-pound wheels of a savory Swiss cheese called Emmental to music—including Led Zeppelin's "Stairway to Heaven," Mozart's "The Magic Flute," and A Tribe Called Quest's hip-hop song "Jazz (We've Got)"—and one control cheese to silence. Each cheese "listened" to its song on repeat inside a wooden crate for six months nonstop until it matured. Then the cheeses were examined by scientists and blind taste-tested by food experts, artists, and politicians.

What They Learned: All of the musically matured cheeses tasted better than the control cheese, but the hip-hop cheese was judged to be the best by far. Wampfler, though, had a loftier take, claiming that the experiment transcended taste: "The cheese can also work as a transmitter between different people who like hip-hop or who like folk or who like rock 'n' roll. So this can also help bring society a little bit together."

....in the San Francisco earthquake and fire of 1906.

AWAY WITH WORDS

Great writers always have the best words...even their last words.

"Go on, get out. Last words are for fools who haven't said enough."

—Karl Marx

"It's been a long time since I drank champagne."

—Anton Chekhov

"I must go in, the fog is rising."

—Emily Dickinson

"DON'T LET THE AWKWARD SQUAD FIRE OVER MY HEAD!"

—Robert Burns

"Take away these pillows, I won't need them any longer."

—Lewis Carroll

"It's me. It's Buddy. I'm cold."

—Truman Capote

"Goodnight, my kitten."

—Ernest Hemingway

"What's that? Does my face look strange?"

—Robert Louis Stevenson

"Here am I, dying of a hundred good symptoms."

—Alexander Pope

"Now, now, my good man, this is no time for making enemies."

—Voltaire

(when asked by a priest to renounce Satan)

"I am sorry to trouble you chaps. I don't know how you get along so fast with the traffic on the road these days."

—Ian Fleming

"I can feel the daisies growing over me."

—John Keats

"I don't think two people could have been happier than we have been."

—Virginia Woolf

YOU'RE MY INSPIRATION

More surprising pop culture origins.

THE PHILADELPHIA EAGLES: One day in 1933, Bert Bell bought an NFL franchise in Philadelphia. But what to name it? While walking around the city that afternoon, he saw a billboard advertising President Franklin D. Roosevelt's National Recovery Administration. Bell was a big fan of FDR's New Deal, which had lifted the country out of the Great Depression. He decided right there to name his football team after the emblem on the billboard: an eagle.

SHURI: On the set of the 2018 movie *Black Panther,* director Ryan Coogler saw Letita Wright, who was playing Shuri, wearing her hair in a "messy double-bun," as she described it. "You look like Princess Leia," Coogler told her. Wright explained that it wasn't the hairstyle that her character—a feisty, young princess—was supposed to wear. "Well," said Coogler, "we'll just make it happen." Result: In Shuri's first scene, she has the same double-bun hairstyle that Carrie Fisher made famous in 1977's *Star Wars.*

"ROCK LOBSTER": The B-52's New Wave party anthem, released in 1978, was inspired by two things—a photo of a lobster, and Yoko Ono. The song's co-writer Fred Schneider was at an Atlanta discotheque: "Instead of having a light show, they had a slideshow...of puppies, babies, and lobsters on a grill, and I thought, okay, 'Rock Lobster,' that's a good title for a song." The whooping vocal refrains in the song were inspired by Ono's eccentric singing style. Two years later, John Lennon heard "Rock Lobster" in a club and loved it. Knowing nothing of its origin, he immediately thought of his wife and was inspired to end his five-year recording hiatus and begin work on what would be his final album: 1980's *Double Fantasy.*

WALL-E: In 2005, while writer-director Andrew Stanton was working at Pixar, "Anywhere from two to a dozen boxes from Amazon showed up at my doorstep every other day." That got him thinking: "Where does all this sh*t go?" Answering that question led to his 2009 Oscar-winning movie about a lonely robot who roams a trash-filled Earth.

THE MARVELOUS MRS. MAISEL: Fans of this Amazon dramedy about a female stand-up comedian in the 1950s often wonder: Was there ever a real Mrs. Maisel? Show creator Amy Sherman-Palladino said there is no real-life counterpart: "She's her own gal." The character was inspired by Sherman-Palladino's father, Don Sherman, who *was* a stand-up comedian in the 1950s. Don's stories about that time formed the basis for Midge Maisel's adventures—including "what it means to try to be funny...and how hard it is to turn that off."

Binding legislation: From 1935 to 1937, Wisconsin restaurants were required to offer free cheese with every meal.

INDIGENOUS TO ENGLISH

On page 96, we told you where the names "Eskimo" and "Inuit" came from. Now for some more words that were invented long, long ago by people we know very little about today.

WORD TO YOUR ANCESTORS

In the 15th century, Europeans sailed the seas in search of trade routes, wares to trade, and new lands to colonize. More often than not, those voyages wreaked havoc on the lives and culture of Indigenous peoples, and for many of them, all that remains are modern versions of a few of their words, including some that might surprise you. For example, you might already know that "teepee," "kayak," and "moccasin" come from Indigenous languages, but so do words like "shack," "bayou," and both parts of "Coca-Cola" (though from different continents). Because it's impossible to trace these words all the way back to their first utterances, historical linguists and anthropologists try to pinpoint when and where they entered English, and then do their best to piece the history together. It's not easy. Here's some of what they've learned so far.

HUSKY

MEANING: Arctic working dogs with thick coats, used for pulling sleds over the tundra

ORIGIN: "Husky," as it pertains to a gravelly voice or a large person, is not an Indigenous word. That word comes from "dry as a husk" (*husk* is a Germanic word for "little house"). The origin of the name of the husky dog breed is much less cut and dry. It most likely came into English via the French, who shortened it from *Esquimaux*, the same word that likely gave us "Eskimo." How exactly "husky" came from "Eskimo" isn't known for sure. One theory: It's a shortened version of "Eskimo dog," which is how the breed was often referred to by outsiders in the 19th century. It could have also come from *Ehuskemay*, a word for "Eskimo" recorded in 1743, or a contraction of *Huskimos*, an alternate version of "Eskimo" once used by English sailors. Making it more confusing: For at least a century, the people *and* the dogs were referred to as "husky" (or "hoskey")—often in unflattering terms, as evidenced by this 1855 account from a British naval officer in Greenland: "The Esquimaux, or 'Huskies,' as the Danes customarily term them, come off in sufficient numbers to satisfy you that you are near the haunts of uncivilized men." It wasn't until the 20th century that "Eskimo" and "husky" diverged and took on their present forms.

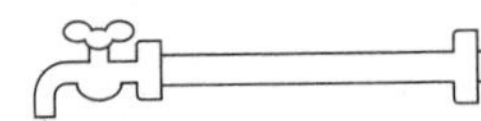

IGLOO

MEANING: Traditionally, a dome-shaped hut made from blocks of compressed snow or ice

ORIGIN: Originally associated with Indigenous people in central and eastern Canada, "igloo" was first recorded by Westerners in 1824. But linguists say that the word itself—or variations of it—goes back 7,000 years or more, to something akin to "uhnloo" that later became "ugloo," a word found throughout many Arctic cultures. Today, in the Inuit language, the word is spelled "iglu" (its plural is "igluit"), and it can be used to describe any small abode. The actual structure you picture when you think of an igloo is called an *igluvijaq*.

BARBECUE

MEANING: As a verb, the act of grilling food (usually meat) over an open fire outside; as a noun, the social event surrounding it

ORIGIN: Spanish explorers in the West Indies encountered a Caribbean tribe called the Taino, who spoke the now-extinct Arawak language. The Taino were the first people that Christopher Columbus met in the New World. He wrote about them in his journal: "They will give all that they do possess for anything that is given to them, exchanging things even for bits of broken crockery." One of the things they shared was food grilled on a raised wooden grate over a fire pit. Based on the Taino's pronunciation, the Spanish called the structure a *barbacoa*. Originally used to describe any small wooden support, over time it became solely associated with grilling and eating meat. In 1755, the word was added to Samuel Johnson's *The Dictionary of the English Language*. "To ba'rbecue: a term used in the West-Indies for dressing a hog whole; which, being split to the backbone, is laid flat upon a large gridiron, raised about two foot above a charcoal fire, with which it is surrounded."

Other Taino words: "hammock," "tobacco," and "hurricane."

HURRICANE

MEANING: A large storm with high sustained winds that forms in the North Atlantic Ocean, mainly affecting the Caribbean, Central America, and eastern North America

ORIGIN: *Hunrakan* was what the Maya called their god of the storm. Since 1500 BC, these Mesoamerican Indians lived in what is now southern Mexico, Guatemala, and northern Belize. From there, the word—with varying forms and meanings—spread throughout the Americas and into the Caribbean, where the Taino people used it to describe their god of evil, whose wrath was felt in those intense storms. In the 1550s, Spanish explorers first recorded the word from the Taino, and it entered that language

as *huracán*. According to the *Oxford English Dictionary*, over the next few decades, its spelling varied significantly, resulting in at least 39 versions (including *herrycano* and *harrycain*) before it finally landed on "hurricane" in the 1630s.

SKUNK

MEANING: A small mammal that defends itself by spraying a noxious odor

ORIGIN: Europe has no skunks. When settlers first encountered them in New England, the natives, known as the Massachusett people, were calling the animals *segonku*. The word entered English in the 1600s with a simplified pronunciation, spelled something like "squuncke." Some etymologies say the Indigenous word meant "urine fox," while others say it's "he who squirts." Either one makes scents.

WOODCHUCK

MEANING: A large, burrowing rodent of the marmot genus known today as a groundhog

ORIGIN: "Woodchuck" is a good example of the guesswork that goes into word origins. Depending on the source, it could come from the Narragansett *ockqutchaun*, the Cree *otchek*, the Ojibwe *otchig*, or another Algonquin word, *wejack*. All of these people hail from the northeastern United States and southern Canada, and it wasn't uncommon for them to have slightly different variations of the same word. Wherever "woodchuck" came from, colonizers gave it a phonetic spelling based on what they heard. When the more descriptive "groundhog" took hold in the mid-19th century (along with the holiday), "woodchuck" was no longer the accepted word for this animal, which has gone by many regional names—including marmot, woodshock, groundpig, whistlepig, whistler, thickwood badger, monax, moonack, weenusk, and red monk. So why is "woodchuck" still around? Blame "The Woodchuck Song" from the early 1900s, which introduced the tongue-twisting conundrum: *How much wood would a woodchuck chuck if a woodchuck could chuck wood?*

DID YOU KNOW?

Woodchucks (aka groundhogs) might not be able to chuck wood, but as the largest members of the squirrel family, they can climb trees. Their favorite activity, however, is digging. To excavate a single burrow, a woodchuck will move up to three tons of dirt.

SHACK

MEANING: A small cabin or hut made of wood—usually hastily and sloppily built

ORIGIN: Dictionaries cite two possible origins, the most likely being the Nahuatl word

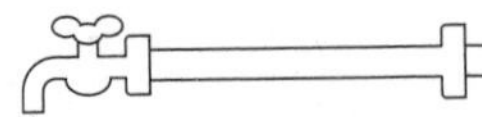

First car with a touchscreen "Graphic Control Center": the 1986 Buick Riviera. The screens were dropped in 1990 after drivers complained they were too distracting.

for "wooden hut," *xacatli.* Like Algonquin, Nahuatl is a group of languages. It was spoken in central Mexico by about 1.7 million Nahua people, who lived there (and some still do) for 13,000 years. Their best known culture: the Aztec people. "Shack" entered Mexican Spanish as *xacal,* which was pronounced "shackal" and got to the southwestern United States in the 1870s as the shortened "shack." (A less-cited theory says it's of European origin, a shortened form of *ramshackle.*)

Other words from Nahuatl languages: "chocolate," "chili," "chipotle," "chia," "tomato," and "coyote."

COYOTE

MEANING: A species of wild dog smaller than a wolf, native to the Americas

ORIGIN: The Nahuatl people called the crafty canine *coyotl,* which meant "trickster." The Spanish first encountered them in the 1650s, after which they went by "prairie wolf," "jackal," and "brush wolf." But the Indigenous word, first written down in 1651, held on. It reached English 200 years later with various spellings, including *cayjotte* and *cocyotie.* The current version, "coyote," took hold in the 1880s.

BAYOU

MEANING: A marshy outlet of a lake or river

ORIGIN: When French colonizers of the Gulf Coast region arrived in what is now Louisiana, they already had words for "river" and "stream." They were less familiar with the slow-moving, swampy waterways that marked the area, so they borrowed the name of a particularly large waterway the Choctaw people were living along called *Bayouk Choupic.* The word entered French as *bayouque,* and then English, first as "buyou," and then "bayou." Today, Bayouk Choupic is known as Bayou St. John, and what's left of it flows through several neighborhoods in New Orleans.

COLA

MEANING: A carbonated beverage traditionally flavored with an extract of kola nuts

ORIGIN: From the 15th to 19th centuries, more than 10 million West African people were kidnapped and taken to the United States via the Atlantic slave trade. When Portuguese slave traders encountered the Temne people of Sierra Leone, the Temne were cultivating rice, cassava, and millet, as well as the nut of an evergreen tree. In the Niger–Congo languages (today, the third-largest language family in the world), it was called *aŋ-kola,* meaning "kola nut." The Temne chewed on the nuts recreationally, medicinally, and for religious ceremonies. They were even used for currency. By the 1850s, after the active ingredient was found to be caffeine, demand

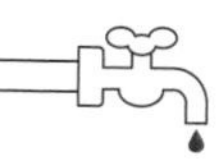

Before plastics came along, the snow in snow globes was made from animal bone chips.

for the kola nut skyrocketed in the Americas and Europe, where chemists and chefs alike began experimenting with it. How did kola the nut become cola the beverage? See the next entry.

COCAINE, COCA-COLA, AND COKE

MEANINGS: A stimulating narcotic, the trademarked name of the world's most popular carbonated beverage, and a nickname they both share

ORIGIN: Along with kola nuts and other native crops like sugar, tea, chocolate, tobacco, and coffee, coca leaves became popular in the United States in the mid-1800s. The word "coca" comes from the Quechua *cuca*, a large shrub that has been cultivated in the Peruvian Andes for at least 5,000 years. Containing psychoactive alkaloids far more stimulating than caffeine, coca was an integral part of Inca culture when the Spanish conquered South America. (They outlawed the leaves for religious use, but gave them to laborers because it increased production.) As with the kola nut, it took Europeans a long time to catch on to coca's mind-altering effects. In the 1870s, a German graduate student named Albert Niemann developed a method to isolate the active alkaloid from the leaf. In his doctoral thesis, he coined the word "cocaine."

In the 1880s, Lieutenant Colonel John Stith Pemberton, an Atlanta pharmacist who was addicted to morphine (he'd been wounded in the Civil War), was looking for a safer substitute with similar effects. Pemberton mixed and matched several ingredients until he came up with a sweet, stimulating tonic that contained cocaine from coca leaves, caffeine extracted from kola nuts, sugary syrup, and carbonated water. Pemberton's bookkeeper, Frank M. Robinson, came up with the name. He liked the idea of two big C's on the label, so he replaced the k in "kola nut" and came up with Coca-Cola. Using Spencerian script, a popular typeface of that time, Robinson designed the logo that to this day is among the best-known logos in the world. (Or, as the *New York Times* called it: "Capitalism's flagship.") Marketed first as a "brain tonic," Coca-Cola retained trace amounts of cocaine until 1929, and in 2016, the kola nut was replaced with synthetic ingredients.

As for the word "coke," it was a slang term for cocaine before it became a shortened form of Coca-Cola, which for a time was nicknamed "Dope" (a term later transferred to drugs). In the early 1900s, as people started calling the soft drink Coke, the beverage company tried to quash it with ads that read, "Ask for Coca-Cola by its full name; nicknames encourage substitution." But consumers insisted on using the nickname, so the beverage company trademarked "Coke" in 1945. Then it introduced Diet Coke in 1982, then Cherry Coke, Vanilla Coke, and many others, keeping alive a little word—*cuca*—that sprouted to life thousands of years ago deep in the Andes mountains...to the best of our knowledge.

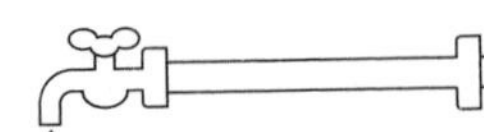

NAME THE OTHER GUY

It seems like every major musical duo has one member who is more famous than the other. For every Hall, there's an Oates; for every Simon, there's a Garfunkel, and so on. Here are some of the biggest two-person acts in rock history. Can you match the name of the duo to its less-famous member?

1. Wham! (George Michael)
2. Tears for Fears (Roland Orzabal)
3. White Stripes (Jack White)
4. Eurythmics (Annie Lennox)
5. OutKast (Andre 3000)
6. Tenacious D (Jack Black)
7. Steely Dan (Donald Fagen)
8. Righteous Brothers (Bill Medley)
9. Pet Shop Boys (Neil Tennant)
10. Erasure (Vince Clarke)
11. Evanescence (Amy Lee)
12. Indigo Girls (Amy Ray)
13. Air Supply (Russell Hitchcock)
14. Run the Jewels (Killer Mike)
15. Roxette (Marie Fredriksson)
16. Yaz (Alison Moyet)
17. The Buggles (Trevor Horn)
18. Sleigh Bells (Alexis Krauss)

a) Walter Becker
b) Chris Lowe
c) Meg White
d) Andrew Ridgeley
e) Emily Sailers
f) Graham Russell
g) Big Boi
h) Vince Clarke
i) Bobby Hatfield
j) Curt Smith
k) Dave Stewart
l) Derek Edward Miller
m) Kyle Gass
n) Andy Bell
o) Ben Moody
p) Per Gessle
q) El-P
r) Geoff Downes

Banner year: In 2015, the UK finally paid off its debt from World War I (1914–18).

STILL MORE CLASSIC ROCK ALMOSTS

Our final batch of stories about how a few twists of fate almost changed the history of popular music. *(Part II is on page 260.)*

FREDDIE MERCURY AND MICHAEL JACKSON ALMOST FINISHED RECORDING A SONG TOGETHER.

Story: The late 1970s and early 1980s saw a slew of chart-topping superstar duets. Paul McCartney and Stevie Wonder on "Ebony and Ivory." Paul McCartney and Michael Jackson on "Say Say Say." Mick Jagger and David Bowie on "Dancin' in the Streets." David Bowie and John Lennon on "Fame." Queen and David Bowie on "Under Pressure." Freddie Mercury and Michael Jackson on "There Must Be More to Life Than This." Never heard of that last one? That's because it wasn't released until after both singers were long dead.

Why It Didn't Happen: According to legend, Jackson's pet llama ruined the recording sessions. That did happen, but there was more to it than that. The King of Pop was a huge fan of Queen, attended several of their shows, and eventually struck up a friendship with Mercury. In fact, it was Jackson who convinced Queen to release "Another One Bites the Dust" as a single in 1980. The band was hesitant, but as Jackson predicted, the song hit number one.

Mercury and Jackson had often talked about working together. By the time their schedules allowed them to collaborate in 1983, "Wacko Jacko," as the tabloids had started calling him, was spending nearly all his time at his home studio in Encino, California, on the sprawling Jackson estate where he grew up. So Mercury had to travel there. The plan was to record three songs: "There Must Be More to Life Than This" (which Queen had started but never finished for 1982's *Hot Space*), "State of Shock," and "Victory."

But they barely completed one song because, as Mercury said in an exasperated phone call to his manager: "Michael's bringing his pet llama to the studio every day! I'm really not used to recording with a llama, and I've had enough. And I want to get out."

Other than Jackson doting over his llama (named Louie), the sessions were reportedly going well until Mercury left. He said he regretted not getting to them sooner: "I think one of the songs would have been on the *Thriller* album if we had finished it, but I missed out."

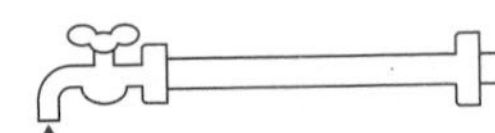

Aftermath: The Queen singer recorded a solo version of "There Must Be More to Life Than This" for his 1985 solo album *Mr. Bad Guy*, but he never got the chance to work with Jackson again. Mercury was diagnosed with AIDS in 1987 and died in 1991.

In 2014, five years after Jackson's death, Queen guitarist Brian May and drummer Roger Taylor finished the song for an album of "forgotten tracks" called *Queen Forever*, bringing in one of the industry's most renowned producers, William Orbit (U2, Prince, Madonna), to combine the original Queen backing track with the separate vocal tracks that Mercury and Jackson had laid down a year later. "Hearing Michael Jackson's vocals was stirring," said Orbit. "So vivid, so cool, and poignant, it was like he was in the studio singing live. With Freddie's vocal solo on the mixing desk, my appreciation for his gift was taken to an even higher level." If you've never heard the duet, be forewarned—it's definitely on the schmaltzy side ("I live and hope for a world filled with love") but definitely worth a listen. What about the other two songs? "Victory" never saw the light of day, but "State of Shock" was re-recorded by the Jacksons in 1984 with lead vocals by Michael Jackson and Mick Jagger. It reached number three on the *Billboard* Hot 100.

PETER FRAMPTON ALMOST JOINED GRAND FUNK RAILROAD.

Story: Another defining aspect of classic rock is the live album. Standouts include the Who's *Live at Leeds* (1970), Led Zeppelin's *The Song Remains the Same* (1976), the Allman Brothers Band's *At Fillmore East* (1971), and Humble Pie's *Performance: Rockin' the Fillmore* (1971), which featured Englishman Peter Frampton on vocals and lead guitar. But the live album that arguably made the greatest impact on classic rock radio stations was 1976's *Frampton Comes Alive*, which yielded three top-15 singles: "Show Me the Way," "Baby I Love Your Way," and "Do You Feel Like We Do."

Ten years earlier, at age 16, Frampton joined a band called the Herd and quickly became one of England's most sought-after guitarists. Then he joined singer Steve Marriott of the Small Faces in one of rock's first "supergroups," Humble Pie. Despite the supergroup status, they weren't chart-toppers. And by the time *Performance: Rockin' the Fillmore* was released in 1971, Frampton had already left Humble Pie to go solo.

Grand Funk Railroad (often shortened to Grand Funk), started out as a blues-rock band from Flint, Michigan. They're known as much for their 10-minute opus "I'm Your Captain (Closer to Home)" (1970) as they are for their roller-coaster career. The band went from breaking a Beatles' ticket-sales record in 1971 (the fastest band to sell out New York's Shea Stadium) to getting sued for everything except their name by their manager (and former friend) Terry Knight. "He had taken all of our money and we were broke," recalled drummer Don Brewer. If they wanted to stay afloat, they'd need a hit. "Rock radio was changing from being the FM underground thing with seven-minute songs," said Brewer. "FM was becoming the hit radio and we needed to

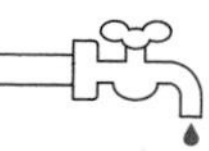

Before getting a driver's license in Sierra Leone, applicants have to play a driving safety board game called The Drivers' Way.

follow that trend. We had done a tour with Humble Pie, and we heard that Frampton was no longer with them and that he was looking for something else."

As one of rock's rare singer-songwriters who could also play blistering guitar solos, Frampton would have been a huge addition to Grand Funk. "It was a phenomenal tour," recalled Frampton, "and I got to know the guys really well. So when I announced that I was leaving Humble Pie, Grand Funk were the first people to say, 'Will you join up with us?' "

Why It Didn't Happen: Though Frampton was "thrilled and honored," he told them, "I've got to stick with my guns and go this solo route."

Aftermath: But by 1975, after five years and four solo albums that garnered better reviews than sales, Frampton must have been wondering if he'd taken the correct route. He paid the bills with session work (his highlight was playing guitar on George Harrison's *All Things Must Pass*). All the while, Frampton toured with his band as often as he could, perfecting his live act, which came to include his signature "voice box" guitar effect.

It all came together one summer night in 1975 at the Winterland Ballroom in San Francisco. "We did this show that's one where you walk off and go, 'Oh, wish we'd recorded that.' Well, we did." *Frampton Comes Alive* hit record stores the following January and took off beyond his wildest dreams, spending 10 weeks at number one on its way to becoming the best-selling album of the year.

Who knows what would have become of Grand Funk if Frampton had accepted their offer? (After Joe Walsh joined the Eagles in 1975, their next album was *Hotel California*.) The Michigan rockers did manage a few hits—most notably 1974's "We're an American Band"—but nothing they did was as successful as *Frampton Comes Alive*. They split up in 1976, re-formed a few years later, split up again, and so on. In 2016, Grand Funk (with two original members) joined the "Rock Legends" cruise ship tour, sharing the bill with headliner Peter Frampton.

A FEW MORE NEAR MISSES

- Before he formed Led Zeppelin, Jimmy Page almost started a band with drummer Keith Moon (who wanted to quit the Who), bassist John Paul Jones, and fellow Yardbird guitarist Jeff Beck. They would have been called the New Yardbirds.
- Blind Faith almost played at Woodstock.
- Simon and Garfunkel's "Mrs. Robinson" was almost called "Mrs. Roosevelt." (The original lyrics were about First Lady Eleanor Roosevelt.)
- Pink Floyd almost did the music for *A Clockwork Orange* and *Caddyshack*.
- Crosby, Stills and Nash almost did a song for the 1983 movie *WarGames*.
- John Lennon almost starred in the 1983 movie *WarGames*.

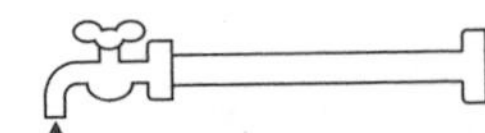

THE PECULIAR PLATYPUS

In 1800, Captain John Hunter of New South Wales sent a platypus pelt to European scientists...who thought it must be a hoax. They were wrong; it was real—really unique, really unusual, and really weird. Meet the platypus.

- Native to freshwater areas in Tasmania and the eastern coast of Australia, the platypus has webbed feet and a bill like a duck, and a large, flat tail like a beaver.
- Like the beaver, it's an aquatic mammal. But unlike most every other mammal, the platypus lays eggs.
- Like other mammal mamas, the platypus's mammary glands produce milk, but instead of a teat, she "sweats" out the milk through a duct on her stomach. There it pools, allowing the *puggles* (that's what baby platypuses are called) to lap it up.
- The platypus is a *monotreme,* the only kind of mammal that locates food with electroreceptors. It emits an electrical field from its snout, which it uses to locate prey.
- Platypuses like to play, pose, and show off.
- The male platypus has barbs on its hind legs that emit a toxin that's chemically similar to snake venom.
- The bill of the "duck-billed platypus" (as it's often called) is hairless and moist, and covered in fine grooves that filter food from water.
- Thanks to double cones in its eyes, a platypus can see better in the dark and sense more subtle movements. (Humans have single cones.)
- What does the platypus have in common with a few species of whales, pangolins, and anteaters? They're the only mammals with no teeth. Inside the bill are jagged pads that perform the same basic function.
- Most mammals' genetic code features two sex chromosomes: two Xs mean female, and XY indicates a male. Platypuses have ten sex chromosomes, and one of its X chromosomes is similar to one found in birds.
- Most mammal GI tracts have separate ducts for urination, defecation, and reproduction. Ever the nonconformist, the platypus foregoes a traditional stomach for an "all-purpose" duct that carries out all those functions, just like many fish have.
- Is the plural of platypus "platypuses," "platypi," or "platypodes"? The first one is considered correct English usage, but the other two have been gaining popularity in recent years.

Most of a wild lion's diet is carrion—the rotting flesh of scavenged dead animals. It will only make about 15 to 20 kills a year.

THE EYES HAVE IT

If you're reading this with the aid of glasses, you may have wondered how they came to be. Here's a timeline.

Circa 750 BC The Nimrud lens, the oldest lens ever discovered, is handcrafted in Assyria (modern-day Iraq) out of polished rock crystal. It's unclear what purpose it served. It may have been used for magnification and reading, or to erase writing on wax tablets by focusing the sun's rays to melt the wax. It could have been used to start fires, or to cauterize wounds. (Ouch!) It's also possible that the lens was purely decorative and served no practical purpose at all. No one knows for sure.

1st Century AD Seneca the Younger (c. 4 BC–AD 65), a Roman statesman, philosopher, and playwright, is said to have read every book in every library in Rome by looking through a globe of water that provided magnification.

c. 1268 The English philosopher and Franciscan friar Roger Bacon notes in his treatise *Opus Majus,* "If anyone examine letters or other minute objects through the medium of crystal or glass or other transparent substance, if it be shaped like the lesser segment of a sphere, with the convex [curved] side towards the eye, he will see the letters far better and they will seem larger to him...For this reason such an instrument is useful to all persons and to those with weak eyes, for they can see any letter, however small, if magnified enough." According to author Richard Corson, this "is the first concrete evidence we have that lenses were or could be used for reading." These lenses were most likely held in the hand, possibly using a handle like a magnifying glass.

c. 1280s Someone (no one knows who), sometime in the years leading up to 1289 (no one is sure when), invents eyeglasses, probably in Pisa, Italy. That year, the Florentine writer Sandro di Popozo writes, "I am so debilitated by age that without the glasses known as spectacles, I would no longer be able to read or write. These have recently been invented for the benefit of poor old people whose sight has become weak." The earliest glasses are "rivet spectacles," little more than two magnifying glasses riveted together at the handles so the lenses can be held over both eyes at once and, possibly, balanced precariously on the bridge of the nose. The lens frames are made of wood, horn, or bone. Centuries will pass before anyone figures out how to make lenses for people who are unable to see things that are

far away (a condition known as nearsightedness or *myopia*) or who have *astigmatism*, blurred vision caused by an irregularly shaped cornea. These earliest glasses only help people who have trouble seeing things up close, either due to age (*presbyopia*) or because they are naturally farsighted (*hypermetropia*).

1280s A Dominican monk named Alessandro della Spina learns the art of making eyeglasses from the original inventor, who has not publicized his invention and wants to remain anonymous. Della Spina makes one pair of glasses for himself, then many more copies that he gives away. Only now, thanks to della Spina, do eyeglasses begin to spread beyond their inventor. Why did the inventor want to remain anonymous? One theory: fear of being persecuted by the Catholic Church. "The Church in many instances encouraged the idea that afflictions sent by God were meant to be endured in silence for the good of one's soul," Richard Corson writes, "and that any mechanical device which counteracted them must perforce be the work of the devil."

1352 Barely 60 years after they are invented, eyeglasses have gone from being a tool of the devil to a status symbol denoting erudition and intellectual achievement. How do historians know this? Portrait artists begin including them in paintings of important scholars. The first example: a posthumous portrait of a French Dominican cardinal and biblical scholar, Hugh of Saint-Cher, painted by Tommaso da Modena in 1352. (Saint-Cher died in 1263, some 20 years before eyeglasses were invented. Though he's the first person in history to be depicted wearing glasses, he never actually did.)

c. 1440 Johannes Gutenberg, a German goldsmith, invents his movable-type printing press, sparking a revolution in publishing. Books become more widely available than ever before. By 1500, some 20 million books have been printed in western Europe alone. As the supply of reading material increases, literacy soars, and so does demand for eyeglasses. Production methods improve, and prices drop. By 1500, they're a common item sold by street peddlers, and cheap enough that virtually anyone can afford them.

Early 1500s Concave lenses, which correct distance vision, become available for the first time. Pope Leo X (1475–1521) is one of the first people to own a pair; he wears them while hunting. "With them I see better than my companions," the nearsighted pope explains. In a portrait painted by Raphael in about the year 1518, Leo is shown holding a pair of glasses in his hand.

The first Christmas card, printed in 1843, depicts a child drinking wine.

Mid to late 1500s Along with increased demand for glasses comes demand for a better way to secure them in place in front of the eyes. One of the earliest practical solutions is frames made of stiff leather instead of bone or horn. The frames include long straps that can be passed over the ears and tied together behind the head.

1604 The German astronomer Johannes Kepler publishes the first accurate explanation of how convex and concave lenses correct vision—they refocus light on a point directly on the retina (the layer of light-sensitive cells at the rear of the eyeball), instead of in front of it, as is the case with nearsightedness, or behind it, which is what happens with farsightedness.

1600s One unintended consequence of eyeglasses becoming so common is that they fall out of favor with the upper classes, who stop wearing them in public (but continue using them in private). For show, the highborn take to wearing a single glass lens like a necklace, tied around the neck with a cord or a ribbon. Called a "perspective glass," the lens is more often intended for distance viewing than for reading and is held up to an eye whenever the wearer wants to see something far away. The English parliamentarian and diarist Samuel Pepys brings his perspective glass to church, as he relates: "I did entertain myself with my perspective glass up and down the church, by which I had the great pleasure of seeing and gazing at a great many very fine women; and what with that and sleeping, I passed away the time till the sermon was done."

In Spain, eyeglasses remain important status symbols. According to one contemporary account, "There are different Spectacles according to different Qualities and Degrees of Men and Women. Proportionably, as a Man's Fortune rises, he increases in the Large-ness of his Spectacle-Glasses, and wears them higher upon his Nose. The grandees of Spain wear them as broad as one's Hand."

1620s Eyeglasses are now available with frames made of brass, silver, gold, or tortoiseshell in addition to wood, bone, and leather. The two lenses are often joined with a somewhat flexible piece of curved metal called a spring bridge, which helps the glasses grip the bridge of the nose. Another alternative, the "forehead frame," a metal band worn around the forehead, is also used to hold the glasses in place. A third option is to suspend the glasses from the brim of a hat. By 1650, a fourth option becomes available: the *spina frontalis*, a metal strap curved to match the shape of the top of the head that is worn beneath a hat.

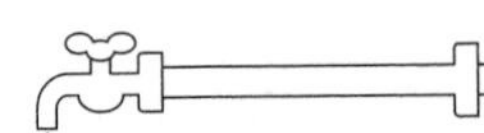

The National Federation of the Blind (USA) estimates that only 10% of blind people can read Braille.

1700s The "quizzing glass," a single lens with a short handle attached, becomes a fashionable alternative to eyeglasses with both men and women. Like a perspective glass, they are often worn around the neck with a cord, ribbon, or chain like a necklace. They remain popular into the 1850s.

Late 1720s Nearly 350 years after the invention of eyeglasses, a London optician named Edward Scarlett begins advertising "temple spectacles"—eyeglasses that are held in place using hinged, rigid side-pieces called *temples* that secure the glasses in place by pressing against the sides of the head. They do *not* extend as far as the ears. Scarlett never claimed to have invented this style of eyeglasses, nor did he patent them; the identity of the inventor is unknown. Scarlett's business card, which dates to around 1730, contains the earliest verifiable illustration of a pair of eyeglasses with rigid side-pieces.

1750s "Scissor spectacles" are invented in Germany. They're similar in design to rivet spectacles except that the lenses are attached to a handle that gives them an appearance similar to a pair of scissors—picture yourself holding a pair of scissors by the blades and peeking through the finger holes in the handles. Often hung on a chain or a cord and worn around the neck, they were popular for more than 150 years, only fading away completely at the beginning of the 20th century. George Washington, the Marquis de Lafayette, and Napoleon Bonaparte all owned scissor spectacles.

1752 A London optician named James Ayscough invents eyeglasses with "double-jointed" sides. The extra-long sides pass over the ears and continue straight past the back of the head, where a second set of hinges allows the sides to bend around the back of the head until they touch—"so contrived," he writes, "as to press neither upon the Nose nor the Temples."

c. 1770 George Adams, a London instrument maker, invents the *lorgnette* (from the French word for "squint")—eyeglasses with the handle mounted on one side. Scissor spectacles required a person to hold their hand in front of their mouth, which proved especially awkward when talking; lorgnettes let a person keep their hand to one side. The handle often doubles as a case that the eyeglasses fold into. Lorgnettes are especially popular at the opera and at masquerade balls.

1784 Benjamin Franklin, who suffers from both myopia and presbyopia, gets tired of carrying two pairs of glasses and having to switch pairs every time he wants to look at something nearer or farther away. His solution:

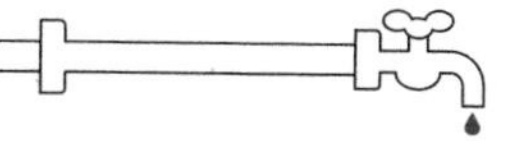

bifocals. "I had the glasses cut and a half of each kind associated in the same circle. By this means, as I wear my own spectacles constantly, I have only to move my eyes up or down, as I want to see distinctly far or near, the proper glasses being always ready," he wrote in a letter to his friend George Whatley. These early bifocals were likely not the very first invented. But after Franklin's death in 1790, Whatley published this and other correspondence in which Franklin discusses the glasses. His name has been associated with bifocals ever since. (There is, however, some evidence to suggest that Franklin wore bifocals as early as the 1750s, which if true, may mean that he really did invent them.)

1820s The quizzing glass, a single lens with an attached handle, loses popularity to the monocle, a single lens that is worn in the orbit, or eye socket, and thus does not need to be held in the hand. Quizzing glasses were popular in an era when lens crafting was more of an art than a science—creating lenses with the appropriate strength for each eye was difficult. For people whose vision varied greatly in each eye, wearing eyeglasses often caused eyestrain and headaches.

Custom-made monocles fit snugly and comfortably; cheaper standard monocles are difficult to keep in place. For this reason, monocles come to be associated with the wealthy, the only people who can afford to have them custom-made. They remain a fashionable men's accessory until World War I, when their association with German military officers ruins their popularity outside of Germany. (Famous monocle wearer: the Penguin from Batman.)

1820s "Pince-nez" ("pinch-nose" in French), glasses that are held in place by—you guessed it—pinching the bridge of the nose, are introduced. The style remains popular into the 1940s. They're usually worn with a cord that attaches to the wearer's vest or another article of clothing, so that the glasses don't fall to the floor if they pop out.

1825 George Biddell Airy, a British mathematician and astronomer, invents the first lens that corrects astigmatism, a condition caused when the cornea or transparent layer forming the front of the eye is oval or spoon-shaped, instead of circular and spherical. Airy's lenses work by reproducing the cornea's spoon shape in the shape of an eyeglass lens, but oriented perpendicular (90 degrees) in relation to the spoon shape in the cornea, causing the irregularities to cancel each other out. About one third of people with poor vision have astigmatism in one or both eyes, and now their vision problems are treatable for the first time.

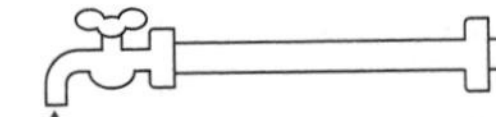

Three cities with the largest German population in 1855: 1) Berlin; 2) Vienna; 3) New York City.

1827 Why stop at *bi*focals? John Isaac Hawkins, a British inventor who is also credited with inventing the upright piano, invents trifocals, which typically correct for near vision (bottom of the lens), arms-length vision (middle), and distance vision (top), all in one pair of eyeglasses. Hawkins is also the guy who gave bifocals their name.

1850s The first eyeglasses with "curl-side" pieces that curve around the ear become available. Modern eyeglasses are born.

1955 After getting his start in the eyeglass business fusing traditional bifocal lenses together in his uncle's lens factory, Irving Rips invents the first commercially viable seamless or "invisible" bifocals that "wouldn't give away the wearer's age with its telltale lines." He founds a company called Younger Optics (because the glasses make you look younger) in Southern California.

1996 Joshua Silver, a British physicist, develops eyeglasses with adjustable, fluid-filled corrective lenses for developing countries, where trained optometrists are few and far between. The wearer simply puts on the glasses, then turns a small dial to adjust the amount of fluid in a lens, thereby changing its shape until the wearer's vision comes into focus. The process is then repeated with the other lens. Silver spent seven years perfecting the design, then introduced the glasses, called AdSpecs (short for "adaptive spectacles") in 2003. To date, more than 100,000 pairs of the glasses have been distributed in 30 developing countries around the world.

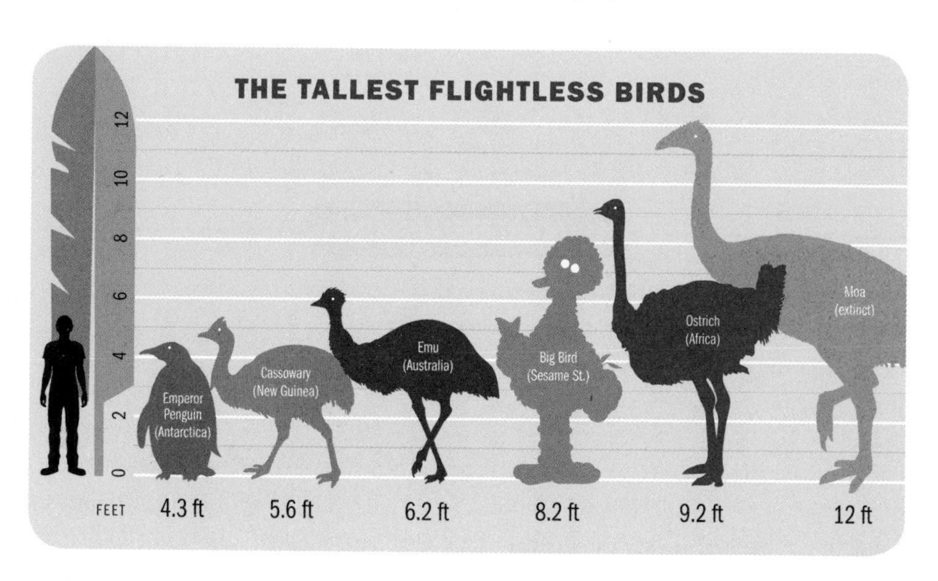

By the time a monarch butterfly finishes its 14-day caterpillar stage, it will weigh 2,000 times as much as it did when it started.

LOVE...LOST AND FOUND

Ever think about a long-lost friend, or someone you knew in school, or an old flame, and wonder where they ended up? Thanks to social media, you can probably find them...unless they changed their name, or maybe you didn't even know their name. And what if you met them under extraordinary circumstances, such as a war? War changes everything and leaves a lot of open wounds, few of which ever heal. Here's a love story that took a 50-year hiatus.

THE ONE THAT GOT AWAY

Vu Thi Vinh was 17 years old in 1968, and her home country, South Vietnam, was mired in war. She got a job as a bar hostess at the Enlisted Men's (EM) Club near the Long Binh Army Post in Bien Hoa. Lots of American GIs had their eyes on the pretty young woman, but one young man in particular, a 22-year-old logistics data worker at the base named Ken Reesing, caught *her* eye. For the next nine months, the two lovebirds went on dates every weekend (because locals weren't allowed on the army base). Then, three months before his deployment was scheduled to end, Reesing was given his orders to return home.

He pleaded with Vinh to come back with him, but she had to remain with her family. On the last day they spent together, Reesing bought her 50 envelopes and promised to return to Vietnam after he received the final letter. Vinh wrote every day until the envelopes ran out, and then she wrote more letters. Reesing wrote back, care of the EM Club, but when the war ended, the bar closed, and their means of communication suddenly stopped. He knew her only by her club name, a pseudonym—Lan. He didn't even know her family name. All he had was a single photograph of her smiling at the club.

LOOKING AND LOOKING

As the years passed, Reesing tried several times to find Vinh, first asking returning soldiers if they knew what became of the hostess at the EM Club. He used the internet in the early 2000s to hire a private investigator based in Ho Chi Minh City. Respecting her privacy, Reesing only wanted to know if Vinh was alive and happy. If he found out she'd died, he thought, he would go to Vietnam and put flowers on her grave. But nothing ever came of the searches. Reesing had gotten married, but it didn't last long. In 2019, he was a divorced 71-year-old, a retired construction worker living in Ohio with his cat...expecting to spend the rest of his life alone.

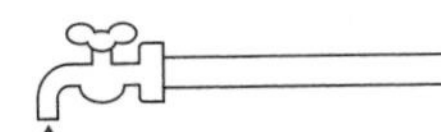

That June, Reesing read an account of another Vietnam veteran who had finally located his own lost love...only to learn that she'd died. On a whim, Reesing decided to share his story in the comment section, where it was read by Robert Frank, an American-Vietnamese journalist living in Ho Chi Minh City. He shared Ken's story on some local and regional pages, and from there it only took a day for one of Vinh's neighbors to post a comment that she knew this woman!

THE REUNION

Vinh was 67, living with her daughter and running a *congee* (porridge) stall, where she'd been working for 30 years. She too had been married, but it hadn't lasted. On their first conversation in half a century, the first thing Reesing said—in Vietnamese—was, "I'm sorry I didn't come back for you." They spent the next two weeks talking every day, and then he booked a flight to Ho Chi Minh City.

At the airport—with family and members of the press on hand—Vinh wore a traditional yellow dress like the one she'd had on when they were last together. Reesing walked up in a green shirt like the one he'd been wearing. They cried and embraced for several minutes. After posing for some pictures, they left the airport, hand in hand. As for the future? "We will let things happen naturally," she said.

* * *

ON HINDSIGHT

"Hindsight. It's like foresight without a future."
—**Kevin Kline**

"There's many a forward look in a backward glance."
—**Evan Esar**

"Of all the words of mice and men, the saddest are 'It might have been.'"
—**Kurt Vonnegut**

"It is easy to be wise after the event."
—**Arthur Conan Doyle**

"Hindsight's a wonderful thing. If we all had it there would be no history to write about."
—**Kate Atkinson**

"Hindsight is illuminating but not always what we want to see."
—**Kylie Minogue**

"The inevitable effect of a biographer's hindsight is to belittle the subject's foresight."
—**Clive James**

"Hindsight is not necessarily the best guide to understanding what really happened. The past is often as distorted by hindsight as it is clarified by it."
—**Amos Elon**

"People change, though, especially after they are dead."
—**Margaret Atwood**

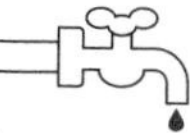

"La Bamba" singer Ritchie Valens's musical career lasted just eight months before he died in the same plane crash that killed Buddy Holly in February 1959.

BIOSPHERE 2: ECOLOGIC BOOGALOO

Where did the communal living and hippie ideals of the 1960s meet futuristic, sci-fi technology? In an enclosed structure in the middle of the Arizona desert.

THE TEACHINGS OF JOHNNY DOLPHIN

John P. Allen did a lot of things. Born in Oklahoma, he studied science at Stanford, served in the U.S. Army Corps of Engineers, trained as a metallurgist, earned a degree in engineering, got an MBA from Harvard, wrote poetry (under the name "Johnny Dolphin"), and—after forming a performance troupe called Theater of All Possibilities—traveled to exotic and remote locales, including the Osun-Osogbo Forest of Nigeria, the Amazon Rainforest, and the Australian Outback. Allen got himself and his actors to those far-flung locales on a ship he built himself.

In 1969, he founded the Synergia Ranch, outside of Santa Fe, New Mexico. In addition to serving as his theater company's headquarters, the 130-acre preserve was also a commune, research facility, and thriving small business. Allen and his fellow "synergists" wanted a place where ecology met technology met commerce—where they could create things that would help the planet but also turn a profit. Scientists at Synergia studied soil fortification, organic farming, and sustainable architecture. In the 1970s, Synergia was hired to build more than 30 traditional adobe-style structures in Santa Fe. In 1983, Synergia went out into the world with "Houses of the Forest," a 1,000-acre project next to a rainforest in Puerto Rico where it studied sustainable forestry.

All of this helped Allen and his acolytes explore the biosphere, the delicate web of how animals, plants, and nature interact to sustain life on Earth, and it would all inform the construction and operation of a new biosphere. Because "Biosphere 1" is the planet Earth itself, Allen's synthetic version would be called "Biosphere 2."

LIFE ON EARTH

In 1984, Allen joined forces with Ed Bass, who was a lot like Allen, only wealthier. The scion of a Texas oil baron, Bass had opened and operated ecologically minded land development projects (he styled himself an "ecopreneur") and a performing arts center in Fort Worth. Allen believed civilization was dying, and Bass believed the planet was dying. Together, taking their cue from terrariums, aquariums, and other sealed environments where life could thrive with no outside help except sunlight, Bass and Allen conceived of an idea to build a massive *vivarium* with people inside. This sealed building would be airtight, and contain several different environments,

The infield dirt at more than two-thirds of Major League Baseball's 30 stadiums is a special blend of dirt that is formulated in Slippery Rock, Pennsylvania.

or *biomes*, that would provide all the oxygen, water, and food they'd need. Allen and Bass even thought that if their sealed world worked, people could live in them on the Moon, on Mars, or right here on Earth (in a post-nuclear apocalypse).

Bass offered up $30 million in initial funding, with which they secured real estate in the Arizona desert, just north of Tucson, and hired crews to start building a planned 3.4-acre complex. Inside the glass, plastic, and steel structure of geodesic domes and pyramids were a miniature rainforest, a desert, a grassland, and a small ocean with a coral reef.

Human waste would be used to fertilize crops and feed algae.

BUILDING THE BIOSPHERE

Bass, Allen, and other planners were attempting the largest experiment of its kind, but theirs wouldn't be the first. The Soviet Union's space program, in researching how to sustain life for cosmonauts in the harsh environment of space, conducted several similar experiments in the 1960s and '70s. The longest placed test subjects in a sealed chamber for six months, and the cosmonauts ate crops grown with hydroponics (without soil) and breathed oxygen generated from algae.

Biosphere 2 planners took some of those ideas, but also focused on the importance of recycling. Human waste would be used to fertilize crops and feed algae, for example. Meanwhile, in a makeshift research facility built next to the Biosphere 2 site, scientists studied crops and fish species to see which might be the easiest to grow and sustain under glass. (Ultimately, 3,000 different plants and animals were approved for use in Biosphere 2.) Another team looked at a waste treatment system that used bacteria to break down animal waste in the healthiest, most efficient way. Organizers also had to decide who would get to live inside Biosphere 2 during its initial run, scheduled at first for 1989 and then pushed back to 1991. Applicants were whittled down to 12, with varied backgrounds in botany, animal husbandry, horticulture, engineering, and medicine, from which eight were finally chosen—four men and four women.

OPENING NIGHT

On the evening of September 25, 1991, Space Biospheres Ventures invited the media and celebrities to a massive launch party on the grounds of (but not inside) Biosphere 2. Then, early the next morning, the eight Biospherians, dressed in blue jumpsuits, posed for photographers one last time, and walked into Biosphere 2, their home for the next two years. The airlock was sealed behind them.

Life inside Biosphere 2 seemed to proceed swimmingly at first. The scientists started working the artificial land for crops (along with hummingbirds and bees brought in for pollination) and recycling their own waste (solid and liquid) into potable water and fertilizer. Their bosses at Space Biospheres Ventures saw huge potential for making money, telling the media that the experiment was going so well

Not what you thought? Sharks, which appeared about 450 million years ago, are much older than trees (they came along 100 million years later).

that they'd re-create Biosphere 2 as soon as 1995—on the Moon. The new, progressive water purification system the Biospherians were working out could be patented, produced, and sold, plus they'd certainly secure contracts to build biospheres for universities and corporations around the world. In the meantime, they generated a modest income by charging busloads of tourists to come to Biosphere 2, walk around, and gawk at the scientists working inside.

THE FIRST CUT IS THE DEEPEST

But just two weeks after the doors of Biosphere 2 were sealed shut, the quality of life inside—and the success of the mission itself—began to wane. It started when Biospherian Jane Poynter sliced off the top of a finger in a rice-hulling accident. Fellow Biospherian Dr. Roy Walford reattached it the best he could, but he so lacked confidence in his work that he sent Poynter out of Biosphere 2 to undergo surgery. Poynter returned to the complex a couple of days later, smuggling in a duffel bag full of computer parts and other items her colleagues needed—a violation of Biosphere 2's declared mission of self-sustainment with no outside help.

It wouldn't be the last time the Biospherians were quietly given supplies to juice the experiment's chances for success or to keep themselves alive. Throughout late 1991, they received quiet deliveries every two weeks, including items like seeds, vitamins, and mousetraps. More bad news: a crew had to install a new air filtration system to manage the facility's alarmingly rising level of carbon dioxide.

CONDITION: CRITICAL

Part of the reason the Arizona desert was selected as the location for Biosphere 2 was the climate—it's sunny more often than not, and sunlight coming through the facility's glass walls and ceilings was vitally important in ensuring healthy crops for the residents' subsistence farming. But that winter, the area grew uncharacteristically cloudy, a pattern that stretched out for months. First the crops were anemic, and then they didn't grow at all. Fearing starvation, the Biospherians reported the problem to superiors, who informed them that they'd stashed away a three-month emergency supply of food.

Then it became hard to breathe. An outbreak of bacteria in the soil consumed huge amounts of oxygen, changing the atmosphere of Biosphere 2. Tests revealed that there was so little oxygen, it was as if the facility sat at an altitude of 14,000 feet. Bosses had to send a truckload of liquid oxygen into the building so the scientists wouldn't die.

But the delivery was too late for some residents. The oxygen shortage killed off the hummingbird and bee populations that had been introduced to pollinate food crops. Without them, many food sources didn't grow, decimating the Biospherians' food supply once again. Then the nematodes and mites attacked what was actually

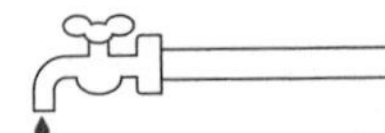

growing. This occurred in the summer of 1992, less than a year into the mission, and at which point Biosphere 2's entire scientific advisory committee quit...but not before issuing a report lambasting Space Biospheres Ventures for a lack of clear goals, for inadequate planning, and for hiring scientists who didn't know what they were doing.

WE'RE DOMED

By 1993, Space Biospheres Ventures was deep in a financial hole, and that was almost entirely because of Biosphere 2. Even without all the extra expenditures, the experiment had cost much more than originally projected. The company now estimated that it would operate at a $20 million deficit for the coming year, so it decided to bring in an investment banker and corporate "fixer" to turn things around. Bass hired a new CEO for the company named Steve Bannon—the same Steve Bannon who would later become chief campaign strategist for President Donald Trump and then get arrested (and later pardoned) for lining his pockets with money diverted from a charity set up to build the Mexican border wall.

Meanwhile, inside Biosphere 2, the scientists had all survived their two-year stint, emerging on September 26, 1993. They'd all lost a substantial amount of weight and hadn't been able to run a self-sufficient, domed community (which would technically qualify the experiment as a failure), but hey, they were alive. In the weeks after, Bannon fired Biosphere 2 cocreator John Allen along with the rest of the executive board. Bannon charged ahead, however, overseeing selection of a new series of Biospherians.

THE GREAT BIOSPHERE BREAK-IN OF '94

The only people who understood what life would be like for the second team of Biospherians—which entered the building on March 6, 1994—were members of the first team, and at least two of them, Abigail Alling and Mark Van Thillo, were so alarmed by the idea that they felt they had to shut the whole thing down. So, just before the sun rose on April 4, 1994, they broke into Biosphere 2, opened all five doors to the facility and smashed several glass panels, breaking the airtight seals and allowing outside air to seep in.

Alling and Van Thillo were hauled away by police, and later told reporters that they'd done it because they feared the new round of scientists weren't safe and would end up struggling to stay alive, just as the first team had, and that they hoped to end the mission.

Nobody left Biosphere 2, at least not when Alling and Van Thillo gave them the chance. A few months later, in August 1994, Bannon ended it, cutting the second Biosphere 2 residency short after advisors declared that life was no longer sustainable inside. Nor was it financially feasible. According to an internal report, it had cost $200 million to build and run Biosphere 2, and all that money had been spent on

Between 1992 and 2012, 10% of all electricity generated in the U.S. was produced from decommissioned Soviet nuclear warheads—about 20,000 bombs' worth.

technology that "failed to generate sufficient breathable air, drinkable water, and adequate food."

LESSON (NOT) LEARNED

Biosphere 2 remains standing in the Arizona desert, a relic of the past devoted to a future that didn't arrive, at least not yet. Shortly before leaving Space Biospheres Ventures, Bannon sold the facility to New York's Columbia University, where scientists used it for research projects somewhat less grand than the preservation of human life in artificial environments. The building changed hands again in 2011, when remaining cofounder Ed Bass donated Biosphere 2 to the University of Arizona, along with a $20 million grant for maintenance.

Ecological study was the overarching goal of the entire Biosphere 2 project and, curiously, most of the scientific research data about the Earth's biomes that was obtained by two teams of Biospherians appears to be lost. When first team member Mark Nelson began work on a book about his experiences, he tried to access any Biosphere 2 data that hadn't yet been published. Space Biospheres Ventures didn't have it, Columbia University didn't have it, and the University of Arizona didn't have it either. A representative of the university told Nelson that they were never even given any research about the earth, ecology, or artificial environments. Not only was the $200 million project unable to support eight people for two years, the Biospherians weren't even able to hang on to the data they'd collected, either. So if anyone ever decides to create another experimental artificial world in the future, there's a good chance they'll have to start from scratch.

However, a few studies based on research conducted by the Biospherians during their brief stay did increase understanding of ecology and the effects of climate change. "We learned lessons to help keep stressed reefs alive and how to protect rainforests," Nelson wrote in 2018. "We worked with our green allies to keep CO2 from getting too high. Our farm showed that high productivity and full nutrient recycling could be done without toxic chemicals. Much of what we learned went unappreciated."

* * *

ORIGIN OF A TV CATCHPHRASE

Ed Helms, who played Andy Bernard on *The Office*, explained how childhood bullies inspired his character's catchphrase. "After they gave me a wedgie or pushed me down... they'd go, 'Roo-doo-doot-da-doo!' as an expression of dominance...It didn't make any sense, and that's what made it even more terrifying." Helms turned the phrase into "something positive. It became Andy's expression of joy."

In 2003, as a class project, some second- and third-graders in Joliet, Illinois, got the governor to proclaim popcorn the state's official snack food.

REALLY DUMB CROOKS

Here are some lawbreakers who probably would have gotten away with it... if not for a really bad screw-up late in the game.

BAD KITTY

In the early 21st century, the FBI's most wanted cybercriminal was a man named Jeremy Hammond, a master hacker who focused on breaking into networks and websites of government agencies, police departments, and corporations who made big money from government contracts. After working as an activist hacker (or "hacktivist") for more than a decade, he was arrested after busting into the digital files of Stratfor, a national security think tank that consults with the U.S. Department of Defense and the Department of Homeland Security. Hammond successfully exploited flaws in Stratfor's computer codes...until the FBI exploited a flaw in Hammond's laptop. Authorities remotely accessed his Macintosh computer in search of evidence by guessing his password: "Chewy123." That's the name of Hammond's cat plus the three most obvious numbers he could have chosen. He's currently serving a 10-year prison sentence.

LETTER OF THE LAW

In January 1999, Virginia man Paul Warner Powell, 21, stabbed and murdered his 16-year-old friend Stacie Reed, allegedly because he disapproved of her boyfriend. He then attempted to kill Reed's 14-year-old sister, Kristie. But Kristie survived, and her testimony helped lead to Powell's conviction for first-degree murder, for which he was sentenced to death. On appeal, the Virginia Supreme Court threw out the verdict due to some irregularities in the case. Powell's sentence was commuted to three life sentences. Powell, who believed double jeopardy laws precluded him from facing the death penalty, then wrote a letter to prosecutors in which he bragged about getting away with his crimes, and described them in graphic detail. Using his confession, prosecutors were able to again indict—and convict—Powell of capital murder. This time the death sentence held: Powell was executed (by electric chair) in 2010.

SPELL CHECK

In October 2019, Robert Berger of Huntington, New York, was sentenced to a year in jail on theft charges. Shortly before he was scheduled to report to prison,

It may not seem like it, but in the U.S., parking spaces outnumber cars by 8 to 1.

however, he committed suicide in New Jersey. Not really—he just tried to make it *look* like he did, enlisting his fiancée to claim he'd died and having her submit a death certificate to the presiding judge and prosecutors. The document looked legitimate, almost exactly like one issued by the New Jersey Department of Health, Vital Statistics, and Registry. Almost. The ruse was exposed when a prosecutor examining the document recognized it as a forgery, and concluded that Berger had faked his own death. Berger's mistake: He'd spelled "Registry" as "Regsitry." Meanwhile, the crook had absconded to Philadelphia, where he was arrested on charges of robbery (again) and providing a false identity to the cops when they busted him.

DID YOU KNOW?

According to the Bureau of Justice Statistics, police in the U.S. make 10 million arrests each year...but only about a quarter of all crimes are solved by arresting the guilty party.

LACK OF COMMON CENTS

In 2018, a Florida man named Shane Anthony Mele was down on his luck. He asked a friend of his, a financier named Michael Johnson, if he could stay in his office for a while. Johnson agreed in exchange for his help on a project. One morning, Johnson arrived to find his office ransacked and Mele gone—as was Johnson's prized coin collection, which he'd inherited from his late father. Police had a pretty good idea that Mele was the culprit after viewing footage of him putting tape over the security cameras prior to the burglary. He was arrested a short time later. Here's the really dumb part. "He easily had $33,000 worth" of commemorative presidential $1 coins, said Johnson, "and he dumped them in a Coin Star machine...so he could buy a couple of twelve-packs of beer."

IN THE BAG

In February 2020, a Florida Highway Patrol officer in Santa Rosa County clocked a vehicle traveling at 95 miles per hour (20 mph over the speed limit), and pulled the driver over. The officer was only planning to issue a speeding ticket, but then decided to run a check on the two men in the car and found that one of them, Ian Simmons, had an active felony warrant over a probation violation. So he requested backup to conduct a search for illegal materials in the vehicle, which is when a drug-sniffing dog uncovered an array of controlled substances, including meth, cocaine, ecstasy, prescription painkillers, and drug paraphernalia. Turns out they didn't really need the dog. All of those narcotics were stashed in a cloth sack labeled "Bag Full of Drugs."

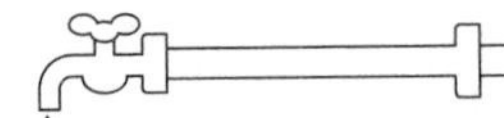

"Anaconda" comes from the Tamil (India) word *anai-kondra*, which translates to "elephant killer."

STRANGE MEDICAL NEWS

The human body is a complicated organic machine, and modern medicine hasn't unlocked all its secrets yet. Here are some of the oddest—and grossest—happenings to befall patients and baffle doctors in recent years.

URINE FOR A SURPRISE

In 2019, a 70-year-old woman in France (not named in news reports) was admitted to a hospital after suffering a stroke. As part of her treatment, she was catheterized and she seemed to be recovering normally...until the tenth day of her stay, when medical staff noticed that the urine collecting in her catheter bag had turned a shade of pinkish-purple. This is a rare but well-documented condition called "purple urine bag syndrome." (Seriously.) It's the result of a chemical reaction when bacteria convert indoxyl sulfate, a chemical present in urine, into red and blue compounds, which combine to make a purple liquid. Purple urine is mostly harmless, though it can indicate a urinary tract infection. Fortunately the patient didn't have that, and after four days of additional hydration, her pee returned to yellow.

A SPICY STORY

Wasabi, a spicy horseradish served as a condiment with Japanese food, is mushy and green, and strongly resembles guacamole, a mild Mexican dip made from mashed avocado. According to *BMJ Case Reports,* a 60-year-old woman attended a wedding reception in Israel in 2019 and ate a large dollop of what she thought was guacamole, but which was actually wasabi. Not only did the sudden kick of intense spice burn her mouth and nose, she felt an instant jolt of pressure in her chest, which spread to her arms. She was immediately taken to the hospital, where doctors diagnosed her with "broken-heart syndrome." The wasabi had triggered a stress response in the patient's body, which caused her heart to beat so fast that the left ventricle temporarily enlarged and then became so weak that it couldn't properly pump her blood, leading to excruciating chest pain. Good news: After a month of observation and a regimen of heart medication, the woman made a full recovery.

IT'S A BLOWOUT

A 63-year-old man from the Jiangsu province of China, identified in news reports as "Mr. Wang," had suffered from bowel obstructions off and on for a year before his body tried to correct the problem itself. One evening in July 2020, he ate a large bowl of wonton soup for dinner, and the next day, he heard a loud "bang" coming from inside his body, as if something had exploded. Then he felt a sharp pain in his abdomen and couldn't stop sweating. His family rushed him to Huai'an Traditional

From 1978 to 1989, the use, possession, and sale of skateboards was illegal in Norway. (Too many skateboard-related injuries.)

Chinese Medicine Hospital, where doctors diagnosed his problem: something *had* exploded—his bowels had blown a 1.2-inch-wide hole in his colon, and sent the bowel blockage into his abdominal cavity. Emergency medical staff removed about 100 ounces of liquid and semisolid waste from Mr. Wang...and he made a full recovery.

TELL US HOW YOU REALLY EEL

There was some kind of foreign object in his stomach, but they couldn't tell what it was.

In June 2020, a man (unnamed in news reports) checked himself into Huangjiang Hospital in China's Guangdong province complaining of severe abdominal pain. Doctors performed a CT scan and determined that there was some kind of foreign object in his stomach, but couldn't tell what it was or where it came from. So, they inserted a camera through his abdominal wall, which is how they figured out what it was: an eel. An emergency surgery revealed that the eel was 16 inches long and had been dead for several days. After the surgery, the patient admitted that he'd been suffering from constipation, so he tried an old folk remedy: he stuck the eel—live at the time—into his rectum. It didn't work—the angry fish apparently burrowed its way through the man's intestines, got stuck in his stomach, and died.

FIRE IN THE HOLE

At a 2019 European Anesthesiology Congress in Vienna, Austria, a doctor presented a case study about a bizarre complication for a 60-year-old heart surgery patient. The man had undergone surgery to repair a life-threatening tear in his aortic artery, which carries blood out of the heart. Because the patient had a history of severe lung problems, doctors administered supplemental oxygen to help ensure he'd survive the surgery. They also employed an electrocautery device, which uses electricity to heat body tissue and prevent bleeding. But electricity can start fires, and oxygen can feed fire. Result: During the surgery, the electrocautery device threw off sparks that, helped by the oxygen, set the surgical gauze in the patient's chest cavity aflame. It was quickly extinguished, and doctors successfully repaired the aortic tear.

A HAIRY SITUATION

Minoxodil is a topical medication used primarily for hair restoration. It's the active ingredient in Rogaine. Another widely available medication is omeprazole, found in products like Prilosec, which is taken orally to help relieve heartburn in adults and stomachaches in children. In Spain, both products are distributed by the pharmaceutical company FarmaQuimica Sur. Because of a packaging error made at FarmaQuimica Sur in 2019, at least 20 children were given a stomach remedy that contained minoxodil, and not omeprazole. Parents only discovered the error in July 2019, when they noticed that the children started growing thick hair on their backs and torsos.

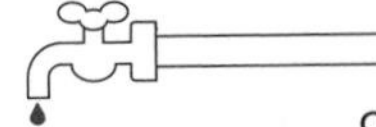

Queen Elizabeth II trained as a mechanic and truck driver for the women's branch of the British Army during World War II.

HUMAN NATURE EXPLAINED

Humans are weird. We're mesmerized by shiny things, we go bonkers for chocolate, and we turn to jelly at the sight of a cute widdle baby...awww! Also, humans are, for the most part, cynical and distrustful. How did we turn out like this? The reasons may surprise you.

BACKGROUND

Biologically speaking, evolution is the process by which cumulative changes occur in a population over several generations. These changes take place on a genetic level, and are often the result of a mutation that, for whatever reason, gives some individuals an advantage over others, allowing for future generations to inherit the genes. The mechanism that drives this process: *natural selection.* Though sometimes called "survival of the fittest," it's not necessarily the biggest and the strongest that make it to breeding age—especially when it comes to that most complex animal: us.

The current consensus among anthropologists and evolutionary biologists is that the first primates to acquire proto-human features showed up about six million years ago. Our species, *Homo sapiens,* showed up between 200,000 and 300,000 years ago during the Middle Paleolithic era, marking the beginning of the Stone Age. "Modern humans" date back to roughly 50,000 years ago in western Africa. And a great deal of who we are today was shaped by the obstacles our prehistoric ancestors had to overcome, and many of those tendencies remain...for better or for worse. Here are some common questions about why we are the way we are, and leading scientific theories that attempt to answer them.

WHY DO SOME PEOPLE HAVE BLOND HAIR?

After early modern humans banded together and ventured north out of Africa to the colder climes of Europe, an Ice Age nearly drove them to extinction. That was about 11,000 years ago. Up until then, all our ancestors had dark skin, dark hair, and brown eyes.

Those unending winters led to longer hunts and fewer hunters returning to the cave, resulting in a shortage of males in northern Europe. According to Canadian anthropologist Peter Frost's 2008 theory, genes for blond hair took hold because of "sexual selection," a concept introduced by Charles Darwin in the 1850s—which Darwin defined as "the advantage which certain individuals have over other individuals of the same sex and species solely in respect of reproduction." During that Ice Age, a rare genetic mutation occurred in some females, giving them blond hair and blue eyes. Frost contends that the fair-haired females "stood out" in a crowded field, and made them more desirable. "Intense female-female competition may explain an

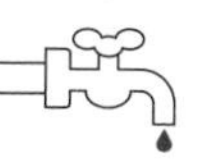

80 percent of plane crashes happen in the first three or last eight minutes of the flight.

unusual convergence of color traits in northern and eastern Europeans," he explains, adding, "Intense male-male competition may explain increased masculinization of body build in highly polygynous [several females for one male] agricultural populations of sub-Saharan Africa." (Translation: Buff guys got more women.)

That wasn't the first time a genetic mutation for blond hair cropped up, but because of the specific set of harsh conditions, the trait caught on, even though it serves no physical advantage. But how much did it really catch on? If it seems like there's an abundance of blondes out there, that's only because they're overrepresented in European and North American popular culture. In reality, only 2 percent of humans alive today have naturally blond hair.

Bonus: Depigmentation of skin color was a separate process that took hold in Europe about 3,000 years *after* blond hair emerged. Lower levels of solar radiation required less natural protection—which dark skin provided—so genes for lighter skin got passed on.

WHY DO WE LOVE SHINY THINGS?

It was once assumed that our adoration of all that glitters is due to its association with monetary wealth, but money is a relatively new addition to the human equation (circa 3,000 to 5,000 years ago). And a love of money doesn't explain why babies prefer shiny objects to dull objects (and are even more likely to put them in their mouths). It also doesn't explain why some indigenous cultures that have no currency are also transfixed by shiny things. Even crows have been observed fighting over shiny things.

According to researchers at the University of Houston and Ghent University in Belgium, ancient humans took a shine to shiny things because they were thirsty. For our nomadic ancestors lost in the desert, a glimmering oasis on the horizon could lead them to life-sustaining water. In 2013, the researchers tested this theory. After first concluding that, in general, test subjects preferred glossy pictures to duller matte pictures, the scientists gave some participants water and salty crackers...and others *only* got the crackers. From the findings: "The thirstier participants got, the more they preferred glossy pictures."

WHY DO WE LIKE TO THROW THINGS?

A major league pitcher can hurl a baseball at 90 miles per hour, hitting a target 60 feet away that's no bigger than the ball itself. Even toddlers can throw objects at a high rate of speed with remarkable accuracy (a skill they sometimes display at the worst possible times). This is notable because throwing is the only thing *Homo erectus* was better at than every one of its predators. They certainly weren't stronger than big cats, wolves, or bears. Or faster. But when our ancestors learned to walk on two legs, that freed up their opposable thumbs to grip objects. Throwing came later.

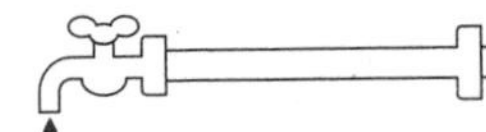

The Washington National Cathedral in D.C. has a gargoyle shaped like Darth Vader.

In 2013, Neil Roach, an anthropologist at the Center for the Advanced Study of Hominid Paleobiology at George Washington University, reported that, two million years ago, a physiological change developed in the ligaments and tendons of *Homo erectus*'s shoulder, giving it more elasticity. This allowed their shoulders to store energy when positioned back, resulting in incredible forward momentum when released. This physiological change, combined with superior mental acuity and stereoscopic vision (which allows for accurate depth perception), gave these cunning primates deadly accuracy. A lone, barehanded *H. erectus* was no match against a saber-toothed tiger, but a small group wielding baseball-sized rocks could easily take out a big cat, or chase away a pack of hyenas from their kill. All of a sudden, there was a lot more to eat. "This dietary change led to seismic shifts in our ancestors' biology," Roach told BBC News, "allowing them to grow larger bodies, larger brains, and to have more children, and it also did interesting things to our social structure. We start to see the origins of divisions of labor around that time, where some would be hunting, others would be gathering new foods."

Roach's hypothesis hasn't been universally accepted, as it's impossible to determine from bones exactly how prehistoric shoulders operated. But whether we got good at throwing two million years ago or much later, we still do it better than every other animal.

WHY DO WE HAVE A SWEET TOOTH?

"Sugar is a deep, deep ancient craving," says biologist Daniel Lieberman of Harvard University. It made a lot more sense in prehistoric times, he says. Whereas modern humans in need of a midday boost can grab a candy bar or an energy drink, nothing packed more of a punch for our early ancestors than a ripe piece of fruit dangling from the canopy. The riper the fruit, the sweeter its meat, and the more vitamins and energy it provided. That was crucial for the survival of these proto-humans, who spent most of their day foraging and hunting, and avoiding constant threats. The primates that ate the most fruit gained an energy advantage, and over time, natural selection yielded a craving for sweets.

When Earth's climate cooled about 1.5 million years ago, a genetic mutation took hold that allowed the sugars in the fruits—which our bodies break down into glucose and sucrose—to be stored as fat. That was good news for our always-on-the-go ancestors, and not such good news for us today. Biologists like Lieberman refer to this as the "evolutionary mismatch concept," meaning our ancient bodies aren't well adapted to our modern environment.

For example, our brains have the same sweet cravings as our prehistoric counterparts, but we lack the active lifestyle of our ancestors, so that fat doesn't get burned. "We have created a kind of positive-feedback loop that I call 'dysevolution,'"

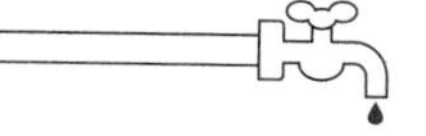

explains Lieberman. "We are eating diets and leading lives that contribute to poor health. Then, when we get sick, instead of treating the causes of those diseases, we treat the symptoms, enabling the disease not only to continue but also to become more prevalent. I think that's why the rates of obesity and Type 2 diabetes and various kinds of cancer are going up—because we are not dealing with the causes of these problems." Here's another way to explain it:

WHY ARE PEOPLE SO PESSIMISTIC?

Even the most optimistic "glass half full" person seems to understand that it takes more than a smile to be your umbrella; one has to prepare for rain. This isn't merely common sense. It's a pessimistic view of life that was hardwired into us long ago. According to psychologist Martin Seligman in his 2018 book *The Hope Circuit,* "The species that [was] going through the Ice Ages had been bred, and selected, through pessimism. The mentality that said, 'It's a beautiful day in San Diego today, I bet it'll be beautiful tomorrow' got crushed by the ice. What got selected for, in the Ice Ages, was bad weather animals, who were always thinking about the bad stuff that could occur. So what comes naturally to people is pessimism."

He further points out that while pessimism helped our ancestors endure long winters, there's an overload of it today that's leading to mass distrust and division. And pessimism isn't something you can overcome just by willing it away. But there is good news, says Seligman, a pioneer in an emerging field called "positive psychology." We can achieve harmony and happiness, but not by *trying* to be happy. His method, which he abbreviates as PERMA, recommends adding more of these things to your life: "positive emotion, engagement, relationships, meaning, and accomplishment." (Go ahead and try it, but it probably won't work.)

WHY DO WE HAVE SUCH BIG BRAINS?

Scientists often refer to the human brain as the "crowning achievement of evolution." It's the reason why only one species out of millions has managed to create enduring cultures and build ships and travel to space. Physiologically, our brain isn't much different from a chimpanzee's or even a mouse's. What we do have are more *glial cells,*

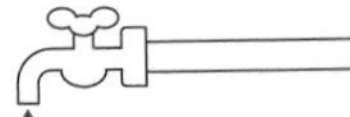

World's biggest coal exporter: Australia. It exports roughly 90% of the coal it produces, accounting for 32% of total global coal exports.

which may be the key to our advantage. They're associated with *brain plasticity*, the ability to react to changing conditions.

It requires a tremendous amount of energy to operate such a big brain, more than can be attained from raw vegetables (unless they're eaten in huge quantities). Richard Wrangham, an English primatologist, realized this while studying the diets of chimpanzees in the 1990s (he studied under Jane Goodall as a grad student). Although chimps share many characteristics with humans, their brains are much smaller than ours, so he wondered, "What would it take to convert a chimpanzeelike ancestor into a human?"

Wrangham compared modern chimps to the fossil evidence of *Homo erectus*, a proto-human primate that lived 2 million to 1.6 million years ago. *H. erectus* was the first ape with a much larger brain—50 percent bigger than that of its predecessor, *Homo habilis*. When *H. erectus* ventured out of the forest for the open savanna, there was less cover and harsher, hotter conditions. This is where brain plasticity comes in. Hunting required cooperation, and cooperation required planning, abstract thought, and being able to quickly change plans to turn defeat into victory. Those cognitive abilities required a complex brain firing millions of synapses per second. Only the most intelligent *H. erectus* survived long enough to procreate.

That explains the behavioral mechanisms that led to a bigger brain, but what happened physiologically? According to Wrangham, the fuel came in the form of calories derived from cooking tubers, which breaks down the raw fibers into energy-packed starches, the ultimate "brain food." It's uncertain how or even if *H. erectus* learned to control fire and cook food, but Wrangham asserts that this is the only diet that could have fueled such rapid brain growth.

Physiologically, our brain isn't much different from a chimpanzee's or even a mouse's.

That laid the evolutionary groundwork for other physical changes first seen in *H. erectus*: smaller teeth and smaller stomachs—like we have. By comparison, a chimpanzee has much larger teeth and would have to eat several pounds of raw tubers per day to get the calories of a cooked one. Studies have shown that chimps prefer cooked food, and some take right to cooking when they're taught, giving credence to Wrangham's theory that *H. erectus* tamed fire.

Other anthropologists contend that cooking didn't begin until a few hundred thousand years ago with the Neanderthals, or even much later. So if not by cooking, then how did *H. erectus* get their brains? Improved hunting techniques expanded their omnivorous diets, which made available large quantities of calorie-rich soft tissue like bone marrow and brain tissue. But however or whenever it occurred, the science does point to a change in diet resulting in a bigger brain, which led to things like language, the wheel, and PTA meetings.

WHY DO WE FIND BABIES SO DARN CUTE?

"Oh my god, your baby is soooo adorable! I could just eat him up!" That's something an otherwise well-adjusted adult might say, and no one would bat an eye. This curiously aggressive response is triggered not just by infants but by any baby animal—especially other mammals, from kittens to baby elephants. But it can also be triggered by tiny tree frogs or fuzzy chicks. The characteristics that trigger this response—a miniature body, miniature head, proportionally larger eyes, smaller nose, and bonus if it's pudgy or furry—make up what Austrian zoologist Konrad Lorenz called *kindchenschema*, or "baby schema," the theory that these combined factors compel us to want to care for the thing.

This response is a by-product of our brain's delayed development. Humans have small heads. If our heads were any larger, they wouldn't be able to fit out of the birth canal. Why wouldn't natural selection yield a larger birth canal? Because humans are bipedal animals, and a wider birth canal would impede walking on two legs. Once our species attained the ability to stand up and see over the top of the savanna grasses, the size of the human birth canal was set.

Because we have the most complex brain in the animal kingdom, and one of the largest in proportion to the body, the brain is still years away from fully developing by the time the fetus's head has grown to its birthing size. This isn't the case when it comes to the young of less-intelligent animals—such as a newborn deer that lands awkwardly on its feet and only requires a few licks from its mom to start stumbling around. In contrast, it takes newborn humans about eight months before they can stand up without any help.

Raising such a helpless creature requires, to put it simply, love. Through natural selection, we gained a fondness for the *kindchenschema* characteristics, which activate the part of the brain associated with motivation and reward. What's the reward? Dopamine. It's the same "feel-good neurotransmitter" our brains release when we're in love (or having dessert). The *kindchenschema* response is so strong that we're even compelled to take care of *other* babies. This gave our ancestors an "it takes a village to raise a child" approach to culture.

But what about the "I could eat you up!" part of the response? This is called *cute aggression.* Though its exact purpose is uncertain, it could be a way for us to "come down" from the cuteness high. Displaying an aggressive emotion counters the effect of all that dopamine, allowing you to quickly return to your well-adjusted self.

According to psychologists, human babies reach "peak cuteness" at five or six months. It's around this time that they pick up on our positive reaction and act even cuter to keep that reaction coming. As early as three years old, toddlers have been observed responding to cuteness in younger babies as well as other fuzzy widdle tings with big puppy-dog eyes. Especially puppies. For that story, feel free to grab a plastic poop bag and take a walk to page 398 for "It's a Dog's World."

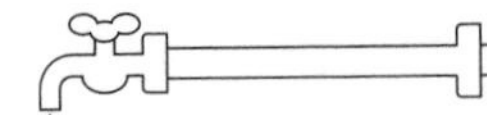

PAUL PIERCE'S PUTRID PANTS

The bizarre story of how a basketball superstar's reputation was, um, soiled.

THE WHEEL STORY

The Boston Celtics won the 2008 NBA Finals over their longtime rivals, the Los Angeles Lakers, in six games. The MVP of the series: Paul Pierce, who averaged more than 21 points and six assists per game for Boston. That outcome seemed unlikely during the third quarter of game one. When Lakers star Kobe Bryant attempted a baseline shot, the Celtics' Kendrick Perkins went for the block and failed, instead ramming into his teammate, Pierce, sending the all-star hurtling to the ground.

As he clutched his leg, some of the other Celtics attempted to carry the apparently injured Pierce off the court—a rare occurrence in the NBA, where even players who suffer a muscle tear or a bone fracture choose to heroically hobble all the way to the locker room. Then the situation seemed to get even more serious—the Celtics' staff made the unprecedented move of calling for a wheelchair to escort Pierce off the court and away from the 20,000 fans in the arena.

The game continued without Pierce, but then, after about just two minutes had ticked off the clock, Pierce reemerged from the locker room, standing up, fully mobile and ready to go back into the game, seeming no worse for the wear. Immediately after subbing back in, Pierce sank a couple of three-pointers and the Celtics ultimately won the game, 98–88, thanks to 13 late points from the guy everybody thought had suffered a season-ending injury. Because of Pierce's dramatic exit, the contest came to be known in NBA lore as "the Wheelchair Game."

A RIPPING TALE

For more than a decade, Pierce held firm to his explanation as to why he suddenly had to leave one of the most important games of his life, and how he so quickly and miraculously recovered from what looked like a serious knee injury. He claimed that Perkins knocked him to the ground, he heard a "pop" come from inside his leg and, fearing it was a devastating ACL tear, he didn't want to walk on it and risk injuring himself even more.

That didn't hold water with fans, though—it all just seemed too pat, which made them suspicious. Basketball fans on the internet wildly speculated on the nature of the incident, with a few suggesting—jokingly at first—that Pierce had to make a quick exit because he'd pooped his pants.

That became the only alternate explanation for the events of "the Wheelchair Game." Not only had Pierce accidentally emptied his bowels in the middle of the

The pope cannot be an organ donor because "his body belongs to the entire Catholic Church and must be buried intact."

game, the theory held, but he had to get to the locker room as quickly as possible without fans—or the TV cameras broadcasting the game to millions of viewers—noticing the telltale physical traces. There are a few stray bits of "proof" that support the theory. For example, Celtics personnel carried Pierce off the court and then into the wheelchair in such a way that his rear end was completely concealed from fans in attendance and the cameras. And video footage of the game just before Pierce's fall and "injury" reveals a perfectly unsullied pair of green shorts.

Still, Pierce never deviated from his take on events—that he thought he was injured and was being extra-careful, that he turned out to be fine, and that he returned to the game as soon as it all shook out. But rumors, particularly ones involving celebrities' embarrassing moments, never really die.

COMING CLEAN

Pierce retired in 2017 and went on to become a broadcaster, co-hosting NBA pregame and halftime shows for ESPN and ABC. On June 5, 2019, Pierce was covering game three of the NBA Finals with sportscaster Michelle Beadle, who remarked that the date happened to be the 11th anniversary of game one of the 2008 NBA Finals—the game in which Pierce provided clutch points for the Celtics despite an interruption when he was carried off the court in a wheelchair, presumably injured. With a nod to the "poop theory," Beadle said Pierce had to exit the game "for reasons he will keep to himself." But then Pierce decided not to keep them to himself any longer. "I have a confession to make," Pierce blurted out. "I just had to go to the bathroom." His co-hosts, former players Chauncey Billups and Jalen Rose, were shocked, amused, and incredulous. "Why did you need a wheelchair to get to the bathroom?" Billups pressed. "Something went down, I had to get to the bathroom," Pierce explained. "You were streaking?" Rose teased.

Beadle moved the broadcast chatter away from the potty talk and back to the game at hand, but a few hours later, Pierce returned to the subject of that messy day in 2008. He took to Twitter and, amazingly, backtracked on everything he'd said on television that day. "Sorry to bust y'all haters bubble," he wrote, "but the only 💩💩💩💩ing I did June 5 2008 was on the Lakers."

Obviously, he couldn't get his story straight. Maybe someday the truth will leak out.

OOPS!

In a January 2007 game between the NBA's Boston Celtics and Indiana Pacers, a referee blew a whistle late in the game, stopping the clock for a while. Any shot wouldn't count, but Tony Allen went for it anyway. He headed up for a slam dunk, and, with nobody guarding him, missed entirely. Adding injury to insult: He landed poorly and tore two muscles in his left knee. Allen had to sit out the rest of the season, missing 48 games.

Speed demons: Sloths can swim three times faster than they walk.

THE ICEMAN KILLETH

The Simpsons *has made fun of almost every aspect of daily life, including video games. Bart is a big gamer, and over 30 years, viewers have seen him (and other characters) playing games on home consoles and at the arcade. Here are the titles of those fake games from the show.*

Super Slugfest

Escape from Grandma's House

Touch of Death

Larry the Looter

Escape from Death Row

My Dinner with Andre

Panamanian Strongman

Bonestorm

Kevin Costner's Waterworld

Cat Fight

Dash Dingo

Virtual Doctor

Sim Sandwich

Yard Work Simulator

Billy Graham's Bible Blaster

Hockey Dad

Rocky III vs. Clara Peller

Earthland Realms

Let's Make a Baby

Astro Blast

Bowling 2000

Triangle Wars

Death Kill City II: Death Kill Stories

Word Jammers

Low-Blow Boxing

Kick the Can

Fruit Shoot

The Iceman Killeth

Tandem Bike Ride with Your Mum

Stickball

Waltz Waltz Revolution

Bar Brawl 4: Final Fracas

Halloween Hit & Run

Cereal Killer

Guts of War II: Entrails of Intestinox

Disembowler IV

Pack Rat

Pack Rat Returns

Devil's Advocate

Nuke Canada

Assassins Creed: Summer of Love

Grand Theft Walrus II

BabyBlast

Marching Band

Built in 1945, ENIAC, the first electronic computer, performed more mathematical calculations over the next decade than all of humanity had up to that point.

HUMAN GUINEA PIGS

On page 111, we told you the grizzly story of how Dr. William Beaumont used his patient, Alexis St. Martin, as a human lab rat. Here are some other people who were the subject of experiments...including one doctor who experimented on himself.

GUINEA PIG: August Hildebrandt, the lab assistant of a German surgeon named August Bier

Experiment: Test the effectiveness of the world's first spinal block anesthesia

Details: Dr. Bier was the surgeon who, in 1898, came up with the idea of injecting cocaine—which has medicinal use as a numbing agent—directly into the spinal column as a means of providing local anesthesia to people who could not tolerate general anesthesia. Bier first tried his theory on six patients, and it worked: the patients felt no pain during their surgeries. But after the procedures were completed, some of the patients complained of side effects such as severe headaches and vomiting, in some cases recurring for a week after surgery. To get a better understanding of why this was happening, Bier wrote, "I decided to perform some investigations on my own body."

That was the plan...but when Bier's assistant, Dr. August Hildebrandt, inserted the needle into Bier's spine, he realized too late that the needle did not fit properly onto the syringe. Result: Most of the cocaine spilled out of the needle, along with quite a bit of Bier's cerebrospinal fluid. "Because of the considerable loss of cerebrospinal fluid, I postponed repetition of the procedure on me until a later occasion," Bier later recalled, "but Dr. Hildebrandt immediately offered to have the same study performed on himself without delay." So Bier injected Hildebrandt instead.

When Hildebrandt became numb below the waist, Bier tested the extent of the numbness with a series of painful stimuli, including pushing a long needle through the flesh in Hildebrandt's thigh and into the bone, "pinching the skin severely and seizing and crushing it in toothed forceps," burning his legs with a lit cigar, yanking out a tuft of his pubic hair, giving him "a strong blow to the shin with an iron hammer," and "strong pressure and traction on the testicles." In each case, Hildebrandt felt mild pressure or, with the cigar burns, a sensation of warmth, but in all cases, he felt no pain.

Aftermath: Both men felt well enough that evening to celebrate with wine and cigars, but the following morning Bier experienced dizziness and a headache, something he attributed to the loss of cerebrospinal fluid. He took to his bed for nine days until the symptoms abated. Hildebrandt complained of headaches and nausea for the next four days and "a mild feeling of weakness that lasted another 2–3 weeks." But they weren't able to do much about these symptoms—and more than a century later, headaches are

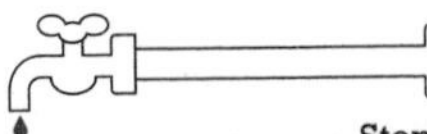

Stephen Hawking's ashes were interred between the graves of Isaac Newton and Charles Darwin in Westminster Abbey's "Scientists' Corner."

still the most common problem following spinal anesthesia and are still attributed to the loss of cerebrospinal fluid.

GUINEA PIG: Werner Forssmann, 25, a newly minted graduate of the University of Berlin's medical school in 1929

Experiment: Test whether a catheter can be threaded through a vein in the arm all the way into the heart

Details: In the late 1920s, the idea that doctors could perform procedures on a heart without opening up the chest was thought to be absurd—the stuff of fantasy. Trying to thread a catheter through an artery or vein into the heart, it was feared, would interfere with heart function and possibly kill the patient. But Dr. Forssmann had seen a photo in a book that showed a similar procedure being performed on a horse, and he didn't see any reason why it wouldn't also work on humans. When he asked for permission to test his idea on a patient, his superiors—understandably—told him no. They forbade Forssmann from attempting the procedure under any circumstances.

Undaunted, the brash young upstart decided to disobey orders and try the procedure on himself. Only problem: Forssmann was so new at the hospital and so low in status that he didn't have access to the locked cabinet where the catheters were stored. So he enlisted the help of a nurse named Gerda Ditzen, who *did* have access to the catheters. But perhaps because she feared for the life of the brand-new doctor, Ditzen insisted that Forssmann perform the procedure on her instead of himself.

Forssmann pretended to agree and strapped Ditzen down on a gurney and went through the motions of preparing her arm for catheterization. Only then did Ditzen look over and see Forssmann inserting the catheter into the crook of his own arm. After feeding it a foot and a half into the vein toward his heart, Forssmann released Ditzen from the gurney and the two of them made their way down the stairs to an X-ray room where they used a fluoroscope (an early type of X-ray imaging device) to check whether the catheter had indeed gone all the way into Forssmann's heart. It was *nearly* there, but not quite, so Forssmann pushed the catheter a few inches further in, about two feet in total, until it entered the right auricle. It was in! And just as Forssmann had hoped, the procedure didn't kill him. He later published his findings in a medical journal.

Aftermath: It's understandable that someone as willful and disobedient as Forssmann might continue to have problems with authority. That certainly was the case: after several more conflicts with his superiors and being fired from more than one job, Forssmann abandoned cardiology in favor of urology, a field in which his reputation as a troublemaker was not as well known. During World War II, he was a member of the Nazi party and served as a medical officer for the German military until he was captured by the Allies and interned in an American P.O.W. camp. After the war, he worked as a lumberjack in the Black Forest for several years before returning to urology.

Nearly half of all phone calls that Americans receive each year are robocalls.

Forssmann was still practicing medicine in 1956 when, one evening after work, he was sitting in a tavern enjoying a beer and his wife called the tavern to tell him that someone with a foreign accent had telephoned the house wanting to speak to him. The call sounded important, his wife explained. But it didn't sound important enough to pull Forssmann away from his beer, and he ignored another similar call after he got home. It wasn't until he got to work the following morning that he realized what the calls were about. They had come from Sweden, where he had just been awarded the Nobel Prize for Medicine for his catheter experiment on himself 27 years earlier. Forssmann shared the award with two other doctors, Andre Frederic Cournand and Dickinson W. Richards, who had read his paper in the medical journal and developed his technique further.

GUINEA PIGS: Robert Shafran, Edward Galland, and David Kellman

Experiment: A "nature vs. nurture" study designed to explore whether heredity or environment plays the bigger role in a person's social development

Details: It sounds crazy today, but when twins were put up for adoption in the 1950s and early 1960s, it was the policy of some adoption agencies to separate them and place them in different homes. The thinking was that if the twins were separated, "early mothering would be less burdened and divided, and [each] child's developing individuality would be facilitated," as a psychiatrist named Dr. Viola Bernard put it.

Separation was the policy of a New York City adoption agency called Louise Wise Services, and in the early 1960s, Peter Neubauer, a prominent child psychiatrist, decided to make use of separated identical twins—and in one case, identical triplets—to study which element played a bigger role in the development of the siblings' personalities: genetics (nature) or family environment (nurture).

Neubauer's study was a carefully guarded secret. And as with all closed adoptions in the 1960s, none of the adoptive families were told whether their child had siblings. Though researchers visited the adoptive homes of the separated twins and triplets every couple of months to observe how the children were developing, the parents were told that the study involved *all* children placed in adoptive homes, not just separated identical twins and triplets, in order to prevent the parents from learning the truth. The researchers visited the children regularly for nearly 20 years, and in all that time they never let slip to any of the families that their adopted child had an identical sibling.

The study might still be a secret today were it not for the fact that in the fall of 1980, a 19-year-old man named Robert Shafran arrived at Sullivan County Community College in Loch Sheldrake, New York, to start college and was startled to discover that many people he'd never met before seemed to recognize him, except that they knew him as someone named Eddy Galland. Shafran soon discovered that Galland was his identical sibling, and that the two had been separated before

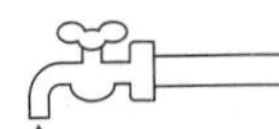

NASA briefly considered sending Big Bird (actor Caroll Spinney, in costume) into space aboard the space shuttle *Challenger*.

being placed with adoptive parents. News coverage of the reunited twins caught the attention of a third adopted 19-year-old named David Kellman, who looked just like Robert and Eddy. He was their identical sibling as well—they were the triplets in Neubauer's study.

When the boys' adoptive parents confronted Louise Wise Services and demanded to know why they hadn't been told about the other siblings, the agency explained their policy of separating twins and triplets and the rationale behind it, but they made no mention of Neubauer's secret study. Another 15 years passed before Lawrence Wright, a reporter for the *New Yorker* magazine, finally uncovered the study in 1995 and revealed to Shafran and Kellman that they and their brother Edward Galland had been a part of it.

Aftermath: As of 2020, the study still has not been published, though no reason has been given as to why. In fact, there's no guarantee that it ever will be published: Neubauer died in 2008, and his research records have been sealed until 2065. Following the release of a 2018 documentary about Shafran, Galland, and Kellman that generated negative publicity for the keepers of Neubauer's records, some of them were released to the brothers. Others have been released to a few sets of identical twins who, like the triplets, had managed only by chance to discover that their siblings existed. In each case, the records that were released were heavily redacted and inconclusive, shedding little light on Neubauer's study.

Shafran, Galland, and Kellman all struggled with mental illness in their teenage years, and in 1995, when they were in their mid-30s, Eddy Galland committed suicide. At least two other siblings who were part of the study committed suicide as well. Some of the biological mothers are known to have had a history of mental illness, including the mother of Shafran, Galland, and Kellman, raising the possibility that what Neubauer was really studying was whether identical siblings put up for adoption by mentally ill mothers would also develop mental illness. But since the study has never been published, it's impossible to know for sure. At least 13 sets of identical twins were used in the study; there may have been more. As of 2020, it's believed that at least four sets of twins still have no idea that they *are* twins, and that their identical siblings are, hopefully, still out there somewhere, waiting to be discovered.

* * *

RANDOM ORIGIN

In the 1970s, NBA player Fred Carter added a variation to the high-five: instead of slapping with an open hand, he gave a gentle tap with his closed hand. He shared this greeting with players on several teams (he got around) and has since been credited as the man who popularized the fist bump.

No pepper? The Palacio del Sal is a 16-room hotel in Bolivia that's made entirely of salt (including all the tables, chairs, and beds).

THEY DON'T BUILD THEM LIKE THEY USED TO

One of the fun things about visiting, or, if you're lucky enough, living in a really old house is that you get to see features that aren't included in new homes anymore. Here are some you may have wondered about.

COAL CHUTES: As late as the 1940s, when most people in colder parts of the country heated their homes with coal, a fuel that was similar in consistency to rocks and gravel, a home might go through a ton or more of it over the course of a long winter. To make delivering and dealing with the dirty fuel a little bit easier, homes were built with a chute or slide that made it possible to deliver the coal straight from the coal truck down to the furnace in the basement. The top of the chute was at ground level and accessed via a small iron door built into an exterior wall of the house. The coal delivery person opened the door and shoveled coal from a wheelbarrow into the chute; it slid down the chute into a coal bin in the basement that sat alongside the furnace. Many furnaces had electric conveyor devices that fed the coal from the chute into the furnace automatically. (If not, it had to be shoveled into a stove or a furnace by hand.) Coal furnaces and coal chutes are no longer being used, but if you look at some older homes carefully, you can still find abandoned coal chute doors, near the driveway, just above ground level.

DUMBWAITERS: A dumbwaiter is basically a miniature freight elevator used to move heavy and bulky items, like firewood, food, and laundry, from one floor to another in a multistory home without having to carry them up and down the stairs. They were especially useful in homes where the kitchen was in the basement and the dining room was on the main floor. The dumbwaiter sat inside its own vertical elevator shaft inside the wall and was pulled up and down using ropes on a pulley. It was big enough for a small child to climb into, which made them dangerous, and the shaft itself provided an easy path for a house fire to spread quickly from one floor to another. These problems, plus changing trends in architectural design—which moved kitchens out of the basement and onto the main floor, adjacent to the dining room—caused them to fade from popularity. (Another popular feature in multistory homes: a laundry chute built into the wall, often in bathrooms, that let people drop their dirty laundry straight down into the basement, where the washer and dryer were located.)

DUTCH DOOR: A Dutch door is a door that's divided into two parts so that the top half of the door and the bottom half can open and close independently of each other. The doors go in and out of fashion today, but in the days when most people lived on farms

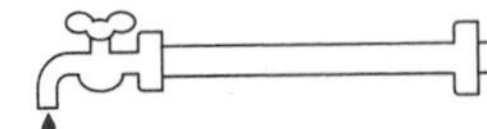

and were surrounded by animals, they were more of a necessity: they enabled residents to open the top half of the door to let in air and sunshine, while keeping the bottom half closed to prevent farm animals from getting in and small children from getting out.

PHONE NICHES: In the early 1900s, telephones were heavier and bulkier than they are today. Telephone service wasn't cheap, and the phones themselves were symbols of the owner's affluence. For all these reasons, phone niches were popular. A niche was a recessed area built into a wall that provided a place to put, and in many cases to show off, the homeowner's telephone. In the days when homes had just one phone, the niche was often in the front hallway or in a parlor or living room where anyone could use it. As telephones got smaller, lighter, more portable, eventually cordless, and so cheap that almost anyone could afford telephone service, the niches lost their purpose and went out of style.

PITTSBURGH POTTY: Uncle John remembers visiting an old house years ago that had a toilet in the basement that sat out in the open next to a crude shower. He never knew what they were for, until now: Popular in industrial towns like Pittsburgh, these crude, unfinished bathrooms provided miners, steelworkers, and people employed in other dirty jobs a place to get cleaned up without tracking dirt and grime upstairs into the rest of the house.

COFFIN CORNERS: Many Victorian and other large old houses have a staircase that rises to a landing and then changes direction before continuing to the second floor, and many of those stairwells have a recessed niche built into the wall at the landing. These niches are called "coffin corners." According to popular legend, they were put there for a practical reason: in the late 1800s and early 1900s when these homes were built, it was much more common for people to die at home, often in an upstairs bedroom, and for the funeral to be held in the downstairs parlor. The custom in those days, at least according to the story, was to carry an empty coffin up the stairs and into the bedroom where the person had died, load them into the coffin, then carry the coffin back downstairs and set it up in the parlor where the funeral would be held.

If you've ever tried to carry a coffin-sized piece of furniture up a flight of stairs that changes direction halfway up, you can understand why it might make sense to build a recess into the landing to make it a little easier to turn it around and carry it the rest of the way up the stairs. For decades people have looked at these niches and assumed that's what they were for, hence the name "coffin corner."

Alas, architectural historians assure us, the story is a myth. And while coffin corners might have occasionally come in handy when carrying extremely bulky items like mattresses, couches, and even a coffin or two down the stairs, the niches are purely for decorative purposes. They gave the homeowner a place to hang a painting, display a vase filled with flowers, or do something else to beautify that spot. That's it.

From 1925 to 1934, French automaker Citroën paid to advertise down one whole side of the Eiffel Tower using 250,000 lights.

PHANTONYMS

A phantonym (a combination of phantom + antonym) is a word whose definition you think you know...but it actually means something completely different. Like these.

ENORMITY
Sounds like: Implies largeness
But it means: Monstrously immoral

DISINTERESTED
Sounds like: Uninterested, bored
But it means: Unbiased, impartial

BEMUSED
Sounds like: Amused
But it means: Confused

FULSOME
Sounds like: Full
But it means: Abundant, or abundant to the point of excess

INFLAMMABLE
Sounds like: Flame-retardant
But it means: Something that is likely to catch fire

ENERVATED
Sounds like: Energized
But it means: Weakened

FORTUITOUS
Sounds like: Lucky
But it means: Accidental

NIGGARDLY
Sounds like: A racial epithet
But it means: Stingy

NONPLUSSED
Sounds like: Unbothered
But it means: Bewildered

NOISOME
Sounds like: Noisy, loud
But it means: Having an offensive or noxious smell

SPENDTHRIFT
Sounds like: Someone who saves money
But it means: Someone who spends money carelessly

PENULTIMATE
Sounds like: Extremely ultimate, better than the best
But it means: Next to last

RESTIVE
Sounds like: Restful
But it means: Impatient

DEFENESTRATION
Sounds like: Something to do with defense or self-protection
But it means: Throwing an object or person out of a window

LACKADAY
Sounds like: Disinterested, lazy
But it means: Regretful

LUXURIANT
Sounds like: Luxurious
But it means: Abundant

CRAPULOUS
Sounds like: Terrible, of poor quality
But it means: Hungover

IRONIC, ISN'T IT?

Another dose of irony to put the problems of day-to-day life into proper perspective.

FROM NOTHING, IRONY: Perhaps the widest divide between people who believe in God and people who don't is how the universe began. Atheists and agnostics who favor science point to the big bang theory, which proposes that the universe began as a very small, dense ball of matter that exploded and is still expanding today. The big bang theory was introduced in 1927 by a Belgian physicist named Georges Lemaître, who also happened to be a Catholic priest.

HARD-HITTING IRONY: In the 1980s, in an effort to reduce head injuries, the National Football League began making helmets out of stronger, heavier materials with more padding inside, along with stronger face masks. According to a study by the American Medical Association, the improved helmets did make it safer to get hit, but they also led to an increase in players using their helmeted heads "as the primary point of contact in blocking [and] tackling," which led to an increase in spinal injuries and concussions.

IRONY UNDER THE INFLUENCE

- A drunk driver "weaving all over the place" in Berkeley, California, one night in 2019 was arrested by California Highway Patrol. The arrest made news because of the electric sign on top of the man's car that read "I should probably get a ride home" and "Buzzed driving is drunk driving." (The National Highway Traffic Safety Administration has a program that pays drivers to carry these rolling public service announcements, though they prefer the drivers to be sober while displaying them.)
- A drunk driver was speeding on a Colleyville, Texas, road late one night in 2014 when he hit another car and flipped over. His SUV then skidded across a parking lot and crashed through a brick wall before finally coming to rest inside Lone Star Collision Repair.

MAKING AMERICA IRONIC AGAIN: Before becoming president, Donald Trump was involved in more than 3,500 lawsuits—a sizable portion of which involved people suing him for failing to pay for goods and services. The plaintiffs included former business associates, independent contractors, resort employees, and later on, several law firms that Trump had hired to represent him in those lack-of-payment suits... which were now also suing him for lack of payment.

Cats show you their rear end to communicate that they're comfortable around you. They're saying, "Have a sniff."

THY NAME IS IRONY: In December 2019, Diana Ortiz met a friend at a bar in the Upper East Side of Manhattan. After drinking only one beer (as she claimed in her lawsuit), Ortiz went to the restroom, which was located at the bottom of a ten-step stairwell, which the lawsuit described as "dangerous, defective, hazardous, unsafe, uneven, broken, worn, poorly maintained, dilapidated, inadequately illuminated and slippery." As Ortiz told the *New York Post*, "Between the second and third step, I just fell down the stairs," which led to "excruciating back and knee pain" (and the lawsuit). The name of the bar: the Stumble Inn.

IRONIC ROLE REVERSAL: Two sisters from Toronto—Jyoti and Kiran Matharoo, known in the tabloids as the "Canadian Kardashians"—made international headlines in 2017 after they were arrested for setting up an internet scam designed to extort money from a Nigerian billionaire.

IRONIK, ISN'T HE? In 2010, a 22-year-old British rapper named James Charters was returning from a gig when two muggers robbed him of his jewelry. In the fracas, according to the BBC, he received a "knife wound to the buttock," which is somewhat ironic, considering that Charters was a vocal anti-knife campaigner. Also ironic: His rapper name was DJ Ironik. He later shortened it—now it's just Ironik.

IRONY DOESN'T DISCRIMINATE: In January 2020, Sauntore Thomas, 44, of Detroit, Michigan, won a lawsuit against a former employer for discriminating against him because he's African American. After Thomas received his sizable settlement check, he tried to deposit it at his bank, where he'd had an account for two years. But the white employees refused to accept the check, believing it to be fraudulent, and called the police. Thomas had to get his lawyer on the phone to convince them that the settlement check was legitimate. He later filed a suit against the bank for racial discrimination.

UNIDENTIFIED FLYING IRONY

- Named after the Greek god of wind, the European Space Agency's *Aeolus* satellite was designed to make wind forecasting much more accurate. After 16 years of development and delays, the project (which was supposed to take only five years) was finally ready to lift off in August 2018. But the launch had to be postponed a day. Reason: It was too windy.
- Despite numerous claims to the contrary, there has *never* been a documented case of a flying saucer from Mars landing on Earth. In 2012, however, when NASA's *Curiosity* rover was making its final descent to the Martian surface, its flat, round, saucer-shaped heat shield fell off, thus becoming the first documented case of a flying saucer landing on another planet.

THE WASHINGTON R*DSK*NS

By the time you're reading this, Washington's football team will probably have a new name. For now, it's simply called...the Washington Football Team. How did it come to this? Here's the controversial history of one of the NFL's most revered franchises.

CANCEL CULTURE

Change was in the air in the summer of 2020. In the midst of nationwide demonstrations for racial justice and equality, a bevy of brands bade goodbye to outdated stereotypes like Aunt Jemima, Uncle Ben, and Mia (the Land O' Lakes girl). All over the country, statues of Confederate leaders and Christopher Columbus were taken down—some by protesters, some by the municipalities in which they stood. In Washington, D.C., outside the abandoned RFK Stadium, workers removed a statue of George P. Marshall, the home team's controversial founding owner. All of a sudden, it was looking like the impossible might actually happen: The Washington R*dsk*ns might finally change their name.

"We'll never change the name, it's that simple. NEVER—you can use caps," team owner Daniel Snyder famously said to *USA Today* in 2013. That was shortly after Snyder received a letter from members of the Congressional Native American Caucus, including Tom Cole (R-Oklahoma) and Betty McCollum (D-Minnesota), who pleaded with Snyder to change the name: "Native Americans throughout the country consider the R-word a racial, derogatory slur akin to the N-word among African Americans." [Editor's note: That's why we've added the asterisks.]

LIFELONG FANS

After the *USA Today* interview, Snyder was called to a meeting with NFL commissioner Roger Goodell, who asked Snyder to reconsider. He wouldn't budge. The notoriously stubborn owner was only 34 years old when he purchased the team from previous owner Jack Kent Cooke's estate in 1998. "My father took me to my first game in 1971," boasted Snyder, "and I fell in love with the R*dsk*ns and the NFL right then. I was hooked. And we didn't even win that game."

Another lifelong Washington fan is Chief Billy Redwing Tayac of the Piscataway Indian Nation, who has long maintained that the name "is a racist term." Like Snyder, Tayac grew up in the D.C. area and had also been attending home games since the '70s. That's when Native Americans—often in traditional dress—began protesting outside the stadium every Sunday. Chief Tayac joined the effort in 1985 and became its most visible member. As he often pointed out, his Piscataway ancestors had occupied the area for thousands of years before it got an NFL team. "The term has only continued to be acceptable because Native people have been

**Classic riddle: Q: What has the eyes of a cat, the fur of a cat, and the paws of a cat, but isn't a cat?
A: A kitten.**

decimated and don't have the political or economic clout to stop it," Tayac said in 1998, a year after the team moved a few miles outside of D.C. into Jack Kent Cooke Stadium in Landover, Maryland. In 1999, after Snyder took over, FedEx bought the naming rights for $7.6 million per year. The R*dsk*ns' home became FedExField. And the protesters showed up there, too.

THE MARSHALL PLAN

Snyder, just like Cooke before him, argued that "R*dsk*ns" can't be racist because it was named by "an actual Indian." According to team lore, when the franchise was still in Boston in 1933, the head coach—a Sioux named William "Lone Star" Dietz—changed the name from the Braves. That was the story Marshall told, but the truth is that Marshall changed it himself to avoid confusion with the Boston Braves baseball team. He wanted to keep the Native connection, though, so he went with another word that people used to describe American Indians. (Interestingly, Dietz wasn't even Native American; he only said he was to avoid the World War I draft, and was jailed for it in 1920.)

When the franchise arrived in Washington in 1937, it became the league's southernmost team. Marshall's plan was to help turn the fledgling NFL into the same kind of entertainment package that college football had become—complete with marching bands, halftime shows, cheerleaders, and fight songs. And he really pushed the Native imagery: "Besides my coach [Dietz]," Marshall boasted, "I've got half a dozen Indian players signed up, and I'm going to have them wearing Indian war bonnets, and blankets, and everything."

WHAT THE HAIL?

Snyder often referenced his team's famous fight song in defense of the name: "We don't say, 'Hurt anybody'...We sing, 'Hail to the R*dsk*ns. Hail victory. Braves on the warpath. Fight for old D.C.' We only sing it when we score touchdowns." (So, not a lot, then.) The lyrics were written by George Marshall's wife. Here's the original second verse:

Scalp 'um, swamp 'um, we will
Take 'um big score.
Read 'um, weep 'um, touchdown,
We want heap more.

At home games in Washington (a city located near the northern boundary of the Confederate South), the lyric "Fight for old D.C." was often replaced with "Fight for old Dixie." Marshall, an outspoken segregationist, was the last NFL owner to integrate his team, and he only did so after Congress refused to let him build a new stadium in Washington in 1961 unless he signed black players. His response: "We'll start signing Negroes when the Harlem Globetrotters start signing whites." In 1961, after

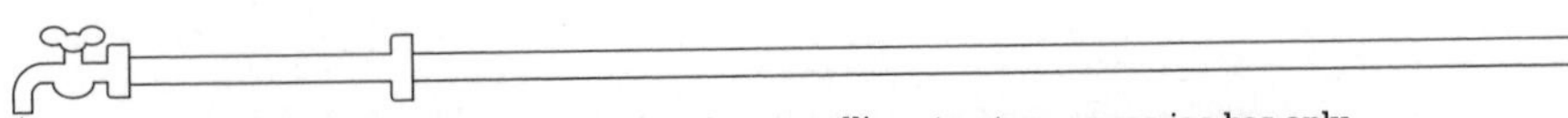

Ice can't incorporate salt into its crystalline structure, so sea ice has only a tenth the amount of salt as seawater. Melt it, and you can drink it.

a debilitating stroke, Marshall sold the team to Cooke; in 1963, he was inducted into the NFL Hall of Fame.

As the civil rights movement gained steam in the mid-1960s, and African Americans had proven that organized activism could bring them new rights and protections, American Indian activists felt more emboldened to air their grievances as well: Europeans had driven them from their homelands; federal, state, and local governments had broken nearly every treaty; and Native people had become relegated to the fringes of society. Most white people knew "Injuns" only as caricatures in films and on television...and as sports mascots.

THE MAN ON THE HELMET

In 1972, Walter "Blackie" Wetzel, a member of the Blackfeet tribe in Montana and president of the National Congress of American Indians, led a delegation to D.C. to officially demand the name be changed. Cooke said no. Seeking a compromise, Wetzel convinced the team to let him design a new logo for the helmet, which, at the time, was a burgundy "R" in a white circle surrounded by gold. Wetzel replaced the "R" with the profile of an American Indian, based on the Buffalo nickel. The image on the nickel was actually a composite of several Indians, one of which was a Blackfeet chief named John Two Guns White Calf, and it's White Calf's profile that became the R*dsk*ns logo.

The second verse of the fight song was toned down from "Scalp 'um, swamp 'um, we will" to "run and pass and score."

Wetzel got the team to make a few other small but significant changes: The miniskirted cheerleaders no longer had to wear braids and feathers (but they were still called the R*dsk*nettes, or as some fans would later call them, the "Pocahotties"). And the second verse of the fight song was toned down from "Scalp 'um, swamp 'um, we will" to "run and pass and score." But the team's name remained intact.

MOUNTING PRESSURE

As the years passed, the protests ramped up. When Washington went to Super Bowl XXVI in January 1992, the American Indian Movement organized a rally of more than 2,000 people who demonstrated outside the Metrodome in Minneapolis. "The fact that a football team in the nation's capital could be named the R*dsk*ns in this day and age shows how pathetically ignorant this country is," Charlene Teters of the Spokane Indian nation told the *Philadelphia Daily News.* "I've had some tell me the team is honoring the Indian people by using that name. I said there are better ways to honor the Indian people."

"I like the name, and it's not a derogatory name," Cooke said in response to the protests. "To me, the name represents pride, courage, adventure, derring-do, and bravery." After Snyder took over, he toed the same line, saying, "The name really

Secretariat won horse racing's Triple Crown in 1973
and set speed records in all three races that remain unbroken today.

means honor, respect." He even had "scientific proof": In 2004, the NFL hired a private firm to conduct a phone poll that asked Native Americans what they thought about the name. According to a statement released by Snyder himself, "The highly respected Annenberg Public Policy Center polled nearly 1,000 self-identified Native Americans from across the continental U.S. and found that 90% of Native Americans did not find the team name...to be 'offensive.'"

THE R-WORD

But was it offensive? Apologists often justify use of the word by insisting that it was actually coined by Native Americans, and there is some scholarly debate over whether that's true. But regardless of who started using it, by the mid-19th century, there was little doubt as to its intended meaning. For example, this announcement ran in Minnesota's *Winona Daily Republican* in 1863:

> The State reward for dead Indians has been increased to $200 for every r*d-sk*n sent to Purgatory. The sum is more than the dead bodies of all the Indians east of the Red River are worth.

Merriam-Webster defines it as "a contemptuous term used to refer to a North American Indian." (There's no second definition mentioning "honor, respect.") Chief Tayac explained it like this: "Just like the hide of a deer is called a 'deerskin,' and the hide of a beaver is called a 'beaverskin,' the scalp of an Indian was called a 'r*dsk*n.'... People want to see us riding horses and living in tepees, but Indians are modern people and we want the same respect that has been applied to other peoples. We are men and women—not animals."

FULL COURT PRESS

A decades-long legal battle ensued in 1992 when Chief Tayac and other activists filed a lawsuit claiming that the federal government cannot protect a trademark if said trademark is a racial slur. The team's lawyers countered that the term is synonymous with "Indian," therefore it is neutral. The case went all the way to the Supreme Court... which the Washington franchise finally won on First Amendment grounds in 2017.

Yet even as Snyder held firm—despite heartfelt pleas from friends, family, and several other team owners—most other teams with that name had ditched it. In the 2013 letter sent to Snyder by the Congressional Native American Caucus, the lawmakers cited the fact that "28 schools in 18 states have dropped that name in the last 25 years." When Miami University switched to RedHawks in 1997, Washington's NFL franchise became the last major U.S. sports team to be called the R-word.

PUBLIC RELATIONS

Feeling the heat, Snyder hired a PR firm to run interference. In 2014, he announced the formation of the "Washington R*dsk*ns Original Americans Foundation."

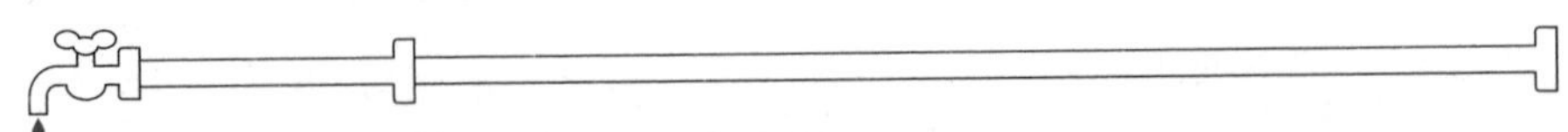

Although the foundation was supposed to "provide meaningful and measurable resources that provide genuine opportunities for tribal communities," *Sports Illustrated* reported in 2020 that Snyder had "cut back his support when public scrutiny waned following the resolution of a lawsuit over the team's trademark." The PR firm also launched a website dedicated to defending the team's name: "It epitomizes all the noble qualities we admire about Native Americans—the same intangibles we expect from Washington's gridiron heroes on game day. Honor. Loyalty. Unity. Respect. Courage."

But Snyder's most effective PR boost came from his hometown newspaper. In 2016, the *Washington Post* conducted a phone poll that resulted in the same "90% Indian approval rating" as the 2004 NFL poll. As the *Post* reported, "The results—immediately celebrated by team owner Daniel Snyder and denounced by prominent Native American leaders—could make it that much harder for anti-name activists to pressure [team] officials, who are already using the poll as further justification to retain the moniker."

FLAWED METHODOLOGY

In response to the *Washington Post* poll, writer and activist Jacqueline Keeler wrote in *The Nation*, "Given that I have 50 first cousins who are enrolled in the Navajo and Yankton Dakota Sioux Nations, none of whom likes the team name, I found the results to be curious. When I looked more closely at the methodology of the poll, I was appalled." Among the flaws Keeler notes: The pollsters asked even fewer "self-identified Native Americans" than the 2004 study had. More than half of those polled couldn't even name what tribe or nation they belong to. "Imagine asking 500 white Americans for an opinion about Europe," she wrote, "and not caring that more than half had no connection to their ancestors' place of origin."

In February 2020, a new study, this one conducted by the University of California–Berkeley, concluded that "57% who strongly identify with being Native American and 67% of those who frequently engage in tribal cultural practices were found to be deeply insulted by caricatures of Native American culture." The study mentioned other personal fouls from the sports world, but the carefully worded conclusion made sure to include "especially the R*dsk*ns."

FOURTH DOWN

By the late 2010s, the team name controversy wasn't even Snyder's worst problem. During his tenure as owner, the R*dsk*ns had gone from Super Bowl contender to perennial bottom-dweller, and most fans blamed him. Amid numerous front-office and player scandals (not to mention some disastrous player trades), in 2019, Snyder was mocked in the press and on social media for flaunting his $2.6 billion wealth by purchasing a $100 million "superyacht" with an IMAX theater.

By this point, the sponsors were jumping ship. Nike's "Salute to Service" gear

Why are the eyes of many albino animals red? Their irises lack pigment and are thus transparent, allowing the blood vessels in their retinas to be visible.

included every NFL team's name...except for the one that more and more news outlets were awkwardly referring to as "the Washington Football Team." Meanwhile, legislators were threatening to deny Snyder permission to build a new stadium in Washington if the team still had that name. He *still* wouldn't budge.

Elsewhere in the sports world, after mounting pressure, in 2019, the MLB's Cleveland Indians retired their cartoonish mascot, Chief Wahoo. Not long after, the MLB's Atlanta Braves and NFL's Kansas City Chiefs announced they would be phasing out the "Tomahawk Chop," a chopping motion popular with fans that has been criticized for reinforcing the stereotype that American Indians are savages.

SNYDER'S LAST STAND

It all came crashing down in the summer of 2020 when the calls to change the name reached a fever pitch. The *Washington Post,* only four years after its controversial phone poll, ran an op-ed titled "Change the name of the Washington NFL team. Now." But Snyder held firm. If he could ride out this latest storm, as he had all the others, then the calls for change would most certainly die down again.

Then, in mid-July, the *New York Times* reported that Snyder had decided to review the team's name. What changed his mind? The stadium's sponsor, FedEx, had threatened to "back out of an $8 million naming rights deal unless the team's name was changed." A few days later, the change was made official. The name was gone. (So was the logo, which upset some supporters of the name change.)

Chief Tayac, now 80, was thrilled. When asked by ABC News why he thought Snyder finally relented, he said it wasn't because the owner suddenly grew a conscience. "Money talks...He realizes that he's fighting a losing battle. And that's the bottom line."

Despite continuing demands (from both inside and outside the franchise) for Snyder to step down, he was still Washington's majority owner as of this writing. When his nameless team took to the field in 2020, they were still wearing their familiar burgundy-and-gold uniforms, but the man on the helmet had been replaced with the player's number, and the once-ubiquitous R-word was nowhere to be seen.

* * *

LITERATURE QUIZ

Q: What famous book (and later movie) character is named Oscar Zoroaster Phadrig Isaac Norman Henkle Emmannuel Ambroise Diggs?

A: The Wizard of Oz. In L. Frank Baum's fourth Oz book, *Dorothy and the Wizard in Oz* (1908), the wizard explains why he goes by that name: "When I grew up I just called myself O.Z., because the other initials were P-I-N-H-E-A-D; and that spelled 'pinhead,' which was a reflection on my intelligence."

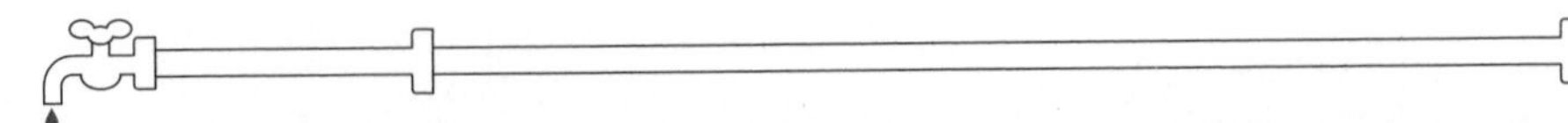

Sharks are buoyant thanks to their big livers, which are filled with oils and fats that are lighter than water.

MAN VS. BUG

Sometimes, the smaller your target, the bigger the collateral damage.

YARD LIFT: "My wife complained that there were a lot of roaches invading our garden," said Cesar Schmitz. The 48-year-old truck driver from Enéas Marques, Brazil, sprayed some beetle killer into the nest, but that just made the cockroaches angry. Then, for good measure, he poured in a cap full of gasoline. Bad idea. Unbeknownst to Schmitz, methane gas from the cockroaches had gathered underground. A home security camera caught what happened next: As his two beagles stood nearby, Schmitz tossed a lit match into the hole and quickly scooted away. Just as he stepped onto the concrete patio—less than five feet from the hole—a subterranean explosion lifted most of the yard several feet off the ground. When the rocks, dirt, and lawn furniture settled, neither Schmitz nor his beagles were injured, but if they'd been a little closer, "It could have been fatal," he said. Also, the cockroaches were still there.

ZAP! BANG!

- An electric fly swatter is just like a tennis racket, with electrically charged strings. An unidentified man in Ilocos Norte, Philippines, was chasing a mosquito through his house when he finally zapped it...in the room where dozens of fireworks were being stored for an upcoming holiday. According to GMA News: "The dead insect fell on rocket fuses...setting off a small fire that eventually lit up the cache of pyrotechnics." The family escaped, but their house burned to the ground.
- An 80-year-old Frenchman (unnamed in press reports) didn't know that a gas canister was leaking in his kitchen. Had he known, he wouldn't have used his electric fly swatter to kill a fly. Had he not done that, the room wouldn't have ignited and burned the man's hand along with a significant portion of his house. But it did.

SLASH AND BURN: In August 2018, three men in Washington state tried (allegedly) to poach a protected big leaf maple from Olympic National Forest. According to court reports, after the timber thieves found a particularly large and potentially lucrative tree, they weren't about to let a massive bee colony stop them from taking it. Working at night, they tried spraying it with wasp killer, but that didn't work. So they tried setting fire to the hive, but instead they set fire to the tree. Unable to extinguish the blaze with their water bottles, the thieves fled as the flames spread. By the time the fire was over, it had cost $4.5 million to extinguish, burned 3,300 acres of old-growth forests on federal and state land, and smothered Seattle in thick smoke for several days. After an investigation, two of the three men, Justin Wilke and Shawn Williams, were charged with a litany of federal crimes (though none for attempted bee-i-cide).

WOODEN'S WISDOM

UCLA men's basketball coach John Wooden (1910–2010) won 10 national titles and mentored hundreds of players with a motivational system he called the "Pyramid of Success." Here are some of his most potent thoughts on how to live a good life.

- "Nothing will work unless you do."
- "Whatever you do in life, surround yourself with smart people who'll argue with you."
- "Happiness begins where selfishness ends."
- "Be more concerned with your character than your reputation, because your character is what you really are, while your reputation is merely what others think you are."
- "If you don't have time to do it right, when will you have time to do it over?"
- "Don't let the peaks get too high and the valleys too low."
- "Don't let yesterday take up too much of today."
- "You are not a failure until you start blaming others for your mistakes."
- "Failure is not fatal, but failure to change might be."
- "You can't let praise or criticism get to you. It's a weakness to get caught up in either one."
- "It's what you learn after you know it all that counts."
- "Success comes from knowing that you did your best to become the best that you are capable of becoming."
- "It takes time to create excellence. If it could be done quickly, more people would do it."
- "Do not let what you cannot do interfere with what you can do."
- "Things turn out best for the people who make the best of the way things turn out."
- "Consider the rights of others before your own feelings, and the feelings of others before your own rights."
- "If you're not making mistakes, then you're not doing anything. A doer makes mistakes."
- "Seek opportunities to show you care. The smallest gestures often make the biggest difference."
- "You can do more good by being good than any other way."

Largest single structure constructed by living organisms: Australia's Great Barrier Reef. (It covers 134,634 square miles.)

THE LATE-NIGHT TV TIMELINE

Here's a history of what Americans have had playing on their TVs while they fell asleep over the last 70 years.

1950 NBC debuts *Broadway Open House*, the first late-night show to use the format that will become the industry standard—a little comedy, a variety of performers (musicians, comedians, dancers), and some lightweight chat. Jerry Lester and Morey Amsterdam alternate hosting duties until Amsterdam leaves. The show is canceled in late 1951.

1954 Innovative comedian Ernie Kovacs becomes one of television's first stars, appearing in shows of various formats that air at different times of the day, on all four networks. *The Ernie Kovacs Show* airs on the low-rated, cash-strapped DuMont Television Network from April 1954 to April 1955, shortly before the network ceases operations.

1954 NBC president Pat Weaver gives late night another shot with *Tonight Starring Steve Allen*, hosted and cocreated by comedian Steve Allen. He further cements the standard late-night format, focusing on celebrity interviews and comedy bits, including one he originates—the "man on the street" taped segment.

1957 Steve Allen departs the renamed *The Tonight Show* to focus on a Sunday night variety show to air against CBS's *The Ed Sullivan Show*, leaving the late-night slot open to the show's next host, Jack Paar.

1960 When NBC censors cut a risqué joke about "the W.C." (short for "water closet," or bathroom) without his knowledge, Paar quits—on the air—the following night and walks off the set. Sidekick Hugh Downs hosts the show for three weeks until NBC lures Paar back.

1962 Paar leaves, and Johnny Carson takes over as host of *The Tonight Show*. During his tenure (along with announcer Ed McMahon and original bandleader Skitch Henderson, with whom Carson frequently banters), the show becomes a must-watch show that destroys the competition for nearly 30 years.

1964 ABC offers an alternative to Carson's brand of breezy entertainment with the confrontational political affairs program *The Les Crane Show*. Hosted by a San Francisco radio host, the show flops. Within months, ABC renames it *Nightlife*, and dumps Crane and politics in favor of guest hosts and a *Tonight Show*–type format. That flops too. The show is canceled in late 1965.

The British royal family is distantly related to Vlad the Impaler, the inspiration for Bram Stoker's character Count Dracula.

1967 ABC tries again with *The Joey Bishop Show.* The talk show is hosted by the Rat Packer and his sidekick, Regis Philbin.

1967 The United Network becomes the fourth broadcast TV network, joining ABC, CBS, and NBC. The organization is troubled from the start and only manages to get one show on the air for the four weeks it broadcast in May 1967: the splashy and dazzling *The Las Vegas Show,* broadcast live from Sin City and starring comedian Bill Dana.

1969 Gregarious singer, songwriter, and game show host Merv Griffin hosts a daytime talk show on NBC from 1962 to 1963. He launches a syndicated version two years later, and then moves it to CBS's 11:30 p.m. slot in 1969. It's the Eye Network's first attempt to dethrone Carson, and its ratings are strong enough to force ABC's *The Joey Bishop Show* off the air…but it can't touch *The Tonight Show.* In 1972, CBS blinks and cancels *The Merv Griffin Show,* which returns to daytime syndication. CBS uses the time slot to air old movies until 1989.

1969 *The Dick Cavett Show* moves from prime time to late night on ABC. The show features in-depth conversations with serious guests, setting it apart from Carson's lighter celebrity interviews on *The Tonight Show,* with people like Noel Coward and Salvador Dalí stopping by instead of Bob Hope and Zsa Zsa Gabor. In 1971, writers and enemies Norman Mailer and Gore Vidal snipe at each other during an episode. It attracts a niche audience, and endures until 1975.

1973 NBC expands its late-night schedule, adding *Tomorrow* with Tom Snyder, airing weeknights at 1:00 a.m., after *The Tonight Show.*

1975 After Johnny Carson forces NBC to stop showing reruns of *The Tonight Show* on Saturday nights, the network hires a young Canadian variety show producer named Lorne Michaels to create a show for the weekly 11:30 p.m. to 1:00 a.m. time slot. He envisions a variety show, commonplace on TV at the time, but with rotating celebrity hosts, hipper musical guests, and edgy comic sketches. The show is called *NBC's Saturday Night,* later renamed *Saturday Night Live.*

1979 During the tense Iran hostage crisis in November, ABC airs a nightly roundup of all the day's developments opposite *The Tonight Show* in a show called *The Iran Crisis–America Held Hostage.* When the hostages are finally freed in 1981, ABC decides that the ratings were so good that they create a Monday-through-Thursday news show hosted by Ted Koppel called *Nightline.*

1980 ABC launches *Fridays,* a sketch comedy show to rival *Saturday Night Live,* except that it's not as popular with audiences and critics (and it airs on Friday nights instead of *Nightline*). It's notable for launching the careers of *Seinfeld* star Michael Richards and *Seinfeld* cocreator Larry David, but it sputters out by 1982.

In 1844, Samuel Morse let a friend's 17-year-old daughter select the first message sent by telegraph. She picked a Bible verse: "What hath God wrought?"

1980 As part of Carson's contract renewal with NBC (ABC tried to poach him during negotiations), he gets *The Tonight Show*'s running time reduced from 90 minutes to 60. To fill the time, *Tonight Show* lead-out *Tomorrow* moves up from 60 to 90 minutes and adds Rona Barrett as a gossip reporter. Host Tom Snyder hates the changes so much (he and Barrett even bicker on air) that he quits the show and *Tomorrow* is canceled by 1982.

1982 NBC allows Carson to determine who will host the show that follows *The Tonight Show.* He picks offbeat comedian David Letterman, who'd hosted a short-lived daytime show on NBC in 1980. Letterman brings an ironic sensibility to TV and introduces goofy segments that become late-night hallmarks, such as "Stupid Pet Tricks" and "The Top 10 List."

1983 Canadian actor and songwriter Alan Thicke (he wrote the theme songs for both *Diff'rent Strokes* and *The Facts of Life*) hosts a daytime talk show so successful in his native Canada that he gets to host a syndicated nighttime version in the United States called *Thicke of the Night.* The show features sketches performed by a cast of regulars, stand-up comedy, and music, but it gets crushed by Carson in the ratings. (TV milestone fun fact: Uncle John appeared on an episode of *Thicke of the Night.*)

1986 In 1983, comedian Joan Rivers was named Johnny Carson's permanent guest host on *The Tonight Show,* filling in a few nights a month during Carson's many vacations. In 1986, the brand-new Fox network hires Rivers to host its first-ever show: *The Late Show,* opposite *The Tonight Show.* Rivers takes the job without telling Carson, causing a rift that lasts until Carson's death in 2005. Very few Fox affiliates are in place at the time, and some refuse to carry it, fearing getting buried in the ratings by Carson. In May 1987, Fox fires Rivers and replaces her with rising comedian—and former *Thicke of the Night* regular—Arsenio Hall. Thirteen weeks later, Fox cancels *The Late Show* entirely.

1989 *The Arsenio Hall Show* debuts in syndication. It's the first show to significantly cut into Carson's dominance of the late-night ratings, pulling away scores of younger and non-white viewers.

1989 With Carson's tenure pushing 30 years, rumors of his impending retirement lead other TV networks to consider their late-night futures. CBS programs *The Pat Sajak Show,* starring the host of *Wheel of Fortune.* Debuting in January as a 90-minute show, it will be reduced to 60 minutes by October, and by early 1990, Friday shows will be guest-hosted...until CBS pulls the plug in April 1990.

1992 Johnny Carson retires, and NBC executives botch the handover of *The Tonight Show* to a new host. The network "promises" the show to both

Tonight's permanent guest host Jay Leno and *Late Night* host David Letterman, not wanting another network to poach either comedian. Leno ultimately gets the gig, and Letterman bolts from NBC.

1993 *The Late Show* with David Letterman premieres on CBS, airing head-to-head with NBC's *The Tonight Show.* For the first time in decades, another show consistently beats *The Tonight Show* in the ratings.

1993 Needing someone to fill the 12:30 a.m. late-night spot, NBC approaches comedians Dana Carvey and Garry Shandling, who both say no. *SNL* producer Lorne Michaels is tasked with finding a host, and he selects a former *SNL* writer named Conan O'Brien, who has no performing experience.

1993 With all the shake-ups and switch-ups in late night, Fox jumps back in again. After singer/actress Dolly Parton declines the job, *The Chevy Chase Show* debuts, featuring the *National Lampoon's Vacation* star and *Saturday Night Live* alum. It receives such a critical drubbing and poor ratings that it's canceled after just six weeks. It's the last late-night talk show Fox will produce.

1995 David Letterman asks *Tomorrow* host Tom Snyder to return to TV to host *The Late Late Show,* which follows *Late Show.*

1995 While Fox declines to participate in weeknight late night, this year it debuts an *SNL* competitor called *MADtv.* Branded after the long-running humor magazine, it runs until 2010.

1996 Debuting on Comedy Central this year is *The Daily Show,* a nightly parody of fluffy news shows like *Entertainment Tonight* and *Inside Edition.* It's hosted by ex-sportscaster Craig Kilborn.

1997 After four years on Comedy Central, *Politically Incorrect,* a panel discussion show hosted by comedian Bill Maher, jumps to ABC. A few days after the September 11 attacks in 2001, Maher makes some controversial comments (he says that the airplane hijackers were "not cowardly"), ratings decline, advertisers pull out, and ABC eventually cancels the show in 2002. A year later, Maher resurfaces with a similar show on HBO called *Real Time.*

1999 Tom Snyder retires, and Letterman's production company asks *SNL* star Norm Macdonald to replace him. CBS overrules Letterman and brings in Kilborn, leaving *The Daily Show* anchor chair empty. Jon Stewart, who'd auditioned for the job won by Conan O'Brien at NBC in 1993, and hosted his own talk show on MTV that year, wins the gig and turns the show into a sharp political and social satire program. Several *Daily Show* correspondents will go on to host their own shows, including Stephen Colbert, Samantha Bee, and John Oliver.

2003 ABC brings in another former Comedy Central star, Jimmy Kimmel (*Win*

Ben Stein's Money), to host a midnight show called *Jimmy Kimmel Live!* After a rocky start—the show's post–Super Bowl premiere episode featured an onstage bar, and guests and audience members got very intoxicated—it goes on to become ABC's first long-lasting late-night show.

2004 Hoping to avoid a repeat of the 1992 chaos in picking a successor to Johnny Carson, NBC tries to get ahead of the situation when Jay Leno decides to retire. As part of a contract renegotiation, NBC announces that *Late Night* host Conan O'Brien will move up to *The Tonight Show*...in 2009.

2005 After Craig Kilborn abruptly retires, CBS installs *The Drew Carey Show* cast member and Scottish stand-up comedian Craig Ferguson (and his sidekick, a robot named Geoff) as host of *The Late Late Show.*

2009 As scheduled, Jay Leno leaves *The Tonight Show* and Conan O'Brien takes over. But neither NBC nor Leno are quite ready for the host to leave. In hopes that another network won't sign Leno to a new talk show to compete with *Tonight,* NBC gives him *The Jay Leno Show,* a *Tonight*-style prime-time show airing at 10:00 p.m. five nights a week. That show proves a low-rated, critical flop, which hurts the ratings of *The Tonight Show* with Conan O'Brien. In January 2010, NBC suggests a plan to turn things around: cut *The Jay Leno Show* to 30 minutes and put it on at 11:30 p.m., thus moving O'Brien's *Tonight* to midnight. O'Brien refuses, NBC buys him out of his contract, and Leno is reinstalled as the host of *The Tonight Show.* (O'Brien, after entertaining offers from multiple outlets, starts hosting *Conan* on TBS in 2010.)

2014 Jay Leno retires...for real this time. Jimmy Fallon moves up from *Late Night* to *The Tonight Show,* and his old *Saturday Night Live* costar Seth Meyers takes over *Late Night.*

2015 David Letterman retires, and CBS replaces him with Stephen Colbert, who for the previous decade hosted Comedy Central's *The Colbert Report* in character as a blowhard cable TV news pundit.

2015 Jon Stewart leaves *The Daily Show.* The show is offered to Chris Rock, Amy Schumer, Louis C.K., and Amy Poehler, all of whom turn it down. The job goes to newly hired *Daily Show* correspondent Trevor Noah.

2015 Craig Ferguson is out at *The Late Late Show,* and English actor James Corden comes in.

2019 *A Little Late with Lilly Singh* debuts on NBC in a new 1:30 a.m. slot. Singh, a Canadian YouTube megastar, becomes the first woman and the first person of color to host her own late-night show on one of the big broadcast networks.

The pineapple is indigenous to South America, where it's pollinated by bats.

JIMI HENDRIX IN BLACK AND WHITE, PART II

It's June 1967 at a concert in California. Jimi Hendrix is ready to take on the world. But can the world take Jimi Hendrix? *(Part I is on page 300.)*

FIRE

"I'm at the Monterey Pop Festival and all of a sudden these three guys come on stage in all these psycho-jello clothes and stuff, and they just looked incredible," said Micky Dolenz, lead singer of the Monkees. The Who had just finished their set by smashing their instruments, only to be upstaged by Hendrix, who lit his Stratocaster on fire (an idea credited to Hendrix's manager, Chas Chandler). After the concert, Dolenz convinced his TV show's producers to have the Jimi Hendrix Experience open for them on their summer tour "because they were very theatrical and *The Monkees* [were] theatrical." Hendrix wasn't sure, having once described the Monkees' music as "dishwater," but their records *were* outselling the Beatles that year. Chandler signed them on to the tour, but after half a dozen shows, Hendrix gave up trying to play over the throngs of teenage girls who wouldn't stop yelling, "We want the Monkees! We want the Monkees!" He flipped off the crowd and quit the tour.

It wasn't just the teenyboppers—a lot of rock music writers didn't know what to make of Hendrix, either. Anthony DeCurtis was one of them, having seen the Experience several times that summer. "I wouldn't say the response was racist," the longtime *Rolling Stone* editor wrote in his 2015 *Medium* article, "Jimi Hendrix: Rocking the Racial Divide," "but it definitely registered on the overwhelmingly white audience that he was black, and that fact sharpened the edge of his presence."

Here was this flamboyantly dressed "negro" (a widely used term back then) with a huge afro. His bandmates were white, as were most of his girlfriends. (In 1967, it was still illegal in 17 Southern states for whites to marry non-whites.) The music press in both England and America described Hendrix in not-so-subtly racist terms—including "the Black Elvis," "Psychedelic Superspade," and "Wild Man of Borneo."

VOODOO CHILD

The reaction to Hendrix from his fellow blues-rock guitarists ranged from admiration to jealousy to outright hostility. Jeff Beck once described his relationship with Hendrix as "difficult."

"Some of their resistance to him was rooted in ego as well as race," journalist John Blake wrote in his 2014 article "How Jimi Hendrix's Race Became His 'Invisible

Legacy.'" Meanwhile, some rock critics accused Hendrix of "stealing white music" from bands like the Who, the Beatles, and the Rolling Stones, ignoring the fact that those bands had "borrowed" quite a bit from black American R&B artists. (Chuck Berry sang "Here come ol' Flat Top" more than a decade before John Lennon took credit for writing it.) That isn't to say Hendrix was fully original. He did copy Pete Townshend's amplifier setup, T-Bone Walker's teeth-playing, and many of Chuck Berry's stage moves, to name a few. And Hendrix wasn't the first guitarist to play with feedback, but he took it where no one else had before.

Looking at the response to his "Star-Spangled Banner" performance at Woodstock, Blake wrote, "Hendrix summoned the sounds of falling rockets and bursting bombs from his guitar, yet others heard something more, a black man's protest. Hendrix played the song at the height of the Vietnam War, where black soldiers were dying in high numbers." Woodstock wasn't a one-off; Hendrix played his version of America's national anthem at more than 60 shows. Each time it got a bit angrier: "Here's a song that we was all brainwashed with, remember this oldie-but-goodie?"

CASTLES MADE OF SAND

To most white rock fans, Hendrix was just another "hippie freak," a label he did not embrace, once lamenting, "You have to be a freak in order to be different. And even freaks, they are very prejudiced. You have to have your hair long and talk in a certain way in order to be with them. And in order to be with the others, you have to have your hair short and wear ties. So we're trying to make a third world happen, you know what I mean?"

To most white rock fans, Hendrix was just another "hippie freak," a label he did not embrace.

By the time he got to working on his third album, *Electric Ladyland*, Hendrix had begun to retreat inward, preferring writing and recording to performing. But he was becoming such a perfectionist—requiring dozens of takes, and constantly tweaking the controls on the mixing board—that his manager, Chas Chandler, thought Hendrix was losing his spontaneity, and quit. That left the Experience under the sole stewardship of Mike Jeffrey, who never had Hendrix's best interests in mind. Over the years, Jeffrey has been accused of everything from embezzling from Hendrix to murdering him for insurance money. What is verifiable is that Jeffrey forced the Experience—the highest-paid act in rock—to tour almost constantly, and he kept most of the profits for himself.

MANIC DEPRESSION

What stung Hendrix more than anything was the refusal of black radio stations to play his songs. Still segregated at the time, white stations played rock, and black

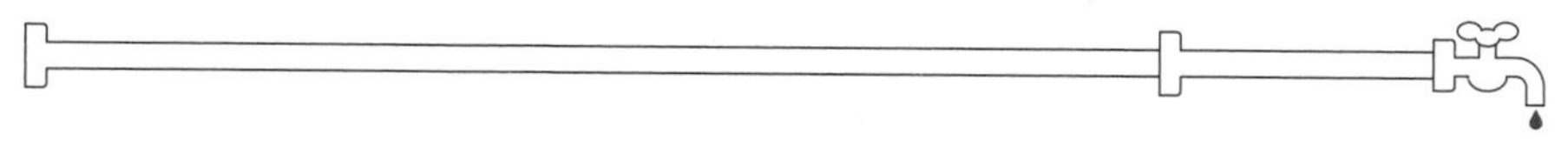

stations played soul and R&B. (In fact, about the only way a black American was likely to hear Jimi Hendrix on the radio in the late 1960s was as a soldier in Vietnam.) Why wouldn't the stations play his music? According to Elijah C. Watson in the 2017 *OkayPlayer* article "The White Erasure and Black Reclaiming of Jimi Hendrix," black people criticized Hendrix for catering "to predominantly white audiences with white bandmates during a time of Black Power and separatism."

As John Blake wrote, Hendrix desperately wanted to "connect with blacks who had dismissed him as a musical Uncle Tom: a black man playing white man's music." Unwilling to become a civil rights speaker, Hendrix nevertheless did try to associate himself with the movement. A few days after Martin Luther King Jr. was assassinated in April 1968, Hendrix played at a tribute show for the slain civil rights leader in New York City with, among others, Buddy Guy and B. B. King. Later that year, following clashes at the Democratic National Convention in Chicago, Hendrix played at a benefit concert for the Chicago Seven activists who'd been charged with starting the riots. But that same year, he was booed by a mostly black audience in Seattle when he made a "triumphant return" to his hometown high school.

In September 1969, two weeks after Woodstock, at the behest of his old bandmates from the Ghetto Fighters, Hendrix played at a street fair in Harlem. "I want to show them that music is universal," he told the *New York Times* ahead of the event, "that there is no white rock or black rock." That kind of talk fared better with wide-eyed hippies; the Harlem crowd booed Hendrix and threw bottles and eggs at him as he opened with "Fire." He then dedicated "Voodoo Child" to the Black Panthers, but the crowd didn't really warm up until Hendrix played R&B songs from his days on the Chitlin' Circuit.

No matter what he tried, he still wasn't truly fitting in. "I don't want to be a clown anymore," he complained. "I don't want to be a rock and roll star."

ASTRO MAN

Retreating into his own world in 1970—one that consisted of "astronomical amounts" of LSD—Hendrix began jamming with an eclectic mix of musicians, including jazz trumpet great Miles Davis, who encouraged him to start experimenting with the "sonic possibilities." But the real world kept creeping in. In March, a *Rolling Stone* interviewer said to Hendrix, in an obvious attempt to egg him on: "One thing that's been written of Hendrix over recent months is that he's forming closer ties with black militant groups, possibly the Black Panthers."

"I heard about that, too," laughed Hendrix. "In *Rolling Stone.* Tell me all about it." Hendrix said he was in favor of equal rights "but not the aggression or violence or whatever you want to call it. I'm not for guerrilla warfare." A few months later, in what turned out to be Hendrix's final interview, he reiterated, "Music has been

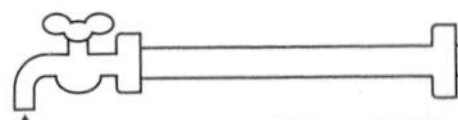

Why did belt sales crash in 2020? The COVID-19 pandemic. According to an industry expert, "Nobody needs a belt when they're not wearing pants."

getting too heavy, almost to the state of unbearable. I have this one little saying, when things get too heavy just call me helium, the lightest known gas to man."

Hendrix gave that final interview in London, where he'd gone to escape the American music industry and learn how to read music and play more instruments. There were plans in the works for him and Miles Davis to record an album with Paul McCartney on bass. What would that have sounded like? We'll never know. James Marshall Hendrix died on September 18, 1970, at age 27. The death was ruled accidental: He "aspirated his own vomit and died of asphyxia while intoxicated with barbiturates." (There are rumors that Mike Jeffrey killed him, but nothing has ever been proven, and Jeffrey died in a plane crash three years later.)

I DON'T LIVE TODAY

Though his fame lasted barely four years, Jimi Hendrix's influence on rock 'n' roll cannot be overstated: For five decades, it's been a rite of passage for every beginning guitar player to awkwardly finger the intro to "Purple Haze." As John Mayer once put it, "Who I am as a guitarist is defined by my failure to become Jimi Hendrix." And not just rock but heavy metal, too: "Listening to his version of 'Star-Spangled Banner,'" said Metallica shredder Kirk Hammett, "I thought, 'I'm going to get a guitar.'"

Hendrix's influence on black music, though not as well documented, might in fact be stronger than it is on rock and heavy metal. "If you had to build a Mount Rushmore to black music, you have to put his face on it," said Lamont Robinson, creator of the Official R&B Music Hall of Fame Museum, which inducted Hendrix in 2015. "It would have to go up there with Michael Jackson, Aretha Franklin—he's right there." He's influenced giants from George Clinton to Andre 3000, from Lenny Kravitz to Frank Ocean, from Kanye West to Pharrell. A 1969 Hendrix jam session with drummer Buddy Miles and Jalal of the Last Poets—which featured the anti-war poem "Machine Gun"—has been called one of the first true rap performances. If you listen to hip-hop, then you've heard Hendrix's music sampled more than you probably realize.

PURPLE RAIN

But no artist since has been compared to Hendrix more than Prince...who never really liked that comparison, often saying, "It's only because we're both black." (Prince maintained that he was more inspired by Carlos Santana's guitar playing.) But the fact remains that both singer-songwriter-guitar-virtuosos were genre-bending forces of nature that altered the course of popular music. And in 2004, Prince did say this: "I learned from Jimi Hendrix. They all wanted him to do the tricks, and at the end of his career, he just wanted to play. I lived longer than he did, and I can see how those pressures can really play with your head."

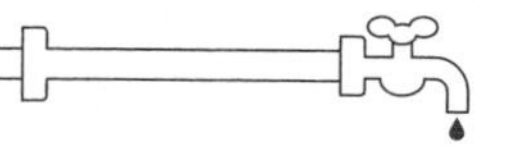

A NEEDLE-TO-KNOW BASIS

Uncle John took up hand sewing in 2020—while he was stuck at home during the pandemic—and he was surprised to discover how relaxing, exciting, and creative this simple art was. He also found out that there are a lot of different types of sewing needles, each with specific features that make them suitable to particular types of sewing jobs.

POINTED HISTORY

In 2016, archaeologists were patiently poking their way into the layers of sediment that made up the floor of Denisova Cave, a large cave in south-central Siberia in Russia, which is known to have been inhabited by humans for tens of thousands of years. There they made an amazing discovery: a sewing needle, made from a bird bone, complete with a tiny hole in one end to poke a thread through. The needle's age: approximately 50,000 years. It is the oldest sewing needle in existence.

Other prehistoric needles have been found across Eurasia and Africa—from eastern China to western Europe, and down to southern Africa. And all of the discoveries correspond to eras when primitive humans were making technological and cultural advances that were bringing them closer to the characteristics that define modern civilization. Consider the role the humble sewing needle played in that story. It allowed primitive humans to make clothing that fit better, and offered better protection from weather extremes, which, in turn, allowed them to move into regions with colder climates, and to live longer in those regions. Later, needles played a vital part in the history of exploration, as it became possible to sew larger sails for ships and boats.

Today, needles are so commonplace that we tend to overlook how important they are, but they represent a basic technology that has been part of human evolution for thousands of years. Naturally, like most technologies, this one has been refined and specialized over those years. Result: There are dozens of types of needles. Here are a few.

QUILTING NEEDLE: Also called *between* needles, or just *betweens*. These are short, sturdy, sharp needles with small, round eyes, commonly used to stitch together the "sandwich" of fabrics—top, batting, and backing fabric—that make up a quilt. The shortness of these needles is important for this job, because this sewing work puts a lot of tension on the needle, and longer needles tend to bend under that pressure. Betweens are also popular with professional tailors, for precise hand stitching on fine clothing.

SHARP: General rule: If you have only one type of sewing needle, it will probably be a *sharp*. They are the most popular type, and can be used for many different kinds of sewing jobs. Sharps are generally medium length, very fine, and, as the name implies, sharp-pointed needles, with a small round eye, about the same diameter as

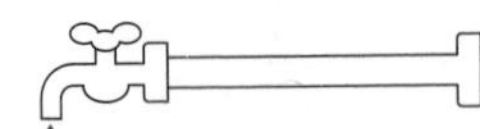

the needle's shaft. The shortness, sharpness, and small eye make sharps easy to glide through fabric without tugs or stops, and the round eye also makes them strong and durable compared to needles with elongated eyes, which are more prone to breaking. Like most kinds of needles, sharps come in different sizes, usually graded from 1 to 12 or higher (there is no standardized numbering system for needle sizes), with the larger numbers representing the smallest needles. Very fine needles, numbered 11 or 12, for example, are meant for very fine fabrics such as silk and nylon, while larger needles, numbered 1 or 2, are more suitable for heavier fabrics such as denim. Sharps are especially suitable for simple sewing jobs like simple dressmaking, fixing a hemline, or replacing a button. (Sharps are also known as *straight point needles.*)

EMBROIDERY NEEDLE: Also known as a *crewel* needle after the crewel style of embroidery, these needles are generally a little longer and thicker than sharps, with large, elongated eyes to accommodate the thick flosses and yarns commonly used in embroidery, and sharp tips to help them make their way through tightly woven embroidery fabrics.

TAPESTRY NEEDLE: These have stout shafts, large, elongated eyes to accommodate thick threads and yarns, and a blunt point, often bent away from the shaft a tiny bit, that allows them to glide through woven and knitted fabrics without piercing or catching on the fabric's heavy threads and/or yarns. It's used for embroidery and needlepoint work, and for adding decorative stitching to loose-weave fabrics.

CHENILLE NEEDLE: Similar to the tapestry needle but with a very elongated eye and a very sharp point, to allow it to be used with tightly woven materials rather than loose-weave fabrics. Primarily used for decorative stitching and particularly for ribbon embroidery—the art of embroidering with ribbon material rather than thread or yarn.

DID YOU KNOW?

What are the scariest kinds of needles? Hypodermics...and they've been around longer than you might think. Ancient Native Americans made them out of hollow bird bones attached to the bladders of small animals and used them to inject medicines beneath the skin.

BEADING NEEDLE: A long (up to 3 inches), thin, and somewhat flexible needle with a very small, round eye, used for stringing beads for jewelry or for attaching decorative items like beading or sequins to fabric. Beading needles have exceptionally tiny eyes and are therefore quite difficult to thread. An option: look for *big-eye* or *wide-eye* beading needles, which are actually two thin, flexible, wirelike needles joined together at their ends. To thread one, simply use your fingernails or tweezers to separate the two pieces and pull them apart a bit. You now have a large "eye" that runs almost the entire length of the needle, and is very easy to thread. (Be careful: These needles are sharp at both ends!)

DARNING NEEDLE: Like beading needles, darning needles are long and thin, but they have a large eye and are used for *darning*—fixing holes in fabric by covering the hole with a series of crisscrossing stitches until the hole is covered. They are most commonly used to darn holes in wool clothing, such as socks and sweaters.

LEATHER NEEDLE: Also known as *glovers* or *wedge* needles, these are strong, stout needles with a small eye and a characteristic triangular point, designed to pierce leather without tearing it. Used to make and/or repair leather clothing and other items. (A *sailmaker* needle is similar to a leather needle, but its triangular point extends farther up the needle's shaft. These are commonly used for canvas boat sails, as well as for thick leather items.)

MILLINERS NEEDLE: Long, thin needles with small, round eyes traditionally used in the art of millinery, or hat making. Most commonly used today for pleating, and in the decorative needlework style known as *smocking*. Also known as *straw* needles.

UPHOLSTERY NEEDLE: These curved needles are used in the repair of upholstery, especially in fixing torn stitching on upholstered furniture, which can be very difficult with a straight needle. (What makes sewing repairs on upholstery so difficult is that the fabric is attached to something, e.g., a piece of furniture, and therefore the repairer doesn't have access to both sides of the fabric, as you would when repairing a pair of pants or a shirt. This is why the curved needle is such a necessity with upholstery repair.) Note: There are also straight upholstery needles, and they can be very long—up to 12 inches. Extra-long upholstery needles are also referred to as *mattress* needles.

BODKIN: Thick, long needles with rounded, blunt points, and one or more long, slotted eyes, used to thread cord, ribbon, or other material through holes or channels in clothing, such as inserting elastic into a waistband. A *ballpoint* is a type of bodkin that has a rounded, ball-shaped nub on its end, which allows it to slide easily through narrow cloth channels.

Bonus: Sewing experts advise against licking the end of a thread to make it pointy and easier to thread through the eye of a needle, because the moisture can cause rust to form in the needle's eye. And if you find a needle that's already rusted, you can polish it up—with your needle strawberry. You've probably seen a "tomato pincushion," a popular style of pincushion that comes in the shape of a tomato. They customarily come with a small, strawberry-shaped bag attached. That bag is filled with fine emery powder—and you're meant to pass your needles through it occasionally to polish them up.

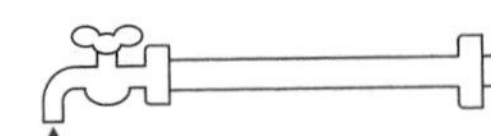

...A: Conquest (white), War (red), Famine (black), and Death (pale green, as a corpse).

RETCH-WORTHY RECIPES

We scoured old cookbooks and the far corners of the internet to find the oddest kitchen concoctions...and we think we succeeded. Warning: These recipes are not for the faint of heart, and if you're actually brave enough to try them, you do so at your own risk.

BEEF FIZZ

Use fresh lemon to make this old-time drink extra special.

Ingredients

- 10.5-ounce can condensed beef broth
- 1 tablespoon lemon juice
- 4 ounces ginger ale

Directions

Combine ingredients, and pour over ice into 3 or 4 glasses.

TUNA AND PEAR PIZZA

Ingredients

- 8-ounce can of tuna in oil
- 2 medium onions
- 2 ripe pears
- 8-ounce can of tomatoes
- Pinch of dried oregano
- Premade pizza crust
- A little oil
- Small can of anchovy fillets
- Pickled walnut slices (found in British shops)

Directions

Drain oil from tuna into a saucepan. Peel and chop the onions and pears. Toss them in the tuna oil. Add tuna and pour in the tomatoes, including the liquid. Add salt as desired. Simmer uncovered about 15 to 20 minutes until firm, then season with oregano. Place crust on a greased 10- or 11-inch round baking sheet. Brush dough with oil and spread tuna mixture over it. Top with anchovy fillets and pickled walnut slices. Bake at 425°F for 10 to 15 minutes, then at 325°F for 10 to 15 minutes. Like revenge, this dish can also be served cold.

HANGOVER TEA

Ingredients

- 1 teaspoon Marmite
- 1 cup boiling water
- Lime juice
- Fried onion, sliced

Directions

Dissolve Marmite in water. Add lime juice to taste. Stir in onion. Chug. (Note: this is a traditional hangover cure in parts of South Asia.)

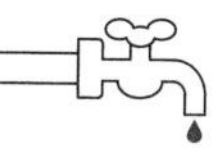

The seven-page itch? In Ian Fleming's 007 novels, James Bond drinks a cocktail an average of every 7 pages.

NO-BAKE MOUNTAIN DEW CHEESECAKE WITH DORITOS CRUST

Ingredients

- 2 cups sugar
- 3/4 cup light corn syrup
- 1 cup Mountain Dew
- 10-ounce bag Nacho Cheese Doritos, crushed
- 5 tablespoons melted butter
- 16 ounces cream cheese, room temperature
- 14-ounce can of sweetened condensed milk
- Green and yellow food coloring, optional

Directions

In a medium saucepan, combine sugar, ½ cup corn syrup, and Mountain Dew. Heat on stove, just hot enough to boil off the sugars. Cool to room temperature. Pour crumbled chips and melted butter into a bowl. Stir with fork. Press "crust" into bottom of a springform pan, or a round pan lined with foil or parchment paper long enough to hang over the sides. Use the bottom of a glass to pack down the crust. Refrigerate about 10 minutes.

In bowl, use a mixer to soften cheese. Pour in condensed milk, and mix. Add remaining ¼ cup corn syrup, and mix. Pour into pan. Refrigerate 3 to 4 hours. Use a butter knife to loosen around the edge of the springform pan and release, or lift out the pie by the paper.

Optional Steps

Reserve some of the mixture and add a drop or two of yellow food coloring. Dye the rest of the mixture with a few drops of green coloring. Spread the green cheese mixture into the pan with a spatula, and firmly tap the pan on the counter to help it settle. Pour the yellow mixture on top and use a spatula to swirl it around decoratively.

PRUNE WHIP

Caution: Eating raw egg with tons of prunes may cause salmonella and/or diarrhea.

Ingredients

- 2 egg whites
- ¼ teaspoon salt
- ¼ cup sugar
- 2 tablespoons lemon juice
- 1½ cups cooked prunes, pureed
- 1 teaspoon vanilla

Directions

Whip egg whites with salt. Once whites are very foamy, add sugar, one tablespoon at a time, and beat. Repeat until soft, shiny peaks form. Mix remaining ingredients separately, and fold into egg whites. Spoon into 4–6 dishes and chill. Garnish with maraschino cherries.

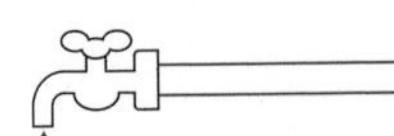

CORN S'MORES

Ingredients

- 2 ears of corn, shucked
- Marshmallow creme
- 3 or 4 graham crackers
- 1 milk chocolate bar

Directions

Grill the corn. Crumble up the graham crackers, and melt the chocolate bar. While corn is warm, spread it with a thick coat of marshmallow creme. Roll it in graham cracker crumbs, and drizzle with chocolate.

LIVER SAUSAGE PINEAPPLE

Polish up on your sculpting skills with this pineapple-shaped monstrosity from a 1953 cookbook.

Ingredients

- 1 pound liver sausage
- 1 tablespoon lemon juice
- 1 teaspoon Worcestershire sauce
- ¼ cup mayonnaise
- 2 tablespoons cold water
- 2 teaspoons unflavored gelatin
- About ¼ cup hot water
- 1 cup mayonnaise
- Stuffed olives, sliced
- 1 pineapple crown (the leafy top of a pineapple)

Directions

Mix first four ingredients and chill well, at least 1 or 2 hours. Mold the mixture around an 8-ounce glass to give it the round shape of a pineapple, and chill another hour. Add cold water to gelatin. Mix in just enough hot water to dissolve it, about ¼ cup. Stir in 1 cup mayonnaise. Chill only until it's the consistency of frosting—not so long that it turns jellylike. Frost the meat mixture "pineapple" with the mayo "icing." Dig a small well on top (to fit the pineapple crown). Chill. Just before serving, score the pineapple with crisscrosses along the sides to give it the texture of a pineapple, and dot each diamond with a sliced stuffed olive. Decorate with pineapple crown.

SMOKER'S COUGH

Ingredients

- 1 shot Jagermeister
- A dollop of mayo

Directions

Drop the mayo on top and down it quickly before you lose your nerve.

* * *

"Ask not what you can do for your country. Ask what's for lunch."

—Orson Welles

The first Mardi Gras celebration in the Americas took place in 1703 in Mobile, Alabama, fifteen years before the founding of New Orleans.

IT'S A DOG'S WORLD

Dogs were the very first animals to be domesticated, so humans might not have become so successful without their help (which came in more ways than you might realize). But throughout history and into the present, our dealings with the family Canidae *have often gone awry. Here's some new research that sheds light on how this connection began, why it's so strong with domesticated dogs, and why it gets so messy with their wild cousins: foxes, coyotes, and wolves.*

Who's a Good Human?

Scene: The Dawn of Man. A band of prehistoric hunters is sitting around a fire eating from the day's kill. Wild animals are hiding far off in the shadows, except for a lone wolf that's sitting just inside the edge of the firelight. She's on her belly—not threatening, not snarling—looking toward the men but not right at them. Not sensing a threat, they continue their meal. At one point, a hunter takes a bite of his food, but is having trouble chewing through the gristle. On a whim, he tosses the scrap over to the wolf. The wolf inches a bit closer and eats it. Then she inches a bit closer...and slightly wags her tail.

Survival of the Friendliest

Scientists can't agree on exactly when or where the wolf (*Canis lupus*) and the dog (*Canis lupus familiaris*) became separate species. The split happened sometime between 15,000 and 40,000 years ago, most likely in Asia. What's really interesting is *how* the complicated relationship between humans and canines began. Recent findings reveal that it wasn't people who domesticated dogs but, according to evolutionary anthropologist Brian Hare, "Wolves largely domesticated themselves among hunter-gatherer people."

The theory, which Hare describes as "survival of the friendliest," explains how such an aggressive carnivore went from being the hunter's rival to eventually aiding in the hunt. "Anyone who has spent time with wild wolves would see how unlikely it was that we somehow tamed them in a way that led to domestication," says Hare, director of Duke University's Canine Cognition Center. Instead, he says, it was the friendlier wolves who risked entering our world (like our fictional account above), and exploited early humans by pulling on their heartstrings. Hare estimates that it took only a few generations of this "self-domestication" to bring about such physical changes as bigger eyes, floppy ears, and fluffy tails.

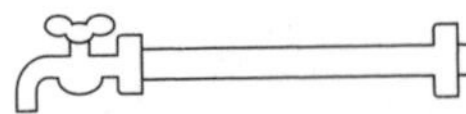

Man's Best Friend...and Child

As agriculture allowed prehistoric people to stay in one place, dogs stuck around, and before long, several other wild animals had been domesticated—including cattle and poultry (and, for some reason, cats). In addition to hunting, domesticated dogs—thanks to selective breeding—aided our ancestors by standing guard at night, pulling sleds through snowy terrain, herding livestock, and protecting sheep from wolves. Today, dogs still guard livestock and property; they help with search-and-rescue operations; they sniff out bombs, contraband, and diseases; they aid people with special needs; and they provide billions of dog lovers with companionship and joy.

No other animal even comes close to interacting with humans in such a wide variety of ways, so there's got to be something very strong at work to make that bond possible. You know how some people say their dogs are like their children? They're not wrong—at least, as it relates to certain chemical reactions in the brain. In all mammal species, when a mother looks into the eyes of her offspring, both of their brains release a hormone called *oxytocin* that, among other things, reinforces feelings of trust and maternal bonding. A 2015 study at Japan's Azabu University discovered that when a dog and its owner gaze into each other's eyes, that hormone is released by both animals. This is the only case where this happens between two different species. "I have three standard poodles," said lead researcher Takefumi Kikusui, "I participated in the experiment, and my oxytocin boosted up after the eye gaze, like 300 percent." In other words, not only did dogs "self-domesticate," but in doing so they altered human behavior as well. To put it another way, says Kikusui, "We co-evolved."

Worlds Apart

Those are just two of numerous studies that show what we don't really need a study to show: our relationship with *Canis lupus familiaris* (dogs) is both profound and unique. What about *Canis lupus*—the wolf? Kikusui also examined people who had raised wolves from pups. The wolves neither gazed back the way dogs do, nor did their brains release any oxytocin. Although it was an ancient species of wolf that evolved into the modern dog, today's wolves cannot be so domesticated. Nor can their canid cousins: coyotes, foxes, jackals, and hyenas.

Although it was an ancient species of wolf that evolved into the modern dog, today's wolves cannot be so domesticated.

Humanity's relationship with the family *Canidae* has always been one of give and take: We take away the wild canines' habitats by developing an area for our own use, which gives them new opportunities to find food and shelter. But when that development goes unchecked, the entire ecosystem can be thrown out of whack. In North America, for example,

The aardwolf looks nothing like an aardvark. It's a relative of the hyena and is native to Africa. It eats insects—termites mostly—and can consume 250,000 in a single night.

indigenous peoples had thrived alongside of gray wolves for millennia. Then in the 1800s, Europeans transformed the New World's flourishing savannas into endless tracts of farmland. In doing so, the government waged a war of extermination on wolves, which even the environmentalist president Theodore Roosevelt described as "beasts of waste and destruction." By the mid-20th century, the U.S. gray wolf population had been reduced from 500,000 to fewer than 300 (near the Canadian border). This widespread endangerment created a "trophic cascade," a change that occurs from the top downward in the food chain when the apex predator is removed.

The Wolves of Yellowstone

A famous example of how a trophic cascade works—in reverse—was documented in Wyoming's Yellowstone National Park after 66 wolves were reintroduced there in 1995. The wolves immediately reduced the overabundance of grazing animals like deer and elk, which had all but decimated the grasslands. Even more important, the wolves' return changed the deer's behavior by scaring them out of the wide-open meadows. This aerated the soil and revived the grasses and wildflowers. Reduced deer numbers also increased the foliage and undergrowth in the forests, which made the trees grow taller—some to five times their previous height. The increased foliage brought back songbirds, and bears enjoyed the bounty of berries. The thicker undergrowth was ideal for smaller animals like mice, weasels, and beavers. The beavers built more dams in the streams, which created even more habitat in the form of ponds for reptiles, amphibians, fish, and waterbirds. That led to more hunting grounds for raptors, and more carcasses for scavengers.

Within a decade, these biological changes had physically altered Yellowstone's geology. With the grasses and undergrowth restored, soil erosion was greatly reduced, which strengthened the riverbanks and reduced silt in the crystal-clear waters. Result: The barren landscape that Yellowstone had become in the 20th century was reborn a thriving, balanced ecosystem that still exists today. All because of 66 wolves.

Public Enemy No. 1

That's great news for the wild animals *inside* Yellowstone's two million acres. Outside the park, the reintroduction of wolves, reported *National Geographic*, "provoked fear, resentment, and even lawsuits among people concerned about their livestock and livelihoods." Subsequent reintroduction programs have brought wolves back to other U.S. states that haven't seen them for nearly a century, sparking even more controversy. And just as humans and wolves have a tenuous connection, so too do wolves and other wild canids. When the wolves retook Yellowstone, they killed off many of the coyotes.

So many attractions at Universal Studios theme parks are based on Steven Spielberg's movies that he earns up to $50 million a year in royalties and fees from the parks.

Outside Yellowstone, coyotes (*Canis latrans*, which means "barking dog") have had an even tougher go of it. Native to western North America, they were first called "prairie wolves" when explorers Lewis and Clark encountered them in 1804. As farmers settled the frontier, coyotes gained a reputation—just as wolves had—for taking livestock. Whereas people feared wolves, they truly despised coyotes. As Mark Twain wrote in 1870:

> The coyote is a living, breathing allegory of Want. He is always hungry. He is always poor, out of luck, and friendless. The meanest creatures despise him, and even the fleas would desert him for a velocipede. He is so spiritless and cowardly that even while his exposed teeth are pretending a threat, the rest of his face is apologizing for it. And he is so homely! So scrawny, and ribby, and coarse-haired, and pitiful.

Thanks to this reputation, coyotes were hunted and poisoned with little if any thought to their well-being. But they proved a lot harder than wolves to get rid of.

Wily Coyotes

The first big misconception about coyotes is that they prey on the same animals as wolves. They don't; they mostly scavenge, but they also hunt mice and rats (which tend to overrun farms when the coyotes are gone). Another misconception is that coyotes behave like wolves, which are strictly pack animals. Coyotes aren't so bound by instinct. As Dan Flores, author of *Coyote America: A Natural and Supernatural History*, explains, "Coyotes evolved alongside larger canids, like wolves, which often persecuted and harassed them and killed their pups. As a result, coyotes developed a fission-fusion adaptation, which human beings also have. This enables them to either function as pack predators or as singles and pairs." If a pack is broken up, coyotes can survive on their own until they find others to pack up with again.

Coyotes have another tactic that's even more impressive: If 70 percent of a local population is killed, then the next season, litter sizes can increase by that same amount to keep their numbers stable. The coyotes' nightly howling and barking sessions serve as a sort of census-taking to keep track of their numbers. Ironically, the nation's coyote population was greatly "helped" by government-funded poisoning campaigns in effect until the 1970s. How? Because the coyotes' efforts to get away from poisoned areas, explained Flores, "was one of the things that kept scattering them across North America."

So, despite a war of extermination that continues to this day—as many as 500,000 coyotes are shot by ranchers or the U.S. government annually—they've managed to inhabit every state in the lower 48. There's even a thriving coyote population in New

U.S astronauts aboard the International Space Station vote using absentee ballots. Their address is listed as "low-Earth orbit."

York City. And it was reported in 2020 that coyotes were inching closer and closer to South America. It will be interesting to see their effect there...especially how they get on with the jaguars.

Outfoxed

There are 12 species of foxes—the genus *Vulpes*—and few have had an easy time with humans. Europeans bred foxhounds specifically to help them hunt the swift creatures for sport. And the fox's soft, red fur was in high demand for centuries, peaking in the 1970s. The fox is no friend to farmers, either, who must constantly reinforce their chicken coops to keep the cunning canines at bay. Yet despite efforts to reduce or even eradicate foxes, their numbers have remained steady.

Nowhere have foxes had a larger impact than in Australia. In the 19th century, when the British Empire spread Down Under, colonizers brought along European red foxes (*Vulpes vulpes*) solely so they could continue hunting them. A century and a half later, Aussies are still trying to correct that mistake. First to go were the indigenous prey animals that proved no match for the clever, nocturnal hunters. Foxes are so effective, in fact, that they exhibit "surplus killing behavior"—taking more animals than they could ever consume. According to the Australian government, foxes "have contributed to the extinction of several species of small mammals and birds." So you'll never get to see a greater bilby, a numbat, a bridled nail-tail wallaby, or a quokka. Foxes also pursue poultry, lambs, baby goats, and, occasionally, cats.

Australia's government estimates the cost of eradicating these "pests" (their official designation) plus the monetary damage to farmers, at around $200 million annually. The taxpayer-funded extermination campaign includes "baiting, trapping, and shooting." Has it worked? Hardly. "The red fox may be the most destructive species ever introduced to Australia," explains Chris Johnson, professor of wildlife conservation at the University of Tasmania, who blames the animal for playing a major part in the loss of at least 20 Australian mammal species.

Two mammal species that do deter foxes happen to be other canids: the domesticated Maremma sheepdog (originally bred in Italy) and the dingo, a feral breed whose ancestors were domesticated dogs. But these canines can only do so much. By the turn of the 21st century, foxes had spread to every corner of Australia, except one...maybe.

Tasmanian Devils

If foxes were to make it to Tasmania, an island state off Australia's southern coast, they could wreak havoc on the local wildlife and farm animals like nowhere else on Earth, according to some experts. But are they there already? According to Australia's

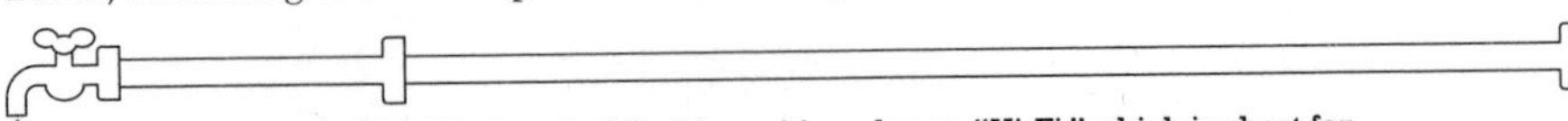

What is "Wi-Fi" short for? Nothing—it's a play on "Hi-Fi," which is short for "high fidelity," a term applied to home stereos beginning in the 1950s.

ABC News, "It has been alleged that hunters smuggled fox cubs into Tasmania around 2000, raised and set them loose in the wild, in order to hunt them." A police investigation failed to find any hard evidence of a fox population, despite reported sightings. Taking no chances, in 2006 the state government initiated the expensive decade-long "Fox Eradication Program" with the goal of eliminating foxes before they could establish themselves or have any impact on the island's animal population. This included utilizing "preventative broad-scale poison baiting." (Game wardens used a toxin called 1080 that affects foxes but not native animals.)

The situation got really ugly when conspiracy theories emerged that government agents had planted fake fox evidence to justify the high costs of the $50 million program, which was abruptly canceled with no real evidence that any foxes had been found or eradicated. Then, in October 2016, the state's Invasive Species Hotline received a call about a dead fox on a street corner in northern Tasmania, renewing the debate in the news and online. One person commented, "I saw a live fox last time I was there. I didn't realize there weren't supposed to be any until I saw a TV program later." At last report, there were "officially" zero red foxes on Tasmania. Hopefully it stays that way, and not just for the sake of the local critters; foxes and coyotes can do harm to people, too—and you don't even have to touch them.

Beware of Dog

The U.S. Centers for Disease Control and Prevention estimates that there are 4.7 million domestic dog bites in the United States every year, with 800,000 requiring a visit to the doctor, and 30 to 50 resulting in fatalities. Other than a mauling, the greatest threat from dogs is rabies, which causes the infected animal to become overly aggressive and likely to bite, thus transmitting the fatal disease to humans. That's one of the biggest risks of exposing domestic dogs to their wild counterparts. Along with bats, skunks, and raccoons, foxes and coyotes are the animals most likely to spread rabies to dogs—as well as other diseases like mange, canine distemper, and CPV (canine parvovirus infection).

Direct attacks of wild canids on humans are rare, but they do happen, as in the case of Norman Kenney. The 88-year-old Mainer was attacked by two foxes in two separate incidents in the fall of 2019. The second fox bit him several times... and he later tested positive for rabies. Without several rounds of painful injections, Kenney would have died. When asked why foxes were targeting him, he answered, "I wish I knew." Kenney's experience aside, very few of these wild dog attacks occur, and only one to three Americans contract rabies in a given year. Coyotes, foxes, and wolves—even the rabid ones—tend to keep their distance when given the chance. And if you're scared of being eaten by a wolf, it's very unlikely. There have been only two documented cases of North Americans being killed by wolves in the last century.

The Volkswagen auto plant in Wolfsburg, Germany, produces more sausages than cars. (The links have their own part number: #199 398 500 A.)

A Wag of the Tail

Canines have had a profound impact on human civilization and the natural environment, much of it positive, some of it negative. But history has proven again and again that we work much better with them than against them—even though this partnership doesn't always end well (as in the case of the foxes). The challenge is to co-exist with these animals when possible, and when necessary, to minimize the damage they do to native species and other living creatures. Either way, dogs—wild or domesticated—are survivors. They always seem to find a way to live on.

* * *

"Be the person your dog thinks you are."

—J. W. Stephens

HOW MUCH SLEEP DO I NEED?

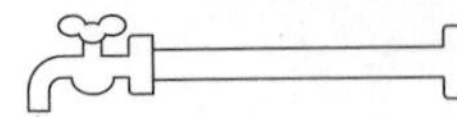

ANSWERS

DOT BOMB *(Answers for page 72)*

1. c; **2.** f; **3.** l; **4.** b; **5.** h; **6.** j; **7.** n; **8.** e; **9.** k; **10.** d; **11.** m; **12.** a; **13.** i; **14.** g; **15.** q; **16.** o; **17.** p; **18.** r

MUSIC AND INDUSTRY *(Answers for page 166)*

1. d) Seattle
2. j) Detroit
3. r) Boston
4. h) San Francisco
5. t) London
6. p) St. Louis
7. o) Stockholm
8. l) Minneapolis–St. Paul
9. i) Phoenix
10. b) New York City
11. k) Houston
12. e) Dearborn, Michigan
13. c) Memphis
14. g) Atlanta
15. f) Athens, Georgia
16. s) Liverpool
17. q) Toronto
18. n) Topeka, Kansas
19. a) Dublin
20. m) Chicago

WHAT AM I? *(Answers for page 219)*

1. A goose
2. A housefly
3. The Moon
4. A map
5. A cloud
6. Tomorrow
7. A kiwi
8. Fire
9. Pac-Man
10. The horizon
11. The letter f
12. A bald head
13. Your legs
14. A pea
15. Milk
16. Sand—it helps people to see because glass is made from it
17. A tree
18. A tap
19. A penny

LEAVE THE GUN. TAKE THE CANNOLI. *(Answers for page 277)*

1. e) *Goodfellas*
2. h) *The Blues Brothers*
3. g) *Smokey and the Bandit*
4. c) *Five Easy Pieces*
5. a) *The Godfather*
6. b) *A Christmas Story*
7. d) *When Harry Met Sally*
8. i) *Pulp Fiction*
9. f) *The Silence of the Lambs*

NAME THE OTHER GUY *(Answers for page 335)*

1. d; **2.** j; **3.** c; **4.** k; **5.** g; **6.** m; **7.** a; **8.** i; **9.** b; **10.** n; **11.** o; **12.** e; **13.** f; **14.** q; **15.** p; **16.** h; **17.** r; **18.** l

* * *

WHAT'S THE DIFFERENCE BETWEEN...

...a Preface, a Foreword, and an Introduction? Any of these items may be found in the opening pages of a book, prior to the actual content. (They're called "front matter" in the publishing world.) A preface is a statement of intent by the author—it explains their goals in writing the book, and can include acknowledgments of others who made it possible. A foreword is a statement by someone other than the author, often a prominent individual extolling the importance of the material in the pages to come. An introduction is the first "real" part of the book, where the narrative begins, with the author attempting to draw the reader into the subject.

- ❒ Uncle John's Bathroom Reader Plunges into the Presidency
- ❒ Uncle John's Bathroom Reader Plunges into the Universe
- ❒ Uncle John's Bathroom Reader Quintessential Collection of Notable Quotables
- ❒ Uncle John's Bathroom Reader Salutes the Armed Forces
- ❒ Uncle John's Bathroom Reader Shoots and Scores
- ❒ Uncle John's Bathroom Reader Sports Spectacular
- ❒ Uncle John's Bathroom Reader Takes a Swing at Baseball
- ❒ Uncle John's Bathroom Reader Tales to Inspire
- ❒ Uncle John's Bathroom Reader Tees Off on Golf
- ❒ Uncle John's Bathroom Reader The World's Gone Crazy
- ❒ Uncle John's Bathroom Reader Tunes into TV
- ❒ Uncle John's Bathroom Reader Vroom!
- ❒ Uncle John's Bathroom Reader Weird Canada
- ❒ Uncle John's Bathroom Reader Weird Inventions
- ❒ Uncle John's Bathroom Reader WISE UP!
- ❒ Uncle John's Bathroom Reader Wonderful World of Odd
- ❒ Uncle John's Bathroom Reader Zipper Accidents
- ❒ Uncle John's Book of Fun
- ❒ Uncle John's Canoramic Bathroom Reader
- ❒ Uncle John's Certified Organic Bathroom Reader
- ❒ Uncle John's Colossal Collection of Quotable Quotes
- ❒ Uncle John's Creature Feature Bathroom Reader For Kids Only!
- ❒ Uncle John's Curiously Compelling Bathroom Reader
- ❒ Uncle John's Did You Know...? Bathroom Reader For Kids Only!
- ❒ Uncle John's Do-It-Yourself Diary for Infomaniacs Only
- ❒ Uncle John's Do-It-Yourself Journal for Infomaniacs Only
- ❒ Uncle John's Electrifying Bathroom Reader For Kids Only!
- ❒ Uncle John's Electrifying Bathroom Reader For Kids Only! Collectible Edition
- ❒ Uncle John's Endlessly Engrossing Bathroom Reader
- ❒ Uncle John's Factastic Bathroom Reader
- ❒ Uncle John's Facts to Annoy Your Teacher Bathroom Reader For Kids Only!
- ❒ Uncle John's Fast-Acting Long-Lasting Bathroom Reader
- ❒ Uncle John's Fully Loaded 25th Anniversary Bathroom Reader
- ❒ Uncle John's Giant 10th Anniversary Bathroom Reader
- ❒ Uncle John's Gigantic Bathroom Reader
- ❒ Uncle John's Great Big Bathroom Reader
- ❒ Uncle John's Greatest Know on Earth Bathroom Reader
- ❒ Uncle John's Haunted Outhouse Bathroom Reader For Kids Only!
- ❒ Uncle John's Heavy Duty Bathroom Reader
- ❒ Uncle John's Hindsight Is 2020 Bathroom Reader
- ❒ Uncle John's How to Toilet Train Your Cat
- ❒ Uncle John's InfoMania Bathroom Reader For Kids Only!
- ❒ Uncle John's Legendary Lost Bathroom Reader
- ❒ Uncle John's Lists That Make You Go Hmmm...
- ❒ Uncle John's New & Improved Briefs
- ❒ Uncle John's New & Improved Funniest Ever
- ❒ Uncle John's Old Faithful 30th Anniversary Bathroom Reader
- ❒ Uncle John's Perpetually Pleasing Bathroom Reader
- ❒ Uncle John's Political Briefs
- ❒ Uncle John's Presents: Book of the Dumb
- ❒ Uncle John's Presents: Book of the Dumb 2
- ❒ Uncle John's Presents: Mom's Bathtub Reader
- ❒ Uncle John's Presents the Ultimate Challenge Trivia Quiz
- ❒ Uncle John's Robotica Bathroom Reader
- ❒ Uncle John's Slightly Irregular Bathroom Reader
- ❒ Uncle John's Smell-O-Scopic Bathroom Reader For Kids Only!
- ❒ Uncle John's Supremely Satisfying Bathroom Reader
- ❒ Uncle John's The Enchanted Toilet Bathroom Reader For Kids Only!
- ❒ Uncle John's Top Secret Bathroom Reader For Kids Only!
- ❒ Uncle John's Top Secret Bathroom Reader For Kids Only! Collectible Edition
- ❒ Uncle John's Totally Quacked Bathroom Reader For Kids Only!
- ❒ Uncle John's Triumphant 20th Anniversary Bathroom Reader
- ❒ Uncle John's True Crime
- ❒ Uncle John's Truth, Trivia, and the Pursuit of Factiness Bathroom Reader
- ❒ Uncle John's 24-Karat Gold Bathroom Reader
- ❒ Uncle John's Ultimate Bathroom Reader
- ❒ Uncle John's Uncanny Bathroom Reader
- ❒ Uncle John's Unsinkable Bathroom Reader
- ❒ Uncle John's Unstoppable Bathroom Reader
- ❒ Uncle John's Weird Weird World
- ❒ Uncle John's Weird Weird World: Epic
- ❒ The Wackiest Joke Book Ever!
- ❒ The Wackiest Joke Book That'll Knock-Knock You Over!
- ❒ Who Knew?
- ❒ Who Knew? Women in History

THE LAST PAGE

FELLOW BATHROOM READERS:

The fight for good bathroom reading should never be taken loosely—we must do our duty and sit firmly for what we believe in, even while the rest of the world is taking potshots at us.

We'll be brief. Now that we've proven we're not simply a flush-in-the-pan, we invite you to take the plunge: Sit Down and Be Counted! To find out what the BRI is up to, visit us at *www.portablepress.com* and take a peek!

GET CONNECTED

Find us online to sign up for our email list, enter exciting giveaways, hear about new releases, and more!

Website: www.portablepress.com

Facebook: www.facebook.com/portablepress

Pinterest: www.pinterest.com/portablepress

Twitter: @Portablepress

Well, we're out of space, and when you've gotta go, you've gotta go. Tanks for all your support. Hope to hear from you soon.

Meanwhile, remember...

Keep on flushin'!

POST CARD

With Greetings

The Moscow subway accepts payment via squat thrusts — only 30 for a free ride!

REAL PHOTOGRAPH

Series.3

Postcards were invente
in Germany
Austria wa
country to p
them to use

Did you know there are more cows in New York State than in Wyoming?

Uncle John

Post Card

ADDRESS.

The U.S. Postal Service processes 160 billion pieces of mail each year! And photographs every single one of them!

UNCLE JOHN

THE BATHROOM

READERS' INSTITUTE

Funshine